HENRY FORD'S WAR
ON JEWS AND THE
LEGAL BATTLE AGAINST
HATE SPEECH

HENRY FORD'S WAR ON JEWS AND THE LEGAL BATTLE AGAINST HATE SPEECH

VICTORIA SAKER WOESTE

Stanford University Press

Stanford, California

Stanford University Press
Stanford, California

© 2012 by the Board of Trustees of the Leland Stanford Junior University. All rights reserved.

Published with the assistance of the American Bar Foundation.

Printed in the United States of America on acid-free, archival-quality paper

Library of Congress Cataloging-in-Publication Data

Woeste, Victoria Saker, author.
  Henry Ford's war on Jews and the legal battle against hate speech / Victoria Saker Woeste.
    pages cm
  Includes bibliographical references and index.
  ISBN 978-0-8047-7234-1 (cloth : alk. paper)
  ISBN 978-0-8047-8867-0 (pbk. : alk. paper)
    1. Ford, Henry, 1863–1947—Trials, litigation, etc.   2. Sapiro, Aaron—Trials, litigation, etc.
3. Trials (Libel)—Michigan—Detroit.   4. Dearborn independent.   5. Anti-Jewish
propaganda—United States—History—20th century.   6. Antisemitism—United States—
History—20th century.   7. Hate speech—United States—History—20th century.   I. Title.
  KF228.F667W64 2012
  346.77403'4—dc23

                                                                                2011052265

Typeset by Newgen in 10/15 Minion

*To my parents, and in particular
to my father, a lawyer who took his profession as his vocation
and sought to make God's work his own*

Like the deer that yearns for running streams,
so my soul is yearning for you, my God.

My soul is thirsting for God, the God of my life;
when can I enter and see the face of God?

My tears have become my bread, by night, by day,
as I hear it said all the day long:
"Where is your God?"

These things will I remember as I pour out my soul:
how I would lead the rejoicing crowd into the house of God,
amid cries of gladness and thanksgiving,
the throng wild with joy.

—Psalm 42

CONTENTS

LIST OF ILLUSTRATIONS

ACKNOWLEDGMENTS

It is a serious pleasure to thank the institutions and people who supported this project. The American Bar Foundation, its director Robert Nelson, and his predecessor Bryant Garth provide a scholarly paradise to all of us lucky enough to work there. I am also indebted to the National Endowment for the Humanities, the Friends of the Princeton University Library, the American Jewish Archives, and the American Philosophical Society for fellowships that underwrote parts of the research.

A veritable stable of students assisted with the project over the years. Megan Birk, Claire Boyle, Mike Foster, Steven Freund, David Harrington, Elisabeth Houseman, Akta Jantrania, Nona Richards, Lisa Simeone, Amy Sturtz, and Tiffanye Threadcraft handled myriad tasks in the field and on-site at the Bar Foundation. I am especially grateful to Betsy Mendelsohn, Susan Barsy, and Daniel Owings, whose dedication, imagination, and initiative measurably contributed to the maturation of my ideas and the maintenance of my sanity.

I spent many happy weeks at the Benson Ford Research Center in Dearborn, Michigan, and at the American Jewish Archives in Cincinnati, Ohio. I laud the expertise and efficiency of Linda Skolarus and John Bowen in Dearborn and Gary Zola, Kevin Proffitt, Lisa Frankel, Camille Servizzi, and Ruth Kreimer in Cincinnati. Linda's and Kevin's ongoing support enabled me to fill gaps without leaving my desk. I also acknowledge the archival help of Gunnar Berg, Lee Greenbaum, Julie Koven, and Fruma Mohrer at YIVO/The Center for Jewish History in New York; Susan Woodward at the New York branch of the American Jewish Historical Society; Susan Powers at the Clarke Historical Library, Central Michigan University; Jennifer Palmer at the Western History Center, University of Missouri–Kansas City; Holly Teasdle at Temple Beth-El, Bloomfield Hills, Michigan; Ben Primer and Dan Linke at Seeley Mudd Library, Princeton University; John Grabowski, Ann Sindelar, and Vicki Catozza at the Western Reserve Historical Society, Cleveland, Ohio; and the staff at the Library of Congress in Washington, D.C., as well as at the National Archives in College Park, Maryland; Chicago; and San Bruno, California.

At Northwestern University Law Library, Lynn Kincaid managed my obscure interlibrary-loan requests with equanimity, and Audrey Chapuis renewed books when I overtaxed the online system, which was often. Bill Benneman of Boalt Hall Law Library, University of California at Berkeley, found the 1911 *Berkeley Gazette* on microfilm for me. Max Wallace sent me his copies of Ernest Liebold's Federal Bureau of Investigation file and the John Bugas memo from the Ford Research Center. Ken Goldstein forwarded historical newspaper coverage of Aaron Sapiro's Canadian work. U.S. District Judge Avern Cohn of Detroit sent me thick envelopes filled with *Detroit Jewish Chronicle* and *Detroit Jewish Herald* photocopies and biographical material on Judge Fred Raymond. Randy Studt and Richard Levy translated the *Völkischer Beobachter*. Margot Canaday retrieved American Civil Liberties Union files from the Princeton Library, sparing me a trip late in the writing process. My aunt and late uncle, Sara and Richard Abowd, hosted me in Detroit, as did Sandra Van Burkleo and the late Edward Wise.

When I began this project, I had no idea how much it would become a biographical story—a trio of stories, to be precise—and that I would come to know members of the Sapiro family so intimately. I thank them for entrusting me with their memories, documents, and photographs. It was my honor to interview Stanley and Marian Sapiro, their daughter Linda Sapiro Moon, and Leland Sapiro. Sam Bubrick, Sylvia Lane, Gail Jacobs Nebenzahl, Jeannette Arndt Anderson, and Jerome and Mary Sapiro were all gracious and welcoming. It saddens me that Stanley and Jerome Sapiro did not live to see this book finished. Gary Milton Sapiro loaned me the papers of his grandfather, Milton Sapiro.

Descendants of the book's other subjects also cooperated with me. Patricia Gallagher Wooten, William Henry Gallagher's daughter-in-law, loaned me his abundant clippings files and his granddaughter Connie Bookmyer, his unpublished memoir. Before his death in 2004, Frank Untermyer, the grandson of Samuel Untermyer, granted me a long interview and access to his files.

The main arguments in this book have evolved substantially since I published my first research findings in 2004. I explored issues related to the origins of group-libel law, the civic status of American Jews in the early twentieth century, and Louis Marshall's role in the outcome of the libel litigation in my article "Insecure Equality: Louis Marshall, Henry Ford, and the Problem of Defamatory Antisemitism, 1920–1929" (*Journal of American History* 91, no. 3 [December 2004]: 877–905). Marianne Constable, Sarah Barringer Gordon, Bonnie Honig, Laura Kalman, Richard S. Levy, Charles McCurdy, David Montgomery, Laura

Beth Nielsen, Mae Ngai, Lucy Salyer, Harry Scheiber, Christopher Schmidt, Stephen Siegel, Joyce Sterling, and Winifred Fallers Sullivan either helped to shape that early formulation or supplied patience and good advice thereafter, or both. At the Bar Foundation, Lucinda Underwood plotted creative communications strategies and Allison Lynch provided capable assistance. I thank Jill Marsal for sending the book to Stanford University Press, for which Jonathan Sarna and Richard Levy were encouraging but exacting reviewers. At Stanford, Norris Pope, Sarah Newman, Emma Harper, and Emily Smith patiently shepherded the book through production; at Newgen, Jay Harward and Katherine Faydash expertly managed copyediting and page proofs. The book is so much better for the intervention of all these wonderful people. Karl Saur, Dave Farrer, Nancy Good, Barbara and William Wester, Sarah Mustillo, Christine Benner, Cadi and Jim Bien, Stephanie Bosma, Carol Brophy, and Peter and Jenny Hulen kept me company along the way.

This book would not be what it is were it not for my family. It has accompanied Helen, Margaret, Joseph, and Phillip through their childhoods. In their earlier years, they rewarded me at the end of each day by bursting into my study and demanding the computer for more diverting pursuits. As they grew, they braced my resolve to finish with smart suggestions for the book's title. Helen gets credit for "Henry Ford's War." I am overjoyed to share this with them and relieved that their adolescence still remains for us to spend together.

Keith Woeste, my husband, makes everything go in our lives. As always, he read and commented on every page of the manuscript multiple times, but that effort seems merely mortal compared to his performance over the twelve years we have lived in Indiana as I worked in Chicago. I do hope that his admirable ability to solo parent, which now greatly outpaces my own, furnishes one intangible reward for the stresses he has had to manage. Perhaps another will be the leisure in which to enjoy the sumptuous life of the mind that he so effortlessly cultivates and shares with me.

V.S.W.

November 2011

Chicago, Illinois, and West Lafayette, Indiana

INTRODUCTION

At the height of the roaring twenties, Aaron Sapiro, a California lawyer leading the burgeoning agricultural cooperation movement, sued Henry Ford and his newspaper, the *Dearborn Independent,* for libel. The *Independent* had published a series of articles accusing Sapiro of leading a Jewish conspiracy to subvert American agriculture. Tried in Detroit, the million-dollar marquee case culminated in a spectacular mistrial after a series of bizarre events derailed the legal process. At Ford's behest, another Jewish lawyer, the renowned civil rights leader Louis Marshall, prevented the case from returning to court by penning Ford's apology to the Jews.

Paradoxically, the apology narrowed the case's legal significance and relegated it to a footnote in Ford's life story. This book argues that what was most important about Ford's apology was not what it said. It is that Ford did not write it. When it was published in July 1927, no one but Ford, his closest advisers, and Marshall knew the truth. Consequently, reactions to Ford's apology focused on its putative author's obscure motives rather than its capacity for ending Ford's career as a purveyor of antisemitic literature or its implications for legal curbs on speech.[1]

Lawsuits are the common coin of conflict in U.S. history. Once in a while, an individual trial commands special attention because it raises issues and concerns that resonate over time and go directly to the heart of how Americans perceive and understand themselves.[2] *Sapiro v. Ford* is one of those cases. The defendant, of course, is an iconic figure in American history. At stake was nothing less than the fundamental equality of an entire group of citizens, certainly, and something else just as important, though more ephemeral: distinct visions of American social and economic development—and, for Marshall and Sapiro, ensuring that Ford's vision did not come to pass. That the two lawyers were at odds in that endeavor is the surprising story behind *Sapiro v. Ford.*

Henry Ford's War on Jews and the Legal Battle Against Hate Speech transforms our understanding of this famous lawsuit and Ford's apology by focusing

Jewish Exploitation of Farmers' Organization

Monopoly Traps Operate Under Guise of "Marketing Associations"

By ROBERT MORGAN

A glimpse at the beautiful Santa Clara Valley, where the most elaborate trial of the Sapiro Plan has been staged, with disastrous results to the prune and apricot growers. These California fruit-growers would like to cast off the Jewish millstone they have tied around their own necks, but they dare not.

I.1. "Jewish Exploitation of Farmers' Organizations." *Dearborn Independent*, April 12, 1924. The first article in the series of seventeen antisemitic articles attacking Aaron Sapiro that ran in Henry Ford's newspaper between April 1924 and May 1925 (University of Chicago Libraries).

on the intricate triangulated relationships that link the three chief characters. This book answers two critical questions: First, what was Henry Ford's vision for remaking American society during the 1920s? Second, how did Aaron Sapiro and Louis Marshall, two men who should have been allies in the fight against antisemitism but were not, almost fail to stop him?

During the late nineteenth and early twentieth centuries, Americans swam in an ocean of polite antisemitism. Whether black or white, Protestant or Catholic, most Americans regarded Jews as different, alien, and inferior. Still, antisemitism in America was muted compared to the more violent expressions of Jew hatred that were the norm in Europe. New World antisemitism was confined mostly to forms of speech and social discrimination: literary stereotypes; pernicious propaganda; explicitly biased advertisements; and beginning around the time of the Civil War, policies discriminating against Jews in hiring and employment. The most notorious example was General Ulysses Grant's General Order No. 11. In 1862, the order declared "Jews as a class" responsible for cotton speculation and smuggling and expelled them from the western war zone. President Lincoln revoked the order after Jews staged an outraged and effective protest, but the precedent stung.[3]

For the most part, de jure (by law) exclusions and discriminations against Jews were rare occurrences in post–Civil War America. Yet Jews suffered plenty of de facto discrimination, the kind that happens in everyday life by dint of custom or casual practice. Concealed under the right of freedom of association, the habit of turning Jews away from schools, clubs, and organizations became ingrained in American social life after the mid-1870s and grew more malicious after 1900. Ford's newspaper engulfed the nation in the logic of antisemitism, liberated it, pushed it beyond private social exchange into open air, and sought to institutionalize it in how Americans thought about their government and society.[4]

Much like the iconic Model T, the *Dearborn Independent* reflected Ford's personality and his vision for the country. He plucked the newspaper from obscurity and rebuilt it to serve as his direct and unfiltered voice to the people. He increased its readership from barely 1,200 to nearly 700,000 at its peak. The paper was sent unsolicited to schools, libraries, and universities across the country. Ford dealers were even required to fill monthly quotas for newspaper subscriptions along with their car sales.[5]

As the otherwise innocuous content of his newspaper portended, Ford envisioned a nostalgic American future. Although he had done as much to usher in an age of technology and consumerism as any other single person, he cherished the idea that Americans would be far better off living on small family farms; eschewing alcohol, cigarettes, and theater; and finding spiritual renewal in Protestant churches and the old-fashioned dances he personally enjoyed.[6] He imagined a nation of mechanization and mobilization, strangely juxtaposed with an idealized, remade rural society. Cars and tractors were supposed to make farming appealing, not induce people to desert their farms for dirty, overcrowded cities and the novel concentration of power they represented. For decades, historians have sought to explain Ford's antisemitic prejudice by rooting it in a narrow-minded populism. But his beliefs were subtler and more complex than that. Ford disliked Jews who he believed exercised disproportionate control over the institutions that were vital to the rural-mercantile economy he wanted to build.[7]

The three men at the center of this legal drama were not so different from one another. Each is an enduring American character. Each reflected important aspects of Progressive Era America; each fought to shape the country according to his vision of what he believed it should represent. Ford personified the rags-to-riches rise of entrepreneurial ingenuity, the triumph of industrial design and marketing, and the transformation of transportation. After him, there would be no going back. Louis Marshall and Aaron Sapiro lived Horatio Alger tales of their own, rising from humble, even destitute beginnings to distinguished careers and national prominence. But what they wanted to accomplish brought them into conflict with Ford—and with each other.

Marshall was the leading constitutional and immigration lawyer of his day and, as president of the American Jewish Committee, the most important secular leader of American Jews of the early twentieth century. Hailing from rural New York, he became a patrician New York City lawyer, the cornerstone of the bar and pillar of Jewish society. He wanted newcomers to become as fully American as he was. In his view, Ford's attacks on Jews endangered what Jews could become, what their future as Americans should be. For Marshall, antisemitism was more than a racial slur, not just a libel against an entire people. It was un-American, an anachronism that had no place in a nation governed by a constitution based on equality.[8]

After enduring a wretched childhood in a San Francisco orphanage, Aaron Sapiro turned to law as the vehicle for self-realization and for achieving social change. Molding a nascent body of law into a field of legal expertise all his

4 THE DEARBORN INDEPENDENT April 19, 1924

All Little Pals Together—To Save the American Farmer!

ALBERT D. LASKER,
Former head of Shipping Board.

AARON SAPIRO,
Organizer of American farmers.

HON. E. MEYER, Jr.,
Former head of War Finance Corporation.

(C) Harris & Ewing
HON. B. BARUCH,
Former head War Industries Board.

Jewish Exploitation of Farmers' Organizations

II. The Story of the Sapiro Boys

By ROBERT MORGAN

THE history of Jewish attempts to seize control of the agricultural and horticultural resources and production of America begins with the employment by the late Harris Weinstock, then head of the California State Market Commission, of a young Jewish attorney, named Aaron Sapiro, as counsel for and legal adviser to the commission. There is nothing to indicate that the commission and Mr. Weinstock could not have used the state's legal department for such business as they had to transact with the courts, but a glance at the names of employer and employe will furnish at least one of the reasons for the opportunity so opened to Mr. Sapiro.

About two years were required by the new legal adviser to grasp the plan by which the co-operative marketing associations of California, then as now under state control, could be "improved." As soon as this plan had become well formulated, Sapiro left the state commission and branched out as "organizing legal counsellor" for co-operative marketing organizations. Despite the statement of Herman Steen, panegyrist for Sapiro, that "nineteen out of twenty of the co-operative marketing organizations" were not functioning properly or profitably prior to the coming of this "counsellor," it is a fact that the farmers in these associations, though prices for their products were lower then than now, received more money, net, acre for acre and tree for tree, for their crops, than they received last year.

Nevertheless, Sapiro was able so to influence the farmers of California, particularly the growers of deciduous fruits, that within two years, he had extended his activities into a dozen states. *Today, he is legal adviser to sixty co-operative marketing associations, with a combined membership of more than 500,000 agriculturists, or approximately one-tenth of all those men who till the soil in the United States.* Back of these half-million owners of farms and orchards are at least two million women and children. These men and women and their sons and daughters are absolutely dependent on the advice, suggestion, direction and control of this attorney. He has had no experience in agriculture or horticulture in any form; he never has produced a dollar from the soil; he knows nothing of the problems which confront the farmer, save what he has read in books; he is not a producer of anything except ideas which require his personal employment by the American farmer. *Yet, seventeen states have altered their laws to conform to his plans of co-operative marketing,* and to enable farmers to fix prices for their crops at his command. *Forty-seven states contain associations whose members have pledged their crops to boards of directors obedient to Aaron Sapiro, and have pledged not one crop, but all the production of their lands for periods of five to seven years.*

Not a dollar can be paid by any purchaser to those American farmers unless the boards of directors of their associations—boards a majority of whose members are selected by Sapiro, or whose selection meets with his approval—permit it to be paid. These farmers must deliver the crops from their own lands, the production of their own supposedly independent and free American labor, when and where and to whom Sapiro directs, and accept for it the price his agents, or his representatives, or his boards of directors have fixed for it. The rapidity with which this young man—he is not yet forty—has worked, and the gullibility with which his propaganda and plans have been swallowed by more than half a million American men who, prior to his coming, had been able to manage their own businesses well enough to make a fair profit therefrom, is little less than the eighth wonder of the world.

Just how Sapiro attained to this eminence in co-operative marketing in so short a time is a story of too much detail to be told here, and is not of especial interest except to students of economic theories and students of the legal aspects of the new development. What is of value, and of the greatest value, to the five million or more farmers of America today, is the present activity of this leader of the greatest agrarian movement ever attempted.

Aaron Sapiro is at present the head of the legal firm of Sapiro, Levy, Hatfield and Hayes, with headquarters in the First National Bank Building in San Francisco, where a suite of twelve elaborately furnished rooms are maintained, and with branches at 1686 Equitable Building, New York, and in the Magnolia Building, in Dallas, Texas. The firm consists, besides Aaron Sapiro, of Milton D. Sapiro, his brother; David L. Levy, George J. Hatfield, Lawrence L. Levy, Boyd Oliver, E. L. Hayes, Frederick B. Wood, Robert Beale and E. T. Korn.

The elder Sapiro spends very little time at the firm's headquarters in San Francisco, on the average, not more than one month out of the year. So great is the business of establishing control and leadership of the co-operative marketing organizations throughout the country that he is on tour of the agricultural, fruit-growing and dairying sections of this country virtually all the time. During his absences, however, the business is well handled by Milton D. Sapiro, who keeps out of the spotlight so continuously thrown around his brother and the two Levys. Milton Sapiro keeps taut the cables with which Aaron has bound the farmers in the associations, and the Levys attend to the legal repairs necessary to prevent breakage in the cables.

Every dollar that comes into this firm from these associations comes out of the pockets of the American farmer, in payment for "services" which he does not need, and for "direction" of his associations which were better directed when the farmer did the directing himself.

The energies of Aaron Sapiro are now being devoted to the organization of the potato growers of this country into state associations, to be followed by a national association. Announcement is made at the Sapiro headquarters that by the time the 1924 potato crop is ready for the market, associations composed of at least seventy per cent of the potato producers of Maine, New Jersey, Virginia, Minnesota, Michigan, Wisconsin, North and South Dakota, Idaho, Colorado, Utah, Nevada and California, will be in operation. The central or national organization will direct the sales policies and sales prices, transportation, distribution, and flow of potatoes to market, as well as name the markets to which the tubers shall be shipped. This is the same plan on which the other Sapiro-controlled co-operative marketing associations are operated, and, to quote Milton Sapiro, "the central body will control the distribution so as to equalize prices and conditions everywhere as a protection for the farmer."

The facts show that the farmer is not protected by these associations to the extent that he receives any more net for his crop than he received before, but that, on the other hand, the charge to the consumer is increased. The economic condition created by the Sapiro plan of control of all the products of the American farm, however, deserves wider consideration later. Let us for the moment pass it by, and consider the other Jewish gentlemen who are concerned in the success of the exploitation of the farmer in the United States.

Bernard M. Baruch, known best, perhaps, for his connection with the Wilson administration, is one of these. So deeply is he concerned with the success or failure of the Sapiro plan, that he signs his name to the official foreword of a book called "Co-operative Marketing, the Golden Rule in Agriculture," by Herman Steen, managing editor of *The Prairie Farmer*. Though this foreword is very like the main text of the book in style and substance, the signature at the end of the foreword leads the reader to believe that Mr. Baruch is responsible for it. In this foreword appears the following appeal (and also warning, if read aright) to farmers to refrain from objecting when the high overhead, heavy salaries and other extravagances take their money:

"Mistakes will be made in co-operative marketing; they are made in all human affairs, and only experience can finally point the approximately perfect way. Here and there will be losses, due to mishaps which cannot be avoided or foreseen. When these arise, the members of the co-operatives should deal with them loyally, practically, and tolerantly; and, if they are led by the high type of business executive which the work demands, they will win through. For it is the man, more than the organization, who will win or lose for the co-operatives, and those farmers *who allow themselves to be agitated by the so-called high salaries paid for co-operative executives are fighting against their own interests.*"

Cotton planter, the steamboat operator and the singing Negro in the cotton fields, all pay tribute to the exploiters of the American farmer when the planter signs away his crop on a co-operative marketing association contract of the kind forced on him by the Sapiro plan.

I.2. "All Little Pals Together—To Save the American Farmer!" *Dearborn Independent*, April 19, 1924. This article linked Aaron Sapiro to prominent Jews and accused all of them of wielding nefarious influence over American public finance and agricultural policy (University of Chicago Libraries).

own, he led a movement to organize farmers into marketing cooperatives that improved their standard of living much as labor unions did for wageworkers. Sapiro built on the conservative legal model of the corporation, but the implications of his idea sounded radical: enabling farmers to come together into powerful collectives that could bargain for better prices for their crops. Sapiro preached the gospel of cooperation; for him, it was a secular religion. If farmers could support their families in the modern industrial economy, they could send their children to school and be productive citizens just like urban families. Unlike Ford, who prized rural over urban, Sapiro envisioned rural and urban as equal partners in modern America.

The conflict that brought these three visionaries to their unlikely encounter took place during what historians call the tribal twenties: a decade of racial and ethnic tension and conflict that followed World War I. John Higham coined the term in the 1950s to describe the rising tide of private social discrimination that spilled into the public realm after the Armistice. This pattern of discrimination affected minorities of all kinds, including women, non-Protestants, and ethnic and racial groups. Conflict bubbled up everywhere after the war; racial animus catalyzed the labor unrest and strikes that nearly paralyzed the nation in 1919. Emboldened by the experience and sacrifice of military service, minorities demanded equal treatment and equal access to jobs and homes. This impertinence met a severe backlash as reactionaries swiftly clamped down to restore economic order and reassert traditional social prerogatives.[9] It is no coincidence that Ford's antisemitic campaign and the rebirth of the Ku Klux Klan occurred within a few years of each other.

To their shock, American Jews were caught up in this swell of racial animosity. They believed that they had embraced American civic ideals, and they considered themselves distinct from nonwhite minorities; still, the dominant culture regarded them as the "white other." Although their color did not mark them as a subordinate class, the tribalism of the postwar era told them they were not full citizens. Pinned by this social construction of racial identity, Jews struggled to mount a public response that would not call into question their social status or civic equality. Elite Jewish American lawyers were, after all, men of their generation, not without prejudices and preconceptions about race. They believed that African Americans needed to have their constitutional rights defined and defended by law. But as white persons, they did not see themselves as similarly situated. Because they did not agree among themselves about the

Jewish Exploitation of Farmers' Organizations

III. Money for Everybody but the Farmer

By ROBERT MORGAN

IF THE impression has been left by preceding articles that Aaron Sapiro, or the Sapiro plan, is responsible for the co-operative marketing idea or its development, allow me at once to correct that idea. Mr. Sapiro did not originate nor develop co-operation. He simply has taken hold of an existing condition, the development of nearly a century, and is engaged in shaping it to his ends, and to the advantage of the bankers, attorneys, promoters and other exploiters of his kind, to the mouthpiece.

Mr. Sapiro in his addresses and in his "educational campaign" among the farmers uniformly tells the agriculturists of what "we" have done in California. Since he thus selects California as the scene of his greatest successes in the promotion of the Sapiro plan, and since it is a fact that more farmers, fruit-growers, poultry-raisers and vegetable-producers have been misled into following that plan in California than in any other state, let us turn to the record and see the results of the application of the plan there.

In the first place, neither Aaron Sapiro nor any of his crowd, have had or now have anything whatever to do with the few co-operative marketing associations which have been markedly successful in California or on the entire Pacific Coast. The California Fruit Growers' Exchange, which handled 27,158 cars of the 43,630 cars of citrus fruits which the co-operatives marketed in 1923, has been in operation for thirty years. Mr. Sapiro never has had the slightest connection with it and has none now. This exchange has 213 local associations (not branches) and marketed $48,647,800 worth of citrus fruits last year.

The California Walnut Growers' Association, which markets about 81.5 per cent of the walnut crop of California, valued at more than $9,000,000 a year, has never had any connection in any way with Mr. Sapiro or his associates, and is operated on a plan and organization altogether different from that offered by the "leader of American agriculturists."

The Sun-Maid Raisin Growers' Association, of Fresno, which has had troubles enough of its own without borrowing any from Sapiro sources, is referred to almost constantly by the promoters of the Sapiro plan as an example of the success of the American farmer, as "an outstanding example of the success of our co-operatives in California." Yet neither Mr. Sapiro nor any of his associates has ever had the slightest connection with the Sun-Maid Association, any of its district or local organizations, or any of its members.

The California Peach and Fig Growers' Association, with headquarters at Fresno, is another which is frequently referred to by the promoters of the Sapiro plan as an example of the success of that plan. The truth of the matter is that Mr. Sapiro has not now and never has had any connection of any kind with this association.

Going farther north, I find that the Tillamook County Creamery Association—one of the most successful of all dairy co-operatives ever organized—was formed when Sapiro was a small boy, and has been functioning without his aid ever since.

The Apple Growers' Association of the Hood River Valley, Oregon, sometimes pointed out by Sapiro's agents as another shining example of the success of their plan, was organized nearly twelve years ago, with A.

W. Stone as organizer and general manager. Mr. Stone is still general manager and has been able to operate the association successfully without a word from the Sapiros or anyone connected with them.

The Fraser Valley Dairies, Limited, of Vancouver, British Columbia, reports that, while successful, it can attribute none of its success to Mr. Sapiro or his organization, since his advice never was asked nor his plan used in any way in any connection with this notably successful co-operative organization.

So this list of those associations in which Sapiro never has had a word to say, but to whose success he "points with pride," could be continued indefinitely without going any farther outside the state of California.

One thing that Mr. Sapiro, Mr. Rubinow and others neglect to mention is that the plan of organization, operation and control of virtually all the successful associations is fundamentally different from the Sapiro plan. Co-operative associations organized or reorganized under the Sapiro plan in California, and in other Pacific Coast states as well, are most conspicuous for the disasters which have overtaken them. As we read, we shall see that virtually all these disasters are due to two factors:

First, simple, yet fundamental errors in the Sapiro plan itself.

Second, bad management, sometimes because of ignorance of the industry, sometimes because of dishonesty on the part of the managers.

The majority of the managers are Gentiles, and all the managers must meet with the approval of Mr. Sapiro, or they do not remain as managers. There is nothing to show that Mr. Sapiro connives when these managers either in their ignorance or their dishonesty,

but as a picker of managers, he has little success with regard to the prosperity or the safety of the farmer.

One of the first of the Sapiro plan fiascos was the California Tomato Growers' Association. Sapiro, with the assistance of Mark Grimes, organized this association some six years ago. Both Sapiro and Grimes received their fees for their services, but the unfortunate tomato growers were left holding the sack for approximately $48,000 at the end of the first year. The association never has been revived.

The Fruit Growers of California, a co-operative green-fruit marketing association, with R. P. Van Orden, a close friend of Sapiro's, as president, has found itself under the necessity of immediate reorganization, and the establishment of a new marketing agreement, according to Van Orden's announcement, made at San Jose, California, on January 28, 1924. The Fruit Growers of California was built on the Sapiro plan fully and completely, and it is the latest of the Sapiro-plan associations to go the way the majority of them have gone—into reorganization either to avert or to remedy disaster.

But between the unfortunate tomato growers and their loss of $48,000, including Mr. Sapiro's fees, and the latest movement of the Fruit Growers of California, lies a long list of wreckage.

In Oregon, no more than three years ago, there was a Dairymen's League which had been working to the satisfaction of its members for some time. They listened to the call of the new era in co-operative marketing, followed the Sapiro-will-o-the-wisp, and, two years ago, were sunk without trace, with heavy individual loss to the members.

Farther north, in Okanagan, British Columbia, there was in existence, until two years ago, the Okanagan United Growers, Ltd., a successful co-operative marketing association, at least its members never had lost any money, and believed they were making more than they would trying to sell individually. Here Sapiro tried his usual scheme of destroying existing methods to make way for his own. The Okanagan growers were lured into the Sapiro plan, their existing organization and its methods were discarded, and the old association forced into the new association, organized on the Sapiro plan and making ready, also, to force to the wall those existing associations near whose members he can obtain control, as he did at Okanagan.

Apparently the Colorado Potato Growers' Exchange has kissed the Jewish fly in the American amber, for on the Pacific Coast, at the end of January, the newspapers gave space to a dispatch that "Aaron Sapiro, the

Every stalk of celery shown in this corner of a large field pays direct tribute to Jewish domination of the co-operative marketing system in this section of the United States.

Every half a year shows drying in the California sun belongs in part to the ring which controls the fixed co-operative marketing associations of the deciduous fruit districts of that state.

Every sack of grain produced in the United States will help to swell the fortunes of those now seeking control and direction of the wheat industry of this country, when the Sapiro plan becomes the method of marketing our grain. Here are barge loads of grain coming down the Sacramento River for shipment to Europe.

danger Ford posed to Jews in the 1920s, it is hardly surprising that historians disagree about the extent to which his newspaper threatened Jews' civic status.[10]

The controversy over Ford's newspaper can be understood, in part, as a result of the uncertainty surrounding speech rights at the time of the dispute. During the war, a series of federal laws suppressed criticism of the government and interference with the war effort. Thousands of people were indicted and hundreds convicted under these laws, and during the Red Scare of 1919 the government unleashed its repressive powers in frightening ways. When cases challenging these statutes reached the U.S. Supreme Court, the justices interpreted civil liberties and free-speech rights cautiously. In a series of decisions, the court ruled that the government could not restrict speech in advance of publication, but it could penalize people if what they said or published posed harm to the public welfare. Dissents by Justices Holmes and Brandeis in *Abrams v. United States* (1919) defended "free trade in ideas" and marked the start of a new awareness of the value of unregulated speech in an industrial democratic society.[11]

It was, however, a mere beginning. Civil libertarians remained in the minority on the Court and in legislatures. Censorship of books, movies, and newspapers continued apace during the 1920s. Sedition laws, which criminalized speech or acts that tended to incite insurrection, and criminal libel statutes, which permitted authorities to prosecute purveyors of ideas that had the potential to cause public disturbances or offend public morals, continued to slow traffic in the free flow of ideas. The American Civil Liberties Union, formed in 1917 to fight laws restricting First Amendment rights, was nearly alone in championing freedom for unpopular or offensive ideas. Yet when Ford's rights as a publisher came under attack from city authorities in 1921, other newspapers threw him their support, not because they agreed with what he published, but because they believed in the principle he was defending (see Chapter 3).

In the judicial midwifery that attended the birth of modern free speech, there was hardly any comment on the subject of what we now call hate speech— speech that attacks groups of people on the basis of their race, creed, or religion. The only statutory development of the era emerged, interestingly, from social discrimination against Jews. In 1913, New York enacted a group libel law, drafted by Louis Marshall, which criminalized printed or published attacks on groups identified by race, religion, or national origin. Six other states had adopted versions of the law by the mid-1920s, but the laws went largely untested in the courts for the following thirty years.[12] In the litigation over free-speech rights that confronted the Supreme Court during the 1920s and 1930s, the justices remained focused on individual, not group, rights. Although it would be decades before the Court arrived at the more absolutist reading of the First Amendment that characterized its postwar speech jurisprudence, the Court was unwilling to carve out an exception before the war that would permit states to regulate speech that stigmatized groups of people on the basis of race or religion.[13]

This book expands the story of the First Amendment's historical development by revealing divisions in the civil liberties community over how to respond to speech that attacked race and religion. Jewish lawyers and activists who were best positioned to react to Ford's newspaper were handicapped not only by the lack of relevant statutes but also by philosophical and political differences among themselves. As a result, when the Ford case finally presented itself, it was staged by a relative outsider—Sapiro—as a conventional individual libel suit rather than a group libel case.[14] The national press, having covered every word Ford uttered on his obsession with Jews since 1915, elided the technical legal distinction between individual and group libel and proclaimed the case a fight between Henry Ford and "the Jews." That characterization amplified the consequences of Sapiro's lawsuit for Jews generally and made Louis Marshall desperate to contain its effects on Jewish Americans' civic status.

This book is about how law shaped events and choices over the course of the litigation. It is not a story about the development of legal doctrine; nor does it rechronicle the lawsuit from Ford's perspective, as his many biographers have already done. Rather, it relates how law provided a common point of reference for all sides in the dispute, even if they sometimes disregarded it. The *Sapiro v. Ford* case became one of the many trials of the century of the 1920s; the promise that Ford would appear on the witness stand kept the press fixated on each day's developments. After the suit was settled out of court, it dropped off the press's radar, but its resolution imposed a continuing duty on Ford to restrain the republication of his antisemitic pamphlet, *The International Jew,* in the United States and abroad.

The measure of Ford's sincerity in apologizing—the true test of Marshall's strategy in handling the case as he did, taking it out of the realm of law and putting it under the dominion of his personal authority—is whether Ford followed through on that duty. In managing the case as a civil rights activist, Marshall unwittingly ensured that his ultimate goal—withdrawing hateful speech from the marketplace of ideas—would not be attained. The literature in the field of American Jewish history, perhaps understandably, soft pedals the divisions within Jewish circles throughout the duration of the Ford matter. Scholars defend Ford's apology as a great victory and a historic repudiation of antisemitism. This book questions those interpretations. On the basis of new archival findings, we can ask what Marshall sought to gain by acting as he did and, more critically, whether he got what he wanted. Moreover, a closer look at the contemporary reaction shows that most Jewish newspapers received Ford's statement skeptically, accepting it gracefully at Marshall's behest to end the ugly mess or, more likely, grudgingly despite Marshall's entreaties because they had no alternative. In the meantime, we learn that Ford never lost control over the legal process, that his subordinates undermined Marshall as he attempted to enforce the apology in 1927 and 1928, and that Marshall did not live to ensure that Ford made good on his promises. Without the authority of law to constrain him, Ford was free to disregard his statement and the promises he made once he and Marshall realized that European publishers who wanted to reproduce Ford's book had law on their side.

This book tells the story of Ford's newspaper, Sapiro's lawsuit, and Marshall's diversion of its outcome. In Part 1, five chapters lay out the context in which Ford waged his war on Jews and establish the triangulated dynamic between Ford, Marshall, and Sapiro. Ford and Marshall's tangle over the *Independent* in 1920, Sapiro and Ford's clash over the second antisemitic series in 1924, and the divisions among Jewish leaders before the trial supply the keys to what follows. Part 2 proceeds chronologically. It gives a narrative account of the trial in Detroit, its unexpected outcome, and its consequences for Jewish civil rights activism on the eve of the 1930s.

By publishing and speaking about his beliefs about Jews, Ford tapped into the strong strain of American nativism and xenophobia that, as Louis Marshall knew, was driving national policy on civil rights, citizenship, and immigration. Recent work in the field portrays Ford as an extremist who had many fans but did not change minds. What this literature fails to capture are the ties between Ford and the prominent men who assumed responsibility for the future of American Jews. The fight of Jewish Americans for civil rights in the 1920s was by no means carefully coordinated or united around a univocal strategy. Moreover, their political power was confined mostly to cities, where they could galvanize protest against the *Independent*. It was among rural conservatives where Ford remained iconic, where his newspaper found its widest readership, and where bigotry against Jews remained robust during the tribal twenties. The fight between Ford and the Jews was many things, but fundamentally it reflected the pervasive split between rural and urban America that has never ceased to characterize the nation's landscape and its enduring social and political divide.

PART I

Parties and Players

MR. FORD SURVEYS THE WRECKAGE

In the early evening hours of Sunday, March 27, 1927, Henry Ford felt restless. Finding nothing to hold his attention in the vast spaces of Fair Lane, his Dearborn residence, he climbed behind the wheel of his favorite custom-built Ford coupe and set out for his office. His destination was the Ford Motor Company's River Rouge headquarters, a sprawling complex one and a quarter miles east of his mansion, just over the Detroit city line. Although Ford had not yet made his plans public, he was working on designs for a new car to replace his beloved—and much maligned—Model T. After spending an hour hunched over blueprints, he decided to return home. By then, it was just after 8:30 p.m. The sun had long since set, and the only illumination was provided by car headlamps reflecting the "fine drizzle" that obscured visibility and coated the streets.[1]

The conditions did not deter Ford. He was just four months shy of his sixty-fourth birthday and his wife "was always fearful of a holdup or kidnapping," but Ford insisted on chauffeuring himself around town. His car was equipped with a special "gear-shift transmission" (in today's parlance, a manual transmission), "extra gears," and unbreakable glass. Unlike cars sold to the general public, Ford's personal machine could achieve a zippy maximum speed of seventy-five miles per hour. It was a car built for a racer, an expert driver, and a control freak. Ford had once been all three, but in truth, now only the last designation applied with any degree of accuracy. His "custom of going about alone at all hours has caused concern to his family and friends," the *Washington Post* noted, but according to company officials, "'no amount of counsel has availed to change it.'"

Ford's route home took him west on Michigan Avenue, also marked State Route 12, a well-traveled road linking Detroit to Dearborn. He approached a bridge spanning the winding River Rouge, which kept him company on his journey from the Ford plant to Fair Lane. When he got to the bridge, he was not far from home. Just as he crossed the river, his car was struck from behind and forced from the road. The Ford coupe spun down a fifteen-foot embankment, narrowly passed between two trees, and was saved from entering "the

River Rouge and its 20 feet of swirling water" only by a happy intersection with a third tree. Ejected from his auto, Ford lay on the ground for an undetermined time, concussed and unconscious. On regaining his senses, he walked, "bleeding and half-dazed," the two hundred yards that remained between him and the gate of Fair Lane. The gatekeeper immediately telephoned Mrs. Ford, who "ran down the graveled path" to meet her husband. "She and the gatekeeper supported Mr. Ford while he walked 200 feet to his home."

Once back at the mansion, Clara Ford assisted her husband into bed and then rang their family doctor. Dr. Roy D. McClure, chief surgeon at Dearborn's Henry Ford Hospital, immediately rushed to Ford's bedroom and attended him there. In addition to his concussion, Ford suffered cuts to his face and contusions to his ribs and back. No one was told about his accident and injuries, apart from the family and a few trusted advisers. The next day, only the federal judge trying the famous case of *Sapiro v. Ford* in Detroit was informed. Police reports in Detroit and Dearborn were "suppressed." Two nights after the accident, Ford's condition worsened, and Dr. McClure quietly admitted him to Henry Ford Hospital, where he spent the next three days with Clara; their son, Edsel; and Edsel's wife and children at his bedside. The story was kept from the public for another day, although Ford was about to be called to the witness stand to face hostile questioning from his opponent's lawyer. Dreading that prospect, Ford "gave explicit instructions to all his associates that not one word should be given to the public," lest people "believe the accident had some connection with the million-dollar Ford-Sapiro libel suit."[2]

That connection was exactly what Ford hoped the public would discern, as news of his mishap emerged through his skillful management of the press. On his first full day in the hospital, Wednesday, March 30, Detroit reporters began asking pointed questions about his whereabouts. Word of his hospitalization "leaked out" that morning, and the press pursued the leak with "persistent inquiry." The Ford family and the Ford Motor Company organization "at first denied that anything had happened to the manufacturer." Then, in the early afternoon, William Cameron, editor of Ford's newspaper, the *Dearborn Independent*—the subject of the lawsuit in which Ford was embroiled—issued a statement. Forced to admit (or given the go-ahead to acknowledge) that Ford was involved in a mishap with his car, Cameron was quick to characterize it as a mere accident and to stress that "'at present Mr. Ford is resting easily and no complications are expected.'" Cameron hastened to add that Ford was convinced that no one intended him harm: "'Mr. Ford strongly deprecates the suggestion that the accident was the result of intent on any one's part.'" No less well-placed a source than Harry H. Bennett, Ford's redoubtable, reliable bodyguard and chief of the Ford "secret service," also contributed an "authentic statement" that no intent to harm or kill was suspected. Bennett "was satisfied that Ford's light car was sideswiped by a hit-and-run motorist driving with one arm about a girl or slightly intoxicated."

The story hit the national press the next day. The suggestion that someone had intended to harm Ford dominated the front-page headlines of all the national newspapers. "Mystery in Ford Death Plot," roared the *Detroit Times.* "Ford Hurt in Death Plot," proclaimed the *Chicago Tribune.* Even the somber *New York Times* piled on: "Plot to Kill Ford Suspected." The next day's papers pushed this theory even more baldly, even as it was announced that Ford was sufficiently recovered to return to his home: "Henry Ford is convinced a deliberate attempt was made to kill him when two unidentified men in a Studebaker touring car forced Ford's coupe down a steep embankment near Dearborn Sunday night."

Indeed, by April 1, five days after the accident, Ford—through Bennett—was feeding the press an elaborate, embellished account of the accident that planted the seeds of an assassination plot at the gate of Ford's home. "When Mr. Ford came out of his home on Sunday night," an official statement declared, "he saw a couple of men in a Studebaker car." The men followed Ford to his office, tailed him as he returned home, and rear-ended his vehicle as he crossed the Michigan Avenue bridge. Although the roads were dark, visibility was poor, and Model Ts came equipped with relatively small rearview mirrors, Ford was certain not only that the Studebaker had purposefully forced him from the road but also that the same men had followed him all the way from the Ford Motor Company's River Rouge headquarters. On April 1, Ford was quoted as saying that he believed that the incident was "a deliberate attempt to kill him." The official line on the accident changed considerably in just one day.[3]

The Ford publicity machine was not foolproof, however. Two young men reported to the police that they had witnessed Ford's car go off the road but had not seen a Studebaker or any other car involved in the mishap. The *Detroit Times* identified the witnesses as Ernest Wilhelmi, twenty years old, and Carl Machivitz, nineteen years old, the driver and passenger on the road behind Ford the night of the accident. Injecting "an element of mystery" into the episode, they "contradicted the motor magnate's version and insisted no other car struck Ford's." They said that Ford's car simply turned abruptly off the end of the bridge, went down the embankment, and landed at the tree. Then, they reported, two men emerged from Ford's car, not one. They observed as "the car was being worked forward and backward. Someone must have been inside shifting the gears, they reasoned." Fearing "a hold-up situation," they left the scene and reported the accident to the police, who interviewed them and inspected their car. What they found, aside from one missing hubcap, was an intact automobile. Machivitz and Wilhelmi were quickly cleared of all official suspicion and released. For Bennett, they created a dilemma: would the public believe Henry Ford or these two kids?

Not everyone in the press was buying Ford's story, and not just because of the credibility of the young witnesses. Some newspapers sent reporters to walk the accident site. What they found led them to contradict the official rendition coming out of Dearborn: "That Mr. Ford's plight had been exaggerated was indicated by a close inspection of the scene," the *Washington Post* observed. "His car stopped fully 60 feet from the bank of the River Rouge and he could not have been in danger of being drowned unless he had lost control of it and headed back in the direction opposite to that in which he was driving." Even more damaging, according to the *Post*, was the fact that had Ford's car failed to hit the tree that stopped its momentum, its next stop would not have been the river. "Had Mr. Ford's machine missed the elm tree he would have had before him the wide, level stretch to the Michigan Central embankment in which to recover control of his car."

Bennett swiftly took charge of a private investigation of the accident, using the considerable resources of the Ford Motor Company. First, he led a citywide search for the Studebaker: "About 150 Ford secret police, under Harry H. Bennett, chief of the Ford secret service department, are making a checkup of all Studebaker cars answering the description of the one seen by Ford." Bennett focused on places that supported the notion of a plot against his employer: "I have looked through several garages but have been unable to find any car corresponding to the one in the mishap. We have gone through the underworld of Detroit, but have obtained no clues." No one seemed to question the spectacle of Ford employees preempting the job of the Dearborn and Detroit city police: "[The Ford detectives] are engaged in making a car-to-car canvass, quietly and without the assistance of public police." The *Detroit Times* even reported that "police know the auto license number of the Studebaker," a "fact" one might assume Bennett planted, because the paper did not publish the license number, thus inhibiting public participation in the search.[4]

Second, Bennett quickly reestablished his boss's control over the public narrative of the accident. This was company tradition. Ford had always carefully controlled what information his company released to the press about his business; he managed the public relations of his accident just as carefully. The press admiringly noted how well that discipline was maintained after the accident: "It has been a rule of long standing that no one in the Ford organization spoke for publication, and even under the stress of the unforeseen condition this has been adhered to." Bennett quickly found a way to explain away what the witnesses had seen. The men working on Ford's car after it landed down the embankment were not Ford and a passenger, Bennett revealed, but "William J. Cameron, editor of Ford's *Dearborn Independent*, and Ray Dahlinger, manager of the Ford farm, who came to the scene afterward." The witnesses, Bennett commented, "being young and emotional, were rather excited," and their stories yielded so many inconsistencies that he was convinced "that they can be of little service in the hunt for the men in the [Studebaker] car." On Sunday, April 3, Bennett announced that he had found the car, identified the perpetrators—whom he did not name—and wrapped up his search. Mr. Ford, the newspapers were informed, preferred not to pursue legal action, and the local prosecutor announced that he would drop the matter. Acting as police, prosecutor, judge, and jury, Bennett assured authorities he "'was convinced it was just an accident,'" whereas "others high in the Ford organization conveyed the information that the convalescent billionaire still insists that he was the intended victim of assassins."[5]

The contradictory messages about whether it was an accident or assassination attempt kept attention focused on Ford's personal well-being and security. Talk of when he would be able to appear in court was met with statements emphasizing Ford's valor and dignity: "Issuance of medical bulletins on Mr. Ford's condition has ceased by his own order. The idea of being put forth to the world as a patient confined to a sick room is said to be strongly distasteful to him." By the following Monday, eight days after the accident, the *Detroit Times* was reporting that Ford was "indignant over stories that his reported injuries are a ruse to escape testifying" and was "willing to go to court splinted and bandaged if called." That resolve lasted the better part of a week, until it became likely that Ford would, in fact, be summoned to the stand by mid-April. Then, head-lines proclaimed that Ford had taken another bad turn and would be unable to appear for a long time: "'Mr. Ford is a very sick man,' said one of the auto king's closest friends. . . . 'Certainly he will not be able to testify in the trial for another month unless he is carried in on a stretcher.'"[6]

The sensational episode—no matter how dubious its truth-value—played to Ford's advantage. While he kept to his Fair Lane sickbed, the trial of *Sapiro v. Ford* proceeded in Detroit's federal court with a seemingly endless cross-examination of the plaintiff. Whether real or staged, the accident diverted everyone's attention from what was going on in court. It also gave Ford exactly what he wanted: an opportunity to survey the wreckage, not of his car but of the libel lawsuit he was desperate to escape. Now he would decide, again with Bennett's help, how to administer the final blow, how to end an engagement over which he had inexplicably lost control to an enemy he once denounced as the scourge of American civilization.

1 FORD'S MEGAPHONE

If Henry Ford's mind is an oyster, I failed utterly to open it.

—*New Republic* reporter, 1923[1]

Henry Ford, the man who had everything, wanted to own a newspaper. In late 1918, as the nation celebrated the end of the Great War, Ford felt besieged. His once-impervious public image took a beating during the conflict. He had not yet recovered from the embarrassment of his failed peace mission to Europe in 1915, he had just narrowly lost a contentious race for a U.S. Senate seat in his own state, and he still faced two prolonged court battles. One was his libel suit against the *Chicago Tribune*, which had called him an "ignorant idealist" and an "anarchist" for opposing U.S. military preparedness on the Mexican border in 1916; the other was a messy battle with minority shareholders of the Ford Motor Company, led by the Dodge Brothers, who were suing to force Ford to pay stock dividends.[2]

The fallout from these missteps and failed initiatives, not to mention the public relations debacle of keeping his son Edsel out of military service, was bruising. Ford blamed the national press, which was, he thought, "owned body and soul by bankers." For years, Ford made the press a useful, effective conduit for promoting his car, his company, and his down-home public image, but in the wake of his wartime blunders, he no longer viewed it as friendly: "'The capitalistic newspapers began a campaign against me. They misquoted me, distorted what I said, made up lies about me.'" What he wanted was access to the hearts and minds of ordinary Americans without having to pass through the biased filter of the mainstream press. He intended to make the paper his voice in the homes of his customers, and he planned to use the paper to do more than just market Model Ts. According to his most recent biographer, Steven Watts, Ford decided to buy the paper during his pacifism campaign, "when he became convinced that a hostile press was controlled by banks and other powerful financial interests."[3] What he sought, in effect, was a paper and print version of a megaphone: an instrument that would amplify—but not alter—what he wanted to say.

It was a common practice for American industrial magnates to start or acquire newspapers. Having a media outlet at one's disposal made for a useful appurtenance to the business, whether it was steel or lumber or cars. As down-home and folksy as Ford portrayed himself to be in the public eye, he was also as savvy a consumer and user of modern media as any entrepreneur of his day. To promote his cars, he courted celebrity for himself, and he became adept at shaping his public image while managing the inquiries of a skeptical—or critical—press corps: "'I am very much interested in the future, not only of my own country, but of the whole world,' said Mr. Ford [in 1918], 'and I have definite ideas and ideals that I believe are practical for the good of all. I intend giving them to the public without having them garbled, distorted, and misrepresented.'"[4]

When Ford entered the newspaper business, he started at the bottom and rebuilt, by buying his small, failing hometown newspaper. In 1918 the *Dearborn Independent* was a sleepy suburban weekly, "a typical small-town publication which had been in business since the turn of the century" but was barely hanging on to one thousand subscribers. Intent on building a "national platform"

1.1. Henry Ford with his first car, Detroit, ca. 1890s (© Corbis).

that could directly reach thousands of ordinary Americans, Ford paid $1,000 for the *Independent*—a steal. The *Independent* suited his purposes. "'We intend getting out a paper that will be of interest to the whole family,'" he announced. "'I believe in small beginnings, and for that reason we are taking the small home paper and building on that.'"[5]

The press greeted Ford's incursion onto its territory with a mixture of disdain, sarcasm, and respectful praise. "[A]s a newspaperman Ford is a great manufacturer of flivvers," a Connecticut editorialist commented dismissively. The *Detroit Times* granted the local hero wider latitude: "If he does as much good with his journal of civilization as he has with his factories, bank, school, farm, and hospital, the world will be better for his 'hunch' that he ought to have a newspaper."[6]

. . .

The culmination of several years' planning and effort, Ford's purchase of the *Independent* and the press on which to print it was the fruit of a necessary collaboration. Ford rarely undertook any major initiative by himself; rather, he relied on top aides to plumb his desires and execute his instructions. Ford's foray into newspaper publishing was no different. It began with a friendship he struck up with a Detroit reporter around 1914 and built into an enterprise that eventually drew in the most trusted members of his staff.

Edwin G. Pipp was a writer and editor for the *Detroit News* when he met Henry Ford. Just a few years Ford's junior, Pipp sprang from the same Michigan roots. His birthplace, Brighton, lies only about forty miles northwest of Dearborn. But unlike Ford, Pipp saw a bit more of the world in his early career, gaining experience as a reporter in Kansas City before returning to Detroit and covering local politics for the *News*. Possessing a "flair for going behind the scenes," he unearthed corruption in the city's Public Works Department and the Detroit United Railway. In sixteen years with the *News*, Pipp served as a foreign correspondent and managing editor before ascending to editor in chief, where his professional visibility and philanthropic accomplishments brought him to Ford's attention. While at the *News*, he began "serv[ing] as the manufacturer's informal public relations counselor during much of the period between 1915 and 1918."[7]

The two forged a partnership on shared philanthropic interests. During the war, Ford felt drawn to Pipp and supported his charitable work. Ford was struck by Pipp's thoughtfulness and intellectualism. Pipp saw Ford as an honest, well-intentioned businessman who dreamed of changing the larger world around him and wanted to help him reach that goal. It could have been only the highest flattery when Ford "made a confidant of [him]," granting Pipp exclusives on the company or on Ford himself. "If Henry Ford had something to talk about that he thought was a good story, he would send for Pipp first," a longtime employee remarked. One such scoop was the announcement of the $5-per-day wage. When that wage offer flooded Detroit with more people than Ford could possibly employ, Pipp reported on the suffering of idle workers and their families and called on the public to help. Ford immediately sent word: "[I] will put $50,000 at your disposal if you will look after caring for those people." "It won't take that much," Pipp replied. During the winter of 1914, Pipp and his staff organized assistance "for 497 families and many single men," and they spent less than 10 percent of Ford's budget.[8]

After their joint relief project, Pipp "saw more of Ford than [he] had seen before and admired him more." Even more significant, "[i]t was not long after that that Ford commenced talking to [him] about coming with his organization and starting a paper." In 1916, Ford and Pipp "confidentially discussed two projects, the purchase of a weaker paper . . . or the founding of a new daily." Nothing came of that venture at the time. After a spat with higher-ups limited Pipp's authority at the *News*, he left Detroit for Washington, D.C., where he spent the rest of the war. Ford was occupied with managing his company's war effort and his battles with the Dodge brothers and the *Chicago Tribune*.[9]

Pipp returned to Detroit at war's end, lured home by his friendship with Ford and by Ford's reignited interest in publishing a newspaper. Just after the peace announcement and Ford's loss in the 1918 Michigan Senate race, "a funny thing happened," William Richards recounted. "An old chap came to [Ford's] office and wanted to sell a Dearborn newspaper." After years of fruitless searching, the *Independent* practically dropped into Ford's lap. Pipp accepted the job of *Independent* editor on the understanding that "it was to be a paper to bring about a better feeling among the races and nations of the earth . . . and I, as its first editor, set about to make it such a paper."[10]

Ford quickly pulled together a crew of newspaper veterans who, under Pipp's supervision, would be responsible for putting the *Independent* before Ford's audience each week. The most significant hire of all, William J. Cameron, was a *News* reporter who came to the *Independent* with Pipp in late 1918. In sixteen years at the *News*, Cameron had "established himself . . . as a facile writer, a columnist of capacity and something of a scholar. His colleagues had nicknamed him the 'walking dictionary.'" The Canadian-born, forty-year-old Cameron was a gifted writer with a tender heart and a tendency to drink. Largely self-taught, Cameron possessed an "evangelical temperament which enabled him to infuse editorials, sermons, radio talks, and brief essays with an inspirational quality."

1.2. William Cameron (from the Collections of The Henry Ford, 90.1.1940.12/ THF101586).

The former "preacher" belonged to "one of the most curious sects on earth, the British Israelites, who believed themselves descendants of the Lost Tribes, and based an esoteric interpretation of history and eternity on data derived from the Great Pyramid." The British Israelites believed "that after Moses, the Israelites were divided into two groups—'Israel and Judah.' The group of Israel (the Anglo-Saxon race) is blessed. The group of Judah (the Jewish people) is damned.'" He believed in a millennialism that dovetailed with Ford's austere, though generally unchurched, religious conservatism. Upon joining the *Independent*, Cameron jumped to the top of the staff, reporting directly to Pipp.[11]

What Pipp found so appealing about Cameron's personality and intellect soon drew their boss's attention. Ford developed the habit of dropping by Cameron's office unannounced. The two established a rapport that went well beyond the intimacy Ford extended to almost all his other employees. Under extraordinary pressure during the *Tribune* lawsuit to explain his public statements, Ford turned to Cameron for what would today be called media training. Cameron astutely recognized the problem:

When I first went out [to work for Ford], the complaint was that Mr. Ford had been misquoted in the papers. That's when they threw the interviewing over to me; that is, I was to be present at the interviews and I found that he had not been misquoted. He had been precisely quoted without understanding what he meant. He spoke in telegrams and epigrams, and they had to be translated. When he would say a thing to a reporter, my major function was to have him explain it, to make it clear.

Soon, it was Cameron who performed the translating and explaining after Ford issued opaque public statements. By then already in his fifties, Ford needed his staff to divine what he meant and communicate that meaning to others for him. Anyone attempting to interview him outside Cameron's presence came away with little material of publishable quality; a reporter for the *Toronto Star* had to phrase a request for a follow-up in diplomatic terms: "I am still groping around in a haze in most of the things we talked about and I should like very much to talk to you again, for my own education if for nothing else." Most of the time, Cameron's abilities spared Ford such impositions, as David L. Lewis has described: "Cameron . . . acquired the ability virtually to read the manufacturer's mind. Often he broke into Ford's conversation with, 'What Mr. Ford means is—' and then proceeded to expound on Ford's views. The manufacturer, as he listened to the flawless presentation of his ideas, would nod pleasantly.

Never, so far as his associates knew, did Ford repudiate his aide's comments." Cameron so completely earned Ford's trust that Ford asked him to ghostwrite the *Independent*'s central feature: a column titled "Mr. Ford's Page" that discussed the day's major issues.[12]

The *Independent*'s business manager, like most of the paper's other staffers and writers, came to work for Henry Ford through a connection to Pipp. Fred Black, a native of Michigan and a college graduate, was working in regional paper sales in Detroit during the war when he befriended Pipp's son Gaylord. One day in 1916, the elder Pipp invited the twenty-five-year-old Black to lunch and explained that he was working secretly to acquire a newspaper and printing press for Ford. "[Pipp] said Mr. Ford did not want it known that he was interested, because it would start a lot of rumors," Black recalled. The conversation led Black to believe that he could sell paper to Ford once the sale went through. Instead, Pipp asked Black to conduct a quiet but intense search for a printing press on Ford's behalf. More than two years later, Black found one, and Pipp invited Black to meet Ford the day it was moved to the *Independent*'s offices. As Pipp looked on, Ford surprised both men by making Black an impetuous offer: "Say, we've got to have somebody run the business end of this thing. How would you like to come out and work on it?"[13] Black's duties included managing the business and operations staff of the newspaper. The most important part of his job description was that he reported not to Pipp, the friend who brought him to Ford's notice, but to Ernest G. Liebold, Ford's private secretary who knew everything about Ford's affairs, business and personal.[14]

Ford may have put Black in charge of the paper's business office, but he appointed Liebold as general manager of Dearborn Publishing Company, the corporate owner of the *Independent*. It was a telling sign to the newspaper veterans that regardless of their professional experience, a Ford insider would always be looking over their shoulders. And Liebold was *the* Ford insider, closer to him at the time than anyone at the company. That fact, by itself, gave Liebold enormous power across the entire Ford organization. Liebold's proximity to Ford, and Ford's trust in Liebold, built a bond between them that ensured what the *Independent*'s true purpose would be long before the likes of Pipp and Cameron ever came to Dearborn.

Born to a German Lutheran family in Detroit on March 16, 1884, Ernest Gustav Liebold took his education from a local business college and then worked as a bank teller. His swift rise to bank officer caught the attention of James

1.3. Fred L. Black (from the Collections of The Henry Ford, 90.1.1940.10/ THF101584).

Couzens, Ford Motor Company treasurer and the man closest to Ford during the company's early years. In 1910, after Ford misplaced a $70,000 check—it eventually turned up in a suit pocket—Couzens persuaded Ford to bring Liebold aboard as his personal bookkeeper. Two years later, Couzens picked Liebold to run the D. P. Lapham Bank in Dearborn, which Ford had purchased to serve his employees, and Liebold performed impressively in that capacity. "From the

1.4. Ernest Liebold, ca. 1925 (from the collections of The Henry Ford, THF23844).

beginning," wrote Nevins and Hill, "he gave complete and expert devotion to his employer—a difficult feat, particularly outside the factory, as the precise wishes of Henry Ford were seldom easy to ascertain."[15]

By the time Ford acquired the Dearborn *Independent*, Liebold reviewed practically every decision Ford made. Throughout the 1910s, Liebold controlled the press's access to his boss, shaped Ford's publicity, and worked on the Fords' personal financial affairs. He kept their checkbook and held their power of attorney. "His main job was to keep in step with Mr. Ford," a newspaper observed upon his death in 1956. "That he did well—even to the point of incurring the dislike of others." According to Albert Lee, David Lewis, and Anne Jardim, Liebold determined whom Ford would see and sat in on any meeting whose outcome he wanted to control. He didn't care whom he alienated, and reporters put off by his brusque manner and thwarted by his ironclad gatekeeping retaliated by doing what they could to embarrass him publicly. Insiders recognized Liebold's loyalty and understood him to be acting on Ford's instructions, particularly when he discharged high-level managers and executives. Fred Black later recounted Liebold's advice on how to move up within the company: "You [need to] be in a position where you don't give a goddamn what happens to anybody." Liebold even directed the Ford for President movement in 1923 and 1924, perhaps hoping to be "the power behind the throne in Washington, as he was then in the company."[16]

For this dedicated service, Ford rewarded Liebold with expanded responsibilities: "There was no task too foreign or too great to dismay him; and to all of them he brought one great attribute—a driving, endless energy." Liebold oversaw the company's acquisition of railroads, mines, and forestland. He ran the complicated negotiations surrounding Ford's attempt to purchase the government-owned nitrate and power plants at Muscle Shoals, Alabama. Most significant of all, as general manager of Dearborn Publishing Company, Liebold managed the *Independent*. Ford's "personal public relations" work shifted gradually to William Cameron as the *Independent*'s antisemitic campaigns revved into high gear, but the press's road to Ford remained blocked by Liebold until after the *Sapiro* libel suit ended in 1927. There was little question that Liebold acted on Ford's behalf and with his authorization; as Fred Black admitted, "Generally, any action Mr. Liebold took reflected Mr. Ford's attitude." But even Liebold could not take foolish chances: "Liebold was fairly careful about covering himself with Mr. Ford. . . . [I]t was generally assumed that he didn't take many chances on running counter to Mr. Ford's opinion."[17]

Scholars have seconded Black's assessment of the Ford-Liebold relationship. Albert Lee, a former Ford Motor Company publicity writer, remarked in 1980, "Ford detested details and day-to-day business." Liebold executed tasks Ford didn't want to touch, firing people "who offended the boss in the slightest manner." He "expanded his authority by exploiting Ford's quirks, such as his dislike of paperwork and refusal to read most correspondence." Despite his unquestioned authority, Liebold did not exactly welcome the new *Independent* employees. Pipp and Cameron were forced to "operate[] under the watchful eye of Liebold, who detested Pipp and barely tolerated Cameron." It is hardly surprising that "considerable friction" arose between Liebold and Pipp, who resented Liebold's efforts to supervise him.[18]

Liebold held the title of executive secretary to Ford until 1944, although the period of his greatest influence and power ran from 1913 to 1933. During that time, no person at the company knew Ford's affairs or his inmost beliefs and convictions more intimately than Liebold. "His greatest talent," according to the Detroit *Times*, "was his ability to translate into action every Ford wish and suggestion." No one was better positioned to exploit the power that talent—and Ford's confidence—conferred. And no one more ruthlessly executed Ford's antisemitic directives, because no one at the company, perhaps including the boss, hated Jews more than Liebold did.[19]

The sources and origins of Liebold's antisemitism are even more opaque than those of his longtime boss. The press and his coworkers ascribed a "Prussian" temperament to him, but that alone does not explain when or how his feelings toward Jews became so visceral. Liebold served as a buffer between Ford and the many individuals who wrote to protest the *Independent*, advising anyone who took issue with the antisemitic campaign to read the articles and understand the "facts" on which they were based. Liebold did little to camouflage his prejudice or to distinguish his views from his boss's. Fred Black later recalled that Liebold often expressed hatred toward Jews: "You could tell it was part of his whole makeup—he was anti-Semitic."[20] Allegedly a German sympathizer during World War I—the government suspected him of spying—Liebold encouraged his boss's latent bigotry.[21] Although it would be going too far to give Liebold sole credit for Ford's antisemitic attitudes, Ford's other subordinates and historians generally agree that without Liebold to run operations behind the scenes and divert criticism from him, Ford's career as a purveyor of propaganda would not have been nearly so broad scaled—or successful.

· · ·

By the time Ford assembled the newspaper, the press, and the staff to write and publish it, he had put himself through a series of experiences that seared several unshakeable convictions into his mind. The war in Europe prompted him to state his antisemitic beliefs publicly for the first time, and his statements brought him into encounters with law and the legal process. His handling of two lawsuits, one over an insulting editorial in the *Chicago Tribune* and the other over control of Ford Motor Company stock dividends, revealed critical patterns of behavior, attitudes, and decision making. The *Tribune* libel suit proved in many ways a dress rehearsal for the *Sapiro* case a decade later, and Ford's loss in the stock dividend case provided an object lesson in how to work around the courts when they ruled against him.

The Great War initially brought out some of Henry Ford's admirable qualities. As the nation's foremost industrial statesman, he was determined to make his views on the evils of war not only public but also influential. He began speaking out against the war in August 1915, a time when many Americans shared his belief that the European conflict did not involve American interests: "I will do everything in my power to prevent murderous, wasteful war in America and in the whole world," he told the *Detroit Free Press*. "I would teach the child at its mother's knee what a horrible, wasteful, and unavailing thing war is. In the home and in the schools of the world I would see the child taught to feel the uselessness of war; that war is a thing unnecessary; that preparation for war can only end in war." Pacifism became Ford's platform for a sustained critique of the major institutions of American capitalism. However ironic that seemed to industrial leaders, politicians, and prominent newspaper editors, Ford pressed ahead in 1915 with a wide-ranging denunciation of "the money-lenders, the absentee owners and the parasites of Wall Street."[22] His declarations attracted the hopes of serious pacifists who began to think that his support would help prevent, or at least delay, the United States' entry into the war.

Some of his executives, particularly James Couzens, who had been with him since the company's founding, did not agree with his outspoken declarations on pacifism, but Ford took direction from no one. Couzens, vice president and treasurer, left the company over Ford's insistence on using company publications, which Couzens supervised, to disseminate his views. Ford then sent word through the editor of the *Detroit Journal* that he and Mrs. Ford were interested in meeting with Rosika Schwimmer, a Hungarian peace activist and a Jew, when she came through Detroit as part of a U.S. tour in November 1915. Coincidentally, Liebold was in California at the time, "on vacation with his family," and unable to prevent the meeting.[23]

The purpose of Schwimmer's tour was to organize support for a peace conference in Europe. When Schwimmer arrived at the Ford Motor Company offices on November 17, she discovered that Ford did not need to be converted to her cause. To her consternation, she also learned that Ford held some views inimical to hers:

Discussing pacifism in general during lunch, Mr. Ford showed himself an absolutely clear and radical pacifist—in entire agreement with my own uncompromising position. . . . All the more astonishing it was to me to hear Mr. Ford, after all his logical and well expressed statements, suddenly say: "I know who caused the war—the German-Jewish bankers." He slapped his breast pocket. "*I have the evidence here. Facts! The German-Jewish bankers caused the war. I can't give out the facts now, because I haven't got them all yet, but I'll have them soon.*"

Schwimmer was horrified to hear Ford simplistically attribute the war to Jewish bankers, but she ascribed that notion to the influence of his advisers who crowded around their luncheon table. Anxious to preserve her peace mission, she declined to engage any of the company on the question of "the responsibilities for the war." Within the week, she accepted an invitation to call on the Fords at their Fair Lane mansion, where she was received "in so friendly and unaffected [a] way that I felt at once at home with them." She found Mrs. Ford to be "virgin soil" for the cause of pacifism and eager to join the Women's Peace Party. The encounter, she knew, was a critical audition, without which Ford would not agree to support the pacifist cause financially or to accompany her to Europe.[24] She earned the approval of both Fords. Henry Ford promptly decided to sail to Europe to bring peace to the warring parties.

He would do it without President Wilson's endorsement. Ford chartered an ocean liner to ferry himself, Schwimmer, and other notables to Norway in time to "get the boys out of the trenches by Christmas." Such "artless" declarations caused the American press, which "was both cynical and pro-British," to turn on him with a vengeance. Everyone of note—from politicians to statesmen to social workers—declined Ford's invitation to join the voyage. Even Thomas Edison, Ford's idol and close friend, refused to accompany him on what was swiftly becoming a circus event. Clara Ford pleaded in vain with her husband not to go. The trip was a disaster. Reporters accompanying Ford, "increasingly bored and liberally lubricated with drink," wrote detailed dispatches on the internal disagreements that percolated among the delegates. Many of the press developed a sincere personal liking for Ford, but the mission was beyond saving after Ford became ill and took to his cabin. After Ford ceased to exercise leadership, Schwimmer was unable to fill the vacuum; delegates found her haughty, sensitive to criticism, and short tempered. Several days after docking in Oslo, Ford was spirited out of his hotel and onto a U.S.-bound vessel, surrounded by bodyguards and "a flying wedge" of local Ford employees. It was Christmas, the boys were still in the trenches, and the true pacifists were left to reconstruct their mission without their famous patron. The peace delegation toiled on in Europe for more than a year before finally dissolving, "demoralized and dissension-ridden," in early 1917.[25]

Ford endured brutal criticism in the press and among political leaders for his failure to broker peace. Typical of the negative reaction was a column in *Our Times*: "After its failure, dying down to an echo of gigantic and exhausted laughter, [the Peace Ship] deprived every other peace movement in the country of force and conviction." Yet Ford again managed to connect with the sentiments of ordinary Americans: "I wanted to see peace," he wrote in *My Life and Work*. "I at least tried to bring it about. Most men did not even try." The Peace Ship may have seemed a farce, as Kenneth Galbraith wrote nearly a half century later, but "possibly it was one of Ford's better ideas. To hope that men and women of good will might mediate a conflict in which the generals had been reduced to marching their men in masses against machine guns was natural if maybe optimistic. In any case, no one had a better plan."[26]

The general public seemed to agree and ignored the press's criticism of Ford. As his popularity soared, there was some discussion of his standing for election to the presidency in 1916; he even won the Republican primary in Michigan and collected a respectable number of votes in Nebraska and Ohio after friends in those states placed his name on the ballot. Disdaining the office, Ford threw his support to Wilson, who rewarded him by inviting him to run for the Senate in 1918 as a Democrat. A willing candidate in that race, Ford lost by a narrow margin. The electoral defeat, like the Peace Ship, only reinforced his public image as the hero of common folk and set the stage for years of speculation about his presidential prospects.[27]

In one of the first biographies to appear after Ford's death, Keith Sward wrote, "[I]n his pacifism Ford was a rebel only for a day." However shallow, Ford's pacifism was grounded in a scorn for a certain kind of capitalist, those who he believed controlled the money supply, and a distrust of political leaders whom he viewed as too entrenched in politics to see the nature of international conflict as clearly as he did. The most striking thing about Ford's pacifism, and what makes it historically significant, is Ford's lack of accountability for it. What it meant, what responsibilities it conferred on him, and how it situated him as a public figure were all issues with weighty consequences that he did not appear to work out, at least not in public view. For example, the onetime pacifist agreed to supply the government after the U.S. entered the war and declared he would take no profits on any government contract. He instructed Pipp to "tell anybody and everybody that I am going to return it all." Pipp publicized that promise throughout Ford's 1918 senate campaign. But Ford never returned any money to the U.S. Treasury; nor did he or his representatives debunk the growing legend that he had.[28]

Not every newspaper in the country had fallen under the spell of Ford's folksy charm and straight-shooting statesmanship. Unimpressed with Ford's showing in the 1916 Michigan presidential primary, the *Chicago Tribune* scolded its neighbors for abandoning all "good sense": "A passion for peace will not save the United States from the consequence of lazy thinking or no thinking. The vote for Ford represents a process of reasoning like this: Mr. Ford is a good man who wants peace. I want peace. Therefore I am for Mr. Ford." The *Tribune* was unafraid to confront Ford editorially during the months when he was proving his appeal at the ballot box, and for some weeks it did so by engaging his ideas directly and refuting them with equally excited counterarguments. In May 1916, the *Tribune* dismissed his folk-hero qualities: "There is no mystery about Ford, except that erroneously attributed to him by the excited literati because of the melodramatic manner in which he has started out to separate himself from a few millions." The *Tribune* took every opportunity to outline its doubts about Ford's fitness to serve as president and to shape public opinion about the nation's security. To illustrate, Theodore Roosevelt was crisscrossing the country at the same time, perhaps positioning himself to win both the Republican and the Progressive Party nominations. The *Tribune* feasted on the contrast between the two.[29]

Like Ford, *Tribune* owner Robert McCormick opposed U.S. entry into the war in Europe. But unlike Henry and Edsel Ford, McCormick joined his state's National Guard and defended the Mexican border against incursions in 1916. In addition, he promised *Tribune* employees that "if they volunteered, their jobs would be secure and wages would be paid during their service." His National Guard unit reported for duty equipped with guns McCormick purchased. Having demonstrated his patriotic commitments, the publisher had little patience for billionaires who preached anti-preparedness on the basis of what he saw as "views . . . not founded on knowledge or shaped by common sense."[30] Yet even McCormick had to take care in attacking Ford. Between January and June 1916, the *Tribune*'s editorial position on Ford acknowledged his status as a cultural icon and simply dismissed the idea that he should influence serious matters of politics and diplomacy.

As summer neared, the battle became more pitched. The *Tribune*, worried about Ford's demonstrated popularity at the polls, continued to pound at the implications of his claim that capitalist interests fed the machines of war and diverted public resources for private gain. When President Wilson called out the National Guard to defend the Mexican border, the *Tribune* investigated what the nation's large manufacturers were doing to support the military. On June 22, the *Tribune* reported that "Ford employees who volunteer to bear arms for the United States will lose their jobs." The story was strangely brief in view of the bombshell it dropped; it neither quoted Ford directly nor named any Ford Motor Company official. Nevertheless, the *Tribune* headlined its next day's editorial, "Ford Is an Anarchist."[31]

The editorial climaxed weeks of carping, criticism, and condemnation directed at Ford. To dismiss employees who chose, or were required, to leave their jobs to perform military service was, in the *Tribune*'s view, to attack the very essence of patriotic citizenship: "Mr. Ford thus proves that he does not believe in service to the nation in the fashion a soldier must serve it." Approximately seventy-five Ford employees stood to lose their jobs if called to the Mexican border that summer: "If Ford allows this rule of his shops to stand he will reveal himself not as merely an ignorant idealist, but as an anarchistic enemy of the nation which protects him in his wealth." For the *Tribune*, Ford's policy struck at the foundation of national self-protection: "Th[e] government is permitted to take Henry Ford himself and command his services as a soldier if necessary. It can tax his money for war purposes and will. It can compel him to devote himself to national purposes." The *Tribune*'s final comment was unsparing: "[Ford] takes the men who stand between him and service and punishes them for the service which protects him. The man is so incapable of thought that he cannot see the ignominy of his own performance."[32] The *Tribune*'s wrath stemmed both from personal dislike and from political differences. McCormick did not want to see such a man elected to the presidency. But the newspaper had its own obligations to fulfill. One was to get its facts right.

This the *Tribune* had not done, according to Ford biographers Allan Nevins and Frank Ernest Hill. Nevins and Hill report that the *Tribune*'s reporter spoke with only one Ford official. A high-level manager named Frank Klingensmith erroneously informed the paper that no Guard reservists would be permitted to return to their jobs and that the company would provide no support to their families in their absence. In fact, the company not only guaranteed reservists their jobs but even gave some of them "better places than they had held before" and provided aid to their families. It was reasonable to criticize Ford's pacifism, but the *Tribune* went too far; Nevins and Hill characterize the "anarchist" editorial as "peculiarly silly and obnoxious."[33]

It was the Ford Motor Company's chief lawyer, former congressman Alfred Lucking, who insisted to Ford that the Tribune's last volley was "intolerable" and should be answered publicly. "Well," Ford is said to have replied, "you'd better start suit against them for libel."[34] Lucking did so in September, 1916, asking for $1 million in damages. The two sides wrangled for two years over pretrial motions, discovery, and pleadings. Trial finally began in Mt. Clemens, a county-seat backwater twenty-two miles northeast of Detroit, in May 1919.[35]

At the time of Ford's dustup with the *Tribune*, American libel law strongly constrained newspaper publishers seeking to expose public figures to the light of public scrutiny in several ways. To "protect the best men," as historian Norman Rosenberg put it, American courts in the late nineteenth century imposed more restrictive limits on editorial and news content than had prevailed earlier in the century. To restrain the power of the "new journalism," which prized exposé-style reports into the private lives of public officials, public employees, and persons with established celebrity reputations, state appellate courts upheld damage awards in cases where juries believed newspapers had gone too far in holding such public figures to ridicule. "Insurgent political movements" such as populism, with their own newspapers and networks, "sought to wrest both the terms and the channels of political debate from the hands of a new political-corporate elite." During this time, legal theory developed a "scientific" law of defamation that helped judges protect the reputations of "honorable and worthy men."[36]

Courts regularly employed the so-called bad-tendency test to penalize newspapers for publishing stories that harmed the public morals or public health. The right to freedom of speech did not carry with it a blanket immunity to say or publish anything at all. As David Rabban has noted, "The judges who decided these cases sometimes made a special point of emphasizing that the press has no greater right to freedom of expression than any individual member of the public." The courts drew a careful distinction between "protected criticism of public officials and libelous attacks on their character." Newspapers could pursue the legitimate purpose of uncovering "'official abuse and corruption,'" but as public critics, they had to be careful about ascribing motives they could not know—or prove—to the conduct they sought to condemn.[37]

Still, an essential and important element of American libel law remained in place from the American Revolution on. Courts and legislatures consistently adhered to the American legal innovation that truth supplied a defense in libel actions. This innovation broke with English common law, which cared not at all whether the published speech was true and generally held newspapers strictly liable for libelous speech. American courts, though committed to giving publishers the chance to defend themselves by proving the truth of what they said in print, were still reluctant to endorse a broad notion of freedom for the press at the turn of the twentieth century. The salacious tastes of yellow journalism should be obliged to respect the service and reputations of officeholders, these judges believed. Because the marketplace of ideas supplied no sense of restraint (and indeed only whetted the symbiotic appetites of publishers and readers), the courts felt bound to step in. The writers of legal treatises by and large agreed. As a result, the general trend toward more protection for published speech during the period between 1890 and 1916 was paralleled by rulings grounded in the fear that character attacks would drive decent men out of public service and politics, even if those attacks revealed less than dignified behavior.[38]

Still, there was no consensus on the scope of privacy to which public persons could feel entitled. As Rabban observes, by the early twentieth century, "the relationship between the First Amendment and the law of defamation had not been clarified[,] and . . . 'judicial decisions had often been narrow, illiberal and confusing.'" What newspapers did know was that they were in trouble if they published false statements, even if they were "'made in good faith, without malice and under the honest belief that they are true.'"[39] The Supreme Court's standard rule during this time was that "free speech did not 'permit the publication of libels, blasphemous or indecent articles, or other publications injurious to public morals or private reputation.'"[40] Some states went so far as to prohibit the publication of newspapers "'devoted largely to the publication of scandals, intrigues, and immoral conduct,'" in an indication of just how widespread the "new journalism" had become and, just as important, how nettlesome politicians found it.[41]

By the time the *Tribune* published its "anarchist" editorial on Ford, newspapers were on notice to watch what they said. Libel lawsuits were frequent occurrences, in part because of the strict liability standards and in part because of the rise of contingent-fee lawyers, who may have inflated the number of defamation suits. Newspapers had already begun staffing their newsrooms with lawyers, to avoid publishing obviously libelous statements. The roiling social and foreign policy issues of the Progressive Era did battle in some newspapers with a desire to steer clear of provoking high-profile defamation suits, because the risk that the newspapers would lose was rather significant. Newspapers and their lawyers were aware of the perils of exercising the freedom of the press.

In short, then, the state of American libel law at the time Ford filed his suit against the *Tribune* neither gave newspapers carte blanche to print anything nor yielded libel plaintiffs a decided edge. Courts were not engaging in absolutist readings of the First Amendment; they were carefully guarding the reputations of the "best men" in American public life from reckless reporting. Plaintiffs alleging libel enjoyed an edge in suits where the publications could be proved false or blatantly malicious. The Dodge stockholders' suit and the earlier Selden patent fight, in which Ford broke George Selden's monopolistic hold on the automobile technology, show that Ford was willing to use the courts to achieve his business aims. In view of the broader political goals that lay behind the Peace Ship and his dalliance in presidential primaries, it is reasonable to think that Ford saw libel litigation against the *Tribune* as an opportunity not only to score a decided victory over a national press he had come to detest but also to establish his public image as an American folk hero more firmly in the wake of the Peace Ship.

Still, the case posed significant risks for Ford. McCormick and the *Tribune* possessed the necessary resources for defending an expensive lawsuit. The newspaper could avail itself of expert libel lawyers rather than rely on general practitioners, as libel plaintiffs of the time tended to do. McCormick's eminent social and political standing compared favorably to Ford's, particularly after the embarrassment of the Peace Ship. To prevail, Ford's lawyers would have to show that they understood the rugged terrain of American libel law and pick a

1.5. Henry Ford in a contemplative mood during the *Chicago Tribune* libel suit, Mt. Clemens, Michigan, July 21, 1919 (from the collections of The Henry Ford, THF23844).

clear path to a favorable judgment, one that maximized the strengths of Ford's legal position while dealing with its weaknesses.

The hamlet of Mt. Clemens, Michigan, "previously known only for medicinal springs beneficial to rheumatic patients," was an unlikely host for a major civil lawsuit. A sleepy county seat, the town was not yet wired for telegraph before the trial filled its modest hotels to bursting with the parties, their teams of lawyers, and dozens of reporters. "Like armed bands establishing rival fortresses," the teams working on behalf of Ford and the *Tribune* established fully equipped offices and got to work. Liebold took charge of the plaintiff's office, which became the off-site "business center" of the Ford Motor Company while the trial lasted. The Ford news bureau at Mt. Clemens was staffed by Pipp, Cameron, Black, and other *Dearborn Independent* employees. Their mission was to counteract the negative publicity from the mainstream press that Ford expected to come his way and, just as important, to supply coverage favorable to Ford to towns whose newspapers could not afford to send reporters to Mt. Clemens.

The editors posted a map on their office wall on which pushpins marked the cities where their paper made inroads against the one-sided coverage that Ford ascribed to the national press.[42]

Ford came to Mt. Clemens armed for battle. More than sixty lawyers, company employees, and "a battery of private detectives" worked on the case in Mt. Clemens. In addition to Albert Lucking, Ford's chief counsel, personal attorney, and corporate lawyer, as well as several of Lucking's law partners, Ford retained local counsel in Mt. Clemens. The plaintiff's side was topped off by the addition of a distinguished figure from the Detroit bench, retired judge Alfred Murphy. According to Nevins and Hill, Murphy earned his fee: "Having come into the case on Ford's insistence, [Murphy] was to miss few opportunities of tossing garlands of purple rhetoric about Ford's neck." It is not clear whether any of these attorneys had tried libel suits of any consequence or possessed the kind of expertise in the area that, according to Norman Rosenberg, conferred legal and strategic advantages on libel plaintiffs.[43]

The *Tribune* trained big guns of its own. Lead counsel Elliott G. Stevenson and partners from his Detroit firm had represented the Dodge brothers in the shareholders' suit, which got Stevenson noticed by the *Tribune*. In that case, Stevenson had nettled Lucking and rattled Ford as he testified. Other lawyers for the newspaper included Weymouth Kirkland and Howard Ellis of the Chicago firm of McCormick, Kirkland, Patterson, and Fleming, who were counsel to the *Tribune* Company. The newspaper, like Ford, covered its bases by hiring additional attorneys in Mt. Clemens.[44]

The *Tribune*'s position was that Ford's pacifism endangered the national welfare and made him fair game for critical editorial comment. Naturally, its lawyers contended that the *Tribune*'s editorials had not libeled Ford. They argued, as McCormick had, that prevailing standards about avoiding defamatory statements about public-minded men did not apply to Ford. In the publisher's view, Ford had not earned his political popularity; he was not equipped by virtue of education or disposition to command public assent or to lead in the formation of public opinion. Thus, Ford was not one of those "best men" whose good name and willingness to serve should be protected from reckless libel. Ford had forfeited that goodwill by sponsoring the Peace Ship and by publishing long essays as paid display advertisements in which he laid out his views against preparedness. Kirkland's summary of the opposing sides was one indication of the contempt with which McCormick regarded Ford's political views:

"Mr. Ford believed that soldiers were murderers, and that those who argued for preparedness were war profiteers. *The Chicago Tribune* believed that those who sought to reduce the force of government in times of national stress were anarchists; for, without force in such times, government cannot exist."[45] The *Tribune*'s unwillingness to settle and avoid the costs (and risks) of prolonged litigation was another such indication.

The legal issues of the case would turn, as was common in libel cases, on the nature and scope of the evidence that the judge permitted the parties to introduce. Because it was Ford's claim that the characterizations of him as an ignorant idealist and an anarchist were libelous and damaging, the court had to hear arguments about the commonsense and legal meanings of those terms. Ford asserted that the word "anarchist . . . meant one who unlawfully seeks to overthrow the government; or, as [he] put it, a bomb thrower." The *Tribune* countered with a less literal definition: "one who advocates a condition of affairs in which the force of government is so inefficient or inadequate that the government cannot properly perform its functions." Those functions included supplying military protection for the lives and property of its citizens. The difference was legally significant. In the key ruling of the trial, Judge Tucker decided to leave it to the jury to determine which definition to apply. This decision enabled both sides to introduce evidence to back up their definition of the words *anarchist* and *anarchy*.[46]

Nevins and Hill argue that Ford's attorneys blew the case. By suing over the entire editorial, rather than just the words *anarchist* and *anarchy*, they opened the door for the judge to exercise discretion as to what evidence the newspaper could bring in to justify its use of those words. "[U]nder the common law," according to Nevins and Hill, "[Ford] would have had an ironclad case, for the courts had already decided that these words could be penalized." In the years since the assassination of President William McKinley by the anarchist Leon Czolgosz, many states took drastic steps to curtail anarchists' publications and crack down on their public speeches. Although figures such as Emma Goldman often successfully challenged such bans, the mood of the country toward their politics was decidedly hostile.[47] To be tagged as an anarchist was serious business; the libel case would turn on how the jury understood what the label meant. Was it sufficient simply to express views that, if enacted, would undermine the government's policies, or did one have to throw bombs and shoot presidents?

Apparently Ford's attorneys were unprepared for an adverse ruling on the issue of the libels' scope. They began their case by using forty witnesses to refute the *Tribune*'s contention that returning reservists would have no jobs at the Ford Motor Company. Special badges were issued to departing soldiers, one Ford executive related, to entitle them to resume employment after their service. Frank Klingensmith denied ever talking to the *Tribune*'s reporter about company policy on reservists, and another executive described the benefits paid to their families while they served. Others attested to Ford's enlightened labor policies, to show that such a progressive employer "would [never] threaten members of the Michigan National Guard with dismissal." Ford's attorneys then disparaged the *Tribune*'s motives in criticizing Ford, first by arguing that the newspaper's support for military action in Mexico was inconsistent with its opposition to American involvement in Europe, and then by claiming that the McCormick family's stock interests in Standard Oil, which obtained crude from Mexico, represented a conflict of interest for the newspaper. Finding proof of that theory insufficient, the judge instructed the jury to ignore it. The plaintiff's weak case concluded in early June when Ford's attorneys could fashion "no other farfetched theories to chase."[48]

Because the jury was to consider which kind of anarchist the editorial had in mind, the defense had to "prove that Mr. Ford was an anarchist in the sense for which it contended." As a result, "all of Mr. Ford's utterances and acts having to do with preparedness or with the affairs of government were material." Tucker's unwillingness to limit the defense meant that the newspaper "could argue that Ford's pacifism and antipreparedness were the essence of the case." The newspaper's attorneys gleefully swore in witnesses who could testify to Ford's involvement with the Peace Ship, his views on the Mexican skirmishes of 1916, his successful efforts to keep Edsel out of uniform during the war, and the Ford Motor Company's munitions production and profits from war contracts. The *Tribune* even brought a band of Texas Rangers to Michigan, keeping them waiting weeks for their turn to appear in court, to "recite the horrors of rape and pillage along the Rio Grande during June of 1916." Their testimony turned out to be irrelevant, but for good measure, Ford's lawyers put on the stand "three times as many Mexicans, who recited equally sordid tales of depredations committed by American troops."[49]

Ford and his ideas were the key to the case for both sides. *Tribune* attorney Elliot Stevenson began Ford's cross-examination on July 14. Ford resisted his attorneys' frantic attempts to prepare him for the relentless questioning he was about to endure. The *Tribune*'s lawyer then "compelled [him] to think aloud for a solid week." It was an ugly recitation for Ford partisans to endure. "Setting verbal traps and playing upon the manufacturer's ignorance in general fields of knowledge, Stevenson essayed to prove that he was totally unqualified to serve as a guide in politico-social fields." Ford identified Benedict Arnold as a writer, placed the American Revolution in 1812, and professed not to understand the phrase "fundamental principles of government." He often answered questions before the judge had time to rule on his attorneys' objections, passing up an obvious escape from difficult spots. The result was soon evident: "Ford, so self-confident, alert, and expert in his own plant, soon became a reluctant, discomfited, and shamefaced witness."[50]

Relentlessly pummeled on the stand, Ford was unable to charm his way out of a public mess for the first time in his life. Still, he found ways to fight back. None too convincingly, Ford evaded a request that he read aloud to the court, claiming he had left his glasses at home. He refused to apologize for his intellectual shortcomings, all but admitting under cross-examination that he didn't mind so much being called "ignorant" and that "his real objection was to the word anarchist."[51] By this point in the case, however, the *Tribune* had related Ford's ignorance to his pacifist views. The newspaper's advantage became clearer as testimony progressed. By giving the *Tribune* ample demonstration of his ignorance on the stand, Ford gave the *Tribune* sufficient grounds to prove the truth of its characterization of him as an "ignorant idealist."

Equally important for later events were Ford's admissions about his relationship to the writer who penned essays on preparedness appearing under Ford's name during the run-up to the Mexican incursions. In newspapers all over the country and in Ford Motor Company brochures, the essays bore the byline of Henry Ford, but they were written by Theodore Delavigne, Ford's "peace secretary." Delavigne's relationship with Ford exactly presaged Cameron's when he later produced "Mr. Ford's Page" for the *Dearborn Independent*. Under oath, Ford described how the essays came to be: "He got the facts together as much as possible, and wrote them off, had them printed; and I paid for them. That is about all I had to do with it. I didn't go over it all; I went over a good deal of it, but not all." This would not be the last time Ford disavowed statements made in his name. Pressed by Stevenson to explain the essays, Ford replied, "I gave authority to my agent to write it; I am responsible for what he did, but when you ask me what I meant by this, you are asking for what goes beyond my knowledge."[52] Ford's "agent" thus had the job of expressing Ford's ideas for him; Ford accepted responsibility for what was written under his name, but he was merely the sponsor of its dissemination. He neither authored the text nor, in some cases, entirely understood what it meant. Then, when pressed in a court of law, Ford did not seem to care about the appearances—or the ethics—of such an arrangement.

The *Tribune*'s attempts to re-create the high emotions of the times three years before the trial produced a mixed result. After deliberating for one day, the jury found the *Tribune* guilty of libeling Ford and fixed damages to him at precisely $0.06. Ford's agents immediately set about interviewing jurors to learn how this bizarre verdict came about. The *Tribune* did not persuade a single one of them that Ford was an anarchist in the figurative sense the newspaper intended. But the jurors disagreed as to whether the *Tribune*'s editorial constituted fair comment; one juror who thought it did commented that the McCormicks, who had served in the military, were "much better Americans than the Fords," neither of whom had ever worn a uniform. Eight jurors wanted to award Ford substantial damages; to win over the other four, they offered a nominal sum.[53] The verdict, though anticlimactic and ambiguous, affirmed one thing: Ford was a public individual, vulnerable to libelous defamation, and no newspaper, however patriotic its intentions, should speak unguardedly, even in matters of war and peace.

Both sides claimed victory. Ford's attorneys downplayed the trivial damage award. Alfred Murphy dismissed the notion that money was an issue for Ford while acknowledging that his client had been forced to defend himself: "[Mr. Ford] stands not only vindicated, but his attitude as an American citizen has been justified after a trial which raised every issue against him which ingenuity and research could present." *Tribune* lawyer Weymouth Kirkland asserted that the trivial damages accurately measured what was left of Ford's reputation: "If a 6 cent verdict had been asked for in this case it would not have lasted three months. It was not what Mr. Lucking had insisted upon. He said a small verdict would be a defeat. We are satisfied if he is."[54]

Ford was livid, not so much at the verdict but at the storm of critical editorials that followed. The *New York Times* closed ranks and endorsed the *Tribune*'s legal position on the meaning of Ford's views: "A genius in his own business, his qualifications as an instructor of the people are not too manifest, and he must feel that his appearances in that role are at an end." The *New York Post* echoed this sentiment: "If *The Chicago Tribune* conducted its defense of the libel suit mainly for the purpose of making an end of Henry Ford as a public character, it undoubtedly succeeded." Editors of many of the country's major dailies congratulated the *Tribune* for exposing the limits of Ford's genius, pro- claiming the end of his public life and arguing that the litigation was worth the expense and time because it produced a socially valuable result. The *New York World* condemned the lawsuit as a "withering indictment of the administra- tion of the law in this country."[55]

Carol Gelderman has called the *Tribune* case "one of America's most absurd law suits." Perhaps the parties had quarreled like children, but the case was not without consequences. Despite the confused state of American libel law, with shifting ideas about free speech and the reputations of public men, and despite the disorganized trial, the jury got the law right. The *Tribune* went too far in labeling Ford an anarchist, but Ford exposed himself to ridicule, not so much with his profession of pacifism as with his performance on the stand.[56]

Although many contemporary editorial writers thought the case would end Ford's career in public life, the opposite occurred. Ford found himself even more in demand, which enabled him to rebuild his public image after the suit and maintain his high profile. His "views on modern society" became and remained "a staple of American public discussion." At the same time, Ford changed his mind about the utility of the courtroom as a place to defend his personal views. Upon departing the courtroom after his testimony, he was reportedly heard to say, "'Never again.'"[57]

Ford made some changes in his legal staff after the case. He gradually sepa- rated Lucking, his longtime chief counsel, from his inner circle and eventu- ally let him go. His biographers agree that of all the momentous events of the decade, it was the decision in the libel suit, which from his perspective failed to conform to his commonsense beliefs, that "mark[ed] the beginning of Henry Ford's isolation, not only from the associates of his rise to power, but from the city of Detroit." What Anne Jardim calls "the narcissistic style," which had already emerged in his obsession to control his company and his pattern of quickly abandoning interests he was once so passionate about (i.e., the Peace Ship), fully matured in his corporate governing style after the *Tribune* verdict.[58]

That style also began to surface in Ford's relationship to the legal process, as discussion of one further lawsuit demonstrates. After 1919, Ford made changes

in his company when cases in which he was involved did not end to his satisfaction. There was nothing much he could do about the *Tribune* suit, which
after all did not directly affect the company financially. But the other lawsuit
in which he was entangled—the Dodge brothers' attempt to force him to pay
stock dividends—struck directly at the heart of the Ford Motor Company and
at his determination to permit no one else to interfere with his management of
it. That suit, Steven Watts observed, "violated Ford's visceral need for control
over his company and its destiny, an impulse that had driven him since his
earliest days in the automobile business."[59]

Filed in 1916, the Dodge brothers' suit revealed Ford at his most ruthless. It
also showed, for the first time, what he was willing to do to elude the reach of
legal authority when he didn't want to perform as commanded. At trial in May
1917, Ford relied heavily on his public persona as a modest man committed to
using his company to serve the public. Called to testify about his company's
expansion plans, he genially denied "experimenting" in risky endeavors with
company funds with the parry that "there wouldn't be any fun in it" if the
company never tried anything new. Opposing counsel tried to avoid giving
Ford the opening to link the construction of cars to the public good, but Ford
proved adept at turning the witness stand into a public platform: "[The Ford
Motor Company is o]rganized to do as much good as we can, everywhere, for
everybody concerned." Making money was "'incidental'" to the company's
operations, he declared, not its central concern. Such testimony helped Ford
in this case, because it enabled him to showcase a business philosophy that
was all about production and expansion and providing jobs, not the maximi-
zation of profits and dividends. But Ford erred in disclosing his intention to
suspend dividends indefinitely rather than for a specified term. The court ruled
against him, ordering the disbursement of a special dividend of 50 percent of
the company's accumulated profits. On appeal, fifteen months later, Ford won
a broader judicial recognition of the Ford Motor Company's right to expand
its business, but the obligation of the company to pay dividends remained:
"[T]he Ford Motor Company was adjudged prosperous enough to expand and
pay large dividends at the same time."[60]

Ford's response to his defeat in the Dodge brothers' suit was to buy out
every shareholder outside the Ford family. By 1919, the Ford Motor Company
reverted entirely to family ownership. Yet Ford had to go deeply into debt to
accomplish this goal, borrowing $75 million from eastern banks to secure his

independence. He made Edsel the company's president, but the title was honor-
ific: "No one . . . doubted that the Ford Motor Company after its reorganization
was an autocracy entirely subject to the whims of its aging, egocentric founder."
The writer Anne Jardim analyzed this move psychologically: "Detached from
concrete objectives, Ford's need for control would now become a need to have
that control recognized, assented to, conformed to, and feared."[61]

Success brought out the baser aspects of Ford's character, but success also
enabled Ford to conceal his character flaws or, when it suited the circumstances,
use them to achieve his business aims. For example, in 1920, Ford faced a sobering reckoning: he owed $25 million on the loan he took to acquire full owner-
ship of the company, he was obliged by the Dodge suit to pay $20 million in
dividends, and he wanted to pay his workers a bonus of $7 million. Unwilling
to finance these expenses, he played a cunning trick on the rest of the industry:
he slashed prices on Ford cars, the largest in the industry's history, and when
demand failed to rebound, Ford halted production at all plants and ordered a
company housecleaning: "[Ford] stripped his production and office forces to
a skeletal crew of managers and superintendents (discharging, in the process,
some of his most capable lieutenants . . .) and relentlessly collected and sold all
useless or surplus material and machinery." The press regarded these decisions
as proof that Ford had lost his Midas touch and spread rumors that foreclosures
were imminent. Ford then recommenced production in February 1921, ordering
dealers to buy and take delivery of seventy-five thousand cars or else lose their
franchises. By forcing dealers to finance the new production, Ford was able to
avoid doing so himself. Two months later, the company was running a surplus.
The *Detroit News* was quick to trumpet Ford's latest triumph, proclaiming that
he had "outwitted the bankers" yet again. The press garnished Ford's image with
glowing praise about this latest David-and-Goliath episode. What Americans
admired about Ford, as the editor of the *Nation* put it, was that, "being rich, he
still hates Wall Street . . . and they do not mind if he frequently turns a trick for
which they would denounce any well-known Wall Street operator."[62] Having
proved his identification with the working person and the ordinary American,
Ford enjoyed an astonishing immunity; criticism of his business decisions did
not penetrate the armor of his folk-hero status.

But to those who knew him more intimately, the modest tinkerer had
become an unlikable boor, the innovative genius an industrial autocrat. The
high stakes game he played in innovation, business operations, and marketing

left Ford with a "compulsion to paint every person near him in business as a monster in one way or another." He trusted few people and isolated himself in his obsessions. His work on the cutting edge of automotive technology did not transform him into a sophisticated thinker; instead, it seemed only to reinforce his parochialism. As much as his fame and fortune relied on a technological revolution, he seemed to want to limit the effects of that revolution on American society. With the passing of time, he increasingly looked to the past for his cultural touchstone. As Collier and Horowitz note, "He had escaped from the farm, but it remained his sole point of reference."[63]

. . .

The war and related events changed everything for Ford. He saw the war as "an economic disaster" that portended death on the battlefront and destruction of productive industries at home. After the war ended, its capacity for destruction remained unchecked. The *Tribune* suit was proof enough of that. As Pipp, Cameron, and Black revved up operations at the *Independent*, Ford and Liebold prepared for war of another kind: a war on Jews.[64]

The *Independent*'s first issue under Ford, dated January 11, 1919, featured literature; political commentary; and, of course, "Mr. Ford's Page." The editorial staff used Ford Motor Company resources to acquire some genuinely respectable literature. Fred Black recalled, "We bought articles from some of the leading English and American authors; articles and poetry from writers such as Carl Sandburg, Robert Frost and Hugh Walpole, the British novelist." In reconfiguring the *Independent*, Ford created a media voice that he alone controlled, one that both spoke in the vernacular of his limited ken and ignored his increasingly unflattering press coverage. The paper created a nostalgic picture of the late-nineteenth-century America in which he had come of age. The family farm, the one-room school, and racial and ethnic homogeneity all dovetailed with a profoundly conservative and Christian fundamentalism. *Independent* articles extolled the virtues of Thomas Jefferson and Abraham Lincoln, superimposing anachronistic aspects of their political ideas on postwar culture. The paper attacked the modernist impulses of its time, inveighing against new cultural trends that Ford personally abhorred: smoking; drinking; jazz; newfangled dancing styles; and what he believed was the disproportionate influence of Jews on politics, culture, entertainment, diplomacy, industrial capitalism, and the state.[65]

As the *Tribune* case concluded, a document was making its way from England to the United States, borne across the waters by Russian royalists hostile to the Russian Revolution and anxious to restore the tsarist regime. The *Protocols of the Elders of Zion*, arguably the most significant antisemitic forgery of the modern era, "presents a Jewish plot to take over the world and to reduce non-Jews to abject slavery." First published in St. Petersburg in 1903, the tract spread to Moscow and other cities before World War I. The Russian Revolution pointed it toward the West like a rocket and lit the fuse. Fear of communism, postwar social and political instability, and economic tumult all fed prejudicial assumptions that the *Protocols* seemed to bring into the light of day. The specific connection between Jews and Bolshevism alone granted the document credibility, not just among pro-tsarist Russian refugees on the Continent but also among British noble and intellectual elites for whom antisemitism was a generally accepted social attitude. In the wake of the radicals' triumph in Russia, the *Protocols* suggested that "[r]esistance to liberal and leftist ideologies was resistance to a malevolent Jewish plot." As émigrés carried it beyond the borders of Russia, it was swiftly translated and published in "all major languages." Within a year of the Armistice, "copies of the *Protocols* were being circulated in the highest echelons of [U.S.] government." Among the prominent Americans who knew of its existence or laid their hands on a copy were Supreme Court Justice Louis Brandeis; former justice and 1916 Republican presidential nominee Charles Evans Hughes; Louis Marshall, American Jewish Committee president; and the members of a Senate committee looking into "German and Bolshevik propaganda activities." It was the height of the Red Scare; fear and suspicion saturated the air.[66]

The *Protocols* came to Henry Ford through a byzantine chain of events and persons that ultimately ran through a former official of the Imperial Russian Government, Boris Brasol-Brazhkovsky. Brasol was living in the United States at the time of the Revolution. The overthrow of the tsar so disgusted him that he resigned his post and remained in exile. After serving as a confidential adviser to U.S. military intelligence during the war, he took a job with the U.S. War Trade Board in 1919, where he made friends with Attorney General A. Mitchell Palmer and important nativists in the War Department. From this perch, Brasol insinuated himself into the office of a military intelligence officer named Harris Houghton, supplied Houghton's assistant with a copy of the *Protocols*, and then helped translate the book into English. Somehow, he and Liebold found each other—no one seems to know just how—but Liebold began bringing Brasol into his confidence and onto the *Independent*'s masthead in early 1919.[67]

Liebold quietly emerged as the architect of Ford's antisemitic campaign. His connection to Brasol brought him into contact with other Europeans— Germans as well as Russians—who were trafficking in the *Protocols* and other forms of antisemitic propaganda after the Russian Revolution and the end of the war. Gradually, Liebold began building a network of links and fellow travelers on whom he could call for corroborating information.

These developments were an express challenge to Pipp and to the direction in which he planned to take the newspaper. Both, however, were vulnerable. The "Fordized" version of a mass-circulation periodical was a bland, unremarkable product. Accepting no advertisements, the paper was sold by street vendors and distributed through Ford dealerships. Some dealers groused that the money would be better spent on improving the Model T. By 1927, the *Independent* would do as badly as the car, losing more than $2 million in all, but Ford did not care. He intended to make the *Independent* the common folks' primer on American culture, literature, and political philosophy. The *Independent* may have offered a window onto Ford's mind, but it failed to make much of a niche for itself in a crowded market, coming across as "a weak, hybrid adaptation of the *Saturday Evening Post, Collier's,* and *Harper's Weekly.*"[68]

Still, Pipp's challenges went beyond merely penetrating the newspaper market in a down economy after the war. He and the boss had serious philosophical differences over the newspaper's function in the wider Ford Motor Company universe. Pipp did not approve of Ford's decision to use the *Independent* to smear Truman Newberry, who defeated Ford in the 1918 Senate race. Further, Pipp resented the intrusion of company rivalries into the *Independent*'s newsroom, rivalries he was powerless to neutralize. But those things were nothing compared to Liebold's designs. Closeted in his private office at the main plant, just next to Ford's, he coordinated the collection of "facts" and "proof" about Jewish warmongering and postrevolutionary plans for world domination. Sometime in early 1920, Liebold procured a copy of the *Protocols* from Brasol in New York and promptly handed it to Cameron to rewrite. Initially, Cameron balked at the assignment. One morning, he confided to Pipp, "Ford has been at me to commence writing on those cursed Jewish articles." Edsel Ford, too, was troubled about what the newspaper was preparing to do. But he could no more countermand his father's orders than Cameron could disobey them.[69]

On May 22, 1920, the *Independent* launched the antisemitic series, purporting to reveal the role of the "International Jew" in world affairs. In ninety articles that ran weekly for nearly two years, the *Independent* excerpted and recapitulated the *Protocols of the Elders of Zion*, adapted and Americanized for its intended audience. The first article labeled the "International Jew" as "The World's Problem" and staked out familiar antisemitic beliefs: "The Jew is the world's enigma. Poor in his masses, he yet controls the world's finances. . . . [H]e has become the power behind many a throne." Ford's newspaper spread this "conspiratorial delusion" to nearly seven hundred thousand readers at the peak of its circulation in the mid-1920s, an increase of more than half a million from 1919. The articles singled out the elite of American Jewry including Bernard Baruch, Eugene Meyer, Paul Warburg, Oscar Straus, Felix Warburg, Albert Lasker, Otto Kahn, Julius Rosenwald, and Louis Marshall. All had distinguished themselves in public service, banking, law, or commerce. By associating them with the *Protocols'* critique of modern state building and by giving antisemitism a national platform for the first time, the *Independent* carried on the ignoble tradition, developed in nineteenth-century Europe, of demonizing Jews in an effort to pressure the state to disavow its relationship with them.[70]

Pipp was not around to witness the opening salvo in Ford's war. He left before it began, fully aware that in a matter of weeks the *Independent* was "going to start in on the Jews." Unable to assert any counterweight against Liebold and unable to talk Ford out of doing the campaign, he quit on March 31: "Conditions here are such that I cannot do my best work or anywhere near my best work. To continue would be doing so merely to get the salary, which I feel I do not care to do." After resigning, Pipp founded *Pipp's Weekly*, based in Detroit. In its pages he conducted a revealing muckraking crusade against Ford for the following three years. Often, an issue of *Pipp's Weekly* refuted claims made in that week's issue of the *Independent*. Pipp could not hope to compete against Ford's mighty, ready-made, mass-circulation machine, but while he was able, and as long as his conscience demanded, he made his newspaper a veritable "mine of fact and commentary on the inner workings of the Ford Motor Co[mpany]."[71]

Even before the "International Jew" series began, several journalists, including Herman Bernstein, editor of the *New York Jewish Tribune*, had been working to discredit the *Protocols*. In 1921, the *London Times* revealed its actual origins in three widely reprinted articles. Undeterred, the *Independent* continued its series, goading its targets with defamatory statements and daring them to sue.

The Ford International Weekly
THE DEARBORN
INDEPENDENT

By the Year *One Dollar*   Dearborn, Michigan, May 22, 1920   Single Copy *Five Cents*

The International Jew:
The World's Problem

"Among the distinguishing mental and moral traits of the Jews may be mentioned: distaste for hard or violent physical labor; a strong family sense and philoprogenitiveness; a marked religious instinct; the courage of the prophet and martyr rather than of the pioneer and soldier; remarkable power to survive in adverse environments, combined with great ability to retain racial solidarity; capacity for exploitation, both individual and social; shrewdness and astuteness in speculation and money matters generally; an Oriental love of display and a full appreciation of the power and pleasure of social position; a very high average of intellectual ability."

—The New International Encyclopedia.

THE Jew is again being singled out for critical attention throughout the world. His emergence in the financial, political and social spheres has been so complete and spectacular since the war, that his place, power and purpose in the world are being given a new scrutiny, much of it unfriendly. Persecution is not a new experience to the Jew, but intensive scrutiny of his nature and super-nationality is. He has suffered for more than 2,000 years from what may be called the instinctive anti-semitism of the other races, but this antagonism has never been intelligent nor has it been able to make itself intelligible. Nowadays, however, the Jew is being placed, as it were, under the microscope of economic observation that the reasons for his power, the reasons for his separateness, the reasons for his suffering may be defined and understood.

In Russia he is charged with being the source of Bolshevism, an accusation which is serious or not according to the circle in which it is made; we in America, hearing the fervid eloquence and perceiving the prophetic ardor of young Jewish apostles of social and industrial reform, can calmly estimate how it may be. In Germany he is charged with being the cause of the Empire's collapse and a very considerable literature has sprung up, bearing with it a mass of circumstantial evidence that gives the thinker pause. In England he is charged with being the real world ruler, who rules as a super-nation over the nations, rules by the power of gold, and who plays nation against nation for his own purposes, remaining himself discreetly in the background. In America it is pointed out to what extent the elder Jews of wealth and the younger Jews of ambition swarmed through the war organizations—principally those departments which dealt with the commercial and industrial business of war, and also the extent to which they have clung to the advantage which their experience as agents of the government gave them.

IN SIMPLE words, the question of the Jews has come to the fore, but like other questions which lend themselves to prejudice, efforts will be made to hush it up as impolitic for open discussion. If, however, experience has taught us anything it is that questions thus suppressed will sooner or later break out in undesirable and unprofitable forms.

The Jew is the world's enigma. Poor in his masses, he yet controls the world's finances. Scattered abroad without country or government, he yet presents a unity of race continuity which no other people has achieved. Living under legal disabilities in almost every land, he has become the power behind many a throne. There are ancient prophecies to the effect that the Jew will return to his own land and from that center rule the world, though not until he has undergone an assault by the united nations of mankind.

The single description which will include a larger percentage of Jews than members of any other race is this: he is in business. It may be only gathering rags and selling them, but he is in business. From the sale of old clothes to the control of international trade and finance, the Jew is supremely gifted for business. More than any other race he exhibits a decided aversion to industrial employment, which he balances by an equally decided adaptability to trade. The Gentile boy works his way up, taking employment in the productive or technical departments; but the Jewish boy prefers to begin as messenger, salesman or clerk—anything—so long as it is connected with the commercial side of the business. An early Prussian census illustrates this characteristic: of a total population of 269,400, the Jews comprised six per cent or 16,164. Of these, 12,000 were traders and 4,164 were workmen. Of the Gentile population, the other 94 per cent, or 153,236 people, there were only 17,000 traders.

A MODERN census would show a large professional and literary class added to the traders, but no diminution of the percentage of traders and not much if any increase in the number of wage toilers. In America alone most of the big business, the trusts and the banks, the natural resources and the chief agricultural products, especially tobacco, cotton and sugar, are in the control of Jewish financiers or their agents. Jewish journalists are a large and powerful group here. "Large numbers of department stores are held by Jewish firms," says the Jewish Encyclopedia, and many if not most of them are run under Gentile names. Jews are the largest and most numerous landlords of residence property in the country. They absolutely control the circulations of publications throughout the country. Fewer than any race whose presence among us is noticeable, they receive daily an amount of favorable publicity which would be impossible did they not have the facilities for creating and distributing it themselves. Werner Sombart, in his "Jew and Modern Capitalism" says, "If the conditions in America continue to develop along the same lines as in the last generation, if the immigration statistics and the proportion of births among all the nationalities remain the same, our imagination may picture the United States of fifty or a hundred years hence as a land inhabited only by Slavs, Negroes and Jews, wherein the Jews will naturally occupy the position of

1.6. Front cover, *Dearborn Independent*, May 22, 1920 (University of Chicago Libraries).

When Louis Marshall learned of the *Protocols* in 1918, he dismissed them as silly and unlikely to be taken seriously; in 1920 he had to step in to stop a prestigious American publisher, G. P. Putnam's Sons, from bringing out an American edition. That year alone, three other publishers issued English-language versions. By the time the refutations appeared, the *Protocols* had already found a receptive audience in the United States.[72]

The *Independent* was not the first such screed to appear in the United States, only the most widely distributed. Before World War I, nativist writings echoing similar themes appeared in such mainstream journals as *McClure's Magazine*, *Harper's Weekly*, and the *North American Review*. Their common purpose was to whip up opposition to Eastern European Jews—as well as Catholics, Greek Orthodox, and other non-Protestants—by casting aspersions on their qualifications for citizenship. Together, this propaganda and the ongoing nativist crusade to restrict immigration imbued American culture with explicitly racialized views of Jews. To contemporary progressives, the antisemitic articles in the *Independent* marked Ford as an ordinary racist with extraordinary resources. By linking Ford's influence and cultural importance to the nativist crusade, the newspaper gave a patina of legitimacy to assumptions about Jewish unfitness and racial inferiority. In the words of Howard Sachar, "the Ford assault represented the single profoundest shock [Jews] had encountered in twentieth-century America."[73] They never saw it coming.

2 MARSHALL FOR THE DEFENSE

I fear that our divisions . . . will be our undoing, unless the better element organizes in some authoritative way that will impose respect and submission.

—Rabbi Max Heller, 1920[1]

The May 22, 1920, issue of the *Dearborn Independent* landed in the offices of Jewish religious leaders, lawyers, intellectuals, and activists like a series of perfectly timed grenades. Cleveland's *Jewish Independent* immediately took up the gauntlet, running front-page editorials that provided week-by-week rebuttals to the Ford articles. Confusion and uncertainty were typical reactions. "Our people are thoroughly aroused," an Ohio rabbi noted irately, but "they do not know what to do." Other observers saw more ominous signs. Rabbi Max Heller of New Orleans warned a friend: "I fear American Judaism is on the eve of an unpalatable battle. Papers like the *Chicago Tribune* and the *Atlantic Monthly* give space to slanders and reflections upon us; . . . the public press has no condemnation [for] even so well proved a dolt as H[enr]y Ford."[2]

Amplifying the voices calling for action from within the Jewish community was the throbbing silence with which the mainstream press greeted the launch of Ford's antisemitic campaign. The *New York Times, Chicago Tribune, Wall Street Journal, Atlanta Constitution, Cleveland Plain Dealer,* and the *Los Angeles Times*—none of these national dailies printed a word about Ford's latest enterprise for weeks or even months after the *Independent* began attacking Jews. The inattention of the mainstream press complicated the politics of answering Ford. The Jewish communities of America were in a total uproar, but no one else seemed to care, at least not publicly. The fact that Ford's latest stunt failed to grab the national spotlight offered cold comfort to the nation's Jewish leaders. They knew that anything Ford did would become news eventually.[3]

Into this vacuum stepped Louis Marshall, lawyer and activist. His law firm, Guggenheimer, Untermyer & Marshall, occupied a prestigious space in a handsome brownstone located at 120 Broadway in lower Manhattan. As the city's oldest Jewish firm, the partnership drew more than the usual corporate and estate business. Like a magnet, Marshall attracted Jewish causes that required legal intervention and advocacy in and outside the courts. The matter of Henry Ford and the *Dearborn Independent* was no different, in Marshall's view, from any of the hundreds of entreaties and dispatches that had come to his desk since he began practicing law in 1877. He had only to glance at the headline of the May 22 issue—"The International Jew: The World's Problem"—before deciding to proceed. He called for his secretary and dictated a telegram.[4]

Marshall addressed his wire to Henry Ford personally. He did not bother to disguise his indignation. The *Dearborn Independent*, he noted, contained "articles which are disseminating antisemitism in its most insidious and pernicious form. The statements which they contain are palpable fabrications and the insinuations with which they abound are the emanations of hatred and prejudice." Marshall was not content merely to describe the articles as prejudicial; he went on to warn Ford that the *Independent* might attract undesirable legal attention: "They constitute a libel upon an entire people who had hoped that at least in America they might be spared the insult, the humiliation, and the obloquy which these articles are scattering throughout the land." He appealed directly to the idea that in America free people should not have to worry about being smeared so intolerably. Marshall pleaded with Ford to assure the country that the newspaper did not represent Ford's own beliefs: "I ask you from whom we had believed that justice might be expected whether these offensive articles have your sanction, whether further publications of this nature are to be continued, and whether you shall remain silent when your failure to disavow them will be regarded as an endorsement of them by the general public." In his final sentence, Marshall spoke for all the nation's Jews: "Three million of deeply wounded Americans are awaiting your answer."[5]

Marshall's majestic voice and ringing argument might have signaled to Ford that a formidable person, one unintimidated by power and wealth, led American Jews. Louis Marshall represented the pinnacle of German Jewish acculturation and socioeconomic attainment. His life was an immigrant success story; like Ford, he was a second-generation American. Suffused with the heady ideals of American constitutional law as a teenager, he extolled them loyally and constantly as an adult, convinced that Jews belonged as Americans.

In his life, work, and faith, Marshall carefully balanced Jewish identity with the obligations of American citizenship. He advised Jews to be Americans first and to maintain their Jewish faith proudly, because he saw no contradiction between secular citizenship and religious belief. "I am not one who believes in distinctions of race, creed or nationality," he declared. "[W]e are all American citizens, of equal rank, character and quality, equal in right and equal in duty and obligation," he reiterated during World War I.[6] This conception of equality, however firmly grounded in American law and constitutional theory, remained elusive in the early twentieth century, as long as white Protestants identified Jews as a separate religious and racial caste. Certainly printed and spoken speech freely articulated the ancient suspicions and hatreds that attended Jews wherever they lived, but American barriers to equality left a bitter aftertaste. Yet Marshall's accomplished career—as well as those of other distinguished American coreligionists—came to embody the best hopes of American Jews for attaining civic equality; for dissolving the offensive beliefs that reinforced discriminatory practices; and most essentially, for finding a way to become fully American while remaining Jewish. By the time the *Independent* appeared, Louis Marshall was the unquestioned leader of American Jewish civil rights activism.

. . .

Born on December 14, 1856, in Syracuse, New York, Marshall was the oldest of six children, the scion of one of the first German Jewish families to settle in upstate New York. Seven years Ford's senior, he held the advantages of education and intellectual sophistication over the automaker when their tangles began. Indeed, it could well have been Marshall, who was one of America's most prominent Jews by the end of World War I, whom Ford intended to bait with the *Independent's* hook.

Like Henry Ford, Marshall rose from humble beginnings. His father, "penniless and barely able to read or write," immigrated to the United States in 1849, after continental political revolution and rising nationalism broke up the insular Jewish communities dotting the German countryside. Louis's mother, Zilli Strauss, also endured the rough two-month Atlantic crossing from Germany, arriving in New York in 1853 at the age of twenty. The two met in Syracuse, married in 1855, and promptly settled into the familiar rhythms of domestic life.[7] To support his wife and their six children, Jacob opened a leather and tanning business that thrived as the town grew before the Civil War.[8]

Louis's childhood was braced by the staple ingredients of the American dream: a stable, intact family; doting parents who primed their son to succeed; and the assuredness and confidence that comes from economic stability and emotional comfort. While her husband fulfilled his responsibilities as a trader and businessman, Zilli Marshall lavished love and intellectual stimulation on her children. Intelligent and self-educated, Zilli saw herself as her children's primary teacher and the caretaker of their heritage. In that vein, she "[kept] alive a spirit of Judaism" and refused to learn English, even for her children. As Marshall remembered, "I spoke German before I knew a word of English, and so long as my mother lived (she died in 1910) I never spoke to her otherwise than in German." As Zilli worked in the family home, her sons read aloud to her, in German, the works of Schiller, Scott, and Hugo; while she rested, Louis recited to her from memory.[9]

Most important of all, Jacob and Zilli encouraged Louis to pursue his education. They recognized his "zest for knowledge" and compensated all they could for the time he spent away from school helping his father. By the age of eight, he was keeping his father's books; as he grew older, he performed more physical labor, "salting hides and calfskins" in the tanning shop. The Marshalls sent him to the Syracuse public schools and also to private German and Hebrew schools. Eventually he learned six languages, including French, Greek, and Latin. Later, when he was well into his fifties, Marshall learned Yiddish to improve communications with the Russian and Polish Jewish immigrant communities in lower Manhattan. Intellectually voracious, he "read everything within reach" and sought out still more diversions.[10]

One of the favorite pastimes of Syracuse teenagers was to form debating clubs. Louis joined at the age of twelve and jumped into the fray with the older students. More often than not, their topic was the U.S. Constitution. Louis immediately developed a passion for the text, its meaning, and its history: "I became engrossed in the creation of this new nation; [I] was eager to learn how its laws had been drawn and its institutions founded." He waxed grandiloquent in his later reminiscences: "I saw the beauty of the American ideal. Its glory illuminated my life. I determined to defend America and American principles with all my soul." Debate club was early training for the legal career he had already decided to pursue.[11]

Marshall's path from debating club to the bar charted the usual route for a nineteenth-century law student. After high school, he apprenticed for two years for a local lawyer. The office afforded a view of a square that had once served as the Syracuse village hay market, where his father's customers parked their wagons when they came to town. Marshall "ran errands, served papers, swept the floors, and built the fire," menial tasks that were essential for the office's smooth operation. He also spent long stretches of time in the office and next door at the courthouse library "zealously read[ing] all the books, even the oldest and dustiest ones and those no longer in use."[12]

His quick study and impressive recall caught the attention of local lawyers and a prominent judge, William C. Ruger, who later became chief justice of the state's highest court, the court of appeals. One day during Marshall's apprenticeship, the firm was in court, trying a case involving the Erie Canal. An old precedent with a complicated set of facts was invoked. Judge Ruger was eager to see the original opinion to compare the two cases, but the court's librarian was unable to locate the volume. A search failed to locate the book. "The lawyers were anxious to go on," a reporter later noted, "but the Judge insisted upon the document." Just then, a "small, earnest Jewish boy got up from a nook in a corner. 'I think, judge,' he said, blinking and swallowing his Adam's apple assiduously, 'I can get you a copy of what you want. . . . It's in some old papers over in Mr. Smith's office.' He grabbed his hat and hustled out. The [lawyers, both] deans of New York State law, sat and looked at each other. When the boy came in, clutching Moore's report and mopping his brow, Ruger took another chance. 'What I'm anxious to get,' he said, 'is [a] reference on struck juries.' 'Oh, yes, sir,' said the boy, 'I've just been looking up struck juries. I'll write you out a list of references. Most of them are here in the library, but they take a little time to find.' He got out his pencil and set to work." The boy was Marshall, whose reputation eventually eclipsed those of everyone else in the room that day.[13]

In September 1876, not yet twenty years old, he matriculated at Columbia Law School in New York City. He did not intend to stay long. Taking the first-year classes in the afternoon and the second-year classes in the mornings, Marshall finished the required two-year course of study in one year. The dry rules of judicial decisions—what most students labored to commit to memory—were for Marshall the raw materials of a mental library he had been building since childhood. Professor Theodore Dwight, head of the law school, quickly learned that he could call on Marshall to supply his class with the case name, citation, and even exact page number for any principle of law decided by any New York court. Because the law school required two years' residence to award a diploma, Marshall never formally graduated. It hardly mattered. Then he encountered another roadblock: he could not sit for the bar examination until he turned twenty-one. While he waited, he freelanced himself to other lawyers, writing briefs to support himself. In early 1878, finally licensed to practice, he returned to Syracuse, where he joined Judge Ruger's law firm.[14]

Marshall quickly established himself as one of the state's leading constitutional lawyers. Between 1878 and 1896, he argued at least 150 cases before the court of appeals, the state's highest court. In 1890, he served on a commission to revise the state's constitutional provision dealing with courts and in 1894 gained election to the state's constitutional convention. In 1915 he would be elected to another. With a "consistency that verged upon inflexibility," he promoted reforms that clarified the jurisdiction of the lower courts and rationalized the appeals process. He worked fifteen-hour days, becoming so familiar with state and federal constitutional cases that he could "dictate a brief, citing cases and quoting from opinions without leaving his desk or looking at a law book." It was a skill entirely of a piece with reciting Schiller's poems for his mother. His local fame was established beyond dispute when he represented a Catholic priest in a proceeding before a tribunal of the Catholic Church. The case required a brief and an oral argument, both rendered in Latin.[15]

The home life in which he found refuge and comfort enabled him to dedicate himself completely to his profession and his clients. During this time, one of his law clerks later observed, "he had little outside interests except his profession." With his material needs and domestic comforts provided for, he was free to put in inhuman hours at the office each day and to remain apparently disinterested in a social life apart from his parents' established routines and contacts. As long as he lived in Syracuse, marriage remained a distant prospect. While he lived at home, Louis continued to observe Orthodox Judaism dutifully with his parents, although while in law school he had embraced the liberalism of Reform Judaism. Social and religious life in Syracuse revolved around Zilli Marshall. His mother's strong influence hardly diminished once Marshall attained adulthood and embarked on his profession; in 1928, he declared, "[L]ooking back seventy-two years I can say without any qualification that she was the greatest influence upon my life." For him, "Syracuse was a comfortable place in which to live, not entirely detached from the rural environment, and with the surrounding hills always in view."[16]

As Marshall's portfolio ranged beyond local corporate matters, he became acquainted with other nationally prominent Jewish lawyers. In 1891, he and a carefully chosen delegation urged President Benjamin Harrison to intercede with Russia on its treatment of Jews, an issue of growing concern after brutal pogroms in 1881. A case involving Jewish philanthropy and a contested will took him to Philadelphia, where he sought out Mayer Sulzberger, the distinguished common pleas court judge, and Cyrus Adler, the first American-trained Ph.D. holder in Semitics, at that time a curator for the Smithsonian Institution. Sulzberger referred Marshall to Randolph Guggenheimer, partner in the New York law firm of Guggenheimer and Untermyer, to help with Marshall's case, but the men had even more to connect them. Guggenheimer's partner and half brother, Samuel Untermyer, had been Marshall's classmate at Columbia; the two had traded cases since leaving law school. At Untermyer's behest, Guggenheimer extended Marshall an offer that changed his life.[17]

In the fall of 1894, Guggenheimer invited Marshall to come to New York City and join his firm. The position offered him higher professional status and greater financial prospects than anything left for him to accomplish in Syracuse. The job promised more than greater material reward, however; it gave Marshall a national platform for his growing interest in Jewish civil rights in a city that was swiftly becoming the epicenter of legal activism. Still, it was a momentous decision. Marshall's contemporaries wondered at his decision to leave Syracuse, the hometown he loved, where his life was so well established and where he stood anointed as the "plumed knight" of the Syracuse bar. But once he arrived in New York in the fall of 1894, in Edith Wharton's New York, with its overt social hierarchies and polite antisemitism, he wasted no time in creating a new domestic life.[18]

Here, too, the firm provided. Samuel Untermyer introduced Marshall to Florence Lowenstein, a young Untermyer cousin. Eighteen years Marshall's junior, Lowenstein was New York City born and bred, the eldest daughter of a Prussian dry-goods dealer and his American-born wife. The courtship proceeded apace. He was wealthy and professionally established; she was well educated and came from a respectable family. By February 1895, the two were exchanging formal notes. Lowenstein assured her suitor that she was "grateful" for his attentions. Marshall proceeded deliberately: "Availing myself of the welcome which you have accorded to me, I must ask you not to deem me too persistent, if I request you to receive me on Saturday evening—I have much to say to you." A week later, he proposed, and her acceptance made him giddy: "My darling Florence: After leaving you last night, I met a picture of my former self coming up the avenue—a poor, untouched, unhappy, former bachelor. No joy of humanity was on his countenance—cold and impassive . . . . How changed a man I am, from the one I was—the one I have just described. . . . Oh that I could at this moment gaze into that *soulful face*, into those loving eyes and pour out my heart in kisses! Impatient to meet once more, I am your Louis." They married on May 6, 1895, Florence's twenty-first birthday. Nearly every day of their engagement, Louis wrote to his intended and pleaded with her to reciprocate "if not for the present, [then] for the sake of the future."[19]

Marshall's hurry was understandable. Thirty-nine at the time of his marriage, he was eager to begin his life as Florence's husband. The new couple moved into a lovely home on the Upper East Side, and Florence joined Louis for services at Temple Emanu-El, New York's oldest Reform congregation and the nation's largest synagogue structure, then located at Fifth Avenue and East Forty-Third Street. The Marshalls swiftly welcomed children, whom they educated at the New York Ethical Cultural School—a departure from the traditional Hebrew schools Marshall attended as a child. James, born in 1897, followed his father into law and joined his father's firm. Ruth, the only daughter and her father's special confidante in his later years, was born in 1898. In 1920, she married Jacob Billikopf, the executive director of the Joint Distribution Committee for the Relief of Jewish War Sufferers. Robert, born in 1901, became an outspoken advocate of wilderness preservation from his post in the U.S. Forest Service. George, born in 1904, earned a Ph.D. in economics and became a pioneer in the American civil rights movement after World War II. He served jail time for refusing to name names before the House Un-American Activities Committee in 1946.[20]

Louis and Florence were proud parents of the children they groomed to accomplishment and distinction. But time was not a friend to them. The Marshalls had exactly twenty-one years together. In 1915, Florence fell ill with breast cancer; in May the following year she succumbed at the age of forty-two. By then, with both his parents gone, Louis was left once again to devote himself entirely to his work and, in time, to enjoy his grandchildren.[21]

After his wife's death, Marshall pursued a solitary, work-focused routine and by all accounts sported a modest outward appearance. "Louis Marshall never lived like the millionaire he was," according to the *New Yorker*. He "never owned an automobile" and wore his hats until the felt gave out. Friends often saw him riding the subway to work and scanning the newspaper for baseball box scores. He gave generously to Jewish philanthropic organizations for relief work in the United States and Europe and was notoriously thrifty: "[H]e would save stamped, addressed envelopes received from businesses . . . and use them

2.1. Louis Marshall with his father, Jacob Marshall, and his son, James Marshall, ca. 1900 (courtesy American Jewish Archives, Cincinnati, Ohio, Collection No. PC-2875).

in his personal correspondence." He kept an extensive home library, where he did the bulk of his reading and writing. One indulgence he permitted himself was the accumulation of a sizable collection of valuable art, which adorned the walls of his residence.[22]

Marshall had an outsized personality to go with his high-powered career. He was a character among his friends; he was a curmudgeon to strangers with the temerity to impose on his time. "Usually kindly, even jovial, his profanity was matchless when aroused. He sometimes even startled banquets and luncheons with purple phrases." Marshall enjoyed writing poetry and delighted in producing sonnets for his granddaughters. "A few of these were published anonymously. He occasionally wrote humorous sketches in dialect and read them to friends." Despite these softer edges, people around him knew better than to cross him or contradict him. His sometimes imperious affect drew the moniker "Louis XIX," and a friend coined the ironic phrase "Marshall law" to describe his imperious, unilateral negotiating style.[23]

With his impressive record, he expected deference and became accustomed to winning. He accepted losses with grace, perhaps because he did not lose often. He embodied, again much like Ford, the values of his time, particularly on economic issues. His specialty was defending corporations from legislative price and wage regulations. That remunerative part of his practice enabled him to take other types of cases on principle: "So devoutly did the noted lawyer revere the Constitution that he regarded anyone who broke an amendment, including the Eighteenth, as practically guilty of treason. A die-hard Republican, he would defend anyone of any party if it were on constitutional grounds." Marshall even defended socialists thrown out of the New York Assembly: "He had no use for Socialists but he did for their constitutional rights. He defended the Civil Liberties Union. Often he took such cases without a fee, and once he said he would be willing to pay for the privilege."[24]

His constitutional values were in accord with the conservative drift of the era and of American law. He did not worry about being out of sync with the direction of institutions and politics, and so he could occasionally champion an idea as radical as civil rights without jeopardizing his professional standing. In the words of Oscar Handlin, Marshall sought "always to elevate laws above men and to avoid the hysteria of mass action."[25] He consistently worked his civil rights activism into the broader fabric of his legal conservatism, defining the rights of immigrants, African Americans, and Jews as part of the larger panoply of the rights inherent in American citizenship. By refusing to countenance racial distinctions, he believed, American law would secure the rights of property and contract exactly where they belonged—at the top of the constitutional pyramid.

There was one issue, however, that Marshall could not entirely resolve. His social position and wealth did not immunize him from the cultural dissonance that Jews—even native-born citizens—experienced in the United States. Marshall, who constantly argued that immigrants had a duty to acculturate swiftly, was himself caught between his ancestral roots and his intense desire to be accepted as unreservedly and wholly American. Marshall dealt with that tension by bringing the influence of German and Jewish culture to bear on his public life and activism. The elite German Jews of New York "looked to Germany as one of the sources of their culture," according to Oscar Handlin. "Yet they were also acutely conscious of the Americanizing influence of their environment and approved of it." They approved of it, perhaps, because they believed that the fundamentally egalitarian thrust of American society offered a real chance for achieving what they had never been able to accomplish in Germany: a fuller integration of social and cultural citizenship.[26]

Marshall spent his career trying to balance the competing loyalties of nation and faith. On the one hand, he proclaimed his civic allegiance in every case he argued before the bar. On the other hand, what his forebears had faced in Germany—the "articulate struggle to live with a plurality of identities and cultures"—was not significantly different from the challenges facing even the "best Jews" in the United States. Most American Jews of German descent saw little contradiction between the requirements of their faith, which was itself undergoing thorough doctrinal and liturgical transformation, and the obligations of citizenship. Marshall consistently preached that there should be no "Jewish bloc" or "Jewish vote" in American elections: "[F]or years I have insisted that there is not and must not be a Jewish vote. . . . [W]henever Jews perform the sacred duties of citizenship it must be as unlabeled Americans. I have vigorously opposed the organization of Jewish political clubs. . . . Jews as individuals should regard it as a solemn duty to take part in elections and to vote according to their personal political convictions." Of course, by the late 1920s, when he made this remark, there was no mistaking the fact that Jews voted in readily identifiable blocs and that both major parties strategized accordingly.[27]

As Cyrus Adler, himself an exemplar of acculturation, noted in 1930, "[I]n the new land in which opportunity was granted, and at a time when freedom was a real ideal, [German Jews] became fervid Americans. Not being morbidly introspective, they found no contradiction between this state of mind and that of deep attachment to their ancestral faith."[28] But Jews faced continual opposition from those who did. Most non-Jewish white people thought that no Jew could ever become fully American. The tendency among elite German Jews to dismiss the notion that Judaism could be perceived as incompatible with American civic loyalty led them, and Marshall in particular, to underestimate the degree of opposition to Jews' full inclusion in society. Thus, the acknowledged champion of the Jewish people in America unintentionally put himself in the strange position of minimizing what it was about Jews that made them prone to discrimination.

. . .

By the time Ford's newspaper began attacking Jews, the dangers they faced had become more real than they had been in Marshall's youth. Everything he had done in his career and all the trappings of his life on Manhattan's Upper East Side—the comfortable home, the book-lined study, the valuable art collection—might have entitled Marshall to think, on some level, that individuals with native gifts and the ambition to realize their potential could achieve success in America. Yet Americans' perceptions of Jews worsened as the nineteenth century drew to a close. Civil rights for blacks took promising shape in the Civil War constitutional amendments, only to wither on the vine as state and federal courts cut back on equality for racial minorities during and after Reconstruction. New waves of immigration from new areas of the world introduced tensions into the Jewish community and heightened the sense of difference that white Americans used to distance themselves from Jews.[29]

Americans' willingness to accept the Jews already in their midst coexisted uneasily with the seemingly immutable concepts of race and color that defined late-nineteenth-century social life. Indeed, white European Americans hedged their acceptance of Jews as political equals by consistently regarding Jews as racially distinct from themselves. In this habit the dominant group acted on long-standing attitudes. Unbridgeable religious differences and perceptions of Jews as preoccupied with money contributed to the widely held view of Jews as unassimilable and thus incapable of becoming loyal American citizens.[30] The perception of Jews as a separate group, religious, racial, and otherwise, was fed by a series of developments in Europe, particularly Germany, that alarmed Jews who felt they had safely established themselves in America, some near society's upper echelons.

The first of these sobering developments was the rise in Germany of an expansive, extended hate literature directed at Jews. This new wave of published bigotry led to the coining of a new word: *antisemitism*, meant "to describe and justify ('scientifically') anti-Jewish propaganda and discrimination." The fact that this racial hatred came out of Germany was particularly disturbing to German American Jews, who made up the vast majority of the Jewish population in the country at the time. According to Jonathan Sarna, "What made this situation even worse was that antisemitism and particularly social discrimination soon spread to America's own shores. Anti-Jewish hatred was certainly not new to America, but Jews had previously considered it something of an anachronism, alien both to the modern temper and to American democracy." The cautious optimism that Jews felt since the Civil War began to ebb, overtaken by an increase in the scale and frequency of social discriminations against them. Hotels, resorts, and theme parks began to turn Jews away after welcoming them for years.[31]

The second development was the wave of violence against Jews in the Russian Empire following the assassination of Tsar Alexander II in 1881. Mobs attacked Jews while the forces of order failed, or failed to try, to stop the pillaging. The destruction of Jews' property and the attacks on their towns, together with Alexander III's renewal of policies designed to make life even more miserable for Jews, unleashed the greatest migration in Jewish history. Jews departing Russia and Eastern Europe for the United States at this time came in numbers large enough to cause alarm in major eastern cities where they initially settled. Between 1881 and 1900, 675,000 Jews entered the United States, more than doubling the number of Jews already living in the country. Significantly, most of these new immigrants came not from Germany or Central Europe but from Eastern Europe, Russia, Russian Poland, Galicia, and Romania. Germany's Jews, having achieved full emancipation and greater economic inclusion, all but stopped coming. The result was that the two great waves of Jewish immigrants—pre– and post–Civil War—shared little aside from their faith. And even that, in view of Reform Judaism's advances among German American Jews and the strength of Orthodox Judaism among the newer arrivals, did not supply the common currency that might have helped smooth the social and cultural transitions of immigration.[32]

These immigration trends led to what Leonard Dinnerstein has called "the emergence of an antisemitic society" between the Civil War and the turn of the twentieth century, a time when stereotypes, racialized perceptions of Jews, and the ancient mythology that fed religious animosity all hardened in American politics and popular culture. Huge groups of Orthodox Jews from outside the usual European points of origin clustered in American cities, living in squalor and earning meager wages as peddlers and traders, pawnbrokers and tailors. The Jewish population in New York City exploded from eighty thousand in the 1870s to nearly 1.5 million by 1915, comprising 28 percent of the city's population and making it the largest urban concentration of Jews in the world. Although whites perhaps all saw the same thing when they looked at Jews, these new arrivals from Eastern Europe were hardly a monolithic bunch; they were divided by religious issues, social tensions, and old prejudices. In the districts of Manhattan where they clustered, Jews lived in "clearly demarcated sub-ethnic districts." They maintained traditional standards of dress and appearance, spoke and wrote in Yiddish, and showed decidedly less inclination to become acculturated than their German predecessors.[33]

Even if such an existence marked for most only a temporary stage in a longer journey, it reinforced stereotypes of Jews that already studded popular literature and the press. Shakespeare's Shylock and Charles Dickens's Fagin supplied Americans with a ready image of Jews as contemptible hucksters and dishonest opportunists. These cultural signals and the new immigrants reawakened the antisemitism of the Civil War era and cranked its volume higher than ever. Anthropologists coined new theories of racial character and identification to substantiate the subordination of Jews to Christian whites, just as they had done to justify the enslavement of blacks earlier in the century. The situation Jews faced in the final years of the nineteenth century was unwinnable: "Most unforgivable was their religion; but also in education, manner of dress, culture, in their very occupations, they were different. . . . In brief, they were nonconformists, no matter how much they wanted to be Americans." Social critics lumped Jews with the Chinese, Hindis, and other East Asians in calling for an end to the nation's open door policy and for new restrictions on immigration. Nativism, religious bigotry, and scientific racism were on the march.[34]

These developments caused a major shift in the status and degree of welcome that established Jews had come to expect in their native and adopted land. Gentiles tended to lump the strange-looking and strange-sounding

Russian immigrants in lower Manhattan with English-speaking German Jews and even native American-born Jews of Western European descent. As a result of white non-Jewish European Americans' disinclination to recognize the many religious, social, linguistic, political, and economic differences among Jews in America, the new impulse toward restrictive immigration and social and economic discrimination hit all Jews, however Americanized they had become. As Judith Goldstein notes, in "housing, resorts, private clubs, and schools, the community-at-large had restricted the choices of American Jews." Jews of German, Spanish, and Portuguese descent who had lived in the United States for decades were increasingly "social[ly] vulnerab[le]" as white Americans reacted to the influx of Southern and Eastern European Jews.[35]

The situation bred resentment on all sides. Jews who traced their families to Western Europe held much more wealth and all of the social status, whereas Russian Jews far outnumbered all other Jewish subgroups in New York City by 1905. German Jews owned many of the factories in which the newcomers found work. The social elites of American Jewry "followed the contemporary model of the Gentile community by excluding the Russian Jews from their clubs, schools, and leadership positions in the A[merican] J[ewish] C[ommittee] and other German-Jewish organizations" that formed shortly after the turn of the twentieth century.[36]

Social exclusion of Jews accelerated after 1880. In particular, the urban upper classes worked to put as much distance between themselves and Jews as they could. Hotels, resorts, private schools, and exclusive communities of summer homes in the Northeast all sided with the upper crust. "By the early 1880s," Leonard Dinnerstein observes, "social discrimination against Jews was obvious wherever prominent members of Gentile society gathered in cities like Los Angeles, New Orleans, Mobile, Portland, Oregon, Cincinnati, Columbus, Akron, Cleveland, Denver, Philadelphia, Rochester, N.Y., and, of course, Boston and New York." Many Jews found these petty practices and discriminations infuriating and said so publicly. Others took refuge in their own institutions, schools, and social circles. The *American Hebrew*, a newspaper reflecting the perspective of "well-to-do, reform-minded Jews," commented editorially that separation appealed to Jews, too: "We have our own social circle . . . we are not desirous of seeking other circles—certainly not when unwelcome there."[37]

From where he worked and lived in New York City, Marshall witnessed the rise of a new wave of racial hatred toward Jews and monitored a growing literature that argued that Jews were racially unfit for inclusion in America. "Many of the upper- and middle-class Americans," Dinnerstein writes, "regarded some of the new immigrants as barbarians." Old and new periodicals, journals, and newspapers produced the muckraking journalism that forced the passage of much-needed federal reforms, but they accompanied these crusades with a torrent of antisemitic publicity and comment that clearly shifted the blame for public corruption and urban decay to Jews, many of them too poor to own property, much less profit from corporate greed. Despite evidence to the contrary, observers insisted on declaring Jews unclean, uneducated, and prone to illness and premature death.[38] Such demeaning descriptions fed white non-Jewish Americans' tendencies to regard Jews as racially inferior. After 1900, their widespread dissemination began to fuel more than mere expressions of denigration.

In 1902, at the height of a long, hot Manhattan summer, the funeral for Jacob Joseph, a prominent Orthodox rabbi, took place on the Lower East Side. That neighborhood had long attracted Jews from Russia and Eastern Europe, and a sharp uptick in new arrivals between 1900 and 1902 increased social tensions in the area. Those who could move out did so; but poorer immigrants lacked mobility. As Rabbi Joseph's bier passed a printing press factory, workers hung out the windows, shouting insults. Eventually they began to throw "screws, bolts, and nuts" at the nearly twenty thousand mourners. Some in the procession burst into the plant, demanding satisfaction; they were "swept out by the use of a fire-hose." Factory managers then called police, who responded by attacking the crowd that had already resumed the trip to the cemetery. The resulting riot pitted Jews against the police, who beat savagely anyone within reach of their clubs while shouting antisemitic slurs. For decades, historians have presumed that Irish Catholics were to blame for the riot, but a more recent examination of census and arrest records shows that the preponderance of workers in the plant and those jailed after the riot were, in fact, of German descent.[39]

New York's various Jewish communities came together over this incident. In public demonstrations, they demanded that the mayor investigate and discipline the police, whom they regarded as abusive and unresponsive to complaints in their neighborhoods. A five-person committee was appointed, and Marshall, the city's most prominent Jew, was included on the panel. Within two months, the committee delivered its report to the mayor, a report Dinnerstein calls "a devastating indictment of the police." The report recommended disciplinary action against rank-and-file officers who had participated in the riot and found the captain whose slurs had inflamed the beat officers guilty of dereliction of duty. Still, the officers were acquitted of criminal charges, and the captain was permitted to resign.[40]

Marshall was satisfied with the results of the oversight process: "[T]he effect has been most salutary, the Jewish people being now protected by the police against similar outrages, where before, their complaints were unnoticed. Moreover, they now receive better treatment in the police courts." Marshall's analysis of the Joseph incident emphasized the symbolic politics of the mayoral commission's report and minimized the continuing brutal treatment that Jews commonly received from police: "[I]t was demonstrated to the satisfaction of the entire world," Marshall wrote in 1902, "that the infamous charges that had been made, that the Jews were the aggressors, were utterly without foundation." He took satisfaction in the condemnation by "the press of the entire country" of those responsible for the violence, because he believed, "[i]n this country public opinion is the greatest power for good." Marshall thought that the strength of public opinion would ensure that "the rights of the Jews will be better safe-guarded than they could be by an army of soldiers."[41] In short, Marshall believed that if Jews could win respect and fair treatment in the province of public opinion—if outrageous charges against Jews could be debunked through spoken and published speech—no further action, legal or otherwise, would be necessary. It was a legal and public relations philosophy that would meet its greatest test from Henry Ford and the *Dearborn Independent.*

Before that test came, Marshall deployed this approach in a number of controversies involving the civil rights of American Jews. In most cases, he was able to manage matters according to his studied preferences of avoiding litigation and other undignified forms of public outrage. Instead, Marshall honed his leadership skills, worked behind the scenes, and maintained throughout that he labored on behalf of the constitutional rights of all Americans—not merely of Jews. The case of Russia's treatment of Jews traveling on American passports ended in triumph for Marshall's strategies and tactics in nearly every respect.

Russia's late-nineteenth-century pogroms ticked off a surge of travel not just to the United States but also back to Russia. American businessmen with commercial interests wanted to inspect their properties in Russia between the periodic outbreaks of violence. Others were anxious to check on family members, perhaps help them emigrate. For years, the tsar's officials had been in the habit of interviewing all American visitors on their arrival. Their intention was to determine which Americans were Jews and deny them entry into the country. This practice violated an 1832 commercial treaty that guaranteed citizens of either nation the right to enter and conduct business "with the same security and protection as natives of the country . . . on condition of their submitting to the laws and ordinances there prevailing." When Russian consular officials in the United States adopted this practice during the 1890s, depriving American citizens of their rights on U.S. soil, Jewish leaders prevailed on successive presidential administrations to condemn it.[42]

Brushing U.S. protests aside, the Russians continued the practice. Then a second, bloodier wave of pogroms "rolled across western Russia" in late 1905 and 1906. More than seven hundred towns and villages were attacked, and more than two hundred thousand people died or were displaced. The violence produced another intense wave of emigration; this time, unlike the 1880s, nearly all of it came to the United States. Jewish Americans sought to help victims of violence and persecution in Russia, but they found it difficult to organize private relief efforts without a central organization or established body to coordinate fund-raising and manage logistics. The violence, particularly the graphic reports emerging from the town of Kishinev in 1903, spurred leading Jews to put together a permanent organization. The American Jewish Committee (AJC) would serve philanthropic and relief causes at home and abroad and defend against antisemitic discrimination wherever it threatened the civil rights of American Jews.[43]

Marshall, ever at the forefront, took advantage of the prevailing mood. Organization "is in the air," he observed. It was also not far from his fingertips. In late 1905, he persuaded his friends to form a national defense organization that would "represent every shade of Jewish opinion in this country, and which [would] fairly represent the consensus of Jewish opinion." Yet it was no less important, as Marshall said, "to avoid mischief" of the sort that arose when too many cooks tried to run the kitchen. The distinguished Philadelphia judge Mayer Sulzberger was elected president, and Marshall accepted the office of vice president, a role that ensured him an influential voice in the new organization's affairs. By ensuring that the AJC drew its members from the same social and professional elites in which he traveled and by squelching rival organizations before they got off the ground, Marshall ensured that his circle of intimates controlled the AJC; how it was run; and most important, how representative it would be.[44]

This last point became a serious bone of contention among Jewish leaders not ten years later, when World War I presented novel questions and tested the cohesion of Jewish leadership in ways unanticipated at the AJC's founding. The group was often criticized as elitist and deaf to the concerns of the majority of American Jews, specifically those from Southern and Eastern Europe. The AJC's critics formed the rival American Jewish Congress in 1918 to be more broadly representative of Jews, whatever their ethnic origins. At the time of the AJC's founding, however, Marshall prevailed in limiting its scope and mission. In February 1906, fifty-seven invited guests from all over the country convened in Philadelphia to organize the AJC. Their plan, in the words of former U.S. ambassador Oscar Straus, was "to aid in securing the civil and religious rights of the Jews in all countries where these are denied or endangered." It could not be claimed that these men (and men only) spoke for the Jewish masses, but the delegates saw themselves as a cross-section of American Jewish leadership. Decision-making authority was vested in an executive committee consisting of the AJC's constitutional officers and regional representatives selected by its president. At the outset, the AJC identified only three issues that merited attention and resources: assisting the victims of pogroms in Europe, pressuring the U.S. government to obtain fair and equal treatment for Jews holding American passports, and raising funds for humanitarian relief and philanthropic purposes. This limited commission, in the words of Jacob Rader Marcus, "proved efficient and successful. [The AJC] reached out to help Jews in Morocco and Turkey as well as Russian refugees. It struggled with some degree of success to fend off anti-immigration legislation and defeated those forces in the United States that had set out to classify would-be Jewish immigrants as 'Asiatics' (the United States had been excluding Chinese since 1882)."[45] Under Marshall, the AJC sought to deploy influence discreetly rather than engage in confrontational politics or lawsuits—with mixed success.

Marshall used that approach to resolve the Russian passport question. Despite the pressure exerted at high levels by Jacob H. Schiff and Oscar Strauss for more than two decades, no American president wanted to abrogate the Russian commercial treaty of 1832. On May 28, 1907, Secretary of State Elihu Root appeared to capitulate to the tsarists entirely when he issued a circular letter informing travelers that no passports would be issued "to former Russian subjects or to Jews who intend going into Russian territory, unless [the State Department] has assurance that the Russian Government will consent to their admission." This policy, Marshall protested to Secretary Root, "withholds from [American Jews] one of the privileges of citizenship if they harbor the intention of visiting Russia without having first secured the consent of the Russian Government. All other citizens, of whatever race or creed, are assured an unlimited passport, and are guaranteed the absolute protection of our flag." This was typical of Marshall's approach: treat all citizens alike, whatever their race or religion, including those who happen to be Jewish. The passport question was not a Jewish question; rather, it was a matter of guaranteeing equal rights to all who traveled under American passports. This lawyerly approach attracted criticism, some of it from within the AJC. In turn, Marshall began to lose patience with people who feared offending the Russians. In 1908, five years after the Kishinev massacre, he complained, "[W]e are getting to be too damned diplomatic."[46]

President Taft, however, was no more inclined to abrogate the treaty than his predecessors, costing him the support of Schiff and other important Jews in 1912. The AJC spent several years internally debating strategy before finally mounting a discreet campaign that involved the use of some public tactics for the first time. In January 1911, Marshall delivered a speech in New York to the delegates of the Union of American Hebrew Congregations (UAHC). In the address, he argued passionately that the passport question affected all Americans. It put "a stain on the honor of our nation and on the integrity of American citizenship," because Russia could willfully disregard the sanctity of a U.S. passport when its holder was a Jew. Still prioritizing trade and property, President Taft continued to rebuff the pro-abrogation forces. The AJC, B'nai B'rith, and the UAHC then went into a full-court press, getting abrogation resolutions introduced in fifteen state legislatures and finally, by the end of 1911, producing a congressional resolution that passed the House by a 300–1 vote (eighty-seven members abstained). Recognizing that the full Congress would abrogate the treaty and vote to override his threatened veto, President Taft finally consented to congressional abrogation and informed the tsar's government of the U.S.'s intentions.[47]

In all his work on the passport question Marshall took care to identify himself as the AJC's representative. Still, he expressed a great personal elation "now that success has crowned my efforts." In legal terms, he saw the abrogation as "the removal of the last civil disabilities to which the Jews of this country have been subjected." It was also a demonstration of the AJC's rising influence with national government, as well as Marshall's. Shortly after this victory, Sulzberger decided not to stand for another term as the organization's president. In 1912, Marshall assumed the position and held it until his death seventeen years later.[48]

Toppling Russia's explicit discrimination against Jews did not guarantee that antisemitic feeling would disappear from American legal proceedings. A worrisome sign of increasing antipathy toward Jews was the ordeal of Leo M. Frank, an Atlanta factory manager who was accused of the 1913 murder of Mary Phagan, a thirteen-year-old girl in his employ. The case was a forensic and prosecutorial mess. Rather than pursue evidence pointing to the guilt of an African American worker, police instead trained their suspicions on Frank, a New York–born and educated Jew. As Frank's trial progressed, the courtroom was infiltrated by hysteria that trapped the judge as much as it did the defendant. Railroaded by Atlanta's newspapers' daily demands for justice, the trial judge suggested to Frank's lawyers that the defendant remain in his cell for the reading of the verdict. After Frank was found guilty, members of the jury told local newspapers that they felt they had had no choice but to return a guilty verdict or suffer lynching themselves. With deliberations so tainted, Frank's friends and advocates in Georgia felt certain they could win on appeal. Fanning northward to spread the news of Frank's trouble and garner support for his plight, they had no trouble convincing Marshall to take Frank's case. Marshall was careful, however, to make it clear to all who asked that he represented Frank in his capacity as a private attorney, not as a representative of the American Jewish Committee. He did not want Frank's case to be identified only as a Jewish cause. But he was overlooking the central dynamic that would determine Frank's fate: the ability of Southern antisemitism to rival Southern antiblack racism in tainting the legal process.[49]

Marshall could not imagine how any appellate court could permit a verdict produced by "a crime against justice" to stand. When mob sentiments and the threat of mob action influenced the work of judges and juries, he believed, the legal system would defend itself and its integrity, not surrender to the intimidation of "mob demonstrations." His optimism, and that of Frank's trial lawyers, proved misplaced. Both the Georgia state courts and the federal courts repeatedly affirmed the guilty verdict. In all, the courts turned Frank away thirteen times between late 1913 and mid-1915. As long as there was a chance for a favorable hearing, Marshall urged friends and fellow activists to lay low. He was worried that any outpouring of sentiment on Frank's behalf, particularly if it originated from outside the South, would only make things worse for his client. As Frank proceeded to lose repeatedly on appeal, it became increasingly difficult for Marshall to control everyone else. *New York Times* publisher Adolph Ochs waged a sustained editorial campaign that awakened Americans to Frank's plight but also, as Marshall feared, stirred up resentment in Atlanta. The *Jeffersonian*, the broadside sheet of Tom Watson, fiery ex-populist turned U.S. Senator, outdid Atlanta's Hearst-owned *Georgian* in stoking antisemitic fears and trafficking in racist stereotypes as the appeals process dragged on.[50]

While the case was pending in the federal courts, Marshall kept his impatience at bay making two successive runs at the U.S. Supreme Court. The first was a direct appeal of Frank's state case in November 1914; the Court declined review within the month. Then, when the federal district court in Georgia turned down Frank's habeas corpus claim in early 1915, Marshall filed again. All the while, Marshall advised Jews to remain discreet, instead prompting Christian ministers and other non-Jewish leaders to publish commentaries in the Southern press in the hope of influencing local opinion in a less inflammatory way. Marshall sought to lay the groundwork for political acceptance of a pardon of Frank; meanwhile, as he cautioned one of Frank's advocates, "we are not as yet out of the courts."[51]

The courts proceeded to disappoint him in every conceivable way. The Supreme Court scheduled argument in Frank's habeas case for late February 1915. Marshall described the hearing's significance to Frank's rabbi, David Marx, in late December: "What we have gained, has been an opportunity to present our cause to the world, before its greatest judicial tribunal. I am satisfied that our legal position is sound, and I have a profound faith that right and justice will in the end prevail." Only two justices, Hughes and Holmes, voted to grant Frank a new trial. Marshall confessed to a "bitter disappointment" over the ruling: "I fear that I shall never again be able to feel that reliance upon the courts in respect to the accomplishment of the ends of justice that I have hitherto entertained." He held out hope that the two dissents, together with his campaign to "bring every possible influence to bear in [Frank's] behalf," would induce either the Georgia Board of Prison Commissioners or Governor John Slaton to commute Frank's sentence. When Slaton mustered the political courage to do so, Frank and his partisans celebrated the possibility they might eventually win a new trial and, eventually, Frank's freedom.[52]

They never got the chance. Shortly after dusk fell on Monday, August 16, 1915, twenty-five of Atlanta and Marietta's leading citizens kidnapped Leo Frank from the state prison in Milledgeville, drove him through the night to a farm adjoining Mary Phagan's birthplace, and hung him from a stately oak tree. Three thousand people came to see the body before it was cut down; the hanging rope was hacked into pieces and sold for souvenirs. One of the leaders of the lynch mob—a sitting judge—prevented the bystanders from desecrating Frank's corpse by arranging its quick removal to Atlanta in a Ford Model T.[53]

Marshall was utterly crestfallen. "No fair-minded man who has studied the record can reach any other conclusion than that of the absolute innocence of Frank," he wrote after the lynching. "Perhaps out of all of this evil some good may eventually come. But how, it is as yet difficult to say." Yet he declined to see antisemitism as the agent of Frank's fate. The case, Marshall insisted, "involved fundamental principles of justice and in which the religious faith of Frank was only an incident which was injected into the situation at one of its later stages." The blame for Frank's death, Marshall believed, rested with the Georgia criminal justice system, which he judged guilty of "judicial murder."[54] Even in this ghastly example of the first lynching of an American Jew, Marshall sought to separate Jewish identity from the denial of legal equality to any American, of whatever race, religion, or creed. To this principle, so sorely tested by Frank's tragic murder, he remained deeply, inflexibly committed.

Other Jews were beginning to stake out different approaches to civil rights activism, however, and after the Frank case they did so in more public ways than the AJC found acceptable. The Anti-Defamation League (ADL) of B'nai B'rith, which was organized in 1913 in response to Frank's arrest, denounced the published antisemitism that was responsible for ginning up public opinion against him in Atlanta. Frank's case was a rare exception to the general pattern of American antisemitism, which remained a localized phenomenon that did not lead to widespread physical violence against Jews. Yet American Jewish leaders had grown nervous, uncertain as to how antisemitic sentiment would manifest itself in American political and civic life. If anything, the Frank case seemed to indicate that Jews were capable of being construed as the moral and social equivalent of American blacks. Lynching, after all, was a punishment meted out by whites on blacks outside the rule of law, with complete impunity.[55]

Compounding that anxiety was the war in Europe, which led Americans to question the loyalty of recent arrivals, regard anyone speaking German with outright suspicion, and renew racial standards for awarding citizenship and welcoming recruits into military service.[56] As great as the obstacles that lay before them were, many immigrants seeking to prove themselves worthy of citizenship—and perhaps give a conclusive answer to the hate and prejudice they encountered—decided to enlist in 1917 when the United States formally entered the war. Jewish soldiers and officers encountered a steady stream of bias and discrimination in the military; Jewish civilians reported to Marshall that their employers, after winning government contracts, fired them for missing work because of religious observances.[57] Brave service and valiant sacrifice did little to change racist perceptions of minorities. The Russian Revolution of 1917 further inflamed hostilities toward Jews and gave conservatives a new argument with which to undermine the civic credibility of Jews. After the revolution, Jews were tagged as Bolshevists by definition, simply because some of them had been prominent in the overthrow of tsarism. "Judeo-Bolshevism," this potent image of guilt by association, gained strength in the 1920s and 1930s; it, too, would turn up in the pages of the *Dearborn Independent*, hurled accusingly at Americans who had just helped their country win a war.[58]

Yet more ominous was the wider circulation in the United States in 1919 of the *Protocols of the Elders of Zion*. Secretly furnished to U.S. military officials during the war, the pamphlet surfaced among civilian readers as Marshall led a Jewish delegation to the postwar Paris peace conference that was deliberating on the rights of religious and racial minorities in Europe. Alarmed at the tract's appearance in the United States and rightfully worried about its impact on antisemitic propagandists, Marshall cut back his high-profile international civil rights work in order not to give currency to the *Protocols'* charges of a worldwide Jewish conspiracy. All he could do was denounce it as "the lucubration of an insane man . . . written on behalf of the Czaristic regime. It is now sought to be employed by those who find it useful to make of the Jew a convenient scapegoat."[59]

. . .

Scapegoating was just what Ford was up to. Marshall's June 3, 1920, telegram to Ford was meant to signal to the automaker that there were national consequences to scapegoating Jews, that Ford's attacks would draw the return fire of big guns. Marshall, naturally, saw himself as the biggest gun of all. Before writing to Ford, he did not consult his friends, the AJC's executive committee, or any other natural ally. The response he received to his June 3 telegram to Ford did not persuade him to reconsider his tactics.

The answer from Dearborn was calculated to reinforce the offensive message of the newspaper. Marshall's private telegram to Ford was delegated to staff. Someone, most likely Ford's secretary Ernest Liebold, sent Marshall an aggressive, condescending, and unsigned response: "Your rhetoric is that of a Bolshevik orator. You mistake our intention. You misrepresent the tone of our articles. You evidently much mistake the persons whom you are addressing. . . . We hope you will continue to read [the articles] and when you have attained a more tolerable state of mind we shall be glad to discuss them with you."[60]

That wire was not the only unpleasant communication Marshall received on June 4. Also in his mail that day was a telegram from Rabbi Leo M. Franklin of Detroit's Temple Beth-El. Franklin had his own ideas for managing the Ford situation. Before the Fords built their grand estate in Dearborn, they lived down the block from the Franklins. Ford often stopped his car at the rabbi's house for impromptu conversations that became the basis of an unlikely friendship. After Ford moved to Dearborn, where Jews were unwelcome until well past midcentury, Franklin seemed intent on maintaining the friendship, and not just because Ford presented him with a new, custom-built Ford sedan each year. Then as now, Detroit was a company town, where wealth and power (if not social status) flowed from the Flyver King. Perhaps Franklin saw his relationship with Ford as a chance to build bridges in a community that was deeply riven by religious prejudice. If anyone believed it was possible to prevail on Ford through a personal appeal, it was Rabbi Franklin. Certainly no one in Detroit had greater reason to want to succeed in ending Ford's campaign. Inundated with hundreds of letters from all over the country urging him to intervene and braced by his own circle of influential Detroit professionals, Franklin decided to seek a personal appointment with the automaker. It took him several days of persistent telephone calls and notes before Ford acceded to his request. The rabbi called at Ford Motor Company headquarters twice in early June, spending a total of nine hours with Ford.[61] Franklin's report of his meetings to Marshall lit a fire in the Jewish community that would burn out of control all summer long.

During the second meeting on June 4, Franklin wrote later that day, he persuaded Ford to sign a statement to clarify the newspaper's purposes in publishing the articles. As Ford dictated this statement to a stenographer, Marshall's furious telegram arrived. In Franklin's view, the telegram completely altered the dynamic of the meeting and sabotaged its outcome. Franklin was the only person not on Ford's payroll to witness his reaction to the wire, and immediately on returning to his office he wrote to Marshall to tell him about it. According to Franklin, after reading Marshall's wire, Ford abruptly adjourned the meeting for lunch. When they returned to the office, Ford reversed himself and refused to sign the letter he had dictated. Franklin never saw Marshall's wire, but he assumed that it was so offensive and upsetting as to cause Ford to change his mind. For spoiling his attempt to negotiate an end to the newspaper's antisemitic campaign, Franklin upbraided Marshall. "It has been my conviction all along that more could be done with Mr. Ford by the people here whom he personally knows and trusts," the rabbi wrote, "than by the bombardment of letters and telegrams that have poured in upon him from Jews in every part of the country." Believing Ford capable of rehabilitation, Franklin set out a defense of Ford that came dangerously close to an apologia: "He is so much of a humanitarian that real hate of any individual or of any group is foreign to his nature." Franklin further declared that Ford "has no anti-Semitic feeling" and was merely "the victim of evil advisors who have somehow put into his head the notion that a group of Jews whom he calls 'the internationalist Jew' control the monies of the world and that it is to the interest of this group that wars should be fomented." He repeated Ford's defense of the articles: "[Ford] claims that it is his idea in permitting these articles to be published in his paper, to bring these unscrupulous Jews and their agents, many of whom are non-Jews, to the surface, to the end that all Jews who suffer through the misdoings of a few may find it to their interest to help in exposing the few who have brought the name of all Jewry into disrepute."[62]

Marshall was furious. Franklin's account made it clear that Ford took full responsibility for the paper and that he justified the publication with a calumny that Franklin unflinchingly recounted. Marshall was not buying a word of Franklin's defense of Ford. "The worst thing that could possibly be done," Marshall replied to Franklin, "would be to let Mr. Ford act under the impression that there are any Jews who will excuse this kind of publication." Throughout the summer, Franklin continually asserted that Ford did not harbor hate toward individual Jews or toward Jews as a race, but Marshall never countenanced this explanation. He dismissed Franklin's offer to intercede with Ford: "I regard these publications as most dangerous, largely because of the fact that Ford has unlimited means, with which he can, if he sets out to do so, poison the minds of those who form their opinions from headlines." Franklin eventually published an article in the Detroit *Jewish Chronicle* condemning Ford's antisemitic beliefs and calling on him to refrain from publishing further "slanderous charges against the Jewish people." Still, the damage was done. Franklin had lost all credibility with Marshall.[63]

Fired by Franklin's inept handling of his encounter with Ford, Marshall turned to the insulting letter from the *Independent*. He sent back a terse message containing a barely veiled threat of litigation: "Your telegram in answer to my personal message to Henry Ford has just been received from which I infer that your answer is authorized by him and betokens his sanction of the articles in the Dearborn Independent to which I have taken exception in words that I shall be able to justify." Marshall's friends, such as the lawyer Max Kohler, sought to cool this impulse: "Mr. Marshall talked about a possible prosecution but I think on sober thought, he will see the futility of such [a] course." Kohler as well as other AJC leaders, including the elder statesman Jacob Schiff, believed that Marshall would adhere to the AJC's long-standing policy— a policy Marshall himself strongly championed—of refraining from litigating antisemitism unless it specifically denied Jews their civil rights. Though offensive, Ford's libelous publication had no such effect, at least not directly. At the time, though, Marshall was bent on swift retaliation. As he told Fred Butzel, a Detroit attorney and AJC member, "It was my view from the beginning, that the only way to deal with an abuse of this kind was to come out into the open and hit it as hard as possible." Such a sentiment led friends to express concern at his contribution to what they saw as an unfortunate escalation of tension during the summer of 1920.[64]

Provoked nearly as much by Franklin as by Ford, Marshall was particularly frustrated by Franklin's apparent complacency and, worse, by his inability to see that any attack on Jews as a group was inherently racist. Marshall found it impossible to finesse Ford's actions; the only possible response was to denounce him unreservedly. But this Franklin was unable to do. His investment in their personal relationship, which seemed greater than Ford's at this point, and his sense of his rabbinical role led Franklin to see Ford as both a powerful patron who commanded social deference and a sinner who should not be abandoned. Whatever optimism Franklin harbored for his brokered resolution soon dissolved with the realization that Marshall would not accept a statement from Ford short of a full apology and retraction. Whether Ford was ever willing to sign such a document will never be known, although evidence suggests that he never planned to do so. Ford sent Franklin a letter after their meeting that did not back off from the published charges and also—just as Franklin had reported in his letter to Marshall—justified the articles as designed to "help and not hurt the Jew" by identifying "those Jews who have been untrue to their own highest ideals and teachings."[65] It was hardly a document that Franklin could offer his friends and fellow rabbis as proof of his ameliorating influence.

As Franklin was beginning to discover, he had other problems besides an inability to produce a letter of retraction from Ford for Marshall. Other rabbis were beginning to tell him their own reservations about his handling of the matter and to urge him to condemn Ford publicly. Louis Wolsey wrote from Cleveland to press Franklin to consider legal action against Ford, only to be told to say nothing in public himself. "I flatter myself," Franklin told Wolsey, "that I am a little closer to Mr. Ford than any other Jew." It was precisely that intimacy that led Wolsey to doubt whether Franklin understood the situation as other Jews did: "That you say that Mr. Ford has not a drop of anti-Semitism in his make-up will very naturally cause a raising of the eyebrows. . . . I very much fear that our faith in Mr. Ford is not quite what yours is." Wolsey's analysis of the *Independent* echoed Marshall's criticism of Franklin: "One who believes that an international group of Jews controls the finances of the world for the purpose of fomenting wars and who believes that the conspiracy is a part of their Jewish character, is an anti-Semite, to my thinking. And when he very carefully fails to qualify his statements and uses the term 'Jew' in a universal sense, he only multiplies the needles on the cactus of his anti-Semitism." Wolsey sought to alert Franklin to the danger of his position, noting the "embarrassment" of the situation to him "personally" but expressing the hope that "the attitude you take will be one concerning which your friends and colleagues will have to make no explanation whatever." Stung, Franklin finally acknowledged that Ford had indeed done a "tremendous injury" to the Jews, but he continued to insist that the antisemitism in the *Independent* came from other people, whose views Ford was merely parroting. Franklin then pointed a finger at Marshall, blaming Marshall's June 3 telegram for changing Ford's mind just when Franklin had brokered an agreement to end the antisemitic campaign. Franklin reacted to the stressful situation by attempting to make Marshall, more than Ford, responsible for the *Independent*'s continued publications. That assertion would prove damaging—to Franklin.[66]

Marshall's and Wolsey's letters warned Franklin he was on thin ice. Franklin then took an extraordinary step, one that demonstrated his recognition that nothing he had said to Ford so far had changed the automaker's course. "With deep regret but after mature deliberation," he wrote to Ford in mid-June, "I feel it my duty to return herewith for such disposition as you may choose to make of it, the special sedan which you so thoughtfully presented to me some months ago." He had "never failed to appreciate" Ford's friendship and generosity; nevertheless, Franklin felt compelled to return the car because of the continued publication of the *Independent*'s series and the harm it was doing to all Jews. Franklin attributed the *Independent* articles to "an unfortunate idea that has taken possession of you" but pointed out that the articles "must inevitably tend to poison the minds of the masses against the Jews." Should Ford "come to realize the enormity of the injury you are doing to a people whose sufferings and sacrifices for the sake of humanity have through the ages been beyond measure," Franklin assured him, their friendship might resume.[67]

The response from Dearborn was, according to Allan Nevins and Frank Hill, swift and shocked.[68] "Astonished" by the gesture, Ford wrote a note to Franklin attempting to explain his intentions: "It is farthest from our thought to make an attack upon the Jew in general. On the contrary we wish to bring out the fact that the Jew has contributed much to what is best in modern civilization. Our quarrel is with those Jews who have been untrue to their own highest ideals and teachings." Franklin hopefully relayed Ford's message to Marshall, only to elicit his disgust: "Th[is] pretense . . . is ridiculous. It is as though a highway robber who planted his revolver against his victim's breast, might seek to excuse the consequences of his act of letting go of the trigger by saying he was merely seeking to frighten the dead man." Even less ambiguous was Ernest Liebold's note to Franklin: "It is of course to be regretted that you have seen fit to thereby sever the relations of friendship which have heretofore existed between you and Mr. Ford. I sincerely hope, however, that conditions will so adjust themselves as to eventually convince yourself that Mr. Ford's position is correct." Liebold readily ended Ford's friendship with Franklin, effectively trumping the only ace Franklin had left to play.[69]

Marshall and Franklin's acrimonious exchange, along with the two rabbis' disagreement, highlighted preexisting divisions in the Jewish community. Franklin and Marshall embodied the regional rivalry that had arisen in the late nineteenth and early twentieth centuries, as the physical center of Jewish leadership moved from Cincinnati to New York. The relocation amplified a shift in the character of leadership as well. The new activist organizations, led by lawyers, supplanted the authority of Jewish religious figures. Marshall and Franklin stood on opposite sides of that divide, and their approaches to the Ford matter reflected their different institutional and cultural roles. While Franklin continued to be conciliatory, Marshall saw the problem as requiring an institutional and organizational response, not as one that could be dealt with, as Franklin urged, through social channels and personal entreaties. Franklin's relationship with Ford and Marshall's exchange with the automaker put them at odds at a critical point in the *Independent*'s activities. Neither one succeeded in ending the "International Jew" articles at that time. Even if they had been able to act collaboratively, they probably would have failed to accomplish their goal, because Ford, with Liebold executing his every instruction—or supplying some of the initiative—then showed no inclination to stop publication. Still, Marshall and Franklin each believed that, but for the other's interference, he would have achieved the desired result.[70]

· · ·

The impasse was of little consequence to Marshall's colleagues at the AJC, who were more concerned about what Marshall might do in the face of the continuing provocation. Marshall's view of the Ford publication as "a libel upon an entire people" and his implicit threat to sue raised the issue of what legal remedy, if any, the Jewish defense organizations should pursue. He and his colleagues may have believed the *Independent* guilty of libelous defamation of Jews as a group and of individual Jews, yet they also knew that existing First Amendment doctrine and libel law protected the newspaper's right to publish what it saw fit as long as what it published was true. After the war, controversies over free speech abounded, with the U.S. Supreme Court eventually embracing a civil libertarian position on unpopular or unpatriotic speech under federal espionage laws. Still, as David Rabban has argued, the contemporary debate over free speech concerned mainly political freedom of expression for individuals. As a result, the hateful, insulting, and defamatory speech appearing in the *Independent* fell outside the concerns of the courts and guardians of free speech such as the American Civil Liberties Union. In most states the only way to challenge Ford's newspaper was to sue, alleging individual libel; the only way to win was to prove the publication was both false and malicious.[71]

Yet, as Marshall knew, a remedy for published defamation of a group existed in New York at the time of Ford's publication. In 1907, after friends were denied accommodations at upstate resorts, Marshall drafted an amendment to the state's civil rights law. Finally enacted in 1913, the law did not require hoteliers to rent rooms to all comers; rather, it prohibited the publication and dissemination of statements that advocated the exclusion of anyone on the basis of race, creed, or national origin. That group libel statute thus offered a potential weapon in the fight against libelous antisemitism by threatening criminal punishment to anyone who "offended the reputation of American Jews as a group." Throughout the 1910s the law remained untried, with Marshall preferring to field inquiries from resort owners about the legalities of their advertisements rather than to file lawsuits. Seven states adopted versions of the New York statute before 1930, making group rights a nascent category in First Amendment law.[72]

If it occurred to Marshall to use the New York group libel law to challenge the Ford articles, he never urged such an approach on his colleagues. As Kohler predicted, Marshall abandoned the idea of suing Ford once it became apparent that no one else in the AJC supported such a move. Jacob Schiff, Cyrus Adler, and other executive committee members were reluctant to come out against Ford directly, although they found the *Independent*'s rehashing of the *Protocols* repugnant. More than one source told Marshall that he had misjudged the situation; a close friend remarked, "I have spoken to several of my friends, non-Jewish, regarding the Ford fulminations, and they are quite generally of the opinion that the entire onslaught should have been ignored." The executive committee decided not to reply publicly to Ford that summer "on the theory that . . . the bringing of the Jewish question into discussion throughout the country is exactly what Mr. Ford was aiming at." Worried that a discussion about the fitness of Jews for citizenship—the meaning of the "Jewish question" in this context—might amplify accusations of conspiracy and warmongering, the AJC adopted a policy of public inaction consistent with the style of its prewar activism. The executive committee instructed Marshall to communicate privately with editors of Jewish newspapers, advising them not to endorse a Jewish boycott of Ford because it "might act as a boomerang and produce a counter boycott in which the Jews would greatly suffer." This strategy of "dynamic silence" would be a mainstay of the AJC's approach to propaganda both before and after World War II.[73]

In those first days of the *Independent*'s campaign, when no one knew how long it would continue or how far it would go, there was as much confusion as decisiveness among those who sought to manage the crisis. Rabbis all over the country were inundated with demands that they denounce Ford from their pulpits. The sentiment that both Franklin and Marshall had expressed—that Ford's "mischief breeding sheet" was best ignored, so as not to dignify his allegations with an answer—was also heard in abundance. Jewish newspapers printed editorials condemning Ford and letters from readers expressing widely varied perspectives on the matter. In short, there was no univocal response from a single Jewish community because, no matter what antisemites claimed to the contrary, there simply was no unified Jewish community; rather, leading and rank-and-file Jewish Americans were divided by Ford's attacks and unclear about how to respond. Certainly, there was no shortage of ideas. Rabbi Wolsey volunteered to collect affidavits for the authorities, because sending newspapers to nonsubscribers violated the postal laws and several of his congregants had reported receiving multiple unsolicited copies of the *Independent*. Fred Butzel recommended that the American Jewish Committee demand a congressional investigation. The Anti-Defamation League raised money for possible litigation and publicized Ford's failed attempt to secure the 1920 presidential nomination of the Third Party Convention, tying his loss of support to bad publicity from the *Independent*.[74] Nothing put much of a brake on the Ford publishing machine.

But the conflict between Marshall and Franklin for control over authority in the Jewish community to negotiate with Ford and speak for American Jews swiftly came to a head. By late summer, Franklin publicly undermined Marshall by taking the lead among those who believed the best answer to Ford was no answer at all. More ominously, he circulated among his correspondents his view that Marshall's June 3 telegram was to blame for the *Independent*'s continued campaign. Quick to press his advantage of having been in the room when Ford was about to sign a statement he believed was a retraction, he neglected to mention the fact that he never saw Marshall's telegram. He assumed, from Ford's reaction, that it had to have been inflammatory: "Mr. Marshall's telegram arrived calling Mr. Ford every name in the calendar of sin. Undoubtedly he deserved all that Mr. Marshall gave him but it was not the proper way of meeting our problem. Anyone who knows Mr. Ford at all would have understood this. As a result, he has become stubborn and I believe means to carry on his foolish fight to the bitter end."[75] Well aware that the letter Ford intended to sign offered nothing approximating a retraction, Franklin was being less than fair to Marshall by blaming him for Ford's apparent change of mind—if indeed one had ever occurred. Like the telegram sent to Marshall, Ford's June 4 letter to Franklin simply asked readers to suspend their indignation until the conclusion of the *Independent*'s series.

Word that Franklin blamed Marshall for the failure of his overture reached Marshall's friends in New York, and the lawyer lost patience. Reaching out to David Brown, a Detroit businessman and AJC member, he dismissed Franklin entirely: "Dr. Franklin was flattering himself as to what he might accomplish. . . . Ford had no more idea of retracting or of discontinuing these articles than he had of becoming a convert to Judaism." What Marshall found less forgivable was the damage Franklin had done to his reputation: "Without flattering myself I may say that I am not a novice and that I have been engaged in a hundred battles with men of infinitely greater ability than Ford and have succeeded in most of my controversies in protecting the honor of the Jews of this country. I therefore regard the underhanded methods that have been resorted to by [Franklin] in attacking the American Jewish Committee, as nothing short of disgraceful." Marshall pointed out to Brown that he had so far refrained from publicly rebuking Franklin because—as so many were advising with regard to Ford himself—he did not wish to bring additional publicity "to his unspeakable tirades."[76] Marshall took pride in his position and authority; he remained certain that he would ultimately lead the movement to answer Ford, and for the time being, he seemed to believe that movement would take place on his territory, in a court of law.

But first he had to contend with Franklin. The rabbi's continued public remarks about Ford and the *Independent* throughout the summer of 1920 not only were at odds with what Marshall knew but also undermined his efforts to put forward a publicly united front. David Brown went to Temple Beth El, showed Franklin a copy of Marshall's June 3 telegram and the Dearborn Publishing Company's reply, and "convinced him that he had made an ass of himself." Marshall invited the rabbi to his New York office in late August, when he asked Franklin whether he could agree that the telegram was "entirely proper and free from objection." Obliged to concede the point, Franklin agreed to withdraw his

statements blaming Marshall for the failure of his negotiations with Ford. Yet
the letter Franklin subsequently wrote to Marshall only prolonged their quarrel, for in it Franklin faulted Marshall for not having copied him on the June 3
wire. Marshall was so angry he cut off all communication with the rabbi and
even withdrew an invitation to Franklin, as president of the Central Conference of American Rabbis, to attend a joint meeting with the AJC in November.
It was Franklin's turn to be furious: "How Mr. Marshall could write as he does
is inconceivable to me. . . . Does he believe that he is God Almighty and that we
Rabbis must bow down to him?" A New York rabbi, Samuel Schulman, intervened separately with both men, patched up relations, and restored Franklin's
invitation. It was too late. The rabbi had lost face with the lawyer. Likewise,
the rabbis' organization was no longer an equal player with the AJC, which
henceforth dominated the process of fashioning the official Jewish response
to Henry Ford and his newspaper.[77]

As the *Independent* continued to churn out articles, AJC members urged
Marshall to join them in crafting a unified response. Cyrus Adler and Jacob
Schiff persuaded Marshall to call a meeting of the AJC executive committee
for June 23. Those present were reluctant to come out against Ford directly.
Many Jewish leaders shared Marshall's dismay over Ford's course; few wished
to mount a public challenge. Instead, they sought a careful, dignified defense
that stopped short of validating the stereotypes the *Independent* presented.
A majority voted against any litigation or investigation into Ford's allegations.
Heeding the wishes of their senior member (and wealthiest contributor), Jacob
Schiff, the AJC adopted a policy of public silence. Marshall was instructed to
communicate privately with editors of the Jewish newspapers, to urge restraint
and tamp down all talk of boycotts.[78]

Marshall continued to search for an active response to Ford that other AJC
members could endorse. Even after Jacob Schiff died on September 25, Marshall
could not persuade the committee of the wisdom of a direct counterattack.
Accordingly, he changed his target, taking aim at Ford's source, the *Protocols*,
to which the *Independent* was giving its widest ever circulation in the United
States among clubs, newspapers, Congress, and "in the hands of thousands
of the social elect." At an AJC executive committee meeting on October 15,
Marshall outlined the relationship between the *Protocols* and the *Independent*
articles. As he intended, the group decided to commission a refutation of the
Protocols. By this time, people close to Marshall such as David Brown and

Fred Butzel had begun to agree that the time had come "to hit and hit hard." The idea of defending themselves against Ford by attacking the *Protocols* also won support at a meeting of national Jewish organizations later that month, momentarily uniting Jews against their nemesis. A statement written by Marshall and Oscar Straus was released to the press in December and mass mailed in pamphlet form. For the following six years, that statement would constitute the AJC's sole public comment on the *Independent*'s campaign.[79]

Marshall's statement, titled "The 'Protocols,' Bolshevism, and the Jews," condemned the *Protocols* as "a base forgery" that constituted "an indictment against an entire people." He labeled the idea that Jews were responsible for Bolshevism as "a deliberate falsehood" and dismissed Ford as an intellectual stooge: "We have refrained from commenting on the libels contained in *The Dearborn Independent*. Ford, in the fulness of his knowledge, unqualifiedly declares The Protocols to be genuine, and argues that practically every Jew is a Bolshevist. We have dealt sufficiently with both of these falsehoods. It is useless in a serious document to analyze the puerile and venomous drivel that he has derived from the concoctions of professional agitators. He is merely a dupe." The AJC released Marshall's statement to the press and mass mailed a pamphlet version across the country.[80] Marshall was pleased with the public response, content to let the mainstream press and its editorial writers transmit the AJC's message discrediting Ford and debunking the *Protocols*.

This result was actually in keeping with Marshall's long-established view on how the AJC and, implicitly, Jews everywhere should handle public controversies involving antisemitism. Years of constitutional litigation over civil rights had convinced him that "the Jewish position in America was sound" as long as Jews embraced the secular ideals of American law and citizenship. His characteristic approach of working behind the scenes rather than provoking "great public controversies" had guided both his work as a lawyer and the policies of the AJC. By furnishing a living example of good citizenship and refraining from retaliation when attacked, he believed, Jews would earn the respect of their fellow citizens. Marshall's initial impulse to go after Ford in court faded entirely by the end of 1920. When an *Independent* article devoted entirely to Marshall appeared a year later, he refused to take the bait and stuck to his renewed resolve not to dignify Ford with a response. Instead, he returned to the main theme of his civil rights activism: "To engage in a debate with the nominees of Ford and Cameron is to imply that there is something to debate about. I deny it. The answer of the Jews of America is their contribution to American citizenship and to the moral, philanthropic, intellectual, industrial, and commercial life of the land of which they are proud to form a component part."[81]

Once the AJC took the lead with Marshall's pamphlet, many (but, of course, not all) Jewish groups fell into line with the AJC's preferred policy on Ford. They began to ignore Ford and his newspaper, declining to mention him or his publication in their meetings and public resolutions. In May 1921, the Union of Hebrew Congregations and Federation of Temple Sisterhoods not only ignored Ford and the *Independent* but also refrained from discussing ongoing developments in Congress, where conservatives were working hard to restrict immigration. Instead, the Jewish groups endorsed resolutions calling on the U.S. government to support the restoration of equal rights "for people throughout the world, and particularly the millions of suffering Jews in Eastern Europe."[82] Marshall could not have been more pleased.

Henry Ford meant for his newspaper to explode with incendiary force. The *Independent* damaged relationships, some already fragile, some permanently, among Jewish leaders who saw themselves as chiefly responsible for protecting their community from so frontal and offensive an attack. In subtle ways, the newspaper permitted Ford to play sophisticated and learned individuals off against one another. He would put that tactic in the field again to good effect before the newspaper published its final issue seven years later. In the meantime, what emerged from Ford's encounters with Marshall and Franklin in 1920 was an unqualified admission that Ford authorized the paper and assumed responsibility for its content. Whether Ford's opponents could turn that admission to their advantage remained an open question.

3 TAKING IT TO THE STREETS

Police bulletins indicate h'nry's new flivver—the Dearborn Independent—has
slipped too far for skid chains, but what about a gas mask for the putout?

—Chicago Tribune, 1921[1]

A wave of favorable publicity greeted the December 1920 publication of the
American Jewish Committee's (AJC) pamphlet, "*The Protocols*, Bolshevism, and
the Jews." It was the first hopeful sign after six months of unrelenting pounding
at Ford's hands. Knowing the end was nowhere in sight, Louis Marshall kept his
relief and exultation under wraps: "Without a discordant note," he confided to
a close friend, "the editorial comment was all that we could have asked it to be."
Newspapers, politicians, and non-Jews were paying attention to Ford, but the
AJC was defining the debate in the larger terms Marshall preferred: attacks on
Jewish civil rights were always attacks on American civil rights in general and
could be defended only as such. To bring Ford's war to an end, Marshall knew
he would need to remind Americans of the danger of impugning one another's
rights as citizens.[2]

As 1921 dawned, Ford renewed his determination to wage war on Jews. He
intended to seize control of the public relations front and stage a new battle on
the streets of U.S. cities to place his newspaper before American readers. But
the battle was soon joined, and Jews found allies to help with the fight. Urban
mayors and police chiefs stepped up to try to stop the onward march of the
Dearborn Independent in 1921. They had a potent weapon of their own. Criminal libel laws targeted publications that disparaged people on the basis of religion, creed, or race. By using criminal libel as the legal basis for banning sales
of the *Independent* on city streets, public officials hoped to serve two aims at
once: assure their Jewish constituents that they took Ford's attacks seriously
and head off the threat of violence on the streets.

For a time, at least, retaking the public relations front would be a daunting
task for Ford. The AJC's pamphlet commanded the attention of the editorial
columns of leading newspapers and magazines well into 1921. Before its appearance, most newspapers left it to others—mostly Jews—to voice the shock and

disgust the *Independent* stirred in reasonable minds. The *Chicago Tribune* paid heed to Ford's newspaper a month after the antisemitic articles appeared, in June 1920, but only briefly and indirectly, by publishing a letter to the editor. After disclosing an initial inclination to remain silent, Rabbi Abram Hirschberg said he felt compelled to label the charges in the *Independent* "falsehoods as black as the blackest night."[3] The *Tribune* was only too happy to publish Rabbi Hirschberg's rebuke of the *Independent*, but not because *Tribune* owner Robert McCormick was particularly concerned about the rights of his Jewish fellow citizens. The *Chicago Tribune* had a reputation for antisemitism long before its dustup with Henry Ford. Hirschberg's letter pointedly referred to Ford's ill-advised libel suit against the *Tribune*, and keeping the memory of that debacle alive gave McCormick no end of pleasure.

Lacking McCormick's personal history with Ford, other newspaper editors paid even less attention to the *Independent*. The *New York Times* first mentioned Ford's antisemitism in September 1920, in a story on a local Yom Kippur sermon. Rabbi Samuel Schulman urged Jews "to repel with indignation the miserable revamped charges against the Jew which were published in the newspaper owned by Henry Ford." The *Wall Street Journal* did not report on the *Independent* for six months. Its first story observed the beginnings of an informal, undeclared boycott against Ford by Jews in Michigan.[4] In those first months, few outside Ford's home state noticed the *Independent*'s tirade. It was the impassioned reaction of Jews that made Ford's attacks a national story—a fact that, in hindsight, lends credence to the idea that silence might have been an effective way to answer him.

An especially prestigious source of condemnation came from former president (and future U.S. Supreme Court chief justice) William Howard Taft. In late December, Taft delivered a speech in Chicago that redeemed his lack of support for the Russian treaty abrogation in 1911.[5] In an address before the Anti-Defamation League, Taft compared the *Independent* to the tales of Baron Munchausen and rebuked Ford for circulating "unfounded and unjust charges." As did so many others, Taft wondered about Ford's personal responsibility for the paper's editorial content, and he spoke memorably about the pernicious effect it would have on American society. "One of the chief causes of suffering and evil in the world today is race hatred," Taft said, "and any man who stimulates that hatred has much to answer for." Speaking not as the sitting president but as a liberated former politician, Taft condemned the idea that Jews did not count as full citizens: "Anti-Semitism is a noxious weed that should be cut out. It has no place in America."[6]

A more significant public condemnation of Ford's campaign followed closely on the heels of Taft's Chicago speech. In mid-January 1921, Taft, outgoing President Wilson, and Wilson's secretary of state joined more than a hundred politicians, church leaders, educators, artists, and literary figures in signing a protest statement. Penned by John Spargo, a socialist reformer and writer, "The Perils of Racial Prejudice" urged "all those who are molders of public opinion . . . to strike at this un-American and un-Christian agitation." Without mentioning Ford by name, the statement expressed "regret" at the spate of recent publications "designed to foster distrust and suspicion of our fellow-citizens of Jewish ancestry and faith—distrust and suspicion of their loyalty and their patriotism."[7] Spargo intended for his petition to supply a rebuttal to Ford from outside the Jewish community. The impressive list of those who signed and helped pay for the petition's appearance in major newspapers included William Cardinal O'Connell, Ray Stannard Baker, Ida Tarbell, W. E. B. DuBois, Jane Addams, Charles Beard, Clarence Darrow, Robert Frost, and Edwin Markham. Some, though, were surprises: Paul Cravath, partner in a white-shoe Wall Street law firm that closed its doors to Jews during the 1920s; John Grier Hibben, president of Princeton University, an institution with a long history of antisemitic practices; and, most suspiciously, David Starr Jordan, Stanford University president and author of a book widely blamed for deepening Ford's antisemitic beliefs.[8] Incoming president Warren G. Harding, pleading the "etiquette" of his office, declined to sign, as did former Supreme Court justice and presidential candidate Charles Evans Hughes; war food administrator Herbert Hoover; Navy Secretary Josephus Daniels; the presidents of Harvard and Yale, A. Lawrence Lowell and Arthur T. Hadley, as well as Harvard's former president, Charles W. Eliot. Not long after this, Harvard and Yale instituted quotas limiting the number of Jews permitted to matriculate, to preserve the "cultural 'like-mindedness'" of the scions of native-born white, Protestant elites in America's top-tier universities.[9]

Still, Taft's speech and the Spargo protest effectively uncorked the bottle of unfavorable publicity for Ford and his newspaper. The first report of a Chicago-area minister preaching from the pulpit against Ford and the *Dearborn Independent* came on the heels of the release of the protest statement. The Reverend Hugh Robert Orr told his congregation that far from being "at the bottom of the trouble in Russia," Jews were nearly unanimously opposed to Bolshevism and 107 leaders of the Russian Zionist party were then sitting in Moscow jails. Within the week, Rabbi Stephen Wise followed suit in New York, declaring the *Protocols* a "deliberate forgery" and responding to Ford's claim that "no Jews are buried in the war cemeteries of Europe" with an unsubtle reminder that Edsel Ford was America's most famous nonvolunteer of the war.[10]

The *Chicago Tribune* pounced in an extended editorial in February 1921, reviewing Ford's history of rash comment and concluding that he had again proved himself wholly unsuited for public life: "We hope Mr. Ford never finds his way into the United States [S]enate or into any other position of public responsibility. . . . He'll be down south next promoting world peace by start-ing a race war. . . . *The Tribune*, realizing the American people think that a man successful in one endeavor must be wise in all, has endeavored to keep Mr. Ford from getting influence over people's opinions. We think that the endeavor was fully justified." The next day, three Jewish organizations in Detroit, led by Rabbi Leo M. Franklin, issued a joint statement demanding that Ford either prove the charges leveled against Jews in the *Dearborn Independent* or withdraw them. The Detroit organizations dismissed as outrageous the idea that had been offered in Ford's defense that he "does not know what is being published in his own organ."[11] Rabbi Franklin had come a long way in eight months. He was now publicly rejecting the justifications and excuses that Ford had proffered in his own defense, but his change of heart was too late for him to lead the national repudiation of Ford.

Just a few weeks later, Spargo brought out his new book, *The Jew and Ameri-can Ideals*. Like the petition and protest that preceded it, the book was less a rebuttal of Ford's articles than a robust declaration of American democratic principles and a passionate argument for Jewish inclusion in that egalitarian vision: "This little book was written without the knowledge of any Jew. It is not a defense of the Jew. It is not a pro-Jewish argument. It is a defense of American ideals and institutions against anti-Semitism; a plea for Christian civilization." Spargo explained to readers that he did not join Ford's Peace Ship expedition because he believed Ford's idealism was being used for "dangerous intrigue," and he sought, somewhat ineffectually, to refute the *Protocols of the Elders of Zion*. The journalist Herman Bernstein, who had just published *A History of A Lie*, his authoritative refutation of the *Protocols*, enthusiastically reviewed Spargo's book in the *New York Times* a few weeks after its release.[12] All these statements, speeches, books, and petitions gave the mainstream press license to go after the *Independent* and, by implication, Ford himself.

Accordingly, about six to nine months into the *Independent*'s campaign, the initial novelty and shock had worn off, and the opposition's counterattack began to gain traction. The growing resolve of anti-Ford forces, braced by the pushback from the nation's Jewish organizations, emboldened municipal officials to respond with greater assertions of public authority. Public libraries that had been receiving the *Independent* without the burden of a paid subscription began to remove the newspaper from their shelves.[13] For a library to remove material to which it had not subscribed seemed to evade, rather neatly, the ethical and legal problems associated with accusations of censorship or banning, not that such scruples greatly restrained public or school libraries of the day. No one seemed particularly bothered about whether banning Ford's paper from city libraries constituted an abridgment of his rights as a publisher, certainly not enough to create a sustained movement of protest against library removals. Nevertheless, irritated at these slight acts of resistance, Ford ordered his employees at the *Independent* to deploy aggressive marketing tactics that quickly outpaced polite debates about library access. The Dearborn Publishing Company (DPC) quickly began expanding the *Independent*'s circulation through direct, on-street sales. It was a marketing strategy intended to give literal meaning to the phrase "fighting words."

Well into the twentieth century, most newspapers relied on newsboys to sell their product on the streets of American cities. The difficult life newsboys led left them vulnerable to all kinds of urban problems. Newsboys typically ranged in age from eight to fourteen and earned between thirty and fifty cents a day. Many of them never finished their formal schooling, some had been abandoned by their families, and others had run away to escape poverty and abuse. They came from a variety of ethnic backgrounds as well. In Cleveland in 1909, for example, fully one-third of newsboys were Jewish. Determined to rise above poverty, many of them formed a local union. Others joined gangs, spent their days gambling near the rail yards, and attracted the concern of local rabbis and social workers.[14]

Such vagabonds as these rebellious and rambunctious children were not the stuff of the compliant labor force to which Henry Ford was accustomed. Instead, for the important work of distributing the *Independent*, the DPC rounded up former and current Ford employees and dispatched them to important cities, including Boston, Cleveland, Columbus, Toledo, Cincinnati, Chicago, St. Louis, and Pittsburgh. (It's not clear whether these were the only cities where Ford employees were selling the *Independent* on the streets or whether these were the only ones that tried to prevent the practice.) Fred Black, the *Independent's* business manager, took charge of the field operations. He reported directly to Ernest Liebold, who supervised the sales operation and kept Ford informed of important developments.[15] Their immediate goal was to put in place a sales network for the *Independent* that was both professional and efficient. That meant replacing local newsboys with a labor force that answered directly and exclusively to *Independent* managers and, even more important, would exercise self-restraint in the face of provocation. It was a smart business plan.

James T. Russell, a twenty-five-year-old from Pennsylvania, had worked for the DPC for two years in Dearborn when Fred Black promoted him to special representative and sent him to Cleveland in February 1921. Black instructed him to oversee all distribution operations in the city, hire a sales force, and coordinate with the home office on everything. Russell arrived in Cleveland on February 16. The first thing he did was to pay a visit to the city's chief of police, Frank W. Smith, and ask whether out-of-state newspaper dealers were required to obtain a license. Russell also wanted to know which local laws "prevented or controlled the sale of the [*Independent*]." Black and Liebold had prepared him well. Chief Smith told Russell that there were no licensing requirements and that he was free to "go ahead and sell."[16]

Russell immediately got to work assembling his sales force. He "was personally very careful to secure as salesmen of mature age, of good character and of a pleasing personality." All of his sales agents were former Ford Motor Company employees who had been "temporarily laid off but not discharged," "due to the slump in the automobile business." The Ford Motor Company had just shut down production in all its plants for the first time in its history, idling thousands of line workers. Most of Russell's hires were locals; he brought in some employees from Michigan as well. They included auto production workers, an accountant, even a banker—all hit hard by the postwar recession and eager to work for the proffered wage of $6 per day. Russell stationed vendors "within a few feet of the stations of police patrolmen," so that should trouble arise, the DPC agents could appeal for assistance. Russell kept a close watch on the sales agents, personally visiting all their posts and checking their "methods of selling." Clevelanders looking to buy the *Independent* could usually find vendors on Public Square, the city's spiritual heart; in front of the public library on Euclid Avenue; and at the intersection of East Ninth Street and Prospect Avenue, about six blocks from the western edge of the city's oldest Jewish neighborhood, the Woodland district. Between February 17 and February 24, *Independent* vendors sold 8,285 copies of the *Independent* on the city's streets, netting $414.25. With sales this brisk, Russell informed his bosses, he saw no need to place the paper for sale on newsstands.[17]

Cleveland's mayor at the time was William Sinton Fitzgerald. A Republican lawyer, Fitzgerald had just ascended to the position by appointment the previous August, when his predecessor resigned to run for governor of Ohio. Facing a November election to win the job in his own right, he was avidly courting the city's Jews. Some of the most prominent members of the city's Republican Party were wealthy Jews who lived in stately mansions on Fairmont Boulevard, where they boarded train lines for daily rides to their downtown offices. The sight of the *Independent* for sale on Cleveland's busiest intersections infuriated them, and they took their complaints directly to the mayor. These businessmen and Republican Party headliners inspired Fitzgerald to take an extraordinary step, one that would enable him to curry favor with a group that, judging from weekly editorials in the Cleveland *Jewish Independent*, the city's leading English-language Jewish newspaper, was furious with Ford's attacks and itching to engage him.[18]

Sometime after James Russell arrived in town, Fitzgerald decided to act on the authority granted to the mayor under section 1770 of the City Ordinances of Cleveland. Passed in 1907, the law banned the publication, exhibition, sale, or distribution within the city of "any indecent, immodest, obscene, scandalous or libelous picture, book, print, newspaper, or publication . . . calculated to excite scandal, or having a tendency to create a breach of the peace." Convinced that the *Independent* and Jewish Clevelanders' response to it met that standard, Fitzgerald signed an order banning on-street sales of the paper.[19]

On February 24, the city began its crackdown. One of the *Independent*'s vendors, Frank Harshman, was escorted to the police station, where a city prosecutor gave him a message: tell your boss to come see me. Russell complied immediately. When he got there, the prosecutor delivered a grim warning: "The Dearborn Independent was a nuisance upon the said streets of the City of Cleveland and that it was likely to cause riots and that [Russell] must cease selling the paper upon said streets of the said city." The prosecutor then took Russell to the city law director, W. B. Woods, who made the city's intent plain: if sales did not stop immediately, the chief of police would order the arrest of anyone "selling or distributing the paper upon the streets."[20]

Russell ordered his sales force to stand down while he sought further instructions from Dearborn. Concluding that the situation was too serious to manage by letter or telephone, Black and Liebold summoned Russell to Detroit. When he reached the DPC's offices, his supervisors questioned him "at great length as to what had occurred in Cleveland." More to the point, Russell hastened to say what had not happened: "there had been no riots, no breaches of the peace, and no trouble of any kind." Russell insisted that he had trained his sales agents to obey all state and city laws in selling the newspaper; moreover, he had told them "to ignore all attempts to engage them in argument and to be very careful not to use any offensive language in calling their wares upon the streets of Cleveland and to avoid every possibility of causing any trouble of any sort." Black and Liebold quickly concluded that the city had gone too far. They dispatched Russell back to Cleveland with instructions to resume sales of the *Independent* on the streets as before. On March 10, Russell arrived in Cleveland and relayed the order to his sales team.[21]

The beat police had their orders as well. The first officer to spot Russell in public directed him straight to the prosecutor's office, where he received yet another warning: stop selling the *Independent* immediately, or he and all his sales agents would face arrest. This time, Russell ignored the city's admonition. But he carefully laid the groundwork for the newspaper to defend itself if the city should follow through on its threat. On March 10 and 11, Russell stationed only one vendor at a time in the entire city so that he could personally and continually supervise his work and the public's reaction, whatever it might be. The vendor worked abbreviated shifts those days, selling the paper only between 2 p.m. and 6:30 p.m. When no arrests took place either day, Russell increased the sales force to three on March 12 and expanded the shift from noon to 6 p.m. It was Saturday, a rainy day. Still, between downpours, the vendors managed to sell 550 copies of the paper's latest issue, which bore the incendiary headline "Jewish Versus American Rights."[22] Clearly, there was a market in Cleveland for what the vendors were selling. Russell and his team resumed work on Monday, March 14. Shortly after taking to the streets, four of Russell's workers were arrested in the act of selling the *Independent* and charged with violating section

1770. Russell sent word to Dearborn about the arrests and continued selling the paper exclusively from newsstands. By the end of March, revenue dropped by more than 80 percent compared to February's robust on-street sales.[23]

The DPC retained the firm of Squire, Sanders, and Dempsey, one of Cleveland's largest and oldest, to represent the vendors in their criminal case. That matter was scheduled for a hearing on March 30, giving the defendants just two weeks to prepare. They did not need that long. On Monday, March 28, Ernest Dempsey strode into Cleveland's federal courthouse to file a request for a temporary restraining order against the city. Instead of merely defending the arrested sales agents, the DPC attacked the mayor's authority to ban the newspaper. "[We claim] that the intent of the city officials is not to prevent a breach of the peace, but to prevent circulation of the Ford paper," the motion asserted.[24]

Dempsey had fought this battle before. In 1917, the distributors of the film *The Birth of a Nation* signed a contract with the owners of the Euclid Avenue Opera House to lease the theater for an indefinite exhibition period. The film had already been shown in the city for four weeks and had been approved by the boards of censors in several states, a dozen cities, and the federal government. Nevertheless, after the film arrived in Cleveland, the city attempted to ban it under section 1770. A state court judge ruled in favor of the film's distributors and enjoined the city from interfering with public showings: "'To admit that this photoplay tends to provoke a breach of the peace is to confess that citizens of African descent are not law-abiding citizens. This I am not willing to admit, as it would be an uncalled-for slander upon these citizens.'"[25]

Four years later, as Dempsey revisited this familiar ground, he made sure to acquaint federal judge David C. Westenhaver with the case by putting a copy of his brief on behalf of the film's distributors in the DPC's federal court file. Mayor Fitzgerald, who had been a member of the city council in 1917, had to have known that the *Birth of a Nation* precedent would make it difficult to prohibit the *Independent*. In 1917 and again in 1921, the city engaged in preemptive acts of censorship that it justified as measures to prevent race riots that had not yet happened. The state judge did not buy this rationale at the height of wartime, when free-speech rights took a backseat to national security and public safety concerns. Would the federal court be receptive to it barely two years after the Armistice?

On March 31, Judge Westenhaver awarded victory to the newspaper. He ordered the mayor and other city officials to appear at a hearing on April 9 to show why a preliminary injunction should not be granted to the plaintiffs. This order effectively threw the burden of proof onto the defendants. Unless the city argued persuasively that its ban was both legal and warranted by fact and circumstance, the court would overturn it. At the same time, in state criminal court, the case against the four Ford employees who had been arrested and charged with crimes for selling the paper on March 14 was set for further hearings on April 13. Everything would depend on the legality of the ban.[26]

Mayor Fitzgerald swore out a statement to explain his action and bolster the city's case. For weeks that winter, he noted, he had been receiving "numerous complaints," not only about the *Dearborn Independent* but also about another newspaper, *Facts*, a Philadelphia-based publication that purported to refute the antisemitic theories in Ford's newspaper. Both papers, the mayor said, were "calculated to excite scandal, or had a tendency to create a breach of the peace." Ford's paper "criticized the Jews and [was] calculated to create racial hatred," whereas *Facts* attacked Henry Ford and thus offended the legions of people who admired him. Accordingly, on February 21, the mayor banned both papers from using on-street vendors. Had he not taken this step, Fitzgerald asserted, sales of these papers would have produced "racial animosity and disturbances of the peace, and [would have been] against the public welfare and interest, and would be in violation of the ordinances of the City of Cleveland."[27] By banning both newspapers, the mayor sought to strike an evenhanded approach in pursuit of the overall goal of preventing potential civic unrest. But his fear of the possibility that citizens might angrily confront one another in public wherever the newspaper was sold was the sum and substance of the city's legal argument. Would it be enough to overcome the Ford organization's careful preparation and the unimpeachable conduct of its employees?

In contrast to the city's sparse legal argument, Ernest Dempsey packed his file with more than half a dozen sworn affidavits. From James Russell on down, each *Independent* vendor gave a consistent account of the work he had been hired to do and the method in which he had been trained to do it. Moreover, Russell personally vouched for the conduct of his employees on the job: "During the entire period when he observed the sales of the said paper there was no trouble of any sort in connection with the said sales; his salesmen were gentlemanly in their conduct and orderly and decent; in calling their wares they used no indecent or offensive language, and that in every respect they were orderly, and that they caused no trouble, no crowds, no blocking of traffic and no interference of any sort with the use of the streets of the City of Cleveland."[28]

Milton Coulson, a thirty-five-year-old bookkeeper from Lakewood, near Cleveland, was one of the four vendors arrested on March 14. He had worked for the Ford Motor Company for more than six years before being laid off in early 1921. Russell stationed him to sell papers at the corner of Prospect Avenue and East Ninth Street, just east of the downtown district. Not only was there no tendency toward a breach of the peace, Coulson said, but crowds had not even tended to form at his post. He had not feared for his own safety, he said, because selling the newspaper never precipitated riots or public disturbances. If violence were to break out, he had been instructed by Mr. Russell not "to fight or resist assaults" but simply to seek police assistance. Coulson further observed that a policeman was always standing nearby when he worked. A traffic clerk, a production clerk, an auto line worker, a bank clerk and war veteran, and a railroad clerk, all in their twenties and thirties, swore out similar statements. Each of them attested to the peaceable environment around them as they conducted their business.[29]

The judge thus had only to compare the city's version of the case, which turned on the as-yet-unrealized possibility of future violence, with Ford's, which offered the sworn testimony of seven white, able-bodied, middle-class men that no violence had occurred for over a month while they sold newspapers. At the show cause hearing on April 9, with the facts not in dispute, the two sides went to the mat over the law. The city, burdened with defending the legality of its ban, relied on the idea that officials had exercised a reasonable degree of discretion while advancing the legitimate goal of protecting public order. It did not take the Ford lawyers long to poke holes in that theory. They attacked the premise of section 1770, described the mayor's order as "'incomprehensible,'" and asserted that Ford had a constitutional right to distribute his newspaper in the absence of any actual violence.[30]

Without evidence of actual riots or disturbances, the city had no leverage to push Judge Westenhaver to uphold the ban. On April 16, the judge gave Ford everything his lawyers asked for. Westenhaver issued an injunction against the city that prevented enforcement of the ban against on-street sales until further court action. "[The ban] was not directed towards preserving the public peace of the city," Judge Westenhaver declared, "and [it] was not in any wise necessary to prevent any breach of the peace." Convinced that the city would not object to the newspaper if it removed the offending articles, he ruled that "the necessary effect of such action is to censor in advance the contents of the newspaper, by preventing its sale in the same manner as all other newspapers are sold." Because the city never interfered with sales of the *Independent* "at news stands and in shops," the judge could conclude only that the mayor's intention was to prevent its distribution on the streets, in clear violation of the First Amendment.[31]

Judge Westenhaver determined that the city acted preemptively in seeking to preserve the public peace. Sales of the *Independent* precipitated no breach of the peace, no public disorder, and no race riots in the city of Cleveland. The judge also agreed with Ernest Dempsey on the relevant precedent. This case was no different, Westenhaver noted, from "certain efforts to suppress the public exhibition of the photoplay called 'The Birth of a Nation.'" Echoing the logic—and language—of the 1917 *Birth of a Nation* decision, Westenhaver described the ban on the *Independent* as an offense against the people it was ostensibly meant to protect: "It would be a libel, it seems to me, on people of the Jewish race to assume that they are imbued with such a spirit of lawlessness." The federal court's ultimate concern lay in the possibility that public officials would use their authority to restrict speech with which they disagreed. Dempsey prevailed in getting the court to see the controversy as a straight-up First Amendment problem, without the complicating factor of public safety. This was a matter of censoring speech one disagreed with, he was convinced, and such speech was exactly what the First Amendment was designed to protect.[32]

Ohio's state courts followed suit a month later. When the Ford newspaper vendors appeared for their state criminal trial, the judge ended the suspense quickly. The men were freed and the charges dismissed, the judge ruled, "on the ground that the affidavit filed by the City Prosecutor was 'insufficient and indefinite.'"[33] In hindsight, the city appears to have offered only a token effort in both the federal injunction case and the state criminal prosecutions.

Once he lost the court cases, Mayor Fitzgerald started putting up a fight in public. Two days after the court enjoined the ban, he appeared at Cleveland's posh Hotel Statler, where 1,500 people gathered to commemorate the fortieth anniversary of the founding of the Hungarian Benevolent and Social Union, a nineteenth-century self-help association created to assist Jews in need. Mayor Fitzgerald declared in ringing tones that "as long as he was mayor he would see that all the people of Cleveland were accorded equal rights regardless of race or religion and that he would continue to oppose prejudice against any group of people." Fitzgerald's full-on embrace of the cause, however sincere, did him little good; he lost his bid for election as mayor in his own right later that year.[34]

The only comfort for Fitzgerald and for Cleveland's Jewish community was that in seeking to ban Ford's newspaper, they were far from alone. They were simply the first. And their efforts emboldened officials in other cities to exercise their own discretionary authority to try to restrict on-street sales of Ford's newspaper.

The trend began to materialize shortly after Cleveland filed its injunction case. During the last two weeks of March, special ordinances aimed at Ford's publication bloomed like the first flowers of spring in a half dozen other Midwestern cities. Cincinnati passed an ordinance prohibiting all sales of the paper in the city as a result of the "very obnoxious" articles that were "an affront to Jewish citizens, who, as a class, are . . . progressive, charitable, . . . and, above all, have proved true, loyal Americans." In Toledo, a public fracas broke out on the steps of the federal courthouse, necessitating police intervention. That melee was an economic squabble among competing newsboys, not a race riot instigated by Jews and other Ford opponents. Nevertheless, the city's chief of police ordered the *Independent* banned from Toledo streets.[35]

The wave of municipal bans and police regulations did not deter Ford. If anything, Cleveland's ban emboldened him to challenge that ordinance and the bans that followed. With his vast resources, he hired workers to sell the paper in open violation of the terms of local regulations, and he then retained lawyers in each city to handle matters in the courts. Ford's lawyers almost certainly knew that the law favored the rights of publishers. Impressed by the theoretical appeal of criminal libel law as a tool for maintaining the public peace, public officials did not expect judges to read the First Amendment as broadly as they did.[36]

The American Civil Liberties Union (ACLU) was keeping tabs on Ford's newspaper and the legal developments it had precipitated. As the Cleveland case wended through the district court, the ACLU seized the opportunity to publicize the broader principle of free speech even in cases when the speech itself was objectionable and offensive. In a circular letter to Fitzgerald and a half dozen other mayors, the ACLU's national chair, Harry F. Ward, and six members of its national committee unconditionally condemned Ford's antisemitic articles, but they equally opposed governmental attempts to "combat this propaganda . . . [by] forbid[ding] the sale of the *Independent* and threaten with arrest those who sell it." Such an exercise of public authority, the ACLU maintained, was "in clear violation of traditional American civil rights" and, once set in motion, had "no logical or practical limit." The ACLU's position was that, because the "freedom to express views of every kind" was essential to democracy, Ford's newspaper, no matter how offensive, must be permitted to circulate freely. The ACLU made no secret of its views, sending the circular letter and a press release to major newspapers and wire services in late March. The mayor of Columbus, Ohio, responded somewhat defensively, informing Ward that on-street sales continued unabated in his city. The only prohibited behavior, he pointed out, was "yell[ing] out on the street . . . for the purpose of creating strife and trouble."[37]

The national press needed no prodding to side with the ACLU. The *Chicago Tribune*, for all its animus toward Ford, quickly assessed the stakes of the First Amendment fight he had caused and threw its editorial weight behind the rights of a free press. Jews should oppose such overreaches of municipal authority, the *Tribune* declared, because to seek recourse to law would only confirm conspiratorial suspicions. That public officials turned to such oppressive uses of public power would "inevitably be ascribed to Jewish influence and will be accepted by many Americans as sufficient evidence that Mr. Ford is justified in charging the Jews with organization to domination." It was hardly a bracing endorsement of civic equality, but the paper did conclude with a regretful comment on the recent "organization of groups and the cultivation of group interests and group consciousness in disregard of our common citizenship and of the basic principles of American liberty and equality. This is, indeed, the evil tendency of the anti-Semitic propaganda." In identifying "group interests" and group identity with the evils of racial prejudice, the paper expressed a common assumption of American liberal individualism: group identifications undermined democracy. The *Tribune* considered group labels dangerous: "[They] mean the disintegration of American nationality and peace, and all intelligent Americans of whatever race, tradition, religious affiliation, party, or condition of life should combat every manifestation of [them]."[38] No wonder the American Jewish Committee eschewed a politics of group identity, even in opposing racism; such a politics would position the AJC in stark opposition to "American nationality and peace."

Despite such paeans to the virtues of free speech, liberty, and equality, Ford's opponents in the halls of city and state law-making bodies continued their efforts to write statutes that would stick. A Michigan state legislator introduced a bill that "would compel" Ford's paper either to "discontinue its slanderous attack on the Jews or cease publication." The bill's sponsor, Representative George Welch, said that his purpose was "to protect all religious sects." Chicago's corporation counsel defended his city's ban as an exercise of "its general police powers with a view to keeping the peace." Cincinnati's leading Republican city council member contended that the *Independent* was "very obnoxious to a great number of respected citizens not only of our own city but of the United States." A Detroit city council member sought vainly to amend the existing city ordinance limiting the sale of publications inveighing "against religious creeds or cults" by adding the term *race* and increasing the fine for violation from $25 to $500. In answer to these attempts to codify newspaper censorship, the ACLU contacted Ford's lawyer in Detroit, asking for information about all pending criminal cases against *Independent* newspaper vendors and enclosing a copy of the March circular letter to show its support for the principle of editorial freedom. William Lucking sent the ACLU a copy of Judge Westenhaver's decision in the *Fitzgerald* case, which he described as "of value on the subject of freedom of the press."[39]

So, for a time at least, Judge Westenhaver's resounding rebuke of Mayor Fitzgerald did not stop others intent on circumscribing the reach of Ford's newspaper and the spread of his message. Westenhaver's robust First Amendment jurisprudence did not trickle down to local officials more directly concerned with—and politically affected by—racial and ethnic conflict that might potentially play out on city streets. World War I–era speech regulations abridging individual rights may have seemed less necessary in peacetime, but police and elected officials remained nervous enough about the possibility of violent strikes and riots that they were willing to ban offensive newspapers first and deal with the courts when forced. They may have been attempting to avoid a repeat of the widespread unrest in U.S. cities and at industrial workplaces during 1919, when violent strikes, interwoven with race riots, tested the capacity of local governments to maintain order. The regulation of morals, alcohol, and literature all helped constitute the larger pattern of social control that was evolving during and after World War I, and local jurisdictions contributed a complicated patchwork of different jurisdictional rules that reflected their unique situations. The Ford controversy reveals how determined different cities were to refight the same battle even after the Cleveland case pointed to the likely result.[40]

In Chicago, the battle over the *Independent* was engaged in the oppressive heat of summer, and it traveled much the same terrain as it had in Cleveland. After the city enacted an ordinance banning on-street sales, the DPC dispatched vendors to defy it peaceably. In July, the police arrested two Ford employees; attorneys for Ford promptly contested the arrests and challenged the city's ban. Taking the constitutional high road, Ford's Chicago distributor, Perley W. Johnson, declared that "the police are interfering with the rights of free speech." He announced that the newspaper would press for a permanent injunction when the county circuit court reconvened in September. Ford's attorneys filed a request for a temporary restraining order against the city in early August. Three days later, the judge granted their request.[41]

No one prosecuting the case for Chicago, it seems, looked closely enough at the statutory language to realize that the Illinois statute and the Cleveland city ordinance both relied on the mere potential for race riots to justify suppressing a publication. If they did, they decided it was worth taking the chance that local conditions would produce a different result. The federal and state courts in Ohio had already ruled that in the absence of proven public disorder, banning on-street sales and arresting newspaper vendors were acts that lay beyond the authority of public officials. Odds were that the Chicago case would not turn out any better for public officials than the Cleveland lawsuit, unless the Illinois authorities could cite some other statutory grounds for their actions—or unless an actual riot broke out.

As in Cleveland, the city of Chicago could produce no riots related to the *Independent*. The unhappiness of Jewish citizens with the *Independent*'s content, however heartfelt, did not induce courts to close down the commerce of speech in which Ford was engaged. The Cook County Circuit Court continued the temporary restraining order against the police from August 1921 into early 1922. In the meantime, Ford's vendors continued to sell issues of the *Independent*, issues that boasted such headlines as "The Press Is Already in Our Hands," "How the Jews in the U.S. Conceal Their Strength," and "The Scope of Jewish Dictatorship in the U.S.," throughout the fall of 1921. The same fate befell Pittsburgh, where a federal judge enjoined the mayor and director of public safety from using the police "to suppress the sale of the *Dearborn Independent* on the streets" there.[42]

Officials in Chicago and Illinois were impatient with this state of affairs. By this point, any successful ban against on-street sales would have provided a potent public relations edge and notched an important symbolic victory for Jewish groups seeking to stop Ford's forward momentum. When the city could make no headway on municipal regulatory grounds, the state of Illinois intervened. In early September, Illinois State's Attorney Robert E. Crowe, an ambitious lawyer with his eye on a larger stage, decided to charge Ford with criminal libel under state law. In the heat of the heightened patriotic fervor of World War I, Illinois made it a crime "to manufacture, sell, or offer for sale, advertise, or publish . . . in any public place in this state . . . any publication or exhibition . . . which . . . exposes the citizens of any race, color, creed, or religion to contempt, derision, or obloquy or which is productive of breach of the peace or riots."[43]

This law did not supply any more promising a basis for banning the *Independent* than Cleveland's vague city ordinance. When Crowe charged in his brief that Ford was guilty of "'publishing articles which cause race prejudice and which might lead to race riots,'" he was merely conjuring the same allegations that Ernest Dempsey had flicked aside in Cleveland. Crowe ordered his assistants to collect back issues of the *Dearborn Independent* as evidence in his investigation and announced plans to impanel a grand jury. Yet he refused to disclose whether he would summon Ford to testify. In the wake of Ford's performance in Mount Clemens, the press found his taking the witness's oath an utterly seductive prospect.[44]

Those speculations and the state's case all came to nothing. In January 1922, Chicago made a last-gasp effort to use criminal libel to censor the *Independent*. Its lawyers embellished their case about the potential for public disturbance with the charge that Ford was engaged in a conspiracy with Ernest Liebold, *Independent* editor William J. Cameron, and DPC distributor Johnson "to engage in propaganda against the Jews which 'will prove disastrous not only to the Jews, but to all citizens of the United States.'" The sole intent of the *Independent*, Chicago Corporation Counsel James W. Breen told the court, was to "mingle truthful and false statements to generate a feeling of hatred and contempt against the Jews." Breen alleged that the nation's social and political stability were threatened: "This propaganda will affect disastrously and prejudiciously all citizens and residents of the United States who enjoy civil liberty and who only enjoy such liberties as long as a spirit of toleration and mutual amity among the people continues and cannot possibly endure if religious hatreds, race, and group antagonisms are generated."[45] It was a valiant effort, but it failed. The court left the injunction against the Chicago police order in place indefinitely.

Ironically, cities wanting to ban the *Independent* needed riots to happen for criminal libel statutes to trump the First Amendment rights of newspaper publishers, even when they held views as repugnant as Ford's. However insulting and offensive the *Independent*'s headlines and stories may have been, everyone on both sides behaved too well to trigger the extreme remedy provided by the law of criminal libel. For all the disputation that had taken place among elite Jews during 1920, the rank and file apparently heeded Louis Marshall well, for they did not engage *Independent* vendors in verbal protests or physical confrontations. The vendors, for their part, were also extremely well trained, particularly in Cleveland and Chicago, where they provoked apparently not a single confrontation. The police in those cities made their arrests preemptively; they acted on the basis of suspicion and dislike, not on the basis of any actual peace disturbance by the *Independent*'s vendors. Amazingly, other cities, even with Cleveland's example before them to notice and not to emulate, fell into the same legal trap. All these efforts to ban on-street sales under criminal libel in 1921 were doomed. Ford won the battle of the streets. No one, not even he, knew what that would mean for the larger war that continued, unabated, on other fronts.

· · ·

Midwestern courts gave Henry Ford unchecked momentum going into 1922. Except for a minor disturbance in Toledo, *Independent* vendors could not be blamed for inciting unrest on any scale. Across the region, convincing legal victories assured Ford the right to sell his newspaper on city streets and gave its objectionable content the full protection of the First Amendment.

Before the final legal judgment was handed down in Chicago, Ford set off on a victory tour of sorts. With Thomas Edison, Edsel Ford, their wives, and a sizable press contingent along for the journey, he departed Dearborn in early December 1921 in his personal railcar for Muscle Shoals, Alabama, the site of a federally owned nitrate plant and waterpower project at Wilson Dam. Ford planned to survey the site as part of a publicity tour, to draw attention to his

3.1. Henry Ford with prize oxen, ca. 1922 (© Bettmann/Corbis).

already-announced bid to purchase the nitrate plants from the government and to produce low-cost fertilizer. His proposal was wildly popular among the nation's farmers, but congressional Republicans were skeptical. The object of the trip was to build political support for his bid.[46]

Muscle Shoals unified the literal plans and symbolic politics of Ford's hopes for the America he intended to build. As Albert Lee commented, "His vision incorporated the creation of a series of small communities along the river, each supplying the work force for a single nitrate plant, and where the part-time farmers could gain the benefits of industrialization without having to live in wicked cities." Manufacturing cheap power and fertilizer would extend his industrial empire and shore up his agricultural constituency. Tying the nation's agricultural sector even more tightly to the Ford name, he believed, would brace his considerable political ambitions. He lost the 1918 Senate race as the Democratic candidate; with President Wilson out of office, Ford was free to run as the Republican he really was, free to appeal to the isolationism and racism that ran deep among political and religious conservatives. Waging the antisemitic campaign, acquiring Muscle Shoals, and testing the presidential political waters from 1921 through 1923 were all means to an end. They all served as machines with which Ford sought to retool the nation's sociopolitical economy.[47]

Ford made no stops while en route to Alabama and gave no interviews until he arrived there on December 3. As ever, when he spoke, he left a lasting impression. Muscle Shoals, Ford said, would be the first step in his grand plan to end all war. By backing national currencies with natural resources other than gold, he intended to break the gold monopoly while bringing cheap power to ordinary people and, at the same time, to ensure national security:

[I]f you went out and knocked at every door along every street and road in the world you would find every grown man and woman in the world [saying], "No, no, God, save us from war." Then if all the families in the world are opposed to war why in the name of Heaven do we have wars, did that question ever occur to you? Well, there is a reason. There is profit in war. I don't mean moral profit, or increased religious interest or spiritual uplift through trial by fire, nor any of that kind of bunk. It is money profit I mean; profits in gold.

For Ford, war boiled down to two things: profit, and those seeking it. Religion, territory, family conflicts, ideological imperatives, and imperial designs utterly disinterested him and did not enter his discernment into the motives of others. Neither history nor politics encumbered Ford's theory: "'There is a group of international bankers, who today control the bulk of the world's gold supply. They have their members or their agents in every country. No matter to what country they, as individuals, claim allegiance, they all play the same game, to keep the gold they have in their own hands and to get as much more as possible. . . . With them the fostering, starting and fighting of a war is nothing more nor less than an active market for money, a business transaction.'" "International bankers" was thinly disguised code language for Jews. The phrase served the same purpose in the *Independent*. Prominent American Jews understood it as such.[48]

Having expressed his view of international conflict in unmistakable terms, Ford then explained that his purchase of Muscle Shoals would break the gold monopoly by enabling the government to back currency with natural resources such as waterpower. Edison's purpose in making the trip was to "indorse" [*sic*] Ford's bid after making an independent inspection of the site. It was important to Ford that Edison, his idol and mentor, validate his political economy; here, too, Edison obliged: "I will recommend to Congress that it complete the dam and give the lease to Mr. Ford," Edison proclaimed as the two departed Alabama on December 5. Moreover, he seconded Ford's beliefs about the villains in the currency system: "It is the money broker, the money profiteer, the private banker, that I oppose. They gain their power through a fictitious and false value given to gold. Gold is a relic of Julius Caesar and interest is an invention of Satan."[49]

The press was eager to get Ford on the record about his newspaper's "anti-Jewish campaign." Ford "explained [its] origin . . . by relating that while on his way to Europe during the war on the famous peace ship he was told wealthy Jews had provoked the war and were carrying it on for their own profit." He brought this intelligence back home, he told reporters, where his own "investigation convinced him the information was correct." He repeated to the press what he had already told Rabbi Franklin and Louis Marshall: "his campaign is only against the 'moneyed Jews' and really is for the mass of Jews."[50]

Even with Edison's support, Ford's Muscle Shoals bid was hardly ensured swift approval. Although the vast majority of the nation's rural voters supported Ford's proposal—mostly on the strength of his promise to use Muscle Shoals to produce inexpensive fertilizer—broad opposition remained in Congress. Ford submitted his bid to Secretary of War John Wingate Weeks in late December, but that was just the beginning of the negotiations. The motor magnate and the government were $15 million apart on price estimates for completing the first two dams on the project, and as Ford's bid was expressed in the form of an estimate, not a solid guarantee, the secretary announced that it would be "necessary to consult Mr. Ford again before an agreement on disputed points could be reached." Ford hoped to conclude the deal quickly, but those expectations were dashed, not least by his own mistakes in the bidding process. Opposition increased in the Federal Reserve, where officials looked askance at Ford's monetary theories.[51]

Scarcely two weeks later, Ford appeared to draw a firm conclusion from these events: the *Independent*'s antisemitic campaign was hurting his pursuit of Muscle Shoals. Early in January 1922, Ford strode into the newspaper's offices and ordered Liebold and Cameron to halt the articles. "One can only speculate as to the extent of Liebold's consternation," the historian Anne Jardim insightfully remarked. Cameron, by all accounts, "was momentarily breathless." Heedless of his staff's reactions, Ford barged on: "Put all your thought and time to studying and writing about this money question. The Jews are responsible for the present money standard, and we want them on our side to get rid of it." Cameron was incredulous: "They won't do it," he replied. "Oh, yes, they will; we can work them," Ford said in dismissal. Liebold sought to reason with his boss: "But we can do both [at the same time]," he said. Ford had the last word: "No, we can't. The Jewish articles must stop, and Cameron must go to work on the money question."[52]

Whatever illusion Ford may have harbored about Jews' willingness to assist him with the "energy dollar" was immediately shattered by no less proximate a Jewish friend than Rabbi Franklin. As soon as Ford announced that the *Dearborn Independent* "would cease its attacks on the Jews after the January 14 issue," Franklin publicly condemned Ford for linking Jews to the creation of "the present financial system" and for calling on them to "aid in constructing a new one." Franklin turned the tables on Ford, demanding that Ford issue a full retraction and admit that "his attacks on the Jews were without foundation and that there is no international Jewish conspiracy" before Jews could have any "confidence in any plan of Mr. Ford or any advances he may make to them."[53]

The announcement that the anti-Jewish articles would cease was by no means a sign of any great change of mind on Ford's part. Nor, as has been speculated, was it merely an "impulsive" move, undertaken as casually as the decision to begin the war of words nearly two years before.[54] The decision represented merely a shift in tactics, from a frontal assault to a more indirect campaign in which Ford intended to make Jews responsible for solving the primary public policy problem with which he associated them: the money standard. Muscle Shoals was to be the vehicle by which the monetary system was changed from a gold-backed currency to an energy- and natural resources–backed currency. It had become Ford's highest nonautomotive policy priority. As long as his bid to acquire control of the Alabama dams and nitrate plants remained alive in Congress, Ford prioritized his financial resources and redirected his public statements accordingly.

Contemporary observers offered different explanations for Ford's abrupt decision to end the *Independent*'s crusade against Jews. One of the more revealing came from the pen of E. G. Pipp, the newspaper's former editor. Writing in *Pipp's Weekly*, Pipp held nothing back: Ford was concerned about the effects of an informal boycott against his dealers, particularly in "Jewish centers of New York, Cincinnati, Cleveland, and other places." According to Pipp, once Ford mastered the concept of the electoral college, which allocated votes to heavily populated states such as Ohio and New York, once it was explained to him "that no man had been elected President in the past sixty years who had lost both Ohio and New York . . . and that the Jews could swing the balance of power in both of [those states]," he immediately made the decision to stop running the articles.[55]

Another, more colorful explanation for Ford's abrupt change of mind comes from the pen of Upton Sinclair, novelist and 1934 candidate for governor of California. In 1937, Sinclair published a highly uncomplimentary yet factually accurate biography of Ford, *The Flivver King*. In it Sinclair describes a Jewish Hollywood film producer, William Fox, the subject of an article about to appear in the *Independent*. Word of the article leaked to Fox, who promptly wired Ford to tell him of a film he had just commissioned: "He had instructed his hundreds of cameramen all over the country to get news of accidents involving Ford cars, and to get pictures of the wrecks with full details, how many people were killed, how many dependents were left, and so on. They were getting experts to swear what defects in each car had caused the accident." Fox was preparing the best clips to include in the newsreels he sent to theater owners each week. On hearing this disclosure, Sinclair said, Ford immediately "sent word back to William [Fox] that he had decided to stop the attacks upon the Jews."[56]

With so many prominent Jews commenting publicly and working behind the scenes to bring Ford's war to an end, where was Louis Marshall, and was he finding it difficult to keep his public silence? Marshall said nothing for attribution while condemning Ford liberally in private. News events soon provoked him to act behind the scenes. In July 1921, after reading newspaper reports that President Warren G. Harding had joined Ford, Edison, and Harvey Firestone on a summer holiday, Marshall sent the president a letter pleading for him to intervene: "The Jews of this country . . . cannot understand why they should be dragged through the mire, why in this land of liberty there should be a recrudescence of that same persecution from which their ancestors had suffered in lands whence they had come to America as a haven of refuge." Harding never responded directly to Marshall, but he complied with his request, sending a personal emissary to Ford a few months later. When Ford announced the suspension of the published attacks, Marshall was pleased to think that his discreet activism proved so quietly effective.[57]

Yet as Marshall himself already knew, Ford's well-publicized decision was disingenuous. The articles lived on in another form. In November 1920, the

Dearborn Publishing Company began to issue the articles in pamphlets sold in sets priced at $1. Titled *The International Jew* (*TIJ*), this collection put the Ford name—and the stamp of approval of American industrialism's towering figure—on the *Protocols*. In its first years in print, *TIJ* sold out of several print runs totaling two hundred thousand copies. That achievement in marketing and sales would please any author then, or now. Adding to its distributive capacity, Liebold purposefully did not copyright the work, thereby permitting all comers to translate and publish it. In short order it appeared in twelve languages on three continents. Aghast at the rising circulation of the *Protocols* and *TIJ*, Marshall authorized the American Jewish Committee (AJC) to finance the 1921 publication of Herman Bernstein's *The History of a Lie*, the first American contribution to the literature discrediting the *Protocols*. The cessation of the *Independent* articles pleased Marshall; before *TIJ* became readily available, he commented publicly that antisemitic agitation had decreased in the United States and that few citizens found the *Independent* articles credible.[58]

So, by early 1922, although the larger battle against antisemitism continued to require constant vigilance, Marshall had reason to believe that Ford's onslaught had been weathered. He managed the organized Jewish response in 1921; he beat back suggestions that Ford's allegations be met in open debate; he and the AJC steadfastly opposed the idea of a congressional investigation into the *Independent*'s antisemitic campaign; and he successfully discouraged prominent Jews named in the newspaper from suing for libel. The campaign had generated widespread adverse publicity for Ford, and although much of it had been generated by the Jewish press, it carried a sting. Parodies such as one that appeared in a 1920 issue of the *American Hebrew* were typical: "Henry Ford Acquires Railroads, Coal Fields, and Timber Lands of Vast Quantity and Wealth. Aims at Great Power. Flivver King's Interests Stretch Out to Control America's Natural Resources. Ford's Desire to Become President Considered a Menace to Nation."[59] With luck, Ford would no longer contribute significantly to the larger antisemitic movement that Marshall and the AJC were fighting to contain.

Despite his careful management of the wider Jewish answer to Ford, Marshall was unable to prevent rogue lawsuits against Ford from popping up in several places. The first was filed in Chicago in February 1921. Morris Gest, a theater owner and producer, set his damages at $5 million after the *Independent* accused him of staging shows that were so salacious in character that patrons snapped up tickets a year in advance. The accusation that he was corrupting the morals of the community probably was not the real insult. Far more offensive to Gest was the *Independent*'s accusation that he neglected his parents, who still lived in Russia. In fact, the senior Gests were well off and did not need their son's assistance; still, as Gest's attorney commented, "a Jewish boy never forgets or neglects his parents." Gest told the *New York Times*, "I'll make that Peace Ship Henry pay dearly for what he has said, and more, too, I'll make him eat his own words." Ernest Liebold immediately replied, "Mr. Gest will be ignored," and indeed, the producer was never heard from again. The suit never came to trial.[60]

A second lawsuit in 1922 put the first cracks in the united front of American Jewish organizations that Marshall was holding together with paper clips. This time, the plaintiff was a person of far greater substance than a theater producer of questionable taste: Herman Bernstein, writer, journalist, and personal friend of Marshall.

As he wound down the *Independent*'s series, Ford threw one final grenade: he fingered Bernstein, who had been a passenger on the Peace Ship, as the source of his information about *The International Jew*. In a widely circulated interview, Ford declared, "The real reason why I printed this matter was because a Jew— Herman Bernstein—told it to me while was crossing the ocean on the Peace Ship. He told me that if I wanted to end the war the way to do it was to see the Jewish financiers who created it. I played ignorant and let him go on. He told me most of the things we have printed." In naming Bernstein, Ford declared him a traitor to his own people. Indignant and offended, Bernstein issued vigorous denials, circulating a statement to every press outlet that reported Ford's interview. Not only did he get no response from Ford; the press did not fully cooperate either. "The International News Service, which sent out the Ford interview, has not sent out extracts from my statement by wire," Bernstein informed Marshall. "They used only a few hundred words. The Evening Post and The Herald published brief extracts from my reply, while the other New York newspapers did not publish it on the ground that they had declined to publish Ford's reference to me."[61]

By drawing Bernstein into the *Independent*'s web of untruths, Ford threatened to undermine the credibility of one of American Jewry's most courageous writers on antisemitism. Bernstein, a novelist and poet of some repute, had won acclaim for his accomplishments in investigative journalism in the 1910s. He was driven "to lay bare the operations of Russian totalitarianism, whether

3.2. Herman Bernstein, 1923 (courtesy American Jewish Archives, Cincinnati, Ohio, Collection No. PC-360).

Czarist or Bolshevist, especially in so far as it affected the fate of Russian Jews." His reporting revealed "the involvement of the Russian secret police in the case of Mendel Beilis, the Jew wrongfully accused of the ritual murder of a gentile boy" in 1911, and he also documented social and political conditions in Russia before and after the Communist Revolution. Bernstein was a prominent figure in American journalism, founding and editing the Yiddish daily *Der Tog* (*The Day*); serving as editor in chief of *American Hebrew*, the leading Jewish weekly, from 1914 to 1919; and, from 1925 to 1929, editing the *Jewish Tribune*. During the early 1920s, he worked in various capacities for Louis Marshall and the American Jewish Committee, which commissioned him to write *The History of a Lie* in 1921.[62] Accusing Bernstein of providing the very calumnies he had just publicly exposed was a brilliant stroke on Ford's (or Liebold's) part. The move not only drew Bernstein into the fray but also, through him, pulled Marshall back in, just when the lawyer thought the ugly episode was finally coming to a close.

As a result, Ford's announcement on January 6, 1922, that he planned to end the *Independent*'s antisemitic series hardly ended matters for Herman Bernstein. Three days later, Bernstein threw all politeness aside. "Today," reported the *Los Angeles Times*, "Bernstein applies the short and ugly word to Ford, and declares that he had no more than fifteen-minutes' talk with Ford on the peace ship, and the Jewish problem was never discussed, except that Ford said he employed quite a number of Jews in his shops and they were good workers." Calling Ford an ass in public was Bernstein's attempt to strip the patina off Ford's shiny public image. It did little good. On January 12, Bernstein decided to "bring suit against Henry Ford for this statement of his and for the article published some time ago in *The Dearborn Independent*, and now reproduced in the third volume of *The International Jew*."[63]

Bernstein immediately turned to Marshall for advice and representation. "I would be very grateful to you if you will be good enough to advise me what lawyer I should consult in this matter. Of course, there is no one who could handle this case as effectively as you or Mr. Untermyer." Marshall immediately declined, not just for himself but also for his law partner: "It would be obviously unwise for me or Mr. Untermyer to represent you in any action that you may desire to bring against Henry Ford or *The Dearborn Independent*." Marshall harbored grave doubts about the substance of Bernstein's suit. He did not believe Bernstein could prove that the newspaper's articles or Ford's statements had caused him legal harm: "The fact that he lied about you and that he attributed to you opinions which you never expressed or harbored does not in and of itself constitute slander or libel." Even more daunting was the choice of jurisdiction in which to file suit. Suing Ford in Detroit, Marshall said, "would be out of the question," whereas serving him with a summons in New York required catching him when he happened to set foot in the state. Then there was the problem of the corporate defendant: "You will probably be unable to get service upon *The Dearborn Independent* in this State. That will necessitate your proceeding against it in Detroit, which, of course, would be out of the question." On that issue, Marshall never wavered; he was convinced that no Detroit jury would ever return a verdict unfriendly to Henry Ford. Nor did Marshall want his firm or anyone connected with it to take the case. When Bernstein persisted, Marshall discouraged Untermyer from representing him, believing it "desirable to select a non-Jewish lawyer." Instead, he recommended Martin W. Littleton, a fellow New Yorker whom he believed might take the case as "a public service" for which he would not expect a large fee.[64]

Littleton took the case, but with little obvious enthusiasm. In April 1922, he reported to Bernstein that without the money to put a detective on Ford's tail, the chances of serving him when he came to New York were slim. Even with AJC member and Detroit businessman David A. Brown alertly watching Ford's announced travel plans, the New Yorkers could gain no traction. Brown advised that the local press was decidedly partial to Ford; in particular, the *Detroit Evening News*, which reached "practically every home in the City of Detroit . . . and could practically swing a verdict one way or another," had not once rebuked Ford or the *Dearborn Independent* for the antisemitic campaign. "The other newspapers I feel sure would not deliberately do anything to hurt Mr. Ford," Brown told Bernstein. "While the people of Detroit are split as to their regard for him, yet there are enough people in the community who would come to his defence if suit were started, especially by a stranger in our midst." Brown confirmed to Marshall that Ford knew of Bernstein's suit "and will fight shy of New York and will even evade Process Service if he comes to New York." Unable to make progress in the case, Bernstein again turned to Marshall for advice and help. Marshall, always generous with the former, declined to extend the latter.[65]

After almost eighteen months of fruitless discovery, Untermyer finally came to Bernstein's aid. At Bernstein's request Littleton willingly relinquished the file to Untermyer in July 1923, having been "not inclined recently to push this case."[66] Together, Bernstein and Untermyer energetically pursued the lawsuit in New York while Marshall renewed his objections: Detroit was "enemy territory," where "it would not be easy to secure competent counsel"; and Ford was building a new plant in Troy, New York, where "a competent process-server should have no difficulty in catching him." Untermyer and Bernstein proved Marshall wrong on the latter point: they were never able to serve Ford with a subpoena. Nor were they able to bring the case to trial. Their victories were more on the order of the symbolic: placing a levy on $115,000 of Ford's money in a

New York bank. The order failed to secure Ford's appearance and was vacated in 1924; moreover, Ernest Liebold asked the bank's officials to honor drafts on the account despite the court order, and they agreed. Bernstein and Untermyer had to content themselves with securing a promise from state officials "to seize whatever copies of the *Dearborn Independent* make their way into the State."[67]

Untermyer delegated the legwork in the case to a young and energetic assistant counsel, Laurence A. Steinhart. The junior partner drafted memoranda; tracked the time he and firm employees spent on the matter; and coordinated the collection of documents, pleadings, and correspondence over the four years of discovery. The firm bore nearly all of the costs of the case while it was in active litigation. Steinhardt, like Marshall, foresaw substantial difficulty in proving that Ford's publications and interviews had actually caused Bernstein legally compensable harm: "Mr. Bernstein has no special damages to plead. He can point to no loss or damage directly traceable to the publication of the article." Steinhardt recommended that Bernstein bring a separate lawsuit over Ford's January interview, which never appeared in the *Dearborn Independent.* It was not going to be an easy piece of litigation for the plaintiff.[68]

Untermyer's entry into the case brought the lawsuit and its plaintiff exactly the sort of attention Louis Marshall hoped to avoid. The announcement of Untermyer's intention to file suit led the *New York Times* to rebroadcast the *Independent*'s allegation that Bernstein had acted as a "spy" for a "mythical combination of international Jewish bankers." Upstanding citizens wrote to tell Bernstein he needn't have bothered:

Well here is where we get busy: Herman Bernstein, editor of the Jewish Tribune is starting suit against our Mr. Henry Ford. Now just such trouble as these aliens are making is what has caused men of World War to investigate conditions in our country. Mr. Ford has called attention to Jews and Catholics as a menace to our country. Our investigations have proven Mr. Ford is right; you don't need take anybody's word for it. Go into any court any day and see for yourself who is making trouble. You will find just what Mr. Ford says. Jews and Catholics are a menace to our country.[69]

As that letter vividly demonstrated, others saw the Bernstein lawsuit as an assault on Ford's very Americanism, which they hastened to defend:

Henry Ford could raise an Army and drive such people as [Untermyer and Bernstein] into the sea. Don't forget for one moment what happened to our Southern

Brothers about one half century ago. When the Hebrews start anything with the American Christain [*sic*] they will learn something the [*sic*] never atempt [*sic*] of or any one else in the History of the World. Henry Ford has in his possion [*sic*] more dope and data about the Hebrew. He is aware of the fact that every Jew goes to his Synogue [*sic*] and vows he will down, cheat, and do every thing in his power to do the Christian. This is un-American, Unconstitutional and against Our Christian Government.[70]

Such ignorant ravings irritated Marshall no end. There was no point in answering them, he knew; but he saw little purpose in precipitating them in the first place.

As the Bernstein suit languished in the New York state courts, Marshall remained publicly silent while privately reminding friends that he opposed it. But it was just one of many unfortunate developments for him that year. Between Muscle Shoals and his rumored presidential aspirations, Ford was never out of the public eye during 1923. *The International Jew* effectively continued where the *Independent* had left off, "'stir[ring] up bitterness against the Jews.'"[71] Indeed, while the Bernstein suit percolated on low heat, Ford laid the groundwork for a second, irreparable breach of Marshall's leadership. This time, Ford selected a target who, unlike Bernstein, had no ties whatever to Marshall, but who, in Ford's two-dimensional rendering, perfectly embodied the danger Jews represented to the America he sought to defend in his ongoing war.

4 THE OUTSIDER

What spirituality and what unwavering vision must a man possess who clings
to some hope of social or commercial opportunities for a family he has not
sufficient income to provide with the bare necessities of life! . . . The justification of
cooperative marketing is that it has been the means of a more progressive form of
living and a superior type of citizenship, as well as an economic remedy.

—Aaron Sapiro, 1923[1]

Aaron Sapiro had few advantages growing up. No one groomed him to take on
the powerful and wealthy. How he came to stand up to Ford is an extraordinary story of perseverance in the face of adversity, a story that has never before
been fully assembled.

Aaron's parents conferred the first of many disadvantages on him by immi-
grating to the United States from Eastern Europe, a place where people tended
to be born poor; to stay poor; and if they were Jewish, to endure persecution.
His mother's parents, the Wascerwitzes, came from Russia, his father's family
from Poland. Both branches of the family tree followed the usual, arduous path
to eventual landing and settlement in the United States. They sought to escape
what God, government, and fate offered them in their native land.

In 1865, the end of the Civil War reopened the nation's doors. That year,
six-year-old Selina Wascerwitz arrived in the United States with her parents,
Gustav and Frederica, and her sisters, Fanny and Amelia. The family came to
the United States by way of England, where they had lived for some time and
where Selina had been born. They first landed in New York, where Fanny and
Amelia met and married their husbands, Simon Ringolsky and Isador Levy,
respectively. The Ringolskys and Levys soon headed to California, where they
established small but profitable businesses, but the elder Wascerwitzes stayed
behind in New York's tenement district with their youngest daughter. Selina
had a suitor of her own, the Polish-born émigré Jacob Sapiro, who had dashing
looks but little to line his pockets. Jacob and Selina married in 1876 and welcomed their first child, a daughter named Hattie, two years later. By then, Jacob

4.1. Aaron Sapiro, ca. 1920 (courtesy American Jewish Archives, Cincinnati, Ohio, PC-3942).

had learned the ropes of American naturalization law. While he marked time establishing residency in New York, his eye on eventual citizenship, he served as a witness for friends and neighbors from the Lower East Side. So invested was he in pursuing naturalization that when the Wascerwitzes decided to join their other children on the West Coast, he declined to make the journey with them. For her part, Selina chose to travel with her parents, although she was again expecting. Her second child, a boy named Philip, arrived in San Francisco shortly after the family did, on a spring day in 1880.[2]

Jacob Sapiro worked as a butcher in New York City while making his run at naturalization in federal court. In the early 1880s, the court summarily rejected his petition, a reversal that finally prompted him to join his family in California. By then, a spare dozen years after the joining of the rails at Promontory, Utah, cross-country railroad travel was both commonplace and reasonably affordable, even for laborers such as Jacob. In 1881, an emigrant-class ticket from Omaha, Nebraska, to San Francisco cost $45; the trip required nine to eleven days.[3] Jacob evidently made his journey sometime in late 1882 or early 1883; on February 5, 1884, Selina gave birth to twin sons. Unable to afford a home of their own, Jacob and Selina shuttled between her sisters' residences, an itinerant existence that doubtless grew more uncomfortable for everyone involved with the growth of the Sapiros' young family: Beatrice in 1887, Saul in 1889, Miriam in 1891, and Milton in 1893. Already in 1884, their circumstances were so desperate that Selina delivered her twins on the floor of Fanny Ringolsky's San Francisco kitchen. One baby lived only a short time. The other, Aaron, survived the difficult birth, as if realizing that the odds would always be stacked against him and that he was already determined to prove himself to the world.[4]

It was a sensibility that became more pronounced as Aaron grew. When he was just a few years old, the family moved across San Francisco Bay to a home in Oakland. The address was 619 Fifth Street, only a few blocks from Oakland's Inner Harbor. Today the street sits in the shadow of an interstate freeway, in one of the heavy industrial districts that line the waterfront. It is hardly a high-rent district now and almost certainly was not then. It was what Jacob Sapiro could afford on his job hauling junk for his brother-in-law, Simon Ringolsky. Although the work was steady, the Sapiro family remained "pathetically poor"—and for a host of reasons.[5]

Jacob's job paid little, and he had no family resources on which to fall back. Selina apparently received little or no financial support from her parents, although her sister Amelia helped by watching Selina's children while she worked. The main reason for the family's economic distress, however, was Jacob's worsening alcoholism. He came home from work drunk and angry, driving his children away. Aaron and his older brother avoided the house for hours once their father returned. "You can't imagine the fear we had of him," he remarked years later.[6]

The rest of the family supplemented Jacob's income with a variety of odd jobs. Selina sewed towels for a local department store. At the ages of ten and six, Philip and Aaron started selling odd items on the Oakland streets before and after school. They began by peddling matches, a dirty and dangerous business. "[P]eddling matches was awfully hard," Aaron remembered. "In those days matches were made in large, square wooden blocks, solid at the base, and with several hundred to the block. . . . They were so heavy that a load big enough to net a profit of fifty cents would weigh twenty-five to thirty pounds." Moreover, in the era before the invention of safety matches, the slightest friction could cause a conflagration. Aaron struggled to manage, keep up with his brother, and make it to school on time.[7]

The boys grabbed the chance to become newsies, a more profitable and less perilous trade. Still, the newspapers were a heavy burden for boys living on the edge of malnutrition. Their tardiness problems worsened, too. In order to recoup what he spent to buy newspapers from the distributor, Aaron stayed on the street corner until he sold every copy. Unaware of his extracurricular activity, his exasperated teacher finally sent him to the principal's office. The principal—the poet Edwin Markham—coaxed the real story out of the boy. Convinced that Aaron was telling the truth, Markham granted him permission to arrive at school whenever he finished selling papers and to make up missed lessons at lunchtime. Kindnesses such as these were rare exceptions in Aaron's deprived youth.[8]

Five days after Aaron's ninth birthday, tragedy rocked the family. Early on the morning of February 10, 1893, Jacob Sapiro was driving a truck with two Ringolsky employees, Antone Juan Correro and Ah Wong. As they were returning from the Oakland Harbor to the Ringolsky junkyard on Franklin Street, their wagon approached a train crossing. A warning bell was ringing, but there were no gates to prevent traffic from moving across the tracks. After one train moved through going in one direction, Sapiro thought the intersection was clear and moved his truck forward. The wagon was then struck by an express train going in the other direction at a high rate of speed. Correro and Wong, seated in the wagon bed, were thrown clear and survived. Jacob Sapiro was dragged under the wreckage until the train could be brought to a stop. Carried to a nearby hospital, he died two hours later. The *Oakland Tribune* briskly passed judgment: "[T]he victims of the disaster were the only ones to blame."[9]

Word quickly reached Selina at home, only six blocks from the scene. She began the trip on foot to see her husband, but never made it to the hospital. Overcome with emotion, she collapsed on the street; friends carried her home. Her children responded with decidedly less grief. Neighbors picked up Aaron and Philip at school and took them to the hospital. They arrived after their father died. "[A]ll I could feel," Aaron reflected, "was that a great fear had been lifted." The weeklong period of mourning was a carefree time. School and work were suspended, the house was lavishly supplied with food, and he and his siblings were showered with attention. An uncle—perhaps Simon Ringolsky himself—bought the children new clothes to wear to the funeral. It was the first new suit Aaron ever owned. When relatives approached with scissors in hand to rend the garments in accordance with Orthodox mourning rituals, Aaron refused to submit. He and Philip took off at a dead run down the street. Eventually, the boys were caught, but Aaron considered it a wasteful gesture, not a tribute to the dead. He found his compensation in "the blessed privilege of eating all [h]e wanted" after the funeral.[10]

Yet with the rites concluded, the family's life became even more desperate. In addition to sewing towels, Selina took another job: sitting with the dead at night for the families of Orthodox Jews. Indeed, death kept its own close vigil on the Sapiro family during this time. In the year after Jacob's death, Selina lost one, perhaps two, of her children, probably to malnutrition or disease or both. The *Oakland Tribune* reported that Jacob left behind a family of eight children. By the summer of 1894, most accounts agree that Selina had only six mouths to feed.[11]

Determined to keep her children together, Selina turned to her sister and brother-in-law, the Ringolskys, in whose employ her husband had met his death. Fanny and Simon were the best off of all the Wascerwitzes. For both those reasons, the family believed that the Ringolskys bore an obligation to assist Selina and her children in some way. The Ringolskys, however, refused to provide any help, a decision that created a lasting bitterness between them and the rest of the clan.[12]

Finally, Selina was forced to make a terrible choice, "a step that almost broke her heart," Aaron said, as if to defend her for having made it. She arranged for the Pacific Hebrew Orphans' Asylum (PHOA) to take the four oldest Sapiro children: Hattie, the oldest at sixteen; Philip, then fourteen; Aaron, ten; and Saul, five.[13] The three youngest—Beatrice, Miriam, and the baby Milton, remained with Selina in Oakland, where she continued to sew towels and sit shivah for money to keep food on the table.

The PHOA was founded in 1870 by the members of San Francisco's Temple Emanu-El and by Joseph and Jesse Seligman, bankers and philanthropists who were among the first waves of forty-niner immigrants to California. Religious groups typically sought to take care of their orphaned children as the western United States grew.[14] The asylum's patrons found a building for their charges on Mason Street between Broadway and Vallejo, enrolled them in the local public schools, and enlisted the volunteer services of friendly physicians to care for the sick. In 1891, the orphanage's board of directors moved the children to a new, majestic Victorian structure on Divisadero Street near Hayes. The new house cost $57,000 to build; initially, twelve people lived there. Demand for space quickly rose over the following decade. By 1905, six thousand Jews had emigrated to the San Francisco Bay area. Children who lost parents to pogroms in Russia were caught up in the tide of immigration and deposited on the steps of institutions like the PHOA up and down the East and West coasts.[15]

State laws required orphanages to accept only those children whose parents had died, not those who had simply been abandoned. Abandonment created a dilemma for the asylum's governors, who wanted all Jewish children to be "rescued and fitted for useful membership [in] this commonwealth." The boys were to be apprenticed out as trade workers, the girls trained as "good housekeepers." Ideally, they would then be placed in the employ of individuals who would care for their "physical welfare and moral culture," but PHOA directors recognized that such placements would be difficult to find. In short, the institution was born of good intentions, yet constrained by the nature of the enterprise on which it embarked. It aspired to shepherd to adulthood those who would otherwise have been lost to poverty. It was not a place for the ambitious, the intellectual, the gifted, or the rebellious. To possess those qualities guaranteed that life at the orphanage would be unbearable.[16]

By the time Aaron and his siblings arrived at PHOA in late summer 1894, the Divisadero Street building housed more than one hundred children. Aaron became "Number 58," the first of a host of indignities he registered. The children lived, Aaron remembered, in "a cold, unfeeling system that tended to squeeze the joy of living and the individuality out of any child." Their food bore little variety and probably less flavor; for lunch they carried pails to school stamped with their orphanage identification numbers and containing a slice of bread and an apple. Their meager meals, numbered lunch boxes, and gray uniforms effectively ostracized PHOA children from other students. The orphanage may have given these children a place to live, but it denied them a sense of normalcy. Few, if any, orphanages at the time strived for such a thing.[17]

Separated from his siblings, Aaron was forced to devise strategies to survive. Punishment for any infraction was a whipping across the hands. In the boys' dormitory, the hierarchies of age and size mercilessly asserted themselves. On his first night at the orphanage, Aaron refused to help an older boy undress and was left "all in a heap." Several more incidents inspired him to try his "first experiment at 'cooperative organization.'" Gathering the young and small boys together, he outlined his plan: all of them would come to the aid of any of them. They sealed their agreement with bloody thumbprints and were delighted when the hoped-for deterrent effect kicked in after only a few demonstrations of their willingness to counterattack.[18]

Aaron's life in the orphanage sealed into him a deep bitterness, a distrust of authority, and a thirst for affection. "If someone could have come in to give us an occasional good-night kiss, or to speak a kind word now and then, it would have meant more to us than all the food in the world." But Aaron was luckier than most orphans. His mother made the arduous trip from Oakland to see her children every Sunday. To save money, Selina Sapiro walked the three miles from the ferry to the orphanage. Once in a long while, she would bring baby Milton along, justifying the expense of a cable-car ride.[19] The regular contact with his mother could only have sharpened Aaron's longing to return home, but that wish was never granted.

As bad as life in Oakland with his father had been, the orphanage could only have been worse. In the dormitory and at school, Aaron had little contact with his siblings, fracturing his sense of family still further. He also lost the autonomy and independence of his role as an income earner. Perhaps the one thing the orphanage might have provided that his home life had not was a closer tie to his faith, but the institution failed him there, too: "Judaism was spoken of, yet never seen. The orphanage stressed the importance of remembering

4.2. Aaron Sapiro (*sixth from right*) and his brother Philip (*fifth from left*) stand with the Pacific Hebrew Orphan Asylum band, ca. 1896 (courtesy Mary and Jerome Sapiro Sr., San Francisco, California).

Judaism without directing its expression."[20] Unimpressed with the outward signs and symbols of the Jewish faith as a child, Aaron's spirituality withered as he grew. The orphanage's lackluster religious training instilled in him a lasting hunger to prove himself.

Aaron quickly found an effective way to do so: he excelled in school. At the age of twelve, he won $250 and a medal for standing first in his class in grade school. That feat earned him a ticket to the city's prestigious Lowell High School, a rare privilege among PHOA boys. At Lowell, Aaron's gifts stood out, and he graduated at sixteen as class valedictorian.[21] The big question then became apparent: what next for so talented and promising a young man?

One of the trustees of the orphanage was Rabbi Jacob Nieto of Sherith Israel, the San Francisco synagogue favored by Polish and Eastern European immigrants and founded around the same time as New York's Temple Emanu-El. Rabbi Nieto used his pulpit to preach on social issues, including capital punishment, which he opposed, and he saw Aaron as a natural candidate for a modern Reform rabbi in the tradition he sought to build at Sherith Israel. For his part, Aaron gravitated toward the charismatic young rabbi, whose social idealism quickened his perception of the world as rife with injustice. His reason for considering the seminary was pragmatic: the rabbinate was a ticket to a better standard of living. So, when Rabbi Nieto approached him with the idea that he go to Hebrew Union College in Cincinnati, Aaron "jumped at the suggestion." It was a measure of Sapiro's ambition and energy that he simultaneously attended the seminary and the University of Cincinnati, receiving his bachelor of arts Phi Beta Kappa in 1904 and a master's degree in history the following year. Then he tutored undergraduate students while pursuing advanced rabbinical training.[22]

By the time he finished his undergraduate degree, Sapiro had encountered new friends who influenced his life in lasting ways. During his summer breaks, he returned to California to visit his mother in Oakland and teach in area synagogues. One assignment placed him in a children's bible class in Stockton, up the Sacramento River delta from Oakland. By 1900, Stockton, an agricultural town, was well on its way to becoming a merchant center; it already reflected a vibrant religious and ethnic diversity. Sapiro's teaching position brought him in contact with one of Stockton's most prominent Jewish families, Michael and Rose Arndt. Michael was a merchant, and Rose, though raised Jewish, had become deeply influenced by Mary Baker Eddy's Christian Scientist Church. Michael and Rose had two children: Stanley, a studious boy, and Janet, a girl who was barely ten in 1905 when chance placed her in Aaron's Scripture class.[23]

Rose Arndt took more than a passing interest in the serious seminarian. She introduced him to Stockton society, broadening his circle beyond the families he met at the synagogue to her own acquaintances in Christian Science. Soon she began inviting him to accompany the family on picnics and day trips around Northern California. Aaron was with Rose and her children in Berkeley on April 18, 1906, when a devastating earthquake struck San Francisco and stranded them in the East Bay for several weeks. Before too long an understanding had emerged: Aaron and Janet were betrothed.[24] Janet, not yet a teenager, apparently welcomed the arrangement; Aaron accepted it as the natural outcome of his relationship with the Arndts.

In Stockton, Aaron seemed to create the family he had never had. The Arndts, intact and robust, offered not only the nuclear structure he idealized but also the intellectual engagement on which he thrived. Rose's turn away from Judaism gave Aaron license to heed his own rebellion, one that had been brewing since the day he concluded that it was irrational to ruin a brand-new suit jacket to mourn his father. Aaron was becoming increasingly disenchanted with the rabbinate. Even the Reformed version was a static institution, he thought, uninterested in promoting social change, too wedded to rules and tradition. The more time he spent in Cincinnati, the more he became convinced that becoming a rabbi required too much intellectual conformity: "I came to believe strongly that any church must be an instrument of social service—to further human welfare—rather than an institution for the preaching of a fixed and changeless creed." Sapiro wanted to change the world. Not even Rabbi Nieto could persuade him to stay.[25]

As he spent time with the Arndts, he became convinced that his future lay outside religious life. He arrived at this decision over a period of some years, probably by 1905, when he finished his master's degree. But he had to return to the seminary each year until he had fashioned an alternative and secured the finances to undertake it. The character traits that came to the surface in this decision-making process had been manifesting themselves since his young adulthood. He did not hide his disdain for authority, particularly when it appeared to him to be unyielding and arbitrary. Nor could he camouflage his high regard for his own ambition and intelligence. He also knew he possessed a burgeoning capacity to rally people to him, from the boys in the orphanage to his students at University of Cincinnati and adults as easily captivated as Rose Arndt. These were his strengths, but he had weaknesses as well, prime among them a craving for emotional intimacy and a poignant inability to sustain professional and personal relationships. This complex personality would play a significant part in shaping the lawyer he became; his career as an organizer of farmers' cooperatives; and most tellingly, the decisions he made that led to his confrontation with Henry Ford.

Once Aaron made his decision to leave the rabbinate, Rose took charge of his postseminary career. She eased his departure from Hebrew Union College with a substantial contribution. Aaron then returned to California, where he enrolled in the law department of the University of California in San Francisco (now Hastings College of the Law) in 1908. During his first year of law school, he apprenticed himself to a local attorney and applied himself to his studies with his accustomed focus and drive. With his betrothal to Janet Arndt already well known, his personal life was equally set.[26]

. . .

Sapiro's return to the city of his stunted childhood brought painful memories to the surface. Unable to contain his anger, he put pen to paper and cataloged his

4.3. Michael and Rose Arndt, their children Stanley and Janet, and Aaron Sapiro, Stockton, California, 1904 (courtesy Jeannette Arndt Anderson, Palo Alto, California).

grievances in a letter to the president of the board of the trustees of the PHOA To his surprise, the board offered him the job of assistant superintendent, "with *real authority* to change the existing order of things." Accordingly, during his first year of law school, Sapiro took up residence in his old orphanage and took revenge on it. He began by firing the cook, an act that must have given him deep satisfaction. He then transformed the house into a model of Progressive Era reform, introducing a nutrition-based diet, regular medical checkups, and self-government by the children. The arrangement must have proved cathartic; stating his grievance resulted in real empowerment and change. It suited Sapiro's needs in other ways as well. The orphanage was a short trolley ride from the law school he attended while running the orphanage. As in Cincinnati, Aaron needed two full-time careers to occupy himself.[27]

Law proved his métier. In earning his degree from Hastings in May 1911, he again distinguished himself academically. As the top graduate in his class, he was selected to address the commencement exercises held at the university's Greek Theater in Berkeley. The title of his speech, "Law as a Training for Citizenship," transmitted his conviction that lawyers played a special role in the civic community. More particularly, he wanted to convey a sense of vocation. Such a profession marked out, he said on that sunny morning, a "prominent and important place . . . in the upbuilding of [the] state," reported the Berkeley *Daily Gazette*. In his "eloquent and forceful speech," Sapiro argued that the standards for professional attainment had shifted: "'A lawyer who wins big cases is no longer considered successful unless he takes an important part in the issues of the day and works for the advancement of the community." As a lawyer, he planned to work for social change.[28]

In the way that fortune often favors the supremely talented, California Governor Hiram Johnson was also seated on the dais that day. Johnson swept into office in 1910 as a barnstorming Progressive reformer. Once in office, he sought out lawyers to help wage what a contemporary journalist called a political revolution in California state government. Just a few months after his law school graduation, Sapiro was offered the position of secretary and legal counsel to the state's new Industrial Accident Board. At a time when victims of dangerous working conditions could expect little help from their employers, the innovation of workers' compensation programs provided real relief. Sapiro, of course, knew firsthand how work-related accidents devastated families.[29]

The board's first task was to implement a new statute setting up a voluntary workers' compensation program, including the administrative forms and processes for handling workers' cases under the new law. The experience of these cases showed the board and its counsel that a voluntary program was inadequate to meet the scope of the problem that workers faced. Sapiro then was assigned to redraft the statute to require employers to participate, guide the bill through the state legislature, and then defend the act in the state courts. Sapiro stayed with the Industrial Accident Board for nearly two years and practiced law on the side with a small firm in San Francisco.[30] Sapiro's departure from the Industrial Accident Board coincided with the culmination of his long engagement to Janet Arndt. On March 24, 1913, Janet turned eighteen, and her wedding to Aaron was set for November 17 of that year. The modest but elegant affair joined him to the family of which he had long been unofficially a part and cemented the personal and professional connections he had been building for years in the Sacramento Delta area.[31]

For it had been through his future father-in-law that he met the person who would provide direction and a career track, things he needed to focus his vague sense of purpose. Sometime in mid-1908, he encountered Harris Weinstock, a wealthy Sacramento merchant who had entered a second career in public service around the turn of the century. Weinstock's daughter, who lived in Stockton, came into contact with Sapiro through the Arndts and served as his conduit to her father.[32]

Weinstock and his half brother David Lubin were wealthy merchants who dedicated their lives to public service and agricultural reform. Both believed in the Jeffersonian vision of agrarian freehold. The idea, as the third U.S. president expressed it, was that democratic values went hand in hand with individual landownership and that agriculture formed the bedrock of civic virtue in American society. The brothers practiced the Jeffersonian ideal. First, in the mid-1880s, they purchased a three-hundred-acre fruit orchard near Sacramento and two wheat farms in a neighboring county. Second, they took the lead in forming the California Fruit Union, an early growers' cooperative that was one of the first organizations to market fruit east of the Rockies. To help realize his twin goals of rural prosperity and world peace, Lubin founded the International Institute of Agriculture in Rome in 1905; sixty-three other nations signed on as members. The organization eventually worked on common projects with the League of Nations in the 1930s and became a part of the Food and Agricultural Organization of the United Nations in 1946. Weinstock stayed closer to home, becoming involved with California state government under Hiram Johnson. Lubin imprinted his zeal for agricultural reform and civic citizenship on his half brother.[33] When Harris Weinstock met Aaron Sapiro, he found a ready-made acolyte of his own.

Aaron's first visit to Weinstock's well-appointed home must have been like getting in to see the Wizard of Oz. Weinstock had accumulated an enormous library of books on farming, agricultural cooperation, and law, some in German and French. Over the course of his visits, Aaron devoured every volume "he had . . . on the subject of world credits and farm marketing, and also [everything] that I could get in the library at the University of California." By the time he arrived at law school, he had constructed a handmade chart of all the laws on the books in the United States on agricultural credits and marketing. On visits to Stockton, Aaron often traveled the countryside with Weinstock, visiting fruit orchards and dairy farms while Weinstock "point[ed] out to [him] a great many things." Sapiro was getting a crash course in the history of agricultural cooperation, and he was a quick and avid student, eager to "[sit] at the feet" of Lubin and Weinstock and "absorb some of their views and vision and some of their sense of service."[34]

The relationship blossomed. Weinstock was already a member of Governor Johnson's administration by the time Sapiro delivered his law school graduation address. That proximity enabled Weinstock to buttress the governor's inclination to hire the young lawyer with a strong recommendation of his own: "There are two classes of men. One you have to drive. On one you have to keep a bridle to hold them back. Aaron Sapiro is one of the latter." But he added a caveat that suggested he knew something of Aaron's intellectual volatility: "He will do excellent work if guided by others and held back to the job in hand."[35] Still, there was no denying Sapiro's commitment to Weinstock and Lubin's platform of economic reform and government service. Lubin and Weinstock's belief that world peace and national prosperity could be secured only through agricultural prosperity gave Sapiro's social justice convictions a concrete underpinning. Soon he would have another opportunity to put those convictions into practice, this time working directly with his mentor, Weinstock, in the field both had studied intensely.

The 1900s and 1910s were a time of real innovation for California's agricultural marketing cooperatives and their members. By that time, California's Central and San Joaquin valleys were chockablock with small fruit and nut farms. Raisins, apricots, plums, cherries, almonds, and many other tree crops were growing by the tidy acre, tended by immigrant families. Armenians, Turks, Greeks, Japanese, Italians, Scandinavians, Hindus, and Northern Europeans all combined in a great agricultural melting pot as California's arid lands turned green under the artificial rain of constructed irrigation works. As fruits and nuts became profitable to produce, growers sought to expand their markets eastward and reach consumers year round. Even before the turn of the century, growers banded together in cooperatives to sell their crops collectively. Still, they encountered difficulties.[36]

The traditional form of cooperative was a loose affiliation of like-minded people, held together by goodwill and the bonds of neighborliness. True cooperatives returned all proceeds to members in proportion to the amount of business each conducted through the organization; they were nonprofit in the fullest sense. In the nineteenth century, such local nonprofit societies proved no match for the corporate brawn of industrial distributors. California fruit growers quickly learned they had to overcome more than geography to get their crops onto the dinner tables of eastern consumers. Packing companies charged an arm and a leg to prepare the fruit for shipping, railroads added their share for transportation, and then the distribution system larded on another surcharge, all before the fruit got to retailers. Informal associations tended to implode when confronted with the competitive forces of the industrial marketplace.[37]

After repeated failures and long, vituperative struggles, growers took a page from their opponents' book. They pooled their crops and then marketed them collectively for the highest price obtainable. Their new cooperatives used monopoly and price-fixing to control the marketing of the state's largest horticultural industries: citrus, dried fruit, and nuts. By 1915, Sunkist oranges, Sun-Maid raisins, Blue Diamond almonds, and Diamond walnuts became multimillion-dollar brand names. These cooperatives looked less like the traditional small-scale organizations of the previous century and more like U.S. Steel.[38] This new model had already drastically reconfigured the relationship of growers to markets by the time Weinstock and, more lastingly, Sapiro became advocates of the cooperative movement.

Johnson and Weinstock considered these developments necessary for agricultural progress. They had witnessed the destruction and misery that accompanied the boom and bust cycles of the previous generation and wanted to help growers make their gains permanent. At the same time, the governor and state legislature wanted to quell public outrage over the high food prices that consumers attributed to these powerful growers' organizations. But the different branches of California's government had different ways of going about this task. In June 1915, the legislature created the California State Commission Market and the position of state market director, who was to "act as a head commission merchant" for all staple goods such as milk, eggs, and flour sold in the state. The legislature's purpose was fairly narrow: to instill a nominal level of state supervision over the market for essential foodstuffs. Johnson appointed Weinstock as state market director, ostensibly to run the market under its enabling legislation. Weinstock had other ideas, and he intended for his protégé, Sapiro, to help execute them.[39]

With Johnson's support, Weinstock proceeded to turn the commission market into a vehicle for organizing marketing cooperatives for California's farmers and, by extension, for making the California model of cooperation the official approach to the state's agricultural economy. Johnson and Weinstock did not want intermediaries and speculators or, worse, financial interests beholden to East Coast investors and interests, to determine agricultural profitability, yet they knew those interests would fight every move the commission made to organize farmers' marketing cooperatives. The commission would need expert help from a well-informed lawyer who shared the governor's commitment to economic and political reform, but the legislature had not provided funds to pay for it. By inviting Sapiro to serve as the commission's staff attorney and paying his retainer personally, Weinstock neatly evaded the legislature's fiscal handcuffs. Further, Weinstock enabled Sapiro to build a substantial private law practice from the referrals he received from the commission. Once the growers formed cooperatives, they then hired Sapiro and his law firm to provide them with legal services.[40]

Sapiro eagerly greeted the parades of growers who traveled the dusty Central Valley roads to his San Francisco office. They came from "all classes of growers," Sapiro later remembered, from "Japanese onion growers and Japanese potato growers and Hindu potato diggers, and then the owners of the Delta lands. We would have conferences with other large growers and quite small growers, with owners and tenants—all different types and growers with different kinds of commodities." After these conferences, growers went back to their farms and their neighbors with what soon became known as the Sapiro plan for organizing a cooperative. This plan was hardly original; rather, Sapiro distilled what worked, carefully culling what did not, from the many elements of cooperative marketing that he had studied. Eventually, this plan made Sapiro famous among California's growers. It also made the commission market controversial for the activist way in which it reorganized the marketing of fruits and vegetables throughout the state.[41]

The Sapiro plan combined elements from many of the successful California cooperatives then in existence, particularly in the raisin-, orange-, walnut-, and almond-growing industries. The most important principle these growers had discovered was to organize by commodity: thus, Sun-Maid sold only raisins and Sunkist only citrus. This kind of specialization enabled cooperatives to invest in all of the operations involved in harvesting, processing, packing, and marketing—including retail branding—for just their members' crops and nothing else. The raisin growers found an innovative device to keep their organization together from one year to the next. To solve the perennial problem of losing members to commercial packers, who easily tempted growers with temporarily higher prices, the California Associated Raisin Company came up with a long-term membership contract that "ran with the land" rather than ending when a farm changed hands. Cooperatives conducted membership campaigns to get growers to sign contracts, and they ran the campaigns with all the fanfare of county fairs and community picnics. In the raisin districts, the membership campaigns coincided with Raisin Day parades. In Southern California, where citrus ruled, anyone who wanted to buy a ten-acre orange grove in 1910 received Sunkist promotional literature along with the land developer's sales pitch. The cooperative members knew that their only hope of maintaining a fair price lay in keeping a majority of growers under the cooperative's umbrella.[42]

Sapiro treated growers as pupils who needed instruction, good care, and expert leadership. Once they were organized into cooperatives run by leaders with good business acumen and armed with the proper legal papers and corporate authority, he felt, growers could live the lives they deserved. Their wives would be able to keep lovely homes, and their children would stay in school, exactly the idyllic life he had been denied.[43] As a lawyer, he believed that quality of life was what social and economic reform could bring about. As a Jew, he was convinced that organized religion had failed to accomplish this end.

The growers who "crowded into the market director's office for help" were largely oblivious to the sense of social mission that inspired Sapiro's work. They asked him to form marketing cooperatives that would hold up in court. In 1916, Sapiro organized his first cooperative for the poultry producers; the following year, he formed the prune and apricot growers' association. The Central California Berry Growers' Association also formed that year; two-thirds of its members were Japanese tenants barred by state law from owning land. After the war, the pear, tomato, olive, milk, and bean industries used Sapiro's plan to incorporate their own associations. Barely five years into his career, Sapiro was earning as much as $80,000 annually practicing in an area of law he was essentially inventing as he went.[44]

By 1917, the nation was at war. The war disrupted and transformed American political and economic institutions. Conscription created an instant army, as young men of every race and ethnicity flowed into the armed forces. The administrative power of the modern American state expanded to regulate the nation's mobilization. In an act that would never have been tolerated in peacetime, the government set up an agency to freeze food prices for the duration of hostilities.[45]

That spring, Sapiro was thirty-three years old, professionally prospering, and socially established. He and Janet already had two young daughters, Jean, born in 1914, and Andreé, born in 1916. Janet was then pregnant with a son, Stanley, who would arrive in January 1918. Aaron was old enough by one year to be legally exempt from the draft, yet he answered the call to duty. Like his contemporary Harry Truman, three months his junior, Sapiro was determined to enter military service. Unlike Truman, who had only to rejoin the National Guard to establish his rank, Sapiro had to start at the beginning. Twice after mobilization, in June and again in August, he applied to Officers' Training Corps. Both times, he was rejected because of color blindness. Sapiro suspected the army of excluding him on the basis of his religion. At the time, the military was as hostile to Jews' serving as officers as it was determined to keep blacks in separate and subservient units.[46]

Finally, Aaron enlisted as a private in the field artillery in June 1918. He left his wife and family and headed to the field artillery school at Camp Taylor, near Louisville, Kentucky, for a month of basic training; the army then sent him to the Thirty-Eighth Field Artillery, Thirteenth Division, at Tacoma, Washington. After two months, Sapiro's regiment sent him back to Camp Taylor to enter the Officers' Training Corps. He was stationed at Camp Meade in Maryland when the Armistice was declared on November 11. After his discharge on December 1, he took the long train ride back to his family and law practice in San Francisco, never having left the country, never having seen action, and not having earned the commission that his talents had finally put within his reach.[47]

Although many returning veterans experienced profound disillusionment over the experience of combat, Aaron Sapiro's disappointment stemmed from other sources. He did not fully share the sense of victory that suffused the nation in late 1918, because he had been denied a chance to help win it. His ambition to prove his civic virtue through military service and sacrifice was thwarted by the military's religious and racial prejudice, he felt. If he aspired to climb from wartime distinction to some higher level of professional attainment, he would have to accomplish those dreams in some other way.

The end of the war thus added to the sense of urgency and missionary zeal that his work with cooperatives had begun to unleash before the war. When Sapiro returned to California, he resumed his work organizing cooperatives, but he no longer needed an official affiliation with the state market director to draw referrals. Indeed, as Sapiro's private practice boomed, Weinstock and the commission became mired in controversy. The public markets Weinstock established in the fish industry, for example, drew accusations that the state was fixing prices and condoning monopolistic tactics. Complicating matters, Hiram Johnson was elected to the U.S. Senate in 1916; his successor as governor, William Stephens, a Progressive like Johnson, did his best to defend Weinstock but had his hands full with radicalism, urban bombings, and labor unrest. Beset with illness, Weinstock resigned under pressure in early 1920. In the meantime, Sapiro began organizing cooperatives outside California, speaking to fruit growers and milk producers in Oregon and wheat growers and the Farmers Union in Washington State in 1919.[48] A larger stage was materializing, and Sapiro was eager to step onto it. His organizations were flourishing, and he was anxious not to be blamed for the collapse of the California State Commission Market.

Sapiro's relationship with Harris Weinstock—who had supplied his foundation of intellectual expertise and professional ascendance—was the most important of his life. Weinstock gave him the job that provided him a standard of living he could not have imagined on leaving the seminary. For the orphaned Sapiro, Weinstock was much more than a friend and mentor; historians describe their relationship as like "father and son." Things were different after the war. Sapiro's renewed focus on building his practice led him to employ tactics that Weinstock would not endorse. The two were involved in a business venture in which Weinstock held stock and for which Sapiro was legal counsel. A dispute over fees led Sapiro to file suit against the company. When he refused to drop the suit, Weinstock dropped him. The break with Weinstock proved final. Once again, a father figure disappeared abruptly, and permanently, from Sapiro's life.[49]

Events in the 1920s would demonstrate that the intense close relationship with Weinstock and its abrupt end were to be a recurring pattern in Sapiro's life, a tangible manifestation of the effects of its sad beginnings. The leadership style Sapiro had tested in the orphanage and perfected in his law practice became the vehicle that took him to glory. It equipped him poorly, however, to handle the political challenges of organizing and running large groups of people and multimillion-dollar business corporations. Every disagreement became a challenge to his authority and beliefs. To prevail meant proving not just that he was right but that everyone else was wrong. Having risen in life through sheer determination, Sapiro never learned the value of negotiating, a professional

handicap. When he encountered disagreements, he severed personal relationships completely, beginning with Weinstock and continuing throughout his life.

. . .

In 1920, Sapiro burst onto the national scene with a two-hour speech at the meeting of the American Cotton Association in Birmingham, Alabama. His vision of
cooperation as a system in which farmers, not the detested middle merchants,
controlled the prices they received for their crops, electrified the delegates. As
one observer wrote, "The whole direction of the movement toward a new control of the cotton industry was changed by one man." The depression into which
agriculture had sunk after World War I led Congress to exempt farmers from
federal antitrust liability, on the assumption that farmers could never create mo-
nopolies with the power to harm consumers. At the same time, Sapiro boldly
claimed monopoly to be the farmers' right: "Only the farmer can have a complete
[and] unlimited monopoly and still be in any measure within the law." Sapiro's
vision was captivating because he did more than preach economic efficiency;
he uplifted "dirt farmers" with an inspiring modernization of the Jeffersonian
ideal of the agrarian citizen. As he wrote in 1923, "The justification of cooperative marketing is that it [is] the means of a more progressive form of living and
a superior type of citizenship, as well as an economic remedy."[50]

Sapiro's fame and popularity among farmers made him the nation's premier cooperative organizer during the 1920s. He became a consultant to
such figures as former War Industries Board chair Bernard Baruch, Illinois
Governor Frank Lowden, and top officials in the U.S. Department of Agriculture. He also became affiliated with the American Farm Bureau Federation,
serving for a short time as legal counsel to the organization. Having finally
caught the attention of national agricultural leaders, Sapiro proceeded to
bring the cooperative movement under his personal supervision and control.
He oversaw the organization of dozens of cooperatives in major staple crops,
coordinating thousands of farmers across many states under long-term contracts. Newspapers hailed him as the farmer's savior: "What John Wesley and
John Knox did for religion, what Oliver Cromwell did for society, Aaron Sapiro
is doing in an economic way for the farmers of this continent. He has liberated
them, through the principles of cooperation, from the clutches of exploiters. . . .
Sapiro went into the tobacco and cotton fields of the South, he went into the
orchards of California, he went to the wheat fields of Canada. And by preaching

4.4. Aaron Sapiro at Saskatoon, Saskatchewan, addressing wheat growers at the opening ceremony of the Canada Wheat Exhibition, July 1926 (University of Saskatchewan Archives, Saskatchewan Wheat Pool fonds, Series 10, Box 141).

the common sense of cooperation, he helped retrieve those areas from a condition of economic dry rot." He moved his practice to Chicago in 1923 and opened offices in New York and Dallas; in his absence, his younger brother, Milton, also a lawyer, ran the firm's San Francisco branch. The national press began to take notice, finding his biography compelling: "He stands as another personal proof that none is too poor to succeed in this country."[51]

As more industries adopted the Sapiro approach, he began to travel in elite circles in government and finance. He became acquainted with Judge Robert W. Bingham, who in addition to being a wealthy tobacco farmer owned and published Kentucky's largest newspaper. Bingham heard Sapiro speak and instantly became a believer, throwing his considerable prestige behind Sapiro's work in the tobacco industry. Sapiro argued the case for commodity-based monopolistic cooperatives to two secretaries of agriculture. Henry C. Wallace remained skeptical, answering a distributor's demand for information about Sapiro with a noncommittal response that neither defended Sapiro nor endorsed his plan. The Farm Bureau split into two camps over the question of whether Sapiro should be retained as counsel. In 1923, when he insisted that he would not assist in any capacity unless he were placed on retainer, the factions engaged in an ugly civil war that ended Sapiro's association with the Farm Bureau and cost his partisans their jobs, including publicity manager Samuel Guard and director of cooperative marketing Walton Peteet. After the highly publicized setback, Sapiro formed the National Council of Farmers' Cooperative Marketing Associations. Ineffective and poorly funded, it did little more than dilute agricultural influence in Congress.[52] Once again, Sapiro had built himself up only to lose to more powerful figures with whom he was unable—or unwilling—to negotiate face-saving solutions.

By far Sapiro's most lasting accomplishment in cooperative marketing was a model statute, written with the help of Judge Bingham, which incorporated the salient features of the Sapiro plan. The statute recognized the legality of monopoly control for cooperatives, the ironclad contract, and the power to sue others for interfering with farmers' shipments to cooperatives. The law guaranteed that cooperatives, their members, and their officers would be immune from antitrust prosecution as long as they conformed to the goal of the statute. Because that goal was to serve the public interest by bringing rationality and order to the marketing of agricultural commodities, it was not an onerous condition. Between 1921 and 1926, thirty-eight states adopted versions of the law, which distributors and warehouses promptly attacked in the courts. Indeed, the most lucrative part of Sapiro's law practice after 1923 was the appellate advocacy he performed in defense of the marketing laws he had helped to pass. He was extremely good at it. In 1923, the North Carolina Supreme Court awarded him a major victory by upholding the statute's broad public purpose in sweeping terms. Victories in a dozen other state high courts followed, topped off by a unanimous U.S. Supreme Court decision upholding Kentucky's version of the act in 1928. It was Sapiro's only appearance before the nation's highest court.[53] In a courtroom, particularly at the appellate level, Sapiro was in his element. When he engaged in advocacy rather than negotiation, he was peerlessly effective.

Stunning as these achievements were, they could not change the stark facts of the 1920s agricultural economy: overproduction and low prices led to continuing cycles of excess supply and lower profits for producers. When some of the crown jewels of Sapiro's cooperative movement collapsed under the pressure of the continued postwar recession, Sapiro came under attack. His unyielding insistence on adherence to his model in all its particulars, some traditionalists complained, caused the cooperative movement's spectacular failures. The difficulty, agricultural leaders and economists insisted, was that the Sapiro model was best suited to California. It was relatively easy to organize fruit growers, according to this critique, because they lived in proximity to one another. In contrast, the nation's major staple crops—cotton, wheat, corn, and tobacco, to name a few—grew across states and regions. Producers in those industries had less in common, shared less of a social identity, and felt less connected to a growers' cooperative that purported to speak for them but remained in many ways more remote and unresponsive to their concerns.[54]

Ultimately, Sapiro-style cooperation proved no panacea. Farmers continued to produce larger crops each year, and cooperatives could do nothing to stop it. Unable to break the continuing cycle of overproduction and depressed prices, many Sapiro cooperatives collapsed by the middle of the decade. Even as they gained the statutory authority to control their markets, cooperatives were undone by the fateful decisions of thousands of individual farmers and the structural workings of national and international economies. Sapiro's career had hit its acme even before Henry Ford trained his sights on him. The movement was already dying when Henry Ford began accusing Sapiro of using cooperative marketing to enslave American farmers.[55]

Sapiro's abysmal childhood unavoidably marked his adult life. In his mind, leaving the seminary, reforming the orphanage, and transforming the cooperative movement each represented an objective triumph over corruption and evil. Circumspection and self-reflection were alien traits; his focus was always turned outward, onto the world he intended to change. Nothing less than complete victory would satisfy him. The engines that drove him conditioned him not to concern himself with costs and risks; instead, he focused single-mindedly on his goals, which he defined in universal terms that brooked no disagreement or debate.

Like many men so animated, his ego was fed less by arrogance than insecurity, less by intellectual certainty than psychological fragility. Yet to admit to either one would have been to capitulate to the social forces he believed he had to contest. As he told an interviewer in 1923, "[T]he gift of leadership is not so much a matter of brains as of *intensity.* If you are so completely saturated with anything that you think it and dream it and live it, to the exclusion of all distracting influences, nothing on earth can stop you from being a leader in that particular movement." For Sapiro, what mattered was to have a vision of the world as it ought to be; persuading others was merely a matter of insisting on his vision as against "all distracting influences."[56] Although he had grown up fearing and distrusting authority, as an adult he became the kind of dictatorial and inflexible authority figure he had always resented and resisted. When reversals began to occur nearly as frequently as triumphs, he never stopped to examine the role his temperament played in the outcome. He approached Ford and the *Independent*'s attacks on him in the same way.

When Sapiro confronted Henry Ford, he was not leading the fight of American Jews against the most pernicious threat to their equal citizenship. Rather, he acted alone, opposed by many of the leading Jewish civil rights activists of the day who did not believe that litigation was the answer to printed insults. It was exactly the sort of fight Sapiro preferred. Although he later complained that no fellow Jews came to his aid, he would never have accepted help if it meant answering to the authority of others.[57]

What led to the legal confrontation between Aaron Sapiro and Henry Ford, then, was a series of gradual alignments that eventually put them on a collision course. Both claimed the mantle of national rural leadership, but they came at that claim from entirely different life courses. Ford saw himself, and farmers saw him, as one of their own; he had grown up on a farm and had lived and worked on his own modest plot before following his dream of building cars. Sapiro's interest in farming, though entirely genuine, did not rise from rural roots; he was an outsider and a professional. By the mid-1920s, Ford had apparently become convinced that the radical implications of Sapiro's work required that it be stopped, for the good of American farmers. Ford believed that twentieth-century farms should operate much as they did when he was a boy: as bastions of individual self-sufficiency, not as the interconnected production units they had become in the mechanized age he had done more to usher in than any other person. Sapiro's forceful advocacy of modern cooperative marketing made him Ford's new target in his war on Jews. In April 1924, the *Independent* launched its next barrage, aimed at Sapiro's supposed attack on Jeffersonian family farming. Now Ford sought to show that Jews intended to undermine the very foundation of American democracy.

5 THE OTHER WAR

As an individual, I was immaterial; but I was there as a representative, first, of the cooperative marketing movement, and second, as a representative of the Jews who were trying in their own ways to bring social light to disorganized industry in America.

—Aaron Sapiro, 1927[1]

By the mid-1920s, the turbulence that gripped the country after the war had dissipated, replaced by a deceptive social peace. The *Dearborn Independent* began its attack on Aaron Sapiro in April 1924, opening an unexpected new front in Ford's war on Jews. This time, however, the *Independent* made key mistakes: its reporting was filled not just with inaccuracies but with outright falsehoods, and it targeted a person who was not inclined to tolerate insults silently. Burdened by their reporter's recklessness and blinded by loyalty to Ford, the *Independent*'s staff delayed grappling with the articles' legal consequences as long as possible.

As the *Independent* undertook this second campaign, Ford continued to pursue a bigger prize: Muscle Shoals. During the fall of 1923, the president and the secretary of war pressed Ford to increase his $5 million bid substantially. The government's engineers reported that "the two nitrate plants, quarry, and steam plant had cost the United States about $85,000,000 and as scrap were worth more than $8,000,000." Nevertheless, in early December, Ford returned to Washington to tell the president that "he had not submitted a new offer for Muscle Shoals and had no intention of doing so." Whether Coolidge made him any promises, or whether Ford offered any political quid pro quo, is unknown; the secretary of war transmitted the unrevised bid to Congress "without endorsement."[2]

The press besieged Ford as he left the White House after meeting with the president. "You fellows are a darned nuisance," Ford snapped, anxious to get away. "So are your flivvers, Mr. Ford," a photographer rejoined. Chastened, Ford paused to pose for pictures. Teased for comment on his presidential intentions, Ford answered coyly: "Humph! That would be funny, wouldn't it?" Although his popularity continued to make him a talked-about candidate, he had little realistic chance of election. Coolidge was the undisputed leader of Ford's Republican Party, and even though the Democrats strongly supported Ford's Muscle Shoals bid, party regulars did not take him seriously as a standard-bearer. Long after his death, Ford's staff argued about his priorities, with those who had been closest to Ford during this time agreeing that the White House was Ernest Liebold's ambition, not their boss's. In any case, Ford announced his support for Coolidge's 1924 campaign within days of their meeting, ending speculation that he would seek the office himself.[3]

Still, if the trail Ford blazed during 1924 is any indication, he was avidly cultivating rural constituents. Such a base would have served both his political ambitions, whatever they were, and his plan to purchase Muscle Shoals. True to Ford's word, the *Independent* published no negative comment about Jews after January 1922—for a time. In the meantime, Liebold and Fred Black secretly commissioned a series of articles designed to burnish Ford's rural image, bolster his Muscle Shoals campaign, and expose the proclivity of trusts and financial combines to take advantage of American farmers.[4]

. . .

Within the *Independent*'s stable of contributors was a freelance writer who was perfect for the job of producing these articles. Harry H. Dunn, a former semipro baseball player living in Berkeley, California, was an obscure writer whose career peaked in 1914, when the *New York Times* picked up his reports on President Victoriano Huerta's reign of terror in Mexico and the U.S. blockade of Veracruz. He then latched onto a hot topic—Germany's infiltration of Mexico during the war—but placed most of his pieces in frivolous journals. His biography of the Mexican freedom fighter Emiliano Zapata was published in 1933, a year after Dunn's death, but John Steinbeck found the book unimpressive.[5]

Dunn and the *Independent* needed each other; what's more, they suited each other. After the antisemitic series on the *Protocols* began, the newspaper still had pages to fill. A writer such as Dunn, who was hungrier for his pay than he was to groom his literary reputation and who would write on any subject, was just what William Cameron and assistant editor Howard W. Roland wanted. Although Dunn was not yet writing about Jews during his first year with the paper, he did cover the subject of race. As the *Independent* wound down its first antisemitic series in January 1922, two pieces appeared under Dunn's byline on the "Japanese problem" in California.[6]

Dunn eagerly accepted the assignment to produce a series of articles on Aaron Sapiro, Jewish involvement in agriculture, and the subversion of the cooperative movement by international Jewish financiers. Sometime in the summer of 1923, Roland sketched the outlines of what Cameron and Liebold wanted and set Dunn to work. At first, the Detroiters worried that Dunn required persuasion: "Don't snicker when I tell you that the Jewish boys are putting the work on the farmers," Roland advised Dunn in August. "It began when Barney Baruch first became interested in Kansas, after Wilson left the White House. Since then there has been a great deal of Jewish interest in the plight of the farmer." Roland bade Dunn to spare no expense and spend whatever time it took to "round the facts up on this." Moreover, the editor recognized the possibility that the other side might return fire: "[I]f you can get it, we'll protect you of course." He saw Dunn's assignment as neatly in sync with the *Independent*'s mission: "I believe that you have an opportunity to do a considerable 'chronicling of the neglected truth' in this case."[7]

Dunn took to the work eagerly. During the following eighteen months, he encountered no lead that pointed away from his quarry. In the summer of 1923, he contacted J. R. Welch, judge of the superior court in San Jose, California. A wealthy grower of prunes and apricots, Welch opposed Sapiro-style cooperatives because he believed that they concentrated too much power in top officers and managers. He told Dunn to contact W. T. McCall of the Idaho Producers' Union (IPU). From information Welch supplied, Dunn concluded that the IPU was "on the rocks" and that its members "attribute[d] their troubles to Sapiro." Dunn relayed the information to Roland, suggesting that the Ford Motor Company put "a man in that section" on the story. Welch furnished information about Sapiro to Dunn throughout the fall of 1923.[8]

The *Independent* heralded its exposé of Aaron Sapiro with a front-page headline in the April 12, 1924, issue: "Exploiting Farm Organizations: Jewish Monopoly Traps Operate Under Guise of Co-operative Marketing Associations." The story ran with an article debunking Wild Bill Hickock's fight with Dave McCanles and another Dunn piece on the redesign of U.S. Navy battleships. Readers were unaware, however, that Dunn wrote "Jewish Exploitation of Farmers' Organizations" and the other nineteen articles attacking Aaron Sapiro that followed over twenty-five months. The *Independent* published them under the pseudonym Robert Morgan. Later, other pieces for Ford's newspaper were likewise disguised under Morgan's byline. These innocuous articles, neither

xenophobic nor antisemitic, were no doubt meant to bolster "Morgan's" credibility as a writer.[9] (To keep the lines of accountability and authorship clear
throughout the text, I refer to Dunn.)

The April 12 article and the next two appearing on April 19 and 26 sketched
out in broad brushstrokes what Dunn described as a menacing Jewish conspiracy in agriculture: "It would require a volume the size of the dictionary
to tell even briefly the schemes that have been used to disrupt, reorganize,
re-finance with various methods of financing, and then hold helpless these local
associations of producers of virtually every crop that comes from the soil in
the United States." Dunn told the story in generalities, adding few details. In
the first three articles, he aimed to give readers the big picture, promising the
substance for later articles: "The writer has reason to know, from sources which
are unimpeachable, that when the farmers of America have been organized into
national associations, the men who control these associations will be united in
one national organization. And the men who control this super-association,
this Jew-directed holding company for all the farmers of America, *will not be
the farmers of America*." The conspiracy branched from state government to
national financial institutions and international relations; it encompassed big
names and prominent agencies. Large photographs illustrated the articles; the
April 12 issue treated readers to bucolic scenes of California's Santa Clara Valley
and an Idaho potato field. The following week, a line of head shots appeared
under the caption "All little pals together—to save the American Farmer!" The
lineup of the accused included not only Aaron Sapiro but also distinguished
individuals such as Albert Lasker, former head of the U.S. Shipping Board;
Eugene Meyer, former and future chair of the War Finance Corporation; and
Bernard Baruch, former head of the War Industries Board.[10]

Dunn's April 19 piece assailed every detail of Aaron Sapiro's career in agricultural cooperation from the moment Sapiro entered public service with Harris Weinstock and the California State Commission Market. All farmers who
sought Sapiro's legal advice and counsel, whether during his work for the state
or after he entered private practice, Dunn concluded, fell victim to Sapiro's
plan to enrich himself at their expense: "Every dollar that comes into this firm
from these [cooperative] associations comes out of the pockets of the American
farmer, in payment for 'services' which he does not need, and for 'direction' of
his associations which were better directed when the farmer did the directing
himself." Moreover, Dunn wrote, Sapiro had no business getting involved in
agriculture because he was not a farmer himself:

He has had no experience in agriculture or horticulture in any form; he never has produced a dollar from the soil; he knows nothing of the problems which confront the farmer, save what he has read in books; he is not a producer of anything except ideas which require his personal employment by the American farmer. *Yet, seventeen states have altered their laws to conform to his plans of co-operative marketing, and to enable farmers to fix prices for their crops at his command. Forty-seven states contain associations whose members have pledged their crops to boards of directors obedient to Aaron Sapiro, and have pledged not one crop, but all the production of their lands for periods of five to seven years.*[11]

The April 19 article condemned every single Sapiro association for failing to obtain a "fair price" for its crops; further, Dunn asserted, the cooperatives' total losses of more than $70 million "were borne by the farmers and not by the bankers or the Jewish directors." Eugene Meyer and Bernard Baruch drew Dunn's ire for publicly defending cooperative marketing and promising government loans to Sapiro-organized cooperatives. The Federal Intermediate Credit Bank, "a new governmental agency for the 'aid of the farmer,'" was also involved in this widening plot, Dunn declared. "[The farmer] will be given the opportunity *to pay more interest on the money he is supposed to receive for his crop.*" Everywhere he investigated, Dunn informed his readers, he found nefarious, nonfarmer Jews taking advantage of governmental largesse and rural naïveté:

Does the American farmer never wonder that of all the leaders of this movement for the exploitation of our agriculture not one has ever been a farmer? Does the American farmer never pause to ask himself why his only "friends" should be an interlocking group of Jews? Does he ask himself why there is not an American farmer in this ring? ... Not one dollar of the money of any of the Jews in San Francisco who are interested in the Sapiro plan is invested in farms, orchards, agricultural lands or agricultural industries.[12]

Dunn's condescension toward farmers was outstripped only by his hatred for Jews. He, too, after all, had never farmed for a living. Nor was he a lawyer with an understanding of the regulatory problems producers faced in trying to set "fair and reasonable" prices for their crops after World War I. And nothing in his prior contributions to the *Independent* evinced knowledge of how government agencies worked, particularly the new national regime put into place during the war to stabilize the economy. What qualified Dunn to write the attacks on Aaron Sapiro were his track record as a writer who produced on spec and the coincidence that he lived in Berkeley, California—across San Francisco Bay from Sapiro's hometown—when the *Independent* commissioned the series.[13]

The third article of the opening salvo laid out the scope of the fraud Sapiro was supposedly perpetrating on farmers and the government. Moreover, when Sapiro organized cooperatives, Dunn reported, he insisted on approving all managers, particularly those who were "Gentiles."[14] But Sapiro's worst sin, as far as the newspaper was concerned, was an alarming pattern: Sapiro made sure that his legal fees were paid ahead of any other expenses a cooperative owed, even if paying his fees pushed the cooperative into reorganization or bankruptcy. As examples, Dunn cited the California Tomato Growers' Association; the Oregon Dairymen's League; the Okanagan United Growers of British Columbia; the Colorado Potato Growers' Exchange; and the melon, alfalfa, honey, rice, potato, and prune and apricot cooperatives Sapiro organized in California. The cost of bringing this information out into the open, Dunn implied, was high: "Some of those who exposed conditions under the Sapiro plan have been terrified—and I mean *terrified*—into silence by their Jewish masters."[15]

After flinging these charges, Dunn's series went on hiatus for three months. Reviews came rolling in to the *Independent*'s offices from approving readers all over the country. A New York City physician conveyed his delighted reaction to the first two articles: "This Sapiro agriculture stuff you are running is *simply great!* . . . [T]he Protocols have a paragraph which just fits all this activity." The owner of a San Francisco advertising agency wrote to Ford with several leads, including independent confirmation of Judge Welch's hostility to Sapiro: Welch led "the fight . . . against this yiddish ring of exploiters in the Prune and Apricot Association." This urban perspective on Jewish involvement in agriculture dovetailed with the *Independent*'s: "[T]he American farmer is rather gullible, you can readily realize how easy it is for the Jew to manipulate him. The Raisin Growers in Fresno is another association that the Jews have their knees on. . . . You will not find one California Farmers Association organized by Sapiro employing a gentile advertising agency." The *Independent* collected dozens of letters from Americans who agreed with Dunn's characterization of Sapiro and his cooperatives.[16]

Advertising executives were not the only interests aligning with the *Independent*. Eastern canners and other food processors eagerly welcomed the newspaper's exposé of Sapiro and cooperatives. One manager wrote to ask, confidentially, whether copies could be "placed in the hands of as many of our farming patrons as is possible and we wish to ask what arrangement could be made with your good selves to this end." Cameron explained the newspaper's purpose to approving readers: "We felt [the agricultural articles] were necessary at this time to awaken the leaders of the farmers' [*sic*] to the very unusual circumstance of four Jews securing control of all our agricultural cooperative institutions. We are doing our best to spread the information as far as possible."[17]

Anyone expressing skepticism or anything approaching disagreement received a chillier response. A member of the Washington State Grange registered what he considered a mild protest:

We believe that . . . agricultural relief must come through co-operation, and the farmers of America will deeply resent your efforts to take out your spite on the Jews by printing such grossly misleading articles calculated to destroy this movement which holds out the strongest hope for Agriculture in America today. If you desire to attack the Jews, why not warn the farmers against injecting Jewish control of their co-operatives instead of joining with the exploiters of the farmers in trying to break down these farmers['] organizations. If such articles continue, we shall be forced to reverse our opinion of the kind of friendship Henry Ford bears for the farmer.

Cameron's rebuke gave no quarter: "I am unable to understand the degree of heat with which you have invested your letter. . . . I agree with you that there are probably fewer Jews engaged in agriculture than in any other occupation in America, and yet the startling fact is that a movement begun by Bernard Baruch, financed with government money through Eugene Meyer, and 'put over' by Aaron Sapiro has practically engulfed the majority of the co-operative organizations in the United States." He then denied that antisemitism lay behind the articles: "It is not the Jewishness of these gentlemen but the dangerous influence of the Sapiro method upon existing co-operating institutions that is in point. . . . As to your threat that Mr. Ford may lose the friendship of the farmers, I am able to say that if telling the farmer the truth that concerns him will lose for Mr. Ford the farmer's friendship, Mr. Ford will simply continue to tell the truth." The chair of the Alabama Division of the Farmers' Educational and Co-operative Union of America contented himself with a simple request: "If you have any better plan it would give me pleasure to have same to present to the Union." That request apparently went unanswered. Newspapers reported that the *Independent*'s first three articles "have drawn the fire of farm organizations in many parts of the country."[18]

Ford's targets fought back, promptly and publicly. As the first rounds continued to fire, Walton Peteet demanded an audience with Henry Ford on behalf of himself and a committee of officials from the National Council of Farmers' Cooperative Marketing Associations (NCFCMA)—the advocacy organization Sapiro formed after he and Peteet left the American Farm Bureau Federation (AFBF) in 1923. He directed his request to Ernest Liebold: "Will you arrange an interview with Mr. Ford for a committee of the NCFCMA to present the aim and purpose of the American cooperative marketing movement and point out the errors and injustice in recent article on this subject in Dearborn Independent." Accompanying him would be Robert W. Bingham, leader of tobacco organizing in Kentucky, and three other prominent cooperative and farm bureau officials. Liebold's rebuff was immediate: "Impossible for Mr. Ford to set time for interview on matter referred to. Suggest you take up matter with our Editor Mr. Cameron or I will gladly make appointment for you with him." Peteet had no interest in anything the *Independent*'s editor had to say: "Sorry Mr. Ford cannot fix time to meet our committee and meanwhile his unjustifiable attack on cooperative marketing by farmers continues. We regard Mr. Ford as responsible for policy of Dearborn Independent toward American cooperative marketing movement and believe no good can come from conference with subordinate." Peteet and NCFCMA officials believed that Ford authorized the attack and viewed him as inseparable from the newspaper.[19]

Cut off from Ford, Peteet characterized Ford's refusal to meet with the NCFCMA leadership as a rejection of farmers' objections to the *Independent*. In a long statement released on May 5, Peteet called Ford's unwillingness to talk to farm leaders a dodge, just like his failure to answer the "many letters and telegrams of inquiry and protest sent to him by representatives of farmers' cooperative associations." None of it made sense to Peteet: "The mere fact that Mr. Ford does not believe in the economic soundness of cooperative marketing is no adequate explanation of these very vicious and vitriolic articles. Nor does the fact that Mr. Ford has a deep-seated hatred and distrust of Jews furnish an explanation consistent with his professed friendship for agriculture."[20] Last, Peteet demolished the *Independent*'s Jewish conspiracy theory. Dunn tagged Bernard Baruch as a coconspirator, Peteet argued, after he wrote the foreword to Herman Steen's book *Cooperative Marketing: The Golden Rule in Agriculture*, which the AFBF published in 1923. Eugene Meyer was included because, as chair of the War Finance Board, he issued government loans to some Sapiro cooperatives: "That is the sole offense for which he is pilloried as a 'Jewish exploiter of American farmers.'" Albert Lasker "is supposed to have some interest in an advertising company which places the advertising for some California cooperatives. That seems to be his sole offense." The banker and philanthropist Otto Kahn was accused because he "gave a dinner to [*sic*] Aaron Sapiro in New York and said some complimentary things about him. . . . It would be to laugh, if the interests so recklessly dealt with were not so precious and vital."[21]

Peteet's public criticism found a seam in Ford's usually impermeable armor. As spring moved toward summer, farmers, cooperative managers, and newspapers friendly to the cooperative movement all registered protests at what they perceived as Ford's hostility to agricultural organization. The first three articles were drawn so broadly that many people came to the same conclusion as Peteet: they thought that Ford meant to attack all farmers and all cooperatives. Unlike Peteet, most of them did not care whether he attacked all Jews or a few. A Kansas wheat grower alerted William Cameron to this problem just two days after the first article appeared:

When the Kansas farmer reads Mr. Morgan's dope they say yes another knock just like what is in the Grain Dealers association paper. One farmer signed up eleven hundred acres on the strength of Mr. Morgan's dope so you see every knock is a boost. The Kansas farmer doesn't need be so well informed about the Jews. They know where all the Jews are on both sides of this game. I think you would do more good[,] Mr. Cameron[,] if you would publish the good things about the wheat association.

In other words, criticizing Jews and cooperation in the same breath only encouraged farmers to rely more on cooperative associations. Judging by the mail, the *Independent* tapped into large veins of rural antisemitism, but many farmers believed that Ford saw no virtue in cooperation whatever.[22]

The *Independent* hastened to clarify. Cameron expressed surprise at the notion that Ford meant to harm rural interests: "There has been no attempt on the part of the Dearborn Independent to attack farmers' cooperative movements whatever. . . . What the Morgan articles set out to do was this—to warn co-operative associations that the Sapiro plan had met with such difficulties in various parts of the country that it behooved successful associations to go varily [*sic*] in accepting it."[23]

Moreover, Peteet and the NCFCMA felt compelled to limit their criticism of Ford in certain ways. The NCFCMA's Executive Committee considered publicly condemning Ford and his bid for Muscle Shoals in a statement to Congress, "in view of his reckless and unfounded attacks upon a movement which means so much to American agriculture." When deliberation time arrived, however, committee members could not take such a step. Muscle Shoals was too important and the NCFCMA too politically weak to take the risk. Agreeing that "it would be a tactical blunder for the National Council to oppose the Ford offer" for Muscle Shoals, Peteet made sure that the NCFCMA's May 5 statement made no mention of the matter. Instead, he delivered copies to Ford's congressional supporters asking that they intercede with him on cooperative marketing: "[D]esigning interests have misled Ford into approving the *Dearborn Independent*'s attack on cooperative marketing. The fact that there are a thousand Jews in the speculative grain and cotton exchanges and in the old dealer system of handling farm products for every one in the Cooperative Marketing Movement very effectually disposes of the pretense that Ford is trying by this attack to save American farmers from exploitation by Jews." Peteet then planned a more extensive "exposure of the falsity and unfairness" of the articles, which he promised would "be given wide circulation."[24]

Meanwhile, the newspaper was preparing a counterattack. To correct the misimpression left by the first wave, Cameron began editing Dunn's pieces to narrow the scope of their message. It was essential to reassure the *Independent*'s main audience—the nation's farmers—that Henry Ford's aim was to protect them, not to destroy agriculture. Subsequent articles would show that Ford's war on Jews was intended to bolster his status as the nation's premier champion of agriculture.[25]

To convey this aim, the enemy had to be precisely identified and, more critically, singled out. It was no longer enough to allege the existence of a Jewish conspiracy, Cameron and his staff realized; all they had accomplished so far was to mislead the *Independent*'s readers. It was their job to name the architect and agent of that conspiracy. When the agricultural articles resumed in the heat of summer, they zeroed in on Aaron Sapiro.[26]

The staff then got a big break. New sources, eager to volunteer information, wrote to Robert Morgan in care of the *Dearborn Independent*. Some of the sources were classic opponents of cooperatives: processors, packers, and transportation interests who did not want to bargain with united groups of farmers. Even more valuable, from the newspaper's perspective, were offers from other rural newspaper editors to supply Morgan with back issues of their publications that documented Sapiro's activities. Volney Hoggatt, editor of Denver's *The Great Divide*, reached out to Dearborn on April 21, alleging that a conspiracy existed between Sapiro and the Jewish owners of a marketing firm:

In my own mind, dear Mr. Morgan, I believe that Sapiro and the two Jewish gentlemen, Weyl and Zuckerman, are in together. You know Weyl and Zuckerman were appointed by the Colorado Potato Growers['] Association to sell the products of these cooperators at $21.50 per car. They are big distributors, big buyers of potatoes; and what a fool thing it seems to me to have a big overhead cooperative association here in Colorado, both district and state, with big overhead salaries for Gentile experts to do not one real thing for the potato raiser but eat up all profits if any were possible.

Dunn quickly spread the word at the *Independent*: "This gives us the inside on cotton, grain and potatoes, from the three letters I have sent you in the past week. If you could arrange to have some one see these men in Minnesota, Mississippi and Colorado, it should be productive of three important exposures of just what the Jews led by Sapiro have been able to do to the producers of three American staple crops."[27]

Hoggatt had an even more valuable lead for Dunn: the name of Joseph Passonneau, who helped Sapiro organize tobacco growers in the early 1920s. After growing disenchanted with Sapiro in 1923, Passonneau accepted the job of director of markets in Colorado, a position established under the Sapiro marketing law just enacted in that state. Hoggatt disclosed that Passonneau left Sapiro on bad terms: "[Passonneau] told me many lies that Sapiro had impinged upon this association down there and [Passonneau] called [Sapiro] a liar to his face—hit him in the nose, I think. Now, he will give you I think valuable information on this Jewish gentleman Sapiro." Realizing that Hoggatt was someone he could trust, Dunn promptly revealed his real identity to him and engaged him in a detailed exchange.[28]

Hoggatt then volunteered to "collect all the material available on the subject." In addition to contacting the Idaho Potato Dealers' Association, Hoggatt set up a meeting with Passonneau for May 23, at which, he predicted, Passonneau "will be only too glad to tell what he knows of [Sapiro]'s actions wherever he goes." The owner of Hoggatt's newspaper, who also happened to own the *Denver Post*, "desires to cooperate with you in your endeavors to get the bottom of what this whole proposition means to the struggling farmers."[29]

Dunn's story on the Colorado potato growers' exchange sought to expose Sapiro's abrasive style. The article focused on Erskine Myer, the attorney for the potato growers. Hoggatt interpreted one incident involving Myer as an embarrassing display of Sapiro's clannishness, and Dunn was easily persuaded. Sapiro retained Myer by telegraph and then reportedly attempted to force him out after discovering that Myer was not Jewish. In the *Independent*, Dunn described Myer as "a young American" who refused to truckle to the "Jewish influence" of Sapiro and the firm of Weyl and Zuckerman. Presented with the resignations of both attorneys, the potato growers' board of directors accepted Sapiro's immediately and rejected Myer's. Sapiro then billed the cooperative for $6,000 in fees. When the cooperative demanded an itemized bill, Sapiro's San Francisco firm filed suit and sought an attachment against the cooperative's assets—namely the potatoes in Weyl and Zuckerman's possession. According to the story, Myer had already obtained receipts from the firm for the sale of the potatoes, thus saving the farmers from the attachment. If Sapiro wanted to recover his fee, the story concluded, he would have to resort to the federal courts and risk "exposure" of his scheme.[30] Because he did not do so, Dunn insinuated to his readers, Sapiro was guilty of malfeasance.

Dunn mailed a draft of the potato article from Denver to Dearborn on June 12, 1924. His original headline for it read, "Beating the Jewish Ring at Its Own Game." The *Independent* published the piece on July 26 under the title "Potato Growers Beat Sapiro at His Own Game." The subtle change was doubly effective: the published headline cast Sapiro as the villain and farmers as heroic figures. Twelve separate references to *Jewish*, *Gentile*, and other explicitly antisemitic words or phrases that Dunn included in his submission were omitted from the published version. Likewise, two general references to Jews were changed to specific mentions of Sapiro, and the word *Gentile* was deleted altogether.[31]

In short, Dunn's draft committed many more acts of group libel than the newspaper's published version, which was in turn more libelous of Aaron Sapiro than the original. Cameron wanted to make it clear that Sapiro, not all Jews, posed the danger to farmers. The new message was that Sapiro perverted cooperation; funneled money to Jewish advertising agencies and bankers; and kept farmers from getting paid on time, if ever. Other powerful Jews supported him, so he did not act alone; but he was the chief threat and, once knocked out, his enablers could be removed more easily. Or so Cameron and Dunn strategized.[32]

Cameron and his assistant, B. R. Donaldson, were anxious for Dunn to resume his contributions. The first three articles had found a wide audience, but judging from the critical letters flowing into Cameron's office and the negative editorial comment in other publications, the *Independent* had not convinced skeptics. After some delays, prodding, and planning, Dunn finally agreed to conduct additional field research for future stories. In mid-May he departed Berkeley for Walla Walla, Washington, where he planned to cover the northwestern grain growers. He was confident of his source there, he informed William Cameron, "but it is probable that I shall have to see other men to confirm what I get from him." From there he planned to travel to Colorado to obtain "all the material on the potato fiasco" from Joseph Passonneau, who might also supply "a good story on the tobacco-associations and their career under Sapiro." Dunn kept his connection to Ford and the *Independent* a secret: "I shall travel under my own name, and shall not let any one know that I am Robert Morgan, unless you would prefer me to do otherwise." When a member of Sapiro's San Francisco law staff called him in May to verify his identity, he acknowledged writing articles for the *Independent* but denied being Robert Morgan.[33]

Dunn envisioned the trip as a long and comprehensive hunt for information on Sapiro's work across the country. From Colorado, Dunn went to Minnesota, whose grain growers, he thought, merited a separate story, because "the Sapiro ring tried a different trick on each one of these rings of growers." His next subject was Sapiro's plan to take over the Boys' and Girls' Clubs of America, a plan hatched in Chicago with the help of Jewish philanthropist Julius Rosenwald, the head of Sears, Roebuck. Sears sponsored a national radio program that supported the Sapiro plan of cooperative marketing, and Dunn suspected that Sapiro intended to use radio advertising to reach the Clubs. From Chicago, Dunn reported to Dearborn, where he filed the Washington, Minnesota, and Chicago stories.[34]

After a short layover in Dearborn, Dunn resumed his work. He visited Winona, Minnesota, and New Orleans to dig deeper in the cotton story and then went to Southern California to investigate the bean growers, who, he noted, had been "virtually ruined" by the "Sapiro scheme." Dunn promised a long slate of articles: "This will give us seven separate stories on the co-operative marketing associations which have met with disaster under the Sapiro Plan." Dunn expressed to Cameron his heartfelt "thanks for this assignment."[35]

But Dunn did not reach Denver until June 11, and by then he had run out of money. He sent the *Independent* twelve stories, but only four of them covered cooperatives. Soon, however, the *Independent* found a way to get Sapiro back onto its pages without the wayward Dunn's help: by publishing Sapiro's testimony before the Royal Grain Inquiry Commission in Winnipeg, Canada. In response to questions about his work organizing wheat growers in western Canada, Sapiro explained how, under the new state laws he had written in the United States, cooperatives secured control over farmers and crops: "We rely upon *the co-operative spirit* for procuring the signature to the [membership] contract. When once the contract is secured, we rely upon *the contractual terms* and if a man is induced to break his contract we proceed exactly as you would under any contract. *We go into the courts and procure enforcement* of these contracts." The *Independent* added emphasis to call attention to a particularly objectionable feature of the Sapiro plan: the power to enforce membership contracts in state courts. Use of the law for the "exploit[ation]" and "enslavement" of American farmers was what the *Independent* and its publisher thundered against.[36]

Beginning in July and continuing into the fall, as Dunn concluded his travels, the *Independent* unloaded on Sapiro with both barrels. Ten articles on allegedly failed Sapiro cooperatives ran between July 19 and September 20. First, readers learned that the wheat growers of the Pacific Northwest lost "two millions a year" under Sapiro's marketing plan. Next, Dunn revealed that the Colorado potato growers escaped much the same fate by cutting ties with Sapiro when he allegedly failed to respond to their requests for legal advice and counsel while on retainer. Likewise, Oregon's hop growers "refused Sapiro's overtures [and] maintained their industry." Hops cooperatives on the Sapiro plan, by contrast, "ate up one-third of the money which the members of the association should have received." The brisk conclusion: "Jewish 'direction' of the American farmer is expensive!"[37]

Next came Sapiro's alleged exploitation of the wool producers in Oregon. In this piece, Dunn began to express specific objections to Sapiro's binding membership contract: it was too one sided. "There is nothing in this contract whereby the farmer who signs it can hold the association or any of its officials, including Sapiro, to market his crop at any fixed cost; to pay him even the current rate which the independent buyer is paying the independent producer; or to pay him at any given date, or within any given time after the product of that farmer's land and labor has been sold." Dunn concealed from readers the contract's reciprocal features binding the association to perform on growers' behalf.[38]

Dunn's exposé on Kentucky tobacco appeared on August 16. It began with the escalated allegation that Sapiro cooperatives were "uniformly disastrous to the non-Jewish member." Effective cooperation began in tobacco in 1921 when Judge Robert Bingham brought Sapiro in to consult on drafting a cooperative marketing law for Kentucky. In 1923, for two months' work organizing the burley and dark-tobacco growers, Dunn reported, Sapiro received $107,845—enough to "pay the salary of the President of the United States for approximately one and one-half years." Dunn alleged that Sapiro exercised a veto power over all employment decisions that the cooperatives made while he was on retainer; the problem with this practice, Dunn asserted, was merely that "in the Sapiro organization, the less a man knows about the work he is supposed to be employed to do, and the more he knows about Mr. Sapiro, the better qualified he is to exploit the American farmer." The article featured a large picture of Joseph Passonneau, but neither quoted him nor attributed any facts to him.[39] The legal consequences of the tobacco piece would soon emerge.

Dunn expanded the saga as he turned to the wheat industry. Playing on the well-worn association between Bolshevism and Jews, Dunn tied cooperative organizing in Idaho, Oregon, and Washington to a rise in Jewish immigration after 1920 and the activities of the Industrial Workers of the World and the Communist Party in all three states. "If a man will take a map of Idaho, Washington, and Oregon," his August 16 article began, "and with a supply of red and white and blue pins set down a red pin wherever there has been an outbreak of Communism, Radicalism, or I.W.W.-ism; stick in a white pin wherever the Jewish farm-exploitation organization has founded one of its so-called California plan co-operative marketing associations; and put in a blue pin wherever one or more such associations have failed—he will find that he has a set of three pins at each point."[40]

The *Independent* repeatedly referred to its "three-pin" theory as it chased down proof of the association among Jews and radicalism in the Pacific Northwest. By the time Sapiro began organizing farmers in 1923, Dunn implied, the influence of radicalism had laid the groundwork for his top-heavy methods: "Reds and Radicals and Communists and I.W.W. agents . . . went out in gangs of three to eight and hammered the weak-kneed, radical, or dissatisfied hay-growers into joining this association." Growers dissatisfied with high marketing costs and huge debt-servicing loads, Dunn reported, were breaking their contracts and selling their crops to independent dealers, essentially daring the hay cooperative to take them to court. "The Northwest Hay Growers' Association, however, is not quite so ready," Dunn finished with a flourish, implying that Sapiro-style cooperatives were too feeble to use the strong-armed tactics at their disposal.[41]

Readers were meant to sense a shift in the logic of Dunn's attack. Until the hay story, the *Independent*'s chief argument was that Sapiro cooperatives were too powerful, that they were the product of far-reaching conspiracies, that they controlled the crop from the moment it entered the processing stream until it reached the retail market. After the August 23 issue, the newspaper emphasized agricultural industries that Sapiro had failed to dominate. Next, the *Independent* ran Dunn's story on Sapiro's rocky tenure with the American Farm Bureau Federation and Sapiro's attempts to establish a joint U.S.-Canadian wheat pool. Because Sapiro had invited Australia and Argentina to join as well, Dunn alleged that Sapiro intended to create an international wheat pool "which will control the wheat crop of the world, and which, in turn, will be controlled by Mr. Sapiro and his Jewish backers."[42]

Dunn positioned the *Independent* as a steadfast friend of the AFBF and those of its cooperative marketing programs formed according to traditional cooperative principles. But the AFBF went awry when it opened its doors to Sapiro and flirted with "absolute . . . subservien[ce] to organized Jewry." For example, the AFBF's publicity director, Samuel Guard, though not Jewish, supported Sapiro: "Mr. Guard is a very radical young man, pro-Jewish in his leanings, and at present a high-salaried employe[e] of Sears, Roebuck & Company, of which Mr. Julius Rosenwald is president." Dunn described a power struggle between Sapiro and Walton Peteet, AFBF director of cooperative marketing, on the one hand, and J. F. Coverdale and O. E. Bradfute, AFBF secretary and president, on the other hand, in early 1923. As a result of this struggle, Sapiro resigned, Peteet was dismissed, and the AFBF's dirty laundry got an embarrassing public airing. Coverdale's statements condemning Sapiro and Peteet made such excellent copy that Dunn simply quoted them verbatim.[43]

In August 1924, Dunn asked Donaldson to approve a story on the California raisin industry. The Sun-Maid Raisin Growers had just emerged from bankruptcy "by abandoning [the] Sapiro plan and adopting methods new to co-operative associations . . . showing that fault is in Sapiro Plan and not in co-operative idea." Dunn did not dig deeply enough to discover that Sapiro had nothing to do with Sun Maid's founding, bankruptcy, or reorganization; nevertheless, he believed that its story "demonstrates clearly that if these Jews really wished to make co-operative marketing a success, they could . . . [follow] the simple plan on which the Orange Growers' Association has been operating for years, and on similar lines to which the raisin men are now proceeding."[44]

Dunn was merely recapitulating the standard lines of contrast between the two models of California-style cooperation between 1895 and 1920. Centralized cooperatives, such as the raisin growers', used corporate authority and a top-down management style, whereas federated cooperatives, such as Sunkist, bundled organizations in local and regional networks. Traditionalists tended to favor federated cooperatives, viewing centralized cooperatives as dangerous concentrations of power in the hands of a few. But how and why cooperatives emerged and what legal form they took were not simple, straightforward processes; rather, they depended on the social relations linking growers, their understandings of cooperation and law, and the economic and biological features of the industries. All these factors varied with time and place. Dunn collapsed what was a complex, prolonged debate into crude terms to argue that "these Jews" were ultimately responsible for cooperation's failures. The raisin story, which appeared on September 20, 1924, was the last of the ten consecutive articles Dunn produced from his spring research trip.[45]

Still, the *Independent*'s retooled message continued to miss its target audience. In September, a North Carolina Ford dealer forwarded a clipping from the *Sumter Daily Item* to Detroit with a cautionary note: "[T]here is a general erroneous impression existing among farmers, as well as some dealers, that the Ford Motor Company, through the influence of Mr. Ford, is opposed to cooperative marketing." The dealer thought the idea posed a danger: "The Sapiro interests are naturally endeavoring to promote this impression since it is the only come-back they can stage." But the Sapiro "interests" were not alone. A Mississippi cotton grower told the *Independent*, "The man who wrote those articles is either on[e] of three things, densely ignorant, a cold blooded liar or so prejudiced against [J]ews, that he is willing to tear down the work of the Farmer's Co-operative organizations that they have taken years to build up and that is absolutely the only salvation for the Farmer."[46]

Indeed, by the fall, some readers began to wonder which mattered more to Henry Ford: protecting farmers or attacking Jews. A Colorado potato cooperative manager put the question directly:

I doubt very much the accuracy of the statements made and I cannot help but feel that your campaign against the Jews is leading you to print things that are not actual facts in order merely to discredit the Jews. . . . [W]hen you drag into the mud all of the principles of cooperative marketing which are advocated by the U.S. Department of Agriculture, I think you are carrying your 'persecution' a little bit too far and furthermore, you are damaging the welfare of the farmers who have secured relief through the operation of these cooperative principles.

Caught off guard, Fred Black replied that he would be glad to have "the history of your own co-operative association as you undoubtedly have based your opinion on the way it has worked out. There is no doubt but what the personnel plays a big part in the success or failure of the association." It was essential to establish Ford's intended message: cooperation was fine, but Aaron Sapiro, who "perhaps has it coming," had to be separated from the movement.[47]

Colorado and Minnesota potato dealers who hated the new cooperative laws poured out their complaints to Ford. They begged him to bankroll litigation in which the U.S. Supreme Court would "no doubt" overturn them. "[W]e supposedly called 'middlemen' cannot fight the law as the promoters and their friends would only use it against us. . . . [W]e cash buyers don't dare oppose any cooperative movement today as the press and politicians are all working the cooperative idea for all it is worth." The cooperative idea was exactly what Ford wanted to save, but his criticism of Sapiro positioned him as its opponent. Growers' willingness to voice their true feelings about cooperation was the *Independent*'s best source of credible feedback. The cotton story elicited a wave of similar responses. J. A. Blanchard, a planter from Perthshire, Mississippi, declared that Dunn "can [not] be complimented too highly . . . [the association] has had more to do with demoralizing our labour conditions than any one thing that has ever happened to our country."[48]

At the same time, growers continued to inform the *Independent* that its facts were wrong. Writing from the heart of the Colorado potato district, O. E. Webb, a trustee of the Colorado Farmers' Union, paired praise of the newspaper's "independent and pearless [sic] views on the vital questions of the day" with a more sober judgment. The July 26 potato article "was so full of misstatements and untruths that it raised the question in my mind as to the veracity of many of the other articles I have read in your paper." Shown a copy of the letter, Dunn fell back on what was becoming his customary defense: Webb had supplied "neither specific instances, nor proof of the untruth of any of my statements." Dunn assured Donaldson that once Webb provided these particulars, "I will be only too glad to prove to him in a detailed letter the truth of every statement I made." In Dunn's view, however, Webb was already a discredited witness: "Dr. Webb is one of the men who attempted to turn the Colorado potato growers to Aaron Sapiro and Weyl & Zuckerman, Sapiro's Jewish sales agents." Still, Donaldson held the door open, promising Webb "definite information" in exchange for "specific instances and detailed charges" in the hope that they might "arrive at a mutual understanding." Other protests over Dunn's potato story met the *Independent*'s characteristic counterdemand that anyone challenging its version of events provide proof of the newspaper's errors. Most sought to comply, only to give up after their attempts to extract information from the *Independent* proved unavailing.[49]

Throughout the summer of 1924, Aaron Sapiro's San Francisco law partners and office staff were hard at work with countermobilization. Leading the way was Aaron's youngest brother, Milton, also an attorney, who was by then running the San Francisco practice for Aaron. Friends, associates, and cooperative officials offered help and moral support; many of these individuals volunteered to provide sources to disprove the Dunn articles. The president of the California Prune and Apricot Growers' Association sent a draft of his refutation to Milton Sapiro for his review, and Milton encouraged him to take an even more categorical position: "[N]o single constructive suggestion has ever come from the Dearborn Independent so as to aid the farmers of this country, and, that, to the contrary, the Dearborn Independent seems to be attempting to tear down the only constructive work that has been done for the farms of the country, and is attempting to throw obstacles in the way of the farmers working out their own independence."[50]

The *Independent* staff continued to focus on its agenda. Convinced that the tobacco industry merited further investigation, Cameron dispatched another reporter to Kentucky in August. Harry E. Barnet had already spent two years looking for "the last piece of evidence" to prove his belief that "the Jews are trying to wreck the thoroughbred industry of the state." But he was more cautious than Dunn; after one interview with a willing source, Barnet told

Cameron, "I could sit down today and write out a good many pages of stuff dealing only with the point you want[;] yet, I feel that some of these statements must be verified. [My source] told me that every statement any writer makes must have the backing of truth, and he asked me to verify what he said, because he's been too close to the affair, and has always been too close." When Dunn's tobacco article came out on August 16, its inattention to detail was immediately brought to Cameron's attention, not by an indignant grower or cooperative official, but by a presumably friendlier figure: a tobacco broker. That broker, R. M. Barker, noted that several major warehouses had not been built at the time the *Independent* article alleged they were purchased by a warehouse company in 1917 and 1918; further, records disproving Dunn's article were on file in the Burley Association's Lexington offices. "If you would be just as willing to publish the facts, as you are to publish a lot of lies," Barker chided the *Independent*, "you would be doing a greater benefit to the farmers than you are by your continual knocking of the greatest co-operative association that has ever been formed, and . . . the fact that you don't like Sapiro is no reason that every co-operative should come under your blasphemous tongue."[51]

Barnet discovered that witnesses' statements evaporated the moment he attempted to confirm them. "We simply have to have this story," he insisted on September 10. Yet hard as he tried, he could come up with little firm evidence: "I chased down a dozen likely leads yesterday, but they were so prejudiced and vindictive I couldn't take them without verification, and when I verified them, they were of small value to us. The 'guts' of the rumors were mainly vindictiveness." Barnet's avid hope of writing two more stories on tobacco was going up in smoke, despite his earnest assertion that the *Independent*'s enemies could never compromise him: "I neither drink, gamble, nor do I pay any attention to the 'sociable' ladies, so there's no chance to 'frame me' that way, and thus destroy the value of my stuff." Nor was he intimidated by the presence of a house detective on the floor of his Louisville hotel—"a Jew hotel, owned by Reutlinger and a lot of Jews." Barnet continued his pursuit of important local bankers and politicians, but they all refused to meet with him. On September 29, Fred Black ordered him to stop work. Cameron had been called away from the office, and the staff had enough on hand to do.[52] More to the point, the editors seemed to have determined that there was not enough material for another tobacco story, whatever the two Harrys—Barnet and Dunn—might have believed. No second tobacco story ever appeared in the *Independent* under either man's byline.

Dunn's hay story, which followed the tobacco article on August 23, caused even greater headaches for the staff. Yakima, Washington, newspapers immediately countermanded the *Independent*'s version of events. L. A. Hunt, manager of the Northwest Hay Association, penned a bitingly satirical response that the *Yakima Valley Farm News* published just after the *Independent*'s article appeared.

As all readers of the "Dearborn Independent" realize, for the last several months the editors under the order of our genial Uncle Henry have been flaying the Jews of America with a merciless lash and for the last few weeks this attack has centered on co-operative marketing and Aaron Sapiro. The reporter assigned to gather ammunition for Ford's anti-Semitic cannon is well suited for his tasks. Results are what count—facts need not be considered so long as the cannon makes a very loud noise.

Hunt sarcastically answered Dunn's assertions: "If this be failure—and Mr. Morgan says it is—let's have more of them." He disproved Dunn's claim that the hay association was afraid to sue the grower and dealer who broke their contracts: "We are forced to conclude that the water at Walla Walla did not agree with Mr. Morgan and that for this, or some other good reason, he was forced to leave town, otherwise he must have learned that the association filed suit against both the grower and the dealer before the car of hay under discussion left the sidetrack." Hunt saved his most scathing words for last:

In the past we have had our doubts as to our worthy Uncle's fitness for the United States senate and confess, with much humility, the error of our judgment. A man of his proven sagacity, untiring energy, and such a keen sense of humor and fully able to hire a fairly minimum corps of reporters with Mr. Morgan's fearless disregard for the truth, cannot fail to be a source of great entertainment in that august body where facts are of little value anyway. Our Uncle has won his spurs—we're for him! We move the nominations be closed.[53]

Ford and the *Independent* staff might have dismissed Hunt's rebuttal as mere spit and vinegar. Yet an impressive figure soon reinforced it: A. C. Cherry, the Northwest Hay Association's attorney. Cherry informed Ford that the *Independent*'s story "contains numerous false and untrue statements—statements known to be false by practically every person in this community." The most important of these, Cherry declared, was the claim that Aaron Sapiro had anything to do with organizing the hay growers. Nor was there "a single Jew connected directly or indirectly with the association." Hay growers organized in response to crushing postwar economic conditions, he explained: "These farmers have been bled and robbed by unscrupulous dealers for years, and it was to obviate this condition that the Association was formed, through the efforts of the Yakima County Farm Bureau." Cherry did not dispute Ford's antisemitism; he merely contended that it spilled onto innocent people: "[I]t does seem very unfair to me for the Dearborn Independent, in its fight against a Jewish organization, to deal in vituperation and falsehood against an organization of farmers which is honestly endeavoring to render a public service." Cherry also denied Dunn's allegation that the hay cooperative harbored radicals: "The association['s] . . . officers and directors are all substantial farmers and business men who carry the respect and confidence of the entire community. . . . No Red, Bolshevik, Radical, IWW or Communist would be permitted for one moment to have any control or connection with the association." Recognizing the weight of Cherry's evidence, Liebold gave him an uncharacteristically respectful reply: "We are making an investigation of the matter referred to and we will be glad to communicate with you again later on."[54]

Other news kept the *Independent*'s staff on the defensive. Walton Peteet sent Ford and the *Independent* a paragraph-by-paragraph refutation of Morgan's wheat article. That piece painted Peteet as Sapiro's puppet in "a conspiracy to communize American Agriculture and deliver it for exploitation to an international group of Jews." Peteet was not writing, as he had in May, to debunk the notion of a Jewish conspiracy or even to come to the defense of his friend and colleague. This time, he wrote to defend himself: "[I]n the most solemn, definite and explicit manner possible, I deny having had any sort of connection with any kind of conspiracy, Jewish or otherwise, to exploit American Agriculture, and I challenge you and anyone else to offer proof to the contrary." Peteet labeled sentences "pure fiction," "fabrication out of whole cloth," and "as false as false can be." Facts, details, and full transcriptions of telegrams contradicted the *Independent*'s assertions: "If the writer of your article had tried to falsify the facts, he could not have succeeded better than he did."[55]

Peteet's conclusion leveled a warning: the *Independent* had committed libel, not just against Jews, not just against individual Jews such as Aaron Sapiro, but against a non-Jew who was personally and professionally associated with Sapiro:

If you had said that I believed in the commodity plan of Cooperative Marketing, . . . and had sought successfully to have it approved by the A.F.B.F., and had recommended the employment of Mr. Sapiro as legal counsel of the cooperative marketing department and that he had been chosen by unanimous vote of the Executive Committee and that I had many months later resigned in open convention because of differences in policy—if you had said these things, I would offer no objection, because that is what happened. But when your paper charges me with being the agent and tool of a foul conspiracy and resorts to falsehood and misstatement to support a baseless accusation it is guilty of an injustice which an honorable man, when he knows the facts, will undo, insofar as a slander can be undone.

Peteet, after all, was not only not Jewish; he was a bona fide farmer and grass-roots organizer. He started as a wheat grower in Texas and rose through the ranks of the American Farm Bureau Federation. If he, with his professional accomplishments, could be discredited and dismissed as a mere "Gentile 'front'" who enabled Jewish conspirators to dupe the guileless, then no one's reputation was safe.[56]

Recognizing that Peteet's latest memo signaled serious trouble, Fred Black immediately sent a copy to Harry Dunn: "Will you please check this and give us the source from which you got your information regarding Peteet and where we can [find] documentary evidence supporting our statements?" While waiting for Dunn, Black asked an AFBF executive committee member for information on Peteet. Black wanted to run down the rumor that Peteet accepted employment with the AFBF on the "*distinct understanding* that he was to recommend the employment of Sapiro." Ford's advertising operatives tracked down Peteet's Texas origins, describing them in essentially the same terms that Dunn reserved for Sapiro: "[H]e has been exceptionally good at promoting, but when such enthusiasm in the promotion of a scheme had been put over he has not had the ability to carry it on, and consequently . . . every undertaking has proven unsuccessful."[57]

Black's inquiry into Peteet's background says something about the *Dearborn Independent*'s significance in the larger Ford empire. The *Independent*'s staff was authorized to deputize Ford Motor Company personnel all over the United States to collect information and investigate people who were the subjects of or took issue with the newspaper's articles. Through much of 1924, Black and Cameron managed this investigation without assistance from company lawyers. Who gave them the authority to use company resources can be guessed—nothing happened there without Liebold's approval—and once that pattern was put in place, it would continue as the controversy grew. The company and the newspaper may have been separate corporate entities, but one wholly subsidized the operations, investigative work, and eventually the legal defense of the other.

After waiting weeks for Dunn to respond to requests for documentation, Black and Cameron were frustrated with what he finally produced. Like his articles, his letters told his bosses what Dunn thought they wanted to hear. "I do hope that you have not given Mr. Peteet any satisfaction as to his claims. Every line that we printed about him is the truth; most of it is less than the truth." The double meaning was clearly unintended; the reporter was stalling for time. He sent no notes, no reports, and no evidence to corroborate what he published. Furious and exasperated, Black recognized Dunn's unreliability but could not cut him loose because Dunn supported the *Independent*'s antisemitic interpretation of what was happening in the cooperative movement.[58] But Black was left with nothing with which to answer the steady stream of protests that poured into the *Independent*'s offices that fall.

As if that were not enough of a problem for the newspaper, Dunn fell ill with kidney disease after his return to California and was unable to work during the fall. The illness so incapacitated Dunn, he said, that he could not furnish Dearborn with proof of what the newspaper had already published. Black had no alternative but to send Dunn "a great many letters" that had come to the office after the publication of the cotton, wool, and prune and apricot stories, accompanied by a terse request: "Will you please go over [these] and advise the writer where we can obtain documentary proof of our statements?" A growing sense of unease began to pervade the staff of the *Independent*.[59]

Henry Ford was preoccupied with other matters. His efforts to capture Muscle Shoals were collapsing just as agricultural cooperative leaders increased their pressure on the *Independent* during September and October. It was the height of the 1924 presidential election campaign. Ford's best hope was to for Coolidge to endorse the deal personally. The president said nothing to indicate he supported Ford's offer, and strong progressive Republicans such as George Norris of Nebraska and Arthur Capper of Kansas remained opposed. Norris was particularly obdurate; without his vote, Ford could not win Senate approval, even after the House voted to accept his bid in March. Rumors that

Ford had agreed not to enter the race in exchange for Coolidge's support infuriated members of both political parties. On October 15, Ford wrote to tell the president that he would no longer pursue Muscle Shoals.[60]

Dispersing the national political pressure over Muscle Shoals did not relieve the tension at the *Independent*. It did not help matters when Dunn informed Black that his health entirely prevented him from traveling to Michigan that fall. Nevertheless, he pressed Black not to disavow his stories: "I am greatly relieved to know that Mr. Peteet has not been told that our statements were erroneous." Yet he could acknowledge, albeit indirectly, the rising suspicions of his superiors. Although he could not appear in Dearborn, Dunn offered to answer "letters of criticism received, or any questions which may arise in your own mind" and "clear up matters to your own satisfaction."[61]

Cooperatives unleashed a publicity campaign that undercut Dunn's efforts to reestablish his credibility. Days after this October exchange, the *Staple Cotton Review* issued a precise refutation of the cotton article. The *Review*, as Black delicately phrased it, "had some effect upon the members toward making them feel that our article was wrong." Without Dunn to provide ammunition, Black could not initiate a second round: "The big trouble we are finding is handling the situation at this end and is due to our lack of documentary proof of the statements we have made," he reminded Dunn. "We would deeply appreciate it if you would suggest to whom we may write for bulletins and reports that will help us compile information that we can give out from this office." Dunn's unavailability and lack of "documentary proof" put Black in a difficult bind. As letters dissecting Dunn's stories continued to arrive, Black had to defend Ford, the newspaper's journalistic integrity, the accuracy of Dunn's reporting, and the cooperative movement without the evidence he wanted.[62]

Dunn's exposé on the potato cooperative yielded another potential source. Sidney G. Rubinow, an agricultural economist and organizer, joined the throng objecting to the potato story. After Rubinow sent Cameron his account of the industry's history, Black challenged Rubinow to "submit accurate facts in connection with those statements." Black reiterated the *Independent*'s position on cooperation: "The Dearborn Independent is not opposed to cooperative marketing, but believes that the farmers themselves should spontaneously organize and control their own associations. We are interested in exposing what we believe to be the attempt on the part of Mr. Sapiro and others to control these farmers' organizations." Rubinow seized the opening, denouncing Dunn as a liar and pointing out that "spontaneous" movements collapsed in spectacular failures in both Maine and Minnesota before he and Sapiro were hired to organize there. After hearing nothing from Black, in November Rubinow offered to write a series of articles for the *Independent* on cooperative marketing "from an entirely different angle."[63] The *Independent* ignored him.

Dunn and the *Independent* published only four more articles on Sapiro, and they ran in October and December 1924 and April and May 1925. The December article covered Sapiro's work with the Southern Rice Growers' Association, work he regarded as so marginal to his overall practice that he had to ask his brother to remind him of the particulars.[64] Trivial or not, Sapiro regarded the rice story as the final provocation. He was ready to break the public silence he had maintained since April and publicly respond to Ford.

. . .

Sapiro mailed a demand for retraction to Ford and the *Independent* on January 6, 1925. Sapiro released his thirty-page letter to the press the same day, thus ensuring that the whole country read his statement probably before the mail delivered it to Ford. As the opening salvo in the civil dispute process, the document served notice of imminent litigation on the likely defendants: Ford; Liebold; Cameron, the *Independent*'s editor; the Dearborn Publishing Company; and the Ford Motor Company, which, as Sapiro acidly noted, "seems to have easy access to the affairs of the *Independent*." More than anyone else, the document addressed Ford, whom Sapiro sought to engage.[65]

Sapiro outlined what he saw as a personal dispute. He indignantly defended his character, conduct, and good name. Yet he never mentioned the offense of group libel. For Sapiro, this dispute began as an individual grievance. He did not see himself as staging a cause of action on behalf of all Jews or as defending all Jews from Ford. At this point, Sapiro intended to protect his professional reputation. As the press reported, "Mr. Sapiro accuses Mr. Ford of approving 'an attempt to destroy my participation in the cooperative marketing movement.'"[66]

In a short preface, Sapiro described how the newspaper harmed him and how the *Independent*'s characterizations of him had damaged the public's perceptions of his work: "It is impossible to calculate the harm done to my standing by your mean libels. Hundreds of thousands of people throughout the United States, who have never seen me or known me, have come to think of me as a dishonorable conspirator, solely because of your libels. These same people have also come to distrust the Jews as a class, because of your pathetic attempts to create the idea of a great Jewish conspiracy to injure them."[67] This was as close as Sapiro came to an explicit denial of the "pathetic" conspiracy allegations. Using the language of individual libel law, he asserted that people who learned about him and his work from the *Independent* viewed him only as a conspirator. That perception harmed him, and it caused a broader harm to the Jewish people, whom Americans now "distrust . . . as a class." As far as antisemitism was concerned, however, this was as close as Sapiro came to a direct refutation. The "factual" basis of Ford's bias, he said implicitly, could not be disproved, in the sense that all prejudice is irrational when it rests on a predetermined inclination to find certain patterns or outcomes in historical and social events.[68]

Then, maintaining a lawyerly demeanor, Sapiro kept his focus on the legal remedies available to him. He contrasted the secrecy of the *Independent*'s stories, right down to the reporter's pseudonym, with the transparency of the "open tribunal of justice," where Ford's "mask" of public respectability would be removed and his "evil motive" revealed. Ford failed to abide by his responsibilities as a publisher, Sapiro argued, and no motive, whatever its purpose, could justify the newspaper's failure to respond to the many reports of factual error. The "truth" had been "unmistakably brought before you," Sapiro wrote.[69] The letter presented Sapiro's side of the story and indicated how law would help him to tell it.

First, Sapiro notified Ford that his grievance met the legal requirements for instituting an action in libel: "It has been made clear to you that your series contained falsehood after falsehood; and that numerous statements had been made in the series which could have been immediately disproved by easy investigation on your part. Nevertheless, you did not have the courage nor the honesty to print a retraction." Then, he sought to shame Ford: "I am not deceiving myself with the thought that this demand for retraction will bring a retraction. Nothing is as stubborn as a malicious bigot. It takes strong honor and a great soul to admit truth and to do penance for a wrong. I would be delighted as well as surprised to find this in you; but I do not deceive myself with wild expectations." Sapiro's purpose was not to convert Ford to enlightened tolerance; rather, it was to defend his "professional integrity and professional ability" before the world.[70]

Sapiro informed Ford that a lawsuit, unless averted by a retraction, would transfer their dispute from the realm of public discourse to the venue of his profession. In the courtroom, he would force Ford to submit to the law: "You have persisted in these attacks and have thereby compelled me to go to the courts to force you to appear under oath on the witness stand." For Sapiro, the prospect of questioning Ford proffered the ultimate prize: "It is sufficient to say that when my attorneys or myself examine you on the witness stand, we will reveal your failure to make a proper investigation of the things you were so ready to print."[71] Law provided the vehicle for Sapiro's professional and personal vindication and for subjecting Ford to the humiliation his newspaper dispensed to others.

After eight pages of fulsome protest, Sapiro specifically listed what he wanted the Ford and the *Independent* to retract. The demand, he wrote, "covers all your charges and insinuations that tend to hold me up to degradation," specifically the ones that "stand out by reason of their bold clearness." He then recited the worst of the antisemitic slurs from each of the *Independent*'s articles, including the names of individual Jews.[72]

Interspersed with blanket refutations of the articles' antisemitic slurs was a significant number of legal land mines for Ford and the *Independent*. Sapiro batted away the entire hops story in one devastating sentence: "In this connection I advise you that I have had nothing whatsoever to do with any organization among the hop growers on the Pacific Coast or elsewhere at any time or for any purpose whatsoever; and every mention of my name in that article is libelious [*sic*] and improper." The wool article was equally vulnerable: "I have had nothing whatsoever to do with the Pacific Wool Growers or with any organization handling wool in Oregon; . . . every mention to me [*sic*], or use of my name in that connection is malicious, improper and misleading." The April 26 allegation that Sapiro organized growers in four California industries prior to the war was incorrect; he "had nothing to do with [those] organization[s]." Similarly, the July 19 article factually erred in attributing the Tri-State Terminal Company to Sapiro's work or his guiding philosophy, because "all . . . so-called cooperative elevators in the northwest were organized under anything but the so-called 'Sapiro Plan.'"[73]

In short, Sapiro claimed that the *Independent* accused him of working with industries and farmers with which he could categorically deny any association. Sapiro knew that libel law favored him here. The newspaper published falsehoods; Sapiro, and others before him, had notified the newspaper of its errors. Under Michigan law, when the newspaper refused to correct the record, it committed an act of malice for which Sapiro could recover damages.[74] Thus, his unconditional denials, which applied to at least eight cooperatives in Dunn's stories, were intended to make it difficult for Ford and the newspaper to assert truth as a defense to the libels Sapiro identified.

Sapiro spent considerable time on the Colorado potato industry article of July 26. It contained, he said, "misstatement after misstatement." Sapiro charged the Colorado Potato Growers' Exchange a $5,000 fee, which the *Independent* alleged he had failed to earn. Sapiro angrily "advised" Ford that the fee covered his services and his law partner's for work on the cooperative's original organizing campaign. Moreover, although Dunn asserted that Sapiro sued to recover that money, Sapiro said that the exchange "paid that entire account without contesting it." Sapiro also declared that he resigned as counsel to the exchange because its directors declined to follow his legal counsel. He furiously dismissed allegations reflecting on his professional conduct, specifically that he did not answer telegrams or other correspondence while under retainer and that "'this is the same condition in which virtually all the Sapiro organized cooperative associations have found themselves.'" Significantly, Sapiro did not deny Dunn's allegation that he dismissed Eugene Myer.[75]

The demand thus reveals what Sapiro thought was at stake in the case. Sapiro knew that Ford would never be converted from his antisemitism, but he hoped that the law would force Ford to accept the legitimacy of his participation in American public life. Sapiro recognized that the legal battleground of the case would be his legal representation of cooperatives. He understood the burden of proof that he assumed in filing suit, he knew the newspaper had to prove the truth of what it published, and he believed he had all the evidence he needed to win on the facts. What the demand does not reveal is how Sapiro intended to defend himself as a Jew and to reassert the integrity of Jewish Americans against Ford's broader prejudice. At that time, he seemed to believe those tasks were avoidable.[76]

From top to bottom, the Ford organization thought it unnecessary to answer Sapiro's demand for retraction, at least not with the courtesy of a direct reply. Fred Black saw no threat in Sapiro's letter. "We are wondering whether to take even this as an indication of any serious intentions on his part. . . . [W]e believe the most effective way to protect the American farmers from his machinations is to further disclose his subversive activities in court." On January 17, the *Independent* published an editorial, "Bingham, Sapiro vs. Co-operation."

The various public rebuttals of the *Independent*'s articles on cooperation meant nothing, in William Cameron's view. Cooperation had not improved the lot of American farmers:

There was one direct and final answer to all that *The Dearborn Independent* has said. They had only to show that the Sapiro system *had worked*, that the hundreds of thousands of farmers held by its contracts *had benefitted*. That answer would have been entirely sufficient, but it has not been made. . . . Instead, men of Judge Bingham's character, who ought to know better, are engaging in the perfectly futile business of misrepresenting *The Dearborn Independent*'s attitude on co-operation in general. . . . The fact that Aaron Sapiro is a Jew has nothing whatever to do with whether his system is workable or is a failure.

Two weeks later, Cameron took the gloves off: "The matter of libel, and what Mr. Sapiro very erroneously alleges to be the personal difference between him and this paper, can take its chance in the courts."[77]

These editorials served to answer Sapiro's demand for retraction. They laid out the newspaper's position: its campaign had not maligned Sapiro because he was Jewish but rather because he failed as a cooperative organizer and defrauded his clients. According to the newspaper, the legal burden fell on him and his defenders to prove his success. The paper also welcomed the chance to defend itself and argue the merits of cooperation in court. Apparently, no one, not even Liebold, consulted a lawyer. The newspaper got the law wrong, reversing the burden of proof: it was not Sapiro's responsibility to prove his cooperatives had succeeded. It was the newspaper's job to document that they had failed.

Nonetheless, morale in Dearborn was high. Cameron bragged to Dunn: "We have done a little checking up but not a great deal. Passoneau (is that the spelling) disagrees a little with our emphasis. Peteet challenges all our statements concerning him. But I see nothing, as far as concerns the essentials, in which we have made any serious error." Cameron imagined a grand concluding article: "I do wish, however, that it were possible to draw the whole country-wide Sapiro picture in one smashing finale, showing as of present date, where all his combines stand. We haven't finished with him yet, but apparently we haven't got across except to the enlightened. The articles, I believe, are being heard of more at the present time than they were at the time of their publication." Finally, Cameron gently pointed Dunn in the direction of his journalistic lapses:

There were apparently a sufficient number of minor digression [*sic*] from correct names, dates, places, to give Sapiro's spokesmen a shyster's platform chance. This was inevitable when we consider the vast amount of material and territory that were covered in a very short time. Having the perspective I now have, I wonder that you did so much and so well. Another once-over, with documentary proof in view, would, I believe, put the Sapiro system where it belongs. If you have any suggestions along these lines, let us have them.[78]

Though reluctant to criticize Dunn's reporting, the editor knew that Dunn's mistakes mattered. If Sapiro filed a lawsuit, the newspaper needed him to get things right as soon as possible.

Dunn replied to Cameron with an air of modest self-deprecation. "It is very fine if you say that the Sapiro articles were well done, the more especially as I thought, sometimes, that they were rather poor mechanically. The statements made in them are all facts, but as I read them over, it occurs to me that the same facts might have been told with more force." Oblivious to legal liability, he discussed the antisemitic thrust of the articles as if it were his own idea: "[T]here is a well-defined Jewish organization whose ultimate objective is control and exploitation of the agricultural industry and products of the United States." Playing to his audience, he told Cameron the *Independent* had actually paid Sapiro too much attention:

My regret has been, and I appreciate that it is largely my own mistake, that so much advertising has been given Sapiro, when, as a matter of fact, it is the Sapiro plan—which might have just as well have been the Levy plan, the Kahn plan, or any other—which is fundamentally unsound. So long as we have crooked Gentiles, who will do the dirty work for Jewish schemers, just so long shall we have exploitation of anything and everything American for the benefit of these Jews.

Dunn breezily claimed that "what we have told in these articles has been the truth." It was not Cameron who needed to be persuaded. It would be Ford's lawyers—and, if worse came to worst, a jury of their peers.[79]

But for the moment, no one in Dearborn seemed bothered by the prospect of litigation. A prudent libel lawyer surely would have been. Although newspapers expected courts to protect them from state-imposed prior restraints on circulation, contemporary libel law expected publishers to take care not to defame public figures. Sapiro had a strong case in individual libel. His demand for retraction contradicted numerous assertions in the *Independent*.[80] The newspaper's refusal to fix its errors after many individuals and organizations identified them, Sapiro was poised to argue, demonstrated the malice required for a damage award. Confronted with so conclusive a refutation, a publisher with less resolve and fewer resources might have backed down. But the Ford forces were determined to fight and confident they would prevail. The *Jewish Daily Bulletin* observed in a February headline that the "'Dearborn 'Independent' Invites Aaron Sapiro to Bring Suit."[81]

Sapiro spent the winter of 1925 preparing for the litigation he was determined to initiate and fielding inquiries from friends impatient for the lawsuit to begin. In March, he retained Detroit's top trial lawyer, William Henry Gallagher. A Michigan native and a graduate of the Detroit College of Law, Gallagher had established a reputation as "a gentleman of dignity and gentleness outside the courtroom" who displayed "the fierceness of a tiger in cross-examination." Even the court reporters were awed: "'I'd put him right up there with Darrow,'" claimed one. Born the same year as Sapiro, he, too, lost his father in childhood and rose from poverty to professional distinction with preternatural intelligence and energy. During the 1920s, Gallagher secured his local fame by winning record damage awards for several clients. The selection of Gallagher, a flamboyant Irish Catholic, surprised Ford, who expected Sapiro to retain "a 'Jew lawyer' from New York," in the words of Ford's bodyguard, Harry Bennett. "Mr. Ford considered Gallagher a 'Christian front' for Sapiro," Bennett recalled, "and after that always spoke of the Catholics as 'tools of the Jews.'" Apparently, Sapiro shared Louis Marshall's belief that representation by a non-Jewish lawyer would effectively neutralize the conspiratorial assumptions of Ford's antisemitism. On April 22, Gallagher filed a ninety-two-page declaration in Detroit's federal court, officially opening the case of *Sapiro v. Ford*.[82]

Unlike Marshall, Sapiro was determined to take his case to Detroit, straight to Ford: "I went into his home town, where his strength is supposed to be greatest; and I brought the suit in U.S. District Court at Detroit," he explained. More than anything else, Sapiro wanted to "force [Ford] to appear as a witness." He requested damages of $1 million, a sum that riveted the press's attention. In 1925, the president of the United States made $75,000 in a year; Henry Ford made $1 million in two and a half days. Sapiro made it a point to ask for exactly the amount Ford demanded when he sued the *Tribune*.[83]

Sapiro could not count on Marshall's support, however. The American Jewish Committee's president publicly dismissed Sapiro's action with the comment that a lawsuit only gave Ford "the publicity which he has craved ever since he embarked upon his attack [on] the Jews."[84] But what the lawsuit gave Sapiro, Marshall, and American Jews was an opening they would all scramble to define and explore in the months—and years—to come.

PART II

Litigants and Losers

6 THE LAWSUIT

This Sapiro affair is truly a momentous one to the Ford organization and since
the time of the trial is drawing near we are naturally keen to close up all the open
questions.

—Fred L. Black, 1925[1]

Nearly two years passed between the time Sapiro filed his libel lawsuit in April
1925 and the day the trial finally got under way in 1927. Both sides used this
period, known as the discovery phase in the civil litigation process, to gather
evidence and depose witnesses. This contentious process also provided the lawyers on both sides with the chance to measure each other's strengths. With few
resources on which to draw, Aaron Sapiro fought a war of attrition. Just making it to trial would constitute a victory of sorts. Sapiro's reward would be the
discovery that Ford had no intention of defending the *Independent*'s outrageous
articles; rather, Ford's lawyers intended to make Sapiro's Jewishness the issue.
They hoped the jurors would find it easy to believe that because he was a Jew,
Sapiro was dishonest and defrauded his clients.

Sapiro's declaration laid out 21 counts and specified 141 separate libelous
statements in the *Independent*. Sapiro and his lawyer, William Henry Gallagher,
steered the case toward conventional individual libel grounds rather than pushing for the vindication of all Jews. The complaint listed each printed statement
that Sapiro deemed libelous, but that did not include every mention of Sapiro,
Jews, or cooperatives. Gallagher wanted to avoid Ford's error in the *Chicago
Tribune* suit: including too much of the publication in the libel complaint.
Instead, perhaps mindful of "the ease with which inexperienced libel lawyers
could unintentionally turn their plaintiff-clients into the *de facto* defendants,"
Gallagher confined his complaint to words that he could prove were libelous per
se. So he listed only those statements the plaintiff viewed as both offensive on
their face and presumably impossible to prove true: the assertions that Sapiro
was part of a "Jewish conspiracy" that sought to "exploit, oppress, impoverish,
control, dominate, or otherwise cause detriment to farmers or producers, or

their organizations." As a result, the declaration was much narrower in scope than Sapiro's demand for retraction.[2]

American libel law placed the burden of proving the truth of these statements on the newspaper, its staff, its editor, and its owner. Developments in Michigan made Sapiro's decision to sue Ford there particularly smart. During the nineteenth century, the state legislature amended the common law rules, seeking to lighten the load for defendants by, for example, excluding noneconomic damages from libel clams when publishers printed retractions or corrections. These attempts to balance the scales fell short, as the state's supreme court repeatedly struck down statutory limits on damages and other reforms favorable to publishers. Even more relevant to Sapiro was a Michigan Supreme Court decision that made it imperative for publishers to distinguish between statements of fact and opinion if they wanted to avoid liability for damages. Anything not labeled as editorial comment, or anything that left doubt in a reader's mind as to where fact ended and opinion began, would be treated as a statement of fact requiring proof and thus subject to a libel claim. A Michigan plaintiff would still have to prove the publisher's intent was malicious, however.[3]

During the discovery process of the *Sapiro v. Ford* litigation, the defense deployed two separate tactics. The first was to carpet the nation with Ford agents, investigators, and lawyers who retrieved evidence, identified witnesses, and took depositions in preparation for trial. The second was to use "Jewish" as a vague label to which no one could reasonably object, thereby exploiting the impossibility of defining the term, and then to categorize anyone, Jewish or not, who associated with Aaron Sapiro in work affecting American agriculture as involved in a malevolent Jewish conspiracy. Ford's staff and lawyers sought to regain the moral high ground by disavowing explicit antisemitism. Yet in holding to the fundamental assumption that any activity involving Jews in agriculture was by nature conspiratorial, Ford's people shared—and acted on—the malicious belief at the heart of Ford's own prejudice. In the end, for both sides, the case was about Sapiro, Jews, and cooperatives. For Sapiro, there was nothing inherently evil about those things; for Ford, nothing good came when they acted in concert.

Still, the declaration overincluded in one respect. The lawsuit mentioned Sapiro's attorney-client relationships only once, but it was a mention Sapiro could not resist. He sued on language from the Colorado potato article that described him as "incompetent to act as legal advisor to said farmers' organizations." He cited Dunn's allegation that he put a lien on the potato crop when the exchange refused to pay his legal fee and text from the April 26 article that referred to whistle-blowers who "have been terrified—and I mean *terrified*—into silence by their Jewish masters." By including the *Independent*'s indictment of his Colorado work in the libel suit, Sapiro opened the door for the defense to examine his conduct as attorney to all the cooperatives he represented.[4]

The *Independent* staff so perpetuated Ford's antisemitic assumptions that they saw no need to defend the articles' prejudicial characterizations of Jews. Ford's lawyers, although they partook of antisemitic assumptions common to that time, took a pragmatic approach to the case. Focusing on facts rather than beliefs, they set out to prove Sapiro's misconduct as a lawyer by showing that the cooperative movement he built was founded on invalid economic assumptions, that he knew his program would never work even before he left California in 1919, and that he was dishonest. Because Sapiro's Jewishness could not be disputed, the defense would maintain that identifying him as such was an innocent act. To point out his connections to other individuals, Jewish and not, was thus a legitimate observation as well and therefore not libelous. For the better part of a year, then, Ford's agents built a theory of conspiracy as any connection between Sapiro and other people. By the time they faced trial, nearly two years after the case was filed, Ford's lawyers were confident they would win. How they attained that confidence was more a function of luck and Sapiro's enemies in the cooperative movement than it was of their skill.

. . .

The *Independent* began the discovery phase of the lawsuit with a lot of attitude and little evidence. After the bravado of the *Independent*'s January 1925 editorials, in which Cameron chastised Sapiro for failing to prove that cooperation worked, the staff accelerated its scramble to assemble documentation for the entire Sapiro series. *Independent* office manager B. E. Larson asked Harry Dunn to return to the *Independent* all their correspondence; Dunn promptly sent all he had from the *Independent* and "from persons interested in co-operative marketing." His helpfulness soon began to wane. Two months after the demand was published, Fred Black politely suggested that it might be an "excellent idea" for Dunn to come to Michigan and review his work with "our Washington man and possibly one of our attorneys." Dunn demurred, pleading money and health problems.

By the end of March, Black pressed Dunn even more urgently to make the trip and to send a list of the documents in his possession so that they could know what he had.[5] Dunn finally showed up in Detroit in early May 1925.

There is no record of what transpired when Dunn met with the *Independent* staff. We can guess that the group in attendance included Cameron, Black, and Liebold. They undoubtedly questioned Dunn at length about the language contained in the declaration and what he could tell them about corroborating witnesses and information. It was the last face-to-face meeting Dunn had with anyone from the Ford organization for more than eight months. After Dunn left the building, the Ford staff decided on their next step.

Meeting with Dunn clarified what the *Independent* staff probably already knew, or guessed at: he could not provide evidence to substantiate his stories. They set urgent plans in motion to travel across the country, retrace his steps, and track down his sources. In early June, Fred Black set out for Oregon, where a witness was willing to testify that Sapiro had written the contract of the raisin growers' organization. That witness also alleged that "Sapiro has never had any standing as an attorney in San Francisco."[6] As he traveled, Black sought out employees at Ford branches and franchise offices whom he could hire as investigators. He talked to workers who could discredit Sapiro's defenders. In his reports, he described publicity favoring cooperation and the Sapiro plan as "propaganda" and dismissed anyone who spoke disparagingly about Ford cars. Finally, he built on the idea, first advanced in Dunn's articles, that Bernard Baruch and Eugene Meyer were connected to everything Sapiro did. One investigator, William Collman, whom Black found at the Seattle Ford branch, confirmed Baruch's role "in the financial end" and described a "whole scheme" that "is extraordinarily complicated and far-reaching." But the trip yielded few real finds for Black and other investigators whom he deputized in the South and on the East Coast.[7]

As the *Independent* ran its investigation, the Ford legal department set to work. Ford's personal attorney, a patrician named Clifford B. Longley, spent the spring and summer of 1925 analyzing the ninety-two-page declaration. As Ford Motor Company (FMC) chief legal officer between 1921 and 1929, Longley held nearly as extensive a portfolio as Ernest Liebold. Longley reincorporated the FMC in Delaware after Ford bought out his minority stockholders in 1920; he oversaw Ford's many acquisitions in railroads, lumber, and mining. The FMC acquired the Lincoln Motor Company in 1922 and began an ill-fated experiment in rubber production in Brazil in 1923 under Longley's guidance as well. By 1924, the legal department consisted of nine staff lawyers in Detroit and numerous attorneys on retainer in other cities and countries. In 1925, Ford appointed him corporate secretary of the Dearborn Publishing Company (DPC).[8]

Memoranda in the files suggest that on receiving word of the lawsuit, Longley put himself through a crash course studying the Dunn articles and what they meant for his client. His first assessment was straightforward: "We defend on the basis of fair comment, criticism and justification, setting up the truth of the articles, all of which I believe can be substantially proved."[9] That, he thought, should have been simple enough.

Longley then composed a laundry list of tasks for the legal department to complete before he would write the defendant's plea, Ford's formal answer to the declaration. On the basis of a review of legal treatises and Michigan case law, Longley concluded that not much had changed since the *Tribune* lawsuit seven years earlier. Courts still deemed some words, such as *anarchist*, libelous per se, or on their face; if a plaintiff complained about the use of those words, it usually meant defeat for publishers. Most other text would be presumed libelous *per quod*, meaning that the language was libelous in context. Both sides would argue over the meaning of *innuendo* and the common understanding that readers were likely to derive from the publication.[10]

Sapiro's decision to file suit in federal court raised important procedural and jurisdictional issues. Longley wondered whether the federal court would be obliged "to follow State decisions in this matter" and, if so, how that would affect the nature of the damages Sapiro could recover. For instance, Longley asked, could Sapiro obtain punitive damages under Michigan law? Was he required to rely on the laws of other states for libel claims involving cooperatives located outside Michigan? Longley brought in Stewart Hanley from the Detroit firm of Lightner, Oxtoby, Hanley and Crawford to help. Together they dispatched junior staff to New York to prepare for depositions there and in New Jersey. William A. Simonds went to Minneapolis and Chicago "to investigate the Wheat Bureau and Passoneay [sic] and then returned to Detroit," where he would "outline the testimony of the witnesses who are to be used on the trial." Longley and F. Hunter Creech of the Ford D.C. office oversaw the Virginia tobacco depositions, and a Mississippi lawyer, Garver Green, managed depositions planned for half a dozen southern states. Once these depositions were completed, Longley would prepare and file the plea.[11]

Investigator William Collman looked in vain for signs of Sapiro's participation in the organization of the New York Dairymen's League. "The Sapiro connection is not there," he reported. "If Sapiro was identified, he must have kept under cover." Because one of Sapiro's sins, in the eyes of Dunn and the *Independent*, was that he craved publicity, to argue that he worked "under cover" would contradict the newspaper. Another field investigator, E. L. McColgin, suggested that they encourage Kentucky tobacco growers to sue to recover payments that the cooperative withheld from members. Similar suits had been instituted in southern Virginia, though not against Sapiro's organizations. McColgin hoped that growers' suits would "put Sapiro on the defense . . . before the world in general." Discrediting Sapiro was essential, McColgin wrote, because the tobacco cooperatives remained popular and well established despite the problems the *Independent* had publicized. "[T]he annoying fact" of the pools' ability to maintain good prices meant, in McColgin's view, that "we cannot expect an uprising on our behalf in the spot where, seemingly, the best defense has been uncovered." Black told Longley he thought the suggestion was "quite interesting," and the Ford lawyers eventually approved it.[12]

Discouraging dispatches arrived in Dearborn in fall 1925. C. E. Dempster of Portland, Oregon, found that Sapiro had "nothing to do with the wool organization." That finding tended to substantiate the declaration's eighth count. Nor could Dempster document Sapiro's role in organizing the Oregon milk producers, so he faulted him for their collapse: "While Sapiro was not responsible for the Oregon Co-operative Dairymen's League, he failed to supply a structure which would enable it to reach dry land." Review of the hop story was equally grim: "Information from reliable sources indicates great distortion of facts in Dunn's article." William T. McCall, a cooperative official recruited to help the Ford investigation, had to conclude that Dunn "evidently shot wide of the mark on the hop article . . . [and] was out of line" on the wool article. Dempster informed his superiors that the hop cooperative did not use Sapiro's crop contract, and he could find "no evidence in Oregon to substantiate assertions in [the hop] article."[13]

The digging in Idaho turned up unexpected gems. By mid-1925, the Washington Wheat Growers' Association's Spokane offices were deserted, so no one objected when assistant Seattle branch manager F. W. Donoghue rifled through abandoned files. Letters documenting Sapiro's influence on the framing of the Washington and Idaho cooperative marketing statutes and the formation of the wheat growers' associations in both states "were dug out of a waste basket." Donoghue pointed out, however, that state legislators would object if they knew the Ford organization had obtained their letters. McCall and Black directed Donoghue to verify the "off-color" reputations of the leaders of the wheat growers' sign-up campaign.[14]

The further Donoghue looked, however, the less he found. Following Black's suggestions, he interviewed A. C. Adams, former secretary-treasurer of the Washington Wheat Growers' Association, and Walter J. Robinson, one of its leading organizers. Dunn had not talked to them in preparing his article, nor did he visit any association office. Having done so, Donoghue relayed a less than rosy story of cooperative organizing in Montana, asserting that the organizers used "misrepresentation and exaggeration" to sign growers up. Losses in 1924 led growers to breach their contracts in droves, and the association agreed to release them rather than sue. All the more reason to wonder, then, why Dunn had done so little legwork: "[I am] convinced that Mr. Morgan based his [wheat] article . . . more or less on hearsay." A month later, Donoghue reported to Longley that he could find no trace of radical influence in either the hay or the wheat associations.[15] In short, the Pacific Northwest operation netted a bunch of salacious letters that might not be usable, no basis for linking cooperative officials to the Industrial Workers of the World (IWW) or the Non-Partisan League, and no proof for the wheat and hay stories. The Montana wheat industry furnished an example of one non-Sapiro cooperative that lasted all of one season.

McCall, who led opposition to Sapiro in the Idaho potato industry, helped build the Ford case in California. At Black's request and at the DPC's expense, he investigated the avocado, poultry, milk, and fruit growers' organizations in Southern California, where witnesses all offered the same somewhat inaccurate report: "Sapiro had nothing to do with any of the Southern California organizations; in fact, very little in any part of California, and was losing prestige in organizations where he did have a part." McCall and a coworker, W. H. Meyerett, interviewed George Farrand, attorney for the California Fruit Growers' Exchange and the California Walnut Growers' Association, two of the state's largest and oldest cooperatives. They found Farrand "non-communicative regarding Sapiro or his operations" but more willing to talk about the subject of cooperative membership contracts. Farrand told Ford's agents that the contract's major features "are all principles that have been in the course of development ever since cooperative marketing began to be practiced, and antedate by many years the time when Mr. Sapiro entered the cooperative marketing field."[16]

McCall and W. T. Sherman dug into Sapiro's California background, compiling a lengthy dossier on his life, education, and career. They focused on his relationship with Harris Weinstock and his work with the California State Commission Market. They discovered that Sapiro had nothing to do with many of the California cooperatives they were investigating, especially in Northern California, where he was not well known outside of San Francisco and Stockton. They also found that some cooperatives that employed Sapiro were satisfied with him and his work. Even the manager of the prune and apricot growers' association, which had fared least well of Sapiro's California organizations, pointed out mistakes and errors in Dunn's piece on his industry.[17]

The news from Texas was no better, Collman conceded: "Evidence to show the control of cotton by an international ring of Jewish bankers is rather difficult to obtain." He wrote an equivocal review of Dunn's cotton article: "Some of these statements may be proved, while others are not exactly in consonance with the facts as I encountered them." He could corroborate that Otto Kahn held a dinner for Sapiro, as reported in the *New York World* on June 18, 1922, and the *American Magazine* in 1923; individuals named as Jews in the *Independent* were actually Jewish; and cooperatives controlled too small a proportion of the crop to control prices effectively. Collman could not prove that speculators ripped off cooperatives or that farmers were personally liable for cooperatives' debts. Still, Collman agreed that farmers were being exploited, if not in the industries he examined.[18]

Dempster worked especially hard to document Dunn's allegation of the relationship between cooperation and radicalism in the Pacific Northwest. All of Dempster's contacts in Oregon—from the state treasurer to the state labor commissioner, the president of Reed College, the head of the Portland "Red Squad," the field officer of the lumbermen's union, and the manager of a Sapiro-organized cooperative—categorically denied the presence of "IWWs, Communists or radicals" in the "organization or conducting of the business of any farm organizations." Each of those witnesses denounced Dunn's "three-pin theory" linking cooperation, communism, and IWW activity. The lumber union official who was to assist Dempster was unable to document the story: "In efforts to get as many producers as possible signed up," Dempster reported, "the organizers did use some strong arm methods. However these could not be linked up with radicalism. . . . I have been unable to get hold of a single lead that would substantiate the Oregon part of the article." Unwilling to surrender the three-pin theory, Black released Dempster from having to prove it:

Upon reading the text of the "three-thumb-tack" statement in the above article you will note that, boiled down, it amounts to no more than a claim of coincidence with the reader being left to assume a tangible connection. *Now we do not have to prove that there was such a connection.* While we would prefer to prove more it would seem as if it will be enough to procure a basis for sworn testimony or proof in court that there were red activities where these Sapiro organizations were affected—merely the coincidence and not necessarily a connection. . . . It would seem as if there is little or no hope of proving anything stronger than a coincidence because *your report indicates that there was no "reds" allied with the Sapiro organizing forces.*[19]

Trial was set for January 1926, he was anxious to put together a body of proof, and he already knew that his theory could not be proved. Still, he would not acknowledge any weakness in Ford's defense.

Although the field investigations were yielding little to verify Dunn's stories, slivers of good news did make it to Dearborn. Gray Silver, president of the American Farm Bureau Federation (AFBF), was willing to state publicly that Sapiro had misrepresented the AFBF's position when he testified to Congress as its legal counsel. The *Independent*'s ace in the hole remained Passonneau, who was willing to talk about what he viewed as Sapiro's mean conduct in the tobacco, potato, and wheat industries. The Ford forces had already picked up another important ally in William McCall, general manager of the Idaho Producers' Union. McCall prevented Sapiro from getting control of that organization several years earlier but could not attest to a larger "connection between Sapiro, Baruch, Meyer and [Albert] Lasker." Like Passonneau, McCall was eager to help Ford and told Black he thought he could substantiate the three-pin theory in Idaho. Black instructed him to "spare no efforts" in getting the "bullet proof facts," because the opposition had formidable allies, too: "Sapiro's recent tendency to align himself and his forces with Secretary [of Agriculture William A.] Jardine makes it imperative that we give him the knockout when this case comes to trial."[20]

McCall's helpfulness was motivated by his own intense antisemitism and dislike of Sapiro. He collected information about the firm of Weyl and Zuckerman, which occasionally marketed crops for some Sapiro cooperatives and did its banking with Jewish-owned institutions. McCall believed that Sapiro put a lien on the crops of the Colorado Potato Growers Exchange when it did not pay his fee promptly, although he had been told that that story was "malicious and absolutely false." Sapiro wrote the Idaho cooperative marketing statute and helped to get it enacted, but McCall was convinced that "the Act could have been written just as well without [him]." Like the *Independent* staff, he shared Ford's attitude toward Jews: "They tried to put Ford out of business, and he outgeneraled them. Personally, I do not blame Mr. Ford for his feelings toward them. The Jews now own the moving picture industry, the clothing industry, the railroads, the lumber and mining industries to quite a degree, and they are by far the biggest factor on the money market today." McCall believed that the *Independent* had injured no one; indeed, it was Sapiro who "should be in the penitentiary, for he has duped the American farmer beyond belief." He thought the *Independent* had done enough to substantiate the articles: "Many of the articles were investigated and found to be substantially correct, hence it was not considered necessary to investigate them all."[21]

Ford's lawyers knew better. Wallace R. Middleton filed separate answers with the court for the DPC and Ford on July 21, 1925. The DPC's plea stated simply that the newspaper intended to prove the truth of what it published. Six months later, after reviewing investigative reports, the lawyers filed amended pleas. McColgin summarized the field agents' findings: despite their "well founded" beliefs, "nothing to support Dunn's voiced suspicions have [*sic*] been brought forward." Longley and Middleton were joined by Ward Choate, Longley's former law partner in Detroit, in addition to Stewart Hanley. Choate was already running depositions in Yakima, Washington, while Hanley was appearing at pretrial hearings in Detroit. The defense claimed that the plaintiff's declaration erred in declaring only some words as libelous. The newspaper would prove at trial that it had "a plain right and duty . . . to publish . . . such comment upon current topics and events and upon the things done or omitted by men prominently before the public as were necessary or desirable for the good of the community." The newspaper intended no malice toward the plaintiff. Rather, it documented the failures of Sapiro-style cooperation for the good of American farmers, and it would prove those failures at trial. The Ford attorneys planned to use the tobacco, potato, wheat, cotton, and prune and apricot industries to document Sapiro's fraudulent methods.[22]

Despite its brash tone, the plea broke no new ground. Pointing out that Sapiro was not a farmer, that he promoted cooperation to enrich himself, and that growers and producers suffered great losses did not refute the libel charges so much as reiterate them. The plea cited no case law and made only one legal argument—that the plaintiff's declaration failed to state a cause of action cognizable in a federal district court.[23] It was a weak shot across the bow.

New analyses from field attorneys in December 1925 did not invigorate the defense. A witness in Denver told Raymond Watson that Sapiro boasted of his access to Meyer and Baruch, sought to fire Erskine Myer as local counsel in Colorado, and initially permitted the potato exchange to set his fee. But the Denver informant "was seriously handicapped" by the discovery that the exchange officers and board were made up almost entirely of "Sapiro men" who "will not appear to testify except by subpoena." With trial looming on January 15, 1926, Longley and Middleton decided to seek expert help. They easily obtained Ernest Liebold's approval and quickly settled on the hired gun who they thought should take charge of the case. In fact, the name came straight from Ford himself.[24]

In early December, Longley asked the company's D.C.-based attorney, F. Hunter Creech, to contact James A. Reed, senior U.S. senator from Missouri. Reed maintained his busy and remunerative corporate law practice out of Kansas City while serving in the Senate; by 1925, he was well into his third and final term. He had been a strong contender for the Democratic presidential nomination in 1924 and was rumored to be interested in running again in 1928. Creech relayed to Longley that Reed was "perfectly willing to enter the case" even though he recognized that "this is a fight between the Jews and Mr. Ford." Longley appeared in Reed's Senate office on December 15. Reed explained to Longley "that it would require a great sacrifice on my part to undertake the work, and that I would have to have a large compensation." Unfazed, Longley replied that "there would be no trouble about that matter," and he promptly arranged for Reed to speak with Ford in Detroit on December 19. After that meeting, where the two "did not discuss the matter of fees at all," Reed returned to the Detroit Athletic Club, where Longley installed him in luxurious accommodations. There, Reed presented his terms for representing Ford: "[A] retainer of $100,000.00 was to be paid, and . . . for services in the case I would charge $200.00 per day." Longley "wanted [Reed] in the case" but needed Ford to

6.1. Senator James A. Reed (Library of Congress, Wilson Papers, Manuscript Division, LC-USZ62-62863).

approve the fee arrangement personally. The lawyers discussed the merits of the case, "particularly the condition of the pleadings," and the need to get a continuance for the January trial date. Longley had only begun to organize the taking of depositions at this point; he had attorneys lined up in three states and thought it would be necessary to do likewise in five or six more states. Reed departed Detroit for Kansas City on December 20 on the understanding that after a final conference with Ford, Longley would wire him a final approval of their arrangement.[25] Everyone involved kept the meetings out of the press.

In retaining Senator Reed, Ford chose one of the nation's highest-profile trial attorneys. At the time, elected officials generally continued practicing their professions after taking office; there were no ethics rules to prohibit them from doing so. Reed instantly brought a commanding presence and an imposing personality to the defense. At sixty-four, he was movie-star handsome, sporting a stately Greek profile and a shock of thick white hair. His stentorian Senate speeches earned him the nickname "Silver-Tongued Orator"; he opposed the League of Nations and was a staunch economic conservative. Reed's principled stands against public corruption earned H. L. Mencken's lavish approval when he retired from the Senate in 1929. His politics were decidedly idiosyncratic: although he opposed child labor laws and the Nineteenth Amendment, he also condemned the Klan and Prohibition. His public denunciation of anti-semitism and a 1916 speech in which he noted the indebtedness of Gentiles to Jews for Christianity, the preservation of learning, and other contributions to world culture probably did much to recommend him as the ideal public face of Ford's defense. It may also have been more than coincidence that Reed owned a summer home in northern Michigan.[26] In any case, Ford and Liebold unhesitatingly approved Reed's retainer and fees. Once Longley persuaded his clients that the case could not be won without a lawyer of Reed's caliber, Ford and Liebold were willing to spend what it took to get him.

. . .

The hire of Reed prized star power over legal expertise. Reed had no reputation in libel law, but he was a masterful litigation strategist. He immediately recognized that Longley had been right to delay trial at every turn. Dragging out the proceedings had been a common device in American libel trials since the late nineteenth century. Both Longley and Reed knew that libel law gave defendants advantages that they needed to exploit while they developed their defenses. After Reed left Detroit, Longley filed a motion for continuance, and Chief District Judge Arthur Tuttle again delayed the trial, this time until March 1926.[27]

Reed then asked Longley for an analysis of Michigan libel law, together with McCall's report on Idaho, Barnet's memo on Kentucky, copies of Sapiro's speeches, and the defense's pleadings filed to date. When Reed got his hands on the declaration, he drafted a list of what he thought the defense could prove, summarizing what Longley's foot soldiers had gathered since April. Reed's notes showed he thought both sides had already made mistakes. The plaintiff's "subpoena [was] too broad," and he would keep as many documents out of the plaintiff's hands as he could. "*Ford's object to protect the farmers,*" Reed thought, competed with "Ford's antagonism to the Jews." Because the "pleadings do charge Jewish conspiracy," the defense would have to prove the fact of a conspiracy. But "don't say we will produce evidence to sustain every charge," Reed strategized, because the presiding judge would hold them to that promise at trial. Most important, Reed decided, "[we] don't want him to establish the matter but to harass and impoverish the plaintiff." He planned to make the discovery process so difficult and expensive for Sapiro that in the end, like so many others who attempted to bring Ford before a judge, he would give up in frustration.[28] Until he could force Sapiro to that point, Reed would make the search for evidence as comprehensive as possible.

In obtaining a continuance, the defense gave the plaintiff additional time to prepare as well. Reed had barely begun to organize his partners and coordinate with Longley when the *Independent* caught wind of an alarming development. Gallagher served Harry Dunn with a subpoena to take his deposition in San Francisco on January 25, 1926. Worried at least as much about his own liability as the *Independent*'s, Dunn sought to make his deposition the concern of Ford's lawyers: "It seems to me that the *Independent* should have legal representation at this hearing," he told Longley anxiously, "and [I] wish you would advise me what steps to take as soon as you can." Dunn also voiced his fear that Sapiro would soon sue him. Longley assured him that he would send "a representative," but the Ford legal team intended to delay Dunn's testimony "until we can prepare our California case for the taking of depositions in our own behalf." Longley also offered Dunn some comforting advice:

I see no reason why it is so inadvisable for you to appear as a witness in this suit. Of course there were mistakes made in the articles. There was also a whole lot of truth told. I doubt however, whether you more than touched upon the whole evil of the situation. We have found things since in our investigations in this case which are hardly believable. This case will not go against us whatever lesser and minor mistakes may have been made in the original publication.

Longley remained confident about the defense's prospects. He knew he lacked evidence to prove the hops story. Still, he "doubt[ed] very much whether they will get very far with it when the whole truth is told." As for the prospect of a lawsuit against Dunn, Longley dismissed that concern:

When we get through with [Sapiro] he will be so thoroughly sick of law suits that I am sure he will not waste further time in attempting to justify something that is impossible of justification. Don't forget this; that you exposed a collosal [*sic*] fraud. Further, that fraud was well covered up with legal fog and a cloak of legality completely surrounds it. Nevertheless, the fraud is there, legal or illegal, and I am sure now that we can prove it beyond any possible shadow of doubt.[29]

Although Longley had not agreed to represent him, Dunn felt "deeply indebted to you for your letter of January 18 . . . [which] cleared up several matters which have not been plain to me." He also asked if his correspondence with the *Independent* might be "exempted" from the records subpoenaed by the plaintiff and whether Longley could get his deposition moved to Michigan, "where your attorneys could be present." His biggest concern, he told Longley, was whether Ford's staff blamed him for exposing them to the lawsuit "without due cause" by "ventur[ing] too far in my stories." He was eager to justify his methods to a sympathetic ear and shift the burden of substantiating his stories to "those who have been deceived and defrauded by this scheme of co-operative marketing which we exposed." He did not say so directly, but he hoped that the Ford organization's legal umbrella would cover him as well.[30]

On that key issue, Longley was noncommittal. He saw Dunn as the defense's "weakest point" and recognized that subpoenaing him would help the plaintiff. Longley recognized that Sapiro "never had anything to do with [the hops] organization" and that "Dunn manufactured the thing out of a blue sky." The wisest thing they could do was to keep Dunn away from opposing counsel for as long as possible: "The real dangerous situation is the taking of Dunn's testimony," Longley told Reed. "What he will testify to I am absolutely unable to say. My judgment of the man is that he is a rather unstable sort of an individual; he will not stay placed. I have the impression that at times he changes his ideas to suit his convenience rather than because of his sincere belief." Longley wrote to Dunn to determine "what sort of a story he will tell." Such an important conversation might warrant Reed's presence. To prepare Dunn properly, give Reed time to participate in that process, and line up the rest of their California witnesses, Longley postponed all depositions planned for that state, including Dunn's, until the summer. The delay gave him time to send Ward Choate from

Washington State, where he was investigating the wheat industry, to interview Dunn in person. Choate's preparation led the Ford lawyers to gain confidence that they could rehabilitate the plaintiff's single most critical witness in time for trial. That event, too, had been postponed; in response to another motion from Longley and Reed, Judge Tuttle set trial for September 14.[31]

The new trial date freed Longley and Reed to plan depositions to their liking in 1926. By late winter, the DPC staff made a full outline of Sapiro's cooperative work and collected all of Dunn's correspondence with the *Independent* for Longley. Depositions were set for Kentucky, Oregon, Idaho, Washington State, Minnesota, Colorado, Kansas, Maine, and Texas between March and August 1926. The punishing schedule forced Gallagher to play catch-up; instead of scheduling his own depositions, he was obliged to attend the defendant's to cross-examine witnesses. Sapiro brought in extra lawyers to help with the workload. Robert S. Marx ("a Jewish gentleman," Ward Choate commented) left a seat on the probate court in Cincinnati to join Sapiro's team. Another assistant counsel, William Lynch, was a junior partner in Sapiro's Chicago office.[32]

Relations between the two sides quickly grew heated. Early on, the defense attorneys asked Gallagher to adjust his deposition schedule to accommodate theirs. An impolitic exchange between Choate and Gallagher at one deposition led Choate to skip a motion hearing in Detroit in March. Defense attorneys then began to insist that if Gallagher wanted to depose Ford's witnesses for his own purposes, he had to do so separately, which "more clearly defines our rights in cross-examination," Longley pointed out. This procedural maneuver, Choate thought, would make it more difficult for Gallagher "to prove the inaccuracies of the articles, outside of the alleged libelous statements." As Gallagher enlarged the scope of the libels during the discovery period, the defense was secretly preparing an amended plea in which it would narrow its burden of proof, eventually "get[ting] it down to what has actually been proved."[33]

In February 1926, Aaron Sapiro delivered a speech in Charlotte, North Carolina, about the lawsuit and its effect on his work. Speaking in a synagogue, Sapiro declared that cooperation was "farmers' salvation," but he doubted he would see its greatest accomplishments: "Ford's attack hurt him, he said, ... but the movement will live. Local men will equip themselves to lead, he said, and take the place of present leaders." He urged local business leaders to continue to support cooperative marketing, because it was "bound to move to a better basis" once the Ford dispute ended. In Dearborn, Liebold shared this "recent public utterance of Aaron Sapiro" with Longley.[34]

In addition to staying on the alert for press coverage of Sapiro, Ford's team monitored the tone and balance of stories about the suit. When Ford attorneys appeared in Western states to take depositions, local newspapers took note. In Spokane, the press deemed it newsworthy that Ford's attorneys subpoenaed seven city residents, overcoming the initial reluctance of the federal court to issue the summonses. Other witnesses included prominent organizers and officials of the Washington Wheat Growers' Association, hay and grain buyers, state officials, and the publishers of local agricultural publications. "Considerable law is involved in the case," Ward Choate told the *Spokane Daily Chronicle*, "and the outcome was not definitely in sight." Choate also argued that "Ford was not opposed to farmers' cooperative movements but was attacking Sapiro." To drive a wedge between Sapiro and the cooperative movement, Choate brought McCall, Idaho's most prominent cooperative organizer, to Seattle.[35]

Two months later in Portland, the press coverage was sympathetic not only to cooperatives but also to the relatively disadvantaged position of the plaintiff in the *Sapiro v. Ford* libel suit. The *Morning Oregonian* summarized the extent of the defense's discovery efforts to date; although the full schedule of hearings had not been announced, "it is known that no expense is being spared to obtain testimony in all sections of the country." That expense, the paper pointed out, was being borne by each party: "The only costs that will be considered by the court in awarding a verdict will be those involved in the actual trial of the case, for which reason the expense of taking depositions in all of these states must be borne by each litigant." Ford's people blamed Sapiro for the failure of three cooperatives: the Oregon Growers' Cooperative Association, the Pacific Co-operative Poultry Producers' Association, and the Oregon Co-operative Dairymen's League. Here, too, the *Oregonian* told another side of the story. According to the former president of the defunct dairy league, "The failure of the league, which was reorganized in 1920 by Sapiro, and similar organizations was due to the post-war depression period."[36]

Meanwhile, McCall and Sherman continued to follow leads in California and Oregon, trying to document Sapiro's break with the prune and apricot growers and verify Dunn's story on the bean growers at Lompoc, in Santa Barbara County. They learned that the president of the Walnut Growers Exchange was willing to testify for Ford, but they also reconfirmed that Sapiro had nothing to do with organizing Sun-Maid or writing its crop contract. The prune and apricot growers copied the raisin contract when they organized in 1917, and Sapiro revised that contract at their request a few years later. But Dunn had erred in claiming that Sapiro originated both contracts, and after March 1926 the Ford team knew it could not prove otherwise. Still, McCall wondered when the attorneys would show up in California to begin taking depositions and nail down other salient points in those articles.[37]

The California situation proved difficult for the Ford attorneys to assess. Farmers and cooperative officials there, as in Oregon, were unwilling to blame Sapiro for the failure of marketing organizations. They were decidedly reluctant to excuse Dunn's mistakes and omissions for Henry Ford's benefit. The vice president of the prune and apricot growers' association, whose collapse had been the subject of a scathing Dunn article, refused to be deposed. Losing "one of our best prospective witnesses in Southern California," was a blow, McCall lamented, but he hoped to find individuals from other associations who would attest that "Sapiro must have known his plan was not working well when he left California and started out to put his plan over in other states as the 'California plan.'" He fell short there as well; those who agreed to go on record "do not care to attack the Sapiro plan in their testimony," McCall explained, "but will show in detail just what the right plan is, and then it will be easy for us to show by argument the differences between the Sapiro plan and the successful plan here." Even these witnesses agreed, however, that when it came to the tomato growers and the California vegetable growers, "Mr. Dunn was somewhat in error."[38]

During the first half of 1926, Dunn remained the defense's greatest liability. Longley wanted to prevent Dunn's deposition from being taken for as long as possible, as late as the trial itself. Longley thought that if Dunn had done his job properly, defending the case would have been easy, because he believed what Dunn wrote was fundamentally right. The Ford team saw it as their job to work around his infelicitous failure to take notes. In Seattle, W. A. Simonds was convinced that Dunn had not even begun to uncover Sapiro's bad motives and results. "In spite of numerous discrepancies which crept into Mr. Morgan's articles, there is an abundance of material to damn Mr. Sapiro in this section a large part of which was not uncovered by Mr. Dunn. Those activities which were not mentioned in the articles which you printed seem to us to be more flagrant than those described."[39]

Longley knew that argument would not be legally sufficient, so he searched for precedent that would excuse Dunn's lack of substantiation and reliance on rumor. One case enabled them to mitigate libel damage claims by showing that the *Independent*'s stories did little more than restate commonly known local facts. Another permitted a defendant to relate the alleged libel to common rumor that he believed to be true. Longley asked Choate to base their defense on these two precedents. After interviewing Dunn, Choate even argued that he could be rehabilitated as a witness: "[J. G.] Bruce and I, also Simonds, are very much impressed with his statement. It is clear, definite, and as far as my knowledge goes from the testimony I have taken is the substantial truth obtained from reliable sources. He really surprised me with his memory of names, figures, places etc. Personally I am very much encouraged on that phase of the case and I do not think we need to worry as much about this as we have."[40]

Other legal experts did not share that optimism. A San Francisco attorney who had been enlisted to help the defense thought their prospects so grim that he suggested they settle the case. Knowing Ford would not consider it, Longley urged his co-counsel to remain focused on the task at hand: "I wonder whether we can't get a little help from you. I am just a bit afraid that you do not fully understand the situation. . . . We wouldn't adjust this case if we could get out of it by paying them fifteen cents. It just can't be done, so there is no use even thinking of such a thing." Longley promptly instructed Middleton to begin contempt proceedings in California to "get some sharply defined definition of the situation in taking testimony in California"—in short, to push Gallagher to commit to a firm schedule for the summer.[41]

The two sides dueled across the witness table all summer long, filing transcripts with the court from Kentucky, Washington, and a half dozen other states in June and July. The Senate session kept Reed in Washington, D.C., for much of the spring and early summer. In May, Longley updated Reed on the progress of the attorneys taking depositions on the West Coast, which he expected to be finished in June. Still to be deposed were witnesses in Texas, Oklahoma, New York, New Jersey, Kansas, and Maine; Creech also had four more states in the South to cover. Longley confided, "it is going to be utterly impossible to take all of this testimony before September 14th unless we can take it at more than one place at a time." Gallagher had agreed "in certain instances" to a speeded-up schedule, and Longley wanted "to force him to come through on this." Word soon reached Detroit that Judge Marx was representing Sapiro at depositions in the western states, and Choate promptly informed Reed's partner Richard Higgins that in view of Gallagher's stated willingness to proceed and Marx's formal entry into the case, "we can ask and insist that [Gallagher] take depositions in two places at once."[42]

That hardball tactic still did not enable the Ford lawyers to meet their court-imposed deadlines. By June, they realized they would not complete their depositions by August 15. With trial scheduled for September 14, Longley and Reed scrambled to arrange a conference in Detroit or Kansas City as the Senate session dragged into late June. Gallagher scheduled a motion hearing that threw off depositions and subpoena dates, and Longley complained that "the other side [is] obstructing progress of California testimony." In preparation for trial, Choate was amassing copies of every Sapiro speech the DPC had on file, together with witness testimony "as to what he said" on other undocumented occasions, to aid Senator Reed in preparing his cross-examination of Sapiro. By June 24, Reed was still unable to leave the Senate, but he informed Longley that if his absence from a conference meant "that Mr. Ford's interests will be jeopardized, I will be there June 24 regardless of my engagements here." That heroic gesture proved unnecessary. The Ford lawyers did not finish their depositions by June 24, and when the Senate adjourned for the traditional July 4 recess, Reed was free to return to Kansas City for the summer. From there and occasionally from Chicago he staged a series of meetings with Longley and the other lawyers in preparation for an August showdown in Detroit.[43] The group resolved to slow the litigation further and throw the blame for the sluggish pace onto the plaintiff and his lawyers.

In mid-July, Longley instructed Middleton to prepare an affidavit accusing Gallagher of causing undue delay in the depositions. Longley told Middleton to document "obstruction tactics of other side; also, all delays due to taking testimony of witnesses for plaintiff; also, all other facts upon which we may base motion for continuance, including schedule giving dates and places where depositions have been taken either on behalf of plaintiffs [sic—there was only one plaintiff] or defendants, and explaining fully all delays of any kind that occurred in connection with depositions." The Ford lawyers bore Gallagher no personal ill will; like many of them, Gallagher was a Detroiter. They did not like William S. Lynch, Sapiro's Chicago partner; they did not care at all for Milton Sapiro, Aaron's younger brother who appeared at some of the California depositions; and they thoroughly detested Robert Marx, whom Middleton described as "nasty" and "cheap." Blaming the other side for obstruction and delay did not buy the defense more time. In late July, Reed went to Detroit, where he and Longley filed their third request for continuance. Reed also instructed that depositions in California and Kentucky should proceed "immediately" and that attorneys in Kentucky should "clear up situation there so that we will either get the testimony or know we are not going to get it."[44]

On July 22, Reed and Longley formally appeared before Chief Judge Tuttle. After a short hearing, the judge and lawyers moved to chambers for a private conference. Tuttle declared that the ruling was completely at his discretion and not subject to appeal. If the defendants would agree to certain conditions, however, he would grant the motion. The conditions, which Tuttle had written out himself, specified a trial no later than March 14, 1927, and no further continuances in the case. Further, Ford was to accept his witness subpoena by September 14, 1926, and pay Sapiro's attorneys $100 per day for each day spent taking depositions, even if they were subsequently canceled.[45]

Following the hearing, Reed returned to Chicago for the weekend and waited for word from Longley. The next day, Longley and Choate drove to Tuttle's farm near Lansing, about 120 miles from Detroit, to meet with the judge. Finding him not at home, they tried his sister's residence, his summer home on a nearby lake, and the county bank where he served as a director. They could discover "nothing of his whereabouts" and were obliged to wait until he appeared at chambers on Monday morning. When the judge arrived, he made it clear to Longley that their Thursday meeting had gone badly: "He immediately launched into a bitter complaint over the treatment we had given him Thursday. He stated that he had never been treated so in his life. He claimed that [Reed] had spit in his waste basket, in his spitoon [sic] and on his rug. He stated that he was not one who should be compelled to clean up tobacco juice after Henry Ford's lawyers. He stated that there was an atmosphere in this case which he had never had in any other case [and t]hat he could not understand the treatment that had been accorded him." Judge Tuttle informed Longley that he saw no reason for Henry Ford to evade acceptance of a witness subpoena and that if Ford wanted a continuance he had to agree to testify. Longley demurred: "I told him that I could not bind Henry Ford to any of the conditions without first consulting with him." Tuttle was not mollified: "He stated whether I could bind him or not, he, Judge Tuttle, could, and that he thought it was a good thing for the community that there was someone in the community who could bind one of Henry Ford's financial standing." To prove to Ford's lawyers that the plaintiff would not put Ford's personal beliefs on trial, Tuttle telephoned William Gallagher, who repeated what he had already told the judge: he planned to ask Ford to testify only about his connections to the DPC and "to make him responsible . . . in the event a verdict was rendered for the plaintiff." Longley suggested that a surety bond could secure Ford's liability in case of a judgment against him, but Gallagher declined to release Ford from testifying without first getting Sapiro's approval.[46] The Ford lawyers were doing everything they could to free Ford from the burden of testifying, whereas the judge was doing everything he could to ensure that Ford would have to appear.

Tuttle regarded the case as a personal humiliation and a threat to his judicial authority. He told Longley that he "had suffered a great deal of embarrassment throughout the case . . . [and] that he had never had so much trouble with any litigation." Longley delicately suggested that the judge might prefer to step aside and let "someone else try the case." Incensed, Tuttle said he "had expected such a suggestion" from the defense, but he would rule on the continuance nonetheless. "He stated voluntarily, that he would only withdraw as Judge in the case when we filed an affidavit [of prejudice against him]." In saying so, he all but invited Ford's attorneys to do just that. Having reached its nadir, the meeting ended on more civil terms. Tuttle assured Longley that "justice would be done;" Longley sportingly agreed. Tuttle noted that if he presided at trial, "there would be no heckling by the other side in their examination of [Ford]. He further stated that what had accured [sic] in the Tribune suit would not occur in this case."[47]

Tuttle may have been trying to maintain cordial relations with the lawyers and reestablish his judicial composure, but Reed wasn't buying it. The senator swiftly resolved not to try the case with Tuttle on the bench. He directed Longley to obtain Ford's signature on an affidavit of prejudice against Tuttle and file it immediately. Longley did so on July 30, after warning Watson in Kansas City that they were "having great difficulty in matter of continuance" and might be "forced to trial in September." Ford's affidavit charged that Judge Tuttle was biased against him because of his wealth. Under the judge's conditions, Ford would have to pay Sapiro's attorneys some $15,000 to obtain the continuance. At the July 22 conference, Tuttle said "he realized this, but that Henry Ford . . . could afford to spend so much money in any case that he has in court, that no poor man could successfully try a case against him. . . . [I]f the case were continued, the said Ford, because of his great wealth, could drag the case along in court for years and wear out and bankrupt his adversary, and that the court in the exercise of its discretion, had a right to take into consideration these facts." Tuttle's answer was to instruct Gallagher to prepare an order denying the continuance, setting the trial for September 14, and relaxing the rules governing the submission of Ford's amended plea. Tuttle signed the order on July 30.[48]

Tuttle then had to step aside as trial judge and recuse himself from ruling on a new motion for continuance that the defendants filed August 3. This motion amplified the defense's earlier pleas for more time with an attack on Robert Marx, accusing him of "an attitude of obstruction, abuse, and delay." But Tuttle did what he could to inconvenience the defense. He refused to tell Longley who the new trial judge would be and "directed [him] in very strong terms to stay away from Judge Denison," whom he called in to rule on the continuance. Reed found those instructions "wholly indefensible" and believed that Tuttle was improperly trying to exercise authority over the case after his withdrawal: "The moment affidavit of disqualification is filed the Judge in my opinion is deprived of jurisdiction to do anything except transmit notice to the presiding judge[;] any attempt on his part to interfere further is I think highly improper." In Reed's view, he and Longley acted simply "to preserve the legal rights" of their client.[49]

Their dedication to Ford's "legal rights" caused Judge Tuttle no small irritation. At the height of summer, finding a substitute judge in the federal circuit to hear the motion for continuance on short notice proved difficult. Telegrams went out to federal court houses in western and northern Michigan and Ohio. Nearly everyone Tuttle asked to sit was impossible to reach; Judge David Westenhaver, still on the bench in Cleveland, declined because he was about to take his "only chance of vacation." The Detroit press sniffed out the story, too, asking Reed to confirm the filing of Ford's affidavit of prejudice on July 30. Anxious to avoid even greater spectacle, Tuttle finally secured the participation of Judge Benson W. Hough of Columbus, Ohio, and set the motion hearing for August 9.[50]

The August 9 hearing was just as contested and angry as the July 22 conference. Reed asked Judge Hough to set a new trial date after March 4, 1927, the end of the coming session of Congress, "so as not to interfere with his legislative work." According to the *Detroit Free Press*, Gallagher "charged that the Ford millions were being used to starve his client into dropping the case, by use of the continuous delays and heavy traveling expenses necessary to the taking of depositions throughout the United States." He produced affidavits showing that Ford attorneys were instigating nuisance lawsuits against Sapiro: "[A] Washington correspondent of the Ford magazine had approached a lawyer of Richmond, Va., and tried to induce him to name Sapiro as one of the defendants in a case in which the lawyer was suing for the recovery of alleged 'stolen profits' of a tobacco firm." The affidavit accused the Ford representative of aspiring to give Sapiro a "'black eye' in the libel case against Ford" and promising the Virginia lawyer Reed's assistance in the tobacco case. Senator Reed rose to his feet to demand proof of his involvement. Gallagher admitted he had none; his point was to show "how the time granted Ford's lawyers for a continuance of the libel case was being used to 'persecute and harass' Sapiro instead of gathering evidence." Gallagher then dropped another bombshell. He was willing to drop all libel charges in the suit except for the allegation that "'Mr. Sapiro is trying to communize the American child, so that when he grows up he will be ripe for Bolshevik doctrine and activity.'" Interestingly, Sapiro was ready to forgo antisemitism and conspiracy as explicit libel charges, maybe to avoid additional depositions. He and Gallagher may have been betting that those published smears would come up implicitly in any discussion of Bolshevism. Reed did not take the bait, however, and Hough listened to seven hours of "argument, wrangling, and considerable personal bickering" before halting the proceedings. He then gave the lawyers until the following morning to agree on a new trial date and produce an order for him to sign, or he would fix "the time, date, place, and method of taking the depositions and fix the trial date without taking into consideration the convenience of either side."[51]

Thus goaded, Gallagher, Marx, Reed, Longley, Watson, Choate, and Higgins hastily drew up Hough's order. It granted the continuance until March 7, 1927, and set out an intricate deposition schedule for September through January. Depositions were to be submitted to the court by March 1; each side would give the other three days' notice plus "the usual and ordinary" rail travel time from Detroit. Finally, the order pledged, "The friendly co-operation of opposing counsel will be expected in order to facilitate the taking of depositions and for the elimination of lost motion in connection therewith." The defendants had until February 1 to file their amended plea. Hough signed the order, believing, as he told Judge Tuttle, that "a good deal of territory had not [yet] been covered in the taking of depositions." But Hough felt certain that the constraints of the new schedule would "serve as a controlling reason why further continuance should not be granted."[52] Reed got nearly everything he wanted from the entire encounter: more time and, just as important, a more pliant judge.

Ford's lawyers had every reason to be satisfied with the results of the August 9 hearing, but their client felt otherwise. Within the month, Ford received a notice from the federal clerk of courts that the trial had been continued and his witness subpoena remained in effect. This unpleasant matter was Liebold's to deal with; he informed the court that Ford had never received a subpoena. It was no longer possible for Liebold to maintain that Ford had not been served, however. Longley sent Liebold a San Francisco newspaper clipping that recounted a letter from Janet Sapiro to her parents in Stockton, describing exactly how Ford was presented with legal papers:

[A] detective secured a newspaper reporter's badge and got himself admitted to an aviation field where Mr. Ford was witnessing some flights by Ford airplanes. The detective approached Mr. Ford and before guards could interfere served the subpoena upon the much sought manufacturer. "Mrs. Sapiro writes that the body-guards of Mr. Ford started to whip the detective, but that others came to the rescue of the officer. The serving of the subpoena was the fruit of an eight-month effort and Ford was furious and tore up the paper, says the letter."[53]

As of September 1926, Ford was legally bound to appear at trial, when it was finally gaveled into session.

. . .

The defense spent its hard-won extra six months running Sapiro's lawyers all over the country. The Ford lawyers also lined up the testimony of dozens of pivotal witnesses who they believed would be crucial to exposing Sapiro's true personality and methods as a cooperative organizer and attorney. Three of the most important were Joseph Passonneau, former tobacco organizer and then Colorado state director of markets; Charles E. Bassett, former head of the U.S. Department of Agriculture's Office of Markets; and Sidney Rubinow, cooperative organizer in Maine and Minnesota. All three worked with Sapiro at various stages in the cooperative movement and then became disaffected with him. In each instance, the Ford team saw parallels with the Sapiro-Weinstock contretemps. As the Ford lawyers discovered, however, it would take more than a common dislike of Sapiro to get these witnesses to produce factually consistent, logically compelling stories about Sapiro's professional misconduct. Much as Harry Dunn did, Passonneau, Bassett, and Rubinow required considerable time and resources from the Ford defense team before they could be certified ready for the witness stand.

Passonneau's biggest liability as a defense witness was that he impeached Dunn's credibility. Dunn interviewed Passonneau in Denver during his swing across the country in 1924 and used Passonneau's information as the basis of his stories. Yet Passonneau, Sapiro's "bitterest enemy," could contribute a firsthand account of behavior and work practices that corroborated the *Independent*'s criticism. In late 1924, Passonneau told Fred Black, "I believe that the unfortunate thing about your articles . . . has been that they contained enough untruths to make them generally more or less uneffective [*sic*] because so many farmers reading them would doubtlessly be impressed with the thought that the Dearborn Independent was against cooperative marketing, and for that reason should be expected to abuse Mr. Sapiro." Black minced no words in telling Longley what Passonneau thought of Dunn's reporting: "Dunn admitted that he was disregarding the facts."[54]

Passonneau certainly had his own version of the story to tell and an agenda to serve as he did so. Wanting to see Sapiro thoroughly discredited without damaging the cooperative movement, Passonneau gave Black a detailed account of Sapiro's work in the Kentucky tobacco industry from Sapiro's appearance on the scene until Passonneau left for Colorado in July 1923. That November, Passonneau wrote a damning indictment of Sapiro in a letter to Illinois's Governor Frank Lowden. In it, Passonneau accused Sapiro of obtaining a $30,000 fee from the Dark Tobacco Growers' Association by falsifying the minutes of its board meeting, hiring unqualified individuals at inflated salaries for jobs with both tobacco associations in Kentucky, and other misdeeds. In January 1923, while both still worked for the tobacco associations, Passonneau and Sapiro had an angry confrontation. Challenged by Passonneau, Sapiro repeatedly called him a "'liar.'" Passonneau responded by punching Sapiro in the face. A few weeks later, Robert Bingham, a Sapiro ally, discharged Passonneau from his job with the dark-tobacco growers on the grounds that he was not performing his duties.[55]

Passonneau insisted that he was not bitter toward Sapiro for his dismissal, but he retaliated by releasing the Lowden letter to the press. It landed explosively in the midst of the AFBF's highly contentious December 1923 meeting, at which Sapiro and Peteet tendered their resignations and their enemy, J. W. Coverdale, was reelected president. The letter also had a paralyzing effect on the agricultural conference Governor Lowden was then conducting with several Sapiro allies to study wheat marketing. Passonneau also placed confidential information with a commercial packers' trade publication, baiting Sapiro into yet another libel lawsuit, this one in Canada.[56] When Harry Dunn visited Colorado in 1924, trolling for damaging information, Passonneau was only too happy to talk.

Passonneau made no secret of his objections to Sapiro's "methods" and "ethics." Yet even as he disavowed personal animus, antisemitic bias shone through: "I have never held it against Mr. Sapiro that he was a Jew. It is not his fault that he was born a Jew, and having been born a Jew, I assume that it is not his fault that his foremost sin in life is to get money and the manner in which he gets it should be given only second consideration." Passonneau believed that Sapiro's "chief interest in cooperative marketing is that of bleeding the farmers as completely as he is able." For the Ford people, that professional opinion would overcome his shortcomings. Watson was "convinced that he will make us a very favorable witness. In fact, I doubt if his cross-examination will detract much from the value of his testimony in chief." Longley needed no persuading: "Passonneau's testimony will be a wonderful help to the defense. I know of no other man who could do as much for us."[57] Both lawyers saw him as the key to their case, despite what he would say about Dunn's methods and credibility.

Another promising witness, Charles Bassett, brought equally impressive expertise to the stand. In addition to five years' federal service, he had worked for seven more as a "director of field organization" across the country. Upon hearing of the demand for retraction, he offered Cameron his assistance. He described Sapiro's work and methods as "*largely selfish and extremely mercenary.*" For example, Sapiro appeared in Idaho to give three speeches, for which he allegedly demanded thousands of dollars, leaving Bassett to do the grassroots organization work for much less money. Bassett also contended that Sapiro "forced" his "Jewish friend[s]," the marketing agents Weyl and Zuckerman, on the Idaho and Colorado potato cooperatives. At the same time, Sapiro was on retainer to another shipping firm, the Federated Fruit and Vegetable Growers, whose owner was "so much afraid of Sapiro's 'influence' that he did not dare oppose him" and thus did not compete with Weyl and Zuckerman for the potato shipments. In placing the potato cooperatives with the San Francisco firm, Bassett noted crisply, "Sapiro was right then playing into the hands of a Hebrew brother, Maurice Zuckerman of California." Bassett's dislike was not merely personal: "It [is] evident that the 'Christ killers' are well organized to stand together and to pluck all the 'fat' that may be had. I have always wondered just why the Jews refuse to eat hog meat, but it must be the fear of being considered cannibals."[58] Such an attitude might have made Bassett too dangerous for the courtroom even for the avowedly antisemitic Ford lawyers.

The third key witness for the defense, Sidney G. Rubinow, served as "Sapiro's chief lieutenant" in Maine and Minnesota. As had Passonneau, he alerted the *Independent* about inaccuracies in its story on Maine long before the litigation began, telling Cameron that the marketing contract had its antecedents in European and American practice long before Sapiro began his career. Finally, Rubinow disputed the newspaper's conspiracy theories: "If there is a 'ring of Jewish promoters and financiers who are today exploiting the American farmer,' then I for one, don't know anything about it." Still, because of his proximity to Sapiro during the crucial phases of organization in the potato industry, Longley approached him in early 1926 to see "whether or not he would be willing to testify in our behalf." A Jewish proponent of cooperation who could indict Sapiro independently of anything said in the *Independent* would make a valuable witness. In August, Longley forwarded the DPC's file on Rubinow to Watson with the request that Senator Reed stop in St. Paul and "line that gentleman up in better shape."[59]

Reed and Watson made the trip, but the meeting did not go well. Rubinow "was not willing to tell us anything concrete," Watson informed Longley on September 4, and he was reluctant to furnish correspondence or other documents at his own expense. What Rubinow wanted was on the order of a quid pro quo: because Sapiro was slowly being displaced as the face of the cooperative movement, he wanted the *Independent* to give him a national platform from which he could establish himself as Sapiro's successor. "Senator Reed made it very plain to Mr. Rubinow," Watson said, "that the defendants in the Sapiro case were not purchasing any evidence, no matter how valuable." The problem was, the lawyers soon realized, that Rubinow's evidence about the 1920 American Cotton Association meeting, the Federated Fruit and Vegetable Growers, and other issues was decidedly valuable. Eventually, Longley decided to let the *Independent* pass on the merits of whatever articles Rubinow submitted in exchange for the opportunity to examine his files. Only one piece by Rubinow on Minnesota's potato cooperatives appeared in the *Independent* before the start of the trial in March 1927.[60]

. . .

Passonneau, Bassett, and Rubinow could all testify about Sapiro's methods as a proselytizer and organizer of cooperatives. What enhanced their value as witnesses was their personal knowledge. They had all worked with Sapiro; befriended him; and, what was best from the Ford point of view, had broken irrevocably with him on what they saw as matters of principle. Together, they painted a picture of an individual who resembled his portrait in the *Independent*: overbearing and bullying, dishonest and grasping. They could speak directly to what one investigator described as his "meanness of disposition."[61] These witnesses could redirect the libel suit away from antisemitism and toward the counterclaim that revealing Sapiro's personality, personal style, and professional habits constituted legitimate public criticism. As a result, the Ford agents dug into the record on how Sapiro set and collected his legal fees; his relations with his law partners in California, Chicago, and New York; and most salacious of all, his personal life.

In addition to the account of how Sapiro supposedly obtained $30,000 from the dark-tobacco growers by falsifying the minutes of their board meetings, Passonneau provided the Ford legal team with correspondence relating to Sapiro's fees with the burley association in 1923. In that situation, Sapiro charged $22,845.40, and the executive committee agreed to pay it, with only one member dissenting. That member told Passonneau that two others had agreed to oppose the fee, only to back down under pressure. The general feeling among burley officials was that if Sapiro's bill for the entire year was "correspondingly high," they would not retain him as counsel. Similarly, William McCall reported from Idaho that Sapiro presented the potato growers there with a bill for $30,000 "for drawing up an association contract and by-laws and making a few speeches." For a single talk in Pocatello, he charged $2,000. McCall corroborated Bassett's account, down to the detail of Sapiro's attaching a lien to the Idaho potato crop to obtain his fee.[62]

Part of the problem lay in how Sapiro negotiated his fees. It was his custom to allow the association to fix his fee after it decided to retain him. "You remember," he told James Pendelbury in Idaho, "that I said you and Mr. Carlson could name any fee you wished for the work that I may do." It was also his custom—and that of his profession, as James Reed demonstrated in his arrangement with Ford—to be paid for his expenses. Here again, he erred on the side of reassuring his prospective clients that their "obligation[s]" to him could be "adjust[ed]" at some future date. If the cooperatives offered Sapiro a reimbursement rate and a fee that he considered less than reasonable, then disputes arose. In Kentucky, if Passonneau is to be believed, Sapiro committed fraud to collect what he thought his services were worth. In Colorado and Idaho, according to Passonneau, Bassett, and McCall, he sued cooperatives to obtain the higher fees he demanded rather than accept the lower fees they were willing to pay. Erskine Myer was willing to testify that Sapiro left the matter of his fee to the Colorado Potato Exchange and to attest to Sapiro's claim that he was tightly connected to Eugene Meyer Jr. and Bernard Baruch, and what Myer perceived as Sapiro's put-down of the farmers at a meeting in December 1923.[63]

Another complaint from officials of failed cooperatives was that Sapiro did not perform services to justify the fees he sought and that he made exaggerated claims about his expertise. The secretary of the Colorado State Farm Bureau recounted that "Sapiro's only services to the Colorado Exchange were the preparation of Colorado forms from the Maine potato forms, two days' speaking tour, writing a few telegrams and letters, sending [attorney] Thomas Chamberlain to Colorado at time the Exchange was incorporated, possibly a few telegrams subsequent to incorporation and his appearance at the December meeting before the Executive Committee." Talking only to the clients produced a skewed perspective on these disputes. What might look unreasonable to the client can represent countless hours of time and years of accumulated expertise. Sapiro could arguably claim to be practicing an area of law he had largely invented.[64]

To document what cooperatives paid their lawyers, in late 1925 McCall conducted a survey on the West Coast. Out of the twenty-six that responded, four that retained Sapiro paid him what he requested. His fees averaged $162 per month. The other twenty-two paid an average of $45 per month for attorney's fees, but the averages in both cases are misleading. Sapiro did not divide his time evenly among his clients, and most of the fees paid to other lawyers were deceptively low—less than $1,000 for more than twelve months' time. The Ford team had little incentive to do an objective valuation of Sapiro's legal services. Had they looked closely, they would have found one measure in their own mail. James Reed and Richard Higgins billed the DPC $200 per day for their legal work on the Sapiro libel suit. Reed invoiced his office assistant's time at $50 per day.[65]

The Ford lawyers also kept an eye out for information on the status of Sapiro's law firm partnerships in San Francisco, Chicago, and New York, as well as his hiring of lawyers to do cooperative organizing work in the field for him. A Chicago lawyer implausibly named Victor Victor agreed to do "publicity work" for Sapiro after the war and worked with peanut growers in Virginia and North Carolina, for which Sapiro promised him $1,500 but paid him only $500. Victor did not believe Sapiro "actually wished to defraud him," but he saw the deed as "evidence of Sapiro's unbearable disposition and lack of business integrity and tact." The real meat, however, lay in the travails of Sapiro's San Francisco law partnership. Black first caught word in September 1925 that the firm of Sapiro, Hatfield, and Levy had dissolved; he asked F. H. Sherman, the San Francisco branch's advertising manager, to confirm the story.[66] He did not hear anything until the following February, but when news came, it was stunning.

Sherman reported that McCall had interviewed H. G. Coykendall and a Mrs. Wallace, both former officials at the prune association. They told McCall that Sapiro had developed "a certain relationship" with a stenographer in his office, but that was all they would disclose. Sherman followed up with David Levy, Sapiro's partner, and another San Francisco lawyer, a Mr. Sargent. Levy refused to talk, so Sherman tracked down Sargent, who had gotten the story from Levy. The young woman's name was Ann Mulligan, and Sargent described her as "'a real flapper, snappy in appearance, a peach, and using plenty of rouge in her make-up.'" Sapiro was "determined" to take her on a cooperative organizing trip to Canada with him in 1924. At the conclusion of the trip, he planned for her to work "permanently in his Chicago office," presumably where she would be out of his family's view. Milton Sapiro, however, objected to these plans, as did David Levy, and both of them told Aaron they would notify Ms. Mulligan's uncle, a Catholic priest, if he did not change his mind. Aaron finally backed down, canceled the Canadian trip, and left for Chicago with Ms. Mulligan in a separate train car. Upon arriving in Chicago, Aaron notified his brother and Levy of his intent to dissolve the San Francisco firm as of January 1, 1925. Levy and Aaron then engaged in a disagreement over shared fees that eventually ended in litigation. Mrs. Wallace's parting shot had to be especially gratifying to the defense: "She really believes that Mr. Aaron Sapiro would be completely wrecked if he learned that we had this story, which is a direct reflection against him personally. She believes that fear of publicity of this matter would cause Mr. Sapiro to drop the Ford suit." But David Levy refused to speak with

Sherman about Sapiro's alleged affair and declared that any testimony he would give would be in Aaron's favor, despite the fact that his dispute with Aaron over fees might have given him reason to be indiscreet and angry. So all that Sherman had on the affair was one secondhand witness. No one in closer proximity to Sapiro would discuss his behavior on the record. Janet Sapiro and her children moved to Chicago from San Francisco in 1924, before the birth of the family's youngest son, Leland.[67]

The Ford team was obsessed with Sapiro's broken attorney-client relationships, his fractured law partnerships, and his alleged infidelity. They overlooked his contributions to the cooperative movement, his ongoing relationships with people such as Walton Peteet, and his functioning law practice. Sometime between 1925 and 1926, the discovery phase morphed into a much larger project than mere documentation of Dunn's statements. It became a mission to destroy Sapiro, to reveal him to the world as a dishonest person, an untrustworthy lawyer, and an adulterous husband. These impressions followed from their perceptions of Sapiro as a Jew. For the Ford lawyers, the litigation had become inseparable from the beliefs that underlay their unreflected antisemitism. When their witnesses mirrored these attitudes and beliefs, they saw it as confirmation of Sapiro's bad behavior and character. In all sincerity and as captives of their own prejudices, they were unable to see their adversary's attributes and achievements.

With so many witnesses telling the same or similar stories about Sapiro's treatment of his farmer clients, particularly where money was concerned, the Ford legal team thought Dunn's stories would ring true in court. Anything in the *Independent* that was literally true they would readily defend. Anything that Sapiro could prove false, like the hay and wool stories, they would assert was so similar to other statements that were true that there was no appreciable legal difference between them. And anything that remained disputed was simply "a matter of interpretation," as Fred Black, who was not even a lawyer, argued.[68] It did not occur to the Ford lawyers that their circular theory of the case and stereotypical view of their opponent might have also distorted their view of the law. In short, they had come to believe in their own creation.

As both sides poured depositions into the court's file between September 1926 and February 1927, the Ford team focused on what its primary task had become. It was imperative to harness the massive amount of factual information that they and their investigators had collected over the previous several years and line it up into a convincing demonstration of the plaintiff's behavior. Then Aaron Sapiro's conduct—rather than the *Independent*'s stories and content—would furnish the defendant's official response to the plaintiff's lawsuit.

As the March 1927 trial date approached, the defense's procedural moves made that strategy patent. An amended answer, 207 pages long and filed in January, demonstrated the reach and depth of the Ford organization's information-gathering ability and efficiency. This new plea was designed to disturb Sapiro and Gallagher, but it succeeded only in confusing the new trial judge, Fred M. Raymond. Judge Raymond had been recently appointed by President Coolidge in 1925 to the federal court in Michigan's Western District, which included his hometown of Grand Rapids. Intellectually, he was not Tuttle's equal, and Gallagher's first encounter with the new judge left him unimpressed.[69]

The defendants' 207-page plea precipitated a highly charged motion hearing on February 28. Because the plea did not go paragraph by paragraph through the plaintiff's declaration, Judge Raymond said he could not tell what defense was being raised: "[I]t is very difficult indeed to analyze the pleadings with any degree of certainty. It would require, I think, as has been suggested here, something like a week to analyze the pleadings, and check the declaration with the plea."

Gallagher urged Judge Raymond to cut to the heart of the matter. The plaintiff alleged the commission of one libel: the allegation that Sapiro was part of "a conspiracy of Jews." The defense, he claimed, was trying to complicate the case unnecessarily and deceptively claiming that it would prove the truth of some but not all the libels it had published. Moreover, the defense failed to say anywhere in its bloated plea that it would prove that such a conspiracy existed. "Without that averment," Gallagher thundered, "there is no justification."[70]

Stewart Hanley professed genuine surprise. "We thought that plaintiff was going to argue that he was not the man that he was said to be in these alleged libelous articles," he said. Pivoting to the theory of the case that then guided the defense, he asserted, "This is not a case for the trial of anything except Aaron Sapiro and his activities, to determine whether or not either or both of the defendants libeled him in the publications that did appear in the *Dearborn Independent*. It is not a trial of Jews, not a trial of Judaism, and we claim that on the part of the plaintiff an effort is being made for the plaintiff to hide behind the claim that this case is a trial of some issue in which Jewism [*sic*] or Jews as a whole are involved. It is not, and cannot be, and we not only have no desire that it should be, but we will use every effort that we can avail ourselves of to prevent the bespattering of any people or of any race."[71]

Gallagher met this statement with sarcastic disbelief: "Mr. Hanley, with an apparent candor that is very, very extraordinary, says to your Honor, 'Why, there is no Jewish question in the case at all. We do not intend to prove there is one.'" Gallagher would not permit Hanley to evade that for which he and Sapiro sought to hold Ford responsible: "That is the very gravamen of the complaint. Henry Ford has spent millions upon millions of dollars trying to convince the American people that such a conspiracy exists. It is about the only purpose to which the *Dearborn Independent* had been put during its entire existence, just to attack the Jewish people and show there is such a conspiracy of international Jews trying to dominate this country . . . and now his lawyers have to stand here and say to your Honor the charge is false and they do not plead the truth of it."[72]

Judge Raymond had more pressing concerns than the Jewish question. He ruled the latest version of the defendant's plea legally defective and gave Ford's lawyers one more week to submit an acceptable version. That decision satisfied neither side. Gallagher knew he wanted to attack the next plea but wouldn't have time to file the necessary motions; Hanley and Longley wanted more time to rewrite their answer. Rather than "be left naked," Hanley grudgingly accepted Raymond's conditions. The judge pointed out that this next plea would be the defense's fourth, and he urged Longley and Hanley to be "diligent and speedy." Both sides spent the final week in a full-out sprint, checking myriad details: Had their witnesses signed their depositions? Had everyone been subpoenaed? Did they know when to come to Detroit?[73] Having given the plaintiff a strategic victory at a critical moment in the litigation, Judge Raymond intended to bring the case to trial and, perhaps thinking wishfully, to conclude it swiftly.

Such a prospect seemed unlikely as the trial's opening drew near. Press speculations abounded that each side planned to call at least 250 witnesses. Despite the defense's attempt to divert the central question of the case from Ford's antisemitism to Sapiro's legal malpractice, editorial writers could not help fantasizing about the prospect of Ford's taking the stand. "We hope that competent psychologists would attend the trial," the *Detroit Jewish Chronicle* asserted, "so that we may be able to learn what mental twists and quirks there are in this man that should have compelled him to crucify a whole people." The tendency to write the narrative of the case in group-libel terms grew more

THE JEWS TRY FORD!

6.2. Broadside headline, *New York Evening Graphic* [March 1927] (courtesy Patricia Gallagher Wooten, Battle Creek, Michigan).

pronounced in newspapers further from Detroit. "Ford will not be permitted to escape the Jewish issue, however, if the petitioner can help it," reported the *Atlanta Constitution*. The tabloid press painted the scene even more graphically: "The Jews Try Ford!" headlined a banner advertisement in the *New York Evening Graphic*.[74] For Ford's defense to ignore the articles' plainly antisemitic language and implications in pretrial motions and pleadings was one thing. The plaintiff and his attorney would have to demolish this approach before the jury.

7 TRIAL AND MISTRIAL

Never lose sight of the fact that Henry Ford stands behind the [*Independent*], gives his thoughts to it to appear on his Henry Ford page, and is responsible for the thoughts which appear in it.

—William Henry Gallagher, 1927[1]

"Legal skirmishes" in Detroit's "Million Dollar Courtroom" filled the days leading to Aaron Sapiro's "Million Dollar Libel Suit." The main federal courtroom was designed to convey the majesty of the law. Built in the 1890s, it featured solid marble walls; mahogany doors; carved grotesque busts; bronze sconces; ornate carvings; and exquisite mahogany desks for the bench, clerks, and lawyers. "The walls are lined with rose-colored marble from Italy of intricate design," wrote the awestruck *Washington Post*, "and the ceilings are elaborately frescoed."[2] In 1934, flush with Works Progress Administration money, the government built a new federal courthouse. Chief Judge Arthur Tuttle saw to it that his courtroom's interior was carefully dismantled and installed in the new building across the street before the old one submitted to the wrecking ball. As a result of his efforts, today one can stand in the same imposing space where the case of *Sapiro v. Ford* was tried in 1927.[3]

In this elegant setting, the defense made a last-ditch effort to avoid trial, and the plaintiff tested the judge's willingness to permit group-libel claims into the case. On March 10, Longley filed a verbatim copy of his original plea, all but daring Judge Raymond to call his bluff and force him to rewrite Ford's answer from scratch. Raymond had to choose between delaying the start of trial or accepting the plea he had already declared defective. He chose to uphold the rules on pleadings, attempting to show that he would not be manipulated, and ordered Longley and Reed to submit an acceptable plea. The new one, 571 paragraphs long, tried everyone's patience; Gallagher angrily described it as "'irrelevant, specious, confusing to the issues involved, and lacking in justification.'" Gallagher and Sapiro responded by trying to force Ford to defend the *Independent*'s explicitly antisemitic statements. They alleged "that the term

'Jew,' . . . on which the suit is based, was used as a term of scorn." But with the start of trial quickly approaching, Raymond spurned their motion, saying that it "only would widen the scope of the case" beyond traditional libel law.[4]

On Monday afternoon, March 14, the plaintiff asked the court to settle the matter of Ford's status as a witness. "'If the Court please,'" Gallagher began, "'Mr. Ford ha[s] denied being served with a subpoena in this case. Attorneys on his behalf have [repeated] these denials. I think we ought to know now what he plans to do. Does he intend to submit to the subpoena or do I have to prepare contempt papers?'" Gallagher produced an affidavit from his process server, an account that corroborated Janet Sapiro's. In August 1926, J. Francis Fitzgerald "tossed" the subpoena and witness fee in Ford's lap as he sat in his car at the Ford Airport in Dearborn. After listening to Gallagher's argument, Senator Reed departed the courtroom, only to be engulfed by reporters. "'I don't think there will be any difficulty about getting Mr. Ford's testimony if the Court wants it,'" Reed said, delicately implying that he would not produce his client merely because the plaintiff asked him to.[5]

From the press's perspective, all of these issues—the possibility of Ford's appearance as a witness, the proposed changes to the plaintiff's declaration, and the defense's willingness to prove the truth of the *Independent*'s stories—made for compelling legal drama. Judge Raymond had yet to rule on whether the words *Jews* and *Jewish* could be sued on as libelous. Nevertheless, the *New York Times* characterized Sapiro's case as a "defense of himself and that of his race against the charges made by Mr. Ford." The *Washington Post*, likewise, predicted that Sapiro and Gallagher would "center the trial on the racial question." On March 15, Judge Raymond swiftly disposed of Gallagher's remaining motions. He declined to restrict testimony to those issues on which depositions had already been taken, meaning that the plaintiff could be surprised by anything the defense cared to introduce. Judge Raymond then settled the matter of the defendant's plea, admitting it and ordering that its defects would be modified "through agreement of opposing counsel" during the trial.[6]

The following order of business was to select the jury. The Ford team had not overlooked this crucial aspect of the case. The federal court announced the names of two hundred individuals in its March jury pool on February 15, giving Ford's lawyers a month to screen them secretly. Someone in the legal office drew up a list of questions for Ford agents to scout. The Ford lawyer instructed the agents not to talk to the prospective jurors while obtaining extensive personal information about them: their ages, their occupations or employers, and whether they were farmers. Had they been heard to comment favorably or negatively about Ford? To what church did they belong? What were their views regarding Jews? Were they Jewish or "related in any manner to Jews?" Armed with printed cards, Ford investigators fanned out and surreptitiously conducted background checks on nearly all the unsuspecting prospective jurors, talking to their neighbors and determining whether they drove Ford cars.[7]

As these reports came to the home office, the Dearborn Publishing Company (DPC) attorneys culled out the unacceptable candidates. A Studebaker sales agent was deemed "doubtful" because "he is working for Jews." A Lansing Ford dealer disparaged another prospect as "no good." Other jurors were marked "ok" if they did "not like the Jews" or thought Ford was "a great man." Still others were deemed toss-ups if the investigators could not obtain sufficient information to make a judgment or felt the decision was too close to call. Most of the forms did not indicate what made a juror unacceptable. Probably being Jewish would qualify; in contrast, Klan membership or owning a Ford car made a juror look sympathetic.[8]

. . .

On Tuesday morning, March 15, the trial officially convened. Judge Raymond, the *New York Times* reported, "regards court proceedings as something as sacred as a service in a cathedral." Working in concert, Judge Raymond, Reed, and Gallagher took four hours to impanel a jury of six men and six women. Gallagher dismissed the wife of a Detroit police officer and a former Klan member. Reed saw to it that the jury included no Jews, excusing two from service after they acknowledged having read the articles. Judge Raymond's main concern was to ensure that jurors had no personal relationships with Ford or his family.[9]

The jury resembled a cross-section of Detroit and its suburbs. Of the men, only one was a farmer. The others came from a variety of occupations in small business and middling professions such as sales and accounting. Three were Catholic, although one of those professed a turn to Christian Science; the others belonged to various Protestant denominations. Observers learned more about the women jurors. Four married women jurors gave their occupations as "housewives"; a fifth, a single woman in her twenties, kept house for her brother; and the sixth was recently widowed. Four of the six were Protestant, the others Catholic; most wore their hair fashionably "bobbed." The hairdos and marital status of male jurors escaped comment. What only the Ford lawyers knew was that one male juror had expressed favorable opinions about Ford and was "radically against" Jews; he and another belonged to the Masons, as did one woman juror's husband. The jury's picture made the papers in Detroit, Washington, and New York. For deciding whether Henry Ford had damaged Aaron Sapiro to the sum of $1 million, the jurors earned $4 per day.[10]

After the jury was sworn in, Gallagher launched into his opening statement. Defining libel as "a written publication concerning a person tending to bring that person into disrepute," he pointed out that publishers reach the limit of "this right of fair comment and criticism" when they "make a personal assault upon the character or the motives of individuals who are involved in the advocacy of the other side of the question." It would be the jury's duty to determine whether Ford and the *Independent* crossed this limit, whether they did so knowingly, and whether in so doing they acted with the malice necessary for an award of damages. Gallagher then addressed the specifically racial character of Ford's attack on Sapiro. "Henry Ford has a perfect right, so far as the law is concerned, to make an attack on the Jewish people and to continue it as long as he wishes; but just as soon as an attack against a race is centered upon an individual of that race, just as soon as an individual is singled out and made the butt of the attack," he declared, "then that individual has the right to come into court and ask for a determination of the justice of that attack."[11]

The *Dearborn Independent*, Gallagher continued, "is merely a means of expression for Henry Ford. It conveys his message and conveys his thoughts, and so he, standing behind it, controlling its policies, giving his thoughts to it, is himself personally responsible for the thoughts that this Independent spreads throughout the country." Ford and his family were the only stockholders in the DPC, and by the time of the suit, Gallagher pointed out, the newspaper owed the Ford Motor Company more than $2 million. He then introduced the parties. "No one need say to a Michigan jury who Henry Ford is," Gallagher said grandly, whereas Aaron Sapiro "is a stranger in our community." But before he could acquaint the jury with Aaron Sapiro, tell much of his story, and demonstrate his bona fides as an American citizen, Judge Raymond took note of the advancing hour and adjourned.[12]

Gallagher resumed the next day, finishing his client's biography and describing the *Independent* articles. Reed objected to the mention of Sapiro's military

7.1. Aaron Sapiro (*left*) and William Henry Gallagher (*right*) at the plaintiff's table in the Detroit federal courthouse, March 1927 (© Bettmann/Corbis).

enlistment as a thirty-three-year-old married man with three children, and Raymond sustained the objection. The details seemed innocuous enough, but the defense wanted nothing in the record that gave Sapiro a patina of patriotism. Gallagher then portrayed the attack against Sapiro as profoundly and thoroughly antisemitic: "There isn't any doubt that he is a dominating figure in American agriculture. But, they make the statement one of libelous character by adding . . . the claim that he dominates American agriculture . . . merely as the instrument and tool of this international body of Jews who have taken him as the instrument of bringing the American farmer under subjection and control." The newspaper charged that "he allied himself, and this body of Jews allied themselves, with Reds and Communists and Bolshevists, worked hand in hand together with the object and purpose of bringing about in this country the same situation that exists in Russia." There was no more explosive political calumny during the isolationist, Russia-phobic 1920s than to be called a communist, unless it was to be called a communist solely by virtue of being Jewish.[13]

7.2. James Reed (*left*) and co-counsel Richard Higgins (*right*) outside the courtroom in the Detroit federal building, March 1927 (© Bettmann/Corbis).

Gallagher promised the evidence would show that charges of a conspiracy involving a network of prominent American Jews were "entirely unfounded... [and] without foundation." The question, as he framed it for the jury, was whether Sapiro was libeled "when he was charged with being a member of a band of international Jews that sought to turn American agriculture over to the international Jews, to spread Communism and Bolshevism among our people and to let the same doctrines seep into the hearts of our children." But as he began reading from the *Independent*, Reed jumped to his feet, objected to the statement as argumentative, and was promptly sustained. Gallagher spent the entire day attempting to walk the jury through each of the 141 libels recited in the plaintiff's declaration as Reed repeatedly interrupted. Finally, Raymond made two key rulings that narrowed the scope of the case. One held "that Mr. Ford's ideas with regard to the Jewish race formed no part of the case built up by Mr. Sapiro." The other ordered that the plaintiff could not prove attacks on himself "'and on his people.'" After adjournment, Reed told the press the two rulings "'put just the interpretation of the case which we have been wanting all along. You can't libel a race.'" Reed may have been pleased, but bored spectators only wanted "the preliminaries" to end and for the lawyers to "begin making faces at each other." The United News Service dressed up its report of the first day in racial terms, describing Gallagher as a "raw-boned Gaelic lawyer."[14]

On the third day of trial, it was Reed's turn to introduce himself to the jury, and he chose the same words that Gallagher used to describe Sapiro: "I, of course, have the disadvantage of being a stranger to you all, and I hope that you will bear with me if I make the same mistakes which strangers are sometimes prone to make." One moment Reed was all charm and self-deprecation, the next he cut brutally to the heart of his case: "[T]he Hebrew race is not here bringing this suit, and . . . Mr. Sapiro has no right to come here and recover damages for the Hebrew race, and put the money in his own pocket, as damage done to himself." Elaborating on Sapiro's Jewishness, Reed stopped to ask for help pronouncing his name: "This is the case, I repeat, of Aaron Sapiro, or Shapiro—I do not know just which way it is pronounced—?" Gallagher corrected him, but the damage was done; the peculiarity of Sapiro's name hung in the air like a profanity. He's not one of us, Reed was telling the jurors. So foreign and removed were Sapiro and his dishonest schemes from the mind of Henry Ford, Reed continued, that Ford had nothing to do with what appeared in the newspaper: "Henry Ford never saw these articles [and] has never read them to this blessed hour."[15]

Reed then dismissed all allegations of libel: "[I]t is no libel to say truthfully of a man who is a Jew that he is a Jew." No antisemitic implications should be read into anything the *Independent* reported, he continued: "[T]his is the same kind of case as it would be if Mr. Sapiro happened to belong to some other race than the Jewish race, and I am casting no reflections upon him because he belongs to that race." Reed deflected Gallagher's characterization of the *Independent*'s statements as antisemitic and insisted that Sapiro, in complaining about them, took "mere sentences or paragraphs" out of context. "[A]ny paper has the right to print . . . the truth, whatever it may be. The law puts no bridle in the mouth of truth. And so we claim here . . . that what has been printed of Mr. Sapiro in all of its real essence was the truth." But just what truths the defense intended to prove still remained a mystery. Late Thursday afternoon, Gallagher requested a conference in chambers to force Reed—and Raymond—to confront the lack of specificity in the defense's opening statement. It paralleled the defects of the defense's plea, Gallagher asserted. But he got nowhere. An hour later, the lawyers emerged, and Reed "was a bit more specific but still he did not take up the libels one by one and show what answer he would make to each." Instead, he painted Sapiro as a conspirator and conniver, out to enrich himself at the ruination of farmers. His presentation was laced with "mockery" and "indignation."[16]

Reed's account of Sapiro's career lacked precision, however. He misidentified the 1920 Montgomery cotton growers' convention as a meeting of dark-tobacco growers and had to correct himself. As his statement went on, he forgot what he had already said and began repeating himself; to his embarrassment, both Gallagher and the judge called him on it. Worst of all, he incorrectly named Sam Guard and Herman Stein, whom he called "Herbert," as Jews and was forced to admit his error. As Reed branched into a litany of "the unprofessional conduct of the plaintiff," Gallagher did his best to rattle him further, interrupting him with objections that he was making arguments rather than simply stating what he planned to prove. Raymond consistently permitted Reed to proceed. Throughout the recitation, Sapiro "sat immobile," although at times "an amused expression flitted over his pale face, made more pallid by the contrasting jet of his hair." At last, on Friday afternoon, Reed concluded his "bitter biography," and the court welcomed its first witness.[17]

William J. Cameron took the stand "determined to protect his employer," in the words of Leo Ribuffo, "even if he had to skate on the edge of perjury." Gallagher sought to treat him as a hostile witness, but Reed and Longley would not cooperate; they knew that Gallagher would attempt to do the same thing with Ford, if he ever took the stand. Nor could Gallagher use Cameron to get at Ford's state of mind with regard to what went into the *Independent*. His attempts to get Cameron to describe his conversations with Ford about "the policy of the paper," "international Jewish banking rings," or Ford's attitudes about anything at all met a solid wall of objections. Raymond upheld Stewart Hanley's argument that the only relevant issue was what appeared in the newspaper, not what Ford and his staff discussed privately. Cameron testified that the paper diverged from Ford's beliefs on war, military preparedness, and "the Russian people's new experiment," toward which Ford was "lenient." Newspapers headlined their stories with that word, as if the day's most important insight was that Ford was soft on Bolshevism.[18]

The trial's slow pace was delaying its main event. Gallagher told the press after Friday's adjournment that Ford "will be called late next week. Mr. Sapiro will testify in advance of Mr. Ford." It had taken nearly a week just to get through opening statements and the first day of Cameron's testimony. Sometimes, however, Gallagher used these gambits to put bits of information before the jury, much to the annoyance of the defense. Unable to get Cameron to testify about the relationship between Ford and the newspaper, Gallagher requested the DPC's business records. "What do you mean by 'all the records?'" Hanley demanded. Gallagher smoothly replied: "I mean the records covering the period since Mr. Ford bought the paper and put the stock in the name of his wife, son, and himself." Hanley objected angrily, but jurors heard what Gallagher wanted them to know, and the *Washington Post* noticed Hanley's loss of composure.[19]

The weekend newspapers profiled the jurors and speculated about the direction in which each side would take the case. Sitting in "rapt attention," the jurors never registered boredom or, for that matter, glee: "When something amusing is said, the jury leaves the smiling to the attorneys." During recesses, the women gathered for "sedate" walks, the men for group smoking sessions. The *New York Times* reported in awed tones that "the jury is making more than the ordinary effort to keep an open mind." The plaintiff's case would consist of the remainder of Cameron's testimony, then Fred Black, Ford, the reading of two depositions, "and the possible examination of the two 'surprise' witnesses." Gallagher estimated he could complete all this testimony, which would largely focus on the *Independent*'s charges linking Sapiro to communism in the Pacific Northwest, in about a week. Senator Reed, he pointed out, had not bothered to mention the "Communist phase of the case" in his opening statement.[20]

The weekend's real news came from the plaintiff. Sapiro emerged from his rooms at Detroit's Book-Cadillac Hotel to give an interview. The

$1 million in fees that Reed alleged he collected, Sapiro riposted, covered the entire period from 1915 to the present and included money paid to all his partners as well as his personal income. At the height of his practice, his firm represented sixty cooperatives, with a total of 750,000 members; those numbers were now down to thirty and 400,000, respectively. "[I]f I had not been attacked by Henry Ford's weekly and suspicion cast upon my integrity, I could have . . . brought even greater benefit to the farmers of the United States." The *New York Times* was sympathetic: "There was no mistaking the earnestness of the speaker. His black eyes snapped and a sharp note came into his voice, usually modulated in low pitch." Sapiro's good humor returned, the reporter observed, when someone suggested that he personally examine Ford on the witness stand. Having raised the prospect in his demand for retraction, he brushed away the idea: "It would be dramatic, wouldn't it? But I don't think it would be in good taste."[21]

American Jewish leaders said nothing during the first week of the trial. When the rabbi of New York's Temple Emanu-El, Samuel Schulman, preached about the lawsuit in his Saturday sermon, Louis Marshall might as well have been speaking. "'Israel does not seek vindication in Detroit,'" Schulman said. "'[T]he reputation of the Jew . . . is safe,'" he declared. "'[N]either the Jewish religion nor Israel as a community can accompany any individual Jew into any court house when he is making a fight for his rights on property and reputation. There he must stand alone.'" Schulman hoped Sapiro would prevail fully in his struggle, but he "'should not identify himself with his people in this matter.'" When he heard about Schulman's homily, Sapiro was surprised and a little angry, as he confided in his friend Lewis Strauss:

What did Schulman mean by taking left-handed cracks at me? I never made any pose of seeking "vindication for my people." But I am trying to compel Ford to be a bit slower in accusing men of being members of a Jewish ring of international Jews who are trying to control the world and are organizing American agriculture in the interest of the Jews and *against* the interest of the farmer. I think Schulman's attack was hardly less than *cowardly* at this critical time.[22]

Rabbi Stephen S. Wise of the Free Synagogue quickly came to Sapiro's defense, praising Sapiro for bringing the suit and urging Jews to stand behind him. The argument was more than semantic. It raised the sticky questions of whether this fight was one with which all Jews could identify and which legal claims Sapiro could make on behalf of Jews generally. If Ford attacked Sapiro, a Jew, at what point did those attacks draw American Jews together? Sapiro thought the line was clear enough: "What I seek," he said in Chicago on March 13, "is vindication in court both for myself and members of my race *who have been libeled by Mr. Ford.*"[23]

Inside court, the rules were clear: legal vindication was available only to those specifically injured. Yet Sapiro was beginning to recognize the case's larger implications: "If I win this case I believe that the people will be fair enough to see the lack of faith that has accompanied Ford's persecution of the Jews." Sapiro believed that Ford's libel of individual Jews stemmed from a "lack of faith" that poisoned the civic community. Whether Jewish or not, Americans would find healing in the justice that only law could dispense. To obtain justice, Sapiro had to face his adversary; counter the press, which was selling the notion that "The Jews" had put Henry Ford on trial; and finally, answer the Jewish religious and secular leaders who refused to connect his case to American civic unity. Thus, this was not simply a matter of group libel for Sapiro. It was a case of individual harm to individual Jews, in which all American Jews had a real stake.[24]

The defense sought to keep the upper hand in the press over the weekend. Clifford Longley issued a statement on Sunday night to whet reporters' appetites on their favorite subject. Ford would take the stand "voluntarily," Longley declared grandly, and he would indeed go into specifics about the "band of Jews": "'Mr. Ford will testify that there was a band, but that the band was made up of Sapiro's friends, his associates in his law office and a few Jews outside of it.'" But there was never any intention to demonize all Jews, he claimed: "'As for Sapiro's interpretation of what the articles mean in their allusions to Jews, it is simply ridiculous.'" No general antisemitism was intended or implied in the articles, Ford planned to say, and Sapiro was wrong to believe he had been targeted: "'Mr. Ford will testify that he never heard of Sapiro . . . [until] the suit was launched.'"[25]

After the weekend recess, testimony resumed with the issue everyone was dying to hear about: how much did Ford know about what was going on in the offices of the *Independent*? The crush of people crowding to get into the courtroom was presenting a serious problem for federal marshals. Back at the witness stand, Gallagher did his best to intimidate Cameron: "Did you ever discuss with Mr. Ford after [April 12, 1924] the contents of this first article entitled 'Mr. Ford's Own Page?'" "No," the witness calmly replied. Gallagher began to

7.3.   Men crowding the hallway of the federal courthouse in Detroit during the libel trial (from the Collections of The Henry Ford, 90.1.1940.7/THF101578).

pick Cameron apart: "When did you first discuss with anybody the publication by *The Dearborn Independent* which would charge Aaron Sapiro with being allied with an international gang of Jews?" Reed objected; Raymond sustained; Gallagher tried again. "Who contemplated placing the farmers of this country under the domination of an international banking ring?" This time Raymond told Cameron to answer: "When this storm of complaint [that the *Independent* had begun to receive in 1924] began to be strong enough to register itself on my mind." The witness maintained that he discussed the matter only with subordinates, and then just to give directions. Gallagher then tried to establish the character of Cameron and Liebold's relationship, but that question drew another objection, promptly sustained.[26]

Gallagher then scored a series of points against the witness with a line of questioning about the carelessness the *Independent* exhibited in framing its allegations about the "band of Jews" involved in the "conspiracy." Over Stewart Hanley's repeated objections, each one overruled by Judge Raymond, Cameron revealed that he did not know the specific names of any bankers allied with the "band," and he was unaware that Sapiro cooperatives had not borrowed money from "any Jewish banking firm." He could not name specific individuals who participated in the band of Jews or the location of the headquarters of the international conspiracy. The only reporter that the *Independent* "employed specifically" to work on these stories, Cameron testified, was Harry H. Dunn, but the defense prevented Cameron from explaining why the paper ran Dunn's stories under a pen name.[27]

Establishing the articles' intent proved difficult. Gallagher introduced H. W. Roland's August 6, 1923, letter to Dunn into evidence ("Do not snicker when I tell you that the Jewish boys are putting their work on the farmers"), at which point Hanley and Reed stopped Cameron from testifying that the *Independent* initially planned "a set of Jewish articles and not a set of Sapiro articles." The judge excused the jury, and Gallagher and Hanley argued the issue for four hours. Gallagher asserted that Michigan law and other precedents supported the idea that "when you libel a certain group of a class, and when particularly when one person of that group is identified by name, then you are responsible to that person, and indeed to the entire group." But none of his cited cases specifically drew on situations in which the libeled group was singled out on account of race. Unwilling to create precedent in the absence of statutory law, Raymond sustained Reed and Hanley's objection to Gallagher's question, effectively stopping him from bringing the issue of group libel into the *Sapiro v. Ford* trial. Later, after the day's session ended, the judge explained his ruling to the press: "'[T]he idea of the race in general would be barred [under this ruling]. Further it means that in this trial Mr. Ford's ideas of the Jews as a whole and his attitude toward them as a people will be barred.'"[28]

Gallagher found more solid footing in letters he subpoenaed from Cameron and the DPC. The jury heard damaging passages from Dunn's correspondence from 1923 and 1924: "As soon as I can prove what I know you will get the story." Two months later, Dunn acknowledged, "[T]here is an almost unanimous opinion that the associations are good things, quite the best method of marketing the fruit growers and vegetable men ever had." The plaintiff and his attorney were seeing these letters for the first time.[29]

In Gallagher's view, the August 6 letter from Roland to Dunn clearly established that the *Independent*'s motive "was anti-Jewish." Sapiro, too, was pleased; on hearing the letter read, he "glanced at the jury and threw back his head with his face wreathed in a smile." His lawyer asserted that this evidence proved his allegations of malice and conspiracy against Ford, Cameron, and the *Independent*. Over Hanley's objections, Gallagher introduced a copy of *The International Jew*, which he displayed for the jury: "They [the defendants] want the world to know that the Jew is the conscious enemy of all that the Anglo-Saxon means by civilization." That demonstration pushed Hanley past his tolerance limits. The first anti-Jewish series, he conceded, was "'unfair and generally anti-Jewish [and] cast aspersions on the whole Jewish race.'" But he argued that it bore no relevance to Sapiro's lawsuit.[30]

Cameron returned to the stand on March 22 for continued examination about his editorial authority. He denied discussing the articles with Liebold, saying they were "entirely in my judgment" as editor. Gallagher pounced: "Who put them in your judgment?" Hanley objected and Raymond sustained; Gallagher could not establish Ford's role from that angle either. The court would not permit testimony on the question of who made Cameron editor of the *Independent*; all Cameron disclosed of his interactions with Ford was Ford's oft-repeated remark: "You are the editor, all you have to do is be sure you are right." Cameron insisted he never specifically discussed the Sapiro articles with Ford, except "probably" at the time the newspaper received Sapiro's demand for retraction. Ford then dispensed his "usual" advice: "get the facts, be sure you are right." That was Dunn's job. Cameron did not reject anything Dunn submitted, and he could not remember whether the magazine conducted any independent investigations to verify Dunn's claim that that U.S. courts had found farmers liable for debts of Sapiro-style cooperatives.[31]

Gallagher then took Cameron through each article, asking whether Cameron could personally confirm individual assertions or supply firsthand knowledge of them. Raymond sustained objections to some questions, but for the most part Cameron had to tell the court that he did not know, independent of Dunn's reporting, how cooperative boards of directors were chosen, how Sapiro's legal fees were calculated, or how Sapiro got control of the potato growers in Colorado, for example. During this line of questioning, the two sides fought over the inclusion and exclusion of letters from people who wrote to dispute facts in Dunn's stories. Focusing particularly on the hay industry, with which Sapiro denied having worked, Gallagher demanded that the defendants produce every letter they received in response to the article. A subpoena to that effect had been served on Cameron two weeks before trial, but he had not turned over the correspondence. Raymond ruled that Cameron could testify

7.4. William Henry Gallagher, co-counsel Robert Marx, and their client Aaron Sapiro stand together during a recess in the libel trial (© Bettmann/Corbis).

about these letters only if the plaintiff put their authors on the stand as well, thus preventing the jury from hearing A. C. Cherry's critical August 21, 1924, letter.[32] Gallagher was thus seriously hampered in his attempt to get Cameron to acknowledge that the *Independent* did not investigate the articles when people told them they were wrong.

The jury might not have heard these letters read into the record, but the newspapers published them. This practice pointedly ignored the judge's pre-trial request that the press not report on excluded testimony and evidence. Raymond could only instruct the jury not to read anything in the newspapers pertaining to the case. The public learned that Cameron did not read much, if any, of the magazine's incoming correspondence questioning the credibility of its trusted reporter. Raymond continued to narrow the scope of Gallagher's questions and prevent him from cross-examining his witness.[33] Neither side was happy when the day ended.

When court reconvened on Thursday, March 24, Gallagher promptly filed a motion to amend the plaintiff's declaration. Hanley then requested until March 28 to examine the amendments. The court gave everyone the afternoon off to read the newly amended declaration.[34]

Testimony resumed with Gallagher attempting to elicit from Cameron a description of the working relationships on the *Independent* staff and Raymond again refusing to permit it. Reed and Gallagher then engaged in another prolonged debate about the admissibility of evidence on "the Jewish question," which Raymond again ruled inadmissible. Gallagher sought to get Cameron to testify about Ford's responsibility for the publication of *The International Jew* and was again stymied, not just by the objections of the defense and the court's insistence on strict adherence to rules on the admission of evidence but also by the technical requirements of libel law. Gallagher could not even ask Cameron about other individuals such as Bernard Baruch or Harold Lasker without Hanley objecting that no evidence had been offered that those individuals were, in fact, Jewish. And because Cameron had been prevented from testifying about what *Independent* staffers knew about the subjects of Dunn's articles, it was impossible for Gallagher to use Cameron to prove anything about the intention behind the Sapiro series, much less get Cameron on record about Ford's attitudes toward Jews. When Hanley commented that Gallagher was "quite well succeeding" in getting passages from *The International Jew* in front of the jury without putting them into evidence, Gallagher replied, with a trace of sarcasm, "I am not succeeding at all."[35]

Hanley was right in one respect: the press was noting the implications of Cameron's fantastic testimony. The *New York Evening Graphic*, which sold its readers the idea that Jews were putting Ford on trial, complained on March 24 that the case was "getting tangled up in such a mass of words that interest is dropping rapidly." With the court keeping the jury and the country from hearing evidence about Ford's attitudes toward Jews and whether he intended to libel them, the *Graphic* concluded that there was little that could be learned from the case itself. The best thing would be for Ford "to announce that after all the Jews in this country are as good citizens as the members of any other race. That would be the *truth*."[36] At the time, no one could imagine Ford doing such a thing, Cameron—his chief defender—least of all.

On Cameron's sixth day, he exhibited the manner of a bored teenager. Ford "dropped in from time to time" at the *Independent*'s offices, he said; "sometimes not once in a week, and sometimes once in a day." They talked about things Ford was interested in at the moment: "I use those occasions to get his thoughts on—well, the philosophical angle of his thoughts in order to prepare the Ford page." He hastened to add, "we do not go into details with him on anything," and he, not Ford, actually wrote Ford's column. But Hanley and Judge Raymond curtailed Gallagher's subsequent questions on the authorship of "Mr. Ford's Page" on the grounds that they related to earlier publications or were "indefinite." Strangely, Raymond continued to permit Gallagher to ask questions about *The International Jew*, despite the objection that it was not mentioned in the declaration and had not been formally introduced as evidence. Cameron danced around the issue of whether he and Ford had ever discussed the Sapiro series. "Not as articles," was Cameron's evasive answer. "It would come up in the way of comment. I have just one definite recollection of one conversation regarding the Sapiro articles, as we called them in the office, and that was at the time of the demand for a retraction. Any conversation before that would be in just the midst of other conversations, comment upon—probably upon comments in the press, or by letter, or by callers. We had numerous—hundreds of people call to see us about them."[37]

That was the longest uninterrupted speech Cameron ever gave on the stand. Hanley kept him from elaborating further. After a prolonged rally in which Gallagher asked Cameron to recount conversations with Ford and Hanley objected each time, Judge Raymond lost some of his judicial calm: "I think the Court is perfectly clear in what I want to ascertain, and that is whether the witness has any memory of recollection of conversations, or the substance of them. I think it could be asked in a very short, simple, direct way, and I think all of us would understand just what is being sought, and I think it is time that we make some progress in this case." Gallagher promptly "subscribe[d] to that proposition." But he could not formulate the question in a way that drew Hanley's approval. When the judge asked Cameron whether he could remember the substance, if not the precise words, of conversations he'd had with Ford, the witness finally put everyone out of their misery with a simple no. Convinced the witness was being purposefully evasive, Gallagher protested and made to continue, but

Hanley complained about "the abuse of this witness at this time before the jury."[38] The judge instructed Gallagher to move on.

Gallagher's following subject was Sapiro's demand for retraction. Hanley stipulated that the DPC received it, but he could not recall on what date. At that point, Cameron did remember a discussion between himself and Ford. "Much to Gallagher's chagrin," Cameron said he told Ford: "For the first time in my newspaper experience I had been called on—the statements that I had been responsible for—I had been challenged by a demand for a retraction." According to Cameron, Ford queried, "On these farm articles that we have been running?" Cameron testified, "I tried to explain it to him and he waived [sic] that off, he apparently did not know what I was talking about." The last clause of that sentence was struck as drawing a conclusion. "I tried to tell him what the thing was and he just passed it off with a wave of his hand. He says, 'Well, if you are wrong, you ought to take it back, and if you are right, you should stand by it.'"[39]

Gallagher then moved to the *Independent*'s investigation of its stories before and after the demand for retraction. Cameron acknowledged that Fred Black "conducted an investigation along some lines," but he could not remember with whom Black talked or where he went to conduct his investigation. Gallagher narrowed the question further: did the DPC appoint or detail "any person to examine the facts set forth in the demand for retraction?" Gallagher wanted to know what effort the newspaper made to check its reporting, particularly because it ran another article after receiving the demand. After the usual arguments and objections, Cameron finally answered: "I think not—my department did not; I gave no orders for anyone else to do it."[40]

Colloquy among Raymond, Gallagher, and Hanley veered toward the absurd when Gallagher tried to use the *International Jew* articles to prove Ford's connection to the newspaper's other Jewish-related content. When he offered the first series as evidence, Hanley countered that those articles never mentioned the plaintiff by name and were thus irrelevant. Gallagher interjected, "[T]hey refer to the international money power and banking ring, which [Sapiro] is later charged with being a member of." Raymond then asked Gallagher, "You do not expect to produce any proof that it was known to either defendant during the publication of these articles that he was a member of any of those various groups?" Gallagher replied, "That would be impossible, if the Court please, [because] it is not a fact." The libels alleged the existence of a conspiracy that never happened, but Raymond expected Gallagher to provide proof of that conspiracy before he could deny its existence. Gallagher was not even permitted to introduce the date of January 22, 1922—the date the first series was suspended—or to connect Ford to the decision to suspend that series or begin the second one.[41]

Gallagher returned his focus to the Sapiro articles, asking Cameron to describe how he edited Dunn's manuscripts for publication. Here again the attorney ran into problems. Asked to explain his markings, Cameron eventually acknowledged that he was trying to restrict the characterization from all Jews to "a few of the financial group." When Gallagher asked him to name names, Hanley objected and Raymond sustained. When Gallagher asked Cameron to interpret his editing, Raymond cut him off there, too: "[The] article speaks for itself and is the best evidence." At this point, because Cameron had not yet produced the original copy of the demand for retraction and all the exhibits that Sapiro had requested, Gallagher suspended his examination of Cameron until he brought the documents to court. The defense deferred its cross-examination until Gallagher completed his direct. Cameron performed admirably in his role as sacrificial lamb, leaving the stand unbowed in his assertion that "he alone was responsible for the *Independent*'s articles and policy."[42]

The following witness was the plaintiff's first "surprise": James Martin Miller, a writer who had worked for Ford in the early 1920s. The relationship soured, and sometime after he was let go, Miller sued Ford in Washington, D.C., where he lived, for unpaid salary. Ward Creech and Ernest Liebold were concerned about the impact of Miller's suit on Ford's Muscle Shoals bid, for good reason. While in Ford's employ, Miller met with Coolidge at Ford's behest, just before the exchange of Ford's presidential endorsement for Coolidge's pledge of support for Ford's bid. If Miller wanted to harm Ford publicly, he needed only to disclose the fact of his meeting with the president.[43]

Miller's testimony did not confirm those fears, but what he said about Ford's knowledge of Sapiro and the cooperative marketing articles was far more damaging. In 1923, Miller was sent to Ford's office, where the two had a memorable conversation: "'Why don't you write an article about the Jews and the Reserve Bank down there, Eugene Meyers [*sic*],'" Ford told Miller, "'and do you know Aaron Sapiro?'" Cameron's claim that Ford did not know Aaron Sapiro had thus been swiftly impeached, but Gallagher was not yet finished: "What did Mr. Ford say?" Miller delivered: "He said that [Sapiro] was organizing the farmers with that bunch of Jews down there, and trying to bilk them." "What else?" "Well, he said, 'We are going to expose him, and I think that the *Dearborn Independent* has a good circulation among the farmers, and we will upset the apple cart.'" Senator Reed rose to his feet with an air of superb unconcern, "tapping his horn-rimmed spectacles against the palm of his left hand": "'You set that claim up in court in Washington and you were defeated?'" "'I lost,'" Miller said "in a very low voice." "'That's all,'" Reed replied. Despite Reed's attempt to undermine Miller's credibility, those "five minutes of brisk new testimony," the *Los Angeles Times* commented, "lifted the trial from the depths of monotony into which it had fallen."[44]

The week drew to a close as Gallagher called Fred L. Black to the stand. Gallagher found Black much more forthcoming in his answers than Cameron, but then Black stayed on safer terrain: the *Independent*'s circulation numbers. Mail subscriptions dropped from 648,009 at the start of the Sapiro articles to 571,575 when the articles ended. Black could not account for the number of copies distributed through car dealers, newsstands, post offices, or "Ford agencies." Nor could he confirm the plaintiff's reports that free copies of the prune article were circulated in California's Santa Clara Valley, the tobacco articles in Kentucky and Tennessee, the hay article in Yakima and Walla Walla, and the cotton article across the South. He acknowledged having had "some part" in the publication of *The International Jew*, although Reed fought to exclude that testimony. Gallagher then introduced Peteet's 1924 correspondence with the *Independent* and asked Black to relate the events surrounding Peteet's September 24, 1924, meeting with newspaper staff. Unlike the *Independent*'s correspondence with A. C. Cherry, however, Raymond permitted Gallagher to enter these letters into evidence. Gallagher asserted that Peteet's letter notified Ford "to stop publishing the Sapiro series." Reed countered that there was "no showing" that the letter "ever came into the hands of Mr. Ford." Gallagher was ready: "I do not maintain that he read it; it probably was read by Mr. Liebold. Mr. Ford reads very few letters. I understand that is part of the job of Mr. Liebold." Judge Raymond stopped the bickering by adjourning until Monday morning.[45]

In its first week and a half, aside from James Martin Miller's revelations, the trial had produced few startling moments. Reed had not yet made much of an impression; he left most of the heavy lifting to Hanley and came to life only briefly, during Miller's and Black's appearances on the stand. The press devoted its coverage of the second weekend's recess to the same subject it had

7.5. Janet and Aaron Sapiro departing the federal courthouse during the libel lawsuit (from the Collections of The Henry Ford, 90.1.1940.13/THF101588).

during the first weekend: the timing of Ford's visit to the stand. Gallagher let it emerge in an interview on Saturday, March 26, that he intended to present his case as quickly as possible to force the defense to put on theirs. Presumably, Sapiro's time on the stand would be limited, and so, too, would Ford's, under the assumption that Judge Raymond would continue to observe the federal rules that prevented attorneys from cross-examining their own witnesses. The defense did not anticipate using Reed, its big gun, on Sapiro; rather, Hanley would cross-examine him. As a result, Gallagher said, he anticipated calling the chief "foes" in the case as soon as Tuesday, March 29. The *New York Times* pointed out that Ford had no reason to worry that he would suffer a repeat of his experience in the *Tribune* case. Sapiro sent his friend Lewis Strauss some press clippings with a sardonic note: "It's *war* here—and I don't know whether I am going to come home on my shield or with it!"[46]

On Sunday evening, the *Los Angeles Times* carried an Associated Press story in which Gallagher said he expected to finish Black's testimony promptly Monday morning, examine Sapiro for an hour, and then call Ford. All indications from the plaintiff, then, were that Ford was likely to be forced to go to the post office, ascend to the fourth floor like any citizen, and swear the witness oath by Tuesday or Wednesday at the latest. Gallagher signaled as much to Longley with a March 28 letter requesting that Ford bring a group of documents when he appeared to testify. But Ford was not just another citizen; he was one of the nation's most "prominent men," and he would come to court guarded by one hundred federal agents. Because he had yet to appear in court, his absence drew no comment on Monday, March 28—the morning after his fateful "accident" on Michigan Avenue.[47]

The trial proceeded with no sign that anything was amiss. The lawyers argued over the admissibility of the amended declaration. Even though Gallagher agreed to drop 54 of the 141 libels from his complaint, the defense countered that all 141 had been read to the jury and evidence had been admitted to substantiate some of the deleted libels. Accordingly, Reed and Hanley argued, the jury would be prejudiced by their exclusion. Raymond ruled that he would accept the amended declaration. The defense, as it had threatened over the weekend, filed a motion for mistrial, which Raymond rejected. Black then returned to the stand, where he discussed several management issues. He could not say for sure whether free copies were sent to Ford dealers in areas targeted by the articles. He always ran all consequential decisions past Liebold. All correspondence addressed to Ford, whether or not marked "personal," went to the mailing office for sorting, and the DPC never made a profit. Reed leapt to his feet at this last statement but was dismissed. Gallagher insisted that the DPC's "poverty" revealed its dependence on "Mr. Henry Ford for his monthly contributions to keep it going." That financial dependence, Gallagher maintained, established that Ford was responsible for what the newspaper published.

Raymond then excluded letters from cooperative officials questioning Dunn's facts and conclusions as the series ran. This correspondence, Gallagher argued vainly, gave the defendants "notice of the unreliable character of Dunn as an informant . . . [thus proving] their malice in continuing publications of which he was the author."[48]

Unable to introduce evidence of protests from outside the Ford organization, Gallagher had to content himself with getting Black on the record as to his own investigations. The witness downplayed the significance of the legwork he conducted before the lawsuit. He acknowledged visiting Chicago; talking to American Farm Bureau Federation officials, including J. W. Coverdale and Oscar Bradfute (two of Sapiro's bitterest enemies); and engaging in the "gathering of documents and various information." But he declared he had not "made any special assortment of letters of that kind." He also hired McCall as a special agent. He could not recall, however, any of the exhibits attached to Sapiro's demand for retraction, nor could he find the complete version of the document as subpoenaed by the plaintiff for trial. Wearily, Hanley agreed to stipulate that all the defendants had been served with the demand for retraction and received the exhibits that came with it. The relevance of this line of questioning became obvious a moment later when Black told the court that he sent the *Independent*'s copy of Sapiro's demand to Liebold rather than to Ford. "Why?" asked Gallagher. "Because I did not take things like that up with Mr. Ford," Black answered. Having heard how the chain of command worked in the Ford organization, Raymond then permitted Gallagher to introduce Peteet's letter to Ford of September 9, 1924—a tactical victory as important as Miller's testimony. Reed demanded to know why: "The evidence thus far is that Mr. Ford never saw this letter." "There is evidence," Judge Raymond ruled, "that it came [in]to the possession of his general secretary." That was sufficient for him. Reed tried to distinguish personal and corporate correspondence, but to no avail; the letter was read to show that Ford knew, as of September 1924, that the published series had raised serious objections in the minds of those it mentioned.[49]

After the court took a two-hour lunch break, Gallagher sought unsuccessfully to admit each of the exhibits that Sapiro attached to his demand for retraction. Finally, Gallagher asked Black whether he had, "during the course of your connection with the Dearborn Independent, . . . from time to time, met Henry Ford?" He had, "occasionally." Had they talked about the *Independent*'s policies? "In a very general way." Had they discussed such policies as related to "the Jewish Exploitation of Farmers' Organizations articles?" "Not prior to the beginning of suit," Black said. He never talked to Ford about the articles, about any of the letters the *Independent* received about the articles, or about any of the exhibits that came across his desk as the articles were published. With that, Gallagher dismissed him. The defense declined to question him. Although the court refused to admit the demand for retraction and its enclosures, Gallagher was then permitted to read at length from the articles themselves, with Hanley objecting frequently. At last, Gallagher rose to his feet. "Mr. Sapiro," he called.[50]

. . .

"The little black-haired, soft-voiced Chicagoan" rose from the plaintiff's table, a rolled-up sheet of paper in his hand, and strode to the witness stand. He turned, faced the court deputy, smiled, and took his oath. The *New York Times* sketched his appearance on the stand:

Naturally, years of court experiences had eradicated any court nervousness in the bearing of the plaintiff. He was calm, but alert—alert with a peculiar quality all his own, sharp, black eyes darting about and never resting long on anybody or anything, color blind eyes by the way; a wan, intellectual face, extremely mobile in registration of the thoughts that seem to be tumbling one after another back of his high, square forehead, and thin-veined hands tensely folded in his lap—hands, for all their repose, that actually suggested that they, too, were vigilant.

The Associated Press echoed that description: "Sapiro, keenly black-eyed, alert, slim, and swarthy, leaned far forward in the witness chair, hands grasping a roll of paper in his lap. A vivid flush spread over his face as he crackled answers to his counsel's volley of questions."[51]

For all he knew, he was the only Jew in the courtroom. He may have preferred it that way. For he alone had taken on Henry Ford. No one had stepped forward to share the burden. The expensive litigation had overwhelmed his considerable financial reserves. A few trusted friends advanced him money to get him through the discovery process. Now, as his attorney approached to begin the rapid-fire direct examination they planned, the spotlight turned solely on him. They would throw off the defense—and finally engage the jury—with the gripping saga of his desperate childhood and his professional success.[52]

Gallagher proceeded to elicit Sapiro's life story efficiently while Reed, sitting "almost at Mr. Sapiro's feet," took notes and Hanley objected at nearly every turn. The defense sought to exclude his military service during the war (which the judge finally admitted), his children (whom he could not discuss), and anything that demonstrated his "fidelity . . . to American principles." Although Sapiro later complained that the judge expunged all talk of his war record, he was in fact allowed to tell the jury how doggedly he sought to put on a military uniform. His calm demeanor on the stand drew rave reviews: "All the time he was polite and courteous and smiling and patient. There was something calm, serene about Sapiro as the story flowed from him in his soft, even, rather high pitched tone. He did not show any resentment, even when Senator Reed tried to block his war record. And as he told it, it was a commonplace thing, nothing to boast about."[53]

Sapiro and Gallagher worked so smoothly and quickly together that it produced a complaint from Reed: the witness supplied answers before defense counsel could register objections. When Reed asked the court to instruct Sapiro to answer more slowly, Gallagher seized the chance: "Either more deliberation or more speed on the Senator," he said, zooming into his next question while Raymond stared stonily at the top of his bench and Reed glanced at the jury. Sapiro ended the day by describing his work organizing tobacco, wheat, cotton, and potatoes. That work, he said, largely ended in 1924, but an explanation for that turn of events had to wait until the next day. Still, Sapiro seemed exultant, "confident that if allowed to explain these affairs in his own way he could show that the attacks on him by the *Independent* were libelous and that he would win the million dollar verdict which has become his goal." At day's end, Gallagher told the press that the rest of Sapiro's direct examination would take only about an hour and a half. After cross-examination—its length, Reed said, depended on Sapiro—Ford would be called next.[54]

On March 29, Sapiro continued to describe the rise of cooperatives under his direction during the early 1920s. The highlights of his career as the movement's premier legal advocate included his appearances in the U.S. Supreme Court and in the supreme courts of fifteen states, as well as his uniform state cooperative marketing statute. Gallagher then led Sapiro through an account of his California organizing days. The witness carefully pointed out that the fundamental principles of cooperative marketing, including such California innovations as the ironclad contract, were not his invention: "I did not evolve any new ideas at all." He acknowledged that it was his insight to organize by commodity rather than by locality. It was also his idea that member contracts should include enforcement clauses, such as "the right of injunction and specific performance." In describing the troubles of the California tomato growers during the war, Sapiro testified, he "appealed futilely to numerous persons for help until Senator Reed was asked to assist." Upon hearing that Reed indeed tendered assistance, Gallagher asked, "Was he one of those 'gentile fronts' referred to in the *Dearborn Independent*?" Before Sapiro could answer, Reed interjected, "I didn't know at the time who I was representing." The courtroom burst into laughter, which an annoyed Raymond quieted with his gavel.[55] The crowd may have found Reed's embarrassment amusing, but it forced Reed to distance himself from the service he rendered to a Jewish constituent.

The press continued to remark on Sapiro's modesty, his lack of anger and bitterness, and composure on the stand. He summarized how the appearance of the articles had damaged his law practice in cooperative organizing: his net income dropped precipitously, only two new farmers' groups asked him to form cooperatives after the series began, and only three established cooperatives continued to retain him. After a lengthy and detailed discussion of Sapiro's legal work, including his extensive appellate practice defending the uniform statute, the court held, again over defense counsel objections, that he qualified as an expert who could testify about the business practices of the associations and the marketing issues associated with the various crops. Gallagher then asked his client to tell the court his annual income over the course of his career. In 1916, he earned $10,000 in fees; by 1920, the year of his stunning performance in Birmingham, Alabama, that amount had tripled. Two years later it doubled again, to $61,000, and held steady at nearly that level through 1924. Thereafter, his income dropped sharply, to $42,300 in 1925 and to $42,900 in 1926. After Sapiro agreed to provide a list of all the cooperatives that had sought or used his services, Gallagher turned to Senator Reed: "You may take the witness."[56]

When the senator took charge of Sapiro's cross-examination, it was the surest outward sign that the Ford legal team knew how considerably the stakes in the case had changed since Sunday night. There was no longer any reason to hold the biggest gun out of action. Ford's lawyers hoped that Reed could break Sapiro.

Reed started by reviewing Sapiro's partnerships, fees, and records. He wanted to know how much Robert Marx and William Lynch were being paid, as they were not full partners in Sapiro's firm. Reed then reviewed Sapiro's practice history, beginning with his admission to the California bar in 1911, trying to rattle him over dates, case names, and exact fee amounts from those early years. Such trivia did not ruffle Sapiro. Reed tried to provoke him when he could not produce account books from those years:

REED: [D]id you destroy or make away with your books of account?

SAPIRO: I have never made away with a book of account in my life.

REED: I did not ask you that. I asked you what you did in this case. You say you have not got them. What became of them?

SAPIRO: I have not any idea.

This accusation drew the first show of anger: "Mr. Sapiro's face flushed and his snapping black eyes fairly blazed. His tone, however, was courteously smooth as he replied." Reed had only twenty minutes with him before the end of the day intervened. Rumors that Ford had been sighted in the courtroom around

7.6. Editorial cartoon lampooning participants in the libel trial, heavily emphasizing Aaron Sapiro's Jewish appearance, and depicting Henry Ford as a hapless victim rather than the powerful instigator, *Detroit Free Press*, March 24, 1927 (by F. S. Nixon, reprinted by permission of the *Detroit Free Press*).

midafternoon—a prank played by local reporters on "gullible court attaches," the *Detroit Times* gleefully recounted—proved unfounded, but not before stirring up spectators and photographers.[57]

Tuesday's restlessness permeated Wednesday's courthouse atmosphere as well. Reed resumed a steady, "grueling" pace in his interrogation, one the witness returned in kind. Tendentiously verifying prior testimony, Reed reviewed Sapiro's legal fees and the dozens of cooperatives from which he had earned them. The issues were dry, technical, and uninteresting to everyone except the principals. Reed sought to parry Sapiro's claim that the articles damaged him by showing, for example, that his income could have declined for other reasons: the cooperatives "had gone out of business"; Sapiro "neglected" his clients; or the entire "plan and scheme" of cooperative marketing collapsed. Indeed, "Senator Reed gave particular attention to bringing out that various farmers' cooperative marketing associations that Sapiro formed have failed." Gallagher seemed unworried. He had so little to do, he told a reporter, "that he had to rise to make an objection to get a chance to stretch his legs." For his part, the plaintiff took seriously the task of defending his organizations and his work. "Sapiro doffed his armor of impetuousness and sparkling temperament," the Associated Press dispatch read, "and met the suave, insinuating thrusts of Reed with an urbane equanimity." The day was "devoid of fireworks," observed the *New York Times*, but the writer was referring to what took place in front of the judge.[58] Outside the courthouse, reporters were getting wind of real fireworks, and those fuses were already lit.

Word of Ford's hospitalization leaked on Wednesday morning. By afternoon, Cameron's statement about the accident was in the hands of a press corps increasingly rabid for information. At 9:15 p.m., Ford's physicians released a terse, three-sentence bulletin about his condition. The following morning, the newspapers led with the story of the accident and pushed the trial to inside pages. Speculation about when Ford would appear at court, and in what condition, ratcheted up the public's emotional investment in the case and its outcome.[59]

Sapiro's third day of cross-examination began with all the appearance of normalcy. Reed picked up from where he had left off the day before. The two attorneys matched each other carefully. Reed kept his questions measured and limited, so as to elicit only the information from the witness that he wanted; for his part, Sapiro used every opportunity to point out when a question was flawed, unanswerable, or required extended explanation. For example, Reed

242 LITIGANTS AND LOSERS

asked Sapiro to confirm that he organized growers into locals that then delivered their crops to larger cooperative associations. No, Sapiro replied patiently, that was not correct. The locals were formed "at the initiative of the growers themselves." What happened after that, he explained, depended on the type of commodity being produced:

SAPIRO: [I]f it were whole milk, for example, that would be localized; if it were a commodity which had to be packed, or which had to be treated in some local way, such as butter or potatoes, then you would form locals and federate the locals.

REED: Now, I am trying to get the first one.

SAPIRO: I am giving you this as a full answer. . . . .

REED: I am simply trying to get this as it is, Mr. Sapiro.

SAPIRO: I am trying to explain it to you as it is.

REED: Yes, but I want to get it my way.

GALLAGHER: Well, I object to the—

REED: I am just trying to be nice with the witness and explain.

THE COURT: I think we are getting along very nicely, if we confine ourselves to questions and answers.

REED: Yes.

Reed was trying to imply that Sapiro proactively appeared on the scene to shepherd growers into cooperatives, wherever they lived and regardless of what they produced. Sapiro deflected that insinuation by distinguishing spontaneous movements by farmers, on the one hand, from the kind of coordinated legal assistance he was called in to provide, on the other hand. After the court's rebuke, Reed ceased arguing with Sapiro over these sorts of answers during this line of questioning.[60]

The brokered peace did not last long, however. When Reed read a letter Sapiro wrote in 1921 to George Jewett about organizing the Northwest Wheat Growers, he inadvertently ignited another sharp disagreement:

REED (*Reading*): "Mailing plan for central agency followed by Rio Grande Growers Exchange which will best suit needs of Northwest Group. Also please go over this with Garrich and adopt."

SAPIRO: "And adapt."

GALLAGHER: Wait a minute.

SAPIRO: I am going to ask you to read it correctly, Mr. Reed.

REED: I what?

SAPIRO: I am going to ask you to read it correctly. It says, "and adapt."

GALLAGHER: It does not say "adopt."

REED: That is true, it is "adapt." What did I say, "adopt"?

SAPIRO: "Adopt."

REED: ["The Senator looked over his tortoise-rimmed glasses at the witness."] Very
well, you distinguish between "adapt" and "adopt"?

SAPIRO: ["Shortly"] Any man does.[61]

Their pointed repartee amused the national press: "Sapiro was too quick
for his questioner, who had difficulty in remembering the long and numerous association titles. The witness, himself a lawyer, smiled indulgently as he
prompted the white-haired veteran of the Senate. In one instance he even suggested a question which he thought would help Reed bring out the point he
had in mind. The senator, however, ignored the proffered aid." Sapiro knew
just what he was doing: "[Reed] had a trick of asking 'double' questions and
he kept me on my guard all the time to cut these double questions in two; and
that would make him pretty 'sore'—for lawyers, including myself, don't like to
have the witness breaking in and correcting them in that way."[62]

Local papers painted a darker picture of the plaintiff's time on the stand.
Harry Bennett, Ford's security chief, was feeding slanted coverage to cronies
at the *Detroit Times*, a Hearst syndicate newspaper. Detroit readers learned, for
example, that Reed's "merciless curiosity" and "oratorical guns" got Sapiro to
admit that he received large fees for securing War Finance Corporation loans
for the wheat and cotton growers. The *Detroit Times* neglected to mention that
Sapiro's fee from the wheat growers, $5,000, represented 1 percent of the total
loan amount. The national papers pointed out that Reed cherry-picked the
record, asking only about organizations that failed, and when it came time for
Sapiro's redirect examination, he would doubtless argue that most of the cooperatives he formed failed "because the rules he laid down were not followed."[63]

The day's big news broke into the trial during the morning. After a brief recess
and a sidebar conference with the lead attorneys, Judge Raymond addressed the
jury. One of the morning papers—he did not specify, but most likely *Detroit
Times*—published a report that "an agent of the U.S. Court" was investigating the relationship between Ford's accident and the libel case. That report,

Raymond declared, "is utterly without foundation," and the jury was to disregard any statement implying that the federal court was involved with any investigation of Ford's accident. Raymond did not sequester the jury in this case, despite its high profile, because, for one reason, it was a civil case, not involving the death penalty; for another, the government was nearly broke. As it was, the district attorney lacked the money even to pay the Ford jurors their daily fees, and the court was relying on their goodwill in proceeding without pay until Congress appropriated funds. Such distractions were minor compared to the question that mattered most: when would Ford come to court? At day's end on Thursday, Gallagher told the press that he intended to seek a court order for an independent medical examination to confirm Ford's condition. Gallagher indicated that he might also demand the defense proceed with its case if Ford could not appear when summoned.[64] If that option was unpalatable to Reed and Longley, they could either take a postponement or keep Sapiro on the stand and forestall Ford's appearance as long as possible.

The defense did not tip its hand the next morning, April 1. Instead, Sapiro and Reed continued their sharp exchanges, with neither side showing any sign of relenting. Reed asked Sapiro to account for his presence in Texas in spring 1921: "You were still down there, were you not?" Sapiro jumped on the adverb: "I was down there, but not 'still,' if you are trying to convey the thought I was down there through the whole period." Reed: "I do not mean to convey any thought except that you were down there in the month of April, 1921." "'Then,' I would say, now, instead of 'Still.'" "Very well," Reed replied; "have it your way." "No," Sapiro responded, "but I want to get it right." At that, Reed turned to the judge: "The witness is constantly haggling over questions here, in a perfectly astounding manner to me, and trying to draw fine distinctions. I have been perfectly plain with him, and I have accepted his corrections, and tried to go on. I want to go on now." Reed's use of the word *haggling* was probably not an accident; it served to remind the jury, unsubtly, of Sapiro's Jewishness. Raymond sought to calm Reed: "I think the question has been answered." But Gallagher would not permit the moment to pass unchallenged: "I do not think it is proper for Mr. Reed to criticize this witness, in this particular instance, especially." Raymond acknowledged that "in this particular instance," Sapiro's clarification was "justified." Reed did not argue with the judge.[65]

Reed spent the day largely on the cotton industry, Sapiro's speech to the 1920 Birmingham cotton meeting, and the location and operation of Sapiro's law offices. "It becomes patent," the *Chicago Tribune* concluded, "that the Ford side is going to show that Sapiro organized some of the large groups, such as cotton growers, under a plan by which their product must be delivered to the association and that the association, disposing of its holdings on a so much a month basis, would borrow from the bankers giving the notes secured by the products on hand. As one of Ford's counsel put it, 'when you've got the output mortgaged to the bankers—who controls it?'" Laying out this complex theory was putting a strain on Reed. At the start of the day, he asked the judge's permission to sit rather than stand while questioning the witness; even granted that privilege, he found himself unable to keep pace with Sapiro's rapid answers, on which he was also taking notes. The testimony was so detailed and technical—different crops required lengthy explanations about how they were grown, processed, and marketed—that Sapiro sought to establish goodwill with the jury: "I do not want to give the appearance of even attempting to evade," he said. But his insistence on clarifying and explaining his answers, rather than simply replying yes or no, added tension to what was an inherently hostile relationship with Reed. Evading usual court protocol, Sapiro addressed Reed directly when he didn't like how something was going:

REED: At this same time that you got the money for them—
SAPIRO: I never got the money.
REED: Now I think we might, if your Honor please, quit quibbling about that.
SAPIRO: I think you should.
GALLAGHER: There is no testimony at all, of course, before us, that he did [get any money].
REED: I submit the witness'[s] conduct is improper.
THE COURT: I think it is more proper to just ask another question and proceed. . . .
   I think everybody in the court room understands the meaning of both parties.

The court adjourned for the weekend early to permit Sapiro to catch a train to Chicago, where he tended to his neglected law practice and visited his family. Just after the trial began, two of his young children contracted scarlet fever.[66]

   Over the weekend, the national newspapers reviewed Sapiro's performance favorably. An Associated Press dispatch that ran in the *Washington Post* and *Los Angeles Times* described his "story of struggle and reward" and his "remarkable accomplishments in a virgin field." The story concluded that Sapiro held his own during cross-examination: "Blunt questions and insinuations have been answered readily, without signs of wriggling by the quick-witted Sapiro, who says his reputation was injured by articles printed in Ford's Dearborn Independent." The ordeal was far from over, bemoaned a *New York Times* reporter: "Something approaching old age may overtake Aaron Sapiro on the witness stand in his suit . . . if the plans for his cross-examination are carried through on schedule." Once Reed finished laying the remains of dead cooperatives at Sapiro's feet, the article explained, Gallagher would "escort the jury over the same thing again" to "clear his client of the 'deaths' of the many cooperatives which have gone out of existence." The issue of antisemitic libel was falling further and further to the side, as the defense kept the focus squarely on Sapiro's law practice and on the amount of money he made in this "virgin field."[67]

The weekend also brought the news that the Wayne County prosecutor, Robert M. Toms, had decided to accept the report of the Ford organization investigators regarding the March 27 accident. Once Harry Bennett's team concluded that the accident was unintentional, "not by design," Toms saw no reason to "duplicate their efforts." "I shall assume that they have made an adequate and thorough investigation," Toms announced, "and I shall accept their findings that it was an accident." In an extraordinary abdication of official responsibility, he deferred to Ford's agents on the grounds that "they had every motive to get at the bottom of the thing." They also had every motive to hide something, or to create appearance of something where nothing existed. Toms's willingness to permit Bennett to draw a sheet over the accident scene meant that there would be no independent inquiry into what happened that night, no official scrutiny of Ford's story, and no corroboration of what the witnesses saw. Everyone in Detroit—from the judge on down—was willing to take Ford's word for it that he had been in an accident, that he had been injured, that the accident was unrelated to the lawsuit, and that he would testify when he deemed himself fit to appear. "Had Mr. Ford been fortunate enough to escape injury he probably would be summoned to the witness chair some day next week," speculated the *New York Times*, estimating that fully ten days would pass before Ford would be well enough to testify. Rumors such as those so enraged Ford, the *Detroit Times* reported on April 4, that he vowed to appear "splinted and bandaged if called." It was the *New York Times*, not the local papers, that reported the presence of Harry Bennett in the federal courthouse on a daily basis during the trial's second week. Ostensibly there to guard the mounting depositions and other documents that were set aside in a room for the defense's use, he was also in charge of "a small army" of "detectives, guards, watch-men, and the like" from the "protective branch of the Ford organization." The detectives "also maintain a watch on the spectators who attend the trial daily. Some of the spectators . . . have become, unwittingly, objects of close scrutiny by the sleuths. So far, no 'suspicious characters' have been located."[68] This cloak-and-dagger characterization suggested that the seriousness of purpose with which the trial began was disintegrating into spectacle as the proceedings dragged on.

On Monday, the session of court began with the admission to local practice of Milton Sapiro, newly arrived in Detroit with his brother's law firm records. After taking his oath, the younger Sapiro joined Gallagher at the plaintiff's table, where the two attorneys listened as Reed continued to hammer away at the matter of legal fees, supposedly an objective measure of how Sapiro "exploited the farmers." All told, between 1922 and 1927 the cotton growers paid Sapiro $70,000; shorn of explanation, that figure seemed huge. Reed "sought to get the witness to admit" that an associate helping him organize New Jersey's wheat growers "had drummed up" a meeting in 1921 and that he refused to represent the New Jersey organization "because [he] did not get any fee." Rather, Sapiro contended, "'I was interested in the welfare of the farmers . . . and I say that in view of all of your insinuations.'" Their interaction grew personal, driving Sapiro to "rebuke" Reed for mispronouncing his name: "'You have used it correctly any number of times. I particularly dislike Sap-eye-ro; there is no such name. I prefer Sap-ee-ro.'" Reed apologized, and at the end of the day he "frankly admitted he was tired." Adding to his burdens, Gallagher publicly confirmed that Ford would be his next witness, news that dovetailed with reports that Ford was quickly regaining his strength. Otherwise it was a "lack-lustre" day, spent reading speeches, letters, and other records into evidence. "'They do no harm, and they do no good,'" Gallagher complained in court. "'They merely clutter up the record. At this rate we will be here for years.'"[69]

On April 7, the Ford lawyers began the day with a private conference with Judge Raymond. They refused to answer questions about the discussion, leading the press to speculate that the meeting concerned Ford's availability. "His physicians," the *New York Times* commented, "were having a hard time keeping him indoors." In contrast, the two Sapiro children remained seriously ill, and their father again left Detroit for Chicago immediately after court adjourned for the weekend to see them.[70]

7.7. Henry Ford and Harry Bennett in Bennett's office at the Ford Motor Company, September 1945 (from the Collections of The Henry Ford, THF24029).

Over the weekend, the Detroit newspapers continued to tell a different story about the trial than the national press. The locals painted Sapiro's testimony in a critical light, showcasing correspondence in which he appeared to threaten to sue the Minnesota potato growers if they did not pay him a "reasonable" fee. Quoting an unnamed source said to be one of Ford's "closest friends," the *Detroit Times* emphasized that Ford remained a "very sick man," unable to walk, and unlikely to attend court for weeks "unless he is carried in on a stretcher." The source was Harry Bennett, who was feeding information to William K. Hutchinson, a Hearst reporter covering the trial for the *Detroit Times*. No other major newspapers ran Bennett's dire reports. Instead, they issued Clifford Longley's update that Ford "makes daily progress and that he is impatient to resume his habit of wandering through his plants 'keeping in touch with things.'" Reporters were growing skeptical: "The fact [is] that only one person, other than members of his family, actually is known to have seen him since [the accident]," the *Los Angeles Times* remarked. "That is Dr. Roy McClure."[71] There was, in fact, another person, not a member of the family, who had been with Ford every day since his accident: Harry Bennett.

Lacking real news about Ford, the national press gave its readers an analysis of what Reed had and had not accomplished as Sapiro began his third week on the stand. The *New York Times* summarized the defense in one sentence: "The objective of the Senator's attack thus far has been to show that Mr. Sapiro harvested fees and that his interest in the agriculturist was commercial and not humanitarian." Would the jury accept that claim as a defense against libel? When testimony resumed, Reed planned to finish his inquiries on the potato industry and then turn to tobacco, "admittedly the field of Mr. Sapiro's greatest labors in the organization of farmers' cooperative marketing associations." As he said in his opening statement, Reed intended to show that Sapiro put together a deal to sell tobacco warehouses to cooperatives for $2 million more than they were worth. But as the discovery process revealed, the warehouses in question did not exist at the time Dunn alleged they were sold. That the defense still sought to prove that allegation promised more excitement.[72]

On Monday, April 11, recognizing that he had so far failed to reveal Sapiro as a ruthless exploiter of naive farmers, Reed decided to provoke a sudden "explosion" with a question about the Indiana Onion Growers' Association. "Now," Reed asked deliberately, "so as not to waste any time on that, did you get some fees out of it?" Sapiro "stiffened" and "a tide of red swept over his pale face" as he snapped: "I won't waste any time on it." Judge Raymond sharply instructed the witness to confine himself to yes or no answers and to cooperate, describing the witness's behavior as "grossly improper." At that, Gallagher leapt to his feet. As his lawyer and judge debated, Sapiro sat stiffly in his chair, seething at the reproof he had drawn, while Reed and the Ford lawyers sat at the defense table, smiling. Asserting that the judge's comments had prejudiced the jury against his client, Gallagher asked for a mistrial, but Raymond refused.[73]

The plaintiff got a measure of revenge the following day. A deputy sheriff served Ernest Liebold with a witness subpoena at last. As had his boss, Liebold had evaded process servers for months. The opportune moment presented itself when, ironically, his Ford sedan stalled while he was on his way to work. He was caught after a "thrilling . . . foot race" down a Dearborn city street. In court, Reed and Sapiro affected civility, but it was short lived. When Reed asked Sapiro to attest to Bernard Baruch's background as a "speculator on the Board of Trade," Gallagher successfully objected. Reed then asked Sapiro to describe Baruch's training as an economist. Sapiro replied that Baruch's service with the War Industries Board constituted "magnificent training," but that comment was stricken. Gallagher objected to the question as unrelated to anything raised on direct examination and was sustained. He also retaliated for the previous day's embarrassment; instead of agreeing to accept copies of documents for the record, as had been his practice so far in the trial, he began insisting on legal originals of everything the defense introduced: "By that method he kept out several letters which under the previous procedure would have gone in."[74]

On Wednesday April 13, the trial returned to what spectators saw as its primary obligation: providing entertainment. The topic was tobacco, the defense's "'biggest gun.'" The fraudulent warehouse transaction, if substantiated, the *Detroit Times* reported, would "prove [Sapiro] exploited American farmers as was charged in the Ford's [*sic*] *Dearborn Independent*."[75]

Instead, the defense mishandled the tobacco evidence and committed its worst mistake of the trial. Reed decided to introduce part of a speech Sapiro delivered in Kentucky in 1921. To the surprise of everyone present, one of the jurors, Amor Durat, rose and asked for the entire speech to "be read in full." Durat, a retired Detroit accountant, was the juror thought to be Catholic by the Ford jury researchers; the *New York Times* reported he had "leanings toward Christian Science." He also owned a Ford car. He never got the chance to explain whether he was merely curious or distrusted the defense lawyers. It is an axiom of American trial practice that jurors do not speak in court. Judge Raymond quickly explained that no juror had the authority to make such a request, but the tide had turned. At his client's urging, Gallagher insisted that the full speech be read, and the judge agreed. Reluctantly, Stewart Hanley and Richard Higgins took turns delivering the speech. It took them three and a half hours; the task left them hoarse and exhausted. The speech triumphantly recounted cooperation's rise in California, the rescue of the fruit industries from near ruin, and the promise of prosperity to the Kentucky tobacco farmers. Delivering it from the defense table not only put the plaintiff's ideas into the record through the mouths of the defense lawyers but also spared the plaintiff an afternoon's questioning. Sapiro's joy enticed him to overstatement: "Before [Hanley] could realize it, he had unwittingly gotten into the swing of it and he was delivering that speech to the jury far more effectively than I could ever have done it." Even the *Detroit Times*, normally sympathetic to Ford, could not comment positively: "The trial rather flivvered during the last week."[76]

"More droning for [the] record" was the *New York Times*'s description of the session. Reed spent the day trying doggedly to show that Sapiro "exploited" the tobacco growers, but Sapiro would not budge. Before the senator could gain further traction, he was interrupted by a pair of pigeons that flew in to the court through a high circular window. "It seemed as if the pigeons sympathized with Mr. Sapiro," the *New York Times* commented, "for every time the Senator raised his voice for a particularly important question the cooing would become almost a crooning." Reed spent two hours reading the minutes of the first meeting of the tobacco association and failed to produce clear proof of malfeasance. Reed further embarrassed himself when he asked Sapiro for documents only to have Gallagher remind him that they had already been introduced on direct examination. Sapiro was confident that his testimony showed that "the operation of the tobacco cooperatives was entirely above board, known to the public, and approved by the farmer members."[77]

The tobacco testimony was supposed to damn Sapiro by disclosing a conspiracy to defraud growers. Reed wanted to show that warehouse owners, rather than tobacco producers, controlled the cooperative and sold the warehouses fraudulently. He also was certain the cooperative was unable to pay Sapiro's fees because of gross mismanagement, not because of the articles. Instead, Sapiro testified that the growers authorized the purchase and conducted the transaction themselves subsequent to their vote. Deeds that Reed insinuated were acts of conspiracy that Sapiro kept secret from the cooperative's rank and file, it turned out, were broadly circulated across Kentucky by newspaper well in advance of the cooperative's 1923 sign-up campaign.[78]

The conflict between lawyer and witness quickly peaked. Reed tried to get Sapiro to admit that he had personally controlled the election of the officers of the Kentucky Burley Tobacco Growers' Association. "That is not so," Sapiro rejoined. Reed took off his glasses and turned in supplication to the court: "Now, if your Honor please, this witness can be more polite than that in his answers." Gallagher moved to strike Reed's remark, and the judge agreed. When Reed attempted to link Bernard Baruch to the conspiracy, Sapiro again defied him: "That is absolutely not so." Reed again complained: "The answer, I insist, is not only impolite, but is insulting and wholly uncalled for." The judge let the answer stand. By this time in the trial, Sapiro and Gallagher were monitoring Reed's nerves by observing how many times he missed the cuspidor and sprayed the female members of the jury. When Reed's spitting was off target two times out of five, Sapiro and Gallagher decided his composure was shot for the day. "You could almost see those women on the jury shudder," Sapiro later remarked; "they all looked like dear, lovely housekeepers, and you could imagine how they felt to see this going on right under their noses all the time."[79]

At the close of Thursday's session, court recessed until Monday, in view of the Good Friday holiday the following day. Everyone scattered for the long weekend. Judge Raymond left for his home in Grand Rapids, Senator Reed departed for Washington, D.C., and Higgins and Raymond Watson, his law partners, took a train to Kansas City. The Sapiro brothers returned to Chicago. The weekend produced little news, other than a prediction that Ford would take the stand within the week and a willingness to connect the accident to his absence from court. On April 18, the *New York Times* reported the "remarkably widespread belief that Mr. Ford would never be heard by the jury." Longley hastened to contradict that rumor, but he and Bennett were working at cross-purposes.[80]

As it turned out, it was not Ford's health that marked the turning point in the case but his chief counsel's. As Senator Reed rode the train back to Detroit on Sunday evening, he "suffered an attack of indigestion." His Pullman car sat atop "'flat wheels,'" making for an uncomfortable ride that disrupted his sleep. Instead of reporting to court the following day, he remained in bed at the Hotel Statler, attended by a Henry Ford hospital physician. The cross-examination had taken a toll on the defense's lead counsel: "Most of the time he has been on his feet and much of the time he has read long documents into the record. At times he has begged the court's consideration while he sat, and associates in the defense of Ford have saved him at others by reading." Although his colleagues insisted that he spent long hours outside of court preparing for trial,

7.8. Women jurors relaxing during a recess of the libel trial. Cora Hoffman, who became the subject of jury-tampering allegations and then gave a newspaper interview that caused a mistrial, stands third from right (from the Collections of The Henry Ford, 90.1.1940.8/THF101580).

Reed reportedly gave dinner speeches in Detroit and once drove to Ann Arbor to address University of Michigan alumni. Speaking through Ford company publicists, the senator downplayed the seriousness of his ailment: "I simply had a little pain in my stomach and felt I should not attend court this morning."[81]

Harry Bennett seized the opening and ordered his "small army" of detectives into action. They supplied reports to Longley and Hanley, who presented them to Judge Raymond. Late on the afternoon of Monday, April 18, a federal marshal escorted juror number 11—Cora Hoffman, "a pleasant-faced woman in her thirties"—into Judge Raymond's chambers. He questioned her for forty-five minutes about the information the Ford detectives had gathered: a relative of hers, who happened to be a Ford employee, heard her say before the trial "that she would not vote for a verdict [favorable] to Mr. Ford no matter how long the case went on." Raymond promptly ordered his marshal to conduct an official inquiry; the marshal notified the Detroit office of the Bureau of Investigation of the U.S. Department of Justice. The bureau opened an investigation. The following morning's papers reported that the defense planned to seek a mistrial.[82]

Back in court on Tuesday morning, Longley reported the lead defense counsel's continuing indisposition and suggested that Stewart Hanley take over the cross-examination in Reed's place. Gallagher would not agree. He wanted the court to address the accusations against Hoffman immediately. Further, he did not intend to give the defense an excuse: "We prefer to have the case stand over until the man in charge of the matter may himself be upon the ground, so there will be no alibi or excuse for the collapse of the defense." At that, a snort issued from the defense table, and Clifford Longley rose to his feet. Judge Raymond then excused the jury, which "had been sitting rather open-mouthed throughout the discussion." After the jury left the room, Longley, red with anger, resumed his protest. "Pardon me just a minute," he said, "but I want an objection on the record to Mr. Gallagher's use of the words 'collapse of the defense,' here." Smiling "benignly," Gallagher gave a withering retort: "Perhaps the defense cannot collapse, when it has never been maintained, so I may be wrong in that respect."[83]

Gallagher had more to condemn on the defense side. Since the trial began, he declared, "the intelligence department of the Ford Motor Company has been very greatly represented in the court room and the corridors of this building." The Ford detectives mingled not only with spectators "but among the jury," Gallagher continued, "and instances have been reported to us where these men were talking with the jury, whether to learn the jury's attitude or to influence the jury's attitude, we don't know." He implored the judge to order the defense lawyers to have all their detectives "refrain from contact with these jurors." "Just a minute," Raymond interjected. "Have you any evidence that anyone has talked with the jurors about this case?" None that he could offer in court, Gallagher acknowledged, merely verbal reports. Reminded that he was obligated to substantiate charges of jury tampering, Gallagher responded that unlike his opponents he did not have an army of staff at his command: "Mr. Sapiro and our associates and I are here alone. We have nobody on the outside. We are here in the court room fighting our battle in the court room and no place else." Although the judge had warned the jurors not to talk, Gallagher argued that they might not realize that a "casual conversation with some bystander" might influence them. To enable Reed to recover, the judge had excused the jury for another two days; Gallagher demanded that the judge use that time to rein in the Ford detectives. Raymond saw the matter in a somewhat different light. Until he saw evidence of such misconduct, the judge was not inclined to issue any order or to declare a mistrial. Gallagher then accused Raymond of discussing the Hoffman matter with Ford's counsel in chambers without him present. Raymond contradicted that account: "Counsel has twice been requested to come to chambers . . . and has refused to come." The judge had no intention of settling that argument in public: "'I do not want to enter into any controversy with you,' returned the judge; 'you are invited now.'" The plaintiff and all the lawyers then moved into chambers, where they remained for about an hour. They met again in chambers in midafternoon. Upon leaving the courthouse, no one involved spoke to the press. "'I have given my word that I would not say anything,' said Sapiro."[84]

Someone else was willing to talk. That afternoon, Cora Hoffman gave an interview to a reporter for the *Detroit Times* who came to her home on Fourteenth Avenue in Detroit. The reporter was William Hutchinson; Harry Bennett had supplied him with her address. The paper published Hoffman's interview that night. Upset about the accusations leveled against her, Hoffman angrily denied ever having expressed prejudice toward Ford and contended that she had maintained her silence throughout the trial. In an indiscrete outburst, she confirmed the defense's fears that it had already lost: "'It looks to me as if certain people were trying to get hold of something to have the case thrown out of court.'" As soon as the night edition hit the streets, the Ford lawyers took a copy to Judge Raymond; he promptly declared that the interview "constituted contempt of court and that he would proceed against the newspaper."[85]

The following day, the defense pursued its mistrial motion with renewed vigor. Longley unveiled fourteen affidavits—all signed by Ford detectives, many of whom also worked as Wayne County deputy sheriffs—alleging a bevy of offenses by Hoffman, including perjury. Instead of owning a plumbing business, one affidavit charged, her husband actually operated a "blind pig," an illegal saloon. She had in fact expressed prejudice against "'Old Man Ford'" but concealed it to be selected for jury service. According to the press, these episodes antedated the start of the trial and were not reported to the court when they were discovered; instead, the Ford counsel reported them to the judge in their private conference with him on the morning of April 7. But if the Ford jury researchers knew these facts before voir dire, they neglected to note them on Cora Hoffman's survey card. All that was recorded about her was that she was "not very well liked among neighbors. Husband [is a] plumbing and heating contractor."[86]

Those issues mattered less than a relationship Hoffman apparently had with Joseph Miller, something the detectives discerned from conversations they observed at the courthouse. In her interview, Hoffman identified Miller as a real estate broker to whom she wanted to sell property she and her husband owned. The Ford agents called him "Kid Miller," a name invented, Sapiro concluded, "to make him sound tough." The agents also decided that Miller was Jewish. Unable to overhear their conversations, the detectives suspected him of offering Hoffman "'thousands.'" One Ford agent, Frank R. Gervaise, visited the "alleged 'blind pig'" and talked to Hoffman's husband, who told Gervaise he advised his wife "to stand out for $15,000" and to treat the exchange as "a real estate transaction." The Ford agents then connected Miller to Sapiro, saying the two had been seen talking at the courthouse during the trial. On March 23, Hoffman accepted a "five pound box of candy" from Miller, presumably at Sapiro's instructions. These allegations, together with the *Detroit Times* interview, were more than enough to get Hoffman into trouble. When she appeared in court on Thursday, April 21, Hoffman "was wan and red-eyed," having spent the previous day undergoing close questioning by Department of Justice lawyers: "A tall, good looking woman, with a quick and pleasant smile, she seemed to have crumpled."[87]

She was not alone in her distress. Sapiro and Gallagher were outraged. Not only was the trial in jeopardy, but the Ford affidavits also alleged that the plaintiff was personally involved in an attempt to tamper with the jury. Hoffman's *Detroit Times* interview, Gallagher conceded, provided just cause for a mistrial, but the rest of the Ford motion, he argued, was based on manufactured evidence. The defense was motivated by "'a desire to stop the case now because it is clearly not going in the way that [they] thought it would go.'" The Ford lawyers resorted to "'desperate means . . . to prevent or postpone the appearance of Henry Ford on the witness stand . . . [because] he dare[s] not face examination on the charges which he has been broadcasting to the world all these years.'" If the mistrial were granted, the extra time would supply another opportunity to "connect" the plaintiff "'with a supposed Jew by the same methods of dark insinuation that have marked much of . . . this trial.'" Sapiro, too, held back nothing: "'This entire matter bears the mark of a perfect frame-up, a desperate method for securing a mistrial at any cost, to defer the appearance of Henry

Ford on the stand and to give the defendants another chance to turn the tide before some other jury.'" In a comment that revealed its sympathies, the *New York Times* added that Sapiro might have encountered Miller as casually as he did the other well-wishers who greeted him at the trial each day. Sapiro filed an affidavit with the court in which he said just that. The *Times* also pointed out that Ford's physician "told newspaper men several days ago that he was fully recovered now [and his counsel] have insisted that he is eager to testify and would come into court at any time."[88]

The following day, Stewart Hanley reintroduced his motion for mistrial by explaining why the defense did not formally challenge Hoffman on April 7. Their suspicions, he said, "were not sufficient to justify any definite action," so they merely brought it to the judge's attention in chambers. It was only after Ford's agents made further investigation and obtained conclusive proof that the lawyers challenged Hoffman's presence on the jury. Hanley contended that the case might have proceeded with eleven jurors had Gallagher been willing to conference privately in chambers rather than discuss the matter in open court as he insisted on Tuesday. Gallagher scoffed. According to the Ford affidavits, Hanley learned of the objectionable circumstances surrounding Mrs. Hoffman on March 24, Gallagher thundered; he waited until April 7 to tell the court, and he never shared the particulars with opposing counsel. "I learned of it," Gallagher reiterated, "upon my way to the Court room [April 20], after it was in flaring headlines in the public press."[89]

After dismissing the allegations against Hoffman as completely speculative, Gallagher put her *Detroit Times* interview in context. When she uttered the phrase that the Ford lawyers believed revealed her prejudice about a verdict, Gallagher argued, she was not talking about Ford at all. She was actually "talking about the charges laid against her, and she had a right to discuss those charges, where the filing of these charges had resulted in this publicity against [her]. It would be a fine state of the law if she could not speak in defense of her own character and honor, in defense of the charges filed against her by the attorneys for [the] defendant in this case."[90]

Gallagher then dismissed the supposed conspiracy afoot among Sapiro, Hoffman, and Miller. He derided the Ford affidavit's description of the "public corridor of the post office building," where Sapiro and Miller supposedly conversed, as "a comparatively obscure and secluded spot." The box of candy was indeed tendered to Hoffman, who shared it with the other jurors; Gallagher himself witnessed them eating it in the jury room during afternoon recess on March 23. But it was not Miller who gave Hoffman the candy. She prevailed in a game of bridge the jurors played during their breaks, and one of the vanquished male jurors handed her the box as her winnings. The Ford detectives mistook the male juror for "Kid" Miller. Gallagher could hardly contain a snicker as he concluded: "Now, if they cannot tell Miller from a juror who has sat in the Court room for five weeks, how can you give any credence at all to any of their statements?"[91]

Gallagher told the judge that the presence of the Ford agents and investigators, notorious to everyone involved in the case, was not unique to this trial. In his preparation, Gallagher studied "the methods employed by the defendant Ford in litigation in which he had an interest." He learned that Ford routinely scouted the jury pool and maintained files on prospective jurors; that Ford commonly investigated witnesses, lawyers, and litigants; and that Ford's agents "make a practice of tapping telephone wires, wiring the private rooms of principals, and even the chambers of Judges; examine sealed mail, examine private baggage, engage merchants in the vicinity of jurors' homes to spread favorable propaganda; go into the homes of the jurors posing as salesmen and issuing propaganda to the families of the jurors; send a note of warning to a juror at his home; and shadow jurors, witnesses, litigants, attorneys, Judges, and visitors, to the Court room." The plaintiff and his lawyer would have to be "asses" to stage "some sort of a conspiracy right here in the Court room . . . knowing these detectives were hanging around there."[92]

Gallagher proceeded to lay out a grand theory of what was going on behind the scenes. He argued that the Ford attorneys staged the Hoffman affair when their tobacco conspiracy theory collapsed on the last day of Sapiro's cross-examination. Sapiro echoed that accusation in his affidavit. The fact that the defense withheld information impugning Hoffman's jury service until April 18—after Reed failed to elicit incriminating admissions from Sapiro on April 14—was all too suggestive to the plaintiff and his lawyer. Court rules governing compromised jurors require lawyers to inform the judge of what they know at the moment of discovery. The Ford lawyers held their knowledge until they suspected that they could not win the case with that jury, Gallagher argued, and should not be permitted to manipulate the rules and the court: "[H]ere we have this client of mine in this hostile territory with hundreds of thousands of Ford sympathizers, with that sympathy reaching so far into the Court room that even the son of the United States Marshal is a Ford employee." It was time for the defense to prove whether it sought justice or delay: "I never have known of a case where justice was not merely blind, but was apparently manacled and chained and gagged." Moments later, however, he gift wrapped the mistrial for the defense: "We want our verdict to be untainted by any suggestion or hint of suspicion. We do not want the court to deny this motion for a mistrial. We want a jury of 11 or 12 or 3 or 4 who are standing before the world unchallenged as to their integrity." Stewart Hanley pounced: "[It] would be impossible to proceed with this case with eleven jurors. It is beyond the serious discussion of sane men that such a thing could now be done." Gallagher got in the last word: "Of course, your Honor is helpless. I am helpless. Mr. Sapiro is helpless. These men have created this situation, and they can take advantage of it. And you or I are powerless to stop it. . . . It is just a question now of whether they want delays and are taking this nefarious way of getting a delay or if they want justice and are willing to try this case." As Gallagher shouted, he pounded the table "under the noses of the Ford attorneys."[93]

The Department of Justice eventually exonerated Sapiro, but it did not matter. Hoffman's published comments about the case made a mistrial unavoidable; she publicly expressed a prejudiced opinion about the case while the trial was ongoing. In his memoirs, Harry Bennett says he engineered the declaration of mistrial by planting the juror-bribing allegations in Hutchinson's hands. But he could not have done it alone. The defense lawyers may have lost the jury, but they got what they wanted from the judge.[94]

Judge Raymond granted the mistrial immediately upon convening court April 21. Apart from granting the interview, Hoffman had done nothing wrong, he made clear; nor was there anything in any of the defense affidavits to support any allegation against Sapiro. Yet under federal rules the case could not proceed with fewer than twelve jurors, and once the press published the allegations against Hoffman he found it "impossible to make further progress with this case." The wave of publicity that crashed on the court after Tuesday's interview, Raymond declared, was truly disheartening. Defense affidavits submitted to the court on Wednesday appeared in the press on Thursday morning before the judge had a chance to read them. "These are the most flagrant violations of the duty which the press owes to the Court . . . that this court has ever known." He had no choice but to disqualify Hoffman from the jury, as both sides agreed that having granted the interview, she was no longer fit to serve. Accordingly, "the case must fall at this time . . . because justice has been crucified upon the cross of unethical and depraved journalism." Just as the trial stumbled to its undignified end, Ford's doctor announced that the auto manufacturer was "completely recovered" and able to testify, "except for a slight stiffness in his back."[95]

8 APOLOGY, RETRACTIONS, AND RECRIMINATIONS

How long will American Jewry and leaders of American Jewry maintain [their] "friendly neutrality" in this unequal contest between the world's richest anti-Semite, a breeder of race hatred, and a man, a Jew, who, at least, has never tried to defame a Gentile, who, at least, has never attempted to sow the prolific seeds of race hatred, who, at least, is willing to face his accuser in an open court of law and lay his whole life open to the eyes of the world?

—*Detroit Jewish Chronicle*, April 1927[1]

The mistrial ended the public drama between Ford and Sapiro, but their battle would continue. Law and the court had provided the arena and the rules for their encounter, and lawyers staged the case before the public. Everyone from the lawyers to the reporters assumed that the parties would return to court. Yet Ford, who had a history of confounding the conventional, decided to finish the dispute outside the legal process. To do so, he enlisted an unlikely ally whose cooperation enabled a sudden, surprising, and anticlimactic conclusion to take place.

The determination of both sides to proceed to trial left Louis Marshall sitting on the sidelines, watching developments impatiently. He was waiting for the chance to "take into consideration an adjustment of the Shapiro [*sic*] case," as he reminded Detroit lawyer Fred Butzel in late June.[2] Before trial, he told Butzel he was eager to assist with a settlement, but there was nothing for him to do. The prospect did not bother him, at least not enough to acknowledge. "I really believe that the game is not worth the powder," he told friends. Despite the evidence brought out at the trial, Marshall remained convinced that Ford's newspaper was popular only with "small, unimportant and ignorant groups that have no influence and [with] the Ku Klux Klan."[3]

When the trial raised the "Jewish question," it reawakened Marshall's concerns about what the *Sapiro* case meant for the larger cause of Jewish civil rights. In late March, he deplored the "loose thinking" the trial generated, insisting that it was merely an "ordinary action for libel." Because the "infamous charges made by Ford against . . . the Jews, as such," had been ruled irrelevant to the

lawsuit, Marshall believed that Sapiro "could not represent the Jews in fighting for their honor." The whole thing was "a personal action of Mr. Sapiro"
and "nobody else's business." The publicity only invited the public to speculate
about how Sapiro should conduct his case and what he should do with $1 mil-
lion if he won. Most of all, Marshall thought the case contradicted the strategy
that he and the American Jewish Committee (AJC) had maintained for more
than six years. He recognized the damage Ford did to Jews, but he seemed to
underestimate the effects of specific unanswered allegations in the press.[4]

In 1927, as in 1920, the AJC president viewed Ford's printed assaults as an
attack on all Jews. He also knew that he could take no direct role in the litigation without the express consent of the parties and their lawyers: "[N]othing
has been further from my mind than to intrude into Mr. Sapiro's litigation,"
he insisted to Fred Butzel. The declaration of mistrial broke open the logjam
that prevented Marshall from getting involved. Now he could try to shape
events and move things along, without "embarrass[ing] Mr. Sapiro" and with
an eye on the larger picture.[5] In short, he could resume his accustomed—and
uncontested—place at center stage.

. . .

In Detroit, the mistrial left loose ends for the judge and lawyers to address. On
April 30, Judge Raymond convened a hearing to discuss a new trial date. Sapiro
and Gallagher pressed for the earliest possible start; Sapiro even volunteered to
"share the expenses of the jury," but that proposal had no chance. Congress had
failed to pass a new appropriations bill to fund federal court expenditures after
July 1, and Judge Raymond was already committed to other cases for the summer. Gallagher pleaded that many of his witnesses were farmers, thus making
a fall trial that conflicted with harvest decidedly inconvenient. He also pointed
out that the contracts of two of Sapiro's tobacco cooperatives were set to expire,
"and unless the Ford charges are disposed of, the Jewish attorney's interests might
suffer." Longley accused him of "playing for publicity" and countered that July
and August "would be 'too warm for court duty.'" Judge Raymond ended the
wrangling by postponing his decision until July 1. He also left unresolved a decision on contempt-of-court charges pending against the *Detroit Times* for the
Hoffman interview.[6]

As soon as the jurors were released, reporters begged them for comment.
Some were more forthcoming than others. The women said only that they

found the case "'interesting.'" Amor Durat, who requested that Sapiro's entire tobacco speech be read aloud in court, asserted, "'The jury almost unanimously believed that the defense had collapsed and that the plaintiff was justified in bringing the suit. He was in a fair way to get a verdict.'" Charles Daly, a Catholic who like Durat owned a Ford car, defended the jury's integrity: "I don't think a fairer jury could be got together. I know that I tried to keep Mr. Ford and Mr. Sapiro on the same level in my mind. We were all sorry for Mrs. Hoffman, and we were ready to go ahead with the case." A retired saloonkeeper, Ernest Schweim, refused to tip his hand: "I didn't see anything on either side."[7]

Sapiro flung himself into a posttrial public relations tour. Immediately after the mistrial declaration, he left Detroit for New York, where he checked into the St. Regis Hotel and spent the weekend visiting friends. After his bruising weeks on the stand, Sapiro found some vindication in the warm welcome he received in New York. He quickly discovered that his new status once again put him in demand as a public speaker.[8]

On May 27, Sapiro gave his first major public speech since the mistrial at Union Temple in Brooklyn. The temple was full, and in the dry, cool spring evening outside, overflow crowds "waited for a glimpse of Sapiro." In addition to declaring his "determination to fight the case to the limit, to vindicate the Jews of America, and [defend] the cause of cooperative marketing," he commented at length on the dramatic developments that punctuated the trial. Ford's accident was "'faked' to keep him off the witness stand." Likewise, Sapiro was convinced that Reed's illness had no physical origins; rather, "'he lost his nerve and his vanity was punctured at the collapse of his case.'" He also asserted that he would "not accept a nickel for himself if he wins the verdict." In a nod to his audience, he complimented "the fairness of the New York newspapers in reporting the trial." Three days later, the Jewish publication *The Day* sponsored his talk at Carnegie Hall, "My Fight Against Henry Ford." Listeners of radio station WMCA heard Sapiro lay out his reasons for continuing the fight: "I want to show the world that [Ford] may be a genius at mass production, but he has distorted [people's] minds and souls when it comes to giving them freedom in religion."[9]

Defense lawyers watched Sapiro's every move, collected press clippings, and hoped he would say something incriminating. The mistrial changed nothing about how they did their jobs, how they viewed their opponent, or how they planned to manage the case. They still did not view the case as putting their employer's ideas on trial; they would continue to attack Sapiro. They harbored only contempt for him, his legal career, and his platform of agricultural reform. Although they underestimated Sapiro and his ideas in the first trial, the Ford lawyers confidently planned no change in strategy as they contemplated their return to court.[10]

Big change, by contrast, was sweeping through the Ford Motor Company. By the time the libel suit came to trial, its venerable brand had endured two years of sluggish sales. The Model T that had once so dominated the American car scene was in its last throes. Between 1925 and 1927, the company hemorrhaged money as Chevrolet and other General Motors models overtook Model Ts on the roads and in the ledger books. In both mechanics and design aesthetics, the Model T had been surpassed, and for months its proud inventor refused to acknowledge what the rest of the industry knew. Finally, however, after Ford dropped tantalizing hints in late 1926 and early 1927, the Ford Motor Company announced on May 25, 1927, that it would design and sell a new car. The next day, Ford greeted the fifteen millionth Model T as it came off the production line in an understated ceremony.[11]

Admitting that the Model T's commercial life had ended was extremely difficult for Ford. He saw the car as an extension of himself: it reflected his austerity, his distaste for frills and customization, his insistence on an unchanging technology. As Ford's lawyers chased Aaron Sapiro and his clients across the country in the mid-1920s, all of those traits left Ford and his company in an unaccustomed position: losing to the competition. Yet Ford stubbornly refused to accept the verdict of the market or the recommendations of top executives who favored a new model. The press assumed that the impending demise of the car led Ford to scuttle the libel case, judging by the timing of his announcement. Many historians have drawn the same conclusion.[12]

That theory is entirely plausible, even likely. But Ford's own executives knew better than to reduce Ford's decision making to simple cause and effect. As Edwin Pipp remarked, "Ford has been doing the unexpected thing for 15 years—ever since I knew him.'" Pipp, Black, and others knew that Ford juggled upward of a dozen major undertakings simultaneously throughout his career, managing and delegating as his attention and interest directed. During the first *Independent* series, he acquired railroads, ironworks, and entire towns in Michigan's Upper Peninsula that he planned to make into model societies built around farming and lumber. During the Sapiro series, he worked to secure

Muscle Shoals, not just to acquire the dam and nitrate mines but also to create, as some in the press described it, a "Detroit of the South." In 1925, he started a project that dwarfed the rest: the acquisition of rubber plantations in Brazil and the construction of a "new America" in the Amazon jungles. Ford was a master of compartmentalization. He generally did not permit events in one part of his life to intrude on his other plans. The mistrial and the announced end of Model T production coincided, but only Ford really knew how the events were connected. From the moment Ford realized he could not avoid testifying, the case ceased to be winnable. Harry Bennett thought that Ford arrived at this realization on the trial's second day, when "Mr. Ford's nerve began to fail visibly" as his lawyers stalled for time.[13] By the day of the "accident," Ford had moved on. All that remained was to create and manage the process by which public events could be made to line up with his private determination.

The deceptiveness that clouded Ford's motives and thoughts during the trial continued to shroud him after it was over. Everyone around him—his lawyers, his private secretary, his corporate executives, his family—believed a new trial would occur. Throughout May and June, the lawyers for both sides prepared for the new trial, although they did not know when it would begin. Taking no one, not even his lawyers, into his confidence, he permitted them to carry on while he, like the mysterious Oz behind the curtain, pulled levers and detonated explosions. While the lawyers continued their work, Ford set in motion a series of events that led several different individuals to believe that each was acting at his behest and in his confidence. And none of those individuals, each working on separate tracks, was talking to Ford's lawyers.[14]

. . .

While the lawyers argued about Gallagher's amended complaint and a start date, Ford put his legal end run into motion. In early May, he summoned *Independent* business manager Fred Black to his office, where he reportedly said, "I want to stop the *Dearborn Independent!*"[15] Because Ford controlled the newspaper, he had only to give Black—and Cameron—instructions to carry out his wishes. He was just planting the first of several seeds. Others he sowed in soil outside the company.

Over the following few weeks, Ford brought several important friends to Dearborn for separate, private conversations. One was the journalist and writer Arthur Brisbane, a prominent figure in the Hearst news organization. His daily column appeared in more than two hundred daily newspapers and eight hundred weeklies in the United States and around the world, "prompting the Hearst chain's public relations department to claim that he was the most widely read writer in the history of the world." Brisbane was one of Ford's closest friends, as close to him as Thomas Edison; Brisbane and his wife socialized with the Fords, one of a very few journalists to enter that select club. In 1921, President Harding used Brisbane as an intermediary when he sought to persuade Ford to end the *Independent*'s first antisemitic series. Though long a Ford admirer, Brisbane did not share Ford's antipathy toward Jews, editorialized against the *Independent* in 1920, and believed that Ford "'did not ever realize the full effect of the articles.'" On May 11, Brisbane visited Ford at Fair Lane, where the two visited privately for the better part of the day. None of Ford's aides, attorneys, or close associates knew about the meeting. Two months later, Brisbane reported that Ford said that day that "'he had made up his mind to discontinue absolutely and permanently all articles such as those that had given offense to Jews.'" Ford also protested that he was not "'an enemy of the Jews'" because he employed thousands of them and respected their accomplishments. Brisbane left Detroit unaware of what Ford planned to do or how he would make his wishes known to anyone. In fact, Ford had already begun to put the gears into motion.[16]

A second figure involved in the Ford end run was Joseph Palma, the former head of the U.S. Secret Service's New York field office. Palma was "an intimate of Harry Bennett's," which may explain Bennett's observation that William Cameron "deeply hated" Palma and did everything he could to separate Palma from the Ford Motor Company. Palma, who would be rewarded for his help in the *Sapiro* case with the Ford dealership on Staten Island, paid a visit to Dearborn shortly after Brisbane. Ford "mentioned that he had been quietly investigating some statements in the *Independent* and was shocked by what he found." Palma confirmed that Ford had offended the Jewish people. According to Palma, Ford replied, "'I wish this wrong could be righted,'" and he accepted Palma's offer of assistance: "'When my real views are explained to the proper people they will know I am prepared to act honorably and to repair the damage as far as I can.'"[17]

A third contact was Earl J. Davis, another Ford friend with federal connections. Former assistant U.S. attorney Davis was then in private practice in Detroit. After answering a call to Fair Lane, Davis went to Washington, D.C., where he sounded out a number of politicians, "including a New York Jew who is a Representative in Congress," about how to "sav[e] Mr. Ford from going on the witness stand in the Sapiro case." Davis also told the unnamed New Yorker that Ford "and his family" wished to "put an end to the controversies and ill feeling" that the *Independent* had aroused. According to the *New York Herald Tribune*, Davis was advised to go to New York and seek out "some prominent member of New York Jewry" on Ford's behalf. When Davis arrived in New York on May 20, he and Palma arranged a meeting with former New York congressman Nathan Perlman, a lawyer and high-ranking official in the American Jewish Congress, established during World War I as a more democratic counterweight to Marshall's American Jewish Committee. Davis and Perlman knew each other from serving together in Washington. The three discussed the *Sapiro* case, Ford's desire to settle, and his benign feelings toward Jews. Davis asked Perlman to suggest "some prominent Jewish leader to whom the Ford agents could go for advice."[18]

In May and June, Marshall was in constant contact with Fred Butzel, who was monitoring developments in the *Sapiro* case for him. With the trial now in abeyance, Fred Butzel saw no reason Marshall should not help. Butzel suggested to Palma and Davis that they contact Marshall once they arrived in New York. Perlman agreed with this suggestion; that way, both Jewish civil rights organizations would be represented in the settlement negotiations. On May 21, Perlman, Palma, and Davis called on Marshall at his office and presented him with Ford's request. Marshall jumped at the chance to orchestrate Ford's historic surrender, believing that he alone acted for the interests of the Jewish people. The mediators conferred three more times before the end of June. Davis and Palma informed Marshall that "Ford was satisfied that those whom he had put in charge of *The Dearborn Independent* had taken advantage of him by publishing a series of articles attacking Jews." Assured that Palma and Davis were authorized to speak for Ford, Marshall presented terms for "the big phase of the subject": "I told [them] that the Jews had been grievously wounded by these libels and that mere words would not heal the injury." But Ford would have to agree to terms: "Particularly . . . there must be a complete retraction of all the false charges made, an apology, a discontinuance of the attacks, and amends for the wrong." On June 16, Davis returned to Detroit.[19]

The involvement of so many people, most of them personally authorized by Ford to represent him, soon generated headaches for Marshall. On June 24 he wrote to Butzel, "I have just learned that we are evidently acting at cross-purposes, that you have been in communication with Mr. Ford and that this is creating a complication in my negotiations which have been advancing with some show of success although one can never be sure until the last minute." Marshall asked Butzel to come to New York so they could discuss the case and so he could "go into details."[20]

Sensing his friend's discomfiture, Butzel called Marshall on the telephone on June 28. Marshall was still uncomfortable about getting involved without some sort of authorization from the plaintiff, or at least without letting him know what was happening. Butzel agreed to contact William Henry Gallagher on Marshall's behalf, but Marshall did not wait to hear from Butzel before ensuring that he was acting with Aaron Sapiro's full knowledge. Sometime between June 24 and June 28, Marshall asked Lewis Strauss to convey a request. Would Sapiro be interested in having Marshall work for him or having him represent his interests in the delicate negotiations then under way?[21]

On June 29, Butzel reported that Gallagher "was quite appreciative of what was being done." Not having spoken to his client in some time—Sapiro was then in Canada at the invitation of the United Farmers of Canada and the Saskatchewan wheat pool—Gallagher was initially "somewhat afraid to act without Mr. Sapiro's consent," Butzel noted. Gallagher finally reached Sapiro by telephone late on the June 28 and briefed him about Marshall's negotiations. Sapiro immediately authorized his lawyer to "approach the Ford attorneys with respect to a settlement immediately." Butzel interpreted Sapiro's instructions to Gallagher as an endorsement of what Marshall was doing, "independently even if simultaneously" of the lawsuit, because Butzel—and Marshall—believed that any statement Marshall negotiated with Ford would make Sapiro better off: "Sapiro feels that the time is extremely right to get his matter disposed of," Butzel claimed, "and that this will not in any sense injure but may help the disposition of the other and larger issues."[22]

It does not appear that either Marshall or Butzel prioritized Sapiro's interests in a new trial during these critical days in late June. Butzel construed what he knew of Sapiro's wishes in a light that reflected favorably on Marshall's work. By June 28, Palma and Davis relayed to Marshall Ford's willingness to accept his conditions, and once armed with that knowledge, Marshall was determined to proceed independent of Sapiro's litigation. On June 30, Marshall reiterated to Butzel that although he was "anxious" to accomplish "a retraction and a settlement which will in other respects be satisfactory" to Sapiro, neither Sapiro's group nor theirs should "interfere with the plans of the other." At the very least, it seems that Marshall equated his role in securing a statement from Ford with Sapiro's stake in the outcome of the litigation.[23]

Evidence exists, however, as to what Sapiro wanted his lawyer to do and how Sapiro related his case to "the other and larger issues." In answering Strauss's telegram containing Marshall's offer to represent him, Sapiro clearly indicated his desires: "Believe Marshall should refer approach to Wm. Henry Gallagher, particularly since Gallagher stood by throughout the fight and is entitled to any prestige of settlement which his courage has earned. Have indicated terms fully to Gallagher . . . [will] waive all personal damages and gladly face my future from my ruins with this accomplished."[24] Besides directing Marshall to defer to Sapiro's attorney of record, Sapiro listed his settlement demands. In addition to a full retraction of the conspiracy charges and the attacks on cooperative marketing, Sapiro wanted payment for his court costs, including Gallagher's fees, and the endowment of an agricultural college scholarship for a Jewish orphan. Whose job was it to ensure that the ongoing negotiations took these wishes into consideration?

The lawyers did not ponder that question. Gallagher apparently saw Marshall's negotiations as Marshall did—as separate from the litigation—and did not intervene. On July 2, Sapiro reported to Strauss that Gallagher had contacted him only to tell him the court set a trial date no earlier than September 12. Marshall, having heard no objections from Gallagher through Butzel, proceeded. On retainer to no party in the case, he technically represented no one. After getting the go-ahead from Butzel, Marshall wrote a statement for Ford to review, consulting Palma and Perlman by phone as he wrote. He was not satisfied until his seventh draft.[25]

On June 30, Palma presented the statement to Ford. To Palma's astonishment, the automaker put his pretty, flowing signature on the last page without reading the document. "This is pretty strong, Mr. Ford, and I suggest you go over it pretty carefully," Palma advised. "Joe, no matter how strong it is it couldn't be too strong," Ford replied. "Let the Jew judge me by my acts in the future." Ford then signed a letter authorizing Davis and Palma to deliver the signed statement to Marshall in New York. Palma promptly telephoned Marshall to inform him that Ford had signed the document and that his only other instruction was that it be released through Arthur Brisbane. Davis and Palma air mailed the paper to New York, where Marshall kept it in his office safe.[26]

Unannounced and unheralded, a signed copy of the statement arrived at Brisbane's office on July 5. That was his first sign that Ford had acted on the ideas they had discussed nearly two months before.[27] It was up to Brisbane to determine how and when he would publish the statement. "Literally, the message I received from Mr. Ford was: 'Here's a statement I have made,'" Brisbane wrote in his column. "'Write around it in any way you like.'" He could have run the statement as a scoop for the Hearst syndicate, but Brisbane chose to release the apology to all the New York newspapers and the wire services on July 7, with the stipulation that it be printed as written. The apology ran under Ford's name. Marshall was mentioned only as having received it from Ford; Marshall's role as its true author was a closely guarded secret. Brisbane also asked that his name go unmentioned, but that request was vainglorious. Hearst's *New York American* published a special with the story of Ford's statement, accompanied by a Brisbane editorial, thus obliging him to deny widespread reports that he had prevailed on Ford to make the statement.[28]

Marshall had much to gain by collaborating with Ford on the apology. He sought to write a fitting end to the ugly episode; to dictate the terms of Ford's surrender gave him enormous personal and professional satisfaction. But he conceded what Sapiro and Gallagher had established at trial: Ford's personal responsibility for the *Independent*. In the apology, Marshall had Ford confess to having delegated the responsibility of running his newspaper to trusted subordinates who betrayed him by publishing articles and editorials that in no way represented his views. Marshall's statement for Ford echoed Cameron's lame testimony: "[I]t goes without saying," the statement read, "that in the multitude of my activities it has been impossible for me to devote personal attention to their management or to keep informed as to their contents. It has therefore inevitably followed that the conduct and policies of these publications had to be delegated to men whom I placed in charge of them and upon whom I relied implicitly." Having discovered the paper's actual contents by finally reading it, Ford was chastened to discover that Jews attributed the paper's content to him and believed that the publication represented his views:

To my great regret I have learned that Jews generally, and particularly those of this country, not only resent these publications as promoting anti-Semitism, but regard me as their enemy. Trusted friends with whom I have conferred recently have assured me in all sincerity that in their opinion the character of the charges and insinuations made against the Jews, both individually and collectively, contained in many of the articles which have been circulated periodically in The Dearborn Independent and have been reprinted in [*The International Jew*], justifies the righteous indignation entertained by Jews everywhere toward me because of the mental anguish occasioned by the unprovoked reflections made upon them.

Having been led "to direct [his] personal attention to this subject," he was "mortified" to discover that the *Independent* had become the "medium for resurrecting exploded fictions." In this way, Marshall reminded readers that Ford's staff had been notified that the *Protocols* had been debunked. "Had I appreciated even the general nature, to say nothing of the details, of these utterances I would have forbidden their circulation without a moment's hesitation, because I am fully aware of the virtues of the Jewish people as a whole, of what they and their ancestors have done for civilization and for mankind toward the development of commerce and industry, of their sobriety and diligence, their benevolence, and their unselfish interest in the public welfare." On its face, this text was incredible. Marshall could not have known that Ford had said essentially the same thing to Arthur Brisbane in May: "'Nobody can accuse me of being hostile to the Jewish people as a race. I employ thousands of them. They include many of my ablest associates. . . . I am hostile to concerns that seek to control others and make money hard to get, no matter what their race or religion, but I am not hostile to Jews.'" Ford then authorized a full retraction in the *Independent* and offered his act of contrition: "I deem it to be my duty as an honorable man to make amends for the wrong done to the Jews as fellow-men and brothers, by asking their forgiveness for the harm I have unintentionally committed, by retracting so far as lies within my power the offensive charges laid at their door by these publications, and by giving them the unqualified assurance that henceforth they may look to me for friendship and goodwill."[29]

The apology was a masterful work of evasion draped in apparent contrition. By incorporating Ford's trial defense in the apology, Marshall permitted Ford to claim that he knew nothing of the *Independent*'s contents until the lawsuit and to place responsibility for the offensive publications on his employees. What Marshall got in return was an important concession: Ford's promise to restrain the circulation of *The International Jew* in the United States and Europe. Stripping the *Protocols* of the power of Ford's name and wealth had been Marshall's aim since 1920. With Ford's name on the statement, and with

Brisbane's gloss that Ford "had expressed deep regret that the articles ever had been published," Marshall believed that he had secured a conclusive, historic victory: he had succeeded in disassociating Ford from the *Protocols*.[30]

In his capacity as the official recipient of Ford's apology, Marshall published a statement, accepting it on behalf of American Jews. In his response, Marshall lectured Ford on the fundamental fallacy of sowing racial prejudice in America: "We [Jews] had fondly hoped that in this blessed republic, with its glorious Constitutions and its just laws, it would be impossible to encounter the hatred and rancor to which our brethren have been and still are subjected in other lands. . . . Happily such excrescences could not flourish on American soil." Still, Marshall continued, the memories of antisemitic prejudice, stereotypes, and falsehoods that Ford's publication brought back to life damaged the good feelings of Jews towards Ford and of Americans toward Jews. Now, however, there was hope for a new beginning:

> The statement which you have sent me gives us assurance of your retraction of the offensive charges, of your proposed change of policies . . . and good-will, of your desire to make amends, and what is to be expected from any man of honor, you couple these assurances with a request for pardon. So far as my influence can further that end, it will be exerted, simply because there flows in my veins the blood of ancestors who were inured to suffering and nevertheless remained steadfast in their trust in God.

The AJC promptly published a pamphlet with Ford's statement and Marshall's letter side by side, lest anyone miss the symbolism of the person to whom Ford sent his emissaries.[31]

The nationwide front-page headlines on July 8 that proclaimed Ford's apparent change of heart confirmed Marshall's sense of victory. Those with different stakes in the matter drew more nuanced conclusions. The plaintiff was still in Canada the day the apology was announced. The Associated Press immediately sought him out for comment on Ford's statement and on rumors that he was about to settle the lawsuit. Sapiro was "'happy to know that Mr. Ford was not going to use his enormous influence and wealth in furthering attacks against Jews.'" Ford's apology, he said, "'justifies all the worry, trouble and expense of the long and bitter suit at Detroit.'" Interestingly, Sapiro agreed that Ford was being "'deceived by subordinates'" but reminded the public that he, Sapiro, was "the agency to bring these things to his attention and thereby to have enabled him to have set himself right as a maker of opinion throughout the world.'"

For comment on the progress of settlement negotiations, Sapiro referred the press to his lawyer. Although Sapiro accepted the cover story crafted for the apology statement, he made it clear in his statement that he held Ford responsible for the *Independent*.[32]

No one in Detroit but Ford knew about the apology in advance. William Cameron was caught completely by surprise when it hit the press and could not answer for the newspaper's new editorial policy: "This is absolutely the first time I have heard of any such statement or intention on the part of Henry Ford," he said. "I most certainly will get in touch with Mr. Ford and find out what is back of this." He seemed compelled to reveal his loss of face: "Mr. Cameron declared he could not believe Mr. Ford would make public such a statement without advising him, inasmuch as he was in control of publication of The Dearborn Independent and would be the first to be notified of any such intention on Mr. Ford's part. 'It is all news to me,' he said, 'and I cannot believe it is true.'" Unnerved, he skipped town on July 8, accompanying Henry and Edsel Ford and a party of engineers as they inspected a railroad in northern Michigan. He left behind a group of stunned *Independent* employees to produce an issue in which no mention was made of the anti-Jewish campaign. "While the presses were operating to-day there appeared to be a tension about the publishing office," the *New York Herald Tribune* reported. "Employees said they had not received official word that a new editorial policy was to be adopted." On his return, Cameron sat in his office and, insulated by Ford "secret service" agents, refused to grant interviews. Liebold was more adroit at avoiding the press. No newspaper got him to comment. Perlman, Davis, and Palma kept their work with Marshall carefully concealed from Ford's top lieutenants, a fact Perlman disclosed with relish on July 10.[33]

The apology publicly humiliated Ford's lawyers. They got advance word of the announcement from Gallagher, their opposing counsel, who got it from Fred Butzel. Longley and Hanley were then put in the awkward position of having to present the statement on Ford's behalf, only to have the Associated Press report that Ford "'did his own talking' and 'played his own hand.'" Marshall confided to Cyrus Adler that he was certain Ford's only advisers in the matter were Davis, Palma, and Edsel Ford. As far as Longley, Hanley, and Reed knew, Ford acted entirely on his own. Their awkwardness stemmed from having to reveal that they had lost control of their client. Longley could tell the press only that he had nothing to do with the preparation or issuance of the statement and that he planned to continue the Sapiro litigation. Hanley sought to disassociate the apology from the litigation, reminding reporters that the Jewish question had been ruled irrelevant to Sapiro's lawsuit: "'I do not see that Mr. Ford's repudiation of the anti-Jewish articles has any connection with the Sapiro case.'" Hanley also asserted that Ford would take the witness stand when the case resumed in September. Because Ford would probably never follow through on that commitment, no one took it seriously. With Gallagher commenting that he expected to settle promptly in light of Ford's statement, Hanley's attempt to finesse commanded little attention.[34]

Senator Reed's fury knew no parallel. In Texas on July 8, he telephoned Detroit with one imperious query: "What in hell is this I see in the Dallas paper?" When a reporter caught up with him on the train to Houston, Reed did not try to contain his shock at being shut out of such an important development: "I was in Detroit when the case was set [on July 1] . . . and so far as I have been advised, we are preparing to go to trial with the case. I might add that I have been where I could be reached constantly and am sure that if any move of this kind was pending I would have been advised." Ever the trial lawyer, he continued to plead his case: "We were prepared to justify [the statements made against Sapiro]—that is, our defense was that the statements were true." A few months later, he contacted Longley to deal with some unfinished business: he had not received the balance of his fee. "In view of the miserable outcome of the case I would like to get the matter settled, and off my mind, and as far behind me as possible. I hardly need say to you that if I had dreamed before entering the case of any such denouement I would not have gone into it for any kind of a fee." Reed assured Longley of his professional and personal regard, "however much I am disgusted with what happened." Longley hastened to reply, reciprocated the compliment, and apologized for the delay. He also confided that he shared Reed's sense of revulsion at the turn of events: "Regardless of the unfortunate turn taken in the case . . . I understand thoroughly how you feel about the outcome of it. No one connected with it felt more disgust at what occurred than I did myself. I am trying to put that part of the recollection out of my mind." Whether the two lawyers were upset at their client's decision to settle or by the fact that he cut them out of the process might be impossible to determine. Several months later, as he geared up for what would be his last presidential campaign, Reed swept all doubts aside for a Kansas audience: "'All I want to say about that case,' said the senator, smiling, 'is that, whatever the amount of the fee, it was not big enough to pay me for a client lying down after I had won my case.'" All told, Reed and his firm billed Ford $118,118.82 for their services.[35]

Edwin Pipp was only too happy to comment after hearing the news. He reminded people that the *Independent*'s antisemitic campaign had been Ford's idea from the start: "[T]he anti-Jewish policy of the publication, now repudiated by Ford's statement, was laid down by the manufacturer himself," Pipp said. "'I don't understand Mr. Ford's retraction at all.'" But in a larger sense, Pipp "was not surprised" by Ford's abrupt switch in policy: "'That formal statement was just Ford's way of pulling the desk out from under one of his employees.'"[36]

Ford's motives, as always, remained inscrutable. Some newspapers, including the *New York World*, asserted that he again had his eye on a presidential run, for which he wanted William Randolph Hearst's support. Others speculated about the Ford Motor Company's "striking loss of business in the last few years" as a key factor. A different perspective came from a "Jewish financier and industrialist" who spoke to the *Chicago Daily Tribune* on condition of anonymity. "'I think that Ford has at last realized that he has been making a boob of himself. He knows Jews won't buy his cars. Even if they did not they are only 3,000,000 out of 118,000,000. But this is a funny country, the majority are inclined to take up for the under dog, and it is very likely that Ford's attacks on Jews did hurt his business with the vast number of Gentiles associated with Jews one way or another.'"[37] Whatever his reasons for ending the litigation when and as he did, Ford's handling of the end game demonstrated his skill at manipulating the parties, the lawyers, and the legal process.

. . .

The apology was the riveting news event of the summer. The mainstream press picked apart Ford's prose in the manner of a critical but constructive schoolteacher. The explanation for the *Independent*'s attacks elicited scorn; the expression of goodwill, in contrast, revealed a general desire that it was heartfelt. As Marshall observed, "The public press has given ample evidence that it does not believe his explanation but is content to accept his retraction and prayer for forgiveness, as sincere." The *New York Times* was not fooled by Ford's weak protest that he had only "'recently'" learned of the objectionable articles in his newspaper. "The fact is, of course, that for several years he has had the matter brought to his notice, both privately and publicly. Till now, he had remained unyielding." But the "complete and handsome" quality of his mea culpa, the

8.1. This antisemitic cartoon by Edmund Gale, published July 12, 1927, interpreted
Ford's apology hopefully. It was printed with the caption, "Ford Isn't Going to Run
'Em Down Any More." "The Jewish People" are depicted in dehumanized form by an
oversized pair of legs that overwhelm and threaten the diminutive Ford (copyright ©
1927 Los Angeles Times, reprinted with permission).

Times wrote, compelled its acceptance: "Mr. Ford has now done the handsome
thing, making the honorable amends to the extent of his power, and there is no
doubt that he will receive a valuable credit in the form of a better opinion of
him by the public in general and even by those whom he has allowed his subordinates to vilify and slander."[38] As it had during the trial, antisemitic imagery
suffused editorial cartoon commentary on the apology. One in the *Los Angeles
Times* portrayed Ford as heroic in capitulation and "the Jewish people" as a
threatening, oppressive presence in victory.

Other press outlets were less lenient. The *Nation* bluntly commented, "In any other man such naiveté would be impossible. . . . Has even an absentee owner of a magazine no responsibility whatever for its contents? That, certainly, would be carrying the doctrine of editorial freedom to lengths which even *The Nation* would hardly indorse." Aside from leaving Ford's personal culpability ambiguous, the case pointed out a larger unfairness: with his vast wealth, Ford could guarantee his First Amendment freedoms. Others were not so fortunate. The editor and business manager of the New York *Daily Worker* faced jail terms for violating indecency and obscenity laws after the newspaper ran a poem of dubious literary quality that indicted American capitalism:

> America is a land of censored opportunity.
> Lick spit; eat dirt.
> There's your opportunity;
> Then you become a big man of business.
> And people take off their hats
> To you
> Because you're a great man;
> A man
> Who robs other men by licking spit and eating dirt.
>
> · · ·
>
> Hell,
> America,
> You can't be liked, spreading hot-air stink.
> You're everything, aren't you, America?
> Of course.
> You're even a neat whore house
> Standing on the sidewalk of the world.
> Two dollars a woman:
> Nice bed
> Warm room.
> But most important:
> A fleshy woman
> To make you feel you're giving away your life water
> For a healthy bastard.
> Why not?[39]

In defending themselves, the *Daily Worker* staff members argued, as had Ford, that they "had never seen" the poem before they published it. The *Nation* contended that the double standard affronted both logic and decency: "The *Worker*'s puerile 'poem' could not conceivably have harmed any one; the *Dearborn Independent*'s long and reckless sowing of race bitterness has spread its poison to millions. Yet Mr. Ford, who is a billionaire, will not go to jail; and the Communist officials of the *Daily Worker* are serving their terms."[40] The *Nation* got the matter right, but not for the reasons it supposed. Ford's newspaper merely insulted a race. The *Daily Worker*'s poem conjured offensive images and impeached the nation's character. American courts had no difficulty finding that the latter was obscene on its face, whereas the former was immune to criminal prosecution.

For the most part, the public did not pause to consider such conundrums. Most people wanted to believe that Ford's gesture might expunge the ugliness of racism from the national conscience. The *Pittsburgh Sun* editorialized, "Let the ugly chapter now be closed. Mr. Ford's retraction is complete and earnestly sincere on its face." The *New York Herald Tribune* approved Ford's statement unconditionally: "[T]here can be no question about the completeness of his present disavowal and apology . . . which handsomely emphasizes his regret and the purpose of his publication to abandon all anti-Jewish propaganda." The *Herald Tribune* also emphasized the "cardinal American doctrine" of constitutional respect for "freedom of faith": "It is not good Americanism to attack anybody on the ground of race or religion."[41] In ending the trial and the lawsuit as he did, Ford masterfully exploited such idealism.

Although anxious for a happy ending, the mainstream press could not quiet all doubt. Many major newspapers could not accept Ford's act of contrition at face value. Beneath the outward praise there lurked a goodly measure of sarcasm and ridicule, some of it subtle, some of it less so. "As for his ordering anti-Semitism out of his paper," the *New York World* waspishly remarked, "it seems likely that he once ordered it in." A Detroit humor magazine commented, "If that is the case, we have been wondering who started the peace ship." The *Chicago Tribune* got digs in at its old adversary: "Mr. Ford advances an empty head to explain his cold feet and the only plausibility is contained in the fact that it took him until advanced years to discover that Benedict Arnold was not a modern writer and that the revolution was not fought in 1812." Colonel McCormick had no sympathy for his fellow journalists on the *Independent*'s staff, either, noting that they had been scooped on the story of what was happening to their own paper: "They may have experienced then the all gone feeling which comes to persons who thought they had their feet on a rock and find it was a soap bubble. . . . It is apparent that the help is now looking for other jobs."[42] These writers found the apology's protestation of ignorance and blamelessness unacceptable.

Parodies of the statement filled newspapers and magazines for months. In a send-up of the statement in the *Detroit Saturday Night*, William Shakespeare confessed that "Bacon *did* write Shakespeare"; Marcus Porcius Cato expressed sincere regret for knocking over Carthage and disclosed that his secretary wrote all his speeches, which Cicero read to the Roman Senate in his stead; and John Hancock declared his shock at discovering that his signature appeared on a document titled "The Declaration of Independence," which he never would have signed if he had known hurt feelings would have resulted. *Life Magazine* ran much the same idea. George III apologized for repressing the American Revolution, not having had the opportunity to learn that America had been discovered. Abraham Lincoln assured his "good friends in the South" that he did not really mean to free the slaves: "Although it has been called to my attention that I signed some sort of Emancipation Proclamation, I hasten to explain that I did not have a chance to read the document, through pressure of other business." Finally, Kaiser Wilhelm had something to get off his chest: "Being much occupied at the time posing for my portrait (you know how these photographers are), I was not aware that a war was in progress. I'm very sorry it happened." Satirical columnists wondered whether a Ford apology to Chevrolet would be forthcoming, observed that a newspaper was "a dangerous plaything," and compared Ford to General George Custer.[43]

America's master humorist could not let this opportunity pass either. Will Rogers's wry gloss appeared in the *Los Angeles Times* and two other papers on July 9:

I certainly was glad to read Henry Ford's statement this morning in the papers in regard to the Jewish people. It was a fine thing for a big man to do. It takes big men to admit a fault publicly, and it has been a lesson to me. From now on I am going to lay off the Republicans. I have never had anything against them as a race. I realize that out of office they are just as honest as any other class and they have a place in the community that would have to be taken by somebody. So I want to apologize for all I have said about them and henceforth will have only a good word to say about them. Mind you I am not going to say anything about them but that is not going to keep me from watching them.

With the scandal essentially over, the *Chicago Daily Tribune* openly mocked the *Independent*: "Who wised Henry Ford to the fact that the Dearborn Independent was full of D.D.'s about the Jews? I never saw anyone read the darn thing." Louis Marshall received a private joke: "Taking Mr. Henry Ford seriously and giving him the benefit of every doubt, it is quite within the range of possibility that he may at some future date, be elected President of the Republic of Palestine."[44] Six weeks after the apology, the Happiness Boys recorded a Billy Rose ditty, "Henry Ford Apologized to Me," in which they proclaimed, "I've thrown away my little Chevrolet / And bought myself a Ford coupé":

> I'm glad he changed his point of view
> And I even like Edsel too,
> Since Henry Ford apologized to me
> My mother says she'll feed him if he calls
> "Gefilte fish" and Matzah balls
> And if he runs for President
> I wouldn't charge a single cent
> I'll cast my ballot absolutely free
> Since Henry Ford apologized to me.

A Chicago theater reviewer found "the verses . . . as good as the title is promising and topical."[45]

Humor and ridicule supplied effective tools for deflecting the deep, lasting hurt that Jewish artists and musicians felt toward Ford. Others, including such luminaries as Nathan Straus and Otto Kahn, continued to employ the studied silence they observed while under attack and declined to comment on the apology. Jewish newspapers, professionally obliged to report on the apology, did their best to accept it at face value. Some deplored what they saw as excessive celebration, however, and editorialized that Jews should not be so quick to accept an olive branch in return for what they viewed as an insufficient declaration of personal accountability. Echoing that position, Marshall urged everyone "not to make Ford a hero" or "go to extremes in thanking and congratulating Ford for his apology."[46]

Still, it was difficult not to express relief that Ford was ending his long war, and in doing so some crossed the line Marshall sought to draw. "We are glad he is getting sensible," said Samuel Phillipson, a Chicago merchant. A Chicago judge praised Ford as "a man of real character," whereas another Illinois businessman hoped that "he will not again be led into harming a people as he has done to the Jews." Rabbi Isaac Landman wrote in the *American Hebrew*, "I am glad Mr. Ford is alive and will reap the joy of righting the almost unforgivable wrong he visited upon the Jewish people." And a prominent Zionist remarked, "Ford has shown himself after all a man of some reason." Clergy across the country extended a conciliatory hand from the pulpit. Ford's act, said a Catholic priest in New York, "will be a great consolation to all right-minded and law-abiding citizens." An Episcopal rector declared that "every decent minded citizen is glad that he is making amends."[47]

Politicians and Jewish leaders followed much the same line of thinking, praising Ford for his change of heart, expressing the wish it had come sooner, and urging him to do more to heal the open wounds his newspaper had left behind. New York Mayor James J. Walker told the *Jewish Day* that it was "gratifying" to hear that Ford had ordered the *Independent* to change its editorial policy and disavowed personal responsibility: "Possibly this incident may influence certain other men in public life to see the light and to eliminate religious and racial rancor from their utterances and publications." The editor of the *Jewish Tribune*, David Mosessohn, spoke of his "profound satisfaction" upon reading the statement and predicted that Jews would "welcome it with deep-felt gratitude to the Heavenly Father of all peoples." Still, Mosessohn pointed out that the *Independent* and *The International Jew* would have a lasting influence as long as they remained in print, and he called on Ford to "counteract that influence with the same energy and enterprise that was employed in his name to spread the ideas he now acknowledges were false." That aim could be accomplished by a "world-wide campaign of education against national chauvinism, religious bigotry and racial antagonism." From Chicago, Julius Rosenwald echoed the widely shared sense that Ford had to have known better: "It is never too late to make amends and I congratulate Mr. Ford that he has at least seen the light. He will find that the spirit of forgiveness is not entirely a Christian virtue, but is equally a Jewish virtue."[48]

Yet Ford did not escape criticism, some of it harsh. "We respectfully suggest that the last sweet dose of love and kisses be ladled out to Mr. Ford's new-found friends by leaving the name Ford off the new car," lectured the *New York Daily News*. "Let it be called instead, let us say, the Solomon Six, or the Abraham Straight-8." The *New York Evening Post* doubted the statement could be believed: "Nobody but Mr. Ford could be ignorant of a major editorial policy of his own publication. Nobody but Mr. Ford could be unaware of the national and international repercussions of this policy of anti-Semitism. Nobody but Mr. Ford could say that he did not 'appreciate even the general nature to say nothing of the details of these utterances' by his own editor. Yet Mr. Ford does make these assertions, and when we remember the almost incredible mental aloofness of his testimony in the Chicago Tribune libel trial, we must feel that we would be unwise to reject even so fantastic a plea of ignorance." The *New York Sun* restated that idea more baldly: "It is hard to imagine Mr. Ford so wrapped in cotton wool that the major activity of his own magazine was unknown to him; that he was as unaware of what the *Dearborn Independent* was doing as if he had been a Tibetan monk."[49]

If Ford had the capacity to register shame from any of these testimonials, the one from the pen of William Allen White might have hit the mark:

A man with the tremendous responsibility that comes with an ownership of a paper like Ford's who would idly or carelessly or ignorantly use his power to pain and humiliate millions of his fellow-men has no qualities as an editor which his fellow-men are bound to respect. His change of opinion is unimportant. The fact that his changed opinion will relieve the Jews of a gadfly's sting does not render the gadfly more intelligent. . . . It is a sad commentary on humanity that Ford's great wealth has not revealed his ignorance, his mental sloth, and his incapacity to think. Man is always inclined to feel that greatness in one field of activity presumes greatness in all activities.

The historian and author Hendrik Willem Van Loon dismissed Ford as "a simple-minded, kindly mechanic who knows a great deal about very efficient and very ugly automobiles . . . who is totally ignorant of everything else." Van Loon termed the *Independent* "the worst garbled and the worst informed sheet it has ever been my pleasure to behold. And now you ask me about his sudden voyage to Canossa on the Jordan, about his retraction of five years of malicious and uninterrupted slander?"[50]

Those raising doubts about Ford's sincerity were not just tilting at windmills. Ford shaped American public opinion; everything he said and did drew press attention. If his newspaper's war against Jews were really over, how would his foot soldiers get the message? As an observer in Washington State pointed out, plenty of *Independent* readers believed its every word. The pastor of "the largest and probably most influential Presbyterian congregation has heretofore vouchsafed for the truth of the charges which Mr. Ford now admits were unfounded." Would individuals firm in their antisemitic convictions follow Ford in his recantation? It was not long before Americans of that stripe made it clear that they had not changed their views. A letter to the editor of *Time* expressed the day's genteel antisemitism:

I don't like the Jews. Why I don't like them is my own business—maybe I am just built that way. But this is a free country and I have a right to my likes and dislikes. I am sure that many Jews feel the same way towards me. When people dislike each other they usually avoid each other and live happily. Why can't the Jews let us alone? Why, when I, and people who feel as I do, make up a club, an association or an organization, do a host of Jews immediately attempt to crash the gates and enter into our midst? . . . Why can't they leave us alone and form their own clubs, hotels and associations where no Gentiles will be allowed. If they did this I believe that there would then be no reason for any Anti-Semitism.

The idea that one statement by Ford could erase deep-seated attitudes such as these, in a society where racial, religious, gender, and class differences were threaded through the fabric of everyday life, was fanciful. But people could not help indulging in visions of tolerant pluralism: "We must all live together in this country," the *New York Evening Post* concluded sententiously, "and we cannot have one part of us attacking another on grounds of race or religion."[51]

. . .

At the time, Americans assumed that Ford wrote the statement himself. Marshall kept his role out of the press, hoping Americans would read the text as an earnest attempt by the bumbling Ford to clear the slate and reestablish himself as the cultural leader they had long believed him to be. The apology expressed contrition to the Jewish community in general and no one in particular. Aaron Sapiro, whose lawsuit precipitated the mission of Ford's representatives to New York, did not rate a single mention. In effect, Ford apologized for the one thing the trial had established that he would never lose on: group libel. Accordingly, both mainstream and Jewish newspapers construed the apology as a victory for Jews and as Ford's admission of defeat.[52]

Marshall hoped to spend July as he usually did, on vacation at his summer retreat in the Adirondacks. The release of the apology and his role as Ford's "confessor," however, obliged him to field inquiries from the wire services for several days at his upstate cabin. The *New York Times* and other outlets erroneously reported that anyone wishing a copy of Ford's statement could request one from Marshall's office, and Marshall's staff politely but firmly redirected scores of requests for several months.[53] Those inconveniences were minor compared to a swift groundswell of competing claims taking credit for the apology.

On July 10, in a front-page *New York Times* interview, Nathan Perlman characterized the apology process as one he initiated after Davis and Palma came to him and in which Marshall's inclusion was an afterthought. Marshall's son-in-law immediately wrote to alert him about Perlman's failure to accord Marshall due deference: "Can something be done to cut off Congressman Perlman's tongue? How those tenth rate politicians in order to get in the lime-light are trying to undo your wonderful achievement in the Ford matter." Marshall turned on Perlman sternly: "[Y]ou telephoned to me saying in substance that Messrs. Davis and Palma had asked you to bring them into communication with me with regard to a possible adjustment of the Ford matter and . . . you had told them that I was the only person who could handle the matter." For six pages, Marshall reconstructed the May and June conferences and contacts in detail, emphasizing his primary role: "Throughout the conversation [with Davis and Palma] I was the spokesman. You were merely a listener and took no part in the discussion." On June 30, Marshall reminded Perlman, he had showed him a copy of the document that Ford was about to sign, at which Perlman "expressed [his] surprise and gratification at what [Marshall] had accomplished." Marshall was particularly offended that Perlman claimed to have represented the American Jewish Congress in the negotiations: "[Y]ou know very well that that organization was never mentioned in any way." Marshall finished with a flourish: "[Y]ou issued a column of fiction in order that you might bask in the lime-light for which you crave and adorned yourself with borrowed plumes to do honor to the occasion."[54]

Confiding in his friend Julius Rosenwald, Marshall took off the gloves: "Perlman merely introduced Davis and Palma, Ford's representatives, to me and then true to his political training sought to make capital of it for himself and the American Jewish Congress by lying." Perlman saw this dispute as another episode in the tense history of the relations between the American Jewish

8.2. Louis Marshall (*center front*) and former New York congressman Nathan Perlman (*standing at right*), pictured in 1928 before an appearance before Congress in support of immigration reform legislation. The two bridged their differences after arguing bitterly over the Ford apology (International Newsreel and American Jewish Archives, Cincinnati, Ohio, Collection No. PC-2875).

Committee and the American Jewish Congress. "I think your letter to me is prompted solely by your antagonistic feeling to the American Jewish Congress," he told Marshall. "I believe that if the newspapers had not mentioned this organization you would continue to have the kindliest regard for me, especially because of my suggestion that you be called into conference on this most important matter." Samuel Untermyer, of counsel to the firm of Guggenheimer, Untermyer & Marshall, was also taking sides, telling Perlman that Marshall "had done [Perlman] an injustice when [Marshall] failed to mention that [Perlman] had participated in these negotiations." Perlman's account bears a ring of truth, but he was outnumbered in his effort to position himself as Marshall's equal. Letters flooded Marshall's office congratulating him on his handling of the matter, not just from friends but also from complete strangers grateful for his intercession: "Your able handling of this matter has again demonstrated why you are the leader of Jewry in America."[55]

Beating back Perlman's grandstanding was a trifling occupation. Marshall had a more serious problem on his hands at the same time, one he had downplayed ever since he first acknowledged it at the moment of Ford's capitulation. Untermyer remained engaged in Bernstein's New York libel suit against Ford. When Marshall decided to act as mediator in the negotiations and write the statement that ultimately served as Ford's public apology, he knew that both Sapiro's and Bernstein's lawsuits were certain to be affected as a result of what Ford—and he—did. Existing legal ethics rules were far too vague to apply to the particulars of this odd situation, but he was far too consummate a professional not to proceed with the utmost care.[56]

When Marshall did not receive Sapiro's permission to represent him in the negotiations, he proceeded to distinguish his work and its consequences from both lawsuits. He did not take a retainer from Ford or establish an employment relationship with him in any other way. He made it clear to those around him, particularly Fred Butzel, that he saw the Palma, Davis, and Perlman discussions as building toward a resolution of the "larger situation," by which he meant Ford's long, seven-year war against all Jews, not the settlement of individual libel grievances. When he talked about Ford's "retraction," he meant the renunciation of Ford's antisemitic beliefs, not specific prejudicial statements. And he reminded anyone who asked that "for more than ten years," he and Samuel Untermyer had not been law partners.[57]

But the "of counsel" designation that Untermyer took in 1912 left a meaningful professional relationship in place between the two lawyers. Otherwise, Marshall would not have felt obliged to contact Untermyer on July 1 and describe to him what happened with Ford's representatives. Marshall also told Untermyer that Ford had signed the statement; that he spoke to Bernstein, who had been "in the office the other day," and that through Butzel he communicated with Gallagher, who in turn informed his client, who was "anxious to get rid of this litigation." Marshall had attempted to see Untermyer "for some days" but "you have been so occupied that I never got a chance." Marshall could not have chosen a more argumentative way to begin this conversation with Untermyer. He implied that it was Untermyer's fault that Marshall was unable to bring him up to date on these events until the ink dried on Ford's signature. Now, with both libel litigants "extremely anxious" to take advantage of the opportunity to settle, Marshall advised Untermyer that Ford was leaving settlement negotiations to his lawyers. Accordingly, he suggested that Untermyer could "secure a very satisfactory adjustment of the Bernstein case." He ended on a note of caution: he hoped that the lawsuits would be settled in a way that would not "interfere with the moral effect upon the public mind here and abroad of this statement of Ford."[58] Instead of minimizing his own impact on his firm's client, he subtly pressured Untermyer to subordinate the lawsuit to the "moral effect" of Ford's apology.

From Atlantic City, New Jersey, where he was spending the Independence Day holiday, Untermyer immediately consulted his client and responded to Marshall: "B[ernstein] insists . . . F[ord] should be required to make retraction and settlement with him simultaneously with issuing statement or at least have it clearly understood that we intend [to] issu[e] statement attacking sincerity his excuse that he was deceived. . . . B[ernstein] says that when you spoke to him you said you were going to counsel me which you should have done and he told you he was willing to leave to me matter of retraction and settlement. I strongly advise against you doing anything until we consult." Further, Untermyer thought "Marshall law" inappropriate for the situation: "By insisting, as usual, on 'going it alone,' I think you have made a mistake. However, if you can arrange so that our statement commenting on this will not be understood and not regarded as a breach of faith by you or me I do not see that I have any right to object. Otherwise I do object—decidedly."[59]

Anxious to preserve Ford's historic confession of wrongdoing, Marshall snapped: "For once I insist that *you* do not interfere. This is a matter affecting the destinies and honor of hundreds of thousands infinitely more important than anybody's lawsuit and there should be no cross-purposes." The entire point, Marshall reiterated, was to make Ford "appear ridiculous" while getting on the record "his desire for settlement [of] both suits coupled with full retractions." The apology eased the way for settling both lawsuits—a key recognition Marshall had not made in any other context and one that he then used to justify his actions. He had another complaint to register: "I tried [to] inform you of proceedings but apparently you had no time for me, besides it was certain what your natural reaction would be and I did not regard your recent treatment conducive to confidences."[60]

This was pushing things too far, in Untermyer's view. He promptly fired back: "[I b]itterly resent your amazing intolerant attitude. [I]t is you who are wantonly inconsiderately interfering in my affairs and autocratically dictating what I shall do without consulting me[,] taking unto yourself credit for [a] situation you did nothing to create and which would not have been created if you had your way." He was taken aback at the accusation that he had been too busy to speak to Marshall: "Your absurd statements about having no time for you and about my treatment of you . . . simply bewilder me." Suspecting that Marshall might shirk his professional obligations to their firm's client, Untermyer tried again: "[I]f you have[,] without consulting me[,] committed me and B[ernstein] as well as unalterably committed yourself[,] I shall have to submit to avoid humiliating you[,] but without such assurance I shall go ahead unless you postpone action until we can confer. [W]hile I agree this is more important than anybody's lawsuit, *I have and you should have obligations in lawsuit which I will not sacrifice.*" In a subsequent wire sent the same day, Untermyer reiterated his position: "Our first duty here is to . . . Bernstein and nothing must be done until he is satisfied nor while Sapiro is [un]satisfied, for to them belongs the sole credit of bringing this thing to a head and I object to anything being done that does not accord them this credit." Raining telegrams on Marshall's Adirondacks retreat, Untermyer wrote on July 5: "[I]f you have bound us hand and foot because you knew I would object why not confess your wrong that is only manly course."[61]

Those words may have forced Marshall to think twice. On the morning of July 7, Marshall directed his son James to ask Arthur Brisbane to hold the apology's release for a few more days. The request came too late.[62]

Marshall separated the apology from the litigation not because ethics rules compelled him to do so but because he believed the politics of the situation demanded it. His reasoning did not persuade those closest to him. However laudable his goal—to extract from Ford the broadest possible apology for what he did to the Jewish people without appearing to interfere with ongoing litigation—Untermyer, Bernstein, Gallagher, and Sapiro believed that the apology was inextricably related to both lawsuits. Marshall saw the matter differently. First, he maintained that his actions had not affected the litigation, telling Julius Rosenwald, "In my opinion, except remotely, neither the Sapiro nor the Bernstein cases had anything to do with the retraction." As he had earlier explained to Untermyer, the apology's importance transcended any mere lawsuit: "I did not desire to have the document intended to set the Jews right in the public mind made a subsidiary to any settlement of a law suit, because it would cheapen the whole matter, but on the contrary that the settlement of the law suits would be subsidiary to the execution of a statement exonerating the

Jews from the libels which had been published in the *Dearborn Independent.*"
Once he entered the negotiations, Marshall believed that his judgment alone
mattered. In his view, obtaining Ford's apology at the expense of the lawsuits
served both justice and the politics of Jewish civil rights activism. He thought
the lawsuits could do nothing to protect the group identity of Jews.[63]

Second, he distanced himself from Untermyer to diminish the appearance of a conflict of interest. Reminding Rosenwald of his opposition to the
Bernstein suit, Marshall casually remarked, "For your information I may say
that I have never had anything to do with that suit. I refused to bring it. It is
Mr. Untermyer's action. As you probably know, we have not been partners for
more than ten years." That statement was true, but only technically. As counsel to the firm of Guggenheimer, Untermyer & Marshall, Samuel Untermyer
and Louis Marshall shared office space, referred clients to each other, and consulted on important cases. Every paper Untermyer filed in the Bernstein case
(and, presumably, other legal actions he filed) bore the name Guggenheimer,
Untermyer & Marshall. The firm was so listed in national law directories until
after Marshall died in 1929.[64] As much as these superficial markers of partnership might have created the appearance of a conflict of interest, they did not
matter as long as the two lawyers kept their finances separate.

The settlement of Bernstein's case was a matter of some negotiation, not
between Ford and Untermyer but among Untermyer, his junior partner Laurence Steinhardt, and Bernstein. When it became clear that they were going to
settle the case, Steinhardt and Bernstein urged Untermyer to accept $60,000
rather than delay the proceedings by holding out for more. Disregarding their
advice, Untermyer induced Ford to agree to $75,000. That sum was divided
equally between the firm and Bernstein. During the litigation, the firm advanced
$6,155.74 on Bernstein's behalf for stenography, staff time, carfare, postage,
telephones, telegrams, photostats, fees for warrants of attachment, filing fees,
advertising, a deposit in the district court, fees relating to depositions and
bonds, fees for services in Detroit, and fees for copies of various legal opinions.
In his accounting to their client, Steinhardt did not include the value of his
time, nor did he venture to guess how much time Untermyer spent in court
and preparing legal papers.[65]

We do know what Untermyer did with the $37,500 he received. He paid Stein-
hardt for his time, reimbursed the firm for its costs, and sent a check for half
the balance to Louis Marshall "as his share in connection with the settlement

of [the] lawsuit against Henry Ford." At the time of the exchange, Marshall informed Untermyer "that he would not use a single cent of that money" but instead reserved it to finance the republication of Bernstein's book debunking the *Protocols*, *The History of a Lie*. By 1933, ill and in debt, Bernstein reissued the book. Yet he never received the money; Marshall had made no provisions before he died in 1929 for Bernstein to obtain it. Marshall's acceptance of remuneration in the Bernstein case cements a professional relationship between him and Untermyer. His role as the author of Ford's apology bore consequences for the legal interests of his firm's client and affected Aaron Sapiro's legal interests. Marshall's handling of that role, particularly his relationship with Untermyer, explains why he was motivated to involve himself in the Bernstein case and to what ends.[66]

. . .

Marshall's July 4 prediction and the press's speculation that the Sapiro and Bernstein cases would soon settle proved correct. Within the month, both libel lawsuits officially ended.

On July 23 Ford published a letter to Bernstein in which he completely exonerated Bernstein and extended him an apology and a financial settlement to "set [him] right in this respect." The AJC publicly credited Bernstein for the welcome development of Ford's apology while downplaying the effect of the Sapiro trial. Its pamphlet featuring Ford's statement and Marshall's letter of acceptance also included Ford's letter to Bernstein and Bernstein's response but said not a word about Sapiro or the trial in Detroit. No allegation of conflict of interest or professional misconduct was ever made against Marshall, but then no one in a position to know the inside story would have dreamed of airing such differences publicly. Untermyer had good cause to be angry, but he kept his feelings to himself. Unlike Sapiro's case, which had come close to a jury verdict, Bernstein's was nowhere near going to trial. The apology, which opened the door to a favorable settlement that otherwise might have taken years to accomplish, was a providential development for Bernstein and Untermyer. Untermyer summoned the grace to patch things up with his law partner: "I approve general plan and believe it will be productive of great results for the Jews the world over." Still asserting he had just been about to "force [Ford's] examination [on the stand]," he permitted himself a moment of crow: "I was right in bringing the Bernstein case against your protest, wasn't I?"[67]

The settlement of the more famous case was less straightforward. The wave of publicity that greeted Ford's statement, together with the fact that the trial cost Sapiro nearly every cent he had, made the option of holding out for a new trial untenable. Telling friends that he had no intention of accepting damages, Sapiro returned from Canada to Chicago on July 10 and prepared to hear from Ford's attorneys. He had already relayed his settlement terms to Marshall through Lewis Strauss, but he soon discovered that while he was in Canada, Gallagher "waived the demand for the orphan's education, because that did not seem to mean anything to him."[68]

Burned by Gallagher's waiver, Sapiro proceeded to negotiate the rest of the settlement himself. The remaining issues were costs and legal fees. In addition to office overhead, which he "worked out mathematically" to be $30,000, Sapiro pegged his costs for depositions and trial expenses at $50,000. He also spent "a great deal of money" on secret investigators to check up on potential Ford witnesses, including $2,800 to investigate Harry Dunn in Berkeley, $1,200 in North Carolina, and $6,000 in several other states. "In view of our statements that we were not using detectives and investigators," he told Strauss, "I could not very well put in these claims." In all, he estimated his costs at $117,000, most of which he expected not to recover.[69]

Ford's attorneys offered $50,000 for Gallagher's fee, and Sapiro requested $5,000 for William Lynch. Believing he had proved himself Reed's equal, Gallagher demanded $100,000. Longley balked, Gallagher held firm, offering to submit the matter to arbitration, but the Ford attorneys would not hear of such an idea. To Sapiro, the apology increased the pressure he felt to settle, and he confided to Strauss that he felt it "unfavorable to me to have the settlement deferred too long after the open retraction on the Jewish issue." Sapiro knew the Bernstein suit was also likely to settle. He suspected that the longer it took him to resolve his case, the more likely people were to draw the conclusion that he was holding out for money. A "thoroughly unfriendly" visit from Joseph Palma added to the pressure, as did signals from Longley to Gallagher that he "felt it his duty to make [the settlement] as cheap for Ford as possible." Recognizing the "strain upon Aaron" that the delay was causing, Gallagher told his client that he would accept $65,000, $50,000 of which would be paid by Ford and $15,000 of which would come out of Sapiro's share. They then agreed to divide the $15,000 between them. As a result, Gallagher received a check from Sapiro for $57,750; after paying Gallagher and Lynch, Sapiro netted $28,800.[70] Not only did Gallagher receive less than Senator Reed, whom he bested at trial, he did not even earn as much as Samuel Untermyer, who did less discovery work and made no courtroom appearance. It was widely reported, over Sapiro's staunch denials, that Ford paid him $140,000.[71]

The parties made the settlement official in an interstate telephone conference. As *Time* described it, modern technology "'hooked up'" the offices of Sapiro and Longley:

Said Counsel Longley, in effect: "Mr. Ford retracts all that the Dearborn Independent has said about you and the Jews."
Said Lawyer Sapiro, in effect: "Because of that I withdraw my litigation."

Judge Raymond's replacement, District Judge Charles Simons, signed a stipulation of discontinuance on July 18. "I am very glad to sign this," Judge Simons said, congratulating both sides. Money did not matter, Sapiro declared, because he obtained the victory he sought: "This trial actually forced Ford to his knees; and the pathetic retraction is a direct result of his dread of facing us under oath on the witness stand. I feel amply repaid for all that this has cost in time, money, and work."[72]

By forgoing the opportunity to get rich from the case, Sapiro believed he placed himself beyond all possible reproach: "I feel that I have done *all* that I should have done, both for my own people and cooperation." He derived his satisfaction from the formal retraction that would be forthcoming in the *Independent*, in which Ford would "recognize cooperative marketing as promising substantial relief to farmers and growers." That retraction appeared on July 30. It was buried deep in the issue, fifth of the issue's six editorials. The actual words of disavowal did not appear until the editorial's third paragraph:

It has since been found that inaccuracies of fact were present in the articles and that erroneous conclusions were drawn from these inaccuracies by the writer. As a result of this, Mr. Sapiro *may* have been injured and reflection cast upon him unjustly. Such statements as *may have* reflected upon Mr. Sapiro's honor or integrity, impugned his motives or challenged the propriety of his personal or professional actions are withdrawn. Likewise the charge that there was a Jewish ring which sought to exploit the American farmer through cooperative associations is withdrawn.[73]

From all accounts, Sapiro was thrilled with the outcome of the lawsuit. He expressed his joy and gratitude to Gallagher for taking "an almost forlorn hope and [making] it over into a glorious victory for truth and justice." Others found reason to be less pleased with his settlement and how he had conducted it. Finding Sapiro's behavior "erratic beyond belief," Fred Butzel criticized his relationship with Gallagher, whom he had urged to remain firm in his fee request. Butzel, who was friends with both Marshall and Gallagher, clearly disliked Sapiro.[74]

On learning of Sapiro's account of the settlement from Lewis Strauss, Marshall was also less than charitable: "He appears to be a strange kind of man. I am afraid that he indicated to his opponents undue eagerness to settle and that they as well as Gallagher took advantage of his state of mind. With the layout that confronted him he did not play his cards well." But Sapiro was not without defenders; both Strauss and Louis Gross, a Brooklyn rabbi and former classmate, believed that his handling of the matter showed "fine character" and revealed the depth of the "sacrifice" he made for the Jewish people. Gross began planning a tribute dinner for Sapiro in New York in late 1927, a gesture Sapiro found deeply touching. Marshall eventually extended an acknowledgment, through Strauss: "Please convey to him my congratulations and the hope that I may become acquainted with him."[75]

Certainly, once the case was finally over Sapiro earned a just share of public praise for what he endured. Compliments from Canada were particularly fulsome: "Aaron Sapiro has rung the death knell of crushing competition in America. He has ushered in the era of organization and co-ordination. And if Aaron Sapiro has helped liberate the farmers of America, he has helped liberate also the Jews of America from the intolerance of bigotry." The *Detroit Jewish Chronicle* acknowledged not only the credit that was due to Sapiro for "his courageous defense of his rights as a Jew and a citizen" but also the lack of public support for him during the litigation. Indeed, there were many "'outstanding Jews' in every community without whom nothing is said or done—[who] were even a little hostile towards the suit." A friend of Lewis Strauss observed, "This generation will never fully appreciate what little Aaron has done to rid this continent of bigotry and racial strife." The *Detroit Jewish Chronicle* evocatively summed up the no-win nature of Sapiro's situation: "In this half-hearted, over-cautious, wishy-washy attitude towards Mr. Sapiro and his libel suit we see one more evidence of the deplorable short-sightedness of Jewish leadership in America."[76]

The apology made it safe for people to acknowledge the embedded hostility toward Sapiro that his lawsuit generated. After the lawsuit was settled, the

Detroit Jewish Chronicle thought it appropriate to publish a letter Sapiro wrote in May, responding both to Rabbi Schulman's April sermon and to a Kansas City rabbi's defense of Senator Reed. Sapiro acknowledged that "quite a few of our wealthy Jews . . . regret that the case was brought." He knew, however, that when civil rights were at stake it usually required one individual to shoulder the burden so that others might benefit:

I believe that any American should be willing to sacrifice himself if he can help advance any great industrial system, such as I have attempted to develop in Cooperative Marketing. I further believe that any American ought to be willing to have himself destroyed, if by his destruction he can help tear down bigotry and give a fair opportunity to other Jews to do the work of idealism in America without the obstacles of hatred, ignorance and intolerance. I further believe that I, as an individual, have a right to show the ignorance and malice behind the attacks on me, as a lawyer, *even though they cannot be separated from the attacks on me as a Jew and as a farm leader.*

For him to have remained silent, Sapiro wrote, would have been "cowardly." Whether he succeeded or failed with the lawsuit, he would have at least "show[n] Henry Ford that one Jew is not afraid to fight him for his bigotry and his malice, right in his own jurisdiction, under his own battlements and in the face of his own horde of detectives and able lawyers."[77] As the tide of opinion turned in his favor, Sapiro took satisfaction in knowing that he had shown up not only Henry Ford but elite Jewish leadership as well.

The Detroit Jewish press seemed to think much the same thing: "We venture to predict that when the whole story of Mr. Ford's retraction and apology is told, it will be found that our acknowledged spokesmen had nothing to do with it one way or another. Their labors consisted in publicly playing the role of the magnanimous forgivers after the apology was made." As if that were not indictment enough of Louis Marshall, the *Detroit Jewish Chronicle* went on to say, "If the present American leadership will not learn the lesson of the 'Ford Incident,' there will surely arise a new leadership—a leadership that will know better ways of meeting the challenge of anti-Semitism than sticking its head in the sand and announcing pompously that there is no anti-Semitism in America." Such matters were not Sapiro's immediate concern. With his law practice "gone to pieces" and his "local Chicago hopes [having] failed to materialize," he had to focus on restarting his life, providing for his family, and starting his career anew.[78]

The most obvious short-term solution was to return to the lecture circuit. In August, Sapiro began a series of engagements in Los Angeles, discussing cooperative marketing and Ford's apology. On October 11, he appeared at Detroit's Temple Beth El, headlined as "the man whose name became a household word in all Jewry." At month's end, he was back in New York for a return engagement at Carnegie Hall, this time under the auspices of Marshall's foe Rabbi Stephen Wise. Three thousand people were denied admittance to the hall after it filled. The *Los Angeles Times* reported that the public learned "nothing new" about the settlement in these talks. Sapiro insisted that he believed Ford's assertion that he knew nothing of the *Independent*'s contents. But he held nothing back when he discussed Senator Reed: "He would refer to me as 'Mister Shippiro'; Sapporo; Sapiro, and in many other ways, so as to bring in all of these cheap plays that he thought the name capable of. . . . Every time a chance came to work up some Jewish prejudice, there was Reed on both feet plugging away as cleverly as he could without daring to say he was against the Jews."[79]

As the year drew to a close, however, Sapiro began speaking more openly. Like Untermyer, he felt Marshall swooped in to steal a victory he had done nothing to earn. As Sapiro traveled and lectured, Marshall reminded rabbis, Jewish organizations, and the press that Ford directed his apology to him and that its most important part was Ford's pledge to withdraw *The International Jew* from circulation. As part of his lecture tour, local organizers hosted tribute dinners for Sapiro. When one such dinner was planned for Marshall's hometown of Syracuse and an invitation describing Sapiro as "'the man who is directly responsible for Henry Ford's retraction'" landed in Marshall's office, he made his disapproval clear to the local rabbi: "I was rather of the impression that I was the man who had done this, and that as a result of what I had done Mr. Sapiro had benefitted in securing a settlement of his litigation. I also had the idea that I was the man who wrote the Henry Ford retraction. . . . I had an idea that at least in Syracuse knowledge of that fact was quite prevalent." Working through intermediaries, Marshall also put an end to Rabbi Gross's plans to organize a dinner for Sapiro in New York City. Sapiro's retaliation was less diplomatic: in speeches, he began to refer to Marshall as "King of the Jews." That barb was received as intended: "The only reason I can surmise is that he is under obligation to me for having dragged his chariot out of the mud," Marshall concluded. "I have never seen him and he has not had the grace to acknowledge what I did for him as Frederick Butzel, of Detroit, and Lewis L. Strauss, Jr. can bear witness. I do not propose to take notice of him."[80]

The insults the two lawyers traded after crossing paths in the Ford case cemented a permanent rift. Their mutual resentments interposed an unbridgeable distance between them after the matter ended, thereby killing the possibility that they might use the case to build a professional relationship. Instead, they never met. Sapiro's grievance against Marshall was rooted in a letter Marshall wrote on March 29 that made the rounds in Detroit during the trial. In it, Marshall emphasized that the lawsuit was Sapiro's "'personal action,'" not a "Jewish issue." Sapiro learned of Marshall's attitude toward his case when the letter passed into his hands during the trial's third week. He knew Marshall was at the vanguard of a group of prominent Jews, including Otto Kahn, Albert Lasker, Julius Rosenwald, and Eugene Meyer, who were withholding financial and public support. To find out that Marshall denigrated all he sacrificed, dismissed the long battle he waged, and obliged him to credit Ford's dubious cover story when he knew it to be untrue was too much to take. All Marshall did, Sapiro said derisively, was "to leap in at the finish perhaps in a desire to seize the laurels of a victory he had not won." Samuel Untermyer agreed.[81]

Sapiro's irritation is understandable. Yet something can be said to explain Marshall's intentions. His consistent aim in his political work was to advance the assimilationist goals of elite American Jews. The apology he wrote signaled other Americans that Jews intended to claim full membership in the community of citizens, that Jews belonged to America, and that Jews made the United States a better nation. For the goal of full membership to be met, the legal interests of the libel plaintiffs had to be sacrificed. Marshall knowingly chose to make that sacrifice. The apology was meant to indicate that the price of accepting Jews into mainstream society was lower than most people feared. Using Ford as his mouthpiece, Marshall staked out his position; his willingness to let Ford's cover story stand made it clear that his approach—and that of many elite Jews—was to avoid confrontation and embarrassment and instead to focus on "friendship and goodwill."[82]

Marshall's interest was the reputation, character, and future of the Jewish people, not the damage done to Aaron Sapiro or any other person. That interest led him to transform Sapiro's case from a libel action into a negotiation in which he secured Ford's disavowal of The International Jew. His goal was to have Ford apologize publicly for his antisemitism and to pull The International Jew out of circulation. He sidestepped the questions of money damages for Sapiro or a personal apology from Ford to Sapiro; ironically, he criticized Sapiro for accepting a settlement that he thought inadequate.[83]

Ford's strategy of evasion continued to be as effective after the trial as it had been during it. He hid behind subordinates who assumed responsibility for the injuries his newspaper inflicted. Then, during the end game of the Sapiro case, Ford exploited the divisions among Jews to escape the authority of the legal process. His request that Marshall write his apology presented the lawyer with what he believed was the chance to rewrite the master narrative of American antisemitism, but Ford never lost control of the outcome.[84]

Marshall construed the apology as a public humiliation for Ford, but it spared the automaker the greater embarrassment of further legal entanglement. For Ford to say he was sorry cost him nothing. Moreover, saying it out of court meant that he was not legally bound by anything to which he signed his name. The responses his statement received from the mainstream and Jewish press, the public, and popular culture suggest that he got what he wanted. Ford used the gesture of an apology as a dodge, not just to extricate himself from the lawsuit but also to give the appearance of taking responsibility without actually doing so. Ford kept one part of his promise to Marshall: the *Independent* published its final issue in December 1927.[85] Although his printed war on Jews ended, Ford controlled the terms of the cease-fire, which left him free to spread his antisemitic beliefs throughout the world by other means. Whether Marshall would be able to counter that spread effectively would depend on his ability to use the apology to force Ford to act in ways that the legal system, for all its formal authority, failed to compel him to do.

9 ENFORCEMENT WITHOUT LAW

Now that Ford has been disposed of we have reached a propitious moment for dealing on a large scale with the crime of anti-Semitism. . . . [S]o long as I live I shall remain in the arena armed for the destruction of the hideous monster with which the Jews have had to contend for so many centuries.

—Louis Marshall, 1927[1]

Louis Marshall's protestations notwithstanding, Henry Ford's apology effectively scuttled the two pending libel lawsuits. The apology then became the foundation for a continuing relationship not between Ford and his libel opponents but between Ford and Marshall. Ford made several promises that Marshall keenly hoped he would perform. As it turned out, Ford kept only one promise without help; he shut down the *Independent*. For the rest, he would require prodding.

In writing the apology, Marshall's transcendent concern was to remove *The International Jew* from circulation in the United States and Europe. *The International Jew* was "the 'Anti-Semites' Bible,'" he told a fellow lawyer in July, and Ford's apology would "neutraliz[e] its effect."[2] Scrubbing the world clean of that particular scourge would prove even more difficult than discrediting its literary ancestor, *The Protocols of the Elders of Zion*. Securing Ford's cooperation in this endeavor drew Marshall into prolonged communications with Ford's staff, which treated Marshall with professionalism and sincerity, at least outwardly. For months, Marshall believed he was making headway and that Ford was helping him with the obdurate European publishers who insisted on selling *The International Jew*.

The situation put Marshall in the position of personally enforcing the apology's provisions. That document, however, had all the legal force of an unwitnessed will. Without a jury verdict or court order to give it the backing of law, the apology represented only an informal expression of Ford's wishes. To prevail on publishers to refrain from marketing a book Ford disavowed, Marshall had to create and implement his own system of private regulation of published speech. The system worked as long as Ford and his staff gave the appearance of cooperating with it. German and South American antisemitic publishers, who never renounced their beliefs, challenged both the terms of Ford's apology and the arguments Marshall constructed to substitute the apology for law.

. . .

Even before the domestic reverberations instigated by Ford's statement began to register, Marshall realized he could use the document to great effect abroad. Because of the constitutional protections accorded to American citizens, he believed that antisemitism had more pernicious effects outside the United States than within. Particularly in Eastern Europe, Jews were subject to vicious official acts of discrimination and violence; during the late 1920s, Romania increasingly ignored protections for the rights of minorities guaranteed by the 1919 Treaty of Paris. On the day the apology was released to the press, Marshall saw to it that Ford's disavowal of antisemitism was circulated to the Romanian government "under the most favorable auspices."[3]

The more Marshall thought about it, the more he became convinced that the real value of Ford's apology lay in the impact it would have in places where Jews still lived in fear of their safety. "[T]he subject is one of life and death to the millions of Jews abroad," he told the *New York Sun*. "*The International Jew* has been translated into the various European languages and has made a deep impression because of Ford's fabulous wealth and the myth that has become prevalent that he is a leader of human thought and a man of high principles." The prospect that Ford would separate his industrial leadership from his anti-semitic literature gave Marshall "more happiness than any action in which I have ever been engaged because I feel that its effect will be far-reaching, especially in Eastern Europe, where anti-Semitism is raging today worse than at any time during this century."[4]

Withdrawing *The International Jew* from circulation was therefore critical not only at home but also in Europe and elsewhere. The book "has become the Bible of European anti-Semites," Marshall told Rabbi Emmanuel Schreiber. "I was officially informed yesterday that Ford had burned five truckloads of this book and intends to carry out in every way his understanding with me that the book shall be withdrawn from circulation. The good effects of this action are already being felt in Roumania [*sic*] and adjoining countries." Word of the book burning came from Joseph Palma, who witnessed the event in Dearborn in mid-August. Marshall took the event as a sign of Ford's commitment to "do whatever lies in his power to suppress that publication everywhere."[5]

Putting a match to copies of the book in the United States was a good first step, but it carried little weight with publishers overseas. On August 17, Marshall received a disquieting delivery in the mail: an advertisement for a new German edition of *The International Jew*. The advertisement's sponsor was Theodor Fritsch, with whom Marshall was well familiar. As the largest circulator of antisemitic literature in Germany, Fritsch had taken the lead in translating *The International Jew* into German and selling the book there through his Leipzig-based publishing company, Hammer-Verlag. Fritsch's investment in *The International Jew* was not confined to his German edition; earlier in 1927, he prepared a Spanish edition. When the apology appeared, Fritsch had a ready explanation for it: "[T]he Jewish bankers had conspired to ruin Mr. Ford and had practically gotten him into such a position that his business was being destroyed and 60,000 employees were on the verge of being impoverished, and that in order to avoid that result he was forced to make the retraction and apology." As Marshall noted to Rabbi Schreiber, Ford's book was a veritable cash cow for the antisemitism industry: "Ford has been regarded as the mainstay of such men as Fritsch and his confreres in their efforts to destroy the Jew."[6]

It was all the more alarming to Marshall to discover that many U.S. newspapers did not print Ford's apology in full and that the paragraph most often omitted contained his pledge to take *The International Jew* out of circulation. Marshall hurriedly distributed copies of the American Jewish Committee's pamphlet with the apology's entire text. But that was not the worst of it, as he told Palma. Fritsch "recently stated that he did not believe that Mr. Ford had made a retraction or apology because he had not interfered with his circulating the [*The International Jew*]." In other words, if Ford had been serious, Fritsch's "rights of publication would have been taken away." It was therefore necessary, in view of the impending publication of the Spanish edition in Spain and elsewhere, to "put an end to any supposed relations between Fritsch and his publishing company and Mr. Ford, whose name is still being used to the injury of Jews and in contravention of world peace." The first order of business was to prevail on Ford to dispose of Fritsch's publication rights, and here Marshall was certain: "[I]f they have not already been withdrawn they will be." Marshall asked Earl J. Davis to prevail on Ford "to induce action which will neutralize the efforts of Fritsch to continue his unholy warfare upon the Jews." Davis came to New York in mid-September, but unable to see Marshall in the short time he was in the city, he left some letters for him with Palma.[7]

The letters consisted of an exchange between Fritsch and the Dearborn Publishing Company. Fritsch's letter, dated July 9, cited a report from that day's *Leipziger Neuesten Nachrichten* (*Leipzig Latest News*) about Ford's "solemn retraction" and the withdrawal of *The International Jew* from bookstores: "We would be grateful for a statement from you of the facts," Fritsch asked Ford, "in order to discontinue the dissemination of the untruthful assertions." In reply, Fred Black confirmed that the German news report "is substantially correct." He observed rather than inquired, "[I]t is your intention to discontinue the dissemination of these articles in European countries."[8] This important correspondence raised the issue that most concerned Marshall: were Ford and the Dearborn Publishing Company prepared for resistance to Ford's new position?

Black's answer to Fritsch, Marshall felt, failed to meet the task laid out for it. It was vague; it failed to deliver a "correct idea of the document signed by Mr. Ford"; and it should have included the full text of Ford's apology so as to leave no doubts as to Ford's intention. "What should have been done was to have demanded in unmeasured terms that Hammer-Verlag and Fritsch should no longer publish or circulate 'The International Jew,'" Marshall advised, "that all existing copies were to be withdrawn, that no further publication was to be made, and that any attempt to do so would be regarded by Mr. Ford as unauthorized and unlawful." Three months after the apology, much to Marshall's consternation, *The International Jew* remained readily available in Germany. Marshall implored Ford's staff to secure a letter from Ford that could be circulated to the Jewish press in Europe "showing the facts" of how Ford desired to withdraw his book from booksellers worldwide.[9]

Two weeks later, Palma took Marshall's recommendations to Detroit, where he met with Frank Campsall. As the *Sapiro* lawsuit collapsed, Campsall replaced Ernest Liebold at Ford's elbow. Liebold and William Cameron remained on the Ford payroll, although the apology called for both to have been dismissed. Campsall authorized Palma to have Marshall draft a plan explaining "just what you want us to do regarding the European situation on the International Jew."[10]

Marshall seized the commission as another chance to summarize, as he had been doing all summer and fall, Ford's legal position regarding his then-discredited publication. Quoting verbatim from the apology, "which was forwarded to me at the instance of Mr. Ford on June 30, 1927," Marshall invoked

Ford's pledge to withdraw the *The International Jew* pamphlets as binding contractual language that required no elaboration. The next step, Marshall indicated, was to "allay" the anxiety of "the Jewish press and the Jews generally throughout the world who, have accepted unreservedly Mr. Ford's retraction." Ford needed to take "active measures" to stop "the misuse of his name," as evidenced by continued distribution of the title "Henry Ford's International Jew." Marshall then attached a plan for suppressing *The International Jew* and ending further republication of the book. The plan urged Ford and the Dearborn Publishing Company to meet Fritsch's objections to the June 30 statement head-on:

In order that there may be no misunderstanding as to my wishes in this regard, you are accordingly notified that whatever rights you have or claim to have to publish "The International Jew" anywhere or in any language whatsoever, are hereby revoked and terminated, and that the publication, sale or other distribution of "The International Jew" and the use of the name of Henry Ford or of the Dearborn Publishing Company in connection therewith, by you or by any person or corporation claiming under you or acting by your authority as agent, licensee or otherwise, are hereby forbidden.[11]

Marshall, an able and experienced lawyer, counted on the fact that Fritsch was not. This language swept the question of legal rights into a category defined solely by Ford's wishes. The fact that *The International Jew* was never copyrighted and that anyone was free to publish it in any form did not count in this reckoning of rights. Marshall wanted Fritsch to believe that publication rights, just like the use of Ford's name, flowed from a grant of permission that Ford now explicitly revoked. Palma thought that Marshall's wording came across too strongly; his cover note to Campsall, to whom he sent Marshall's plan on October 17, suggested he revise the statement.[12]

Campsall saw no need. Marshall's letters to Fritsch and Hammer-Verlag were retyped on company letterhead, signed by Ford, and mailed to Germany on November 1 as originally written. Marshall released the text to the press two weeks later at the AJC's annual meeting. He explained that rumors abounded in Eastern Europe that Ford's signature on his apology—as well as Marshall's on his letter of acceptance—had been faked, in an ominous sign of "the power of the 'International Jew.'" Having received press reports of Ford's June statement and Ford's revocation of the publication rights, Fritsch should not have been under any illusions about Ford's intent. But he was not about to go quietly. His next actions signaled an intent to assert law in defense of his own rights.

In late November, Hammer-Verlag announced to the European press that it intended to continue sales of *The International Jew* "in accordance with legal rights already held." Fritsch denied receiving Ford's November 1 letter and dismissed press reports that he had as "not reliable."[13]

That bluff could be maintained for only so long, and Fritsch knew it. On December 1, he wrote a long, impassioned letter to Ford, asking him to reconsider and pleading the case for the logic and truth of the antisemitic convictions he believed they both held:

Your decision of November 1st, whereby you forbid me any further distribution of the book "The International Jew," is deeply regrettable. Not so much because a considerable trade-value is being destroyed thereby (as about 9400 copies of the German and Spanish publications are depreciated), but because inestimable mental goods are lost for mankind by this fact. It is not so that the book published under your name shows "unjustified contents"; on the contrary it contains facts and truths that offer very sharp weapons in the conflict of the honourable mankind against the tyranny of a formidable might of money and lies.

The book, he continued, "is a most valiant action and a battle-axe of the truth against the bulwark of lies of a shameless and brutal society of conspirators." Its publication "remains the most important action of your life," outstripping "your great economical works." Then Fritsch launched into an extended attack on those who "want to see the book suppressed," "the financial might of the Jews," and those who secretly harbored the "real soul of the Judaism." The true mission of Jews, Fritsch believed, was to destroy the state in any society in which they lived: "The Jewish law isn't a moral doctrine of ideas, but in truth it is a political constitution which joins all Jews of the world to a uniform State, and therefore hindering the Jew to sincerely belong to any other foreign State."[14]

Fritsch's conception of the danger Jews posed to the nation-state made him "a pioneer of the [Nazi] movement" as well as "one of the few successful antisemitic publishers of the imperial and Weimar eras." But he was "a lonely prophet," in the words of the historian Richard Levy, because at the time few were willing to follow the implications of his ideology to the ends Fritsch preached: a constitutional dictatorship that eliminated all "'left-wing criminals and Jews.'" His entreaty to Ford bears the ring of one who thought he had found his soul mate only to experience cruel and inexplicable rejection: "There was a time when all thinking and honest men throughout the world full of expectation had looked up to you, Mr. Ford, as a Redeemer. Ford the highly-gifted and mighty spirit of enterprise, he who is invincible by finance—will break the chains, he will bring the liberty to all men! Such was the expectation! And now this catastrophe!" Fritsch believed that Ford had not pushed his antisemitic convictions to their fullest. There was no point in appealing to the conscience of "good" Jews, Fritsch thought; instead, Ford betrayed himself and his followers by thinking all Jews could be reformed. He had capitulated to "the core of the Jewish danger."[15]

Hammer-Verlag responded to Ford with a formal assertion of its legal rights. The publishing company consulted a "recognized authority about the copyright questions involved," and that authority rendered the following advice: "[N]o German copyright permits that a regular conferred right to distribute the book . . . in the German language and to have it translated into other languages can be withdrawn arbitrarily by a one-sided declaratory act of the author." As a result, Fritsch and Hammer-Verlag stood on solid ground in German copyright law. They notified Ford that they "regret very much to be obliged to decline your order to withdraw from sale the German and Spanish translations we have made." They were willing to make one concession: they would add Ford's June 30 statement to future copies of the book so that every reader "[would] be in the position to know the altered position of the author." Should this course not satisfy Ford, he was free, according to German law, to compensate Fritsch and Hammer-Verlag for the destruction of all 9,660 German and Spanish copies and for the withdrawal of French and Italian manuscripts from publication. Hammer-Verlag pegged the total value of these books at 40,060 German marks and supplied the name of Fritsch's bank and account number to facilitate the transaction. Upon receipt of the money, Hammer-Verlag would immediately cease selling the book and give wide public notice of that fact.[16]

Fritsch did not keep the matter between Ford and himself. He gave copies of his exchange to Adolf Hitler, leader of the Nazi Party and editor of Munich's *Völkischer Beobachter* (*The People's Observer*). Hitler published the correspondence on December 7 under the headline "An Open Word about Ford's Subjugation to the All-Jewish High Finance." When the magazine arrived in Marshall's office, he immediately alerted Ford and his staff: "[T]he notorious Adolf Hitler is one of the most virulent anti-Semites that the world has ever known. . . . He and his followers have resorted to libel, slander and violence of the most pernicious character, and throughout the civilized world he is regarded as a menace to society." Fritsch "is seeking to make it appear that you were forced by Jewish bankers to make reparation for the anti-Jewish articles published in the Dearborn Independent." Marshall asked to see all the letters to draft "what I believe would be a desirable answer to his unwarrantable remarks."[17]

The situation was serious enough to compel the astonishing: Ford, on a trip east to make arrangements for his new car and his Brazilian rubber enterprise, requested a personal interview with Marshall. On January 10, Ford came to Marshall's office, where the two "spent a most interesting hour together." As Marshall dryly observed to his son Robert, "The office was in an uproar of excitement." Ford told Marshall that "he felt better now that he had relieved his mind of the burden of the 'great mistake and blunder that he had made' in his anti-Jewish publications.'" Assured that Ford would put his name to anything Marshall prepared for him, Marshall was convinced that Ford was sincere in his repentance. What really made Marshall a believer was Ford's dismissal of Fritsch, "the effect [of which] has been to bring consternation into the ranks of the European anti-Semites." In a final goodwill gesture, Ford invited Marshall to Detroit to see the new Model A and to pick out one for himself. This act of generosity Marshall politely declined, expressing his "devotion to pedestrian locomotion." A few weeks later, Marshall relayed to Herman Bernstein that Ford was "carrying out his promises in every way," and the press interpreted the meeting as "'the final scene in the reconciliation between American Jewry and Henry Ford.'"[18]

But as battle on one front closed down, it began to heat up on another. Fritsch's invocation of German copyright law put the matter beyond Campsall's expertise, so he referred the file to Clifford Longley for review. Longley acted carefully, telling Campsall to provide Marshall with copies of the Fritsch correspondence together with an invitation to provide "any suggestions which he has to offer us." Campsall sent Marshall Fritsch's letters and inquiries from publishers in Berlin and São Paulo, Brazil, regarding Russian and Portuguese editions. Those publishers also wanted compensation in exchange for their willingness to discontinue or refrain from selling the book.[19] Marshall supplied more than a few "suggestions." He drafted a letter for Ford to send to Fritsch, provoked by Fritsch's "extraordinary communications." Marshall thought it unwise to permit Fritsch's "various insinuations and charges . . . to remain unanswered." He did not explain his thinking to Ford, but he felt silence in the face of published antisemitism in the highly charged European context was much more dangerous than it was in the United States. He denied the allegation that Ford acted under pressure from Jews or financial interests and derided the idea that Ford had been "made the catspaw of others."[20]

But when it came to countering Fritsch's legal claims, Marshall was on less certain ground. Again, he elided the distinction between the use of Ford's name, to which Ford had every right to object, and the republication of an uncopyrighted work, to which Ford had no right of legal ownership:

I have the absolute right to forbid the distribution of these books because of the fact that the articles were contrary to the truth and had a tendency to occasion irreparable injury to innocent people. For you to persist in the fact of these conditions in circulating these books and in using my name in connection there with, offends against the public welfare and contravenes sound public policy. With these facts brought to your attention there can be no legal or moral support for your insistence in the face of my protest.[21]

Just what "sound public policy" Marshall relied on here he left vague. If Ford were to prevail on Fritsch to refrain from publishing materials that "occasion[ed] irreparable injury to innocent people," then private negotiation, not law, would have to be their mutual guide. Unlike Fritsch, who pointed to a specific German copyright statute, Marshall could cite no provision of American law, state or federal, to support his position. Instead, he called on magisterial phrases such as "absolute right" and "sound public policy" in the hope that they would elicit the desired effect. It was all he could do; he had no other weapons—not international law, not even the threat of a lawsuit—at his disposal. Just as in November, the letter Marshall drafted was promptly sent, without any changes, to Fritsch. Another version was mailed to the Berlin publisher who held the Russian translation with the added comment that no compensation would be paid for copies of The International Jew left on hand. A third letter, also drafted by Marshall, was eventually sent to São Paulo. Campsall relied entirely on Marshall's legal advice in dealing with these foreign publishers; Longley watched from the background, only directing Campsall to consult with Marshall in December 1927 and thereafter deferring to the New York lawyer.[22]

Before long, Marshall received information from Berlin confirming that Fritsch had no intention of honoring Ford's wishes. Hammer-Verlag continued to place advertisements in trade publications announcing that Ford had refused to pay him not to sell The International Jew; as a result, he considered himself free to continue to sell it under German law. The ad noted that in six years one hundred thousand copies had been sold and that the *Independent* controversy had only increased demand for the book, a fact that could only have irritated Marshall. The *New York Times* even called Ford's office for comment. With Ford temporarily out of the country, not only was the press obliged to wait; so, too, was Marshall, who held Fritsch's taunts for more than a month before Ford and Campsall returned from Brazil. Marshall was finally beginning to recognize that Fritsch's legal claims could not be defeated under German copyright law. Marshall's next statement for Ford sought only on to get Fritsch to stop the unauthorized use of Ford's name. The draft said nothing about requiring Fritsch to desist from publishing the book.[23]

Upon his return to the United States, Campsall had more pressing matters to bring to Marshall's attention. He sent Marshall a letter from a German journalist—and Nazi agent—working in the United States, Kurt Lüdecke, who sought to intercede with Ford on Fritsch's behalf. Lüdecke minced no words: "According to the legal rights of German publishers, Mr. Fritsch is absolutely justified in demanding the re-purchase of the books in question." He pointed out that since the *Independent* and *The International Jew* were uncopyrighted, Ford had "no juridical power whatever" over their translation and sale. Ford could control only the use of his name; he could not invoke a "moral right" against Fritsch to stop sales. Lüdecke dismissed the apology: "It is too ridiculous to waste one word over Mr. Ford's statement and apology to the Jewish people. There are enough witnesses who know that Mr. Ford knew very well what was going on in the Dearborn Independent and what is written in the 'International Jew.'" If the matter was not settled within a month, Lüdecke said, sales of *The International Jew* would resume "and the matter brought before the public."[24]

Lüdecke was no stranger to Longley. Ford's lawyer first encountered him during the *Sapiro* trial, which Lüdecke covered for several German newspapers, including Hitler's *Völkischer Beobachter*. He had a checkered past; in the early 1920s he escaped prosecution for fraud, swindling, and blackmail in Germany by fleeing to the United States, where he presented himself to sympathetic German Americans and raised money for the Nazi Party at Hitler's personal request. One of his intended targets was Henry Ford, with whom he met in January 1924. Lüdecke had several connections to Ford and the *Independent*. Lüdecke first met William Cameron in 1921, Cameron introduced Lüdecke to Senator Reed during the *Sapiro* trial, and the closure of the *Independent* at the end of 1927 deprived Lüdecke of a $300 commission for two articles he wrote that the newspaper never published. On the strength of Lüdecke's presence in Dearborn during the 1920s, historians have speculated for decades whether Ford contributed to Hitler, but I have found no evidence of a monetary relationship between Ford and the Nazis, at least not during the time he published the *Independent*.[25]

For opponents of antisemitism, Lüdecke was a dangerous figure, the very presence of unsavory German extremism on American soil. When he reappeared on Longley's radar a year after the trial, the lawyer's instinct was to ignore him and deal directly with Fritsch. Longley so counseled Marshall in a courteous note. On his copy of Marshall's April 3 letter to him, urging quick action on both Fritsch and Lüdecke, however, Longley scribbled a note to Campsall: "Frank—While you were away this came to me from the leader of The Chosen People with whom we have been dealing—My answer attached—C.B.L."[26]

Longley's snide note gives the first sign that Ford's staff was tiring of the seemingly incessant demands emanating from Marshall. The second was that Ford, with Campsall in tow, left the country again without authorizing a response to any of the letters written in February and March. Marshall was particularly eager that Ford issue a new statement for the European press, because he had learned more about the public's tepid reception of the apology from a well-informed friend on the continent. Most European papers did not run the full apology, did not print Marshall's follow-up letter, and ignored commentary from the Jewish press, with the result that many people never saw "the very favorable expressions . . . concerning the Jews." And a few, like Fritsch, refused to believe Ford because they had read the apology only in the "Jew Press." Editorial comment in the mainstream European press opined that the whole thing was merely a stunt to whip up publicity for the new Ford car, not unlike some suspicions voiced in the United States. Finally, the friend noted, Fritsch's highly publicized plans to continue selling *The International Jew* made Ford look ridiculous: "People are laughing because the great auto-king finds himself powerless against the small owner of the Hammer-Verlag and allows himself to be defied by Fritsch." In the face of this opposition, even some Jewish voices expressed skepticism about Ford's motives and sincerity. The friendly source urged Ford to undertake an advertising campaign in Jewish newspapers in Europe to counterbalance his heavy ad presence in the mainstream press and give credence to the friendship for Jews he professed in his apology. The ad should consist of Ford's original statement and a new one that proclaimed that the apology had "absolutely nothing to do with his business interests, but was actuated by purely ethical and moral considerations and was prompted solely by Mr. Ford's conscience and his recognition that he had been misled and deceived."[27]

Ford was finished issuing statements, however. Marshall's April 3 letter—the one on which Longley scribbled his dismissive remark—went unanswered. On May 12, Marshall wrote what would be his last entreaty to Ford on the subject: "I sincerely trust that definite action may be taken along the lines which I have suggested, which will surely have good results." He asked for a reply before he left for London in three weeks: "You will, of course, understand that my anxiety in this direction is due to the fact that I regard it as highly important that the work which you have so well begun may find fruition in accomplishment."[28] In that spare sentence, Marshall recognized that for all their exchanges, nothing had changed. *The International Jew* remained readily available in Europe. Unwilling to reimburse publishers for their lost profits, Marshall had no other leverage to apply to entrepreneurs unwilling to bend to "Mr. Ford's wishes." Once Kurt Lüdecke made it clear that Fritsch intended to rely on his rights under German copyright law, Ford's staff lost interest in fighting the battle if they ever harbored any. Ungrounded in any law on which these unlikely allies could rely, the apology set up that battle on unwinnable terms. Marshall was simply the last to concede the point.

Without compensation to induce him to stop or a legal injunction to force him to, Fritsch continued to publish *The International Jew* in German and Spanish and introduced new editions in French and Italian. What had begun as an overwhelming public victory with Ford's abject apology in 1927 ended in quiet defeat for Marshall in 1928. Publicly, he continued to assure people that the entire matter had been properly handled: "We flatter ourselves that the policy which we pursued with regard to the publications of Henry Ford was correct." When subsequent protests from European publishers seeking compensation in exchange for their Italian and Russian translations arrived at Ford's office, no one bothered to answer them.[29] Ford took no further action on his promise to withdraw *The International Jew* from circulation abroad. At home, the subject was dropped just as discretely. Many American pundits saw Ford's retreat as proof positive of the salutary effects of consumer protests and a humiliating lawsuit. But overseas, where Marshall feared the inbred, ingrown culture of antisemitism far more than he did in the United States, the perception that a

Jewish boycott brought Ford to his knees was taken as simply another demonstration of Jews' overweening strength.

. . .

Marshall and Ford exchanged no significant correspondence during the following year and a half. German antisemites cooled toward Ford for a time after the events of 1927, and the continued circulation of *The International Jew*, though rankling for Marshall, was a small annoyance compared to his other overseas concerns. Negotiations with Zionists over Palestinian land claims called him to Europe in 1928 and 1929. Working with his son-in-law Jacob Billikopf and AJC member David Brown, he raised hundreds of thousands of dollars for relief in Russia, Poland, and Romania.[30]

Marshall also paid attention to national politics during the presidential race of 1928. He supported Herbert Hoover enthusiastically and made many speeches and public appearances for him. He also continued to counsel Jewish Americans on the undesirability of kicking up a public fuss about the occasional encounter with antisemitic discrimination. "It is far better to exercise patience," he told a young New Yorker in September 1928, "than to indulge in an outburst which will only have the effect of hypnotically suggesting to others . . . the desirability of adopting a hostile attitude." After the *Independent*, American antisemitism remained something best ignored in a country where Jews "enjoy[ed] political equality" and had access to "vast resources and opportunities which at some time are likely to knock at your door and result in prosperity."[31]

Marshall's confidence in that careful approach nearly evaporated weeks before the 1928 presidential election. In late September, officials in Massena, New York, a small upstate town, accused Jews of abetting in the kidnapping of a child to use her blood in sacrificial rituals—a reiteration of the ancient, horrific charge of blood libel. It appeared to be another situation tailor made for Marshall's intervention. It happened on his turf, and everyone involved knew who he was and for what he stood. Instead, as events unfolded, the Massena blood libel incident showcased the limits of his ability to negotiate unilateral resolutions by apology when the integrity of the Jewish people was at stake.

Massena was an unlikely place for an outbreak of the worst sort of antisemitic prejudice. Settled by white Anglo-Saxon Protestants, the small town underwent an industrial and demographic transformation in the late nine-teenth century. By 1920, a largely Catholic labor force brought to Massena "a polyglot population with immigrants from more than fifty countries." Jews were but a small fraction of the new wave; the sole Jewish synagogue, Adath Israel, boasted fewer than two dozen families. Still, the racial tensions of the 1920s found Massena, remote as it was. When four-year-old Barbara Griffith disappeared on the afternoon of September 22, 1928, among the town residents searching for her were members of the Ku Klux Klan.[32]

The New York State police took over the investigation that night. As the search spread, so, too, did an ugly rumor. In 1928, the Jewish Day of Atone-ment fell on September 24. Yom Kippur is the most important day in the Jewish religious calendar. Someone in the community mentioned the holiday, sug-gested that Jews used human blood in their rites, and connected the notion to the child's disappearance. Whispers grew more audible in the dark that she "might have been murdered by Jews for ritual purposes." Fueled by the rumor, the state police began to single out Massena's Jewish residents for questioning and inspected their homes and businesses without search warrants. After talk-ing to other members of Adath Israel, Jacob Shulkin, the congregation presi-dent, decided the situation was "serious enough to place a long distance call to the home of Louis Marshall." Roused in the middle of the night, Marshall immediately dispatched Boris Smolar, a Ukrainian-born reporter for the Jew-ish Telegraphic Agency, to Massena on the next train.[33]

The accusation of ritual murder trailed Jews throughout history and often incited violence and mass murder against them. It frequently appeared in twentieth-century Europe and America. In 1913, Mendel Bellis was arrested in Kiev, Russia, and charged with murder for the purpose of conducting blood rituals. Prosecutors attempted to use historic Jewish documents and books to convict him, to no avail; Bellis was acquitted. Two cases were reported in Europe around the time Barbara Griffith disappeared. Six cases that amounted to no more than rumor occurred in the United States, mostly in the northeast, between 1913 and 1928. Still, that was too close for comfort for American Jews. For Marshall in particular, the blood libel represented the worst kind of threat to all that Jews had won by their hard work and accomplishment in the new world. Accordingly, when he hung up the telephone in his home, he knew he had to act, "fearing . . . that a blood libel might be in the making." Jews had been tortured, tried, and judicially murdered in Europe over these accusations without proof or due process. Sending a reporter from the Jewish press to learn more was a reasonable first step; Marshall did not want to start a press stampede or a general Jewish outcry before he knew the facts.[34]

Events in Massena unfolded faster than the train could bring Smolar's help. Local leaders believed the rumors; the mayor, W. Gilbert Hawes, continued to manage the investigation after it passed into the state's jurisdiction. Hawes ordered State Trooper Harry M. McCann to bring in the local rabbi for questioning. Offended at this disturbance on the eve of Yom Kippur, Berl Brennglass refused to go to the town hall, telling McCann he would appear in a few hours to make a statement. When he got there, "a mob of several hundred was awaiting his arrival in a state of unusual excitement." The mayor and McCann interrogated him for more than an hour. McCann asked whether it was customary for Jews to obtain the blood of Christian children in their observation of Yom Kippur and whether this might explain the girl's disappearance. Brennglass indignantly declared that the Jewish faith forbade the use of blood of any kind. McCann hastened to say that "a foreigner" supplied them with the idea and that the mayor and he felt compelled to check out all possible leads. As he left city hall, Rabbi Brennglass declared, "This is a . . . slander against the entire Jewish people!" The rabbi was so upset by his encounter with official Massena that on his return home, he summoned the synagogue's leaders to tell them about it. Not yet having heard from Marshall, Brennglass and his group sent him another, more detailed letter. They also decided to wire Rabbi Stephen Wise of the American Jewish Congress. They had no idea what trouble they just unleashed: "Massena's Jews could not anticipate the 'diplomatic' fiasco that would ensue from seeking assistance from the two giant egos of American Jewry."[35]

Around 4 p.m, just as Smolar, the Jewish Telegraphic Agency reporter, arrived at Rabbi Brennglass's home, Barbara Griffith walked out of the woods less than half a mile from her home and into the arms of two teenage girls who had been looking for her. Word of her rescue spread across the village as Massena's Jews were arriving at the synagogue for Kol Nidre services at 6:00 p.m. They felt overjoyed at her safe return, yet bruised by the unjust accusation their neighbors had leveled. They spent Yom Kippur in a state of "mental agony," horrified that "the accursed blood accusation" had followed them to the United States. The following day, Mayor Hawes and Trooper McCann came to the synagogue to apologize in person, but the matter had escalated:

they replied that they would accept no apology.[36] Though Barbara Griffith had come home, the town's ordeal was not over.

Predictably, Marshall and Wise began working the matter independently of each other. But for once, Wise outdrew Marshall. As the historian Saul Friedman points out, it was Stephen Wise who informed the state's top officials of the troubling incident. Wise was close friends with Governor Al Smith and the state superintendent of police, John Warner, Smith's son-in-law. As it happened, Smith was the Democratic nominee for president that fall. On September 28, Wise urged Warner to look into the state police's role in fomenting the blood-libel incident in Massena; four days later, Wise phoned the governor in Albany and briefed him on the accusation. Smith immediately informed the American Jewish Congress that a "thorough" investigation of the state trooper's conduct would be made: "There will be no toleration of an attempt by any public official to give countenance to the grotesque accusation of ritual murder, or any equally baseless indictment against a whole people by the citizenship of America, at least not in this State, while I am its Governor."[37]

Employing his usual methods, Marshall wrote sharply worded letters of protest to Mayor Hawes and Police Superintendent Warner on October 1. Just as when he telegraphed Henry Ford in June 1920, Marshall did not stop to consult anyone else. It was imperative for Marshall to establish the AJC's authority over its rival in this matter. Marshall gave the public officials a learned history of "blood libel," criticized them for subjecting the rabbi to a "shameless interrogat[ion]," and condemned them for thinking that "the Jews of Massena were engaged in a conspiracy to murder an innocent Christian child so that her blood might be used in an unholy rite." He then made a series of nonnegotiable demands. Mayor Hawes had to apologize, immediately, for this attack on Jews and "their honor" and for "the abuse of [his] official position" in permitting Rabbi Brennglass to be questioned on such an offensive premise. The apology had to be presented on "such terms *as will meet with my approval,*" Marshall insisted. Once the mayor made satisfactory repentance, then the self-appointed arbiter of the case would submit it to the scrutiny of public opinion. Marshall also demanded Hawes's resignation and the firing of Trooper McCann. If one or the other condition were not met, Marshall would pursue remedies available under New York's Public Officers' Law relating to acts of official misconduct. Marshall sent his letters to the Jewish Telegraphic Agency, which promptly released them to the *New York Times*, which published them on October 3.

Marshall's letters unleashed a fury in the press that transfigured an outbreak of local prejudice, however ugly, into a matter of national import.[38]

Once Wise alerted the governor, the process moved beyond what letters of apology could accomplish. Smith was in the delicate position of having to take immediate action without appearing to seek political capital from the incident. Accordingly, Marshall's sturm und drang notwithstanding, the state police inquiry proceeded in Albany on October 4 behind closed doors. Warner presided and the Massena town officials attended as "voluntary witness[es]." Also present were Rabbi Brennglass, Adath Israel president Jacob Shulkin, the Massena village attorney, Rabbi Wise, and American Jewish Congress Executive Secretary Bernard G. Richards. After the hearing, the mayor and state trooper issued fulsome apologies to the rabbi and Massena's Jewish community. "I have committed a serious error of judgment," the mayor said. "I have no hesitation in affirming that . . . I should have repelled [the blood-libel suggestion] with indignation and advised the State trooper to desist from his intention of making inquiry of the respected rabbi . . . concerning a rumor so monstrous and fantastic." It was as "unthinkable," he then knew, to suspect Jews of ritual murder as it was to suspect any Christian. "I write this word of heartfelt apology because I would do justice not only to the Jewish people of Massena, but because I desire to offer complete and unreserved amends to that great people which has given to the world the God I worship and the religion I love." He also had an answer for Marshall's threat to seek his dismissal: he did not apologize out of fear he would be removed from office but because he was sincerely remorseful: "I know that the citizens of Massena, including its Jewish members, will not seek to dishonor me through removal from office because of an error in judgment which no one deplores more than I do." Likewise, Trooper McCann apologized to Rabbi Brennglass for questioning him about "a rumor which I should have known to be absolutely false." McCann was reprimanded, suspended without pay, and served out the rest of his career in obscurity. Shulkin and Brennglass issued statements declaring that they considered the matter satisfactorily resolved.[39]

Only then did Mayor Hawes answer Marshall's October 1 letter. He confessed he was "totally ignorant" of the history of blood libel. Had he understood the meaning of such an accusation, he assured Marshall, he never would have permitted the police to approach Rabbi Brennglass. He explained, "by way of palliation," that owing to "excitement occasioned by the disappearance of the child," he ordered the police to investigate every lead. He ended with language he gave Marshall liberty to use if such an accusation ever resurfaced: "I now formally extend my unqualified apology not only to the Jews of Massena, whom I have always found to be good and honorable citizens, but also to Jews everywhere, for the wrong that I have done, and request them to accept this expression of my repentance."[40]

Marshall was at his office, meeting with two Jewish residents of Massena, when he learned that the hearing was under way. Furious at Warner, Hawes, and Wise for their subterfuge, he wrote another portfolio of letters admonishing them for proceeding without him. He accused Warner of ignoring the fact, broadcast in the newspapers, that he "had been requested by the Jewish Congregation of Massena to represent it in this matter." The speed with which the hearing was called and conducted told him all he needed to know about the state's motives in proceeding. Marshall was certain that Warner and the mayor rushed the hearing to narrow its scope, to benefit Smith politically, and to keep from engaging with "the enormity of the offense committed," which he said was "perpetrated not only upon the Jews of Massena, but, I repeat, upon every Jew." The mayor's apology was insufficient because Hawes neglected to address it to the wider Jewish community and because he failed to get Marshall's approval in advance. In a pitch-perfect replay of the Ford matter, Marshall sent Hawes a drafted apology that "I feel that I have a right to ask you to sign and return to me." There would be no negotiating its phrasing. Only if unconditional surrender were made on his terms would Marshall grant Hawes the full absolution of the Jewish people. Unfortunately, Marshall's draft of Hawes's apology has been lost.[41]

Marshall was not finished doling out indignation, rage, and corrections in equal measure. He reserved special scorn for Shulkin, who had telephoned him on the evening of September 22 only to shut him out of the hearing once Wise spoke with Governor Smith. Shulkin, like the mayor and the state police superintendent, did not know how to handle this delicate, explosive situation: "[Y]ou undertook without submission to me," Marshall lectured him, "to accept the apologies of the Mayor and the Corporal, disregarding the important condition that I had made in my letter to the Mayor that any apology that he might make should be in a form approved by me." Shulkin had, after all, violated one of the primary tenets of Marshall's policy on antisemitism in the public realm: "You knew very well that resort to the courts was the very last thing that I desired." Going to official authorities for hearings and resolutions rather than allowing Marshall to adjudicate the terms of a proper apology—or secure the removal of an obdurate mayor from office according to statute—undermined Marshall's authority as AJC president.

More than that, Marshall felt personally humiliated. He took exception to Shulkin's call to close the matter, which "practically dismisses me from the case and decides an important proposition which in no manner concerns you." What Marshall meant by this, he said, was what "the attitude of the Jewish people as a whole should be toward this episode." Why Shulkin, as a Jew at the epicenter of the controversy, should have nothing to say about how the episode was resolved Marshall did not explain. He was unaccustomed to gleaning intelligence from third parties while the principals met in secret and to being dismissed, practically or otherwise, once his services were engaged. The mayor's flawed apology sent him into a tailspin; he judged Hawes "guilty of the most serious offense ever perpetrated in this country upon the Jewish people, infinitely worse than anything that Henry Ford ever did."[42]

That comment is a measure of just how much the Massena incident disturbed Marshall. But the difference between this blood-libel accusation and the half dozen other outbreaks on U.S. soil, for Marshall, could have been simply temporal. In other words, Massena represented a setback because it occurred after Henry Ford apologized for antisemitism—an apology Marshall handcrafted—and because the methodology that seemed to bring Ford to heel was useless against far less inimitable opponents. For such offenses against Jews, Marshall would not accept anything other than an apology dictated by Jews—meaning, of course, by Marshall himself. The apology he wrote for Ford was terribly flawed, but luckily, the world remained unaware of those flaws. The apology he wrote for Mayor Hawes never saw the light of day.

The degree to which Massena had become all about Marshall quickly became clear. He alone refused to accept the mayor's apology. As Saul Friedman observed, "It seemed as if everyone in the country had been placated by Hawes's apology but Marshall." The national press and many Jewish publications agreed with Brennglass and Shulkin that it was appropriate to let the matter drop. The *New York World* believed that Hawes's statement "should put an end to a deplorable incident." The *American Hebrew* remarked that "any further pressure exercised by American Jews would savor of vindictiveness." The Yiddish papers *Morning Journal* and *Der Tog* proudly editorialized on the events in Albany, and in New York City rabbis agreed that the state had taken proper corrective steps. There were also calls for "leniency and understanding" from religious and academic leaders on the Permanent Commission on Better Understanding between Christians and Jews in America, which declared that the "blood accusation is a cruel and utterly baseless libel on Judaism."[43]

With this kind of public reaction—Hawes's repentance was treated as more genuinely made than Ford's—continuing to target the mayor began to backfire. Working separately, Rabbi Brennglass and Shulkin asked Marshall to stop dunning Hawes for another apology. The mayor and his family were receiving threatening telegrams and letters from all over the country, a state assemblyman was preparing to institute proceedings for his removal, and Shulkin feared "if the matter is continued it may have a very unfavorable reaction upon our people." He believed that Hawes had been "sufficiently punished and humiliated." On that point Marshall did not agree, but he evidently conceded that little would be gained by pressing for a signature on the apology he drafted. He never heard from the mayor again. In November at their annual meeting, Marshall and the AJC contented themselves with a public acknowledgment of the apology Marshall had deemed completely unacceptable. In contrast, the American Jewish Congress feted Massena's rabbi and Jewish leaders at its convention later that month.[44]

Marshall's inelegant handling of the Massena controversy did not go unnoticed in the Jewish press. *Der Tog* wryly observed that "the story begins with Marshall and ends with Wise . . . and must make an unpleasant impression." The *Canadian Journal Review*, commenting on "The Reign of Louis M," took an editorial scalpel to Marshall's tendency to act as "absolute ruler of four million Jews of the United States of America" in the style of a king of France or a Russian tsar. Even its praise was Janus faced: "One cannot but admire the beauty of his character. [Yet i]n his day people loved and admired Caesar. Even the last Wilhelm was not without certain attributes of greatness." And then there proceeded a catalog of critiques, culminating in an analysis of recent events: "[W]hen Ford made his overtures to the Jewish people, did it not strike sensitive Jews that Marshall was somewhat arrogant in snapping so readily into the role of a plenipotentiary for the Jewdom of the world? Aaron Sapiro was the soldier who fought the battle. Marshall, at a moment's notice, began to act the statesman, taking advantage of the soldier's victory."[45] For saying essentially the same thing, Sapiro had been frozen out of Marshall's personal and professional circles.

The Canadian writer also found Marshall's conduct in the Massena affair less than admirable. The critique of Marshall was not that he was misguided or that his motives were suspect; it was that he acted on presumption and without consent of the governed: "We entertain no admiration for a state of affairs which permits any individual to presume to act in season and out of season, as the anointed head of the Jewish people." Massena was the straw that broke open the bale. In refusing to accept the mayor's apology, Marshall's authoritarian style and arrogance shone through the events he sought to control and laid him open to public criticism such as he had never before experienced. When unsympathetic observers connected the dots from the Ford matter to Massena, they found a disturbing pattern, not enough to topple Marshall from his high platform but enough to crack his previously impervious facade.[46]

Marshall's insistence on the right kind of apology as the antidote to antisemitism proved ill advised. The Massena affair moved beyond his ability to manage and into the realm of official state processes, steered there by the very organization that opposed Marshall's unilateralism and aversion to courts. The faux-legal document he penned for Ford was unequal to the task he set for it. Perhaps nothing could have contained the menace, once unleashed, of *The International Jew*. The book's lack of a copyright was Ernest Liebold's everlasting gift to his fellow antisemites. *The International Jew*'s lack of legal ownership also undermined Marshall's belief that informal methods would enable him to induce Ford to see that every copy was returned to Dearborn and burned. There was no putting that toothpaste back into its tube. The value of Ford's name, influence, and wealth added power, credibility, and longevity to a text that had no basis in fact. In the end, Marshall's prestige, organizational acumen, and professional standing could not substitute for the authority of law, and neither Ford nor stubborn publishers nor hapless village officials would bow to anything less commanding than law. In the end, though, nothing in Ford's history of antisemitic activity demonstrated whether law could countermand prejudicial speech.

. . .

Louis Marshall did not live to see *The International Jew* thrive among European readers in the 1930s—nor did he witness Hitler's acquisition of power in

1933 and Germany's passage of the first disabling discriminatory laws against its Jewish citizens. Marshall died on September 11, 1929, in Zurich, Switzerland, of a swift pancreatic infection that resisted doctors' efforts to save him. Marshall was in Zurich to attend the sixteenth Zionist Congress, at which he brokered an agreement among Zionists, non-Zionists, and European and American Jews to form the Enlarged Jewish Agency for Palestine. The Jewish Agency, which was to work on the establishment of a Jewish national home in Palestine, promptly elected Marshall its chair. That Marshall breathed his last in the service of the world's Jews justifiably burnished his legend as a hero to his people and added a degree of pathos to the outpouring of grief at his passing.[47]

Marshall's unexpected death elicited tributes and eulogies from newspapers across the world, the official organs of nearly every organized religion in the nation, and civil rights organizations of every kind. In death he rose above the particular, and sometimes petty, and he was embraced as the true patron of American citizenship that he had worked for, and spoken out on behalf of, all his life. Among the thousands of expressions of praise and sympathy at his death was a short note by W. E. B. DuBois in *The Crisis*: "This great constitutional lawyer repeatedly turned aside from his appointed tasks and his lucrative practice to give time and counsel to the National Association for the Advancement of Colored People. He considered the cause of Negro freedom to be the cause of human freedom, and he helped accordingly. His death is a mighty loss for the American Negro." As did Marshall, DuBois believed in the general nature of citizenship claims. In that vein, the Catholic vice president of America's Good Will Union remarked, "With the passion for liberty and justice which inspired the founders of our Republic, and for the old-fashioned American ideals written into our federal constitution, he battled with tireless energy to arouse the minds and consciences of our citizens to realize what the spirit of America truly means."[48]

In their eulogies, his fellow lawyers trumpeted his accomplishments as a Jewish leader and his lasting contributions to New York and U.S. law. They hardly referred to the Ford matter, noting only Marshall's role as confessor, and entirely passed over Massena. The instances in which Marshall fell short were forgivable sins of overreaching; they stemmed from an admirable imperfection his friends and allies preferred to overlook after his death. "Marshall law" became, for Cyrus Adler, Max Kohler, Jacob Billikopf, and all those who worked closely with him, something they valued more highly once it was gone.

Indeed, as with many other great men, the lionization of Louis Marshall began in earnest with his death and grew in intensity with time. Today, Jewish students learn that Marshall was the finest Jewish lawyer never to sit on the Supreme Court and that he was the foremost patron of Jewish civic equality. In 2003, Samuel Untermyer's grandson Frank did not mince words: "Louis Marshall was a saint," he said.[49]

After the praise of the famous faded to echoes, however, important questions remained. It is necessary to look more closely at what Marshall law left in its wake. Marshall's belief that he could personally contain the spread of antisemitism was unwise. Trying to stop the spread of an idea, even one so pernicious, is like trying to capture smoke. Marshall failed to grasp the limits of his approach, in part because he found countervailing methods messy and undignified and in part because the nineteenth-century legal culture in which he trained never led him to challenge the assumption that most wrongs done to Jews did not require legal remedies. Marshall thought he had beaten back antisemitism with the Ford apology, but Theodor Fritsch and Massena revealed that error. He did not live to witness how perniciously the ideas represented in *The International Jew* and the *Protocols* would take root in Europe or that the Nazis would make law an instrument of antisemitic policy.

After 1929, it was left to Marshall's friends and successors at the AJC to maintain pressure on Ford whenever *The International Jew* resurfaced in connection with the growing international antisemitic movement. In 1934, Lewis Strauss asked William Cameron to secure a "restatement" of Ford's position when the book emerged in an antisemitic campaign in Argentina. B'nai B'rith approached Ford through Rabbi Leo Franklin, who was pleased to assist. As Franklin pointed out, even when antisemitic publishers included the 1927 Ford-Marshall exchange in their reprints of *The International Jew*, they always added the disclaimer that Ford did not "specifically deny the truth of the articles." A group called the Defenders of the Faith, led by the Reverend Gerald B. Winrod of Wichita, Kansas, was selling *The International Jew* without the 1927 correspondence, which it dismissed as the work of "powerful Jews." Ford authorized Frank Campsall to write the desired letter, but that was as far as he was willing to go. James Rosenberg, an AJC member and New York attorney, suggested inviting Ford to address a memorial dinner for Louis Marshall in 1934 as a way to obtain a more direct statement from the automaker, but Ford would neither take part nor send a letter to the group.[50]

Ford's enthusiasm for corralling copies of *The International Jew*, if it ever amounted to much, dissipated during the 1930s. Aside from Campsall, by that time no one remained in Ford's inner circle with any connection to the lawsuit or the apology. Clifford Longley left the Ford organization in 1929 and went into private practice, although he remained a consultant to the Ford Motor Company and the Fords personally. Ernest Liebold's star, which began to fade with the fall of the *Independent*, dropped precipitously in 1933, when he suffered a nervous breakdown brought on by the banking crisis and disappeared without a word to his family or employer. He resurfaced thirty-six hours later, near the northern tip of Michigan, pleading that he only needed rest, but his relationship with Ford was never the same. He remained on the Ford payroll in a marginal capacity, his influence steadily diminishing until Harry Bennett finally forced him out in 1944. Bennett did not last much longer than Liebold. The face of Ford's violent union-busting policy during the 1930s, Bennett brutally usurped Edsel Ford, who died prematurely in 1943, and fired other top executives. He was easily the most hated man at the company during the last fifteen years of Ford's life. Upon assuming the presidency of the company in 1945, Henry Ford II's first act was to fire Bennett.[51]

None of the individuals closest to Henry Ford during his career as an antisemitic publisher was inclined to exert a restraining influence on him. They either shared his views or they were more concerned about keeping their jobs. It was never part of company culture to oppose how its founder deployed its resources, not even in private. Compared to the millions Ford put into banks, rubber, railroads, ironworks, and other industrial projects, the $2 million he lost on the *Independent* and the *Sapiro* lawsuit hardly registered on the company balance sheet. The purveying of antisemitic ideas, of course, was never meant to turn a profit.

What Ford learned from the episode was how easy it was to sign his name to nonbinding agreements and statements of sentiment that did not reflect his inner convictions. In the early 1940s, he finally wrote the letter that Strauss asked him to produce a decade before, but he had already conclusively revealed himself. In 1938, on his seventy-fifth birthday, the German consuls of Cleveland and Detroit came to his office and presented him with the Grand Service Cross of the Supreme Order of the German Eagle, the highest award that Hitler's government could bestow on foreigners. The Grand Cross was more of a lifetime achievement award for Ford; it had not taken long for Hitler, the Nazis, and antisemites in Europe and elsewhere to rationalize away the apology and resurrect *The International Jew* as a treasured resource. Much of Detroit joined Ford on July 30 for a celebration at the state fairgrounds, where 8,000 school-children sang "Happy Birthday," and a more intimate crowd of 1,500 sat down to dinner at the Masonic Temple that night.[52]

Protests from Jewish comedians and veterans' groups over Ford's accep-tance of Hitler's medal went unanswered. The national mood was less confron-tational than a decade before. And antisemitism remained, for the most part, still just words on paper. The Anschluss, the German occupation of Austria and its vicious treatment of Vienna's Jews in March 1938, had yet to register with Americans. Barely three months after the German consuls draped their red sash over Ford's chest, the Nazis ordered the destruction of Jewish syna-gogues, businesses, and homes on November 9, 1938, an event thereafter known as Kristallnacht—the night of broken glass—touching off a wave of pogroms that resulted in the deaths of almost a hundred Jews and the incarceration of thousands more in concentration camps. American isolationism resurfaced as the Nazis consolidated power and gobbled up their neighbors in the late 1930s. At that time, no one seemed willing to go to war to protect European civilians, let alone imperiled Jews, from Hitler. After the war began, few were inclined to see the fate of the Jews under Nazi aggression as deserving special attention. Only after it was all over, when films of the liberation of the concentration camps were released and survivors began to tell their stories, did Americans begin to grasp the extent of the human carnage of Hitler's war.

Henry Ford attended a showing of one such film at the Ford plant on the River Rouge in late May 1945. We know nothing of his reaction to it. By then he had suffered a series of increasingly debilitating strokes—the first coming just weeks after his seventy-fifth birthday—and his mental competence was so much in doubt during the war that the government considered nationalizing the Ford Motor Company to get production contracts for motors and airplanes delivered on time. Only much later would his doctor describe his condition that year as "a pleasant vegetable." By late September 1945, the Ford women—Clara and Eleanor, Edsel's widow—prevailed on the old man to step down at last. After his grandson replaced him as company president, Henry Sr. had little to do but go for daily rides with his chauffeur and walk in Fair Lane's gardens with Clara. In the waning years of his life, Ford took evident pleasure in recognizing friends on these outings; some days, however, he seemed not to know anyone.[53]

On April 7, 1947, spring rains caused the River Rouge to flood, wiping out the generator that supplied electricity to Fair Lane. Ford spent the day inspecting the damage around Dearborn, surprisingly alert and cracking jokes. By early evening, power was restored, but only for a while; the Fords spent a few hours listening to the radio before retiring to their bedroom in darkness around 9 p.m. Two hours later, Henry awoke, complaining of a headache, and Clara asked for the doctor to be called. While they waited, she cradled her husband and offered him water, but Ford died before the doctor could attend him. The cause was a massive cerebral hemorrhage that was probably set in motion by the simple act of bending over to untie his shoes.[54]

The *Sapiro* case did not materially affect the course of Ford's life. Ford was never obliged to demonstrate repentance in any meaningful way, his acceptance of the Grand Eagle from the Third Reich poked a thumb in the eye of anyone who had taken his apology seriously, and he continued to use company staff and resources as a dodge. After 1927, he simply went underground with his antisemitic views, quietly supporting platforms of other public intolerants. William Cameron staged a weekly radio show in the 1930s that essentially continued his work for the *Independent*. Ford money also subsidized the radio programs of Father Charles Coughlin, an antisemitic Detroit priest who built a large following later in the decade. Ford's friendship with Charles Lindbergh, as Max Wallace has documented, was based on their common antipathy toward Jews and their shared admiration for Germany's authoritarian state. More recently, historians have begun to debate whether Ford permitted Hitler to nationalize his Berlin plant for the production of munitions—a war crime by any definition—based on newly discovered evidence in the National Archives.[55] Whatever Ford meant by putting his name on Marshall's statement in 1927, his subsequent actions raise serious doubts about his intentions, his sincerity, and his probity.

. . .

Sapiro's life changed the most as a result of his encounter with Ford and Marshall, and not for the better. In 1928, he and his family relocated to Scarsdale, New York, where they lived in a large suburban home with three maids, a butler, and a nurse. Sapiro aimed to start his career "with a clean slate," as he told Lewis Strauss in July 1927, with nothing but his dignity and his good name as collateral.[56] That tableau of domestic bliss belied a continuing, and troublesome, propensity for encountering professional difficulty.

The settlement of the Ford suit marked a turning point in Sapiro's career. His identity as the man who successfully sued Henry Ford followed him wherever he went. Shortly after he arrived in New York, he petitioned the state bar association for admission to practice as an attorney in good standing. The state's Committee on Character and Fitness thought otherwise. Ignoring the *Independent*'s retraction, the committee chair contacted the Ford organization as part of its investigation into Sapiro's application. Despite the terms of the settlement, "we cannot regard such a termination as a complete refutation of the charges that were made against Mr. Sapiro." The committee suspected the case was settled to avoid controversy with the "Jewish race" rather than "because of Mr. Sapiro's innocence." Mercifully, the Ford organization did not put the *Independent* staff in touch with the bar committee, and Sapiro obtained his New York law license with no other apparent difficulty.[57] But the letter made it clear that Sapiro would not be able to shake off the lawsuit—and the *Independent*'s libels—as if they had never happened. The fact that Ford had apologized for group libel, in some minds, did not clear Sapiro of the taint of misconduct.

The most important thing that Sapiro associated with the case seemed indelibly tarnished in his mind. His career as a promoter of farmers' cooperatives, which was on the wane at the time he filed suit, came to a slow and unheralded end, at least in the United States. He remained an active consultant to the movement in Canada, where a more radical offshoot attempted to enforce compulsory pooling in the wheat industry. After the stock market crashed in 1929, accusations of profiteering proliferated in such essential commodities as milk and bread during the first years of the Depression, and Sapiro was called on to advise state and federal officials and agencies struggling to reconcile longstanding deference to free markets with pressing public need.[58]

Sapiro also broadened his New York law practice beyond agriculture. The eastern urban setting set him on a quest for new causes to promote. Convinced that individual operators of all kinds were increasingly disadvantaged in an intensely competitive marketplace, he served as legal counsel to labor and trade groups. After establishing a law office on William Street in lower Manhattan, he organized associations of taxicab drivers, dry-cleaners, milkmen, motion-picture exhibitors, and a variety of similar clients in major cities, simultaneously or in quick succession, in a pattern that would characterize the rest of his career.[59] Sapiro never found an industry that offered him the sort of wide-ranging influence, visibility, and authority that he had enjoyed during his career in cooperative marketing. Instead, his efforts to establish himself as a leader in modern urban industrial and trade organizations would compromise him professionally.

For example, Sapiro maintained contacts and clients in Chicago, where he found excellent opportunities for organizing small-scale businesses, trades, and workers. Law enforcement in that city, overwhelmed with organized crime and corruption, cracked down against efforts to set prices and wages regardless of who was orchestrating them. The purge swept legitimate professionals such as Sapiro, University of Chicago economist Benjamin Squires, and Chicago alderman Oscar Nelson together with gangsters Al Capone and Murray Humphries in a 1933 indictment with seventeen other codefendants. The charge was conspiring to restrain trade in the cleaning and dyeing, laundry, carbonated-beverage, and linen-supply industries. The trial was the longest and most expensive criminal proceeding in Cook County history. One scholar of the rackets trial has explained it as an anachronistic attempt to criminalize forms of economic organization that the New Deal had recently legitimated. Aware of the damage that would follow a conviction, Sapiro fiercely but unsuccessfully resisted extradition. For four long months, the Chicago newspapers linked him to gangsters and racketeering. Sapiro eloquently defended himself, again outperforming opposing counsel on the witness stand; all the defendants were acquitted. But the prosecution stained his name.[60]

A more substantial blow came on the heels of that acquittal. In July 1934, Sapiro was indicted in New York on charges of jury tampering. The issue was whether Sapiro had committed professional misconduct in a 1933 criminal mail fraud case, in which he advised defense counsel on jury selection. The defendant, Murray Harwood, heard that "professional jurors" often sat on federal cases, and he urged his trial counsel, Charles L. Kahn, to investigate the backgrounds of the jurors chosen for his case. Kahn consulted Sapiro, who agreed that such inquiries could be made by someone who would not identify himself or his business and who would avoid all direct contact with jurors. For this delicate work, Sapiro recommended Sam Roth, a trusted business associate.

Roth made inquiries on Kahn's behalf and found that the circumstances of three of the jurors raised questions about their prior jury service. By this time, however, the trial was well under way. Sapiro believed that the information Roth gathered was relevant to the trial regardless of the stage at which it was brought to light, as it showed that jurors had lied during voir dire examinations, and just as in his own case against Ford, they could supply grounds for a mistrial. Kahn disagreed and suppressed the information. Two weeks later, when the judge in the mail-fraud case announced in court that one of the jurors had reported being approached by a defense representative, neither Kahn nor Sapiro associated the event with Roth's inquiry. Harwood was convicted and sentenced to four years in prison. Letters he wrote from prison denouncing Sapiro and Kahn provided grounds for prosecuting both for jury tampering. Harwood's cooperation helped the prosecution of Kahn but did not secure Sapiro's conviction.[61]

Feeling betrayed and discredited by the New York courts and forced into bankruptcy by his legal problems, Sapiro returned to California with his family in 1935. The Sapiros settled in Pasadena, just outside Los Angeles, but Sapiro could not escape his troubles. Judge John Knox and the New York state bar authorities decided that his conduct in the Harwood case required disciplinary action. An assistant U.S. attorney brought disbarment proceedings against Sapiro in early 1936, with Knox presiding. In the midst of the court's fact-finding, Sapiro requested several delays to travel to California after his wife was hospitalized. Doctors described her condition as "'not serious,'" but the true nature of her illness quickly became apparent. Five months later Janet Sapiro died of breast cancer at the age of forty-one.[62]

Judge Knox handed down his decision disbarring Sapiro from practice in the federal courts of New York in 1937. Meanwhile, Sapiro threw himself into the internecine struggles wracking San Francisco's maritime unions. His engagement with maritime labor brought him into contact with the charismatic Australian-born labor leader Harry Bridges, an alleged communist, and led Sapiro to aid the Immigration and Naturalization Service (INS) in its efforts to deport Bridges in the late 1930s. Beginning in 1934, when maritime workers paralyzed the port of San Francisco and inspired workers throughout the city to join them in a general strike, Californians feared the militancy of waterfront labor activists. As workers struggled to use their collective power to improve conditions in dangerous occupations, businessmen's and citizens' groups decried the workers' actions as detrimental to California and its economy. During the Depression, public resentment toward the maritime unions increased, and their activities were branded as anarchistic and un-American. Groups like the American Legion waged a vigorous campaign to goad the Department of Labor into investigating the influence of communism in the maritime unions. Aided by local police and some fervent antiradicals, the INS began, first warily and then with increasing zeal, to try to build a case sufficient to deport Bridges and other foreign-born organizers active on the Pacific Coast.[63]

Sapiro viewed Bridges's leadership of the labor movement with increasing dismay. Bridges was the more established organizer. Still, Sapiro attained a prominent position in the maritime struggle by representing and advising a number of the major maritime unions, including the Sailors' Union of the Pacific, and serving as defense attorney to the Modesto boys, a group of seamen charged with possession of dynamite and intent to destroy property belonging to Standard Oil during a 1935 tanker strike. Sapiro appreciated Bridges's genius, admired his accomplishments as a labor leader, and bailed him out of difficult situations. In December 1936, Bridges hit a young cyclist who darted in front of his auto and was jailed on charges of involuntary manslaughter. In short order, Sapiro secured his release, got the charges dropped, and urged the International Longshoremen's Association to protest Bridges's treatment.[64]

Certainly Bridges, who emerged as a leader in the 1934 strike, commanded broad allegiance among seamen, a power he then sought to use to unite the maritime unions under his authority. He warned workers against following anyone who did not rise from the rank and file. Bridges was also a political radical. Publicly, he denied being a member of the Communist Party, but he secretly belonged to the national central committee of the Communist Party in the United States.[65] Bridges's covert communism and dismissive attitude toward other labor leaders eventually alienated Sapiro.

After one particularly unpleasant encounter with Bridges in 1937, Sapiro offered his assistance to the INS. That November, Sapiro gave a deposition detailing his knowledge of Bridges's union and communist activities. He described Bridges as an opportunist and egotist whose personal ambition and private aims portended disaster for the maritime unions. What he objected to was not Bridges's communism, Sapiro said. He respected an honest revolutionary. Bridges was dangerous to the labor movement because he was committed to the cause of communism while pretending to espouse and advance the cause of American workers. Sapiro helped the INS identify others who might testify against Bridges and encouraged agents to call on him for help. In addition to testifying against Bridges in his 1939 deportation hearing, Sapiro continued to oppose Bridges and to check the spread of the Congress of Industrial Organizations, of which Bridges was the western regional director. But Sapiro's word, even against a known communist, was undermined by his past record. The government lost its deportation case against Bridges; moreover, James M. Landis, the federal trial examiner, pronounced his testimony not credible, citing Sapiro's federal disbarment.[66]

The end of Sapiro's work in the maritime labor movement also marked the end of his career as a lawyer in public service. For the following two decades, he practiced law quietly, occasionally providing free legal services to distinguished friends, including John Barrymore and Igor Stravinsky. In his last years, Sapiro suffered horribly from arthritis. The disease so crippled his hands that he could write only with an enormous pencil. After a short second marriage in the mid-1950s ended in divorce, he died at the age of seventy-five on November 23, 1959. His will specified that his body be donated to the University of California–Los Angeles medical center for arthritis research, which disappointed competing schools. What was left of his grand household—an art collection, extensive library, elegant furniture, antiques—was sold at auction. His obituaries paired mention of the fact that he was the man who sued Henry Ford for $1 million with the sadder note of his fall from professional grace.[67]

No funeral was held for Aaron Sapiro. He told his son Stanley that if one were held, he would return and haunt him for the rest of his days. That did not stop friends from remembering him. Nathan Straus published a letter in the *New York Times*: "That he ended his life in obscurity should not dim the memory of his outstanding services to our country in former days." Lewis Strauss, probably Sapiro's closest friend during the Ford matter, wrote movingly of their personal relationship, their professional collaborations, and "the most piercing eyes I ever saw." He acknowledged what few were willing to say: the Ford case made Sapiro "a marked man. . . . Some of his friends while willing to concede that his suit had brought the fortunate end to an unsavory and dangerous period in social relationships nevertheless did not want to associate with him publicly." Strauss conceded that Sapiro "had never succeeded in reestablishing himself" after the Ford case, but he concluded on an optimistic note: "History, I am sure, will in time give him his due."[68]

CONCLUSION

We cannot know what the *Sapiro v. Ford* jurors would have decided had the opportunity to deliberate come to them. Yet we can speculate: what might have happened had the suit run its course? A jury verdict and damage award in Sapiro's favor might have been personally gratifying, but they would have further alienated Sapiro from Marshall and the Jewish civil rights establishment and perhaps divided Jews at a time when they could not afford it. How would people have reacted to a large damage award? Would Sapiro's reputation have suffered, as Marshall and others suggested, if he appeared to be profiting from Ford's libels against all Jews? Or had he been sufficiently brutalized during the trial that the public would believe he deserved compensation from Ford? His public image aside, the money would have helped Sapiro regain his footing professionally. Whatever else may be said about him, he deserved better than he got.

The jurors' post-mistrial interviews indicate that they retained a healthy skepticism toward Ford and the allegations against Sapiro. They recognized that Sapiro had made mistakes and that the cooperative movement was flawed, but they did not believe that a conspiracy was responsible for the misfortunes of farmers. The jurors were neither impressed with nor intimidated by Ford's wealth, and their judgment reflected the attitude of the country generally. Ford had been unable to convert his money into political power. Brandishing antisemitism as a weapon improved neither his prospects nor his image. The *Sapiro* case should have ended his public career. The theatrical gesture of the apology made him look momentarily ridiculous, but it bought him viability. It also helped that Ford's antisemitism was exceptionally broad and extreme, and it was easy for him to apologize for those excesses. Antisemitism continued to flourish in American society in myriad tacit ways after the *Sapiro* case, remaining an acceptable, respectable prejudice as long as adherents didn't shout it from the rooftops.[1]

The amazing thing about the *Sapiro* case is that it provides a prolonged demonstration of the ease with which Ford drew people into his gravitational pull—and how long he kept them there. With the benefit of hindsight, present-day Americans can recognize that Ford's *amende honorable* was not so honest or sincere after all. He manipulated the legal process and everyone involved to evade responsibility for an ugly situation that he, more than anyone else, created. He did not, however, get away clean. His historical reputation was tarnished and remains so, especially compared to contemporaries who were just as antisemitic as he: Thomas Edison, Charles Lindbergh, George Bernard Shaw, and most politicians of the day. The *Sapiro* lawsuit was only the most public manifestation of Ford's lifelong demonization of and perseveration over Jews. But it was only a momentary engagement; once the moment had passed, it lost its appeal for him, and he tossed it aside with little care, nearly as if it had never happened. Marshall, who should have known better than anyone to keep a safe distance from Ford's magnetism, neatly enabled this outcome.[2]

Largely forgotten were the heroism and bravery Sapiro displayed in confronting a national bully. He saw the fight through to the end, despite what it cost him; more than anyone else involved, he put his faith in law and got the least in return. The case nearly bankrupted him. The apology did not mention his name, nor did it grant Sapiro the satisfaction of a direct vindication. The *Independent* apologized to Sapiro and published a mealy-mouthed retraction in July 1927, but many fewer people were paying attention after the thunderclap of Ford's apology died away. Sapiro was too experienced and learned an attorney to expect a lawsuit to provide healing; he knew better than to believe he would be made whole. He did harbor the belief that in having the law on his side he would find satisfaction, if not justice. Even if the trial did not erase antisemitism from American society, Sapiro believed it was important for Jews to defend themselves in public and take their chances on the good sense of their fellow Americans. From everything he said and wrote after the case, it appears he was content with what he had achieved. Family members say he never discussed the case, but not because he was bitter. Toward the end of his life, he joked that the only car he enjoyed riding in was his son's Thunderbird.[3]

Marshall had his priorities in handling the case, as we now know. He viewed the *Protocols* as a continuing danger to the future of the Jewish people, because discrediting the book in 1921 had failed to stop its dissemination. *The International Jew* only amplified that danger. The continuing accessibility of the *Protocols* and *The International Jew* on the Internet today feeds the apparently widespread psychological demand for ideological certainty in uncertain times and maintains their literary authority despite their repeated repudiation. The *Protocols*—and Ford's endorsement of them—have validated every fear that Marshall expressed about them.[4] The irony is that, despite Marshall's perspicacity, his efforts to destroy *The International Jew* came to nothing. Ford's promise to do all he could to revoke permission for publishers to continue printing the book proved empty. Marshall's death in 1929 ended serious efforts by the Ford Motor Company to make good on Ford's promise, which, unsecured by law, he and his lawyers thereafter disregarded.

In a sense, Marshall wrote the apology to establish a permanent place for immigrant Jews in America's industrial future. In his view, Sapiro did not represent that future, nor would he ever lead the battles that Jews would have to fight over immigration reform, better employment, access to higher education, and other measures of economic mobility that were closed not by dint of law but by social practice and prejudice. What Sapiro represented—the corporate organization of American agriculture—meant less to Marshall, was less valuable to future of the Jewish people in America, than what Henry Ford represented and had to offer. The future for Jews, as Marshall saw it, was Ford's future. As odious as Ford was, Jews needed him. They didn't need agriculture. History was on Ford's side.

Ford managed to take the powerful farmers' movement and make its success a story about who Jews were and the legitimacy of their participation in public policy, agriculture, and public life. By reframing the account of the cooperative movement so thoroughly and enlisting Marshall in that process, Ford succeeded not in discrediting the cooperative movement, but in marginalizing Aaron Sapiro.

The case's resolution outside the arena of formal law prevented it from clarifying the confusion it generated over group and individual libel. Newspapers trumpeted the news when Judge Raymond prevented Sapiro from including claims on behalf of Jews generally in his lawsuit. Yet later, when the apology made headlines, the irony that the apology recognized the grievances of Jews in general and ignored the harms done to Sapiro individually apparently escaped everyone's notice. Sapiro took one for the team, but only the team got the atonement. Moreover, having gotten the nation's foremost purveyor of group libel to recognize his offense—and repent—gave Marshall a potent weapon of his own. Why did he do so little with it? Marshall did not use the apology to instill group libel in American law or to expand protection of Jews from defamation. Instead, he confined its use to a focused, yet futile attempt to retrieve Ford's antisemitic book from European publishers. Perhaps if Marshall had lived to witness the events that unfolded in Germany during the 1930s, he might have resolved to deploy that weapon in a different mode—if not directly in the courts, then maybe by pushing for statutory declarations along the lines of New Jersey's 1935 pathbreaking hate-speech law.[5]

Worried about the presence of the German North American Bund within the state and particularly the Bund's establishment of camps for indoctrinating children with Nazi propaganda, the New Jersey legislature prohibited the publication or circulation of propaganda inciting racial or religious hatred. Also barred were books, photographs, flags, or other symbols conveying such hatreds, as well as the use of the radio to broadcast speeches conveying prohibited messages. Anyone renting facilities to groups that broke the law was also guilty of a crime. The law declared that such materials interfered with the rights of citizens to "pursue and obtain safety and happiness and enjoy freedom of conscience in the matter of religious worship." Like the earlier criminal libel laws that supplied Midwestern cities' only recourse against Ford and the *Independent*, the New Jersey law's justification lay in the state's interest in preserving the public safety and public peace. And as in those earlier cases, the New Jersey courts refused to countenance so great an intrusion into free speech in the absence of actual violence, overturning the law in 1941.[6]

World War II changed the stakes for group libel in American law. The war, the widespread suffering of so many people, and the systematic mass murder of the Final Solution made Americans aware of the uses to which extremists could put group labels, group identity, and group consciousness. This was particularly the case for Jews, but the war also opened the floodgates for racial equality for African Americans. Tensions over housing and integration exploded into race riots in the Chicago area in 1951, and when the U.S. Supreme Court upheld Illinois's criminal libel law the following year in the *Beauharnais* case, it took judicial notice of the violence. The state was justified in banning the circulation of advertisements encouraging landlords not to rent to African Americans, the Court concluded, because the offensive language of the ad could easily instigate more riots: "If persuasion and the need to prevent the white race from becoming mongrelized by the negro will not unite us," the leaflet read, "then the aggressions . . . rapes, robberies, knives, guns and marijuana of the negro, surely will."[7]

The Supreme Court's recognition of group libel in 1952 marked an important exception in its developing First Amendment jurisprudence. The Court deferred to state legislative determinations of what constituted harmful speech, and it acknowledged that individual rights flowed from identification with a collective. Even more significant was the Court's declaration that insults—mere words—hurt an individual's economic rights. Here, group libel that interfered with access to housing was just as unconstitutional as a contractual agreement not to sell to black Americans.[8]

Just as the Supreme Court opened the door to group libel, civil rights groups decided not to walk through it. Fearing the possibility that group libel would be used against not just offensive speech but also unpopular groups, the American Jewish Committee, the NAACP, the American Civil Liberties Union (ACLU), the Anti-Defamation League, and other advocacy organizations abandoned group rights claims in favor of legal strategies that emphasized robust individual constitutional liberties for everyone. As a result, the civil rights movement, the feminist movement, and other social movements during the 1960s surrendered the nexus between group identity and economic rights established in *Beauharnais*. The leading American proponent of group libel theory during the 1940s, the law professor David Riesman, later changed his mind and threw his support to the ACLU when it defended the rights of neo-Nazis to march in Skokie, Illinois, in the late 1970s. The NAACP's critical victories in the freedom-of-association cases—the right of people to join organizations without having their names revealed to state officials—did not empower the organization so much as protect individuals. The wave of college and university on-campus regulations during the 1990s barring offensive language directed at race, religion, culture, sex, and sexual orientation might have resurrected the logic of group libel, but by then the American commitment to individual speech rights was firmly set. Courts struck down campus hate-speech codes after civil libertarians and political conservatives alike attacked them. Those who oppose any curbs on free speech as well as those who advocate for regulation in the interest of protecting group identity might consider etiquette a useful resource; it functions as a different, though no less potent, belief system for limiting speech than law.[9] Etiquette cannot, however, substitute for law; it guides behavior but cannot constrain it. Those wishing to use speech to cause purposeful offense are those members of society least interested in self-regulation.[10]

In the twenty-first century, according to First Amendment scholars, the United States remains a remarkable exception in its dedication to preserving free-speech rights for citizens. European nations have criminalized speech denying the Holocaust and have jailed famous Holocaust deniers. In the United States, the Supreme Court has struck down state laws making the act of cross burning a crime, and the idea of criminalizing Holocaust denial is simply unthinkable. Just as repugnant would be the suggestion that the U.S. government prohibit the publication of images of the prophet Muhammad, but after cartoons of the Prophet appeared in a Danish newspaper in 2006, indignant Muslims demanded legal remedies and plotted to assassinate the cartoonist. Instead of extending the law of Holocaust denial to the desecration of Islam, however, Europeans have asserted free-speech claims in support of reporters, illustrators, and publishers. It is not so much that the United States is the exception in a world willing to censor speech; rather, it may be that Holocaust denial is the exceptional subject when it comes to free speech.[11]

Justice Louis Brandeis once memorably recommended that the answer to objectionable speech is more speech, but effective counterspeech does not always reach the original audience. Today, Internet booksellers offer dozens of editions of *The International Jew*, many under Henry Ford's byline. Rare and difficult to find are a complete run of *Pipp's Weekly* and James Martin Miller's unflattering biography of Ford, both of which Ford bought up in large quantities and destroyed during the 1920s. In the *Sapiro* case and in many similar cases, hate speech has a long half-life. For everyone in the *Sapiro* case, except perhaps Ford, victory was elusive. Louis Marshall was not so naive as to believe that Ford had truly repented. By substituting his own authority for law, however, he permitted Ford to evade a more lasting judgment.

LIST OF ABBREVIATIONS USED IN THE NOTES

BFRC	Benson Ford Research Center, The Henry Ford, Dearborn, Michigan (formerly Henry Ford Museum and Greenfield Village), Dearborn, Michigan
acc.	accession
acc. 1	Fair Lane Papers (Ford Family Personal Papers)
acc. 48	The Aaron Sapiro Case
acc. 285	Henry Ford Office Correspondence, 1921–1952
acc. 1740	Clifford B. Longley Papers
EMP	Eugene Meyer Papers, Library of Congress, Washington D.C.
HBP	Herman Bernstein Papers, YIVO Institute for Jewish Research, New York, New York
JARP	James A. Reed Papers, Western Missouri Historical Society, University of Missouri, Kansas City
LLSP	Lewis Lichtenstein Strauss Papers, American Jewish Historical Society, New York
LMFP	Leo M. Franklin Papers, Temple Beth-El, Bloomfield Hills, Michigan
LMP	Louis Marshall Papers, Jacob Rader Marcus Center, American Jewish Archives, Cincinnati, Ohio
LOC	Library of Congress, Washington, D.C.
MDSP	Milton D. Sapiro Papers, Collection of Gary Milton Sapiro, Alamo, California
NARA-CP	National Archives and Records Administration Headquarters: College Park, Maryland
-GL	Great Lakes Branch: Chicago, Illinois
-PCR	Pacific Coast Region: San Bruno, California
RG	Record Group
RG 16	Records of the Secretary of Agriculture
RG 21	Records of the U.S. District Courts
RG 165	Records of the War Department, GS Military Intelligence, Division Correspondence, 1914–1941
RBP	Robert Bingham Papers, Library of Congress, Washington D.C.
SC	Small Collections, American Jewish Archives
SGMML	Seeley G. Mudd Manuscript Library, Princeton University
SUP	Samuel Untermyer Papers, Collection of Frank Untermyer, Evanston, Illinois (transferred to American Jewish Archives,

	Jacob Rader Marcus Center, Cincinnati, Ohio, after Frank Untermyer's death)
WHGP	William Henry Gallagher Papers, Collection of Patricia Gallagher Wooten, Battle Creek, Michigan
WRHS	Western Reserve Historical Society, Case Western Reserve University, Cleveland, Ohio
YIVO	YIVO Institute for Jewish Research, New York, New York

NOTES

INTRODUCTION

1. Many Judaic scholars argue that the term *anti-Semitism* is linguistically and historically misleading. I follow those who prefer the unhyphenated, uncapitalized word form and use it as it is commonly understood, as a description of acts and words that convey hatred of Jews, although this form and use only imperfectly resolve the semantic problem of grouping all Semitic peoples under the term *anti-Semitism*. See David A. Gerber, "Anti-Semitism and Jewish-Gentile Relations in American Historiography and the American Past," in *Anti-Semitism in American History*, ed. David A. Gerber (Urbana: University of Illinois Press, 1986), 3–54, esp. 3n1.

2. See, e.g., Edward Larson, *Summer for the Gods: The Scopes Trial and America's Continuing Debate over Science and Religion* (New York: Basic Books, 1997); James E. Goodman, *Stories of Scottsboro* (New York: Pantheon Books, 1994); Irene Quenzler Brown and Richard D. Brown, *The Hanging of Ephraim Wheeler: A Story of Rape, Incest, and Justice in Early America* (Cambridge, Mass.: Belknap Press of Harvard University Press, 2003).

3. Jonathan Sarna, *American Judaism: A History* (New Haven, Conn.: Yale University Press, 2004), 120–22; Howard M. Sachar, *A History of the Jews in America* (New York: Knopf, 1992), 78–80; Leonard Dinnerstein, *Antisemitism in America* (New York: Oxford University Press, 1994), 32.

4. On rights in the post–Civil War era, see, e.g., William E. Nelson, *The Fourteenth Amendment: From Political Principle to Judicial Doctrine* (Cambridge, Mass.: Harvard University Press, 1988); Robert M. Cover, *Justice Accused: Antislavery and the Judicial Process* (New Haven, Conn.: Yale University Press, 1975).

5. Ford Motor Company circular letter, date redacted [c. 1926], file 5, box 138, LMP; Fred L. Black, trial testimony, *Aaron Sapiro v. Henry Ford and the Dearborn Publishing Company, a Michigan Corporation*, Case No. 7522, U.S. District Court, Eastern Division of Michigan, Southern Division, Transcript of Proceedings, 15 Mar. 1927, pp. 998–1005 (hereafter Trial Transcript), file 4, box 43, accession 48, BFRC; Dinnerstein, *Antisemitism in America*, 81–83; Anne Jardim, *The First Henry Ford: A Study in Personality and Business Leadership* (Cambridge, Mass.: MIT Press, 1970), 139–40; Carol W. Gelderman, *Henry Ford: The Wayward Capitalist* (New York: St. Martin's Press, 1981), 218–20; David L. Lewis, *The Public Image of Henry Ford: An American Folk Hero and His Company* (Detroit, Mich.: Wayne State University Press, 1976), 140; Allan Nevins and Frank Ernest Hill, *Ford: Expansion and Challenge* (New York: Charles Scribner's Sons, 1954), 125, 262, 316. Nevins and Hill peg the total losses incurred by the Dearborn Publishing Company between 1918 and 1930 at $4,795,000. Ibid., 311.

6. Steven Watts, *The People's Tycoon: Henry Ford and the American Century* (New York: Knopf, 2005); Douglas Brinkley, *Wheels for the World: Henry Ford, His Company, and a Century of Progress, 1903–2003* (New York: Viking Press, 2003).

7. In addition to Nevins and Hill, *Expansion and Challenge*, 311–23, see, e.g., Watts, *People's Tycoon*, 381–84; Gelderman, *Wayward Capitalist*, 218–21; Jardim, *The First Henry Ford*, 139–42. Neil Baldwin's *Henry Ford and the Jews: The Mass Production of Hate* (New York: Public Affairs, 2001) recapitulates the well-documented history of Ford's antisemitism. Baldwin's main contribution is the argument that Ford's antisemitic views could be traced to his childhood exposure to the McGuffey Readers, a primary school text used in the late-nineteenth-century United States, but Albert Lee made that connection more than twenty years before, in his book of the same name (Lee, *Henry Ford and the Jews* [New York: Stein and Day, 1980], 147).

8. See, e.g., Marshall to Editor, *NYT*, 17 Jan. 1916, in Charles Reznikoff, ed., *Louis Marshall, Champion of Liberty: Selected Papers and Addresses* (Philadelphia: Jewish Publication Society of America, 1957), 1:275.

9. On tribalism in the 1920s, see John Higham, *Strangers in the Land: Patterns of American Nativism, 1860–1925* (New Brunswick, N.J.: Rutgers University Press, 1955); Kevin Boyle, *Arc of Justice: A Saga of Race, Civil Rights, and Murder in the Jazz Age* (New York: Henry Holt, 2004); Mae M. Ngai, *Impossible Subjects: Illegal Aliens and the Making of Modern America* (Princeton, N.J.: Princeton University Press, 2004); Lucy E. Salyer, *Laws Harsh as Tigers: Chinese Immigrants and the Shaping of Modern Immigration Law* (Chapel Hill: University of North Carolina Press, 1995); Richard Slotkin, *Lost Battalions: The Great War and the Crisis of American Nationality* (New York: Henry Holt and Company, 2005); Nancy MacLean, *Behind the Mask of Chivalry: The Making of the Second Ku Klux Klan* (New York: Oxford University Press, 1994); Christopher Sterba, *Good Americans: Italian and Jewish Immigrants During the First World War* (New York: Oxford University Press, 2003).

10. On postwar antisemitism, see Dinnerstein, *Antisemitism in America*; and Nathan C. Belth, *A Promise to Keep: A Narrative of the American Encounter with Anti-Semitism* (New York: Times Books, 1979), 58–114; on Jews as the "white other," see Matthew Frye Jacobson, *Whiteness of a Different Color: European Immigrants and the Alchemy of Race* (Cambridge, Mass.: Harvard University Press, 1998), 52–90; Eric L. Goldstein, *The Price of Whiteness: Jews, Race, and American Identity* (Princeton, N.J.: Princeton University Press, 2006). For the argument that elite Jewish civil rights activists subscribed to a "racial hierarchy" that explained their divergent strategies for African Americans and Jews, see David Levering Lewis, "Parallels and Divergences: Assimilationist Strategies of Afro-American and Jewish Elites from 1910 to the Early 1930s," *Journal of American History* 71 (Dec. 1984): 543–64.

11. *Abrams v. United States*, 250 U.S. 616, 630 (1919); Melvin I. Urofsky, *Louis D. Brandeis: A Life* (New York: Pantheon Books, 2009), 545–63; David Rabban, *Free Speech in Its Forgotten Years* (New York: Cambridge University Press, 1997), 342–55; Geoffrey Stone, *Perilous Times: Free Speech in Wartime from the Sedition Act of 1798 to the War on Terror* (New York: Norton, 2004), 135–234.

12. Act of 11 Apr. 1913, ch. 265, sec. 40, 1913 N.Y. Laws 481; Evan P. Schultz, "Group Rights, American Jews, and the Failure of Group Libel Laws, 1913–1952," *Brooklyn Law*

Review 66 (Spring 2000): 71–145, 96; Dinnerstein, *Antisemitism in America*, 73–74; Nathan C. Belth, *A Promise to Keep: A Narrative of the American Encounter with Anti-Semitism* (New York: Times Books, 1979), 23–26. The laws went unconstrued in state courts before World War II, with one exception: New Jersey's 1935 hate-speech law, which the state Supreme Court struck down in *State v. Klapprott*, 22 A.2d 877 (N.J. 1941). The U.S. Supreme Court went the other way in 1952, upholding Illinois's criminal libel law in *Beauharnais v. Illinois*, 343 U.S. 250 (1952). Since that decision, the Supreme Court has backed away from its endorsement of group libel, instead reading the First Amendment as conferring speech rights on individuals and effectively gutting libel as a way to curb what newspapers can publish. See, e.g., *New York Times v. Sullivan*, 376 U.S. 254 (1964). This "preferred position" status further undermined group libel after the civil rights movement.

13. Anthony Lewis, *Freedom for the Thought That We Hate: A Biography of the First Amendment* (New York: Basic Books, 2007); Cass R. Sunstein, *Democracy and the Problem of Free Speech* (New York: Free Press, 1993). In the early 1940s David Riesman alone argued for an expanded commitment to group status claims under the First Amendment. Riesman, "Democracy and Defamation: Control of Group Libel," *Columbia Law Review* 42 (1942): 727–80; Riesman, "Democracy and Defamation II: Fair Game and Fair Comment," *Columbia Law Review* 42 (1942): 1085–1123; Riesman, "Democracy and Defamation III," *Columbia Law Review* 42 (1942): 1282–1318. Within a decade, Riesman changed his mind, abandoning his endorsement of group libel. Riesman, "The 'Militant' Fight Against Anti-Semitism," *Commentary* 11 (1951): 11–19; Samuel Walker, *Hate Speech: The History of an American Controversy* (Lincoln: University of Nebraska Press, 1994), 79–81, 99.

14. Michigan did not carry a group libel statute on its books at the time the case was litigated. Such a bill passed the lower house of the state legislature in 1921 only to stall in the Senate on constitutional objections. *NYT*, 22 Apr. 1921, p. 24.

PART I

1. For the time of sunset on the night of the accident, consult "Monthly Sunrise Sunset Times for Detroit, Michigan, March 1927," accessed May 12, 2009, http://www.sunrisesunset.com/calendar.asp?comb_city_info=Detroit,%20Michigan;83.1;42.3;-5;1&month=3&year=1927&time_type=0&use_dst=1&want_mrms=1&want_mphase=1.

2. Ford's sister, Margaret Ford Ruddiman, describes Dr. McClure as Ford's "very intimate friend" whom he appointed as his hospital's first surgeon in chief. Margaret Ruddiman, "Memories of My Brother Henry Ford," *Michigan History* 37 (Sept. 1953): 225–75, 225.

3. E. B. White, "Farewell, My Lovely," *New Yorker*, 16 May 1936, humorously pointed out that rearview mirrors were not standard equipment on Model Ts. It is possible that Ford's car was customized with a larger rearview mirror, but in view of the auto industry's inattention to safety and visibility during its early years, this seems unlikely.

4. Bennett wrote in his memoirs that Ford told him that he was not in the car when it went down into the river. Harry H. Bennett, *We Never Called Him Henry* (New York: Gold Medal Books, 1951), 53. For a consideration of Bennett's credibility, see Chapter 7 of this volume.

5. Efforts to locate original police records of official investigations under the Freedom of Information Act have proved futile. The Dearborn Police Department reports having no extant records on the incident (correspondence with author on file).

6. In addition to sources in the previous notes, this narrative of Ford's accident is reconstructed from accounts in the *CDT, DT, NYT,* and *WP* from late March through April 1927, and from Allan Nevins and Frank Ernest Hill, *Ford: Expansion and Challenge, 1915–1933* (New York: Scribner, 1957), 319–20.

CHAPTER 1

1. Robert Littell, "Henry Ford," *New Republic,* 14 Nov. 1923, pp. 303–4, quoted in David L. Lewis, *The Public Image of Henry Ford: An American Folk Hero and His Company* (Detroit: Wayne State University Press, 1976), 222.

2. *CDT,* 23 June 1916, p. 6; Keith Sward, *The Legend of Henry Ford* (New York: Rinehart and Company, 1948), 70–74; Allan Nevins and Frank Ernest Hill, *Ford: Expansion and Challenge* (New York: Charles Scribner's Sons, 1954), 116–24, 130–42.

3. Ford quoted in Nevins and Hill, *Expansion and Challenge,* 124 (citing *PW,* 5 Feb. 1921, p. 1; ibid., *PW,* 17 Sept. 1921, pp. 1–15); Steven Watts, *The People's Tycoon: Henry Ford and the American Century* (New York: Knopf, 2005), 273 (quoting *DN,* 22 Nov. 1918). Albert Lee echoes this view in describing Ford's reaction to losing the *Tribune* case: "The financiers had beaten him again, he concluded, this time by using their prestige to control the press." Lee, *Henry Ford and the Jews* (New York: Stein and Day, 1980), 159. On Edsel's military deferment, his mother's refusal to permit him to serve, and the public criticism that rained down on the family as a result, see, e.g., Sward, *Legend of Henry Ford,* 93–95.

4. *NYT,* 23 Nov. 1918, p. 13, quoted in Nevins and Hill, *Expansion and Challenge,* 124 (quoted in turn by Lee, *Ford and the Jews,* 15; Lewis, *Public Image of Henry Ford,* 135; Robert Lacey, *Ford: The Men and the Machine* [Boston: Little, Brown and Co., 1986], 196; Douglas Brinkley, *Wheels for the World Henry Ford, His Company, and a Century of Progress, 1903–2003* [New York: Viking Press, 2003], 238; Carol W. Gelderman, *Henry Ford: The Wayward Capitalist* (New York: St. Martin's Press, 1981), 243 [citing no one]). Nevins and Hill render the last two words as "or misquoted," probably relying on a different original source than the *Times.* On Ford's public image and his media-savvy skills, see Watts, *People's Tycoon,* 64–82, 159–77.

5. Lacey, *Men and the Machine,* 194; William C. Richards, *The Last Billionaire: Henry Ford* (New York: Charles Scribner's Sons, 1948), 255; *WSJ,* 13 Mar. 1918, p. 8; *NYT,* 23 Nov. 1918, p. 13.

6. *Bridgeport* (Conn.) *Telegram,* 16 Dec. 1918, quoted in Lewis, *Public Image of Henry Ford,* 135–36; *DT,* 22 Nov. 1918.

7. 1920 Federal Census Schedule, Detroit, Wayne County, State of Michigan, Ancestry.com, accessed 28 Oct. 2009, http://search.ancestry.com/iexec/?htx=View&r=an&dbid=6061&iid=4311643-01099&fn=Edwin+G&ln=Pipp&st=r&ssrc=&pid=65539872; *NYT,* 8 Nov. 1935, p. 23; Baldwin, *Ford and the Jews,* 70 (quoting *DN,* 7 Nov. 1935); Lewis, *Public Image of Henry Ford,* 130; Watts, *People's Tycoon,* 175. Baldwin gives a birth year of 1868 for Pipp (*Ford and the Jews,* 69); the Detroit Public Library catalog says 1864, but his *NYT* obituary suggests 1867.

8. Nevins and Hill, *Expansion and Challenge*, 124; Fred L. Black, "Oral Reminiscences," p. 138, box 6, acc. 65, BFRC; Edwin Gustav Pipp, "Henry Ford—Both Sides of Him," *Pipp's Magazine* (1926): 47–48, 49–51.

9. Pipp, "Both Sides of Him," 51; Nevins and Hill, *Expansion and Challenge*, 124.

10. Richardson, *Last Billionaire*, 96; *PW*, special edition (Jan.–July 1921), 9; see also Pipp, "Both Sides of Him," 68.

11. *PW* (Jan.–July 1921), 11; Sward, *Legend of Henry Ford*, 142; Nevins and Hill, *Expansion and Challenge*, 125–26; [unknown publication], "M-Day at Dearborn, Part Two: Race Hatred and Violence Go Hand in Hand in Ford-Dominated Dearborn," 19 Apr. 1940, p. 14, vertical file, Ford's Antisemitism, BFRC; Black, "Reminiscences," 138. Nevins and Hill note that Cameron's alcoholism was well established by the time he joined the *Independent*; Lee points out that Ford looked the other way on Cameron's drinking precisely because he was so valuable in press work and public relations. Nevins and Hill, *Expansion and Challenge*, 489–90; Lee, *Ford and the Jews*, 18. Lewis, *Public Image of Henry Ford*, 130, notes Cameron's rising influence in Ford's press relations and the Ford Motor Company's as well.

12. William J. Cameron, "Oral Reminiscence," p. 17, box 11, acc. 65, BFRC; Lewis, *Public Image of Henry Ford*, 221–22, (quoting C. A. M. Vining to Ford, 7 Sept. 1922, box 79, acc. 285, BFRC).

13. Nevins and Hill, *Expansion and Challenge*, 125 (quoting *PW*, 5 Feb. 1921, p. 1; ibid., 17 Sep. 1921, pp. 1–15).

14. Black, "Reminiscences," 1–3, 6.

15. *DT*, 5 Mar. 1956, p. 2; *DFP*, 5 Mar. 1956, p. 1; Nevins and Hill, *Expansion and Challenge*, 12–13; Lee, *Ford and the Jews*, 20–22. The date of Liebold's hire is in some dispute. Max Wallace relies on Liebold's "Oral Reminiscences," in which he names a hire date of 1911 (Wallace, *The American Axis: Henry Ford, Charles Lindbergh, and the Rise of the Third Reich* [New York: St. Martin's Press, 2003], 23, 401n73). Liebold was born in Michigan to German-immigrant parents, but a Detroit newspaper later reported that someone took a red pen to his original birth certificate so that his father's nationality read "American." "M-Day at Dearborn," p. 14. Neil Baldwin says that Liebold began at the Ford Motor Company in 1910, citing no direct source but probably relying on a *Detroit Times* article in a later note (*Ford and the Jews*, 24, 356n10); Nevins and Hill mention Liebold's 1912 appointment at the Lapham Bank but do not say exactly when he came on board as Ford's executive secretary (*Expansion and Challenge*, 12–13). Obituaries for Liebold in the *Los Angeles Times* and the *New York Times* (5 Mar. 1956, p. 19, and 5 Mar. 1956, p. 23, respectively), however, both cite a start date of 1910, almost certainly relying on the same Associated Press dispatch as the Detroit papers.

16. *DFP*, 5 Mar. 1956, p. 3; Lee, *Ford and the Jews*, 21; Lewis, *Public Image of Henry Ford*, 129–30; Jardim, *First Henry Ford*, 208; Black, "Reminiscences," 130–31, quoted in Jardim, *First Henry Ford*, 209; Black, "Reminiscences," 134, quoted in Jardim, *First Henry Ford*, 211; and Lee, *Ford and the Jews*, 43 (incorrectly citing Lewis, *Public Image of Henry Ford*, 211).

17. *DFP*, 5 Mar. 1956, p. 3; Watts, *People's Tycoon*, 272; Lewis, *Public Image of Henry Ford*, 129–30; Black, "Reminiscences," 26.

18. Lee, *Ford and the Jews*, 21; Leo P. Ribuffo, "Henry Ford and *The International Jew*," *American Jewish History* 69, no. 4 (1980): 444; Black, "Reminiscences," 24.

19. *DT*, 3 Mar. 1956, p. 2; Lee, *Ford and the Jews*, 20; Ernest G. Liebold, "Reminiscences," 1951, pp. 444–46, 456–61 (accusing Pipp of commissioning the first antisemitic article from Cameron), vol. 6, acc. 65, BFRC; Watts, *People's Tycoon*, 384–90; Lewis, *Public Image of Henry Ford*, 129–30; *DN*, 5 Mar. 1956, p. 1; *DFP*, 5 Mar. 1956, p. 1.

20. Lee, *Ford and the Jews*, 20 (quoting Black, "Reminiscences" [no pinpoint given]); ibid., 21 (quoting Bennett, *We Never Called Him Henry*, 47); Wallace, *American Axis*, 24; Gelderman, *Wayward Capitalist*, 223 (quoting Liebold to Schwimmer, n.d. [but 1922], Research Files, box 8, acc. 572, BFRC; see also Liebold to Marshall, 5 June 1920, file 5, box 4, LMP; also in file 1, box 4, LMFP).

21. Unknown colonel, General Staff, to A. Bruce Bielaski, Chief, Bureau of Investigation, 21 Jan. 1918, file 10104-379; "Information from Files of Military Intelligence Division Requested by F.B.I.," 22 Apr. 1941, file 2801-445-123, both in box 1854, entry 65, RG 165, NARA-CP. Max Wallace discovered these files and published them first (*American Axis*, 24–26). The documents in the files do not prove conclusively that Liebold spied for the German government against the United States, however, only that he was suspected of sympathizing and was reported to the authorities as a potential subject for further surveillance.

22. Watts, *People's Tycoon*, 227 (quoting *DFP*, 22 Aug. 1915); Sward, *Legend of Henry Ford*, 83.

23. Rosika Schwimmer, "The Humanitarianism of Henry Ford," *B'nai B'rith News*, Oct.–Nov. 1922, pp. 9–10, file 414, box 14, HBP; Baldwin, *Ford and the Jews*, 61; Liebold, "Reminiscences," 254–57.

24. Schwimmer, "Humanitarianism of Henry Ford," p. 10 (emphasis in original); Schwimmer, "When Henry Ford Was a Pacifist," undated manuscript (typescript), p. 2, file 317, box 10, HBP. Schwimmer writes admiringly of Mrs. Ford: "In showing me to the bathroom, Mrs. Ford brought some towels and remarked: 'I bring them myself, because we have no help except the cook. The maid left recently and no white servant wants to work with our Chinese cook. We don't want to dismiss him, and prefer to wait until we get a servant willing to work in the same home with a yellow man.' I am not in the habit of easily falling on people's necks, but mentally I did hug Mrs. Ford for these words. And I took the towels from her hands with respect for her simple personality as if she had handed me one of her many millions" (ibid., 3).

25. Sward, *Legend of Henry Ford*, 86, 87, 88–93; Watts, *People's Tycoon*, 233; Jardim, *First Henry Ford*, 128–29; James J. Flink, *The Car Culture* (Cambridge, Mass.: MIT Press, 1975), 94; Nevins and Hill, *Expansion and Challenge*, 49–50. Most biographers overlook the work of the Neutral Conference for Continuous Mediation, the conference that Peace Ship travelers organized to continue their work after Ford's departure; Nevins and Hill report that once President Wilson made his "peace without victory" speech, Ford apparently came to believe that "Wilson was doing all for peace that he could, and more than anyone else could do," and withdrew his financial support for the conference. When Germany escalated its submarine attacks in 1917, Ford recognized that U.S. entry into the war was a realistic possibility. Nevins and Hill, *Expansion and Challenge*, 51–54 (quotes on 52); Watts, *People's Tycoon*, 234–35.

26. Nevins and Hill, *Expansion and Challenge*, 52, 53 (quoting Mark Sullivan, *Our Times: Over Here: 1914–1918*, in *Annals of the American Academy of Political and Social*

Science 172 [1934]: 183–85, 183; and William L. Stidger, *Henry Ford: The Man and His Motives* [New York: George H. Doran Co., 1923], 25); John Kenneth Galbraith, "The Mystery of Henry Ford," *Atlantic Monthly*, Mar. 1958, 41–47, at 42.

27. Watts, *People's Tycoon*, 240–41, 242–49; Galbraith, "Mystery of Henry Ford," 43.

28. Sward, *Legend of Henry Ford*, 287; Nevins and Hill, *Expansion and Challenge*, 82; Galbraith, "Mystery of Henry Ford," 42.

29. *CDT*, 7 Apr. 1916, p. 6; ibid., 23 May 1916, p. 1; ibid., 21 May 1916, p. 4. For samples of the *Tribune's* Ford criticism, see, e.g. ibid., 14 Apr. 1916, p. 8; ibid., 26 Apr. 1916, p. 8; ibid., 24 May 1916, p. 8; ibid., 25 May 1916, p. 8.

30. Lisabeth G. Svendsgaard, "McCormick, Robert Rutherford," *American National Biography Online*, accessed 17 Feb. 2006, http://www.anb.org/articles/16/16-02435.html; *CDT*, 11 Apr. 1916, p. 8.

31. Ibid., 22 June 1916, p. 3; and ibid., 23 June 1916, p. 6; Nevins and Hill, *Expansion and Challenge*, 129. Sward mistakenly claims that Ford was quoted in the story; *Legend of Henry Ford*, 100.

32. *CDT*, 23 June 1916, p. 6.

33. Nevins and Hill, *Expansion and Challenge*, 129–30.

34. Quoted in Nevins and Hill, *Expansion and Challenge*, 130; also in Watts, *People's Tycoon*, 266. Apparently it took some time to persuade Ford to sue, according to Liebold, who provided this account of the Lucking-Ford conversation in his Reminiscences, 295, cited by Watts, *People's Tycoon*, 563n38; and also by Nevins and Hill, *Expansion and Challenge*, 635n23.

35. McCormick quoted in Nevins and Hill, *Expansion and Challenge*, 130; Sward, *Legend of Henry Ford*, 100–101; Nevins and Hill, *Expansion and Challenge*, 130.

36. Norman L. Rosenberg, *Protecting the Best Men: An Interpretive History of the Law of Libel* (Chapel Hill: University of North Carolina Press, 1986), 178–92, 205, 200.

37. David Rabban, *Free Speech in Its Forgotten Years* (New York: Cambridge University Press, 1997), 155 (quoting *Negley v. Farrow*, 60 Md. 158, 177 [1883]).

38. Ibid., 160; Rosenberg, *Protecting the Best Men*, 187.

39. Rosenberg, *Protecting the Best Men*, 191; Rabban, *Free Speech*, 163 (quoting *Coleman v. MacLennan*, 78 Kan. 711, 716–18 [1908]). Common restrictions on speech included reporting on "scandal, criminal news, and immoral conduct." Rabban, *Free Speech*, 164.

40. Rabban, *Free Speech*, 164 (quoting *Robertson v. Baldwin*, 165 U.S. 275, 281 [1897]). Rabban and Rosenberg locate this pattern in lower federal court rulings by Taft and in Holmes's opinions for the Massachusetts Supreme Judicial Court. In *Burt v. Newspaper Advertiser Co.*, 154 Mass. 238 (1891), for example, the "publication of libelous 'facts [that] are not true'" received no privilege of immunity, because "the traditional doctrine of strict liability still applied" (*Protecting the Best Men*, 201). Critics of this rule were in the minority in the judiciary and among treatise writers (ibid., 202).

41. Rosenberg, *Protecting the Best Men*, 193 (quoting *In re Banks*, 56 Kan. 242 [1895]). He notes also that California banned "publication of pictures or caricatures of any living persons, except state officials or convicted criminals"; the press was also required "to identify the author of every article that was libelous on its face." Rosenberg, *Protecting the Best Men*, 193.

42. Nevins and Hill, *Expansion and Challenge*, 130, 131–32; Black, "Reminiscences," 7. "Ford knew that there were thousands of newspapers too small to afford to send reporters to Mount Clemens and that these were the very papers most likely to be friendly to him" (Gelderman, *Wayward Capitalist*, 158).

43. Sward, *Legend of Henry Ford*, 101; Nevins and Hill, *Expansion and Challenge*, 132; Rosenberg, *Protecting the Best Men*, 197–206.

44. Nevins and Hill, *Expansion and Challenge*, 132; Weymouth Kirkland, "Some American Causes Celebres: Henry Ford vs. the Tribune Co.," *American Bar Association Journal*, 9 (February 1923), 90–92, 90n.

45. Kirkland, "Some American Causes Celebres," 90. One such advertisement appeared in the *Washington Herald* on May 1 and impelled the Navy League (a nongovernmental organization) to sue Ford for libel for alleging that the league was "deceiving the country." *WP*, 7 May 1916, p. A4.

46. Kirkland, "Some American Causes Celebres," 91.

47. Nevins and Hill, *Expansion and Challenge*, 131; Rabban, *Free Speech*, 205; Rosenberg, *Protecting the Best Men*, 193.

48. Gelderman, *Wayward Capitalist*, 164–65; Nevins and Hill, *Expansion and Challenge*, 135; Kirkland, "Some American Causes Celebres," 92.

49. Kirkland, "Some American Causes Celebres," 91; Gelderman, *Wayward Capitalist*, 166–67.

50. Sward, *Legend of Henry Ford*, 103; Nevins and Hill, *Expansion and Challenge*, 135–36, 137–38; Watts, *People's Tycoon*, 268.

51. Kirkland, "Some American Causes Celebres," 91. For extended excerpts of Ford's testimony, see Gelderman, *Wayward Capitalist*, 175–85.

52. Gelderman, *Wayward Capitalist*, 176.

53. Ibid., 190–91; *CDT*, 15 Aug. 1919, p. 1; see also Nevins and Hill, *Expansion and Challenge*, 139; Sward, *Legend of Henry Ford*, 105; Watts, *People's Tycoon*, 270; Lewis, *Public Image of Henry Ford*, 106–8. Gelderman's discovery of the interviews that Ford operatives conducted with jurors went unnoticed by subsequent writers.

54. *CDT*, 15 Aug. 1919, p. 1; Kirkland, "Some American Causes Celebres," p. 92.

55. *CDT*, 21 Aug. 1919, p. 12; and 18 Aug. 1919, p. 10 (*Montreal Star, Peoria Star, Peoria Transcript, Cincinnati Times-Star*, and *New York Sun*); *New York World* quoted in *CDT*, 21 Aug. 1919, p. 12.

56. Gelderman, *Wayward Capitalist*, 156.

57. Watts, *People's Tycoon*, 271; *NYT*, 16 Mar. 1927, p. 1; Sward, *Legend of Henry Ford*, 105 ("never again" in quotes but no source cited).

58. Gelderman, *Wayward Capitalist*, 191; Jardim, *First Henry Ford*, 158.

59. Watts, *People's Tycoon*, 255.

60. Nevins and Hill, *Expansion and Challenge*, 98–100, 104.

61. Jardim, *First Henry Ford*, 99–110, 112.

62. Lewis, *Public Image of Henry Ford*, 111–12 (quoting *DN* and Oswald Garrison Villard, *Prophets True and False* [New York: A. A. Knopf, 1928], 297–98).

63. Brinkley, *Wheels for the World*, 55; Peter Collier and David Horowitz, *The Fords: An American Epic* (New York: Summit Books, 1987), 37.

64. Watts, *People's Tycoon*, 236.

65. Black, "Reminiscences," 20.

66. Michael Hagemeister, "Protocols of the Elders of Zion," in *Antisemitism: A Historical Encyclopedia of Prejudice and Persecution*, ed. Richard S. Levy (Santa Barbara: ABC-CLIO, 2005), 2:568; Richard S. Levy, "Introduction," in *A Lie and a Libel: The History of the Protocols of the Elders of Zion*, ed. Binjamin W. Segel, trans. Richard S. Levy (Lincoln: University of Nebraska Press, 1995), 3; Howard M. Sachar, *A History of the Jews in America* (New York: Knopf, 1992), 312–13; Robert Singerman, "The American Career of the 'Protocols of the Elders of Zion,'" *American Jewish History* 71 (Sept. 1981): 48–78, 51–52.

67. Baldwin, *Ford and the Jews*, 82; Sachar, *History of the Jews*, 312; Singerman, "American Career of the Protocols," 56–58; Boris Brasol, "The Bolshevik Menace to Russia," *DI*, 12 Apr. 1919, pp. 12, 14; *PW*, Jan.–July 1921, p. 10.

68. Jardim, *First Henry Ford*, 139–40; Lewis, *Public Image of Henry Ford*, 140; Nevins and Hill, *Expansion and Challenge*, 127. During its first year under Ford's ownership, circulation rose modestly to about seventy-two thousand. Leonard Dinnerstein, *Antisemitism in America* (New York: Oxford University Press, 1994), 81.

69. Nevins and Hill, *Expansion and Challenge*, 312, 314; Jardim, *First Henry Ford*, 143–46; Sward, *Legend of Henry Ford*, 148 (citing *PW*, 5 Mar. 1921, p. 2); Lee, *Ford and the Jews*, 19.

70. *DI*, 22 May 1920, p. 1; Transcript of Proceedings, *Sapiro v. Ford*, 28 Mar. 1927, file 2, box 44, acc. 48, BFRC, 997. On the first antisemitic series, see Levy, "Introduction;" and Victoria Saker Woeste, "*Dearborn Independent* and *The International Jew*," in *Antisemitism: A Historical Encyclopedia*, ed. Richard S. Levy, 1:162–64; on the demonization of Jewish participation in state building and public governance in Europe and the United States, see Benjamin Ginsberg, *The Fatal Embrace: Jews and the State* (Chicago: University of Chicago Press, 1993); and Sander L. Gilman, *Difference and Pathology: Stereotypes of Sexuality, Race, and Madness* (Ithaca, N.Y.: Cornell University Press, 1985).

71. Lee, *Ford and the Jews*, 17 (quoting Liebold, "Reminiscences," 441); Edwin G. Pipp to Henry Ford, 31 Mar. 1920, file 3, box 10, acc. 48, BFRC; Sward, *Legend of Henry Ford*, 148.

72. Herman Bernstein, *The History of a Lie: "The Protocols of the Wise Men of Zion": A Study* (New York: J. S. Ogilvie Publishing, 1921), 3–15; Levy, "Introduction," 14–17, 55–56, 24–27; Louis Marshall to Fred M. Butzel, 11 Oct. 1920, file 5, box 4, LMP; Cyrus Adler to Marshall, 20 Oct. 1920, ibid.; Henry Sachs to Marshall, 3 Nov. 1920, file 6, box 57, LMP; Isaac Landman-Marshall correspondence, Nov. 1920, file 3, box 55, LMP; Marshall to Henry Sliosberg, 18 Aug. 1927, file 9, box 1599, LMP. The United States is one of the few places where the *Protocols* have never been out of print.

73. John Higham, *Strangers in the Land: Patterns of American Nativism, 1860–1925* (New Brunswick, N.J.: Rutgers University Press, 1955), 265–70; Sachar, *History of the Jews*, 310–15, esp. 315; Lewis, *Public Image of Henry Ford*, 135–41; Collier and Horowitz, *The Fords*, 79–83; Jardim, *First Henry Ford*, 137–47.

CHAPTER 2

1. Max Heller to Louis Marshall, 11 July 1920, file 5, box 4, LMP.

2. Louis Wolsey to Leo M. Franklin, 4 June 1920, file 4, box 4, LMFP; Heller to Marshall, 11 July 1920, file 5, box 4, LMP; *JI*, 4 June 1920, pp. 1, 4, WRHS.

3. Steven Watts, *The People's Tycoon: Henry Ford and the American Century* (New York: Knopf, 2005), 175–77.

4. *DI*, 22 May 1920, p. 1; Louis Marshall to Henry Ford, 3 June 1920, in Charles Reznikoff, ed., *Louis Marshall, Champion of Liberty: Selected Papers and Addresses* (Philadelphia: Jewish Publication Society of America, 1957), 1:329.

5. Louis Marshall to Henry Ford, 3 June 1920, file 5, box 4, LMP.

6. Jerold Auerbach, *Rabbis and Lawyers: The Journey from Torah to Constitution* (Bloomington: Indiana University Press, 1993), 111; Louis Marshall to the editor, *NYT*, 17 Jan. 1916, in Reznikoff, *Champion of Liberty*, 1:275; Louis Marshall, "Lawyers of Foreign Birth or Parentage," *NYT*, 19 Jan. 1916, p. 10.

7. Morton Rosenstock, *Louis Marshall, Defender of Jewish Rights* (Detroit: Wayne State University Press, 1965), 24; Bernard G. Rudolph, *From a Minyan to a Community: A History of the Jews of Syracuse* (Syracuse, N.Y.: Syracuse University [Press], 1970), 16–17; Cyrus Adler, "Louis Marshall: A Biographical Sketch," *American Jewish Year Book* 32 (1930–1931): 21–55, 21. Zilli hailed from Württemberg, according to Jonathan Sarna, "Two Jewish Lawyers Named Louis," *American Jewish History* 94, nos. 1–2 (2008): 1–19, 1. On the origin of Marshall's name, see Reznikoff, *Champion of Liberty*, 1:6.

8. Oscar Handlin, "Introduction," in Reznikoff, *Champion of Liberty*, 1:ix–xliii, x; Henry Wollman, "The Young Louis Marshall," *Jewish Tribune*, 10 Dec. 1926, p. 12, Marshall File, SUP; Rudolph, *From a Minyan to a Community*, 17.

9. Adler, "Louis Marshall," 22; Marshall to Charles Schwager, 17 Dec. 1928, file 13, box 1600, LMP; James C. Young, "Marshall Looks Back over 70 Years," *NYT*, 12 Dec. 1926, p. SM18; Handlin, "Introduction," xi; Wollman, "The Young Louis Marshall," 12.

10. Max J. Kohler, "Louis Marshall," in *Dictionary of American Biography*, Base Set, American Council of Learned Societies, 1928–1936, ed. Dumas Malone (New York: Charles Scribner's Sons, 1933), 7:326–28 (reprinted in part in Reznikoff, *Champion of Liberty*, 1:3); Handlin, "Introduction," xi; Young, "Marshall Looks Back," SM18; Wollman, "The Young Louis Marshall," 12.

11. Handlin, "Introduction," xi; Young, "Marshall Looks Back," SM18.

12. Young, "Marshall Looks Back," SM9; Handlin, "Introduction," xi; Adler, "Louis Marshall," 23.

13. Adler, "Louis Marshall," 23, quoting John K. Mumford, "Who's Who in New York—No. 18," *NYHT*, 15 June 1924, sec. 2, p. 3.

14. Handlin, "Introduction," xi; Kohler, "Louis Marshall," 3; Marshall to Harold R. Medina, 9 Mar. 1929, in Reznikoff, *Champion of Liberty*, 1:8; Sarna, "Two Jewish Lawyers," 3–4; Adler, "Louis Marshall," 23–24.

15. Kohler, "Louis Marshall," 3; Handlin, "Introduction," xii, xvii, xi; William S. Jenney to Samuel Untermyer, 25 Sept. 1929, in Reznikoff, *Champion of Liberty*, 1:9; Handlin, "Introduction," xi; Sarna, "Two Jewish Lawyers," 4.

16. Jenney to Untermyer, in Reznikoff, *Champion of Liberty*, 1:9; Marshall to Charles Schwager, 17 Dec. 1928, file 13, box 1600, LMP; Kohler, "Louis Marshall," 3; Handlin, "Introduction," xii–xiv; Rosenstock, *Defender of Jewish Rights*, 24–25; Adler, "Louis Marshall," 21–55, 22; *NYT*, 23 Jan. 1910, p. 11; ibid., 28 Feb. 1914, p. 9; Louis Marshall to Julian Mack, 5 Mar. 1914, box 1583, LMP; Rudolph, *From a Minyan to a Community*, 17.

17. Handlin, "Introduction," xiv, xiii; Rosenstock, *Defender of Jewish Rights*, 25; Adler, "Louis Marshall," 25–26; Ira Robinson, "Adler, Cyrus," *American National Biography Online*, accessed 11 May 2006, http://www.anb.org/articles/08/08-00012.html.

18. Adler, "Louis Marshall," 24; Edith Wharton, *The Age of Innocence* (New York: Oxford University Press, 2006); see also Sven Beckert, *The Monied Metropolis: New York City and the Consolidation of the American Bourgeoisie, 1850–1896* (New York: Cambridge University Press, 2001). On the social networks of Jewish lawyers and activists, see, e.g., Handlin, "Introduction," esp. xiv–xvii; Auerbach, *Rabbis and Lawyers*, 93–122; and Robert W. Gordon, "'The Ideal and the Actual in the Law': Fantasies and Practices of New York City Lawyers, 1870–1910," in *The New High Priests: Lawyers in Post–Civil War America*, ed. Gerard W. Gawalt (Westport, Conn.: Greenwood Press, 1984), 51–74.

19. Florence Lowenstein to Louis Marshall, 28 Feb. 1895, file 4, box 10, LMP; Marshall to Lowenstein, 28 Feb. 1895, ibid.; Marshall to Lowenstein, 7 Mar. 1895, ibid. (emphasis in original); Marshall to Lowenstein, 28 Mar. 1895, ibid.

20. Marshall to Florence Lowenstein, 6 May 1895, ibid.; Inventory to the Jacob Billikopf Papers, Manuscript Collection 13, American Jewish Archives, accessed 6 Feb. 2009, http://www.americanjewisharchives.org/aja/FindingAids/Billikop.htm. For a history of Temple Emanu-El, see http://www.emanuelnyc.org/simple.php/about _history, accessed 5 Feb. 2009. Ruth Marshall Billikopf, like her mother, died young, in 1936, leaving her husband and two young children. *NYT*, 9 Aug. 1936, p. N7. Robert died at thirty-eight of leukemia. Ibid., 12 Nov. 1939, p. 50; James M. Glover, "Marshall, Robert," *American National Biography Online*, accessed 20 Oct. 2003, http://www.anb .org/articles/13/13-01879.html. James Marshall lived to the age of ninety, serving as head of the New York Board of Education under Mayor Fiorello H. LaGuardia. *NYT*, 13 Aug. 1986, p. D20; ibid., 18 June 2000, p. 32.

21. Handlin, "Introduction," xvi, xxviii; Rosenstock, *Defender of Jewish Rights*, 26; Jerome C. Rosenthal, "The Public Life of Louis Marshall" (Ph.D. diss., University of Cincinnati, 1983), 337; Marshall to Ruth Marshall Billikopf, 4 Jan. 1927, file 2, box 1599, LMP; Marshall to Ruth Marshall Billikopf, 1 Mar. 1927, file 4, box 1599, LMP.

22. "Lawyer and Philanthropist," *New Yorker*, 21 Sept. 1929, pp. 19–20; Handlin, "Introduction," xviii.

23. "Lawyer and Philanthropist," 20; Auerbach, *Rabbis and Lawyers*, 111. According to a Canadian newspaper, the writer and Zionist Israel Zangwill coined the moniker. *Canadian Journal Review*, 19 Oct. 1928, file 8, box 6, LMP.

24. "Lawyer and Philanthropist," 20.

25. Handlin, "Introduction," xvii.

26. Handlin, xv; Paul Mendes-Flohr, *German-Jews: A Dual Identity* (New Haven, Conn.: Yale University Press, 1999), 3.

27. Ibid.; Marshall to Harry Friedenwald, 3 Nov. 1928, file 12, box 1600, LMP.

28. Adler, "Louis Marshall," 22.

29. Eric Foner, *Reconstruction: America's Unfinished Revolution, 1863–1877* (New York: Harper and Row, 1988); Richard Kluger, *Simple Justice: The History of* Brown v. Board of Education *and Black America's Struggle for Equality* (New York: Vintage, 2004); Sarah Barringer Gordon, *The Mormon Question: Polygamy and Constitutional Conflict*

in Nineteenth-Century America (Chapel Hill: University of North Carolina Press, 2002); Gordon, "The Ideal and the Actual;" Charles W. McCurdy, "The 'Liberty of Contract' Regime in American Law," in *The State and Freedom of Contract*, ed. Harry N. Scheiber (Stanford, Calif.: Stanford University Press, 1998), 161–97.

30. Robert Singerman, "The Jew as Racial Alien: The Genetic Component of American Anti-Semitism," in *Anti-Semitism in American History*, ed. David A. Gerber (Urbana: University of Illinois Press, 1986), 103–28, 103–8. Singerman explicitly challenges John Higham's claim that "Jews were traditionally identified only as Caucasians," ibid., 103–4; see John Higham, "Social Discrimination Against Jews, 1830–1930," in *Send These to Me: Jews and Other Immigrants in Urban America* (New York: Atheneum, 1975), 170–71. On Jewish "whiteness," see Eric L. Goldstein, *The Price of Whiteness: Jews, Race, and American Identity* (Princeton, N.J.: Princeton University Press, 2006); Matthew Frye Jacobson, *Whiteness of a Different Color: European Immigrants and the Alchemy of Race* (Cambridge, Mass.: Harvard University Press, 1998) Michael Alexander, *Jazz Age Jews* (Princeton, N.J.: Princeton University Press, 2001); and Nathan C. Belth, *A Promise to Keep: A Narrative of the American Encounter with Anti-Semitism* (New York: Times Books, 1979).

31. Sarna, *American Judaism*, 133; Belth, *A Promise to Keep*, 24–26; Leonard Dinnerstein, *Antisemitism in America* (New York: Oxford University Press, 1994), 39–41.

32. Rosenstock, *Defender of Jewish Rights*, 12–13; Sarna, *American Judaism*, 122–34; Arthur Liebman, "Anti-Semitism in the Left?" in Gerber, *Anti-Semitism in American History*, 329–59, 334–35; Belth, *A Promise to Keep*, 26–29.

33. Dinnerstein, *Anti-Semitism in America*, 35; Jonathan Sarna, *American Judaism: A History* (New Haven, Conn.: Yale University Press, 2004), 153, 157; Auerbach, *Rabbis and Lawyers*, 78.

34. Belth, *Promise to Keep*, 26–57 (quote on 28); Singerman, *The Jew as Racial Alien*, 116; Louise A. Mayo, *The Ambivalent Image: Nineteenth-Century America's Perception of the Jew* (London: Associated University Presses, 1988), 148–78. On immigration trends generally and legal responses to newcomers during this period, see Lucy E. Salyer, *Laws Harsh as Tigers: Chinese Immigrants and the Shaping of Modern Immigration Law* (Chapel Hill: University of North Carolina Press, 1995); and Mae M. Ngai, *Impossible Subjects: Illegal Aliens and the Making of Modern America* (Princeton, N.J.: Princeton University Press, 2004).

35. Judith S. Goldstein, *The Politics of Ethnic Pressure: The American Jewish Committee Fight Against Immigration Restriction, 1906–1917* (New York: Garland Publishing, 1990), 61–65 (quote on 64).

36. Goldstein, *Politics of Ethnic Pressure*, 61–62, quoting Arthur A. Goren, *New York Jews and the Quest for Community: The Kehillah Experiment, 1908–1922* (New York: Columbia University Press, 1970), 17.

37. Dinnerstein, *Antisemitism in America*, 40–41.

38. Dinnerstein, *Antisemitism in America*, 59–61, 62 (on Jewish poverty in major U.S. cities).

39. Sarna, *American Judaism*, 182–83; Dinnerstein, *Antisemitism in America*, 71; Reznikoff, *Champion of Liberty*, 1:10. For the revisionist appraisal, see Edward T. O'Donnell, "Hibernians Versus Hebrews? A New Look at the 1902 Jacob Joseph Funeral

Riot," *Journal of the Gilded Age and Progressive Era* 6, no. 2 (April 2007): 209–25, esp. 220–21.

40. Dinnerstein, *Antisemitism in America*, 71–72; Sarna, *American Judaism*, 183. O'Donnell contends that the police in New York were not singling out Jews; rather, the treatment the Joseph funeral mourners received from police was part of "a long-standing pattern of violence against crowds, be they socialist, black, Irish, or Jewish." O'Donnell, "Hibernians Versus Hebrews," 219.

41. Marshall to R. E. Carey, 23 Jan. 1905, in Reznikoff, *Champion of Liberty*, 1:10–11; Marshall to Editors, *Jewish Gazette*, 29 Dec. 1902, in ibid., 11–12.

42. Rosenstock, *Defender of Jewish Rights*, 71 (quoted language); "The Passport Question," *American Jewish Year Book* 5672 (1911–1912): 19–128; Jacob Rader Marcus, *United States Jewry, 1776–1985* (Detroit: Wayne State University Press, 1989), 3:213.

43. Naomi W. Cohen, *Not Free to Desist: The American Jewish Committee, 1906–1966* (Philadelphia: Jewish Publication Society of America, 1972), 3–4; John D. Klier and Shlomo Lambroza, eds., *Pogroms: Anti-Jewish Violence in Modern Russian History* (Cambridge: Cambridge University Press, 1992); Heinz-Dietrich Löwe, "Antisemitism in Russia and the Soviet Union," in *Antisemitism: A History*, ed. Albert S. Lindemann and Richard S. Levy (New York: Oxford University Press, 2010), 166–95, especially 177–79; Nathan Schachner, *The Price of Liberty: A History of the American Jewish Committee* (New York: American Jewish Committee, 1948), 3.

44. Marshall to Cyrus Adler, 30 Dec. 1905, in Reznikoff, *Champion of Liberty*, 1:19–20. For example, Marshall induced Rabbi Judah L. Magnes, his brother-in-law, to drop plans for a rival organization by including Magnes in his own group. See Marshall to Adler, 30 Dec. 1905, in Reznikoff, *Champion of Liberty*, 1:20.

45. Gregg Ivers, *To Build a Wall: American Jews and the Separation of Church and State* (Charlottesville: University Press of Virginia, 1995), 37; Cohen, *Not Free to Desist*, 9–16, 220–21; Goldstein, *Politics of Ethnic Pressure*, 9–10; Schachner, *History of the American Jewish Committee*, 12–28 (quote on 16); Marshall to Henry W. Pollock, 11 Feb. 1911, in Reznikoff, *Champion of Liberty*, 1:28–30; Marshall to Judah L. Magnes, 10 Oct. 1908, in ibid., 32–35; Jacob Rader Marcus, *The American Jew, 1585–1990: A History* (Brooklyn, N.Y.: Carlson Publishing, 1995), 234.

46. Marshall to Elihu Root, 1 Feb. 1908, in Reznikoff, *Champion of Liberty*, 1:50–51 (quoting Root circular); Rosenstock, *Defender of Jewish Rights*, 72; Marshall to Herbert Friedenwald, 4 Feb. 1908, in Reznikoff, *Champion of Liberty*, 1:53.

47. Naomi W. Cohen, "The Abrogation of the Russo-American Treaty of 1832," *Jewish Social Studies* 25, no. 1 (1963): 3–41, 13, 19–37; Louis Marshall, *Russia and the American Passport: Address of Louis Marshall to the Delegates at the Twenty-Second Council, Union of American Hebrew Congregations, Thursday, January 19, 1911* ([New York]: The Union, 1911); reprinted in Reznikoff, *Champion of Liberty*, 1:59–71 (quote on 60); Marcus, *American Jew*, 235–36; Rosenstock, *Defender of Jewish Rights*, 76–77.

48. Marshall to Oscar Straus, 18 Oct. 1911, in Reznikoff, *Champion of Liberty*, 1:99–102; Marshall to Benjamin Stoltz, 22 Dec. 1911, in ibid., 103; Marshall to Benjamin Stoltz, 22 Dec. 1911, Reznikoff, *Champion of Liberty*, 1:103; Cohen, *Not Free to Desist*, 28. Whether abrogation was a positive or negative step continues to be a matter of debate among historians. Marshall's biographer echoes his view that abrogation was politically and

symbolically necessary (Rosenstock, *Defender of Jewish Rights*, 78–79; see also Sarna, *American Judaism*, 199–200), whereas other scholars contend that despite abrogation, Russia did not change its policies (Naomi Cohen, *Encounter with Emancipation: The German Jews in the United States, 1830–1914* [Philadelphia: Jewish Publication Society of America, 1984], 238).

49. Marshall to David Marks [*sic*], 2 Sept. 1913, file 9, box 1582, LMP; Steve Oney, *And the Dead Shall Rise: The Murder of Mary Phagan and the Lynching of Leo Frank* (New York: Pantheon Books, 2003), esp. 460–66 (on Marshall's handling of Frank's appeal); Leonard Dinnerstein, *The Leo Frank Case* (New York: Columbia University Press, 1968), 77–106; Ivers, *To Build a Wall*, 41.

50. Marshall to Milton Klein, 9 Sept. 1913, file 9, box 1582, LMP; Marshall to Herbert Haas, 14 June 1915, file 6, box 1584, LMP; Oney, *And the Dead Shall Rise*, 397–400.

51. Marshall to Lasker, 8 Dec. 1914; Marshall to Benjamin J. Shove, 30 Dec. 1914, file 12, box 1583, LMP; Marshall to Kraus, 12 Dec. 1914, ibid.

52. Marshall to David Marks [*sic*], 30 Dec. 1914, file 12, box 1583, LMP; *Frank v. Mangum*, 237 U.S. 309, 326 (1915); Marshall to Julian Mack, 24 Apr. 1915, file 4, box 1584, LMP; Marshall to Samuel Untermyer, 10 May 1915, file 4, box 1584, LMP; Marshall to James R. Day, 21 June 1915, ibid. Eight years later, the Supreme Court overturned the *Frank* decision in *Moore v. Dempsey*, 261 U.S. 86 (1923), a decision Marshall described as "a great achievement in constitutional law." Marshall to Walter White, 12 Mar. 1923, in Reznikoff, *Champion of Liberty*, 1:316.

53. Oney, *And the Dead Shall Rise*, 561–71.

54. Marshall to Darius E. Peck, 21 Sept. 1915, file 9, box 1584, LMP; Marshall to John M. Duncan, 22 Sept. 1916, file 9, box 1584, LMP; Marshall to Peck, 21 Sept. 1915, file 9, box 1584, LMP. The *New York Times* shared Marshall's view, editorializing after the lynching that antisemitic feeling in Georgia exploded into the public conversation only after it became imperative to arrest and convict someone for the heinous murder. *NYT*, 20 Aug. 1915, p. 4.

55. On the rebirth of the Klan, see Nancy MacLean, *Behind the Mask of Chivalry: The Making of the Second Ku Klux Klan* (New York: Oxford University Press, 1994); Philip Dray, *At the Hands of Persons Unknown: The Lynching of Black America* (New York: Modern Library, 2003). On the construction of Frank as racially black (and progressively so as the case proceeded), see *The People v. Leo Frank*, Ben Loeterman Productions for *Frontline* and PBS (dir. Ben Loeterman, 2009).

56. Richard Slotkin, *Lost Battalions: The Great War and the Crisis of American Nationality* (New York: Henry Holt and Company, 2005), 73–75. See also Joseph Bendersky, *The "Jewish Threat": Antisemitic Politics of the U.S. Army* (New York: Basic Books, 2000).

57. See Marshall incoming correspondence, 1917–1919, box 155, LMP. One such complaint came from Aaron Sapiro, whom the army twice rejected for Officer Training School in 1918. See Chapter 4.

58. See, e.g., *DI*, 17 July 1920, p. 8; Singerman, "The Jew as Racial Alien," 115; Dinnerstein, *Anti-Semitism in America*, 58–77; Ngai, *Impossible Subjects*, 19–20.

59. Wallace, *American Axis*, 13–16; Matthew Silver, "Louis Marshall and the Democratization of Jewish Identity," *American Jewish History* 94, nos. 1–2 (2008): 41–69, 49–51; Rosenstock, *Defender of Jewish Rights*, 121–27; Handlin, "Introduction," xxxiii. On the

Protocols' arrival in the United States, see Singerman, "The American Career of the *Protocols*," 48–78; and Richard S. Levy, "Introduction," in *A Lie and a Libel: The History of the Protocols of the Elders of Zion*, ed. Binjamin W. Segel, trans. Richard S. Levy (Lincoln: University of Nebraska Press, 1995), 24–27; Marshall to Leo M. Franklin, 7 June 1920, file 1, box 4, LMFP. Marshall became aware that the *Protocols* was circulating among people in the federal government and the press as early as 1917; he noticed its use, for propaganda purposes, in the English antisemitic press just before the *Independent*'s campaign began. Ibid.; Marshall to Harry Schneiderman, 6 May 1920, box 1590, LMP; Silver, "Louis Marshall and the Democratization of Jewish Identity," 56n55.

60. DPC to Marshall, 5 June 1920, file 5, box 4, LMP; also in file 1, box 4, LMFP. For Marshall's reaction to the DPC telegram, see Marshall to Julius Rosenwald, 5 June 1920, in Reznikoff, *Champion of Liberty*, 1:330; Marshall to David A. Brown, 13 August 1920, in ibid., 330–33.

61. David L. Lewis, *The Public Image of Henry Ford: An American Folk Hero and His Company* (Detroit: Wayne State University Press, 1976), 511n39; Robert A. Rockaway, *The Jews of Detroit: From the Beginning, 1762–1914* (Detroit: Wayne State University Press, 1986), 132; Franklin to Ford, 27 May 1920, file 2, box 2, acc. 572, BFRC; Leo M. Franklin, "Some Untold Tales of Detroit and Detroiters," unpublished memoir (1947), 117–22, LMFP.

62. Franklin to Marshall, 4 June 1920, file 1, box 4, LMFP; also in file 5, box 4, LMP.

63. Marshall to Franklin, 7 June 1920, file 1, box 4, LMFP; Marshall to Ford, 3 June 1920, file 5, box 4, LMP; Franklin to Marshall, 9 June 1920, file 5, box 4, LMP; Leo M. Franklin, "Henry Ford and the Jews," typescript of *DJC* editorial, n.d., file 5, box 4, LMP.

64. DPC to Marshall, 5 June 1920, file 5, box 4, LMP; Marshall to DPC, 5 June 1920, ibid.; Max J. Kohler to Simon Wolf, 10 June 1920, file 4, box 4, LMFP; Marshall to Fred Butzel, 20 Sept. 1920, file 5, box 4, LMP. For his part, Fred Butzel thought that if the Jewish press had refrained from paying attention to Ford, then few people would have noticed the *Independent*, which at the time was circulated primarily among Ford employees. Butzel to Marshall, 25 Sept. 1920, file 5, box 4, LMP. In Cleveland there were reports that the *Independent* was circulating illegally through the mail to people who never subscribed to it. Louis Wolsey to Leo Franklin, 4 June 1920, file 4, box 4, LMFP.

65. Ford to Franklin, 4 June 1920, file 4, box 4, LMFP.

66. Franklin to Wolsey, 4 June 1920, file 4, box 4, LMFP; Wolsey to Franklin, 10 June 1920, ibid.; Wolsey to Franklin, 7 June 1920, ibid.; Franklin to Wolsey, 10 June 1920, ibid.

67. Franklin to Ford, 14 June 1920, file 2, box 2, acc. 572, BFRC.

68. Supposedly, Ford himself "innocently" telephoned the rabbi to inquire, "What's wrong, Dr. Franklin? Has something come between us?" Nevins and Hill, *Expansion and Challenge*, 315, citing *Pipp's Weekly*, 12 June 1921, vol. 1, p. 1. This one-sided exchange, which historians have repeated nearly verbatim through the years, is almost certainly apocryphal. The Benson Ford Research Center, which owns the complete run of *Pipp's*, reports that there is no issue dated 12 June 1921, and marked volume 1 (Linda Skolarus, e-mail message to author, 9 Nov. 2009). An article in *Pipp's Weekly*, 12 June 1921, vol. 2, p. 6, confirms the return of the car but bears no mention of any telephone conversation, which subsequent writers have quoted without citing an original source. See, e.g., Peter Collier and David Horowitz, *The Fords: An American Epic* (New York: Summit Books, 1987), 104; Watts, *People's Tycoon*, 391 (citing Baldwin); Neil Baldwin, *Henry Ford and the*

Jews (New York: Public Affairs, 2001), 133 (citing Belth); Belth, *A Promise to Keep,* 77–78 (citing Nevins and Hill). The earliest appearance of the quote in print appears to be Keith Sward, *The Legend of Henry Ford* (New York: Rinehart, 1948), 147 (citing *Pipp's*), but Nevins and Hill do not credit him for the *Pipp's* lead, which I consider unverified.

69. Nevins and Hill, *Expansion and Challenge,* 315; Ford to Franklin, 4 June 1920, file 4, box 4, LMFP; Marshall to Franklin, 7 June 1920, file 1, box 4, LMFP; Liebold to Franklin, 23 June 1920, file 2, box 2, acc. 572, BFRC.

70. Michael A. Meyer, *Hebrew Union College–Jewish Institute of Religion: A Centennial History, 1875–1975* (Cincinnati: Hebrew Union College Press, 1976), 53–54; Marshall to Julius Rosenwald, 22 July 1927, in Reznikoff, *Champion of Liberty,* 1:381–82; Judson C. Welliver to Marshall, 12 Sept. 1923, ibid., 364n.

71. Marshall to Ford, 3 June 1920, file 5, box 4, LMP; David Rabban, *Free Speech in Its Forgotten Years* (New York: Cambridge University Press, 1997), 1–9; David Riesman, "Democracy and Defamation: Control of Group Libel," *Columbia Law Review* 42 (1942): 727–80. Despite Riesman's call for broad restrictions on "offensive racial and religious speech," group-libel laws have never furnished the basis for a widespread movement against discriminatory or defamatory publications. Norman L. Rosenberg, *Protecting the Best Men: An Interpretive History of the Law of Libel* (Chapel Hill: University of North Carolina Press, 1986), 230, 243n18; Samuel Walker, *Hate Speech: The History of an American Controversy* (Lincoln: University of Nebraska Press, 1994), 1–16, 79; Anthony Lewis, *Freedom for the Thought That We Hate: A Biography of the First Amendment* (New York: Perseus Books, 2007).

72. Act of 11 Apr. 1913, ch. 265, sec. 40, 1913 N.Y. Laws 481; Evan Schultz, "Group Rights, American Jews, and the Failure of Group Libel Laws, 1913–1952," *Brooklyn Law Review,* 66 (Spring, 2000): 71–145, 96; Dinnerstein, *Antisemitism in America,* 73–74; Belth, *Promise to Keep,* 23–26. Schultz points out that the law was in fact "an amendment to a law that already prohibited hotels from banning Jews from their premises" ("Group Rights," 96), but Marshall construed the law as not interfering with the rights of property owners to rent to whom they pleased, only from proclaiming their discriminatory practices in print. The New York group-libel law was easily circumvented by the use of code words to signal a selective clientele and thus may not have effectively banned "public insults." Schultz, "Group Rights," 90–100, esp. 99.

73. Simon Fleishmann to Marshall, 27 Nov. 1920, file 12, box 55, LMP; Executive Secretary, AJC, to David Brown, 30 July 1920, file, 5, box 4, LMP; Cyrus Adler to Jacob Schiff, 15 June 1920, file 1, box 55, LMP; Minutes of the Executive Committee, American Jewish Committee, 23 June 1920, file 5, box 55, LMP; Marshall to David Brown, 30 July 1920, file 5, box 4, LMP. On the use of dynamic silence in response to published antisemitism, see Victoria Saker Woeste, "American Jewish Committee," in *ABC-CLIO Encyclopedia of Antisemitism, Anti-Jewish Prejudice, and Persecution,* ed. Richard S. Levy (Santa Barbara, Calif.: ABC-CLIO, 2005), 1:16–17.

74. Marshall to Henry Ford, 3 June 1920, file 5, box 4, LMP; Butzel to Marshall, 25 Sept. 1920, file 5, box 4, LMP; Wolsey to Franklin, 4 June 1920, file 4, box 4, LMFP; Butzel to Marshall, 25 Sept. 1920, file 5, box 4, LMP; Leon Lewis to Franklin, 30 July 1920, file 4, box 4, LMFP; news release, Chicago Anti-Defamation League, 16 July 1920, ibid.

75. Franklin to Philipson, 18 June 1920, file 4, box 4, LMFP.

76. Marshall to David A. Brown, 13 Aug. 1920, in Reznikoff, *Champion of Liberty*, 1:332–33.

77. David A. Brown to Louis Marshall, 3 Aug. 1927, file 2, box 155, LMP; Franklin to Marshall, 6 Nov. 1920, file 4, box 4, LMFP (quoting Marshall to Schulman, 3 Nov. 1920, not extant); Samuel Schulman to Franklin, 4 Nov. 1920, file 1, box 4, LMFP; Franklin to Schulman, 6 Nov. 1920, ibid.; Franklin to Marshall, 6 Nov. 1920, ibid.; Marshall to Franklin, 8 Nov. 1920, ibid.; Franklin to Marshall, 9 Nov. 1920, ibid.; Schulman to Franklin, 10 Nov. 1920, ibid.

78. Cyrus Adler to Jacob Schiff, 15 June 1920, file 1, box 55, LMP; Minutes of the Executive Committee, 23 June 1920, file 5, box 55, LMP; Marshall to David Brown, 30 July 1920, file 5, box 4, LMP.

79. Marshall to Fred Butzel, 20 Sept. 1920, file 5, box 4, LMP; Minutes of the Executive Committee, American Jewish Committee, 15 Oct. 1920, file 5, box 55, LMP; Dinnerstein, *Antisemitism in America*, 102; David A. Brown to Jacob Billikopf, 30 Oct. 1920, file 8, box 55, LMP; Henry M. Butzel to Brown, 12 Nov. 1920, ibid.; Minutes of the Executive Committee, American Jewish Committee, 12 Dec. 1920, file 5, box 55, LMP; Marshall, "The 'Protocols,' Bolshevism, and the Jews," in Reznikoff, *Champion of Liberty*, 1:343–50.

80. Marshall, "The 'Protocols,' Bolshevism, and the Jews," 344, 347, 349; Dinnerstein, *Antisemitism in America*, 102; Minutes of the Executive Committee, American Jewish Committee, 12 Dec. 1920, file 5, box 55, LMP. In addition to the AJC, signatories included the Zionist Organization of America, the Union of American Hebrew Congregations, the Union of Orthodox Jewish Congregations, the United Synagogue of America, the Provisional Organization for American Jewish Congress, the Independent Order of B'nai B'rith and the Anti-Defamation League, the Central Conference of American Rabbis, the Rabbinical Assembly of the Jewish Theological Seminary, and the Union of Orthodox Rabbis of United States and Canada. Reznikoff, *Champion of Liberty*, 1:343n**.

81. Marshall to Charles Ritch Johnson, 10 Sept. 1921, in Reznikoff, *Champion of Liberty*, 1:366; Dinnerstein, *Antisemitism in America*, 104 (quoting Rosenstock, *Defender of Jewish Rights*, 277); DI, 26 Nov. 1921, pp. 8–9.

82. *NYT*, 27 May 1921, p. 24.

CHAPTER 3

1. *CDT*, 30 Mar. 1921, p. 8.

2. Louis Marshall to Richard Gottheil, 5 Mar. 1921, in *Louis Marshall, Champion of Liberty: Selected Papers and Addresses*, ed. Charles Reznikoff (Philadelphia: Jewish Publication Society of America, 1957), 1:343n**.

3. Abram Hirschberg, "Voice of the People: Henry Ford and the Jews," *CDT*, 16 June 1920, p. 8.

4. *NYT*, 23 Sept. 1920, p. 12; *WSJ*, 24 Jan. 1921, p. 3.

5. *NYT*, 24 Dec. 1920, p. 4. As president, Taft passed on the opportunity to put Louis Marshall on the U.S. Supreme Court in 1910. Leonard Dinnerstein, *Antisemitism in America* (New York: Oxford University Press, 1994), 83; Morton Rosenstock, *Louis*

Marshall, Defender of Jewish Rights (Detroit, Mich.: Wayne State University Press, 1965), 55. See Chapter 2.

6. William Howard Taft, *Anti-Semitism in the United States* (Chicago: Anti-Defamation League, 1920), 3, 23; *NYT*, 24 Dec. 1920, p. 4.

7. *NYT*, 17 Jan. 1921, p. 10; Herbert Shapiro, "Spargo, John," *American National Biography Online*, Feb. 2000, accessed 11 Nov. 2010, http://www.anb.org/articles/15/15-00634.html.

8. According to Marshall, Jordan's book argued that "Jewish bankers were responsible for all modern wars" (*Unseen Empire: A Study of the Plight of Nations That Do Not Pay Their Debts* [Boston: American Unitarian Association, 1912]); Marshall to John Spargo, 31 Dec. 1920, in Reznikoff, *Champion of Liberty*, 1:354. Marshall did not make clear the basis for his belief that Ford was specifically influenced by Jordan's writing.

9. Rosenstock, *Defender of Jewish Rights*, 156; Richard Slotkin, *Lost Battalions: The Great War and the Crisis of American Nationality* (New York: Henry Holt and Company, 2005), 460 (referencing "The Jews and the Colleges," *World's Work*, Aug. 1922, pp. 351–52); Harold S. Wechsler, *The Qualified Student: A History of Selective College Admission in America* (New York: Wiley, 1977); Marcia G. Synnott, "Numerus Clausus (United States)," in *Antisemitism: A Historical Encyclopedia of Prejudice and Persecution*, ed. Richard S. Levy (Santa Barbara, Calif.: ABC-CLIO, 2005), 2:514–15.

10. *CDT*, 17 Jan. 1921, p. 10; ibid., 25 Jan. 1921, p. 7.

11. *CDT*, 15 Feb. 1921, p. 8; ibid., 16 Feb. 1921, p. 13.

12. John Spargo, *The Jew and American Ideals* (New York: Harper and Brothers, 1921), vii, 2, 10–46; Herman Bernstein, "The New Anti-Semitic Workings," *NYT*, 3 Apr. 1921, p. 43; Herman Bernstein, *The History of A Lie: "The Protocols of the Wise Men of Zion," A Study* (New York: J. S. Ogilvie Publishing, 1921).

13. *NYT*, 26 Feb. 1921, p. 7; ibid., 27 Feb. 1921, p. 3. Elsewhere, libraries reached opposing conclusions; in Pittsburgh's Carnegie library, a public institution, Ford's paper remained available, because "it is much in demand." Ibid., 28 Mar. 1921, p. 3.

14. Lloyd P. Gartner, *History of the Jews of Cleveland*, 2d ed. (Cleveland, Ohio: Western Reserve Historical Society and Jewish Theological Seminary of America, 1987), 192–93.

15. The *Independent*'s files for the early years of its operations are not extant, but the relationship among Black, Liebold, and Ford is definitively laid out in their oral reminiscences and in correspondence relating to pretrial discovery in the *Sapiro* case. See Chapters 1, 5, 6, and 7.

16. Affidavit of James T. Russell, *Dearborn Publishing Company v. W. S. Fitzgerald, W. B. Woods, and Frank W. Smith*, 31 Mar. 1921, U.S. District Court, Cleveland, Equity Case Files, Case No. 621, RG 21, NARA-GL, 2.

17. Russell Affidavit, 1, 2, 4, 6; Affidavit of John N. Gwin, 31 Mar. 1921, p. 2; Affidavit of Frank Edward Harshman, 31 Mar. 1921, p. 2; Affidavit of Charles E. Stuehr, 31 Mar. 1921, p. 1; Affidavit of Milton A. Coulson, 31 Mar. 1921, p. 1; Affidavit of James A. Burns, 31 Mar. 1921, p. 1, all in *DPC v. Fitzgerald et al.*, RG 21, NARA-GL.

18. "Fitzgerald, William Sinton," *Encyclopedia of Cleveland History*, accessed 29 Jan. 2009, http://ech.case.edu/ech-cgi/article.pl?id=FWS. Maurice Maschke, county Republican Party chair, owned a lovely home on Guilford Road in Cleveland Heights, just off Fairmount Boulevard; from 1924 to 1932, he served as a member of the Repub-

lican National Committee. *Encyclopedia of Cleveland History*, accessed 10 Apr. 2009, http://ech.case.edu/ech-cgi/article.pl?id=MM1.

19. "Ordinances of the City of Cleveland," 1 Jan. 1907, ch. 22, Misdemeanors, Disturbances, section 1770, in *DPC v. Fitzgerald et al.*, RG 21, NARA-GL; *Dearborn Publishing Company v. Fitzgerald*, 271 F. 479 (1921), 480.

20. Russell Affidavit, 3.

21. Ibid., 4, 3.

22. Ibid., 5; *DI*, 12 Mar. 1921, pp. 1, 8–9.

23. Russell Affidavit, 3. Sales for the week of March 21 to 28 netted $80. Ibid., 6; *CDT*, 30 Mar. 1921, p. 8.

24. *JI*, 1 Apr. 1921, p. 1; Show Cause Order, 1 Apr. 1921, *DPC v. Fitzgerald*, RG 21, NARA-GL.

25. *Epoch Production Corporation v. Harry L. Davis, Mayor of Cleveland, et al.*, Memorandum for Argument, 5 May 1917, Court of Appeals, Cuyahoga County, Ohio, in *DPC v. Fitzgerald et al.*, RG 21, NARA-GL; *Epoch Producing Co. v. Davis*, 19 Ohio N.P. (N.S.) 465 (1917); *DPC v. Fitzgerald*, 484.

26. Show Cause Order, 1 Apr. 1921, *DPC v. Fitzgerald et al.*, RG 21, NARA-GL; *JI*, 1 Apr. 1921, p. 1.

27. Affidavit of William Sinton Fitzgerald, 8 Apr. 1921, *DPC v. Fitzgerald et al.*, RG 21, NARA-GL.

28. Russell Affidavit, 4–5.

29. Affidavit of Milton Coulson, 31 Mar. 1921, *DPC v. Fitzgerald et al.*, RG 21, NARA-GL; Affidavits of Charles E. Stuehr, Clem D. Nussell, John N. Gwin, and James A. Burns, 31 Mar. 1921, *DPC v. Fitzgerald et al.*, RG 21, NARA-GL.

30. *JI*, 15 Apr. 1921, p. 7.

31. *DPC v. Fitzgerald*, 481, 483.

32. *DPC v. Fitzgerald*, 483.

33. *NYT*, 11 May 1921, p. 7.

34. *JI*, 22 Apr. 1921, p. 1. In 1919, the group changed its name to HBSU and opened membership to all Jews regardless of national origin. "HBSU," *Encyclopedia of Cleveland History*, accessed 7 Apr. 2009, http://ech.cwru.edu/ech-cgi/article.pl?id=H; William Ganson Rose, *Cleveland: The Making of a City* (Cleveland, Ohio: World Publishing Company, 1950), 780.

35. *NYT*, 24 Mar. 1921, p. 10.

36. *NYT*, 25 Mar. 1921, p. 29; ibid., 30 Mar. 1921, p. 20; *JI*, 15 Apr. 1921, p. 5; *NYT*, 29 Mar. 1921, p. 9; ibid., 24 Mar. 1921, p. 10; *WSJ*, 21 Mar. 1921, p. 12.

37. John Haynes Holmes et al. to James J. Thomas, 29 Mar. 1921, microfilm, reel 26, vol. 185, ACLUP; Holmes et al. to J. Galvin, 29 Mar. 1921, ibid.; Holmes et al., circular letter, 30 Mar. 1921, ibid.; Roger N. Baldwin to Federated Press, *New York Call, The Survey, New Republic*, 30 Mar. 1921, ibid.; James J. Thomas to Harry F. Ward, 1 Apr. 1921, ibid.

38. *CDT*, 12 May 1921, p. 8.

39. *JI*, 15 Apr. 1921, p. 1; *NYT*, 24 Mar. 1921, p. 10; ibid., 7 Apr. 1921, p. 27; Albert DeSilver to William Lucking, 5 May 1921, microfilm, reel 25, vol. 183, ACLUP; William Lucking to ACLU, 10 May 1921, ibid. The Detroit prosecutor dismissed his criminal case against the *Independent* vendor who was Lucking's client. Ibid.

40. On the riots and strikes of 1919, see Slotkin, *Lost Battalions*, 435–43.

41. *CDT*, 2 Aug. 1921, p. 11; ibid., 5 Aug. 1921, p. 17; *LAT*, 5 Aug. 1921, sec. 1, p. 4.

42. *DI*, 11 Sept. 1920, pp. 8–9; ibid., 9 Oct. 1920, pp. 8–9; ibid., 4 Dec. 1920, pp. 8–9; *LAT*, 9 Sept. 1921, p. 11.

43. Illinois Revised Statutes, ch. 38, para. 471, sec. 224a (1949; enacted 29 June 1917). The statute went untouched by the legislature until the early 1950s, when a case involving a white supremacist seeking to keep African Americans out of Chicago went to the U.S. Supreme Court. *Beauharnais v. Illinois*, 343 U.S. 250 (1952); James A. Scott, "Criminal Sanctions for Group Libel, Feasibility and Constitutionality," *Duke Law Journal* 1, no. 2 (June 1951): 218–33, 218, 230. On Crowe's role in the Leopold and Loeb case, see Jeffrey S. Adler, review of *For the Thrill of It: Leopold, Loeb, and the Murder That Shocked Chicago*, by Simon Baatz (New York: HarperCollins, 2008), H-Law, H-Net Reviews, April 2009, accessed 18 Apr. 2009, http://www.h-net.org/reviews/showrev.php?id=23887.

44. *CDT*, 9 Sept. 1921, p. 5; *NYT*, 10 Sept. 1921, p. 22.

45. *CDT*, 6 Jan. 1922, p. 15.

46. *NYT*, 3 Dec. 1921, p. 8; Albert Lee, *Henry Ford and the Jews* (New York: Stein and Day, 1980), 67. Muscle Shoals became the site of the New Deal's Tennessee Valley Authority. See Allan Nevins and Frank Ernest Hill, *Ford: Expansion and Challenge, 1915–1933* (New York: Scribner, 1957), 305.

47. Lee, *Ford and the Jews*, 67–68; Leo P. Ribuffo, "Henry Ford and *The International Jew*," *American Jewish History* 69, no. 4 (1980): 437–77; Steven Watts, *The People's Tycoon: Henry Ford and the American Century* (New York: Knopf, 2005), 246–49, 253–54, 271–75; John Kenneth Galbraith, "The Mystery of Henry Ford," *Atlantic Monthly*, Mar. 1958, 41–47.

48. *NYT*, 3 Dec. 1921, p. 8; ibid., 4 Dec. 1921, p. 1; ibid., 5 Dec. 1921, p. 33.

49. *NYT*, 6 Dec. 1921, p. 6.

50. *WSJ*, 5 Dec. 1921, p. 2. By 1921, Ford publicly confined his knowledge of Jewish involvement in the war to what he learned aboard the Peace Ship, although Rosika Schwimmer contended that his suspicions antedated the cruise. See Chapter 2.

51. *NYT*, 15 Dec. 1921, p. 26; ibid., 20 Dec. 1921, p. 34; Nevins and Hill, *Expansion and Challenge*, 307–11; Anne Jardim, *The First Henry Ford: A Study in Personality and Business Leadership* (Cambridge, Mass.: MIT Press, 1970), 147–50.

52. Jardim, *First Henry Ford*, 146; Nevins and Hill, *Expansion and Challenge*, 316; Lee, *Ford and the Jews*, 41–42 (quoting dialogue from Jardim and Nevins and Hill where exact, and omitting paraphrases). Nevins and Hill cite to the *DI*, Mar. 1922, and *PW*, 28 Jan. 1922, but do not supply exact page references.

53. *NYT*, 6 Jan. 1922, p. 9.

54. Nevins and Hill, *Expansion and Challenge*, 316, echoed in Jardim, *First Henry Ford*, 146. Albert Lee spends considerable time trying to discern Ford's reasons for starting the second campaign. Lee, *Ford and the Jews*, 41–42.

55. E. G. Pipp, "Henry Ford: Both Sides of Him," *Pipp's Magazine* (1926), 70. Admittedly, Pipp was hardly an unbiased observer, but he could still write balanced commentary on Ford. See, e.g., ibid., pp. 53–59 (on Ford's relationship with his family). For writers crediting the effects of the boycott on Ford's decision making, see, e.g., Lee, *Ford and the Jews*, 38; Neil Baldwin, *Henry Ford and the Jews: The Mass Production of Hate*

(New York: Public Affairs, 2001), 299; Carol W. Gelderman, *Henry Ford: The Wayward Capitalist* (New York: St. Martin's Press, 1981), 341.

56. Upton Sinclair, *The Flivver King: A Story of Ford-America* (Station A, Pasadena, Calif.: Privately printed, 1937), 126–27. Albert Lee dismisses this story as improbable, but it carries a ring of authenticity; Ford was in the habit of leading people to believe that they were responsible for a decision he made or that their importunities influenced him accordingly. It kept the public and close observers alike confused about his motives and intentions; it led people to believe they had more influence with him than they actually did; and it maintained an air of uncertainty about him and what he was liable to do that he continually exploited.

57. Marshall to Warren G. Harding, 25 July 1921, in Charles Reznikoff, ed., *Louis Marshall, Champion of Liberty: Selected Papers and Addresses* (Philadelphia: Jewish Publication Society of America, 1957), 1:361–63, esp. 363; Evan P. Schultz, "Group Rights, American Jews, and the Failure of Group Libel Laws, 1913–1952," *Brooklyn Law Review* 66 (2000): 71–145, 100–11; Samuel Walker, *Hate Speech: The History of an American Controversy* (Lincoln: University of Nebraska Press, 1994), 19–21. The official announcement of the end of the antisemitic campaign alluded neither to President Harding's intercession nor to the influence of public opinion. *DI*, 7 Jan. 1922, pp. 1, 9; *DI*, 14 Jan. 1922, pp. 1, 8; Lee, *Ford and the Jews*, 43.

58. Lee, *Ford and the Jews*, 14; Jardim, *First Henry Ford*, 144–45; Nevins and Hill, *Expansion and Challenge*, 316; *The International Jew: The World's Foremost Problem*, 4 vols. (Detroit: Dearborn Publishing Company, 1920–1922); Bernstein, *History of A Lie*; *NYT*, 13 Nov. 1922, p. 11; Victoria Saker Woeste, "*Dearborn Independent* and *The International Jew*," in *Antisemitism: A Historical Encyclopedia of Prejudice and Persecution*, ed. Richard S. Levy (Santa Barbara, Calif.: ABC-CLIO, 2005), 2:162–64.

59. Rosenstock, *Defender of Jewish Rights*, 165–68; *American Hebrew*, 23 July 1920, p. 251 (quoted in ibid., 172).

60. *NYT*, 2 Feb. 1921, p. 13; ibid., 3 Feb. 1921, p. 3; Rosenstock, *Defender of Jewish Rights*, 169; Lee, *Ford and the Jews*, 43.

61. Allan L. Benson, interview with Henry Ford, 5 Jan. 1922, file 413, box 14, HBP; "Statement by Herman Bernstein in Answer to Henry Ford's Accusation," n.d. [but Jan. 1922], file 5, box 63, LMP; *LAT*, 10 Jan. 1922, sec. 1, p. 1; Bernstein to Marshall, 12 Jan. 1922, file 5, box 63, LMP. Benson was willing to testify on Bernstein's behalf; see affidavit, Allan L. Benson, n.d. [but 1922], file 413, box 14, HBP.

62. Gert Buelens, "Bernstein, Herman," *American National Biography Online*, Feb. 2000, http://www.anb.org/articles/16/16-00118.html; Bernstein, *History of a Lie*; see Bernstein to Marshall, 18 Oct. 1921, file 332, box 11, HBP; Marshall to Bernstein, 1 Oct. 1921, file 332, box 11, HBP, crediting Bernstein's book for undermining the *Protocols* in the United States: "One thing is certain—that the Protocols have been absolutely destroyed. The disclosures of the London Times have been most valuable, but they must be read in conjunction with the facts set forth in The History of a Lie."

63. *LAT*, 10 Jan. 1922, sec. 1, p. 1; Bernstein to Marshall, 12 Jan. 1922, file 5, box 63, LMP. In 1921, Bernstein published his own account of the voyage, in which he implied that his conversations with Ford aboard the vessel were more numerous and

prolonged than a fifteen-minute chat. *Los Angeles Examiner*, 7 Mar. 1921, file 317, box 10, HBP. See also *Boston American*, 25 Feb. 1921, file 317, box 10, HBP; "Bernstein Believes Ford 'Dangerous' and 'Menace to America,'" [*Jewish Tribune?*], n.d. [but Mar. 1921], file 357, box 10, HBP.

64. Bernstein to Marshall, 12 Jan. 1922, file 5, box 63, LMP; Marshall to Bernstein, 14 Jan. 1922, file 413, box 14, HBP. In an article that defends Marshall's handling of the Sapiro-Ford matter, Robert Rifkind argues that "Marshall did not express any doubt that Bernstein had been harmed by Ford's words." Robert S. Rifkind, "Confronting Antisemitism in America: Louis Marshall and Henry Ford," *American Jewish History* 94, nos. 1–2 (Spring 2009): 71–90, 81.

65. Martin W. Littleton to Bernstein, 18 Apr. 1922, file 5, box 63, LMP; David Brown to Jacob Billikopf, 29 May 1922, file 5, box 63, LMP; Brown to Bernstein, 27 Apr. 1922, file 413, box 14, HBP; Brown to Jacob Billikopf, 29 May 1922, file 5, box 63, LMP; Bernstein to Marshall, 22 Apr. 1922, file 5, box 63, LMP. Littleton reported that Ford's attorney had been close to accepting service of process on Ford's behalf, "but afterward changed his mind about it." Littleton to Bernstein, 18 Apr. 1922, file 5, box 63, LMP.

66. Bernstein to Marshall, 11 July 1923, file 332, box 11, HBP. Rifkind observes that Littleton "ran up considerable expenses that Bernstein could ill afford" ("Confronting American Antisemitism," 82). Marshall suggested in 1922 that Littleton would take the case pro bono; although nothing in the file indicates the exact financial arrangement, in one letter Littleton requested that his client advance the $1,000 needed to tail Ford, but Bernstein "could not afford to do that." Bernstein to Marshall, 11 July 1923, file 332, box 11, HBP.

67. Marshall to Bernstein, 8 July 1923, file 332, box 11, HBP; Attachment Order, *Bernstein v. Ford*, 30 Aug. 1923, file 413, box 14, HBP; *NYT*, 24 Feb. 1924, sec. 2, p. 14; Press Release, 31 Aug. 1923, file 413, box 14, HBP; Liebold to Corn Exchange Bank, 20 Aug. 1923; Frederick T. Martin to Liebold, 22 Aug. 1923, both in file C21, box 156, acc. 285, BFRC.

68. Laurence A. Steinhardt to Herman Bernstein, 9 Aug. 1927, file 413A, box 14, HBP; Memorandum, Steinhardt to Samuel Untermyer, 23 July 1923, file 413, box 14, HBP.

69. *NYT*, 9 July 1923, p. 17; ibid., 19 Aug. 1923, p. 2; James J. Davis to Bernstein, 9 July 1923, file 413, box 14, HBP.

70. Unsigned to *New York Evening World*, Samuel Untermyer, and Herman Bernstein, 10 July 1923, file 413, box 14, HBP.

71. *Hearst's Magazine*, announcement of Norman Hapgood's series on Ford, quoted in Bernstein to Marshall, 22 Apr. 1922, file 5, box 63, LMP.

CHAPTER 4

1. Aaron Sapiro, "True Farmer Cooperation," *World's Work*, 46 (1923): 193–210.

2. George Jacobs, unpublished memoir, furnished to author by Gail Nebanzahl, 22 Feb. 2008 (on file); see also Gail Jacobs Nebanzahl, unpublished Sapiro family tree, n.d. [but ca. 2001] (on file); Max Herschberg, Petition for Naturalization, 9 Oct. 1880, U.S. District Court, New York, Soundex Index of Naturalization Petitions, New York City, 1792–1906, NARA, accessed 23 Nov. 2010, http://search.ancestry.com/iexec?htx= View&r=an&dbid=1629&iid=31194_120955-05835&fn=Max&ln=Herschberg&st=r&s

src=&pid=6243514; 1880 U.S. Federal Census Schedule, San Francisco, San Francisco County, State of California, Ancestry.com, accessed 23 Nov. 2010, http://search.ances-try.com/iexec?htx=View&r=an&dbid=6742&iid=4239989-00210&fn=Phillip&ln=Sap iro&st=r&ssrc=&pid=15925080. George Jacobs, father of Gail Nebanzahl, was the son of Miriam Wascerwitz Jacobs and great-nephew of Fanny Ringolsky and Selina Sapiro.

3. Jacob Sapiro, Petition for Naturalization, Alphabetical Index of Petitions for Naturalization, U.S. District Court, Southern District of New York, 1824–1941, M1676, NARA, accessed 26 Feb. 2008, http://www.footnote.com/image/4499244; Central Pacific Railroad Photographic History Museum, enlarged 1881 rates of fare timetable, accessed 18 Aug. 2008, http://cprr.org/Museum/Ephemera/CP-UP_Timetable_1881/1881_TT _Fares_2.html. The court did not explain its decision.

4. Nebanzahl, unpublished Sapiro family tree; *LAT*, 5 Nov. 1982, pt. 2, p. 4; *San Francisco Chronicle*, 23 Dec. 1958, p. 16; Merle Crowell, "Nothing Could Keep This Boy Down," *American Magazine* (Apr. 1923), 16–17, 136–46, 136. Family members recall that Aaron was one of a set of twins and that the other twin did not survive. Gail Jacobs Nebanzahl, interview by author, San Francisco, 30 Mar. 2005 (transcript on file); Jerome and Mary Sapiro, interview by author, San Francisco, 30 Mar. 2005 (transcript on file). Aaron's twin, whom Aaron never mentions in his 1923 interview with Merle Crowell, "died very young," according to George Jacobs; see Jacobs, unpublished memoir.

5. Crowell, "Nothing Could Keep This Boy Down," 136; Jacobs, unpublished memoir.

6. Jacob Sapiro's alcoholism is mentioned in Grace H. Larsen and Henry E. Erdman, "Aaron Sapiro: Genius of Farm Co-operative Promotion," *Mississippi Valley Historical Review* 49, no. 2 (1962): 242–268, 243; Aaron alludes to it in his *American Magazine* interview; see Crowell, "Nothing Could Keep This Boy Down," 136, 138.

7. Crowell, "Nothing Could Keep This Boy Down," 136–38.

8. Ibid., 138. On Markham, see William R. Nash, "Markham, Edwin," *American National Biography Online*, Feb. 2000, accessed 17 June 2008, http://www.anb.org /articles/16/16-01058.html.

9. *Oakland Tribune*, 10 Feb. 1893, p. 1.

10. Ibid., p. 1; Crowell, "Nothing Could Keep This Boy Down," 138.

11. Ibid., 138; Nebanzahl, unpublished family tree; Jacobs, unpublished memoir.

12. Jacobs, unpublished memoir.

13. Crowell, "Nothing Could Keep This Boy Down," 143. Aaron does not provide a date of death for Saul, but he says there were seven children in 1894 and that he, Philip, one sister, and "a brother who has since died" were sent to the orphanage. George Jacobs also mentions Saul in his memoir.

14. Andy Altman-Ohr, "JFCS: Nurturing 40,000 in Its 150th Year," *Jewish News Weekly*, 3 Mar. 2000, accessed 14 Dec. 2010, http://www.jweekly.com/article/full/12681/jfcs-nurturing-40-000-in-its-150th-year/; "Joseph Seligman," *Jewish Encyclopedia.com*, accessed 4 Feb. 2008, http://www.jewishencyclopedia.com/view_friendly.jsp?artid=454&letter=S.html. See, e.g., "To Protect the Poor and Fatherless," in *Jewish Voices of the California Gold Rush: A Documentary History, 1849–1880*, ed. Ava F. Kahn (Detroit: Wayne State University Press, 2002), 226–33.

15. Leo Eloesser to Congregation Serith Israel, 30 Sept. 1872, in Kahn, *Jewish Voices of the California Gold Rush*, 228; Altman-Ohr, "JFCS: Nurturing 40,000 in Its 150th Year."

The orphanage moved to larger quarters on Ocean Avenue in 1921, and the Divisadero building was torn down. Ibid.

16. S. W. Levy, Eighth Annual Report to the Patrons and Members of the Pacific Hebrew Orphan Asylum and Home, September 1879, in Kahn, *Jewish Voices of the California Gold Rush*, 232–33.

17. Crowell, "Nothing Could Keep This Boy Down," 143. For good histories of nineteenth-century American orphanages, see Kenneth Cmiel, *A Home of Another Kind: One Chicago Orphanage and the Tangle of Child Welfare* (Chicago: University of Chicago Press, 1995); and Hyman Bogen, *The Luckiest Orphans: A History of the Hebrew Orphan Asylum of New York* (Urbana: University of Illinois Press, 1992).

18. Crowell, "Nothing Could Keep This Boy Down," 143.

19. Ibid.

20. Arno G. Weinstein, "Aaron Sapiro vs. Henry Ford: The Events Prior to, during and following the Confrontation" (M.A. thesis, Arizona State University, Tempe, 1986), 6.

21. Crowell, "Nothing Could Keep This Boy Down," 143; Lowell High School Class of June 1900, class roll, accessed 23 June 2008, http://www.sfgenealogy.com/sf//schools/lhsj00.html.

22. Andy Altman-Ohr, "Sherith Israel's Legacy: Its Outspoken Rabbis," *Jewish News Weekly of Northern California*, 8 Oct. 1999, accessed 14 Dec. 2010, http://www.jweekly.com/article/full/11758/sherith-israel-s-legacy-its-outspoken-rabbis/; Crowell, "Nothing Could Keep This Boy Down," 144; Jacobs, unpublished memoir; Ava F. Kahn and Ellen Eisenberg, "Western Reality: Jewish Diversity during the 'German' Period," *American Jewish History* 92, no. 4 (2004): 455–79, 460–61; Larsen and Erdman, "Genius of Farm Co-operative Promotion," 243. Rabbi Nieto served Sherith Israel for thirty-eight years and led his congregation through difficult times; the temple survived the 1906 San Francisco earthquake and subsequent fire and was used by the city as a municipal courtroom for two years.

23. Jeannette Arndt Anderson, interview by author, Palo Alto, Calif., 31 Mar. 2005, p. 14 (transcript on file). Janet Arndt Sapiro was born March 24, 1895, making her eleven years Aaron's junior; Janet Sapiro, Certificate of Death, 4 June 1936, no. 7502, County of Los Angeles, State of California, Department of Public Health. Stanley Arndt became a lawyer who wrote at least one article on agricultural cooperation and practiced law for a time with his brother-in-law. Anderson interview, 7; Stanley Arndt, "The Law of California Co-operative Marketing Associations," *California Law Review* 8 (1920): 281–94.

24. Anderson interview, 13–14; Earthquake and Graft Prosecution Timeline, 1906–1907, Virtual Museum of the City of San Francisco, accessed 26 June 2008, http://www.sfmuseum.org/hist/timeline.html#top; Linda Sapiro Moon, interview by author, Huntington Beach, Calif., 23 Sept. 2002, pp. 4–5 (transcript on file). On the practice of Jewish families betrothing their young daughters through the late nineteenth century, see Sydney Stahl Weinberg, *The World of Our Mothers: The Lives of Jewish Immigrant Women* (Chapel Hill: University of North Carolina Press, 1988), 23–24.

25. Crowell, "Nothing Could Keep This Boy Down," 144; "Aaron L. Sapiro: The Man Who Sued Henry Ford, a Picture Story," *Western States Jewish Historical Quarterly* 13, no. 4 (1981): 303–312, 304; Jacobs, unpublished memoir ("Rabbi Nieto pleaded with him to no avail").

26. Victoria Saker Woeste, "Sapiro, Aaron," *American National Biography Online*, Apr. 2004 update, accessed 5 Jan. 2005, http://www.anb.org/articles/11/11-01215.html; Moon interview, 11; Aaron L. Sapiro, Transcript of Proceedings, *Sapiro v. Ford*, 28 Mar. 1927, file 2, box 44, Acc. 48, BFRC (hereafter "trial transcript"), 1146, 1148.

27. Crowell, "Nothing Could Keep This Boy Down," 144 (emphasis in original); 1910 U.S. Federal Census Schedule, San Francisco, San Francisco County, State of California, Ancestry.com, accessed 18 July 2008, http://search.ancestry.com/cgi-bin/sse.dll?indiv=1&db=1910USCenIndex&rank=1&new=1&MSAV=1&msT=1&gss=angs-d&gsfn=Aaron&gsln=Sapiro&dbOnly=_83004006|_83004006_x,_83004005|_83004005_x&uidh=x85&pcat=35&fh=0&h=1615724&recoff=10+12 (listing Aaron Sapiro as an assistant superintendent living at 600 Divisadero Street).

28. *Berkeley Daily Gazette*, 17 May 1911, p. 1.

29. Robert Cherny, "Johnson, Hiram Warren," *American National Biography Online*, Feb. 2000, accessed 18 July 2008, http://anb.org/articles/06/06-00315.html; trial transcript, 1148. On the legal history of workers' compensation, see, e.g., Lawrence Friedman and Jack Ladinsky, "Social Change and the Law of Industrial Accidents," *Columbia Law Review* 67 (1967): 50–82; Arthur F. McEvoy, "Freedom of Contract, Labor, and the Administrative State," in *The State and Freedom of Contract*, ed. Harry N. Scheiber (Palo Alto, Calif.: Stanford University Press, 1998), 198–235; and John Fabian Witt, *The Accidental Republic: Crippled Workingmen, Destitute Widows, and the Remaking of American Law* (Cambridge, Mass.: Harvard University Press, 2004).

30. Roseberry Act, 1911 Cal. 399 (participation voluntary for employers); Boynton Act, 1913 Cal. 176 (compulsory participation); trial transcript, 1148–50. The compulsory participation act that Sapiro drafted remains the foundation of California's workers' compensation system. Sapiro's nephew and son attest to his authorship of the Boynton Act. Sam Bubrick, interview by author, Los Angeles, California, 23 Sept. 2002 (transcript on file); Leland Sapiro, telephone interview by author, June 1998. Ironically, the California workers' compensation law could well be Sapiro's most lasting legacy. See Glenn Merrill Shor, "The Evolution of Workers' Compensation Policy in California, 1911–1990" (Ph.D. diss., University of California, Berkeley, 1990).

31. Moon interview, 5.

32. Larsen and Erdman say they met in 1905 ("Genius of Co-operative Promotion," 244), but this account contradicts Sapiro's trial testimony.

33. Olivia Rossetti Agresti, *David Lubin: A Study in Practical Idealism* (Boston: Little, Brown and Co., 1922), 267–79; Michael Magliari, "Lubin, David," *American National Biography Online*, Feb. 2000, accessed 29 May 2008, http://www.anb.org/articles/15/15-00979.html. Jefferson expressed these ideas most fully in his *Notes on the State of Virginia*. See his *Writings*, ed. Merrill D. Peterson (New York: Viking Press, 1984).

34. Larsen and Erdman, "Genius of Farm Co-operative Promotion," 245; trial transcript, 1153–54; Aaron Sapiro, "An Experience with American Justice," *Free Synagogue Pulpit* 8, no. 5 (1927–1928): 3–40, 5.

35. Quoted in Larsen and Erdman, "Genius of Farm Co-operative Promotion," 244.

36. Victoria Saker Woeste, *The Farmer's Benevolent Trust: Law and Agricultural Cooperation in Industrial America, 1865–1945* (Chapel Hill: University of North Carolina Press, 1998), 17–24.

37. Ibid., 24–36.

38. Crowell, "Nothing Could Keep This Boy Down," 136 (quoting Sapiro, who made the analogy at a dinner in 1923 at which Judge Gary, head of U.S. Steel, was also a guest).

39. Steven Stoll, *The Fruits of Natural Advantage: Making the Industrial Countryside in California* (Berkeley: University of California Press, 1998), 212n61; Woeste, *Farmer's Benevolent Trust*, 197; Arthur F. McEvoy, *The Fisherman's Problem: Ecology and Law in the California Fisheries, 1850–1980* (New York: Cambridge University Press, 1986), 169; Larsen and Erdman, "Genius of Farm Co-operative Promotion," 245.

40. Sapiro was already on retainer as Weinstock's personal attorney; see Larsen and Erdman, "Genius of Farm Co-operative Promotion," 245; on Sapiro's not receiving an official state salary, see trial transcript, 1154.

41. Trial transcript, 1155; Woeste, *Farmer's Benevolent Trust*, 197; McEvoy, *Fisherman's Problem*, 170.

42. Woeste, *Farmer's Benevolent Trust*, 117–31; Catherine Merlo, *Heritage of Gold: The First 100 Years of Sunkist Growers, Inc., 1893–1993* (Los Angeles: Sunkist Growers, 1993), 1–58.

43. "'I want to see every farmer in this country make money enough to live decently. I want to see his boy have shoes and stockings, and be able to get a good education without suffering what I have suffered. I want his home to be provided with a bathtub and all the ordinary comforts of life. I don't want his wife to have to work as hard as my mother had to work.'" Crowell, "Nothing Can Keep This Boy Down," 146.

44. Larsen and Erdman, "Genius of Farm Co-operative Promotion," 247; trial transcript, 1156–60, 1168; Weinstein, "*Aaron Sapiro v. Henry Ford*," 8. On alien land laws, see Charles J. McClain, ed., *Japanese Immigrants and American Law: The Alien Land Laws and Other Issues* (New York: Garland Publishers, 1994).

45. Richard Slotkin, *Lost Battalions: The Great War and the Crisis of American Nationality* (New York: Henry Holt and Company, 2005), 1; Woeste, *Farmer's Benevolent Trust*, 139.

46. Trial transcript, 1162–65; *NYT*, 17 Mar. 1927, p. 1; David McCullough, *Truman* (New York: Simon and Schuster, 1992), 104–5; Joseph Bendersky, *The "Jewish Threat": Antisemitic Politics of the U.S. Army* (New York: Basic Books, 2000), 33–46; Slotkin, *Lost Battalions*, 35–212. Sapiro's military file is no longer extant. It was apparently destroyed in a 1973 fire at the National Personnel Records Center in St. Louis, Missouri. John O'Hanlon to author, 10 Sept. 2008 (on file). Marshall busily fielded reports of discrimination and brutal treatment in the military and from companies doing business on government contracts; he issued a steady stream of written pressure from his office to Washington throughout the war in protest of the general pattern he saw. His response to these individuals was less than helpful, as he told them that there was little he could do and that they should simply do their best to serve under the conditions imposed on them. See Reznikoff, *Champion of Liberty*, 1:281–94.

47. Trial transcript, 1165–66; "Sapiro, Aaron," *Who's Who in America*, 15 (1928–1929), 1831; Orville Dwyer, "Sapiro Reveals Life," *CDT*, 29 Mar. 1927, p. 8.

48. Cherny, "Johnson, Hiram Warren;" trial transcript, 1169; Grace Larsen, "A Progressive in Agriculture: Harris Weinstock," *Agricultural History* 32, no. 3 (July 1958): 187–193, 193; McEvoy, *Fisherman's Problem*, 170.

49. Larsen and Erdman, "Genius of Farm Co-operative Promotion," 250. Weinstock also apparently criticized Sapiro for overcharging clients, a criticism that resurfaced when Sapiro took his practice nationwide. Ibid., 250–51.

50. Woeste, *Farmer's Benevolent Trust*, 198 (quoting Robert H. Montgomery, *The Cooperative Pattern in Cotton* [New York: Macmillan, 1929], 74, and William C. Brooker, *Cooperative Marketing Associations in Business* ([New York: Privately published, 1935], 69); Silas Bent, "Three City-Bred Jews That the Farmer Trusts," *Outlook* 134 (8 Aug. 1923): 553–56, 555; Sapiro, "True Farmer Cooperation," *World's Work* 46 (1923), 85–96, 96. At the time, however, local newspapers entirely ignored his speech. See, e.g., *Birmingham Advertiser*, 1–20 Apr. 1920.

51. *Vancouver Sun*, 11 Aug. 1927, editorial page, file 5, box 70, LSSP; Bent, "Three City-Bred Jews," 554; *NYT*, 30 Mar. 1927, p. 16.

52. Henry C. Wallace to E. L. Mack, 8 Feb. 1924, Correspondence of the Secretary of Agriculture, drawer 455 (1924 Marketing), RG 16, NARA-CP; see also Sapiro to Edwin T. Meredith, 1 Sept. 1920, Correspondence of the Secretary of Agriculture, drawer 521 (1920 Marketing), RG 16, NARA-CP; Meredith to Sapiro, 4 Sept. 1920, ibid.; Robert P. Howard, *James R. Howard and the Farm Bureau* (Ames: Iowa State University Press, 1983); James Shideler, *Farm Crisis: 1919–1923* (Berkeley: University of California Press, 1957).

53. *Tobacco Growers Cooperative Association v. Jones*, 185 N.C. 265 (1923); *Liberty Warehouse Co. v. Burley Tobacco Assn.*, 276 U.S. 71 (1928); Woeste, *Farmer's Benevolent Trust*, 203–6.

54. Larsen and Erdman, "Genius of Farm Co-operative Promotion," 260, 263–68; Grant McConnell, *The Decline of Agrarian Democracy* (Berkeley: University of California Press, 1953), 60–61; William E. Ellis, "Robert Worth Bingham and the Crisis of Cooperative Marketing in the Twenties," *Agricultural History* 56 (1982): 99–116.

55. Robert Morgan, "Jewish Exploitation of Farmers' Organizations," *DI*, 19 Apr. 1924, p. 4. In one of the lionizing biographies he commissioned, Ford claimed that he supported agricultural cooperation in principle but criticized Sapiro-style cooperation as unnecessary in a free market. Henry Ford with Samuel Crowther, *Today and Tomorrow* (Garden City, N.Y.: Garden City Publishing, 1926), 214–22, esp. 219.

56. Crowell, "Nothing Could Keep This Boy Down," 146.

57. Sapiro, "Experience with American Justice," 32.

CHAPTER 5

1. Aaron Sapiro, "An Experience with American Justice," *Free Synagogue Pulpit* 8, no. 5 (1927–1928): 10.

2. Allan Nevins and Frank Ernest Hill, *Ford: Expansion and Challenge, 1915–1933* (New York: Scribner, 1957), 308, 305; *CDT*, 7 Sept. 1923, p. 16; *WSJ*, 4 Dec. 1923, p. 6; *NYT*, 4 Dec. 1923, p. 4.

3. *NYT*, 4 Dec. 1923; *Boston Daily Globe*, 4 Dec. 1923, p. 12. On Ford's interest in the presidency, see Nevins and Hill, *Expansion and Challenge*, 301–11; Albert Lee, *Henry Ford and the Jews* (New York: Stein and Day, 1980), 141–42; Anne Jardim, *The First Henry Ford: A Study in Personality and Business Leadership* (Cambridge, Mass.: MIT Press, 1970), 211; Steven Watts, *The People's Tycoon: Henry Ford and the American Century* (New York: Knopf, 2005), 240–42, 248.

4. See, e.g., Judson C. Welliver, "Henry Ford Reveals Himself: A Character Sketch and Interview," *AC*, 1 Nov. 1921, p. 15; ibid., 2 Nov. 1921, p. 13; ibid., 3 Nov. 1921, p. 11; ibid., 12 Jan. 1922, p. 1; *NYT*, 17 Jan. 1922, p. 6; Henry Ford, with Samuel Crowther, *My Life and Work* (Garden City, N.Y.: Doubleday, Page and Co., 1922). Leo P. Ribuffo reports that antisemitic comments began to reappear in November that year, primarily relating to the presidential race and the case of Army Captain Robert Rosenbluth, wrongly accused of shooting his commanding officer. Ribuffo, "Henry Ford and *The International Jew*," *American Jewish History* 69, no. 4 (1980): 437–77, 462.

5. *NYT*, 24 May 1914, p. 13; Harry H. Dunn to Fred L. Black, 22 Oct. 1924, Dunn and Dunn/Morgan File, box 19, acc. 48, BFRC. William A. Simonds described Dunn as "a former Hearst newspaperman whose previous work had been found accurate." Simonds, *Henry Ford: His Life, His Work, His Genius* (Indianapolis, Ind.: Bobbs-Merrill, 1943), 210; 1930 U.S. Federal Census Schedule, San Diego, San Diego County, State of California, Ancestry.com, accessed 10 Jul. 2009, http://search.ancestry.com/cgi-bin/sse. dll?indiv=1&db=1930usfedcen&rank=1&new=1&MSAV=1&msT=1&gss=angs-d&gsfn =Harry+H&gsln=Dunn&msydy=1930&msypn__ftp=San+Diego,+San+Diego,+Cali fornia,+USA&msypn=69169&msypn_PInfo=8-|1652393|2|3249|7|2598|69169|&cpxt=0&c atBucket=r&uidh=x85&cp=0&pcat=35&fh=0&h=92157035&recoff=7+8+9; Harry H. Dunn, "The Kaiser's Trail in Mexico," *Cartoons Magazine* 11: 4 (Apr. 1917): 504–8; H. H. Dunn, *The Crimson Jester: Zapata of Mexico* (New York: R. M. McBride and Co., 1933); Brian Railsback and Michael J. Meyer, *A John Steinbeck Encyclopedia* (Westport, Conn.: Greenwood Press, 2006), 411.

6. H. W. Roland to Harry H. Dunn, 6 Aug. 1923, Dunn and Dunn/Morgan File, box 19, acc. 48, BFRC; Harry H. Dunn, "Yellow Metal That Defies the Melting Pot," *DI*, 7 Jan. 1922, pp. 10–11; Dunn, "How Is California to Be Saved?" *DI*, 21 Jan. 1922, pp. 6–7, 15.

7. H. W. Roland to Harry H. Dunn, 6 Aug. 1923, Dunn and Dunn/Morgan, box 19, acc. 48, BFRC.

8. Harry Dunn to H. W. Roland, 24 Sept. 1923, Dunn and Dunn/Morgan, box 19, acc. 48, BFRC, citing Welch to Dunn, 13 Sept. 1923 (not in file).

9. Robert Morgan, "Jewish Exploitation of Farmers' Organization: Monopoly Traps Operate Under Guise of 'Marketing Associations,'" *DI*, 12 Apr. 1924, pp. 4–5; Walter Nobel Burns, "The Greatest Single-Handed Fight in American History," *DI*, 12 Apr. 1924, pp. 3, 14; Dunn, "'Alphabet Four,' Forerunner of Present Navy," *DI*, 12 Apr. 1924, pp. 10, 14. The extant Dunn-*DI* correspondence sheds no light on the decision to use a pseud-onym for Dunn; there is a gap in the files between the summer of 1923 and May 1924.

10. *DI*, 12 Apr. 1924, pp. 4, 5 (emphasis in original); Morgan, "Jewish Exploitation of Farmers' Organizations, II: The Story of the Sapiro Boys," *DI*, 19 Apr. 1924, pp. 4–5.

11. *DI*, 19 Apr. 1924, p. 4 (emphasis in original). Morgan erred in stating that "forty-eight states" enacted Sapiro's uniform cooperative marketing statute; by 1927, thirty-eight states had done so.

12. *DI*, 19 Apr. 1924, p. 5 (emphasis in original).

13. Elizabeth Sanders, *Roots of Reform: Farmers, Workers, and the American State, 1877–1917* (Chicago: University of Chicago Press, 1999); Gerald Berk, *Alternative Tracks: The Constitution of American Industrial Order, 1865–1917* (Baltimore: Johns Hopkins University Press, 1994).

14. Morgan, "Jewish Exploitation of Farmers' Organizations III: Money for Everybody but the Farmer," *DI*, 26 Apr. 1924, pp. 4–5. Dunn was far from the first to make this criticism of Sapiro; indeed, Sapiro's own published work anticipated the point. See, e.g., Aaron Sapiro, "Cooperative Marketing," *Iowa Law Bulletin* 8 (1923): 193–210; and Sapiro, "The Law of Cooperative Marketing Associations," *Kentucky Law Journal* 15 (1926): 1–21.

15. *DI*, 26 Apr. 1924, p. 5.

16. Harris Houghton to William M. Cameron, [April] 1924, file 1, box 32, acc. 48, BFRC (emphasis in original); E. W. Cahill, S.F., to Ford, 26 July 1923, ibid. See also "A Friend to Robert Morgan," 23 April 1924, ibid.; A. C. Baker to *DI*, 12 June 1924, ibid. ("I am suspicious that the Department [of Agriculture] has placed a Jew in position to know and dictate what is going on with reference to their interests as a race. The only source to which the American people can hopefully appeal for news concerning their despoilers is The Independent and I solemnly hope you will uncover their every diabolical plot"), and other letters in file.

17. B. C. Olney to Business Editor, *DI*, 12 June 1924, file 2, box 32, acc. 48, BFRC; William Cameron to E. C. Vick, 23 Apr. 1924, file 1, box 32, acc. 48, BFRC.

18. A. S. Goss to *DI*, 15 Apr. 1924, file 1, box 32, acc. 48, BFRC; Cameron to Goss, 23 Apr. 1924, ibid.; W. E. Hotchkiss to Editor, *DI*, 17 Apr. 1924, ibid.; *Plymouth (Ind.) Pilot*, 5 May 1924, file 4, box 29, acc. 48, BFRC.

19. Peteet to Liebold, 25 Apr. 1924, file 7, box 122, acc. 1, BFRC; Liebold to Peteet, 25 Apr. 1924, ibid.; Peteet to Liebold, 26 Apr. 1924, ibid. For the backstory on Sapiro's and Peteet's departures from the AFBF, see Peteet, "Memoranda [*sic*] for Mr. Henry Ford," n.d. [but 24 Sept. 1924], 11–15, file 4, box 29, acc. 48, BFRC; Robert P. Howard, *James R. Howard and the Farm Bureau* (Ames: Iowa State University Press, 1983), 198–203; and James Shideler, *Farm Crisis: 1919–1923* (Berkeley: University of California Press, 1957), 251–54.

20. Walton Peteet, "The Cooperatives Reply to Henry Ford," 1, n.d. [but May 1925], file 7, box 122, acc. 1, BFRC; *Plymouth (Ind.) Pilot*, 5 May 1924, file 4, box 29, acc. 48, BFRC.

21. Herman Steen, *Cooperative Marketing: The Golden Rule in Agriculture* (Garden City, N.Y.: Doubleday, 1923); Peteet, "The Cooperatives Reply to Henry Ford," 7–8.

22. F. S. Trusler to Cameron, 21 Apr. 1924, file 1, box 32, acc. 48, BFRC; J. R. Hutchinson to Robert Morgan, 17 May 1924, ibid.; G. H. Kirk to Donaldson, 10 June 1924, ibid.

23. Cameron to F. S. Trusler, 29 Apr. 1924, file 1, box 32, acc. 48, BFRC.

24. Walton Peteet, Special Report on Ford's Attack, 8 May 1924, Peteet file, box 46, BFRC. Newspapers in California picked up Peteet's reply; see Peteet to Milton Sapiro, 21 July 1924, MDSP.

25. H. H. Dunn, "Beating the Jewish Ring at its Own Game," typescript, 12 June 1924, file 1, box 30, acc. 48, BFRC.

26. See, e.g., Robert Morgan, "Wheat Farmers Drop Two Millions a Year: Story of the Northwest Growers Record in Costly Marketing," *DI*, 19 July 1924, pp. 6, 14; Morgan, "Potato Growers Beat Sapiro at His Own Game: $2,000,000 Crop Regained After Organization by 'Cooperatives,'" *DI*, 26 July 1924, pp. 6, 14; Morgan, "To Save an Industry from Sapiro Hands: A $3,000,000 Crop Is Being Kept Out of the Hands of Exploiters," *DI*, 2 Aug. 1924, pp. 4, 15; and Morgan, "The Sapiro Burr in Oregon's Golden Fleece: Another Chapter on the Exploitation of the American Farmer," *DI*, 9 Aug. 1924, pp. 6, 14.

27. Volney Hogatt to Robert Morgan, 21 Apr. 1924, file 1, box 30, acc. 48, BFRC; Dunn to B. R. Donaldson, 28 Apr. 1924, ibid.

28. Volney Hogatt to Robert Morgan, 21 Apr. 1924, file 1, box 30, acc. 48, BFRC.

29. Ibid.

30. *DI*, 26 July 1924, pp. 6, 14.

31. H. H. Dunn, "Beating the Jewish Ring at Its Own Game," 12 June 1924, typescript, potato file, box 30, acc. 48, BFRC. Compare Morgan, "Potato Growers Beat Sapiro at His Own Game."

32. Several explanations have been offered for the *Independent*'s changed message. Leo Ribuffo suggests the most persuasive, and my research confirms his argument. Ribuffo speculated that Fred Black, along with "other members of the Independent staff," was locked in a struggle with Liebold over the series' emphasis. Black wanted the articles to address the failings in Sapiro's marketing plan, a conclusion Ribuffo bases on the oral "Reminiscences" of Black and Liebold (but not of William Cameron). According to Ribuffo, Black lost this editorial struggle. Had he prevailed, the newspaper's legal liability for individual libel would have been much narrower. As published, the newspaper specifically and individually libeled Sapiro; the larger issue was whether and to what degree it committed group libel as well. Ribuffo, "Ford and *The International Jew*," 464. The legal significance of this point will become clear as we proceed.

33. Dunn to Cameron, 15 May 1924, Dunn and Dunn/Morgan, box 19, acc. 48, BFRC; Ella Scherneck, memorandum, 5 May 1924, MDSP.

34. Dunn to Cameron, 15 May 1924, Dunn and Dunn/Morgan, box 19, acc. 48, BFRC; H. H. Dunn to B. R. Donaldson, 11 June 1924, ibid. Dunn was careful to tell Cameron that he was saving money as he planned his railroad travel, but Fred Black did not trust Dunn's estimates of his expenses—"around $100 a week"—and requested weekly updates on his spending (request quoted in Dunn to Donaldson, 11 June 1924, ibid.).

35. Dunn to Cameron, 15 May 1924, Dunn and Dunn/Morgan, box 19, acc. 48, BFRC.

36. H. H. Dunn to B. R. Donaldson, 11 June 1924, Dunn and Dunn/Morgan, box 19, acc. 48, BFRC; *DI*, 5 July 1924, p. 15 (emphasis in original); *DI*, 26 Apr. 1924, p. 4.

37. *DI*, 19 July 1924, pp. 6, 14; ibid., 26 July 1924, pp. 6, 14; ibid., 2 Aug. 1924, pp. 4, 15 (quote on p. 15).

38. *DI*, 9 Aug. 1924, pp. 6, 14 (quote on p. 6).

39. Morgan, "Sapiro Invades the Tobacco Field: What Will-o'-the-Wisp Marketing Costs the Farmer," *DI*, 16 Aug. 1924, pp. 5, 14. Yet the earlier letter suggests Dunn was going to use Passonneau as his main source on the tobacco story, and there is little doubt that the story is told from Passonneau's perspective. On tobacco, see William E. Ellis, "Robert Worth Bingham and the Crisis of Cooperative Marketing in the Twenties," *Agricultural History* 56 (1982): 99–121; Christopher Waldrep, *Night Riders: Defending Community in the Black Patch, 1890–1915* (Durham, N.C.: Duke University Press, 1993); Victoria Saker Woeste, "*Dearborn Independent* and *The International Jew*," in *Antisemitism: A Historical Encyclopedia of Prejudice and Persecution*, ed. Richard S. Levy (Santa Barbara, Calif.: ABC-CLIO, 2005), 2:96, 199, 203, 263n2.

40. Morgan, "Sapiro Rust in the Northwestern Hay Crop: Thousands of Tons Lie Rotting in Fields Through Not Finding Buyers," *DI*, 23 Aug. 1924, pp. 10, 14 (quote on p. 10).

41. Ibid., 10, 14. For documentation of raids against suspected communists in the Pacific Northwest in the early 1920s, see Richard Merrill Whitney, *Reds in America* (New York: Beckwith Press, 1924).

42. Morgan, "Sapiro's Dream—An International Wheat Pool: How He Tried and Failed to Control American Farm Bureau Federation; Joseph's Grain-Control Advice to Pharaoh Repeated—With Variations," *DI*, 30 Aug. 1924, pp. 6, 14 (quote on 6).

43. *DI*, 30 Aug. 1924. On Sapiro and the AFBF in 1923, see, e.g., Victoria Saker Woeste, *The Farmer's Benevolent Trust: Law and Agricultural Cooperation in Industrial America, 1865–1945* (Chapel Hill: University of North Carolina Press, 1998), 202; Shideler, *Farm Crisis*, 251–53.

44. Dunn to Donaldson, 19 Aug. 1924, Dunn and Dunn/Morgan, box 19, acc. 48, BFRC.

45. Morgan, "Sapiro and Raisin Growers," *DI*, 20 Sept. 1924, pp. 10, 14; Woeste, *Farmer's Benevolent Trust*, 64–76, 93–107. For an example of the traditionalist critique, see Edwin G. Nourse, "The Economic Philosophy of Co-operation," *American Economic Review* 12 (1922): 577–97.

46. P. P. Erwin to DPC, 20 Sept. 1924, file 1, box 32, acc. 48, BFRC; W. R. Baughman to *DI*, 20 Sept. 1924, ibid. Among other things, the *Daily Item* article opined: "In South Carolina there are no Jews on the board and no Jewish counsel to arouse Mr. Ford's distrust and we are sure that throughout the cotton belt the affairs of these associations are in the hands of Southern cotton farmers of Christian faith. . . . Mr. Ford never produces a car that he sells at a loss but he is willing to advise cotton farmers to revert to their old system of marketing that has caused them to produce many, many crops at a loss and has burdened our Southland with debt, illiteracy and poverty" ("Replies to Attacks of Henry Ford," *Sumter Daily Item*, 15 Sept. 1924, file 1, box 32, acc. 48, BFRC).

47. W. O. Sauder to *DI*, 29 Sept. 1924, file 1, box 32, acc. 48, BFRC; Black to Sauder, 10 Oct. 1924, ibid.

48. K. W. King and Co. to *DI*, 13 Sept. 1924, file 1, box 32, acc. 48, BFRC; J. A. Blanchard to Morgan, 14 Sept. 1924, "Dearborn Independent Correspondence" file, box 5, acc. 273, BFRC; see also C. H. Butler to *DI*, 11 Oct. 1924, ibid. For letters opposing Sapiro, see file 1, box 30, acc. 48, BFRC.

49. O. E. Webb to *DI*, 7 Sept. 1924, file 1, box 30, acc. 48, BFRC; Harry H. Dunn to B. R. Donaldson, 16 Sept. 1924, ibid.; B. R. Donaldson to O. E. Webb, 23 Sept. 1924, ibid. The file contains no response from Webb. For a fruitless exchange, see D. W. Aupperle to F. L. Black, 15 Nov. 1924, ibid.; Black to Aupperle, 25 Nov. 1924, ibid.; Aupperle to Black, 15 Dec. 1924, ibid.

50. Milton Sapiro to R. H. McDrew, 23 Aug. 1924, MDSP; see also Richard Gutstadt to Milton Sapiro, 28 Apr. 1924, MDSP; Milton Sapiro to Gutstadt, 6 May 1924, MDSP; W. A. Fenny to Milton Sapiro, 17 July 1924, MDSP; Milton Sapiro to Fenny, 19 July 1924, MDSP; R. H. McDrew to Milton Sapiro, 12 Aug. 1924; MDSP; Lawrence L. Levy to Aaron Sapiro, 19 Aug. 1924, MDSP; California Prune and Apricot Growers to Dearborn Publishing Company, 19 Aug. 1924, MDSP.

51. Harry E. Barnet to William J. Cameron, 19 Aug. 1924, Barnet File, box 10, acc. 48, BFRC; R. M. Barker to *DI*, 22 Aug. 1924, ibid. See also Barnet to Cameron, Wednesday noon [27 Aug. 1924], ibid.: "The only man in this region I can trust on this enclosed

stuff read it, and said I had the situation more thoroughly in mind than he had, and he's lived here more than 40 years. You can bank on stuff in this copy, except where I say 'it is reliably reported,' or something like that. I expect to confirm a lot of stuff in Louisville and Hopkinsville, and Mayfield. . . . It is my honest opinion that you may wish to have two Sapiro stories instead of one concerning tobacco." A grocer from Midway, Kentucky, in contrast, thought that Morgan "has not exaggerated his subject in the least and I want to congratulate you in having the courage to present the facts." B. R. Wallner to *DI*, 26 Aug. 1924, "DI Correspondence" file, box 5, acc. 273, BFRC.

52. Barnet to Cameron, 10 Sept. 1924, Barnet file, box 10, acc. 48, BFRC; Barnet to Cameron, Tuesday morning [Sept. 1924], ibid.; Barnet to Cameron, 23 Sept. 1924, ibid.; Barnet to Cameron, 10 Sept. 1924, ibid.; Barnet to Cameron, 18 Sept. 1924, ibid.; Black to Barnet, 29 Sept. 1924, ibid.

53. *Yakima Valley Farm News*, 24 [?] Aug. 1924, p. 1, file 4, box 42, acc. 48, BFRC.

54. A. C. Cherry to Ford, 21 Aug. 1924, file 7, box 122, acc. 1, BFRC; Cherry to *DI*, 21 Aug. 1924, ibid.; E. G. Liebold to A. C. Cherry, 27 Aug. 1924, ibid. Cherry noted that he subscribed to the newspaper. His anxiousness not to be identified with Jewish organizers and to disavow any connection with Jews could point to a degree of sympathy with Ford's goals and prejudices, or it might indicate a desire to put distance between himself and Jews such as Sapiro in order not to be perceived as a lackey.

55. Walton Peteet, "Memoranda for Mr. Henry Ford," 24 Sept. 1924, pp. 1, 2, 8–9, 19, file 4, box 29, acc. 48, BFRC.

56. Peteet, "Memoranda for Mr. Henry Ford," 24; Dunn to Black, 14 Oct. 1924, file 4, box 29, acc. 48, BFRC.

57. Black to Dunn, 30 Sept. 1924, file 4, box 29, acc. 48, BFRC; E. F. Murphy to William Cameron, 4 Aug. 1924, ibid. (emphasis in original); Black to E. F. Murphy, 10 Oct. 1924, ibid.; Smyter Atwell to Dearborn Publishing Company, 29 Dec. 1924, ibid. The letter did not elaborate on these unsuccessful "undertakings."

58. Peteet, "Memoranda for Mr. Henry Ford," 24 Sept. 1924, p. 21; Dunn to Black, 14 Oct. 1924, file 4, box 29, acc. 48, BFRC. Black again demanded documentation from Dunn in late 1924; Black to Dunn, 11 Nov. 1924, file 3, box 19, acc. 48, BFRC. Black wrote a memo for Dunn's signature responding to Peteet. "Report on Article Appearing in the August 30th Issue of the Dearborn Independent," n.d. [but 1925], file 4, box 29, acc. 48, BFRC. This memo shows how the *DI* staff refracted everything Sapiro and the AFBF did through the lens of bias; every organizational difficulty was attributed to the Jewish conspiracy and Gentiles' willingness to serve as its agents.

59. Harry H. Dunn to Fred L. Black, 22 Oct. 1924, Dunn and Dunn/Morgan file, box 19, acc. 48, BFRC; Black to Dunn, 11 Nov. 1924, ibid.

60. *WP*, 5 Dec. 1923, p. 1; Watts, *People's Tycoon*, 347.

61. Dunn to Black, 22 Oct. 1924, file 3, box 19, acc. 48, BFRC.

62. Black to Dunn, 11 Nov. 1924, file 3, box 19, acc. 48, BFRC. Black specifically requested that Dunn supply additional sources for the published assertion that cooperatives were paying bonuses to their agents.

63. S. G. Rubinow, "Commodity Potato Marketing on the California Plan and Sapiro Contract; The Plan; What It Will Do; What It Means to You" pamphlet (St. Paul, Minn.: State Organization Committee, n.d. [but 1924]), file 1, box 30, acc. 48, BFRC; Rubinow

to W. J. Cameron, 9 Sept. 1924, ibid.; Black to Rubinow, 7 Oct. 1924, ibid.; Rubinow, sworn statement, 19 Oct. 1924, ibid.; Rubinow to Black, 13 Nov. 1924, ibid. Rubinow was general manager of the Minnesota Potato Growers Exchange.

64. Aaron Sapiro to Milton Sapiro, 22 Dec. 1924, MDSP; Morgan, "Who Spilled the Beans at Lompoc? Where Heavy Loss and Even Bankruptcy for the Farmer Followed the Application of the Sapiro Plan of Co-operative Marketing," *DI*, 4 Oct. 1924, pp. 9, 11; Morgan, "When Co-operation Has No Strings to It: How Southern Rice-Growers Made a Big Success When Sapiro Was Left Out," *DI*, 13 Dec. 1924, pp. 4, 14; Morgan, "World Cotton Control by Sapiro Plan," *DI*, 11 Apr. 1925, pp. 4, 15; Morgan, "Sapiro's Peach and Fig Growers," 2 May 1925, pp. 18, 22–23, 31.

65. Aaron Sapiro, "Demand for Retraction," 6 Jan. 1925, file 6, box 122, acc. 1, BFRC (hereafter "Demand"), 3. The demand for retraction was required under Michigan law; Sapiro to Milton Sapiro, 25 Mar. 1925, MDSP. By this time, the Fords had transferred all of their DPC stock to the Ford Motor Company, but they and Liebold remained the DPC's only officers. Nevins and Hill, *Expansion and Challenge*, 125, 319. Press coverage of the retraction demand followed Sapiro's emphasis on individual libel and entirely avoided the issue of group libel. See, e.g., *Owensboro* (Ky.) *Messenger*, 8 Jan. 1925, clipping, file 2, box 32, acc. 48, BFRC.

66. Ibid.

67. Demand, 6–7.

68. Ibid. On the psychology of antisemitic conspiracy thinking, see Norman Cohn, *Warrant for Genocide: The Myth of the Jewish World-Conspiracy and the Protocols of the Elders of Zion* (New York: Harper and Row, 1969).

69. Demand, 6–7.

70. Ibid., 3, 8, 1–2.

71. Ibid., 5, 32.

72. Ibid., 8–28 (quote on 8).

73. Ibid., 14, 15, 24–25.

74. On the requirements for winning damages under libel law in the 1920s, see "Direct Proof of General Damage by Defamation," *New York Law Review* 2 (Aug. 1924): 305–16; and William G. Hale, *Law of the Press: Text, Statutes, and Cases* (St. Paul, Minn.: West Publishing, 1923).

75. Demand, 26.

76. Aaron Sapiro to Milton Sapiro, 25 Mar. 1925, MDSP.

77. Fred Black to J. H. Bishop, 16 Jan. 1925, file 1, box 32, acc. 48, BRFC; *DI*, 17 Jan. 1925, p. 8; ibid., 31 Jan. 1925, p. 8.

78. Cameron to Dunn, 3 Jan. 1925, file 3, box 19, acc. 48, BFRC.

79. Dunn to Cameron, 8 Jan. 1925, file 3, box 19, acc. 48, BFRC.

80. These included the hops growers, the Turlock Melon Growers, the California Alfalfa Growers Exchange, the California Honey Producers Cooperative Association, the California Rice Growers Association, the Texas cotton associations, and the Sonoma–Marin County Potato Growers Association, "which you referred to as the important beginning from which 'the exploiters of the farm conceived the idea of organizing all the potato growers of the United States'" (Demand, 25). Although he had nothing to do with raisins, the *Independent* played that one both ways—holding raisins up as an

example of Sapiro-less cooperation that worked and also blaming Sapiro for the California Associated Raisin Company's monopolistic contract, which he did not write but used as a model for other associations. Woeste, *Farmer's Benevolent Trust*, 196–202.

81. [Clifford B. Longley], "What We Can Prove," memo, n.d., file 2, box 1, acc. 48, BFRC; Demand, 15, 20, 22–28, 31–32; *Jewish Daily Bulletin*, 8 Feb. 1925, p. 2, ibid.

82. Harry H. Bennett, *We Never Called Him Henry* (New York: Gold Medal Books, 1951), 49; Marshall to Bernstein, 8 July 1923, file 332, box 11, HBP; Milton Sapiro to Aaron Sapiro, 31 Mar. 1925, MDSP; Aaron Sapiro to Milton Sapiro, 25 Mar. 1925, ibid. (noting that he paid Gallagher a retainer of $2,500 and a per diem); *DN*, 23 Feb. 1964, p. 4B; "William Henry Gallagher," *Detroit Legal News*, Oct. 1995, p. 53; Declaration, *Sapiro v. Ford and the Dearborn Publishing Company* (U.S.D.C. E.D. Mich.), 22 Apr. 1925, Case No. 7522, RG 21, NARA-GL.

83. Sapiro, "Experience with American Justice," 11–12; Michael Nelson, ed., *Congressional Quarterly's Guide to the Presidency* (Washington, D.C.: Congressional Quarterly, 1989), 830. Sapiro was able to sue in federal court because the Constitution granted that right to a citizen of one state who sued a citizen of another. U.S. Const. art. 3, sec. 2.

84. Lee, *Ford and the Jews*, 71 (quoting Marshall to G. Lowenstein, 29 Mar. 1927, in Charles Reznikoff, ed., *Louis Marshall, Champion of Liberty: Selected Papers and Addresses* [Philadelphia: Jewish Publication Society of America, 1957], 1:372).

CHAPTER 6

1. Fred Black to C. E. Dempster, 14 Dec. 1925, file 5, box 29, acc. 48, BFRC.

2. Declaration, *Sapiro v. Ford and the Dearborn Publishing Company* (U.S.D.C. E.D. Mich.), 22 Apr. 1925, Case No. 7522, RG 21, NARA-GL, 9–11, 14, 91–92 (hereafter "declaration"); Norman L. Rosenberg, *Protecting the Best Men: An Interpretive History of the Law of Libel* (Chapel Hill: University of North Carolina Press, 1986), 224.

3. *Park v. Free Press*, 72 Mich. 560 (1888); *McGee v. Baumgartner*, 121 Mich. 287 (1899); *Eikhoff v. Gilbert*, 124 Mich. 353 (1900); William G. Hale, *Law of the Press: Text, Statutes, and Cases* (St. Paul, Minn.: West Publishing, 1923), 135, 137–39, 212–13, 216–17.

4. Declaration, 12, 20–21; *DI*, 26 Apr. 1924, p. 4. Sapiro denied forcing the potato growers to use the San Francisco–based marketing firm of Weyl and Zuckerman (allegedly a party to the conspiracy) and ignoring telegrams seeking legal advice. Declaration, 28–33.

5. B. E. Larson to Harry Dunn, 14 Jan. 1925, file 1, box 19, acc. 48, BFRC; Dunn to Larson, 21 Jan. 1925, ibid.; Sen. Res. 329, 68th Cong., 2d sess. (9 Feb. 1925); Fred Black to Dunn, 10 Mar. 1925, file 1, box 19, acc. 48, BFRC; Dunn to Black, 21 Mar. 1925, ibid.; Black to Dunn, 30 Mar. 1925, ibid.

6. Fred Black, report on Northwest travels, n.d. [but 1925], file 3, box 10, acc. 48, BFRC. Both assertions were wrong. The raisin growers' contract was written in 1913, before Sapiro entered state government in 1915, and he was professionally well regarded in San Francisco. The *Independent* knew by this point that Sapiro was not connected with the raisin growers' organization, but Black embraced the possibility that this witness could verify such a link. Victoria Saker Woeste, *The Farmer's Benevolent Trust: Law and Agricultural Cooperation in Industrial America, 1865–1945* (Chapel Hill: University of North Carolina Press, 1998), 117–18.

7. Black travel memos, 13–14 Aug., 15 Aug., 19 Aug., 22 Aug., and 24–27 Aug. [1925], file 3, box 10, acc. 48, BFRC; Black [memo], 19 Aug. 1925, file 3, box 10, acc. 48, BFRC; Collman to Black, 3 Aug. 1925, file 3, box 12, acc. 48, BFRC. A 1923 article in *The Outlook* linking Sapiro, Meyer, and Baruch presaged the *Independent*'s conspiracy charges. Silas Bent, "Three City-Bred Jews That the Farmer Trusts," *Outlook* 134 (8 Aug. 1923), 553–56.

8. Ford R. Bryan, *Henry's Lieutenants* (Detroit: Wayne State University Press, 1993), 178; Greg Grandin, *Fordlandia: The Rise and Fall of Henry Ford's Forgotten Jungle City* (New York: Henry Holt, 2009), 55–119.

9. [Clifford B. Longley,] "The Scheme," n.d. [but 1925], file 1, box 33, acc. 48, BFRC; "First Count," n.d. [but 1925], file 1, box 33, acc. 48, BFRC; "Legal Memoranda-Sapiro Case," n.d. [but 1925], file 1, box 33, acc. 48, BFRC; "IV," n.d. [but 1925], file 1, box 33, acc. 48, BFRC; Longley to Wilfrid E. Rumble, 5 Jan. 1925, file 1, box 76, acc. 48, BFRC.

10. "Memorandum of Work to be Done in the Ford case," n.d., file 4, box 76, acc. 48, BFRC; accessed 5 Jan. 2010, http://legal-dictionary.thefreedictionary.com/Per+quod: "Words that are actionable per quod do not furnish a basis for a lawsuit upon their face but are only litigable because of extrinsic facts showing the circumstances under which they were uttered or the damages ensuing to the defamed party therefrom."

11. "Legal Points," undated memo, file 4, box 76, acc. 48, BFRC; untitled memo, n.d., ibid.; see also "Memorandum of Work to be Done in the Ford case," n.d., ibid. Simonds was the only nonlawyer included in these assignments; he was Seattle branch advertising manager, where he came to Fred Black's attention. Bryan, *Henry's Lieutenants*, 245–46.

12. Collman to Black, 29 Aug. 1925, file 3, box 12, acc. 48, BFRC; E. L. McColgin to F. L. Black, 19 Sept. 1925; Black to Longley, 21 Sept. 21 1925, both in file 1, box 76, acc. 48, BFRC.

13. C. E. Dempster, report, Pacific Cooperative Wool Growers, n.d. [but 1925], file 5, box 29, acc. 48, BFRC; R. A. Ward, General Manager, Pacific Cooperative Wool Growers, Portland, Ore., to *DI*, 30 Oct. 1924, file 6, box 122, acc. 1, BFRC; declaration, 40–43; Dempster, report, Oregon Dairymen's Co-operative League, n.d. [but 1925], file 5, box 29, acc. 48, BFRC; Black to Sherman, 30 Oct. 1925, ibid.; Dempster, report on hop industry, 19 Nov. 1925, file 5, box 29, acc. 48, BFRC; Dempster to Black, 5 Dec. 1925, ibid. E. Clemens Horst, one of Dunn's major sources, was denying that he had provided information. McCall to Horst, 7 Nov. 1925, ibid.; W. T. McCall to Black, 7 Nov. 1925, ibid. C. E. Dempster reported that Dunn had concealed the subject of his article (the hop growers' association) and his true identity from one of his interviewees. Dempster to Black, n.d. [but Nov. 1925], ibid.; E. Clemens Horst to McCall, 9 Nov. 1925, ibid.

14. F. W. Donoghue to C. B. Longley, 28 Oct. 1925, file 2, box 57, acc. 48, BFRC; McCall to Donoghue, 23 Nov. 1925, ibid.; McCall to C. E. Dempster, 23 Nov. 1925, ibid.; Ford Motor Company assistant manager to McCall, 24 Nov. 1925, ibid.

15. Donoghue to C. B. Longley, 16 Sept. 1925, file 2, box 33, acc. 48, BFRC; Donoghue to DPC, 8 Oct. 1925, ibid.

16. Report of Investigations made by W. T. McCall and W. H. Meyerett on California Avocado Producers' Exchange, Poultry Producers of Southern California, Southern California Milk Producers' Association, Poultry Producers of San Diego, Milk Producers of Central California, Mr. H. H. Warner, American Fruit Growers, Los Angeles, n.d. [but Sept. 1925], file 2, box 57, acc. 48, BFRC. The contract's features included "the principles of pooling, of assessing liquidated damages against members who fail to deliver

to the association in accordance with the terms of the contract, and the provision[s] for requiring specific performance of the contract, and providing for an injunction to prevent further breach of contract." McCall-Meyerett Report, ibid.

17. Report No. 2, n.d. [but late Sept. 1925], interview with Alec Johnston, former secretary of California State Farm Bureau (disassociating Sapiro from Northern California cooperatives), file 2, box 25, acc. 48, BFRC; Report No. 3, 30 Sept. 1925, ibid.; "Another Falsehood Nailed," NuLaid News, September [1925], p. 4 (note stapled to article: "This will probably be used as evidence by Sapiro"), ibid.; Report No. 33, 24 Oct. 1925, interview with M. Ljongeneel, Crop Production Dept., California Packing Corp., ibid; Report No. 28, 22 Oct. 1925, interview with Frank Swett, ibid.; Report No. 29, 16 Oct. 1925, interview with Mr. Shaw, California Prune and Apricot Growers Association, ibid.

18. Collman to Fred L. Black, 21 Nov. 1925, file 3, box 12, acc. 48, BFRC; Collman, report attached to 21 Nov. 1925 letter, ibid. "'The Jewish financial organization, working with and through an association organized, dominated and controlled by another Jew, is exploiting the American farmer.' This statement is quite true; the farmer is being exploited in the manner stated, as shown in the cotton, onion and tomato growers organizations and others." Ibid.

19. Dempster to Black, 7 Dec. 1925, report on "Radicalism in Oregon," file 5, box 29, acc. 48, BFRC; Black to Dempster, 14 Dec. 1925, ibid. (emphasis added).

20. Gray Silver, statement to congressional committee, n.d. [but Oct. 1925], file 7, box 23, acc. 48, BFRC; Black, travel report, Aug. 1927, file 3, box 10, acc. 48, BFRC; William T. McCall to Fred Black, 11 Dec. 1925, file 8, box 23, acc. 48, BFRC. For the Ford team's perspective on Passonneau's likely testimony, see Passonneau file, box 29, acc. 48, BFRC, and text below at n. 54ff.

21. F. H. Sherman to Black, 16 Jan. 1926, file 1, box 57, acc. 48, BFRC; C. J. Hurd to McCall, 30 Nov. 1925, Oregon file, box 78, acc. 48, BFRC; McCall to Hurd, 22 Dec. 1925, ibid.; McCall report on Idaho Potato Growers' Exchange and Idaho Wheat Growers' Exchange, 23 Nov. 1925, ibid.; McCall to Hurd, 22 Dec. 1925, ibid. Founded in Los Angeles in 1905, Weyl and Zuckerman conducted wholesale trade and shipping in potatoes and onions. Most of the firm's employees were Jewish "and have from $5,000 to $10,000 invested in stock in the corporation." The firm also owned 2,700 acres near Stockton, where it grew potatoes, corn, and wheat. F. H. Sherman to Black, 16 Jan. 1926, file 1, box 57, acc. 48, BFRC.

22. Separate Plea of the Dearborn Independent Publishing Co., 21 July 1925, Case No. 7522, RG 21, NARA-GL; Separate Plea of Henry Ford, 21 July 1925, ibid.; Docket Entries, Case No. 7522, General Dockets, 1846–1943, vol. U, p. 33, RG 21, NARA-GL; E. L. McColgin to W. R. Middleton, 18 Nov. 1925, file 1, box 76, acc. 48, BFRC (pointing out that the plea also misidentified an AFBF official); Bryan, *Henry's Lieutenants*, 177–78; *NYT*, 24 Nov. 1939, p. 23. Choate was a former county prosecutor. Like Gallagher, Hanley was Catholic; he was also a Democratic assistant prosecuting attorney and Wayne County probate court judge. Albert Nelson Marquis, ed., *The Book of Detroiters*, 2d ed. (Chicago: A. N. Marquis, 1914), 220.

23. Separate Plea of Dearborn Independent Publishing Company, 6, 11.

24. Watson to Clifford B. Longley, 16 Dec. 1925, file 1, box 76, acc. 48, BFRC; Longley to Raymond Watson, 9 Dec. 1925, ibid. Potato exchange officials would not permit

Watson to examine records without a subpoena, either; however, another exchange attorney provided Watson with copies of "hot telegrams and letters" documenting Sapiro's work for the organization. Watson to Longley, 16 Dec. 1925, ibid. Dossiers of witnesses and lists of evidence that the DPC was prepared to produce as of December 1925 may be found in Watson to Black, 11 Dec. 1925, ibid.

25. Creech to Longley, 16 Dec. 1925, file 1, box 76, acc. 48, BFRC; Lawrence H. Larsen, "Reed, James Alexander," *American National Biography Online*, Feb. 2000, accessed 15 Dec. 2010, http://www.anb.org/articles/06/06-00549.html; James A. Reed, memorandum, "Shapiro [*sic*] v. Henry Ford and Dearborn Independent," 22 Dec. 1925, file 1, box 34, JARP; Reed, memorandum, "In re Shapiro [*sic*] v. Ford, et al.," 28 Dec. 1925, ibid.; Longley to Reed, 22 Dec. 1925, file 1, box 76, acc. 48, BFRC. Longley apparently misunderstood about the $200-per-day charge; he thought it only covered Reed's appearance in court, but Reed intended to receive $200 per day apart from the retainer and initiated an exchange of letters to clarify. See Reed to Longley, 2 Jan. 1926, file 2, box 76, acc. 48; Longley to Reed, 11 Jan. 1926, file 1, box 122, acc. 1, BFRC; Reed to Liebold, 16 Jan. 1926, ibid.: "I acknowledge receipt of your check for $100,000.00 on account of retainer in the Sapiro case. I beg to assure you that the case will receive very careful attention." See also Longley to Reed, 6 Jan. 1926, file 1, box 34, JARP (making Reed's hire official).

26. H. L. Mencken, "James A. Reed of Missouri," *American Mercury*, April 1929, accessed 23 Jan. 2010, http://pages.prodigy.net/krtq73aa/ownman.htm; "James Alexander Reed," *Dictionary of American Biography, Supplement 3: 1941–1945* (New York: Charles Scribner's Sons, 1973), 621–23; Reed, "The Jew," speech delivered 27 Feb. 1916, typescript (ms.), file 8, box 122, acc. 1, BFRC; Lee Meriwether, *Jim Reed, "Senatorial Immortal": A Biography* (Webster Groves, Mo.: International Mark Twain Society, 1948), 242, 264.

27. Rosenberg, *Protecting the Best Men*, 224; docket entry, 28 Dec. 1925, Case No. 7522, RG 21, NARA-GL.

28. Reed to Longley, 3 Jan. 1926, file 1, box 34, JARP; "Memorandum of Facts Proven and to be Proved," n.d. [but early 1926], file 1, box 34, JARP; handwritten notes, n.d. [document 105], ibid. (emphasis in original).

29. Dunn to Longley, 6 Jan. 1926, file 2, box 76, acc. 48, BFRC; Longley to Dunn, 18 Jan. 1926, ibid.

30. Dunn to Longley, 25 Jan. 1926, file 2, box 76, acc. 48, BFRC.

31. Longley to Reed, 15 Jan. 1926, file 1, box 34, JARP; Choate to Longley, 16 Apr. 1926, file 2, box 76, acc. 48, BFRC; docket entries, 27 Feb. 1926 (motion for continuance to Nov. 1926); 23 Mar. 1926 (order allowing amendment of declaration), General Dockets, Case No. 7522, RG 21, NARA-GL.

32. B. E. Larson to Longley, 9 Feb. 1926, file 4, box 23, acc. 48, BFRC; Larson to Longley, 17 Mar. 1926, ibid.; Black to Longley, 4 Feb. 1926, file 7, box 23, acc. 48, BFRC; Longley to Reed, 9 Jan. 1926, file 1, box 76, BFRC; Choate to Higgins, 19 May 1926, file 1, box 34, JARP.

33. Longley to Middleton, 1 Jan. 1926, file 1, box 34, JARP; Longley to Choate 27 Feb. 1926, file 2, box 76, BFRC; Choate to Richard J. Higgins, 21 May 1926, ibid.

34. *Charlotte Observer*, 7 Feb. 1926, file 6, box 122, acc. 1, BFRC; Liebold to Longley, 16 Feb. 1926, ibid.

35. *Seattle Post-Intelligencer*, 19 Feb. 1926, file 2, box 32, acc. 48, BFRC; *Spokane Daily Chronicle*, 9 Feb. 1926, ibid.

36. *Portland Morning Oregonian*, 22 Apr. 1926, file 2, box 32, acc. 48, BFRC. The *Oregonian* mentioned that depositions had been taken in Kentucky, Colorado, Idaho, and Minnesota; after Oregon, the Ford attorneys went to California, Maine, Virginia, North Carolina, Texas, and Mississippi.

37. Black to Longley, 4 Feb. 1926, file 7, box 23, acc. 48, BFRC; McCall to Black, 11 Feb. 1926, ibid.; McCall to Black, 29 Mar. 1926, file 1, box 24, acc. 48, BFRC; McCall to Black, 23 Mar. 1926, file 7, box 23, acc. 48, BFRC.

38. McCall to Black, 29 Mar. 1926, file 1, box 24, acc. 48, BFRC.

39. Clifford B. Longley to Middleton, 24 May 1926, file 2, box 76, BFRC; W.A. Simonds to DPC, attn. F. L. Black, 3 Nov. 1925, file 2, box 33, acc. 48, BFRC.

40. Clifford B. Longley to Choate, 27 Feb. 1926, file 2, box 76, acc. 48, BFRC; Choate to Longley, 16 Apr. 1926, ibid. J. G. Bruce was another Ford investigator collecting evidence on the West Coast.

41. Longley to W. F. Williamson, 28 June 1926, file 2, box 76, acc. 48, BFRC. Williamson immediately replied that he never suggested settling the case. Longley was relieved to hear it: "I am glad you feel as you do. This case is going to necessitate a vigorous and forceable action on our part in dealing with Sapiro's counsel." Williamson to Longley, 3 July 1926, file 3, box 76, acc. 48, BFRC; Longley to Williamson, 12 July 1926, ibid.

42. Docket book entries for 2 June, 22 June, 2 July, 10 July, 14 July, 20 July, and 21 July 1926, Case No. 7522, RG 21, NARA-GL; Reed to Longley, 18 June 1926, file 1, box 34, JARP; Reed to Longley, 18 June 1926, ibid; Choate to Higgins, 19 May 1926, ibid. Gallagher denied ever agreeing to such an arrangement but, in the spirit of collegiality, offered to consult his client and attempt to be present at the Kansas depositions set for June. Gallagher to Choate, 21 May 1926, file 4, box 76, acc. 48, BFRC.

43. Hanley to Reed, 2 Mar. 1926, file 1, box 34, JARP; Longley to Reed, 18 June 1926, ibid.; Choate to Higgins, 7 June 1926, ibid.; Choate to Higgins, 2 June 1926, ibid.; Reed to Longley, 18 June 1926, ibid.; Choate to Higgins, 19 May 1926, ibid.; Higgins to Choate, 21 May 1926, ibid.; "Notes on Cross Examination of Sapiro," n.d., file 2, box 76, acc. 48, BFRC; Reed to Longley, 18 June 1926, file 1, box 34, JARP; Reed to Longley, 2 July 1926, ibid.; Higgins to Hanley, 3 July 1926, ibid.; Hanley to Higgins, 3 July 1926, ibid.; Higgins to Longley, 10 July 1926, ibid.; Reed to Yates, 14 July 1926, ibid.; Longley to Wallace R. Middleton, 15 July 1926, ibid.

44. Longley to Middleton, 15 July 1926, file 1, box 34, JARP; Reed to Longley, 25 July 1926, file 1, box 34, JARP; James A. Reed, Affidavit, 22 July 1926, *Sapiro v. Ford*, Case No. 7522, box 28, ATP; also in Case No. 7522, RG 21, NARA-GL. "Set out in detail contempt proceedings and misconduct of witness and connection of attorneys for plaintiff therewith, including presence and conduct of Milton Sapiro." Middleton to Longley, 15 July 1926, file 3, box 76, acc. 48, BFRC.

45. Docket entries, 22 July 1926, RG 21, NARA-GL; Reed, Affidavit, "Petition Alleging the Disqualification of Honorable Arthur J. Tuttle," 28 July 1926, *Sapiro v. Ford*, file 7522, box 28, ATP; "Exhibit A," attached to ibid.; Longley to Reed, 29 July 1926, file 1, box 34, JARP.

46. Reed to Longley, 25 July 1926, file 1, box 34, JARP; Longley to Reed, 26 July 1926, ibid.

47. Longley to Reed, 26 July 1926, file 1, box 34, JARP.

48. Longley to Watson, 26 July 1926, file 3, box 76, acc. 48, BFRC; "Petition Alleging the Disqualification of Honorable Arthur J. Tuttle," 2–3, file 7522, box 28, ATP; Longley to Reed, 29 July 1926, file 1, box 34, JARP; Higgins to Longley, 30 July 1926, ibid.; Longley to Reed, 30 July 1926, ibid.; Order, 30 July 1926, *Sapiro v. Ford*, file 7522, box 28, ATP.

49. Defendant's Motion for Continuance, 3 Aug. 1926, Case No. 7522, RG 21, NARA-GL; Longley to Reed, 30 July 1926, file 1, box 34, JARP; Reed to Longley, 30 July 1926, ibid. Tuttle filed the Gallagher-drafted motion setting trial for September 14 on July 31—the day after he agreed to step aside as presiding judge. Docket book, 31 July 1926, Case No. 7522, RG 21, NARA-GL.

50. D[avid] C. Westenhaver to Arthur Tuttle, 5 Aug. 1926, file 7522, box 28, ATP; Tuttle to Maurice Donahue, n.d., ibid.; Donahue to Tuttle, 6 Aug. 1926, ibid.; [Benson W. Hough] to Tuttle, 6 Aug. 1926, ibid.; Western Union to Tuttle, n.d., ibid.; Benjamin F. Osborne, court librarian, to Tuttle, 5. Aug. 1926, ibid.; B. C. Miller, Clerk, to Tuttle, 5 Aug. 1926, ibid.; Mrs. Smith Hickenlooper to Tuttle, 9 Aug. 1926, ibid.; City Editor, Detroit Free Press, to Reed, 30 July 1926, file 1, box 34, JARP; Hough to Arthur Tuttle, 17 Aug. 1926, file 7522, box 28, ATP; "Entry," 9 Aug. 1922, ibid.

51. *DFP*, 10 Aug. 1926, in file 2, box 32, acc. 48, BFRC.

52. Order, U.S. District Court, Case No. 7522, *Sapiro v. Ford*, 9 Aug. 1926, file 3, box 76, acc. 48, BFRC; also in file 7522, box 28, ATP; Hanley to Watson, 27 Aug. 1926, file 3, box 76, acc. 48, BFRC; William Henry Gallagher, affidavit, n.d. [but Mar. 1927], file 1, box 1, acc. 48, BFRC; Hough to Tuttle, 17 Aug. 1926, file 7522, box 28, ATP.

53. Elmer W. Voorheis, clerk of courts, USDC, E.D. Mich., to Henry Ford, 9 Sept. 1926, file 6, box 122, acc. 1, BFRC; Liebold to USDC, 11 Sept. 1926, ibid.; Longley to Liebold, 22 Sept. 1926, ibid.: "We quote below a copy of clipping sent to us from our San Francisco Branch: 'Henry Ford is served subpoena in Sapiro case.'" The newspaper was not named. The court's docket book contradicts this account: "Subpoena issued April 27, 1926, returned not served on Henry Ford, filed" (docket book entry, 15 Sept. 1926, Case 7522, RG 21, NARA-GL). The docket was far from accurate; the case file contains several motions and affidavits not recorded on the docket. Ford's separate pleas, filed on July 21, 1925, for example, were omitted from the docket, as was plaintiff's notice of issue, dated August 5, 1925. Ibid.

54. DeLancey Nicoll Jr. to Clifford Longley, 8 Nov. 1926, file 5, box 56, acc. 48, BFRC; Passonneau to Black, 27 Dec. 1924, file 2, box 29, acc. 48, BFRC; F. L. Black to C. B. Longley, 4 Nov. 1925, file 4, box 23, acc. 48, BFRC.

55. Fred L. Black to Clifford B. Longley, 4 Nov. 1925, file 4, box 23, acc. 48, BFRC; Passonneau to Lowden, 28 Nov. 1923, file 2, box 29, acc. 48, BFRC; Passonneau, undated memorandum, ibid.; Robert Bingham to Passonneau, 12 Feb. 1923, ibid.; Executive Order, Governor of Colorado, 23 July 1923, ibid.; see also Passonneau to Shay, 23 Oct. 1923, file 2, box 57, acc. 48, BFRC. Charles Bassett, hardly an unbiased source, repeated the story of the altercation to William Cameron (8 Jan. 1925, file 1, box 32, acc. 48, BFRC).

56. *NYT*, 9 Oct. 1923, p. 39; see also Bassett to Cameron, 8 Jan. 1925, file 1, box 32, acc. 48, BFRC; Passonneau to Thomas C. Jones, 5 Mar. 1924, file 2, box 29, acc. 48, BFRC.

In 1924 or 1925, Sapiro filed a lawsuit against two Canadian newspapers for publishing Passonneau's letters to Governor Lowden. Ford's lawyers obtained a copy of Sapiro's deposition in this case from Chicago-based lawyers who were assisting the defense. In his deposition, Sapiro apparently made admissions that Reed found useful, specifically that Sapiro had sold tobacco warehouses to cooperatives for more than they were worth and forced cooperatives to sell them at a loss. Still, the deposition hardly substantiated everything the *Independent* had published. After losing at trial in the Canadian suit, Sapiro prevailed on appeal, much to Longley's consternation. Judgment, *Sapiro v. Leader Publishing Co. Ltd.* and *Sapiro v. Star Publishing Co. Ltd.*, Court of Appeal, 3 May 1926, file 6, box 122, acc. 1, BFRC; Raymond E. Watson to Clifford Longley, 7 May 1926, ibid.; Longley to Watson, 10 July 1926, file 3, box 76, acc. 48, BFRC. For his victory in the Canadian case, Sapiro accepted a simple apology from the offending newspapers and payment only for his expenses (Aaron Sapiro to Milton Sapiro, 28 Jul. 1926, MDSP).

57. Passonneau to Thomas C. Jones, 5 Mar. 1924, file 2, box 29, acc. 48, BFRC; Passonneau to Black, 27 Dec. 1924, ibid.; Watson to Longley, 4 Sept. 1926, file 6, box 56, acc. 48, BFRC; Longley to Raymond Watson, 7 Sept. 1926, file 2A, box 76, acc. 48, BFRC.

58. Bassett to Cameron, 8 Jan. 1925, file 1, box 32, acc. 48, BFRC (emphasis in original); Bassett to Passonneau, 19 Nov. 1923, file 4, box 42, acc. 48, BFRC.

59. Longley to Reed, 15 Jan. 1926, file 1, box 34, JARP; Sidney Rubinow to Cameron, 9 Sept. 1924, file 1, box 30, acc. 48; see also Rubinow to Editor, *Great Divide*, 8 Dec. 1923, ibid.; Choate to Longley, 3 Feb. 1926, telegram file, box 77, acc. 48, BFRC; Longley to Choate, 25 Aug. 1925, file 6, box 56, acc. 48, BFRC; Longley to Watson, 27 Aug. 1926, ibid.

60. Watson to Longley, 4 Sept. 1926, file 6, box 56, acc. 48, BFRC; Longley to Raymond Watson, 7 Sept. 1926, file 2A, box 76, acc. 48, BFRC; Watson to Longley, 20 Sept. 1926, ibid.; Longley to Watson, 7 Dec. 1926, file 6, box 56, acc. 48, BFRC; S. G. Rubinow, "'Burned Spuds'—How It Happened," *DI*, 6 Feb. 1926, p. 14.

61. A. H. Ashley, Report #14, 6 Oct. 1925, file 2, box 25, acc. 48, BFRC.

62. Thomas C. Jones to Passonneau, 8 Dec. 1923, file 2, box 29, acc. 48, BFRC; McCall, report on Idaho Potato Growers' Exchange and Idaho Wheat Growers' Exchange, 23 Nov. 1925, Oregon file, box 78, acc. 48, BFRC.

63. Sapiro to James Pendlebury, 10 May 1923, file 7, box 23, acc. 48, BFRC; Watson to Longley, 16 Dec. 1925, file 1, box 76, BFRC: "At the December [1923] meeting, when a member of the Executive Committee questioned Sapiro's position on a certain point, Sapiro said: 'Don't you farmers contradict me.'" Watson also annotated testimony covering the Colorado potato industry and the Sapiro-Meyer-Baruch connection. See also G. W. Hamilton to *DI*, 16 Jan. 1926, file 7, box 23, acc. 48, BFRC (same arrangement for inland Washington state hay association); Passonneau to Cameron, 25 Apr. 1924, file 1, box 57, acc. 48, BFRC.

64. Watson to Longley, 16 Dec. 1925, file 1, box 76, acc. 48, BFRC.

65. McCall to Donoghue, 30 Nov. 1925, file 2, box 57, acc. 48, BFRC; Reed to Longley, 10 Feb. 1927, file 1, box 34, JARP. Sapiro's clients and the fees he was paid included the Wenatchee District Cooperative Association, $2,000 for two weeks; California Pear Growers Association, $5850 for eighty-two months; Colorado Potato Growers' Exchange, $5,000 for seven months; and the Northwest Hay Association, $2,000 for two months. McCall to Donoghue, 30 Nov. 1925.

66. DeLancey Nicoll Jr. to Longley, 8 Nov. 1926, file 5, box 56, acc. 48, BFRC; Black to Sherman, 16 Sept. 1925, file 1, box 24, acc. 48, BFRC.

67. Sherman to Black, 16 Feb. 1926, file 7, box 23, acc. 48, BFRC; Gail Nebanzahl, Sapiro family tree, n.d. [but ca. 2001] (on file with author).

68. Fred L. Black, "Report on Article Appearing in the August 30th Issue of the Dearborn Independent," n.d. [but 1925], file 4, box 29, acc. 48, BFRC.

69. Amended Separate and Substituted Plea of the Dearborn Publishing Co. and Amended Substituted Notice, 31 Jan. 1927, RG 21, NARA-GL; Longley to Higgins, 19 Feb. 1927, file 4, box 76, acc. 48, BFRC; William Henry Gallagher, *Family Memoir*, tms. (typescript, 1974–1979; furnished to author by Connie Bookmyer; copy on file).

70. Preliminary Motions on Pleadings, Transcript of Proceedings, 28 Feb. 1927, p. 45, file 3, box 43, acc. 48, BFRC.

71. Preliminary Motions, 114–15.

72. Preliminary Motions, 128, 129.

73. Preliminary Motions, 167, 168; Watson to Passonneau, 21 Jan. 1927, file 4, box 76, acc. 48, BFRC; Watson to Joe Bellamy, 2 Feb. 1927, ibid.; Watson to Longley, 23 Feb. 1927, ibid.

74. *DJC*, 11 Mar. 1927, p. 6; *AC*, 14 Mar. 1927, p. 1; *New York Evening Graphic*, [March 1927], clippings file, Gallagher Papers.

CHAPTER 7

1. *DJC*, 18 Mar. 1927, last p.

2. *WP*, 20 Mar. 1927, p. M3; *CDT*, 15 Mar. 1927, p. 7.

3. "Federal Building," accessed 23 Feb. 2010, http://buildingsofdetroit.com/places/post.

4. *CDT*, 15 Mar. 1927, p. 7; *LAT*, 15 Mar. 1927, p. 1.

5. *NYT*, 15 Mar. 1927, pp. 1, 2; *LAT*, 15 Mar. 1927; *CDT*, 15 Mar. 1927.

6. *NYT*, 15 Mar. 1927, p. 1; *WP*, 15 Mar. 1927, p. 1; *NYT*, 16 Mar. 1927, p. 3.

7. *Daily Ypsilantian-Press*, 15 Feb. 1927, file 1, box 39, acc. 48, BFRC; Term calendar, U.S. District Court, Eastern District of Michigan, Southern Division, June term 1927 (juror list stapled to inside front cover), ibid.; memo, "Traverse Jurors," n.d. [but Feb. 1927], ibid.; Juror surveys, Amor Durat; Earnest Schwain, Charles Daly, Cora Hoffman, Grace Stiles, Emma Clarkson, Charles Parkhurst, Grace Jewel, Anna Konen, Herbert Schornhals, Carl Haag, Ann Brown, Juror file, ibid.

8. Juror surveys: Patrick Sloan; J. B. Van Riper; Ann L. Taylor; Chester Westerman; William J. Stewart, Kranich, all in juror file, box 39, acc. 48, BFRC.

9. *NYT*, 20 Mar. 1927, p. 3; *DJC*, 18 Mar. 1927, last p.

10. *DJC*, 18 Mar. 1927; *NYT*, 16 Mar. 1927, p. 1; *LAT*, 16 Mar. 1927, p. 2; *NYT*, 20 Mar. 1927, p. 3; *WP*, 18 Mar. 1927, p. 5. The jury's photo can be seen in *DT*, 19 Mar. 1927, p. 1; *WP*, 19 Mar. 1927, p. 3; *NYT*, 20 Mar. 1927, p. 3. The Mason-affiliated jurors were Herbert Schoenhals ("radically against" Jews), Charles Parkhurst, and Grace Jewell's husband. Juror file, box 39, acc. 48, BFRC.

11. Transcript of Proceedings, *Sapiro v. Ford*, 28 Mar. 1927, file 2, box 44, acc. 48, BFRC (hereafter "trial transcript"), 3, 6, 12–13, 15; *DT*, 17 Mar. 1927, p. 2; *NYT*, 16 Mar. 1927, p. 3.

12. *LAT*, 16 Mar. 1927, p. 1; trial transcript, 13–15.

13. *NYT*, 17 Mar. 1927, p. 1; trial transcript, 28.

14. *CDT*, 17 Mar. 1927, p. 1; trial transcript, 29; *NYT*, 17 Mar. 1927, pp. 1, 14; *AC*, 17 Mar. 1927, pp. 1, 3; see also *LAT*, 17 Mar. 1927, p. 1.

15. Trial transcript, 152, 153.

16. Trial transcript, 155, 332; *AC*, 18 Mar. 1927, p. 7; *NYT*, 18 Mar. 1927, p. 1; *WP*, 20 Mar. 1927, p. M3.

17. Trial transcript, 197, 305–7, 326–27, 334; *NYT*, 18 Mar. 1927, p. 1.

18. Leo P. Ribuffo, "Henry Ford and *The International Jew*," *American Jewish History* 69, no. 4 (1980): 437–77, 466; trial transcript, 338, 343, 350; *NYT*, 19 Mar. 1927, pp. 1, 2; *WP*, 19 Mar. 1927, p. 1. By federal civil trial rules, attorneys could not cross-examine their own witnesses in order to impeach their testimony. That was the plaintiff's goal here, however, and to accomplish it, he needed the defense's cooperation. Only if defense counsel agreed to cross-examine Cameron could Gallagher re-cross-examine; Reed and Longley would not. Reporters quickly deduced that Gallagher would be unable to use this strategy to treat Ford as a hostile witness. John Henry Wigmore, *A Treatise on the System of Evidence in Trials at Common Law* (Boston: Little, Brown, 1904), 774.

19. *NYT*, 19 Mar. 1927, p. 1; *WP*, 19 Mar. 1927, p. 3.

20. *NYT*, 20 Mar. 1927, p. 3.

21. *NYT*, 20 Mar. 1927, p. 1.

22. Ibid., p. 3; Aaron Sapiro to Lewis Strauss, 22 Mar. 1927, file 5, box 70, LLSP (emphasis in original).

23. *NYT*, 21 Mar. 1927, p. 2; ibid., 14 Mar. 1927, p. 8 (emphasis added). The qualifying phrase has been omitted by historians writing about the case. See, e.g., Ribuffo, "Ford and *The International Jew*," 437. Read in context, however, Sapiro's intent is clear: he meant to come to the defense of those Jews who, like him, had been named in the newspaper. Sapiro was not yet making the group-libel claim that the press was making for him.

24. *NYT*, 14 Mar. 1927, p. 8.

25. *NYT*, 21 Mar. 1927, p. 1.

26. *WP*, 20 Mar. 1927, p. M3; trial transcript, 381, 387, 390–92.

27. Trial transcript, 401–3, 404–13, 415–16.

28. Trial transcript, 426, 435–52 (Gallagher); 452–63 (Hanley); 463–71 (Gallagher rebuttal) (quote on 468); H. W. Roland to Harry H. Dunn, 6 Aug. 1923, Dunn and Dunn/Morgan file, box 19, acc. 48, BFRC; *CDT*, 22 Mar. 1927, p. 8. The major precedent on which Gallagher relied, *Watson v. Detroit Journal*, 143 Mich. 430 (1906), held that, by saying derogatory things about trading stamp companies without mentioning plaintiff by name, the defendant publication did not cause harm. The defense thought the case helped its side because the Michigan Supreme Court held that no libel could be upheld against a class of persons, only against individuals. The case also supported Sapiro's libel suit, as the *Independent* specifically mentioned Sapiro in each article and the *Watson* court held that libel judgments should issue for plaintiffs who were mentioned by name as belonging to the defamed class. *Watson*, 435.

29. *NYT*, 22 Mar. 1927, p. 1; *CDT*, 22 Mar. 1927, p. 8; Dunn to Rowland [*sic*], 7 Nov. 1923, trial transcript, 473, 478. The quoted letters were not retained in the *Independent*'s files.

30. *AC*, 22 Mar. 1927, p. 2; *NYT*, 22 Mar. 1927, p. 18.

31. Trial transcript, 485–89 (quote on 489), 493, 495, 508–9.

32. Trial transcript, 509–718, 723–30. A copy of Cherry's letter is in the Ford files; file 7, box 122, acc. 1, BFRC.

33. *DT,* 24 Mar. 1927, p. 2; trial transcript, 731–42, 772–97.

34. Trial transcript, 801–6.

35. Trial transcript, 823–43, 870, 874–75, 872.

36. *New York Evening Graphic,* 24 Mar. 1927, WHGP (emphasis in original).

37. *NYT,* 26 Mar. 1927, p. 4; trial transcript, 881–82; 884, 902, 918–19; *LAT,* 26 Mar. 1927, p. 1.

38. Trial transcript, 923, 927, 928.

39. Trial transcript, 930–31; 932, 933; *LAT,* 26 Mar. 1927, p. 2.

40. Trial transcript, 936, 937, 939.

41. Trial transcript, 942, 944–47.

42. Trial transcript, 964, 977, 987–90; *LAT,* 26 Mar. 1927, p. 1.

43. James Martin Miller, *The Amazing Story of Henry Ford, the Ideal American and the World's Most Famous Private Citizen: A Complete and Authentic Account of His Life and Surpassing Achievements* (Chicago: M. A. Donohue and Co., 1922); F. Hunter Creech to Ernest G. Liebold, 14 Apr. 1924, file 124, box 217, acc. 285, BFRC; *LAT,* 26 Mar. 1927, p. 1. Miller does not specify when he filed his lawsuit, and the newspapers do not supply that detail.

44. Trial transcript, 991–93 (quote on 992–93, 993), 994, 995; *NYT,* 26 Mar. 1927, p. 4; *LAT,* 26 Mar. 1927, p. 1.

45. Trial transcript, 1000–2, 998, 1004, 1007–8, 1010–14, 1015–34; *NYT,* 27 Mar. 1927, p. 4. Ribuffo, "Ford and *The International Jew,*" 471, names the top three subscribing states as Ohio, Michigan, and Pennsylvania to buttress an argument that *Independent* readers were probably not fading veterans of the Populist Party. The fourth- and fifth-ranked subscribing states, Illinois and Texas, however, were hotbeds of populist activity during the 1890s. I do not see Ford as a full-throated populist; he just hated banks, and he tapped into popular resentment of financial and political institutions not because he shared it but because he sought to use it to shape public opinion. Likewise, as the *DI* subscription data show, whether or not Americans harbored populist sympathies, many of them found Ford's economic ideology appealing in the post–World War I era.

46. *NYT,* 27 Mar. 1927, p. 4; *WP,* 27 Mar. 1927, p. 3; *CDT,* 27 Mar. 1927, p. 22; Aaron Sapiro to Lewis Lichtenstein Strauss, 27 Mar. 1927, file 5, box 70, LLSP (emphasis in original).

47. *LAT,* 28 Mar. 1927, p. 5; William Henry Gallagher to Clifford Longley, 28 Mar. 1927, file 7, box 122, acc. 1, BFRC; *NYT,* 28 Mar. 1927, p. 7; *DT,* 28 Mar. 1927, p. 1. See the preface for an account of Ford's accident and its aftermath.

48. Trial transcript, 1035–58, 1058–62 (quote on pp. 1061, 1062), 1070; *CDT,* 28 Mar. 1927, p. 6.

49. Trial transcript, 1077–78, 1076, 1083, 1088–89, 1090–94 (quote on 1090).

50. Trial transcript, 1100–20 (quotes on 1120, 1121), 1122–43.

51. *CDT,* 27 Mar. 1927, p. 22; *NYT,* 29 Mar. 1927, p. 1; *WP,* 29 Mar. 1927, p. 1.

52. Aaron L. Sapiro, "A Retrospective View of the Aaron Sapiro-Henry Ford Case," *Western States Jewish Historical Quarterly* 15, no. 1 (Oct. 1982): 79–84. The people who gave Sapiro money were Lewis Strauss, the New York investment banker; Harry J. Louis;

and Robert Bingham, publisher of the *Louisville Courier Journal* (ibid., 83). Leland Sapiro recalls that during the trial, "a Canadian farmer sent [his father] a small cash contribution to defray expenses, together with regrets that he couldn't sent any more." Leland Sapiro to author, 11 Nov. 2001 (on file).

53. *NYT*, 29 Mar. 1927, p. 1; trial transcript, 1161; *CDT*, 29 Mar. 1927, p. 8. Sapiro felt that Judge Raymond was decidedly biased: "They let Senator Reed get in all of that sort of stuff [alleging that Sapiro was responsible when a cooperative employee took bribes] to the jury without interruption from the Judge; but, as for us, we couldn't even bring in a legitimate war record to offset the charge that I was trying to subvert the US government with the aid of the Industrial Workers of the World." Aaron Sapiro, "An Experience with American Justice," *Free Synagogue Pulpit* 8, no. 5 (1927–1928): 20. But see *NYT*, 29 Mar. 1927, p. 1, 4; *CDT*, 29 Mar. 1927 p. 8.

54. Trial transcript, 1166–67; *AC*, 29 Mar. 1927, p. 5.

55. *NYT*, 30 Mar. 1927, p. 16; trial transcript, 1179–81 (quote on 1179), 1191; *LAT*, 30 Mar. 1927, p. 3.

56. *WP*, 30 Mar. 1927, p. 1; trial transcript, 1279–80, 1281; *NYT*, 30 Mar. 1927, p. 1, 16.

57. *NYT*, 30 Mar. 1927, pp. 1, 16; *DN*, 30 Mar. 1927, p. 1.

58. Trial transcript, 1301–1431 (quotes on p. 1364); *CDT*, 31 Mar. 1927, p. 2; *WP*, 31 Mar. 1927, p. 3; *NYT*, 31 Mar. 1927, p. 2; *LAT*, 31 Mar. 1927, p. 2.

59. *CDT*, 31 Mar. 1927, pp. 1, 2; *LAT*, 31 Mar. 1927, p. 2; *NYT*, 31 Mar. 1927, p. 2; *CDT*, 31 Mar. 1927, p. 2.

60. *NYT*, 1 Apr. 1927, p. 4; trial transcript, 1460, 1461–62.

61. Trial transcript, 1473–74; editorial descriptions from *NYT*, 1 Apr. 1927, p. 4.

62. *LAT*, 1 Apr. 1927, p. 4; *CDT*, 1 Apr. 1927, p. 13; Sapiro, "Experience with American Justice," 25.

63. *DT*, 1 Apr. 1927, pp. 1, 2; *NYT*, 18 Apr. 1927, p. 10; trial transcript, 1482–89.

64. Trial transcript, 1506–7; *DT*, 31 Mar. 1927, p. 2; ibid., 3 Apr. 1927, p. 4; *NYT*, 31 Mar. 1927, p. 2; *LAT*, 1 Apr. 1927, p. 4.

65. Trial transcript, 1640–41.

66. *CDT*, 2 Apr. 1927, p. 12; trial transcript, 1632, 1685–86; *LAT*, 2 Apr. 1927, p. 2; *NYT*, 2 Apr. 1927, p. 4; ibid., 9 Apr. 1927, p.4; *DT*, 5 Apr. 1927, p. 1; Sapiro to Strauss, 9 Apr. 1927, file 5, box 70, LLSP; "The Press: Ford Mistrial," *Time Magazine*, 2 May 1927, accessed 21 Dec. 2010, http://www.time.com/time/magazine/article/0,9171,751677-1,00.html.

67. *WP*, 3 Apr. 1927, p. M3; see also *LAT*, 3 Apr. 1927, p. 7; *NYT*, 3 Apr. 1927, p. 21.

68. *WP*, 3 Apr. 1927, p. M3; *NYT*, 3 Apr. 1927, p. 21; see also *DT*, 3 Apr. 1927, p. 1; ibid., *DT*, 4 Apr. 1927, p. 1; *NYT*, 3 Apr. 1927, p. 21.

69. *NYT*, 5 Apr. 1927, p. 29; *WP*, 5 Apr. 1927, p. 4; *NYT*, 5 Apr. 1927, p. 29; *LAT*, 5 Apr. 1927, p. 11.

70. *NYT*, 9 Apr. 1927, p. 4.

71. *DT*, 8 Apr. 1922, p. 2; ibid., 10 Apr. 1927, p. 1; Harry H. Bennett, *We Never Called Him Henry* (New York: Gold Medal Books, 1951), 53–54; *NYT*, 10 Apr. 1927, p. 19; *LAT*, 12 Apr. 1927, p. 2. Bennett spells the reporter's name *Hutcheson* and identifies him as a "Washington correspondent."

72. *NYT*, 10 Apr. 1927, p. 19.

73. Ibid., 12 Apr. 1927, p. 3; *LAT*, 12 Apr. 1927, p. 2.

74. *CDT*, 13 Apr. 1927, p. 19; *WP*, 13 Apr. 1927, p. 3; *NYT*, 13 Apr. 1927, p. 14; trial transcript, 2747–48.

75. *DT*, 15 Apr. 1927, p. 2.

76. Juror file, box 39, acc. 48, BFRC; *NYT*, 20 Mar. 1927, p. 3; ibid., 14 Apr. 1927, p. 16; *CDT*, 14 Apr. 1927, p. 17; trial transcript, 2786, 2788–91, 2792–2928; Sapiro, "Experience with American Justice," 27–28; *DT*, 15 Apr. 1927, p. 2. Sapiro spells the juror's name *Duarte* ("Experience with American Justice," 26); it appears as *Duart* and *Durat* in the sources consulted here.

77. Trial transcript, 3034. 2942; *NYT*, 15 Apr. 1927, p. 9; *DT*, 18 Apr. 1927, p. 2.

78. *LAT*, 15 Apr. 1927, p. 5; trial transcript, 2996–3003.

79. Trial transcript, 2939, 3030–31; Sapiro, "Experience with American Justice," 25.

80. *CDT*, 15 Apr. 1927, p. 18; *NYT*, 15 Apr. 1927, p. 9; *LAT*, 16 Apr. 1927, p. 3; *NYT*, 18 Apr. 1927, p. 10.

81. *WP*, 19 Apr. 1927, p. 3; *NYT*, 19 Apr. 1927, p. 12; *DT*, 18 Apr. 1927, p. 1.

82. *NYT*, 20 Apr. 1927, p. 1; *WP*, 20 Apr. 1927, p. 5; *NYT*, 21 Apr. 1927, p. 1.

83. Trial transcript, 3039–40; *NYT*, 20 Apr. 1927, p. 4.

84. Trial transcript, 3041, 3042, 3043, 3044; *NYT*, 20 Apr. 1927, p. 4; *WP*, 20 Apr. 1927, p. 5.

85. Bennett, *We Never Called Him Henry*, 54; *DT*, 19 April 1927, p. 1; e.g., ibid., 22 Apr. 1927, pp. 1–2 (includes reprint of 19 Apr. 1927 interview); *NYT*, 21 Apr. 1927, pp. 1, 3.

86. *NYT*, 21 Apr. 1927, p. 3; Hoffman jury card, juror file, box 39, acc. 48, BFRC. It is not clear when the Ford team first suspected that Hoffman might have perjured herself during voir dire or when it occurred to the defense to accuse her of the offense.

87. Sapiro, "Experience with American Justice," 30; *NYT*, 21 Apr. 1927, pp. 1, 3; ibid., 22 Apr. 1927, p. 2.

88. *NYT*, 21 Apr. 1927, p. 3. The affidavits are reproduced in the trial transcript (3062–66). Sapiro denied ever meeting Miller. *NYT*, 21 Apr. 1927, p. 3.

89. Trial transcript, 3048, 3049, 3050.

90. Trial transcript, 3053.

91. Trial transcript, 3057, 3059–60.

92. Trial transcript, 3060, 3061.

93. Trial transcript, 3066–73 (quote on 3069, 3070, 3072–73), 3079, 3089; *NYT*, 22 Apr. 1927 p. 1; *LAT*, 22 Apr. 1927, p. 3.

94. Bennett, *We Never Called Him Henry*, pp. 53–54; trial transcript, 3038, 3041–44, 3090–98; *DT*, 19 Apr. 1927, pp. 1–2; ibid., 22 April 1927, pp. 1–2; *NYT*, 22 Apr. 1927, p. 1. For the results of the investigation into the jury-tampering charges, see Henry Ford's Federal Bureau of Investigation file, *U.S. Department of Justice, Freedom of Information Act*, accessed 23 Dec. 2010, http://foia.fbi.gov/ford/ford1a.pdf.html, p. 79.

95. Trial transcript, 3093, 3095; *LAT*, 22 Apr. 1927, p. 3; *NYT*, 22 Apr. 1927, p. 2.

CHAPTER 8

1. *DJC*, 29 Apr. 1927, p. 4 (reprinted ibid., 5 Aug. 1927, p. 4).

2. Louis Marshall to Fred M. Butzel, 24 June 1927, file 7, box 1599, LMP.

3. Marshall to M. J. Abrams, 15 Feb. 1926, in Charles Reznikoff, ed., *Louis Marshall, Champion of Liberty: Selected Papers and Addresses* (Philadelphia: Jewish Publication Society of America, 1957), 1:371.

4. Marshall to G. Lowenstein, 29 Mar. 1927, in Reznikoff, *Champion of Liberty*, 1:371–72.

5. Marshall to Fred Butzel, 30 June 1927, file 7, box 1599, LMP; see also American Bar Association, *Canons of Professional Ethics*, canon 6 (Baltimore: s.n., 1908), p. 5 (*The Making of Modern Law*, Gale Cengage Learning, accessed 11 Mar. 2009, http://galenet .galegroup.com.turing.library.northwestern.edu/servlet/MOML?af=RN&ae=F151846384& srchtp=a&ste=14).

6. *DT*, 30 Apr. 1927, pp. 1, 8; *WP*, 1 May 1927, p. 3.

7. *NYT*, 22 Apr. 1927, p. 2.

8. Ibid., 25 Apr. 1927, p. 3. During the trip, Sapiro gave an interview that ran in the Kansas City papers and the Omaha *Jewish Press* but not the New York papers. Curious about this lacuna, Senator Reed asked Dearborn Publishing Company employees to track down the reports for use in the next trial. J. G. Bruce to Richard J. Higgins, 18 May 1927, file 1, box 34, JARP.

9. *NYT*, 28 May 1927, p. 14; ibid., 27 May 1927, p. 1; ibid., 30 May 1927, p. 8; ibid., 31 May 1927, p. 21.

10. Bruce to Higgins, 18 May 1927; Higgins to Hanley, 15 June 1927, file 1, box 34, JARP.

11. Allan Nevins and Frank Ernest Hill, *Ford: Expansion and Challenge* (New York: Charles Scribner's Sons, 1957), 414–15, 431–32. The company manufactured a total of 15,458,781 Model Ts, as demand rose sharply in response to the announcement that production would be discontinued. Ibid., 432.

12. The press did not draw this connection until July, after the apology was announced. See, e.g., *CDT*, 9 July 1927, p. 10. For the historical interpretation, see, e.g., Nevins and Hill, *Expansion and Challenge*, 322; Neil Baldwin, *Henry Ford and the Jews: The Mass Production of Hate* (New York: Public Affairs, 2001), 224, 232–33; Douglas Brinkley, *Wheels for the World: Henry Ford, His Company, and a Century of Progress, 1903–2003* (New York: Viking Press, 2003), 346.

13. *AC*, 10 July 1927, p. 5; Greg Grandin, *Fordlandia* (New York: Metropolitan Books, 2009), 65, 90–96; Harry Bennett, *We Never Called Him Henry* (New York: Gold Medal Books, 1951), 50–52.

14. Motion for Leave to Amend Declaration, *Sapiro v. Ford and the DPC*, No. 7522, 10 June 1927, file 1, box 34, JARP; Stewart Hanley to Higgins, 19 June 1927, ibid.; Higgins to Hanley, 15 June 1927, ibid.; *NYT*, 25 Apr. 1927, p. 3.

15. Fred Black, "Reminiscences," p. 50, box 6, acc. 65, BFRC, quoted in Steven Watts, *The People's Tycoon: Henry Ford and the American Century* (New York: Knopf, 2005), 395; and Carol W. Gelderman, *Henry Ford: The Wayward Capitalist* (New York: St. Martin's Press, 1981), 233.

16. Joyce Milton, "Brisbane, Arthur," *American National Biography Online*, Feb. 2000, accessed 21 Jan. 2006, http://www.anb.org/articles/16/16-00182.html; Nevins and Hill, *Expansion and Challenge*, 317; Baldwin, *Henry Ford and the Jews*, 233, 235 (original source not provided); *NYHT*, 9 July 1927, p. 2. Bennett says in his memoir that Ford did not decide to "quit publishing antisemitic material" until after Herman Bernstein returned from a fact-finding tour in Europe on June 9, 1927, and presented Ford with

"documentary evidence that [the] *Independent* had indeed hurt a great many people." Bennett, *We Never Called Him Henry*, 55. This could be an example of Ford's leading many people to believe they were the agents behind his actions, making his decision making difficult to trace. As I argue in the text, verifying Bennett's account is difficult.

17. Keith Sward, *The Legend of Henry Ford* (New York: Rinehart, 1948), 157; Bennett, *We Never Called Him Henry*, 55; William C. Richards, *The Last Billionaire, Henry Ford* (New York: Bantam Books, 1956), 99. The accuracy of Richards's account is buttressed by an interview Palma gave to the *New York Times*, in which many of these quotes appear nearly verbatim. *NYT*, 5 Nov. 1927, p. 19.

18. *NYHT*, 9 July 1927, p. 1; *NYT*, 11 July 1927, p. 8; ibid., 10 July 1927, p. 18.

19. Marshall to Fred M. Butzel, 30 June 1927, file 7, box 1599, LMP; *NYHT*, 9 July 1927, pp. 1–2; *NYT*, 10 July 1927, p. 18; ibid., 11 July 1927, p. 8.

20. Marshall to Fred Butzel, 24 June 1927, file 7, box 1599, LMP.

21. Butzel to Marshall, 29 June 1927, file 2, box 1599, LMP; Sapiro to Strauss, 29 June 1927, file 5, box 70, LLSP.

22. Butzel to Marshall, 29 June 1927, file 2, box 1599, LMP; *NYHT*, 9 July 1927, p. 2.

23. Marshall to Butzel, 30 June 1927, file 7, box 1599, LMP; *NYT*, 10 July 1927, p. 18.

24. Aaron Sapiro to Lewis Strauss, 29 June 1927, file 5, box 70, LLSP.

25. Sapiro to Strauss, 2 July 1927, file 5, box 70, LLSP; Marshall to Ford, n.d. (labeled "No. 7"), SC 3516; *NYHT*, 9 July 1927, p. 2.

26. Henry Ford statement, 30 June 1927, SC 3515; also in file 7, box 122, acc. 1, BFRC; Richards, *Last Billionaire*, 99; Ford to Earl J. Davis, 30 June 1927, SC 3515; Marshall to Brisbane, 19 July 1927, file 4, box 155, LMP. According to the *New York Times*, Davis returned to New York bearing the signed statement (10 July 1927, p. 18). Bennett says that it was he who read the statement to Ford over the phone and that Ford instructed him to sign Ford's name and release it without changing a word. Bennett, *We Never Called Him Henry*, 56. It appears Bennett put himself in Palma's place. No independent evidence places Bennett in New York City in June 1927.

27. Compare *NYHT*, 9 July 1927, p. 2, with Bennett, *We Never Called Him Henry*, 55–56 (asserting that Brisbane, Samuel Untermyer, and Marshall together drafted Ford's statement).

28. *NYHT*, 9 July 1927, pp. 1–2; *NYT*, 8 July 1927, p. 1; ibid., 11 July 1927, p. 8; ibid., 12 July 1927, p. 12; ibid., 14 July 1927, p. 26; Marshall to Butzel, 24 June 1927, file 7, box 1599, LMP; Marshall to Nathan Perlman, 18 July 1927, file 8, ibid.; Marshall to Arthur Brisbane, 19 July 1927, ibid.; Perlman to Marshall, 27 July 1927, file 2, box 155, LMP; Bennett, *We Never Called Him Henry*, 56; "Races: Apology to Jews," *Time*, 18 July 1927, accessed 23 Dec. 2010, http://www.time.com/time/magazine/article/0,9171,730744,00.html.

29. Ford statement, 30 June 1927, SC 3515; *NYHT*, 8 July 1927, pp.1–2; ibid., 9 July 1927, p. 2; *NYT*, 8 July 1927, p. 1.

30. Ford statement; *NYHT*, 8 July 1927, p. 1.

31. Marshall to Ford, 5 July 1927, file 2, box 155, LMP; also in file 5, box 70, LLSP, and in Reznikoff, *Champion of Liberty*, 1:379–80; Minutes of AJC Executive Committee, 18 Sept. 1927, file 1, box 75, LMP.

32. *NYHT*, 9 July 1927, p. 2; *CDT*, 8 July 1927, p. 1. For press reaction treating the apology as a victory for Jews, see, e.g., *CDT*, 17 July 1927, p. 3; *NYT*, 9 July 1927, p. 1; *LAT*,

11 July 1927, p. 3. The *Washington Post* rejoiced more tentatively, perhaps prompted by the local response: one Orthodox congregation voted to reject the apology, 37 to 23. See *WP*, 14 July 1927, p. 1.

33. *NYT*, 8 July 1927, p. 10; *NYHT*, 9 July 1927, p. 2; *AC*, 10 July 1927, p. 1; *NYT*, 11 July 1927, p. 8; *CDT*, 8 July 1927, p. 1; *WP*, 10 July 1927, p. 4.

34. Richards, *Last Billionaire*, 100; *WP*, 10 July 1927, p. 4; Marshall to Cyrus Adler, 10 July 1927, in Reznikoff, *Champion of Liberty*, 1:380; *NYT*, 10 July 1927, p. 18. *Time Magazine* lauded Edsel for having "taken a true measure both of his father and of himself" in helping to produce the surprising outcome in the case. *Time*, "Races: Apology to Jews," 18 July 1927. In 1948, William Richards asserted that Ford did not consult anyone around him, including Edsel (*Last Billionaire*, 100).

35. Richards, *Last Billionaire*, 101; *WP*, 9 July 1927, p. 1; *New York Evening Post*, 9 July 1927, WHGP; James Reed to Longley, 27 Sept. 1927, file 6, box 1, acc. 1740, BFRC; Longley to Reed, 15 Oct. 1927, ibid.; clipping, dateline Topeka, Kansas, 22 Feb. [1928], file 7, box 122, acc. 1, BFRC; Reed to Longley, 10 Feb. 1927, file 1, box 34, JARP; Higgins to Longley, 11 June 1927, ibid.; Statement, Reed, Holmes, Higgins, and Taylor to Henry L. Ford and Dearborn Independent, 16 Aug. 1927, ibid. (Reed's final bill included his $100,000 retainer). According to the billing records, Reed counted two full weeks—from April 18 to May 1—as sick leave for which he was not paid. Ward Choate received $7,000 (or $7,500) and Stewart Hanley $9,500; Liebold approved these payments. Longley's fees were not separately itemized. C. A. Zahnow to J. Tattan, 18 May 1927; Tattan to Ernest G. Liebold, 14 Mar. 1927, both in file 298A, box 206, acc. 285, BFRC.

36. *AC*, 10 July 1927, p. 5.

37. All quoted in "Races: Apology to Jews," *Time*, 18 July 1927.

38. Marshall to Julius Rosenwald, 22 July 1927, in Reznikoff, *Champion of Liberty*, 1:382; *NYT*, 9 July 1927, p. 12.

39. David Gordon, "America," *Daily Worker*, 12 Mar. 1927, sec. 2, p. 2.

40. *The Nation*, 20 July 1927, p. 47. See also *NYT*, 1 Apr. 1927, p. 13; ibid., 30 June 1927, p. 30; and ibid., 11 Dec. 1927, p. 27. For the criminal prosecutions in the *Daily Worker* case, see *People v. Gordon* and *People v. Daily Worker Publishing Co.*, 247 N.Y. 593 (1928), affirming *People v. Dunne et al.*, 222 App. Div. 726 (1927); *People v. Gordon*, 222 App. Div. 726 (1927). Signers of the 7–0 decision of the court of appeal included judges Benjamin Cardozo and Irving Lehman.

41. Quoted in *DJC*, 22 July 1927, p. 8, and in *NYHT*, 9 July 1927, p. 2; ibid., 9 July 1927, p. 8.

42. *New York World*, 8 July 1927, WHGP; *Detroit Saturday Night*, 16 July 1927, WHGP; *CDT*, 9 July 1927, p. 4.

43. *Detroit Saturday Night*, 16 July 1927, WHGP (emphasis in original); *Life*, "In the Henry Ford Manner," 90 (28 July 1927), p. 10; George Rothwell Brown, "Post-Scripts," *WP*, 31 July 1927, p. 1; Harry Carr, "The Lancer," *LAT*, 13 July 1927, p. A1.

44. Will Rogers, "Will Rogers Remarks," *LAT*, 9 July 1927, p. 1 (republished in *NYT*, 9 July 1927, p. 15; and *WP*, 9 July 1927, p. 3); *CDT*, 13 July 1927, p. 10; David Rosenbaum to Marshall, 8 July 1927, file 2, box 155, LMP.

45. The Happiness Boys, "Since Henry Ford Apologized to Me," track 10, disc 2, *From Avenue A to the Great White Way: Yiddish and American Popular Songs from*

1914–1950, Columbia/Legacy, 2002; David L. Lewis, *The Public Image of Henry Ford: An American Folk Hero and His Company* (Detroit: Wayne State University Press, 1976), 147; *CDT*, 29 July 1927, p. 23. The song may be sampled at http://new.music.yahoo.com/happiness-boys/tracks/.

46. *DFP*, 15 July 1927, WHGP.

47. "Races: Apology to Jews," *Time*, 18 July 1927; *New York World*, 9 July 1927, pp. 1–2, WHGP.

48. *New York World*, 9 July 1927, pp. 1–2, WHGP.

49. "Races: Apology to Jews," *Time*, 18 July 1927; *Jewish Daily Bulletin*, 11 July 1927, p. 4, file 2, box 155, LMP.

50. "From William Allen White," *The Outlook*, 20 July 1927, p. 373; *DJC*, 22 July 1927, p. 8. Canossa is the Italian site where Henry IV of the Holy Roman Empire stood barefoot in the snow for three days in 1077 as penance for his excommunication. I. S. Robinson, *Henry IV of Germany, 1056–1106* (Cambridge: Cambridge University Press, 1999), 160–64.

51. *The Outlook*, 20 July 1927, p. 373; "Letters: Dislikes Jews," *Time*, 5 Sept. 1927, accessed 26 Dec. 2010, http://www.time.com/time/magazine/article/0,9171,723234,00.html; *Jewish Daily Bulletin*, 11 July 1927, p. 4, file 2, box 155, LMP.

52. *DJC*, 15 July 1927, p. 1; *CDT*, 9 July 1927, p. 4; *NYT*, 8 July 1927, p. 1; ibid., 9 July 1927, p. 1.

53. "Races: Apology to Jews;" *Time*, 18 July 1927; *NYT*, 8 July 1927, p. 10; Marshall to Perlman, 18 July 1927, file 8, box 1599, LMP. See correspondence in files 2 and 4, box 155; and file 8, box 1599, LMP. The wire services assumed that when Marshall instructed his son James to supply copies of Ford's statement for their use, he intended to perform that service for anyone.

54. Jacob Billikopf to Marshall, 11 July 1927, file 2, box 75, LMP; Marshall to Perlman, 18 July 1927, file 8, box 1599, LMP. Lewis Strauss later asked to see this letter. Strauss to Marshall, 23 July 1927, file 2, box 155, LMP.

55. Marshall to Julius Rosenwald, 22 July 1927, file 13, box 1599, LMP; Perlman to Marshall, 27 July 1927, file 2, box 155, LMP; S. E. Goldstein to Marshall, 14 July 1927, file 4, box 155, LMP. See also Henry H. Klein to Marshall, 8 July 1927, file 2, box 155; Samuel Bettelheim to Marshall, 11 July 1927, file 2, box 75, LMP.

56. The American Bar Association first addressed lawyers' ethical obligations in 1908, producing thirty-two canons to govern lawyers' behavior on subjects ranging from advertising their services to the unauthorized practice of law. They went largely unchanged until a model code of professional responsibility was produced in 1983. The 1908 canons do not specify how the conflicts of interests provisions apply to of-counsel situations. American Bar Association, *Canons of Professional Ethics*, canon 6 (Baltimore: s.n., 1908), p. 5 (*The Making of Modern Law*, Gale Cengage Learning, accessed 11 Mar. 2009, http://galenet.galegroup.com.turing.library.northwestern.edu/servlet/MOML?af=RN&ae=F151846384&srchtp=a&ste=14).

57. He told Perlman and Julius Rosenwald. Marshall to Perlman, 18 July 1927, file 8, box 1599, LMP; Marshall to Rosenwald, 22 July 1927, in Reznikoff, *Champion of Liberty*, 1:381.

58. Marshall to Untermyer, 1 July 1927, in Reznikoff, *Champion of Liberty*, 1:374–75.

59. Untermyer to Marshall, 3 July 1927, SC 3516.

60. Marshall to Untermyer, 4 July 1927, in Reznikoff, *Champion of Liberty*, 1:376 (emphasis added).

61. Untermyer to Marshall, 4 July 1927, SC 3516 (emphasis added); Untermyer to Marshall, 5 July 1927, ibid.; Untermyer to Marshall, 5 July 1927, ibid.

62. Marshall to James Marshall, 7 July 1927, folder 2, box 155, MS 359, LMP.

63. Marshall to Rosenwald, 22 July 1927, in Reznikoff, *Champion of Liberty*, 1:381; Marshall to Untermyer, 1 July 1927, ibid., 375. Joseph Palma apparently misunderstood, thanking Marshall effusively for his "splendid work and friendly efforts in bringing about th[e Bernstein] settlement." Palma to Marshall, 25 July 1927, file 4, box 155, LMP.

64. Marshall to Rosenwald, 22 July 1927, file 8, box 1599, LMP; motion, 21 Feb. 1924, *Bernstein v. Ford and the Dearborn Publishing Company*, file 413, box 14, HBP; *Martindale's American Law Directory* (New York: Martindale's American Law Directory, Inc., 1925), 1214; ibid. (New York, 1927), 1287; ibid. (New York, 1928), 1364; ibid. (New York, 1929), 1405; ibid. (New York, 1930), 1347.

65. Laurence A. Steinhardt to Herman Bernstein, 9 Aug. 1927, folder 413A, box 14, RG 713, HBP.

66. Bernstein to David A. Brown, 17 Oct. 1933, folder 627, box 24, RG 713, HBP; see also Bernstein to Adler, [1933–1934], file 623, box 24, HBP.

67. Henry Ford to Bernstein, 23 July 1927, SUP; *Henry Ford's Retraction and Apology to the Jews* (New York, [1927]), American Jewish Committee pamphlet, file 413A, box 14, HBP; Untermyer to Marshall, [5] July 1927, SC 3516.

68. Sapiro to Strauss, 18 July 1927, file 5, box 70, LLSP; Aaron Sapiro, "A Retrospective View of the Aaron Sapiro-Henry Ford Case," *Western States Jewish Historical Quarterly* 15 (1982): 79–84, 80.

69. Sapiro to Strauss, 18 July 1927, file 5, box 70, LLSP; Sapiro to Gross, 15 July 1927, ibid.

70. Butzel to Marshall, 21 July 1927, file 5, box 70, LLSP; Sapiro to Strauss, 18 July 1927, ibid.; Sapiro to Gallagher, 17 July 1927, ibid.; William Henry Gallagher, *Family Memoir*, tms. (typescript, 1974–1979; furnished to author by Connie Bookmyer, on file), 19. Gallagher does not mention his $100,000 demand, the $65,000 figure, or the $7,750 he received from Sapiro. Ibid. Sapiro gave Strauss a higher estimate of his costs and losses ($117,000). Sapiro to Strauss, 18 July 1927, file 5, box 70, LLSP. After Gallagher accepted Sapiro's retainer, Ford offered him work on a separate matter that he declined: "'I felt that the prosecution of Mr. Sapiro's claim was little short of a public duty.'" *DJC*, 29 July 1927, p. 4.

71. *NYT*, 19 July 1927, p. 13. The fee distribution raises the question of why Longley acceded to Untermyer's demand for more money but not Gallagher's.

72. "Races: No Jewish Ring," *Time*, 25 July 1927, accessed 26 Dec. 2010, http://www.time.com/time/magazine/article/0,9171,736785,00.html; *CDT*, 19 July 1927, p. 3; *DJC*, 22 July 1927, p. 1; Sapiro to Louis D. Gross, 15 July 1927, file 5, box 70, LLSP.

73. Sapiro to Strauss, 18 July 1927, file 5, box 70, LLSP; Aaron Sapiro, "An Experience with American Justice," *Free Synagogue Pulpit* 8, no. 5 (1927–1928): 36; *CDT*, 19 July 1927, p. 3; *DI*, 30 July 1927, p. 11 (emphasis added).

74. Sapiro to Gallagher, 17 July 1927, file 5, box 70, LLSP; Butzel to Marshall, 21 July 1927, ibid. Butzel's information biased Marshall, who wrote Strauss on July 22 calling

Sapiro "erratic" and labeling him "disgusting" for praising Ford after the apology. Marshall to Strauss, 22 July 1927, file 11, box 68, LLSP.

75. Marshall to Strauss, 25 July 1927, file 5, box 70, LLSP; Gross to Strauss, 14 Dec. 1927, ibid.; see also R. J. Cromie to Strauss, 7 Dec. 1927, ibid.; Sapiro to Strauss, 7 Dec. 1927, ibid.; Marshall to Strauss, 25 July 1927, ibid. Strauss sent Sapiro's July 18 letter to Marshall so that Marshall might appreciate what Sapiro conceded in the negotiations, but Marshall evidently did not interpret the letter as Strauss hoped. Lewis Strauss to Marshall, 23 July 1927, file 2, box 155, LMP.

76. *Vancouver Sun*, 11 Aug. 1927, file 5, box 70, LLSP; *LAT*, 21 July 1921, p. A4; *DJC*, 22 July 1927, p. 4; R. J. Cromie to Strauss, 7 Dec. 1927, file 5, box 70, LLSP ("little" modifies "Aaron," not "what"; Cromie's intention was to compliment Sapiro while affectionately referring to his stature).

77. *DJC*, 5 Aug. 1927, p. 1 (emphasis added).

78. *DJC*, 5 Aug. 1927, p. 4; Sapiro to Strauss, 18 July 1927, file 5, box 70, LLSP.

79. *LAT*, 20 Aug. 1927, p. A1; *DJH*, 30 Sept. 1927, pp. 1, 8; *LAT*, 31 Oct. 1927, p. 5; *NYT*, 31 Oct. 1927, p. 24; Sapiro, "Experience with American Justice," 24. Crowd size estimates varied widely; the Los Angeles *Times* said three thousand attended, whereas the *New York Times* claimed that only one thousand were turned away (*NYT*, 31 Oct. 1927, p. 24).

80. Marshall to Benjamin Friedman, 22 Nov. 1927, file 12, box 1599, LMP; Marshall to Lee Frankel, 16 Dec. 1927, file 13, ibid.; Sapiro to Strauss, 7 Dec. 1927, file 5, box 70, LLSP. Sapiro reportedly so referred to Marshall in Philadelphia in early 1928, but Marshall heard of earlier references. *Jewish Times*, 20 Jan. 1928, file 2, box 155, LMP; Marshall to Harry Schneiderman, 20 Dec. 1927, file 13, box 1599, LMP.

81. "Aaron Sapiro v. Henry Ford," n.d., Sapiro Miscellaneous File, SC 10835; Sapiro, "Retrospective View of the Aaron Sapiro-Henry Ford Case," 82; Marshall to Harry Schneiderman, 20 Dec. 1927, file 13, box 1599, LMP; Marshall to Isaac W. Frank, 11 July 1927, file 8, ibid.; Jacob Billikopf to Marshall, 11 July 1927, file 2, box 75, HBP; Marshall to Franklin, 31 July 1927, file 4, box 14, LMFP; Franklin to Marshall, 4 Aug. 1927, ibid.; Marshall to Rosenwald, 22 July 1927, file 8, box 1599, LMP.

82. Marshall to Rosenwald, 22 July 1927, file 8, box 1599, LMP; Samuel Fisher to Marshall, 13 July 1927, file 6, box 75, ibid.; Ford statement, 30 June 1927.

83. Marshall to Strauss, 22 July 1927, file 11, box 68, LLSP; Marshall to Franklin, 31 July 1927; Marshall to Rosenwald, 22 July 1927.

84. Marshall to Frank Campsall, 23 Jan. 1928, file 5, box 4, LMP; Marshall to Longley, 3 Apr. 1928, file 14, box 122, acc. 1, BFRC. On the relationship between Marshall and Ford's staff after the apology, see Chapter 9.

85. Ford dealers stopped taking subscriptions in July. *WSJ*, 29 July 1927, p. 4.

CHAPTER 9

1. Louis Marshall to Henry Sliosberg, 18 Aug. 1927, file 9, box 1599, LMP.

2. Marshall to Isidore Wise, 11 July 1927, file 8, box 1599, LMP.

3. Marshall to Julian W. Mack, 21 July 1927, file 4, box 155, LMP; *NYT*, 14 Nov. 1927, p. 23; Matthew Silver, "The Democratization of Jewish Identity," *American Jewish History* 94, nos. 1–2 (2008): 41–69, 59, 67.

4. Marshall to H. I. Phillips, 17 Aug. 1927, file 9, box 1599, LMP; Marshall to Emanuel Schreiber, 18 Aug. 1927, ibid.

5. Marshall to Emanuel Schreiber, 18 Aug. 1927, file 9, box 1599, LMP; Marshall to Joseph Palma, 17 Aug. 1927, file 9, box 1599; Marshall to Earl J. Davis, 25 Aug. 1927, file 8, box 1599, LMP; Marshall to Jacob Landau, 17 Aug. 1927, file 9, box 1599, LMP.

6. Marshall to H. I. Phillips, 17 Aug. 1927, file 9, box 1599, LMP; Marshall to Martin Ansorge, 20 Sept. 1927, file 4, box 155, LMP; Marshall to Emanuel Schreiber, 18 Aug. 1927, file 9, box 1599; Jacob Landau to Marshall, 16 Aug 1927, file 4, box 155, LMP.

7. Marshall to Jacob Landau, 17 Aug. 1927, file 9, box 1599; Marshall to Schreiber, 18 Aug. 1927, file 8, box 1599; Marshall to Joseph Palma, 17 Aug. 1927, file 9, box 1599, LMP; Marshall to Davis, 6 Sept. 1927, file 4, box 155, LMP; Davis to Marshall, 13 Sept. 1927, ibid.; Marshall to Palma, 17 Sept. 1927, file 10, box 1599, LMP.

8. Fritsch to Dearborn Publishing Company, 9 July 1927, in Martin Ansorge to Marshall, 19 Sept. 1927, file 4, box 155, LMP; Black to Fritsch, 16 Aug. 1927, ibid. Martin Ansorge was Ford's New York lawyer.

9. Marshall to Martin Ansorge, 20 Sept. 1927, file 4, box 155, LMP; *Jewish Daily Bulletin*, 20 Sept. 1927, ibid.; Marshall to Ansorge, 22 Sept. 1927, file 2, box 155, LMP. Marshall pointed out that the German Jewish press was already raising questions about Fritsch's assertions questioning the apology and asking Ford to respond.

10. Palma to Marshall, 10 Oct. 1927, file 4, box 155, LMP. Allan Nevins and Frank Ernest Hill, *Ford: Expansion and Challenge, 1915–1933* (New York: Charles Scribner's Sons, 1957), 321 (noting that Liebold and Cameron were discharged from their posts at the *Independent* but remained at the Ford Motor Company).

11. Marshall to Palma, 14 Oct. 1927, file 11, box 1599, LMP, also in file 13, box 122, acc. 1, BFRC; Marshall to Ford, 14 Oct. 1927, ibid.; draft, Ford to Fritsch (Hammer-Verlag), n.d., attached to Marshall, "Plan for the Discontinuance of the Publication and Circulation of 'The International Jew,'" n.d. [14 Oct. 1927], ibid.

12. Palma to Frank Campsall, 17 Oct. 1927, file 13, box 122, acc. 1, BFRC.

13. Ford to Fritsch, 1 Nov. 1927, file 13, box 122, acc. 1, BFRC; *NYT*, 14 Nov. 1927, p. 23; *Springfield (Mass.) Republican*, 24 Nov. 1927, file 13, box 122, acc. 1, BFRC; *NYT*, 26 Nov. 1927, p. 17 (Fritsch denied receiving a letter from Ford); ibid., 14 Nov. 1927, p. 23; *LAT*, 26 Nov. 1927, p. 4.

14. Fritsch to Ford, 1 Dec. 1927, file 13, box 122, acc. 1, BFRC.

15. Richard S. Levy, "Theodor Fritsch," in *Antisemitism: A Historical Encyclopedia of Prejudice and Persecution*, ed. Richard S. Levy (Santa Barbara: ABC-CLIO, 2005), 1:249–50; Levy, "Antisemitism and Political Murder," in *Antisemitism in the Modern World: An Anthology of Texts*, ed. Richard S. Levy (Lexington, Mass.: D. C. Heath, 1991), 191; Fritsch to Ford, 1 Dec. 1927, file 13, box 122, acc. 1, BFRC; Theodor Fritsch, *Hammer: Blätter für deutschen Sinn*, 68 (1927): 613–17, 615.

16. Hammer-Verlag to DPC, n.d. [6 Dec. 1927], file 13, box 122, acc. 1, BFRC.

17. *Völkischer Beobachter*, 7 Dec. 1927, p. 6; Louis Marshall to Ford, 21 Dec. 1927, file 13, box 122, acc. 1, BFRC. The term *völkischer* can be translated literally, as here, or rendered more interpretively, as "racial," as Richard S. Levy has suggested. The phrase was apparently racialized at the time and was intended to convey an exclusive sense of "people."

18. Marshall to Robert Marshall, 11 Jan. 1928, in Charles Reznikoff, ed., *Louis Marshall, Champion of Liberty: Selected Papers and Addresses* (Philadelphia: Jewish Publication Society of America, 1957), 1:388–89; see also Marshall to President, Der Vorsitzende des Central-Vereins, Berlin, [Feb. 1928], file 5, box 4, LMP; Marshall to Mrs. Benjamin Marshall, 11 Jan. 1928, file 2, box 1600, LMP; Marshall to Ford, attn. Campsall, 10 Jan. 1928, file 13, box 122, acc. 1, BFRC; Marshall to Bernstein, 21 Feb. 1928, file 3, box 1600, LMP; *NYT*, 16 Jan. 1928, p. 15; ibid., 17 Jan. 1928, p. 5.

19. Longley to Campsall, 4 Jan. 1928, file 13, box 122, acc. 1, BFRC; Campsall to Marshall, 5 Jan. 1928, file 5, box 4, LMP; Campsall to Marshall, 10 Jan. 1928, file 13, box 122, acc. 1, BFRC; V. Kessler to Ford, 22 Dec. 1927; Alexandre F. de Runge to Dearborn Publishing Co., 19 Dec. 1927, both in file 13, box 122, acc. 1, BFRC.

20. Marshall to Ford, attn. Campsall, 10 Jan. 1928, file 13, box 122, acc. 1, BFRC, also in box 4, file 5, LMP; Ford to Fritsch, 20 Jan. 1928, file 13, box 122, acc. 1, BFRC.

21. Ford to Fritsch, 20 Jan. 1928, file 13, box 122, acc. 1, BFRC.

22. Campsall to Marshall, 20 Jan. 1928, file 5, box 4, LMP; Ford to V. Kessler, 17 Jan. 1928, file 4, box 155, LMP. Marshall suggested to Campsall that Ford and the DPC pay de Runge, the Brazilian publisher, the $532 he requested not to publish the Portuguese version, as that was a small price to pay to keep the book out of Portugal, "virgin territory" for antisemites; however, Campsall informed Marshall that the Ford staff decided against doing so because de Runge could simply retain a copy and use it to extort money from Ford in the future. Marshall agreed and drafted a letter for Ford to send to de Runge refusing to pay for the cancelled publication rights. Ibid.; Marshall to Campsall, 17 Jan. 1927, file 5, box 4, LMP; Marshall to Campsall, 23 Jan. 1928, file 14, box 122, acc. 1, BFRC; DPC to de Runge, 2 Feb. 1928, ibid.; Campsall to Marshall, 3 Feb. 1928, ibid.

23. Marshall to Ford, 21 Feb. 1928, file 14, box 122, acc. 1, BFRC, also in file 5, box 4, LMP; undated typed telephone message, *NYT*, file 14, box 122, acc. 1, BFRC; Marshall to Ford, 21 Feb. 1928, ibid.; also in file 5, box 4, LMP; "To the Public," n.d. [21 Feb. 1928], file 5, box 4, LMP. The trade ad appeared in *Börsenblatt für den deutschen Buchhandel*, a weekly German book trade magazine.

24. Kurt G. W. Lüdecke to Clifford B. Longley, 12 Mar. 1928, file 14, box 122, acc. 1, BFRC.

25. Arthur L. Smith Jr., "Kurt Lüdecke: The Man Who Knew Hitler," *German Studies Review*, 26, no. 3 (Oct. 2003): 597–606, 599; Neil Baldwin, *Henry Ford and the Jews: The Mass Production of Hate* (New York: Public Affairs, 2001), 188–89; Kurt Lüdecke, *I Knew Hitler: The Story of a Nazi Who Escaped the Blood Purge* (New York: Scribner's, 1937), 192, 197–200, 309. Lüdecke was introduced to Ford by Siegfried Wagner, son of Richard Wagner (ibid., 191), and he admits that Ford declined to give him money for Hitler. Ibid., 197–201, 273.

26. Longley to Marshall, 5 Apr. 1928, file 14, box 122, acc. 1, BFRC; Marshall to Longley, 3 Apr. 1928, file 14, box 122, acc. 1, BFRC.

27. "Memorandum on the Effect in Europe of Mr. Ford's Statement of June 30, 1927 and by What Methods Its Usefulness May Be Enhanced," n.d. [3 Apr. 1928], file 14, box 122, acc. 1, BFRC.

28. Marshall to Ford, 12 May 1928, file 14, box 122, acc. 1, BFRC; also in file 6, box 1600, LMP.

29. Marshall to Blumenthal Brothers, 15 May 1928, file 6, box 1600, LMP; Luigi Crosciato to Ford, 11 July 1928, file 14, box 122, acc. 1, BFRC; V.A. Kessler to Ford, 23 July 1928, ibid.

30. Oscar Handlin, "Introduction," in Reznikoff, ed., *Marshall, Champion of Liberty*, xliii. There was one brief exchange in January 1929 after Marshall invited Ford to contribute to the American Society for Jewish Farm Settlements in Russia, but apparently nothing resulted from that overture. Marshall to Ford, 14 Dec. 1928, file 13, box 1600, LMP; Frank Campsall to Marshall, 16 Jan. 1929, file 1, box 141, LMP; Marshall to Ford, 17 Jan. 1929, file 2, box 1601, LMP.

31. Marshall to Louis M. Brockman, 18 Sept. 1928, file 10, box 1600, LMP.

32. Marshall to W. Gilbert Hawes, 1 Oct. 1928, file 11, box 1600, LMP; Samuel J. Jacobs, "The Blood Libel Case at Massena: A Reminiscence and a Review," *Judaism* 28 (1979): 465–74, 466, 467; Saul S. Friedman, *The Incident at Massena: The Blood Libel in America* (New York: Stein and Day, 1978), 1–29. The newspapers spell Barbara's name without an *s*, as do Louis Marshall and the *Jewish Telegraphic Agency* reporter in his 1978 story, whereas historians spell it *Griffiths*. I use the contemporaneous spelling. See Boris Smolar, "Blood Libel," *Jewish Week-American Examiner* 188, no. 26 (26 Nov. 1978): 36.

33. Jacobs, "Blood Libel Case at Massena," 467–68; Smolar, "Blood Libel," 36.

34. Albert S. Lindeman, *The Jew Accused: Three Anti-Semitic Affairs (Dreyfus, Beilis, Frank), 1894–1915* (New York: Cambridge University Press, 1991), 183–88; *LAT*, 4 Oct. 1928, p. 7; Abraham G. Duker, "Twentieth Century Blood Libels in the United States," in *The Blood Libel Legend: A Casebook in Antisemitic Folklore*, ed. Alan Dundes (Madison: University of Wisconsin Press, 1991), 233–60; Smolar, "Blood Libel," 36. The German counterpart of the Anti-Defamation League counted no fewer than 120 stories of ritual murder in the antisemitic press between 1891 and 1900; several led to sensational trials. Hillel J. Kieval, "Ritual Murder (Modern)," in Levy, *Antisemitism: A Historical Encyclopedia*, 2:605–8.

35. Jacobs, "Blood Libel Case at Massena," 469; Marshall to John A. Warner, 1 Oct. 1928, file 8, box 6, LMP; Friedman, *Incident at Massena*, 116 (repeating verbatim the phrase "unusual excitement"), 118, 121–22. Marshall did not know the informer's name.

36. Friedman, *Incident at Massena*, 124; Jacobs, "Blood Libel Case at Massena," 469; Marshall to Warner, 1 Oct. 1928. Friedman reports that mobs terrorized small groups of Jews, staged commercial boycotts, and threatened individuals (146–47, 173–74), but Jacobs argues that he dismissed contrary evidence and recollections. Jacobs, "Blood Libel Case at Massena," 470–73.

37. Friedman, *Incident at Massena*, 154, 155–56; Alfred E. Smith to Stephen E. Wise, 3 Oct. 1927, quoted in Friedman, *Incident at Massena*, 155. Friedman notes that the strong language of Smith's condemnation did not appear in the version of the letter released to the press on Oct. 3. Ibid.

38. Smolar, "Blood Libel," 36; Marshall to Hawes, 1 Oct. 1928; Marshall to Warner, 1 Oct. 1928 (emphasis added); *NYT*, 3 Oct. 1928, p. 34; *AC*, 4 Oct. 1928, p. 7; Friedman, *Incident at Massena*, 159–60. The mayor and trooper declined to comment on Mar-

shall's letters, knowing that they would appear the next day before state officials. *NYT*, 3 Oct. 1928, p. 34; ibid.

39. *NYT*, 5 Oct. 1928, p. 27; Friedman, *Incident at Massena*, 169; *NYT*, 6 Oct. 1928, p. 13; Marshall to Shulkin, 6 Oct. 1928, file 11, box 1600, LMP.

40. Hawes to Marshall, 4 Oct. 1927, file 8, box 6, LMP.

41. Marshall to Warner, 6 Oct. 1928, file 11, box 1600, LMP; Marshall to Hawes, 6 Oct. 1928, ibid. Friedman confirms the lack of an extant copy of Marshall's draft of the mayor's apology (*Incident at Massena*, 170); he believes Hawes destroyed the original, but there is no copy in Marshall's files.

42. Marshall to Shulkin, 6 Oct. 1928, file 11, box 1600, LMP.

43. All but last quoted in Friedman, *Incident at Massena*, 172–73; *NYT*, 6 Oct. 1928, p. 13.

44. Shulkin to Marshall, 9 Oct. 1928, file 8, box 6, LMP; Friedman, *Incident at Massena*, 174–75.

45. Friedman, *Incident at Massena*, 175–76; *Canadian Journal Review*, 19 Oct. 1928, file 8, box 6, LMP.

46. *Canadian Journal Review*, 19 Oct. 1928. As Friedman has pointed out, Marshall's biographers have drawn a veil of silence around his behavior surrounding Massena (*Incident at Massena*, 175). Since Friedman's book appeared, that silence has been maintained; indeed, reinterpretation of Marshall's handling of the Ford matter has been dismissed out of hand. See, e.g., Richard Rifkind, "Confronting Antisemitism in America: Louis Marshall and Henry Ford," *American Jewish History* 94, nos. 1–2 (Spring 2008): 71–90; and Matthew Silver, "Louis Marshall and the Democratization of Jewish Identity," ibid., 41–69. For a recent lionizing treatment, see Herbert Alpert, *Louis Marshall, 1856–1929: A Life Devoted to Justice and Judaism* (New York: iUniverse, 2008).

47. Cyrus Adler, "Louis Marshall: A Biographical Sketch," *American Jewish Year Book* 32 (1930–1931): 21–55, 52–53; *NYT*, 27 Aug. 1929, p. 4. His funeral was the first liturgy ever to take place in the brand-new Temple Emanu-El, sited at Fifth Avenue and Sixty-Fifth Street in New York. The $8 million building was not complete at the time of Marshall's death. *NYT*, 17 Sept. 1929, p. 30; ibid., 4 Oct. 1929, p. 3.

48. W. E. B. DuBois, "Marshall," *Crisis* (November 1929), 386, Marshall File, SUP; *Catholic News*, 21 Sept. 1929, file 11, box 68, LLSP. DuBois noted with satisfaction that the chief executive official of the NAACP was asked to serve as one of Marshall's honorary pallbearers. "Recognition," *Crisis* (November 1929), 386.

49. See, e.g., Max Kohler, "Louis Marshall," in *Dictionary of American Biography*, Base Set, American Council of Learned Societies, 1928–1936, ed. Dumas Moore (New York: Charles Scribner's Sons, 1933), 12:326–28 (reproduced in *Biography Resource Center* [Farmington Hills, Mich.: Thomson Gale, 2006], accessed 12 May 2006, http://galenet.galegroup.com.turing.library.northwestern.edu/servlet/BioRC); Adler, "Louis Marshall;" Frank Untermyer, interview by author, Evanston, Ill., 14 Jan. 2003 (transcript on file).

50. Lewis Strauss to William Cameron, 26 Apr. 1934, file 1, box 32, LLSP; Franklin to Strauss, 23 May 1934, ibid.; Franklin to Ford, 17 May 1934, ibid.; James Rosenberg to Lewis Strauss, 31 May 1934, file 9, box 69, LLSP. On Winrod, see Peter R. D'Agostino, "Gerald B. Winrod," in Levy, *Antisemitism: A Historical Encyclopedia*, 2:772–73.

51. Steven Watts, *The People's Tycoon: Henry Ford and the American Century* (New York: Knopf, 2005), 526–27; Ford R. Bryan, *Henry's Lieutenants* (Detroit: Wayne State University Press, 1993), 178, 32–34; *NYT*, 1 Mar. 1933, p. 4; *DN*, 5 Mar. 1956, p. 1; *DFP*, 5 Mar. 1956, p. 1; *NYT*, 5 Mar. 1956, p. 23; Peter Collier and David Horowitz, *The Fords: An American Epic* (New York: Summit Books, 1987), 162, 163–68. Longley drew up Henry Sr.'s and Edsel's wills in 1936 establishing the Ford Foundation to maintain family control over the company after Henry's death. Bryan, *Henry's Lieutenants*, 180.

52. Max Wallace, *The American Axis: Henry Ford, Charles Lindbergh, and the Rise of the Third Reich* (New York: St. Martin's Press, 2003), 358; *CDT*, 31 July 1938, p. 6.

53. Carol W. Gelderman, *Henry Ford: The Wayward Capitalist* (New York: Dial Press, 1981), 375; Watts, *People's Tycoon*, 526–27; Allan Nevins and Frank Ernest Hill, *Ford: Decline and Rebirth, 1933–1962* (New York: Charles Scribner's Sons, 1963); 260; Collier and Horowitz, *Fords*, 164–67. Gelderman says the film was shown in May 1945; Wallace dates the showing to May 1946 (*American Axis*, 358).

54. *NYT*, 8 Apr. 1947, p. 1; Ford R. Bryan, *Clara: Mrs. Henry Ford* (Dearborn, Mich.: Ford Books, 2001), 296–97; Collier and Horowitz, *Fords*, 226; Watts, *People's Tycoon*, 532–33.

55. Wallace, *American Axis*, 325–52; Ken Silverstein, "Ford and the Fuhrer," *Nation*, 24 Jan. 2000, pp. 11–16. Watts does not find Silverstein's evidence "persuasive;" nor does he agree with Neil Baldwin that the Ford Motor Company bears moral responsibility for the actions of Ford-Werke in Berlin. Watts, *People's Tycoon*, 589n24; Baldwin, *Henry Ford and the Jews* (New York: Public Affairs, 2001), 313–15. The Ford Motor Company commissioned two scholars to respond to Silverstein's accusations. Simon Reich and Lawrence Dowler, *Research Findings About Ford-Werke Under the Nazi Regime* (Dearborn, Mich.: Ford Motor Company, 2001), accessed 20 Jan. 2011, http://media.ford.com/events/fw_research.cfm.

56. 1930 U.S. Federal Census Schedule. Scarsdale Village, Westchester County, State of New York, Ancestry.com, accessed 27 Jan. 2011, http://search.ancestry.com/iexec?htx=View&r=an&dbid=6224&iid=NYT626_1665-0574&fn=Aaron&ln=Sapiro&st=r&ssrc=&pid=47108285; Sapiro to Lewis Strauss, 18 July 1927, file 5, box 70, LLSP.

57. Burton C. Meighan, Supreme Court Appellate Division, Office of Committee on Character and Fitness, New York State, to John K. Ormond, 23 May 1928, file 7, box 122, acc. 1, BFRC.

58. *NYT*, 6 Oct. 1929, p. E1; ibid., 25 Aug. 1930, p.1.

59. See, e.g., *LAT*, 26 May 1929, p. 11.

60. Andrew Wender Cohen, *The Racketeer's Progress: Chicago and the Struggle for the Modern American Economy, 1900–1940* (New York: Cambridge University Press, 2004), 273–76; H. Rooney, Character Investigation, Aaron Sapiro, 21 Dec. 1926, Document 62-8878-662, file 40-3875, Federal Bureau of Investigation, U.S. Department of Justice ("reputation as to character and integrity excellent") (hereafter "Sapiro FBI File"); [name redacted], Deputy U.S. Marshall, Case Report, 22 May 1941, Document 62-61509-8, ibid ("attorney of doubtful repute").

61. Report on Sapiro and Knox, 11 May 1937, Sapiro FBI File.

62. *NYT*, 8 May 1937, p. 8; John C. Knox, *Order in the Court* (New York: Charles Scribner's Sons, 1943), 258–60; *NYT*, 18 Feb. 1936, p. 2; *LAT*, 14 Jan. 1936, p. A3; death certificate, Janet Arndt Sapiro, No. 7502, 4 June 1936, Los Angeles County, California.

63. See James L. Houghteling to Arthur J. Phelan, 19 Apr. 1939, file 4, box 3, RG 85, NARA-PCR, and other correspondence in boxes 3, 4, 5, 10, and 18. On the anticommunist movement in California, see Robert Cherny, "Anticommunist Networks and Labor: The Pacific Coast in the 1930s," in *Labor's Cold War: Local Politics in a Global Context*, ed. Shelton Stromquist (Champaign: University of Illinois Press, 2008), 17–48.

64. On the Modesto case, see Bruce Nelson, *Workers on the Waterfront: Seamen, Longshoremen, and Unionism in the 1930s* (Urbana: University of Illinois Press, 1988), 171n.

65. Harper L. Knowles to Paul Armstrong, 20 May 1937, quoting San Francisco *Examiner*, 15 May 1937, file 9, box 4, Papers Relating to Harry Bridges, RG 85, NARA-SB; Robert W. Cherny, "Bridges, Harry Renton," *American National Biography Online*, Feb. 2000, accessed 26 Dec. 2010, http://www.anb.org/articles/15/15-01146.html; "The Comintern's Open Secrets," *American Spectator* 25, no. 12 (December 1992): 34–43, 34–35.

66. Official Report of Proceedings Before the Immigration and Naturalization Service of the Department of Labor, in the Matter of Harry Bridges, Deportation Hearing, Docket No. 55973/217, 19 July 1939, pp. 1243, 1269–70, 1277–82, 1313–27, Boalt Hall School of Law, University of California at Berkeley.

67. Sam Bubrick, interview by author, Los Angeles, 23 Sept. 2002, p. 30 (transcript on file); Aaron Sapiro, last will and testament, 28 Oct. 1957, probate file P423693, Los Angeles County, California; *LAT*, 17 Jan. 1960, p. 23; *NYT*, 25 Nov. 1959, p. 29; *LAT*, 25 Nov. 1959, p. B2.

68. Linda Sapiro Moon, interview by author, Huntington Beach, California, 23 Sept. 2002, p. 9 (transcript on file); *NYT*, 4 Dec. 1959, p. 30; Lewis Strauss, "Aaron Sapiro, n.d. [1960], ms., file 5, box 70, LLSP.

CONCLUSION

1. For scholarly dissections of public apologies and their cultural meaning, see, e.g., Nicholas Tavuchis, *Mea Culpa: A Sociology of Apology and Reconciliation* (Stanford, Calif.: Stanford University Press, 1991); and Keith Michael Hearit, *Crisis Management by Apology: Corporate Response to Allegations of Wrongdoing* (Mahwah, N.J.: Lawrence Erlbaum Associates, 2006). Antisemitism in governmental hiring ran rampant throughout the New Deal, and attitudes did not begin to change until after World War II. Peter Irons, *The New Deal Lawyers* (Princeton, N.J.: Princeton University Press, 1993), 126–28. For a brilliant cinematic capture of the social awakening that then took place, see *Gentleman's Agreement* (Twentieth-Century Fox, 1948; dir. Elia Kazan).

2. On Edison, see Neil Baldwin, *Henry Ford and the Jews: The Mass Production of Hate* (New York: Public Affairs, 2001), 89; on Lindbergh, see Max Wallace, *The American Axis: Henry Ford, Charles Lindbergh, and the Rise of the Third Reich* (New York: St. Martin's Press, 2003), 239–66; for a careful reading of Shaw's difficulties with distancing himself from antisemitism, fascism, and eugenics, see Gareth Griffith, *Socialism and Superior Brains: The Political Thought of George Bernard Shaw* (London: Routledge, 1993), 264–67.

3. Linda Sapiro Moon, interview by author, Huntington Beach, Calif., 23 Sept. 2002, p. 3 (transcript on file); Samuel Bubrick, interview by author, Los Angeles, 23 Sept. 2002, p. 10 (transcript on file). Bubrick says that Sapiro never rode in Ford cars and was upset when anyone he knew bought a Ford. Ibid.

4. Richard S. Levy, "Introduction," in *A Lie and a Libel: The History of the Protocols of the Elders of Zion*, ed. Binjamin W. Segel, trans. Richard S. Levy (Lincoln: University of Nebraska Press, 1995), 4–6, 35, 37; Segel, *Lie and a Libel*, ed. and trans. Levy, 63; David I. Kertzer, "The Modern Use of Ancient Lies," *NYT*, 9 May 2002, sec. A, p. 39.

5. New Jersey Laws (1935), ch. 151, §§1–8, pp. 372–78.

6. Ibid., §1, p. 372; *State v. Klapprott*, 22 A.2d 877 (N.J. 1941).

7. *Beauharnais v. Illinois*, 343 U.S. 250, 252 (1952).

8. *Shelley v. Kraemer*, 334 U.S. 1 (1948).

9. *Patterson v. Alabama*, 357 U.S. 449 (1958); *Bates v. Little Rock*, 361 U.S. 516 (1960); Phillipa Strum, *When the Nazis Came to Skokie: Freedom for Speech We Hate* (Lawrence: University Press of Kansas, 1999); Samuel Walker, *Hate Speech: The History of an American Controversy* (Lincoln: University of Nebraska Press, 1994); Timothy C. Shiell, *Campus Hate Speech on Trial* (Lawrence: University Press of Kansas, 2009); Judith Martin, *Miss Manners: A Citizen's Guide to Civility* (New York: Random House, 1999).

10. *Snyder v. Phelps, et al.*, No. 09-751, U.S. Supreme Court, decided 2 Mar. 2011, slip op. accessed 11 Dec. 2011, http://www.supremecourt.gov/opinions/10pdf/09-751.pdf.

11. Mark Landler, "Austria Frees Holocaust Denier from Jail," *NYT*, 21 Dec. 2006, http://www.nytimes.com/2006/12/21/world/europe/21holocaust.html?_r=1&scp=1&sq=DeboraD%20Lipstadt%20David%20Irving%20Dec.%2021,%20 2006&st=cse, accessed 9 Jan. 2011; *R.A.V. v. St. Paul*, 505 U.S. 377 (1992); *Virginia v. Black et al.*, 538 U.S. 343 (2003); "Newspapers Reprint Prophet Mohammed Cartoon," http://www.cnn.com/2008/WORLD/europe/02/13/denmark.cartoon/index.html, accessed 22 Apr. 2011.

INDEX

Italic page numbers indicate material in tables or figures.